TERRORISM LAW
Materials, Cases, Comments

Sixth Edition

Jeffrey F. Addicott, BA, JD, LLM, SJD

Distinguished Professor of Law & Director,
Center for Terrorism Law
St. Mary's University School of Law

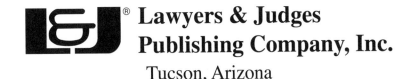

**Lawyers & Judges
Publishing Company, Inc.**
Tucson, Arizona

This publication is designed to provide accurate and authoritative information in regard to the subject matter covered. It is sold with the understanding that the publisher is not engaged in rendering legal, accounting, or other professional service. If legal advice or other expert assistance is required, the services of a competent professional person should be sought.

—From a Declaration of Principles jointly adopted by
a Committee of the American Bar Association
and a Committee of Publishers and Associations.

The publisher, editors and authors must disclaim any liability, in whole or in part, arising from the information in this volume. The reader is urged to verify the reference material prior to any detrimental reliance thereupon. Since this material deals with legal, medical and engineering information, the reader is urged to consult with an appropriate licensed professional prior to taking any action that might involve any interpretation or application of information within the realm of a licensed professional practice.

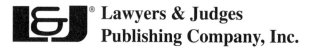 **Lawyers & Judges**
Publishing Company, Inc.

P.O. Box 30040 • Tucson, AZ 85751-0040
(800) 209-7109 • FAX (800) 330-8795
e-mail: sales@lawyersandjudges.com
www.lawyersandjudges.com

Library of Congress Cataloging-in-Publication Data

Addicott, Jeffrey F.
  Terrorism law : materials, cases, comments / Jeffrey F. Addicott. -- 6th ed.
      p. cm.
  Includes index.
  ISBN-13: 978-1-933264-82-0 (casebound : alk. paper)
  ISBN-10: 1-933264-82-9 (casebound : alk. paper)
  1. War on Terrorism, 2001-2009. 2. Terrorism. 3. War (International law) 4. Rule of law. 5. Human rights. I. Title.
  KZ6795.T47A33 2011
  345'.02--dc22

                        2010033384

Printed in the United States of America
10 9 8 7 6 5 4 3 2 1

R.B. Thieme, Jr. (1918-2009)—

pivot of the nation, theologian, soldier, educator, patriot

Contents

Table of Cases

Acknowledgments

The author wishes to acknowledge the invaluable support of Ms. Deborah E. Addicott and Bill Piatt, Dean (1998-2007), St. Mary's University School of Law. Recognizing that "[t]errorism law is an emerging legal discipline critical to understanding the complex balance between global security and civil justice," St. Mary's University established the Center for Terrorism Law in 2003 in order to examine current and potential legal issues related to terrorism in light of the challenge of achieving and maintaining a proper balance between global security and civil justice. In 2005, my sister, Debby Addicott provided a generous financial gift which funded the construction of a state-of-the-art research facility equipped with student offices, training classroom, and conference center where the Center's goal is pursued through teaching terrorism law courses; engaging in professional exchanges such as symposia and consultations; writing, commenting on and publishing written materials; training; and ensuring access to extensive information resources regarding terrorism (www.stmarytx.edu/ctl).

Among the colleagues, students and friends who expertly dealt with editing and conceptual, bibliographical, and organizational problems are Faithe Campbell, John Hicks, Kelly Culpepper, Ema Garcia, David Irwin, R.C. Rondero De Mosier, Sareta Davis, Kristy Eddings, Robert Guerra, Christian Hack, Stephanie Hoppas, Jason Lemons, Grace Uzomba, Javier Rocha, Andre Ranadive, Arzoo Rajani, and Amanda Carter. The author also wishes to acknowledge with appreciation the University of Kentucky Law Journal; Barry Law Review; University of Richmond Law Review; University of Florida Journal of International Law; Houston Journal of International Law; Military Law Review; Israeli Defense Forces Law Review; The Scholar: St. Mary's Law Review on Minority Issues; Carolina Academic Press (Legal Issues in the Struggle Against Terror); The Texas Review of Law and Politics; Pace Law Review; and The Review of Litigation for permission granted to reprint segments of materials previously published.

Introduction

In any civilized society the most important task is achieving a proper balance between freedom and order. In wartime, reason and history both suggest that this balance shifts to some degree in favor of order—in favor of the government's ability to deal with conditions that threaten the national well-being.

—William H. Rehnquist

Be it the Middle Ages or the Renaissance, the Great War or the Cold War, the trends of human history have always been characterized by epochs or eras. While it is sometimes difficult to find the exact chronological line separating one era from the next, some eras are born in a single dramatic event of such enormity that the very date overshadows the general theme of the times. As December 7, 1941, was to the World War II generation, so too was September 11, 2001, to the new era that many believe has now arrived on the stage of history. Arguably, the post-Cold War period has indeed given way to a new time in history labeled by many commentators as the "War on Terror" or alternatively as the "Global War on Terrorism." Although terrorism is not new, the intensity and frequency of al-Qa'eda and al-Qa'eda-styled militant Islamic terrorism has engulfed the entire civilized world and given rise to new methodologies for combating the rising threat.

With the tenth anniversary of the attacks of September 11, 2001, much has changed—both in law and policy. With the destruction of the al-Qa'eda terror bases in Afghanistan and the removal of the brutal regimes of the Taliban in Afghanistan and Saddam Hussein in Iraq, the United States and the world has faced a plethora of legal and policy challenges. Indeed, the central challenge that the United States is facing, as is the rest of the civilized world, is to realistically fight and win the War on Terror under a democratically based rule of law. Clearly, the protection of human rights and civil liberties is a greater obligation in times of increased security than in times of peace.

The government has crafted a variety of robust antiterrorism responses designed to disrupt the terrorist networks and prevent future terrorist attacks from occurring. Including the passage of the Uniting and Strengthening America by Providing Appropriate Tools Required to Intercept and Obstruct Terrorism Act (USA PATRIOT Act); the creation of the Cabinet level post of Homeland Security; and the establishment of United States Northern Command, in Colorado, the United States has also engaged in even greater controversial actions such as the preemptive use of military force against the Iraqi regime of Saddam Hussein and the indefinite detention of certain suspected illegal alien terrorists and unlawful enemy combatants. These solutions focus on various pressure points of the problem, but will not prove adequate if America hopes to significantly blunt the scourge of global militant Islamic terrorism. As in all wars, the enemy must be clearly understood and then the battle must be brought to the enemy. Unfortunately, America has not rooted out the reconstituted al-Qa'eda network in Western

Pakistan. Due to the universalist designs of al-Qa'eda and al-Qa'eda-styled militant Islam, the combination of traditional law enforcement with the more muscular use of military force is essential. The one-dimensional use of the criminal justice system, used so ineffectively in the 1990's, cannot confront an ideology of hate able to recruit tens of thousands of followers and field terrorist cells throughout the world. Although many in the world community (and some in America) still consider the War on Terror against al-Qa'eda and associated forces as a criminal justice matter only, the United States still views the struggle as a real "war" against the al-Qa'eda fanatics. Accordingly, in tandem with the use of domestic federal criminal law tools, the United States utilizes the legal rules associated with the law of war.

Without question, shifting the tactical focus from punishing those individuals, organizations, or nations who commit terrorist crimes or engage in aggression to broad new methodologies designed to thwart such criminal acts in the first place has caused some to challenge these governmental measures as illegal or at least as inconsistent with American values. Despite the fact that the War on Terror is now ten years old, a deep fissure continues to run through the legal community. On the one side are those who steadfastly maintain that no or very minor changes need be made to existing laws and processes, while others advocate that significant changes must be implemented to alter the traditional focus of our current legal system from punishing completed crimes to a more aggressive approach capable of preventing crimes, e.g., stopping suicide terrorist attacks before they occur. Understandably, the pivot in every discussion centers on where the balance should rest between protecting fundamental freedoms associated with civil liberties and providing adequate safety to the nation from the threat of future al-Qa'eda-styled terrorism.

Considering, for instance, that a nuclear truck bomb could obliterate an entire American city and cause a "panicky stampede into truly oppressive police statism, in which measures now unthinkable could suddenly become unstoppable," a 2003 Brookings Institute report aptly argued that "[s]tubborn adherence to the civil liberties status quo would probably damage our most fundamental freedoms far more in the long run than would judicious modifications of rules that are less fundamental." Indeed, should a major weapon of mass destruction event occur in America, a Pandora's box filled with draconian security measures would truly be opened; we might eventually close it again but we could never get everything back in.

A fundamental obligation of any State is to protect its citizens from external as well as internal threats to person and property. Nowhere is this obligation more difficult to perform than in the realm of militant Islamic terrorism, particularly when one considers the apocalyptic horrors that might be unleashed through the terrorist use of weapons of mass destruction. In the War on Terror, the United States is concerned not only with those renegade States which might commit or sponsor terror attacks using weapons of mass destruction, but also there is deep consternation about how to best deal with international or domestic terrorist groups, and even individuals.

For those who follow the studies and trends, the lethality of terrorism continues to grow. The number of serious international terror incidents more than tripled since 2004. According to the State Department there were 655 significant terror attacks in 2004, up from 175 in 2003. The increase in 2004 reflected the rise of terrorism in Iraq, but included large scale events in Spain and Russia as well. The National Counterterrorism Center records approximately 14,000 terrorist attacks across the globe for 2007, resulting in over 22,000 deaths. Of the 355 casualty attacks that killed 10 or more people, 87 percent occurred in the Near East and South Asia. In 2008 there were 11,770 attacks resulting in 15,765 deaths.

Of course, such studies are rather inconsequential when one considers the aftermath of a terrorist directed nuclear, biological, chemical, radiological, or cyber attack in an urban area of the United States. The attacks of September 11, 2001, could very well pale in comparison. Furthermore, to the mass casualties and devastating economic disruption, one must add the troubling impact such an event might have on future civil liberties and freedoms that Americans now enjoy. Considering that al-Qa'eda-styled terrorists have targeted the United States more often than any other country in the world, save Israel, the specter of weapons of mass destruction terrorism demands top priority in our thinking and planning.

Karl von Clausewitz once observed that "[e]very age has its own kind of war, its own limiting conditions and its own peculiar preconceptions." One characteristic of the War on Terror is undeniable: the United States stands as the world's bastion of stability and as the foremost sphere of power and influence. It is absolutely critical that America's national strategy for winning the War on Terror successfully accomplish three things. First, the United States must fully identify and appreciate the threat of the new breed of al-Qa'eda-styled militant Islamic global terrorism. These Islamo-fascists are dedicated murderers who are absolutely convinced that their religion compels them to kill all those that do not accept their worldview. Second, the rule of law—domestic and international—must undergo a major metamorphosis in order to better bring the battle to the terrorists and to the nations that harbor them. Third, particularly in the context of the new Afghani and Iraqi governments, America must unabashedly promote and sustain a dedicated democracy building campaign in order to drain the totalitarian swamps in which all mega terrorist groups breed. This does not mean that American troops need be stationed on the ground indefinitely, but it does mean that America must stay engaged.

This third factor is extremely ambitious and will require decades of commitment. In short, it involves embracing a new paradigm that is intuitively simplistic and yet absolutely vital to winning the War on Terror. Simply put, since democracies do not engage in terrorism, the United States must concentrate resources to do more to promote the normative values of democracy, pluralism, and human rights throughout the community of nations. The United States of America must continue to advocate policies which enhance global stability and encourage, at whatever level, a steadfast adherence to established, well-defined norms of international behavior, i.e., promoting a rule of law rooted in democratic principles. This democracy building initiative must be the basis for a new and dynamic paradigm whose application points to a more effective way to war and terrorism avoidance, especially in regard to State-sponsors of aggression and terrorism. Despite the fact that many elements of militant Islam are migrating from "physical space" to "cyberspace," al-Qa'eda terrorists and their like cannot successfully operate without host nation support from a totalitarian regime.

At the end of the day, terrorism, like crime, can never be completely eradicated. Nevertheless, the new specter of al-Qa'eda-styled terrorism can be better contained. The purpose of this introductory text is to survey the dominant characteristics of the War on Terror and to highlight some of the evolving legal and policy implications that confront the United States with special emphasis on the importance of developing capable law-based responses on the one hand, and promoting democracy as a long term solution to terrorism avoidance on the other. In this context, even if one is cynical enough to believe that the world politic is ruled primarily by the application or threat of force, it is nevertheless of critical importance from both a national and an international perspective that America rubricate its leadership role by thoughtful concerns for the positive advancement of the rule of law and the protection of cherished civil liberties.

Since the War on Terror is a war between law-abiding nations and lawbreakers, the world's most precious commodities—the promotion of democratic values and human rights—must not become casualties in the War on Terror. Indeed, these are the very tools that will prove of ultimate value in winning the War on Terror. There are moral constants across time and space that are common to all mankind. These powerful forces cannot be defeated.

Finally, as the title of this book indicates, a new body of law called *terrorism law* has emerged to deal with myriad legal issues associated with terrorism. As set out in the table of contents, this text covers the basic components of terrorism law. It is absolutely vital that lawyers skilled in terrorism law become involved in the national effort to protect the homeland and civil liberties.

Selected Bibliography

Brookings Review, *Rights Liberties and Security*, Vol. 21, Issue 1, 2003 WL 11169678, Jan. 1, 2003.

Rehnquist, William H. ALL THE LAWS BUT ONE 222, 1998.

Uniting and Strengthening America by Providing Appropriate Tools Required to Intercept and Obstruct Terrorism Act (USA PATRIOT Act) of 2001, Pub. L. No. 107-56, 115 Stat. 272. Oct. 26, 2001.

U.S. Department of State. *Country Reports on Terrorism 2009*. August 5, 2010.

Chapter 1

What is Terrorism?

The goal of the terrorist is to kill one and frighten 10,000.

—Chinese proverb

Things must be properly defined before they can be intelligently discussed. Although many trace the etymology of the word *terror* to France's "reign of terror" under Robespierre and the Jacobin Committee of Public Safety (*regime de la terreur*), the employment of terror is a phenomenon that has been around for a very long time in human history. Notwithstanding the fact that terrorism is the antithesis of the rule of law, there exists no consensus on a precise definition of terrorism either in the international community or in the United States. This is due in part to the tensions of the Cold War era when West and East could agree on precious little, but also continues today under the postmodernist cliché, "one man's terrorist is another man's freedom fighter." For instance, a Palestinian suicide bomber in Israel who intentionally kills innocent Jewish civilians may be considered a "hero" by certain segments of the Palestinian population and a terrorist by others.

1.1 Defining Terrorism

The concept of terrorism is now firmly embedded in the daily lexicon. Yet there is still no specific international definition. Recognizing the politics associated with reaching an acceptable global definition for terrorism, the United Nations has very often elected to avoid the term terrorism altogether, use it in a general sense only, or carefully carve out very specific acts in selected international treaties to characterize as "terrorism." Not only do debates turn on whether a State or just individuals can engage in terrorism, but the issue of using violence in so-called wars of "national liberation" remains a perennial stumbling block. In fact, definitional agreement seems always hindered by whether or not terrorist events are viewed as working for or against one's own national, political, or religious interests. Five examples serve to illustrate this delinquency among the 192 member States of the United Nations.

1

First, the International Law Commission's 1954 Draft Code of Offenses Against the Peace and Security of Mankind contained the following proposed language in Article 25 to define terrorism: "[T]he undertaking or encouragement by the authorities of a State of terrorist activity in another State, or the toleration by the authorities of a State of organized activities calculated to carry out terrorist acts in another State." Even though the proposed sentence failed to define the term, no agreement could be reached. As of this writing, over fifty years later, the United Nations General Assembly has still not been able to reach agreement on a final version of the document.

Second, the latest attempt by the United Nations Sub-Commission on Human Rights to come up with a definition of terrorism has met similar troubles. The first draft report of February 2001 listed three essential elements of terrorism. A terrorist act: (1) must be illegal, violating national or international law; (2) must be intended to harm the State for political reasons; and (3) must be capable of generating a state of fear in the general population. However, in order to reach consensus amongst the committee members on its first progress report, the special rapporteur had to delete the entire definition relating to terrorism.

Third, perhaps the greatest missed opportunity for the United Nations to establish a firm international definition of terrorism as it relates to States that sponsor or support terrorists occurred in its failure to employ the word "terrorism" in the context of the key 1974 United Nations General Assembly resolution defining aggression as it relates to when a nation may engage in armed self-defense under Article 51 of the United Nations Charter. The United Nations chose to classify the activities of States that send, organize, or support "armed bands, groups, irregulars, or mercenaries, which carry out acts of armed force against a State," as simply engaging in unlawful aggression in direct violation of the U.N. Charter. It failed to refer to any of these activities as engaging in terrorism. Terrorism, of course, could have certainly fit into this expression of unlawful aggression, but it was not used.

Currently, there are twelve international conventions related to terrorism and ten criminal acts identified as terrorism in various United Nations conventions and protocols. The identified acts are: hijacking, aviation sabotage, acts of violence at airports, acts of violence regarding maritime navigation, acts of violence against fixed platforms, crimes against internationally protected persons, unlawful taking and use of nuclear material, hostage taking, terrorist bombings, and supporting front organizations serving as financial conduits for terrorists groups. Obviously these ten do not cover terrorism in all its manifestations, but until the international community can form a universal definition, one can certainly reference these documents regarding specific acts of terrorism.

Fourth, in the wake of the September 11, 2001, terror attacks on the United States, the Ad Hoc Committee on Terrorism proposed a definition of terrorism for the General Assembly. This definition was not adopted, however, due to strong opposition from the 56-member Organization of Islamic Conference. In short, the Organization of Islamic Conference wanted the definition to exempt so-called wars of national liberation against foreign occupation, e.g., the Israeli occupation of certain areas in Palestine captured as a result of defensive armed conflict.

Fifth, on September 28, 2001, the Security Council adopted Resolution 1373. The resolution's legal requirements were meant to create a common legal basis for all States to take effective action against terrorists by criminalizing terrorist fundraising and blocking terrorist assets. Quite impressive on paper, Resolution 1373 requires all member States to "[r]efrain from providing any form of support, active or passive, to entities or persons involved in terrorist acts;" "take the necessary steps to prevent the commission of terrorist acts;" "deny safe haven to those who finance, plan, support, or commit terrorist acts;" and "prevent those who finance, plan, facilitate, or commit terrorist acts from using their respective territories for those purposes against other States or their citizens...." To implement these obligations, a Counter-Terrorism Committee (CTC) was created to receive hundreds of State reports on progress in each of the mentioned areas. Amazingly, the CTC has not yet managed to name a single terrorist organization, individual, or State sponsor of terrorism.

Since the victims of terrorism are invariably innocent civilians, it appears fundamentally logical that a definitional approach should concentrate on the act and not the political, religious, or social causes which motivate the act. Under this regimen, the use of violence on a civilian target with intent to cause fear in a given civilian population for ideological purposes is easily classified as a terrorist act. In other words, to the common understanding of the general public, terrorism is immediately associated with violence that is directed at the indiscriminant killing of innocent civilians in order to create a climate of fear. Thus, in the 1980s, acts of bombings and the public murder of civilians (by burning them in tires) by the "Spear of the Nation," the armed wing of the African National Congress, were acts of terrorism. The ends—getting rid of apartheid—can never justify the means.

In this light, bombing public places, sending letter bombs or poisons through the mail, hijacking aircraft, hostage taking, and so on, are all acts of terrorism regardless of the underlying cause said to justify the attack, or whether the attack occurs in peacetime or during war. In a sense, terrorism can simply be described as making "war" on civilians. Former United States Senator George Mitchell defined terrorism in February 2002 as follows: "Terrorism involves the deliberate killing of randomly selected noncombatants for political ends. It seeks to promote a political outcome by spreading terror and demoralization throughout a population."

In summary, if a universal definition is not practicable, one can at least list four key characteristics of terrorism that better reflect the activity:

1. The illegal use of violence directed at civilians to produce fear in a target group.
2. The continuing threat of additional future acts of violence.
3. A predominately political or ideological character of the act.
4. The desire to mobilize or immobilize a given target group.

Although never adopted by the United Nations General Assembly, the Secretary General of the United Nations, Kofi Annan, offered this wonderfully succinct 2005 definition:

[A]ny action constitutes terrorism if it is intended to cause death or serious bodily harm to civilians or non-combatants, with the purpose of intimidating a population or compelling a Government or an international organization to do or abstain from doing any act.

In the United States, the difficulties in definition are not related to a reluctance to use the term terrorism, but rather they rest in the sheer number of different government instrumentalities and federal statutes that have offered independent interpretations of terrorism which, while similar, are not identical. One of the latest American efforts to define terrorism is found in Section 411 of the USA PATRIOT Act, which was signed into law with overwhelming bipartisan support in November of 2001.

Actually, the USA PATRIOT Act provides similar definitions for "terrorist organization," "domestic terrorism," and "international terrorism." A terrorist organization is defined as one that is:

(1) designated by the Secretary of State as a terrorist organization under the process established under current law; (2) designated by the Secretary of State as a terrorist organization for immigration purposes; or (3) a group of two or more individuals that commits terrorist activities or plans or prepares to commit (including locating targets for) terrorist activities.

Domestic terrorism is defined in the USA PATRIOT Act with a slightly different emphasis. Domestic terrorism is the "unlawful use, or threatened use, of force or violence by a group or individuals based [in the United States]…committed against persons or property to intimidate or coerce a government, [or] the civilian population…in furtherance of political or social objectives."

International terrorism is set out in the USA PATRIOT Act as follows:

International terrorism involves violent acts or acts dangerous to human life that violate the criminal laws of the United States or any state, or that would be a criminal violation if committed within the jurisdiction of the United States or any state. These acts appear intended to intimidate or coerce a civilian population, influence the policy of a government by intimidation or coercion, or affect the conduct of a government by assassination or kidnapping. International terrorist acts occur outside the United States or transcend national boundaries in terms of how terrorists accomplish them, the persons they appear intended to coerce or intimidate, or the place in which the perpetrators operate.

1.2 The Goal of Terrorism

Despite the lack of a fixed universal agreement defining terrorism, the essential goal of terrorism is readily identifiable. As the root word implies, the goal of terrorism is to instill fear in a given civilian population by means of violence. In the oft-repeated Chinese proverb, the objective of the terrorist is to kill one and frighten 10,000. While specific acts of terrorism may appear to be mindless and irrational, terrorism is the exact opposite of confused behavior. Terrorism is a goal-directed, calculated, premeditated use of force. Unfortunately, all too often, terrorist tactics prove effective when those who are targeted respond in a way that reinforces the demands of the terrorists. The March 11, 2004, series of coordinated train bombings in Spain by al-Qa'eda-linked terrorists not only killed just over 200 people, but the attacks caused the newly installed Spanish government to withdraw its military forces from the American-led coalition in Iraq, a coalition that was combating some of the very same forces of terror that attacked Spain. On the other hand, sometimes the use of terror tactics can result in unintended consequences for the terrorist network. The al-Qa'eda terror group certainly did not seek the destruction of its primary base of operations in Afghanistan when it attacked the United States on September 11, 2001. At most, al-Qa'eda hoped to spark a massive social and political revolution in the Middle East that would bring to power al-Qa'eda-related governments.

1.3 Terrorism and Weapons of Mass Destruction

Apart from the traditional weapons used by terrorists, one must now add weapons of mass destruction as a special definitional subset. Although current federal statutes take an extremely broad view of what constitutes a weapon of mass destruction (to include a car bomb), an early and still relevant definition comes from Section 1403 of the National Defense Authorization Act for fiscal year 1997. Weapons of mass destruction are defined there as "any weapon or device that is intended, or has the capability, to cause death or serious bodily injury to a significant number of people through the release of toxic or poisonous chemicals or their precursors, a disease organism, or radiation or radioactivity." Thus, in its true sense, weapons of mass destruction include not only nuclear material, but the full range of biological, chemical, and radioactive agents.

The December 2008 Congressionally mandated report by the Commission on the Prevention of Weapons of Mass Destruction Proliferation and Terrorism found that:

> Terrorists are determined to attack us again with weapons of mass destruction if they can. Osama bin Laden has said that obtaining these weapons is a "religious duty" and is reported to have sought to perpetrate another "Hiroshima." The Commission believes that unless the world community acts decisively and with great urgency, it is more likely than not that a weapon of mass destruction will be used in a terrorist attack somewhere in the world by 2013.

As is true for any terrorist event, there are three general sources from which a weapon of mass destruction terrorist attack can emanate—States, sub-State groups, or individuals. Tragically, in the so-called information age, all three categories have demonstrated a willingness to use weapons of mass murder in the physical world and there can be no doubt that this thirst for violence will soon spill over into the cyber world as well. States that engage in terrorism and have the potential of using weapons of mass destruction are further divided as either State-sponsors or State-supporters of terrorism.

1.4 State-Sponsored and State-Supported Terrorism

Perhaps the most easily identifiable category of terrorism is the State-sponsored terrorist attack. In recent times, the international community has been shocked to learn that certain renegade States, such as Saddam Hussein's Iraq, have shown an unabashed willingness to use deadly nerve gas to kill thousands of men, women, and children (the Kurds). It can be argued that all totalitarian States pose an ever-present threat for the use of weapons of mass destruction at any given time—both against their own people and against other nations. Each year, the U.S. State Department designates certain countries as State sponsors of terrorism. This list generally includes a small handful of States such as: Cuba, Iran, and Syria. In fact, regarding weapons of mass destruction, the number is always larger. For instance, in 1999 John A. Lauder, Director of the Central Intelligence Agency's Nonproliferation Center, testified before Congress that a dozen countries "now either possess or are actively pursuing offensive biological weapons capabilities for use against their perceived enemies, whether internal or external." Lauder's statement is still true today.

In the context of a State's use of weapons of mass destruction in a terrorist attack, several commentators seek to distinguish a State-sponsored terrorist act from a State-supported terrorist act. State-sponsored terrorism exists when a State directly but secretly uses its own resources to sponsor acts of terrorism against another country. Since accountability for such acts are denied, the aggressor-State seeks to avoid responsibility. On the other hand, State-supported terrorism refers to the practice of a State providing resources or finances to a terrorist group for training and logistics, as occurred in Afghanistan, where the terrorist group headed by Osama bin Laden once took open refuge. In contrast to the State-sponsored scenario, the State-supported terrorist group generally operates in a more independent fashion from the host State.

A classic case of a State-sponsored act of terrorism occurred in 1986 when Libyan government agents bombed an American frequented discotheque in then West Berlin, Germany. This secretive act of terror was followed by a second State-sponsored act of terror in 1988, when Libyan government operatives bombed Pan Am Flight 103 over Lockerbie, Scotland, killing 278 people.

In the final analysis, it is difficult to make a practical distinction between State-sponsored and State-supported terrorism. The terms really speak only to the degree of culpability. Nevertheless, if the rule of law has any force, States that allow terrorist groups to operate with impunity on their soil should never be able to escape the attendant lawful consequences. While it is subject to legal debate whether a particular terrorist act committed apart from the support or sponsorship of a State would be considered an "act of war" under international law, a terrorist attack with the support or sponsorship of a State could very well be deemed an "act of war."

The early days of concern regarding terrorism and the use of weapons of mass destruction saw most of the emphasis focused primarily on the actions of the totalitarian State. Because many believed that ready access to weapons of mass destruction material was limited, sub-State terrorist groups and individual terrorists were generally given less attention. For these later categories of terrorism, the international community generally concentrated on making specific overt acts international crimes, e.g., airline hijacking or hostage taking. In regard to renegade States, however, the major issue turned on the proper application of appropriate sanctions against the State that sponsored or supported the terrorist incident.

1.5 The Diplomatic Bag

A particular early concern, which demonstrates the depth of the debate regarding how to deal with a weapon of mass destruction terrorist event *vis-à-vis* international legal sanctions, was the use of the "diplomatic bag" to import and export with impunity assorted prohibited and illegal items into receiving and transit States. The diplomatic bag issue continues to stir disagreement even today. Modern international practice has witnessed the use (or attempted use) of the diplomatic bag to transport illegal foreign currency, illegal drugs, weapons, and even people. While all *malum in se* acts committed under the cover of this diplomatic shield are sorely objectionable, the most insidious and disconcerting activities are those in which the diplomatic bag might be used as a vehicle to commit clearly defined acts of terrorism, especially those related to the employment of a weapon of mass destruction.

Currently, the diplomatic privileges and immunities accorded to the diplomatic bag under treaty and customary international law are set out in Article 27 of the Vienna Convention on Diplomatic Relations. In short, the diplomatic bag is deemed by international law to be inviolable and not subject to detention or search. The central thrust of those who periodically call for a change to the Vienna Convention argue that the protected status given to the diplomatic bag must be significantly revised to account for the legitimate security interests of the receiving State. Again, the major concern is that the diplomatic bag could be used by a foreign actor to commit an act of terrorism with a weapon of mass destruction.

Perhaps the most widely publicized abuse of the diplomatic bag to date, and one which clearly illustrates the controversy over the status of the bag, was committed by the Libyan government of Colonel Muammar al-Qaddafi. In April of 1984, two Libyans gunned down 11 demonstrators and one British constable as they stood outside of the Libyan embassy in London. Despite substantial suspicions that the weapons and other evidence connected with this heinous act of terrorism were put inside of Libyan diplomatic bags, the British authorities allowed the Libyans to carry the diplomatic bags out of the country without searching or scanning them. This incident caused a chorus of protest that the rules of diplomatic immunity were obsolete.

Responding to public fears that diplomatic privileges could be used as a vehicle to commit State-sponsored terrorism related to weapons of mass murder, then Secretary of Defense Caspar Weinberger publicly indicated in 1986 that the entire doctrine of diplomatic immunity should be greatly limited. Arguing that State-sponsored terrorists were abusing the doctrine, Weinberger called upon "diplomats, with the assistance of the legal profession" to define new limits that would help solve the problem of diplomatic privileges being extended to those States who were connected with terrorists. Weinberger's call to action was not heeded.

No one can argue that all conventional terrorist acts fade in significance when compared to fears that the diplomatic bag might be used illegally to transport weapons of mass destruction. In the wake of the large-scale destruction that would result from even a single weapon of mass destruction event, the demands for security safeguards would seem to far outweigh any status quo that the international rules might seek to maintain. In short, if ordinary weapons can be neatly and easily sent into the receiving State via the diplomatic bag, why not a weapon of mass destruction? One terrorist from a hostile country, for example, could smuggle in a vial of lethal biological material for insertion in a city water supply in the United States. Although this argument is true enough, the privileged status of the diplomatic bag has never been successfully curtailed. This is true for three reasons.

First, most people understand that if the diplomatic bag privilege is limited then the determined terrorist will find yet another way to smuggle materials for mass murder into the United States. In an open society, such as the United States, the State-sponsored terrorist, or any terrorist, can obtain much, if not most, of the needed materials on the domestic open market and, more importantly, can do so without leaving a signature.

Second, since nations have an inherent right of self-defense to search out and otherwise protect themselves against viable threats to their national security, the State which sponsored such blatant aggressive behavior takes an inordinate risk by using the diplomatic bag in such a manner. Deterrence would keep the renegade State in check.

Third, like all international agreements, the Vienna Convention can never hope to maintain any form of functional integrity unless it is strictly adhered to. Nations who demand inspection of even the most suspicious diplomatic bags must do so only at the risk of having their own bags subjected to the same process by the sending State. And that practice would quickly undermine the entire process of free diplomatic intercourse. The only real guarantee that other nations, friendly or otherwise, will generally follow international rules rests in this reciprocity analysis—the red thread of international law. We follow the rules because the other guy follows the rules.

As discussed in Chapter 2, the way to deal with a State-sponsored terrorist attack, if linkage is established, is to seek redress under the rule of law—financially, judicially, or militarily. Historically, if a State sponsors a terrorist act, the United States has generally demonstrated that it has the capability and willingness to retaliate under the well-recognized venue of self-defense. Unlike other international disputes between nations, terrorist attacks should never be handled by a third-party in the context of dispute resolution. The renegade State must be neutralized in a legitimate manner and forum. Ultimately, the aggrieved State can turn to the classical rules of self-defense, depending on the severity of the terrorist incident. Realistically, if the United States had hard evidence that a State was behind a terrorist attack, it would likely respond under the traditional notions of self-defense and forcible self-help. This, of course, is precisely what occurred in response to the September 11, 2001, attack on the United States. Any nation will certainly do what is necessary to protect itself from illegal acts of violence or the imminent threat of aggression.

1.6 Sub-State Terrorism

Sub-State terrorist groups can either be domestic or international terrorist organizations and are generally categorized by either religious or political ideologies. In 1995, for example, a RAND study found that "25 of 58, or 42 percent of known, active, international terrorist groups had a predominately religious component or motivation." In addition, from a rule of law perspective, sub-State terrorist organizations do not operate with the approval or sponsorship of the host nation, they operate in secrecy.

The first significant use of a weapon of mass destruction by a sub-State group occurred on March 20, 1995, when members of the Aum Shinrikyo religious cult (now called Aleph) in Japan released a lethal nerve agent, sarin, in a Tokyo underground subway. This weapon of mass destruction attack killed twelve people and injured 3,000 others, clearly demonstrating that the scenario of terrorists using a weapon of mass destruction was not the stuff of fiction.

While attacks by sub-State groups against United States interests have yet to use weapons of mass destruction (as of this writing), many groups have shown a viciousness and disregard for human life that clearly points to a willingness to use such weapons in the future. For instance, an Islamic radical group with ties to al-Qa'eda and headed by Ramzi Ahmad Yousef conducted the 1993 bombing of New York City's World Trade Center in an attempt to topple one of the twin towers onto the other to kill thousands, an act clearly in the spirit of a weapons of mass destruction event. In fact, it has been reported that those behind the 1993 World Trade Center bombing were also gathering the ingredients for a chemical weapon that could have brought the death toll into the tens of thousands. Some early reports indicated that the bombs used in the attack might have been laced with cyanide, but the poison burned up in the detonation.

In early 2000, United States and Israeli intelligence sources reported that HAMAS, the militant Palestinian terrorist group, was experimenting with chemical weapons in their rocket attacks against Israeli targets. Although no radical Islamic group has yet to use chemical or biological agents in their terror attacks on Israel, the potential for such an event certainly exists. With the increasing availability of high-tech weapons and nuclear materials from former Communist countries and the ease with which some chemical and biological agents can now be manufactured, there is growing concern that sub-State groups will now actively cross over into the weapons of mass destruction domain. Indeed, the fear also exists that one of the world's dictators might simply give weapons of mass destruction to a sub-State terrorist group. This was certainly a major consideration for the United States-led preemptive attack on Saddam Hussein's regime in 2003 and continues to be an issue in the quest to stop the radicalized Iranian regime from developing nuclear weapons.

1.7 Individual Terrorism

Perhaps the most troubling aspect of weapons of mass destruction terrorism is one not often heard in the War on Terror. It is the prospect of an individual not directly affiliated with any terror organization setting off a weapon of mass destruction in a major urban area. Because they operate on their own, without affiliation to any known group or State, individuals who engage in "lone-wolf" terrorism are far harder to predict, track, or deter.

To demonstrate the seriousness of individual terrorism, on March 3, 1999, William C. Patrick, III, a leading American expert on biological warfare, walked through the security check system at the Rayburn House Office Building in downtown Washington, D.C., carrying 7.5 grams of powdered anthrax, enough to kill everyone in the building, in a small plastic bottle. Not only was he rubricating the ease with which a single determined terrorist could breach security systems and target, in this case, a major federal government installation, Patrick's action certainly should have provided the needed wake up call to United States government officials and the public at large. Unfortunately, it did not.

Patrick told a Congressional committee that he was trying to show how a hostile or aggressor State could smuggle powdered anthrax in to the United States in a secure diplomatic pouch. What Patrick was really demonstrating, however, was the ease with which any individual terrorist—domestic or international—could unleash untold bioterrorism horror, almost at will. In his testimony, Patrick related that he had also carried other similar deadly materials and, "like Sherman went through Georgia," had "been through all the major airports, and the security systems of the State Department, the Pentagon, and even the CIA, and nobody stopped me."

The most notorious example of an individual terrorist attack in the United States occurred in April 1995 with the bombing of the Murrah Federal Building in Oklahoma City by Timothy McVeigh. The bomb killed 167 people, including women and children. Although McVeigh did not employ a weapon of mass destruction in his attack, his actions clearly raised the issue of individual domestic terrorism in the context of weapons of mass destruction. While one can ponder the bizarre "anti-government" sentiments that motivated McVeigh, the greater issue really revolves around individual access to material which can cause widespread damage of life and property.

Furthermore, not all individual terrorism can be associated with fanatical political or religious ideologues. Individual terrorism can be committed by persons seeking personal rather than political gain, or by individuals who are mentally ill. The 2001 anthrax-tainted letter attacks that killed five people and traumatized the nation was said to have been carried out by an anthrax researcher at the U.S. Army's biodefense laboratory in Maryland. The suspect, Bruce Ivins, committed suicide in July 2008. Considering the number of "Bruce Ivins" in any given society, the prospect of individuals obtaining access to weapons of mass destruction is chilling and will unfortunately continue to grow with time.

1.8 Al-Qa'eda-Styled Terrorism and Militant Islam

Al-Qa'eda (the Base) is an umbrella organization founded in 1989 by a Saudi Arabian named Osama (or Usama) bin Laden. Osama bin Laden formed the group out of elements of the Maktab al-Khidamat, an organization founded by Osama bin Laden and Abdallah Azzam (a member of a group called the Palestinian Moslem Brotherhood) in the early 1980s to provide money, equipment, and manpower to the Afghan resistance against the Soviet Union's occupation of Afghanistan. With the withdrawal of the Soviets in 1989, bin Laden started al-Qa'eda in order to redirect his efforts to "attack the enemies of Islam all over the world." The religious view embraced by militant Islam is a fixed, comprehensive ideology that targets for death anyone that disagrees with its very narrow set of mandates. In 2004, Jordanian Abu Musab al-Zarqawi proclaimed his allegiance to Osama bin Laden and headed al-Qa'eda in Iraq. He specifically targeted Muslims and their houses of worship, killing them by the hundreds.

From the early 1990s until the end of 2001, the al-Qa'eda operated openly in the country of Afghanistan with the complete support of the Pashtun-dominated Taliban government. During the tenure of the Taliban regime, the relationship between the Taliban and the al-Qa'eda terrorist organization provided a seminal example of State-supported terrorism. In fact, under the Taliban, Afghanistan became a terror training ground for tens of thousands of Arab and non-Arab al-Qa'eda militants including Saudis, Kashmirs, Chechens, Uzbeks, Uighurs, and others (including a number of Americans). These training camps sent cells of well-trained terrorists into numerous countries where they were encouraged to recruit additional members and carry out terrorist attacks on command. While al-Qa'eda has tens of thousands of supporters and low-level operatives worldwide, only carefully selected Muslim males are offered full membership. Interestingly, the al-Qa'eda leadership does not allow volunteers to join the group. Instead, al-Qa'eda seeks out candidates for full membership. These recruits must sign an oath of allegiance called a *bayat*, swearing to carry out the dictates of al-Qa'eda leaders on penalty of death. They are then indoctrinated and trained extensively in assassination, kidnapping, explosives, small arms, hijacking, and torture.

The War on Terror is predominantly focused on defeating the al-Qa'eda terrorist network, although the United States is now targeting well over a dozen Islamic terror groups. Since the release of the Department of Defense's 2005 National Military Strategic Plan for the War on Terrorism, America has recognized that the number one terrorist threat to the United States is Islamic extremism. The "poster-child" for militant Islam is still the al-Qa'eda organization which is a new type of terrorism that combines almost all of the forms of terror identified in this chapter. They were, at one time, State-supported by the Taliban government of Afghanistan and continue to be State-supported by any number of radical regimes including Iran, the Palestinian territories, Syria and so on. They also qualify as a sub-State terrorist organization because they have secretly infiltrated and established "sleeper" terrorist cells in various nations throughout the world including the United States, Canada, Britain, France, Spain, Italy, Australia, Germany, etc.

Furthermore, the virus of al-Qa'eda ideology also influences individual or lone-wolf terrorism. Their ideology of hate and intolerance has reached the minds of individuals who, although not directly tied to the organization, choose to commit terrorist acts because they have adopted the general theme and goal of the al-Qa'eda mindset. Illustrations of this fact are many, but the most shocking case occurred in the shooting murder of 13 soldiers at Fort Hood, Texas, in November 2009, by an Army medical officer named Nidal Malik Hasan. Although there can be no doubt that Hasan was motivated by radical Islamic ideology when he shouted "Allahuy Akhbar" as he opened fire on his unarmed victims, government officials and subsequent high-level military investigative reports downplayed the impact that radical Islam had as the motive for the attack. In reality, the slaughter committed by Hasan represented the first major terror attack inspired by radical Islam in the United States since 9/11 (an Army recruiter was murdered by a radical Muslim in Little Rock, Arkansas, prior to this attack).

Some have described the al-Qa'eda terrorist group as an entirely new type of entity in the world—not just a terrorist group but a "virtual-State" that normal criminal law processes simply cannot curtail. The virtual-State description is fundamentally valid. The al-Qa'eda virtual-State exhibits many of the characteristics of the classic nation-State, but is able to walk in and out of the shadows of international law because it has no fixed national boundaries. For instance, the al-Qa'eda virtual-State certainly has a political arm and media section that directs its policy, a military composed of thousands of devoted killers, a treasury that raises funds across the globe, a large number of supporters and adherents, and direct and indirect links to the leaders of other nation-states. Indeed, for this reason, the United States has been obliged to reach beyond the tools of normal domestic law enforcement and utilize its military power to make war with this virtual-State. This new approach, employing the law of war, has resulted in numerous legal challenges in both domestic and international law.

Certainly, the War on Terror demands that the United States fully come to grips with the *modis vivendi* of the al-Qa'eda as well as all sister Islamic militant groups that seek to wage war by conducting large scale terrorist attacks on America. Again, America must know the enemy if it is to ever defeat it. In this context, there are three basic reasons why the al-Qa'eda virtual-State and al-Qa'eda-styled militant Islam is vastly different from all previous terror groups that civilized nations have had to cope with.

First, threatened by the normative values of democracy, freedom, and human rights, al-Qa'eda and like-minded militant Islamic terror groups are dedicated to the destruction of the West and all those who adopt Western ideals, including those moderate Muslim and Arab governments that refute their view of Islam. The religious based fanaticism runs so deep that they are eagerly willing to commit suicide in the furtherance of their cause. Unlike previous terrorist groups, al-Qa'eda suicide bombers have no "exit" strategy to save themselves, making it almost impossible for law enforcement to stop them. (The failed al-Qa'eda-styled plot to detonate liquid explosives on as many as ten U.S. bound airplanes coming from London in August 2006 provided an intelligence bonanza for British and American law enforcement.) The predominantly young male suicide bombers are lured into death (euphemistically called martyrdom) by the religious promise of automatically securing a place in Paradise for themselves where they will receive "fleshly delights [virgins] and the expectation that they will be allowed to choose seventy friends and family members to join them in heaven." The radical clerics base this belief on Qur'anic passages such as Qur'an 9:111, which promises Paradise to those who "slay and are slain" for Allah.

Furthermore, democracies offer a plethora of targets that can easily be attacked, particularly if one is not concerned with surviving the assault. There are, for example, over 1,000 nuclear reactors, and 15,000 chemical plants, refineries, and hazardous material sites in the United States. With almost 1,000 of these sites located near large population centers, the death toll from a terror attack could easily total in the tens of thousands. Thus, employing suicide as the method of choice to inflict terror, a dedicated terrorist can target almost any public place; in New York City there are 468 subway stations, and in Chicago there are over 2,000 bus stops. Tragically, these new terrorists have successfully used the openness of the democratic society to attack from within, placing great strains on civil liberties.

Second, militant Islam has learned to use the super highway of modern technology to establish ties across the globe and provide logistical support for terror cells in practically every country in the world. In fact, the next generation of fanatics will be far more adept at using the Internet and will no doubt engage in cyberterrorist attacks to disrupt, for instance, power plants, airports, banking institutions, and even nuclear power plants. Even now, militant Islamic terrorists use the Internet to assist in recruiting and organizing. Moreover, cyberterrorism is unique because it makes normal physical security measures totally irrelevant. There are no borders to sneak across, no security cameras to avoid, and no bombs to manufacture. Terrorists can use a medium of attack that is virtually risk free.

Third, al-Qa'eda and their like have shown an intense desire to obtain any and all forms of weapons which can inflict mass casualties on civilians, including weapons of mass destruction. Their appetite for killing knows no limits. Again, the greatest fear is that a terrorist will obtain a nuclear weapon and smuggle it into an American port of entry. In fact, such a weapon can be smuggled into the United States with very little risk of failure. With 5,525 miles of border with Canada, 1,989 miles of border with Mexico, and a maritime border of 95,000 miles of shoreline, only a tiny fraction of the millions of people (400+ million), cars (130+ million), trucks (12+ million), rail freight cars (2+ million), and maritime containers (8+ million) entering the U.S. each year at over 3,700 terminals and 301 ports of entry are ever subjected to inspection of any kind.

1.9 Why They Hate

Some terrorists have tried to depict the current War on Terror as a war against Islam (*see* Chapter 9.2). This is obviously not true. The War on Terror is against those militant Islamic groups that have declared "war" on the United States, such as al-Qa'eda, the Taliban, and associated forces. The ideological motivations of these militant Islamic terror organizations are focused on the advancement of cult-like "religious" objectives rather than the more typical aspirations of traditional old-styled terrorist groups that are primarily concerned with the achievement of political or territorial goals. Driven by extremist pseudo-Islamic radicalism, the new breed of terrorists are bent on destroying through violence those individuals and things which are deemed to be outside of a very narrow *weltanschauung* (world view). Since the establishment of the new Iraqi government in 2004, well over 500 car-bombs driven by al-Qa'eda operatives and other jihadists have murdered in excess of 10,000 innocent civilians, mostly fellow Muslims. Abu Musab al-Zarqawi, the former leader of al-Qa'eda in Iraq (he was killed by U.S. firepower in June 2006), believed that "slaughtering fellow Arabs who followed different forms of Islam was as important as killing Westerners."

The 2004 National Commission on Terrorist Acts Upon the United States, better known as the 9/11 Commission Report, found that the United States is facing a loose confederation of people, maybe numbering in the tens of thousands, who believe in a perverted strain of Islam and are busy building the groundwork for decades of struggle. Although militant Islam is not restricted to just the al-Qa'eda-styled belief system—the current Iranian theocratic regime has its own radicalized view of Islam—the roots of al-Qa'eda come from a narrow radicalized strain of Islam known as the Wahhabi movement. The movement arose in the eighteenth century under Mohammed Ibn Abd al-Wahab in the desert of Najd in the Arabian Peninsula. Ibn Abd al-Wahab converted a group of illiterate Bedouins under Muhammad Ibn Sa'ud and declared himself the religious leader, or *Sheik*, and Sa'ud the political leader, or *Emir*. Amazingly, one of al-Wahab's first acts was to issue a *fatwa*, a religious decree, casting all non-Wahhabi Muslims as apostates and idol worshippers. In this way, Sa'ud's men were now all cast in the role of fighters for *jihad* (holy war) against anyone not in the new Wahhabi movement, including other Muslims whom they killed in large numbers.

Originally funded in large part by Saudi Arabia, the Wahhabi movement has spread across much of the Islamic world. In fact, the greatest achievement of the sect has been to present Wahhabism to a large segment of the Arab world as an accepted part of Islam, even as the "true" Islam. At its heart, the most extreme segment of Wahhabism adopts the same ideology of the fascists and Communists except that it cloaks itself by manipulating the Islamic religion to gain political power and social domination. Militant Islam is truly an anachronistic mind set, in complete conflict with modern concepts of plurality, human rights, and democracy. The rich tradition of religious tolerance in America is the antithesis of militant Islam. Speaking in 2003 before the Senate Subcommittee on Terrorism, Technology and Homeland Security, Alex Alexiev, Senior Fellow at the Center for Security Policy noted:

A key postulate of Wahhabi's teaching asserts that Muslims who do not believe in his doctrines are ipso facto non-believers and apostates against whom violence and Jihad were not only permissible, but obligatory. This postulate alone transgresses against two fundamental tenets of the Quran—that invoking Jihad against fellow-Muslims is prohibited and that Muslim's profession of faith should be taken at face value until God judges his/hers sincerity at judgment day. This extreme reactionary creed was then used as the religious justification for military conquest and violence against Muslim neighbors of the House of Saud. Already in 1746, just two years after Wahhabism became Saud's religion, the new Saudi-Wahhabi state proclaimed Jihad against all neighboring Muslim tribes that refused to subscribe to it. Indeed, well into the 1920s the history of the House of Saud is replete with violent campaigns to force other Muslims to submit politically and theologically, violating yet another fundamental Quranic principle that prohibits the use of compulsion in religion.

There are numerous terrorist organizations that fit the mold of militant Islam, although not all of the militant groups are at "war" with the United States. The State Department's 2010 list of foreign terrorist organizations (FTO) contains 45 groups; at least 19 of these FTOs cloak themselves in a militant view of Islam. The list includes: Abu Sayyaf Group, Al-Aqsa Martyrs Brigade, Ansar al-Islam, Armed Islamic Group, Gama'a al-Islamiyya, HAMAS, Harakat ul-Mujahedin, Hizballah, Islamic Jihad Group, Jaish-e-Mohammed, Jemaah Islamiya Organization, Libyan Islamic Fighting Group, Moroccan Islamic Combatant Group, Mujahedin-e Khalq Organization, Palestinian Islamic Jihad, and al-Qa'eda. As previously noted, a 1995 RAND-St. Andrew's Chronology of International Terrorism study revealed that "25 of 58, or 42 percent of known, active, international terrorists groups had a predominately religious component or motivation." Many of these radical Islamic groups are associated with Islamic fundamentalism spewed from radicalized *madrasas* (religious schools) which operate with impunity in such countries as Saudi Arabia, Pakistan, and Iran. In fact, in the case of many militant Islamic terrorist organizations, direct links have been established to various *Deobandi* religious schools, which are known for openly advocating the most violent forms of terrorism against Western interests. In addition, radical clerics in Western nations also preach this brand of hate to their followers. For instance, many terrorists associated with the July 7 and 21, 2005, bombings in London had direct links to the infamous Findsbury Park Mosque in London (Muslim cleric Abuy Hamza al-Masri was subsequently arrested on suspicion of terrorism links).

The number of adherents of militant Islam is large and growing, easily reaching into the hundreds of thousands if one counts the strongly messianic strain of Twelver Shiism in Iran (belief that the twelfth legitimate successor of the prophet Muhammad who is said to have disappeared in the tenth century will return to reign over a world where Islam is universal). Pakistan and other Middle Eastern nations teem with al-Qa'eda sympathizers. The most chilling hallmark associated with the spread of militant Islam is not the operation of terror training camps for the terror jihadists, but rather the established methodology of inculcating an ideology of hatred into the minds of innocent children from the moment of birth. In the homes, communities, and the *madrasas*, countless numbers of children are brainwashed each and every day of their lives with no opportunity to escape. The radical *madrasas* are like conveyor belts of death where an unlimited number of suicide bombers emerge convinced that their religion demands the murder of Westerners, Jews, or anyone holding a contrary worldview. Up to 20 percent of all *madrasas* may be actively spreading radical ideologies.

Simply stated, the goal of al-Qa'eda-styled militant Islam is to conquer the world. In 2006 alone, Ayman al-Zawahiri and Osama bin Laden made almost 20 videotaped pronouncements on the global war. In August 2006, Zawahiri told his followers: "All the world is a battlefield open in front of us." This idea of global *jihad* is one of the defining threads that bring together suicide murders from Baghdad to Bali. In this light, al-Qa'eda is both a cohesive terror organization and a source of inspiration for all like-minded fanatics. In an April 24, 2006 tape, Osama bin Laden declared: "It is the duty for the Umma [nation] with all its categories of men, women and youths, to give away themselves, their money, experiences and all types of material support....Jihad today is an imperative for every Muslim. The Umma will commit sin if it did not provide adequate material support for jihad." The never-ending struggle is encompassed in their view of the seventh-century jihad—the spread of Islam by force of arms. Unless and until they are shut down, the War on Terror cannot be won. Then Secretary of Defense Donald Rumsfeld made this point in an October 2003 memorandum he sent to General Richard Myers, Chairman of the Joint Chiefs of Staff, entitled: Global War on Terrorism. In the memorandum, Rumsfeld asked, "Are we capturing, killing or deterring and dissuading more terrorists every day than the madrassas [sic] and the radical clerics are recruiting, training, and deploying against us?"

Ultimately, of course, this means that only Muslims can provide the cure to militant Islam. In the aftermath of the July 7, 2005, bombing in London that killed 52 people, this theme was echoed by both the British and some Muslim leaders in England. The key to winning the conflict is addressing the ideological aspect regarding how terrorists recruit and indoctrinate new followers. Interestingly, the suicide foot-soldiers defy simplistic political, sociological, or psychological profiling. They come from extremely diverse educational, economic, and social backgrounds. The only common red thread that binds them together is an unrelenting devotion to their radicalized Islamic belief system. *United States v. Koubriti*, 199 F. Supp. 2d 656 (E.D.Mich. S.D. 2002):

> Wahhabis, Takfiris, and Salafists…These groups regard the Islam that most Muslims practice today as unpure and polluted by idolatry and Western influence.…These radical fundamentalist-Islamic groups see the world divided in two spheres; that is, Dar-al-Islam (House of Islam or Islamic Zone), where peace reigns (Sallam), and the Dar-al-Harb (House of War or War Zone), which prevents a true Islamic state. The latter is viewed by these radical fundamentalist-Islamic groups to include all infidel areas that must ultimately be conquered. Global jihad is the constant effort to achieve this goal.

Perhaps one of the most chilling revelations of the vicious mindset of militant Islam is found in the "bin Laden videotape," released to the public on December 13, 2001. The tape clearly illustrates the twisted religious machinations of the al-Qa'eda terrorists and their like who pervert religion to justify the mass murder of innocent civilians. In the conversation between bin Laden and Sheik Khaled al-Harbi (who surrendered to Saudi officials in 2004) regarding the attacks of September 11, 2001, numerous references are made to "Allah," "Muhammad," the "*fiqu* [holy war] of Muhammad," and so on. At one point, bin Laden boasts that the attacks were beneficial to a "true" understanding of Islam. "The attacks made people think (about true Islam), which benefited them greatly." The video closes with the guest praising bin Laden in the name of Allah, "By Allah my Shaykh [bin Laden]. We congratulate you for the great work. Thank Allah."

Osama bin Laden and his followers are not simply another isolated sub-State religious terror cult like Japan's Aum Shinrikyo. According to a thought provoking special report from 2001 *Newsweek* entitled, "Why Do They Hate Us," these terrorists "come out of a culture that reinforces their hostility, distrust and hatred of the West—and of America in particular." Incredibly, a Gallup poll taken in late February 2002, indicated that a majority of the Arab world condemned the September 11, 2001, attack on the United States, but believed that Arabs did not carry it out. This opinion was shared throughout the region despite the fact that all nineteen of the hijackers were Arabs.

Similarly, these Islamic zealots are far different from mere criminals. Unlike criminals, they are not in it for monetary gain. They do not wish to circumvent the system; rather they desire to destroy the system. Their fantastic goal is to create an Islamic caliphate that controls the world. Still, al-Qa'eda has cited numerous grievances against the United States to justify their use of terror including American support of "puppet" Arab governments, importation of oil, support for Israel, support for the new Iraq and Afghanistan, Westerners living in Arab lands, morally corrupt Western culture, and so on. These complaints are hollow. Like all enemies of freedom and pluralism, be it the German Nazis or the Stalinist Communists, the radical Islamic terrorists attack the West for what it is, not for what it has done. In a nutshell, whether the anti-Americanism is motivated by religious enmity, radical idiosyncrasies, or just blind hatred, militant Islamic terrorist groups have no regard or respect for human life let alone the human rights and fundamental freedoms of others. In this light, the overall problem is not the acts of terror but the mindset of those behind the terror attacks. To be sure, the U.N. Charter's rule of law and expression of human rights are viewed as hateful concepts of Western domination and not self-evident truths pointing the way to the betterment of mankind.

Related to the inherent dangerousness of al-Qa'eda-styled terrorist groups, is the fact that States providing support to these people suffer from the scourge of totalitarianism and open hostility to America and the West. This is an important phenomenon not only because terror groups could probably not flourish into sophisticated networks without the overt support of a State, but also because they can use those States to launch catastrophic terror attacks that will far exceed the horrors of September 11, 2001. Essentially, time is not on the side of civilized nations, as renegade regimes will sooner or later provide weapons of mass destruction to the radical disciples of hate. More terrifying is the realization that, unlike the situation in the Cold War, terrorists in the post-9/11 world do not require a sophisticated delivery system. The suicide terrorist bomber is the delivery system. In addition, with the advent of modern technology, the power to wage large scale destruction has now passed from the arena of the nation-state into the realm of the terrorist.

Conversely, a topic covered later in this book argues that democracies do not sponsor or support terrorism, dictatorships do. There exists an abundance of empirical evidence that stable democracies do not engage in international terrorism, instigate war, engage in democide (genocide and mass murder), or abuse the human rights of their people. As Anthony Lake, a Clinton era special assistant to the president for national security affairs, related in an address at John Hopkins University: "Democracies tend not to wage war on each other and they tend not to support terrorism—in fact, they don't. They are more trustworthy in diplomacy and they do a better job of respecting the...human rights of their people." Certainly, in the preamble to the U.N. Charter and in Article 1 of the Charter, it is evident that the drafters also understood that nations who respect human rights and fundamental freedoms are less likely to engage in terrorism. This truth is axiomatic and democracies should be much more critical of totalitarian regimes. In fact, the very structure of the United Nations is flawed as any nation—dictator or democratic—is eligible for membership.

1.10 Questions for Discussion

1. *One man's terrorist is another man's freedom fighter.* "The causes of terrorism or the political motivation of the individual terrorists are relevant to the problem of definition." Under this proposition, many have argued that acts of violence against "colonialism" or in wars of "national liberation" fall outside of the definition of terrorism. Hence, the dilemma of "[o]ne man's terrorism is another man's heroism." *See* John Norton Moore & Robert F. Turner, NATIONAL SECURITY LAW SECOND EDITION, (2006).

2. *International definitions.* U.N. Sec. Coun. Res. 1368 (Sept. 12, 2001). The Security Council resolution uses the word terror or terrorism six times in the short one page document. Like all other United Nations efforts in this area, SC 1368 uses the term terrorism but offers no definition of terrorism other than to affirm that the September 11, 2001, attacks on the United States was a "horrifying terrorist attack." Is it possible for the international community to reach an agreement on the definition of terrorism? What benefit would a totalitarian regime have for agreeing to an international definition for terrorism?

3. *Congressional definitions of terrorism.* The provision of the United States Code referenced in the USA PATRIOT Act, defines international terrorism as "terrorism involving citizens or the territory of more than one country." 22 U.S.C. § 2656f (d)(1). Furthermore, "terrorism" is defined as "premeditated, politically motivated violence perpetrated against noncombatant targets by sub-national groups or clandestine agents." 22 U.S.C. § 2656f(d)(2). Section 411 of the USA PATRIOT Act defines "terrorist activity" at length, as well as what it means to "engage in terrorist activity." 8 U.S.C. § 1182(b)(3)(B). Does the language in the different provisions of the United States Code listed above leave gaps in interpretation? In what way might the provisions be inadequate?

4. *Who is the enemy?* Following the failed August 2006 plot by British Muslims to blow up more than ten jetliners bound for the United States, President Bush said that the foiled plot was a "stark reminder" that "the nation is at war with Islamic fascists." Following the failed bombing of an American aircraft on December 25, 2009, President Obama declared "We are at war against al-Qa'eda." Are these appropriate characterizations of the enemy in the War on Terror?

5. *Hatred in the classroom.* Learning why some come to hate the United States and its allies can be gleaned from what is taught in some Pakistani religious schools. In *PREACHERS OF HATE: ISLAM AND THE WAR ON AMERICA*, Kenneth R. Timmerman writes:

In third grade, children learn hate through vocabulary. "The Zionist enemy — attacked — civilians with its aircraft." (*Our Arabic Language for Third Grade*) In sixth grade, hate became a drill. "Who is the thief who has torn our homeland?" (*Our Arabic Language for Sixth Grade*) By seventh grade, students are expected to have internalized anti-Semitism so they can recite it on their own. "Why do the Jews hate Muslim unity and want to cause division among them?" "Give an example of the evil attempts of the Jews, from events happening today." (*Islamic Education for Seventh Grade*) In ninth grade students are told, "One must beware of Jews, for they are treacherous and disloyal." (*Islamic Education for Ninth Grade*).

What is the best way to combat this dissemination of information? Is it right to do so?

Selected Bibliography

1954 Draft Code of Offenses Against the Peace and Security of Mankind, 9 U.N. GAOR Supp. (no. 9) at 11-12, U.N. Doc. A/2693. 1954.

Albright, Madeleine. THE MIGHTY AND THE ALMIGHTY, 2006.

Bergen, Peter L. THE OSAMA BIN LADEN I KNOW, 2006.

Carr, Caleb. THE LESSONS OF TERROR: A HISTORY OF WARFARE AGAINST CIVILIANS, WHY IT HAS ALWAYS FAILED AND WHY IT WILL FAIL AGAIN, 2002.

Chasey, William C. THE LOCKERBIE COVERUP, 1995.

Cohen, William S. *Preparing for a Grave New World*, WASH. POST, July 26, 1999, at A19.

Combating Terrorism: Threat and Risk Assessments Can Help Prioritize and Target Program Investments, U.S. GAO Report to Congressional Requesters, Apr. 1998.

Gabriel, Mark A. ISLAM AND TERRORISM, 2002.

Ganor, Boaz. THE COUNTER-TERRORISM PUZZLE, 2005.

Gerges, Fawaz A. JOURNEY OF THE JIHADIST, 2006.

Gold, Dore. The RISE OF NUCLEAR IRAN, 2009.

Graham, Bob, et al., WORLD AT RISK, THE REPORT OF THE COMMISSION ON THE PREVENTION OF WMD PROLIFERATION AND TERRORISM, 2008.

Guiora, Amos N. GLOBAL PERSPECTIVES ON COUNTERTERRORISM, 2007.

Hartigan, Richard Shelly. LIEBER'S CODE AND THE LAW OF WAR, 1983.

Lesser, Ian O., Bruce Hoffman, John Arquilla, David Ronfeldt and Michele Zanini. COUNTERING THE NEW TERRORISM. Santa Monica, CA: Rand, 1999, at 17.

Lifton, Robert Jay. DESTROYING THE WORLD TO SAVE IT: AUM SHINRIKYO, APOCALYPTIC VIOLENCE, AND THE NEW GLOBAL TERRORISM, 2000.

Loeb, Vernon. *Anthrax Vial Smuggled In To Make A Point At A Hill Hearing*, WASH. POST, Mar. 4, 1999, at A1.

Michel, Lou, and Dan Herbeck. AMERICAN TERRORIST: TIMOTHY MCVEIGH AND THE TRAGEDY AT OKLAHOMA CITY, 2001.

Moore, John Norton, and Robert F. Turner. NATIONAL SECURITY LAW, SECOND EDITION, 2006.

Nelson, William. *Opening Pandora's Box: The Status of the Diplomatic Bag in International Relations*, 12 FORDHAM INT'L L. J. 494 (1989).

Rollins, John, *Al Qaeda and Affiliates: Historical Perspective, Global Presence, and Implications for U.S. Policy*, Congressional Research Service, R41070, Feb. 5, 2010.

Sun-tzu, THE ART OF WAR, Ralph D. Sawyer trans., 1994.

THE COMPLETE WORKS OF FLAVIUS JOSEPHUS, William Whiston trans., 1981. The Hebrew Zealots conducted random acts of assassination against the occupying Romans in Judea prior to Jerusalem falling to the Roman legions under Titus in 70 A.D.

USA PATRIOT Act of 2001, 115 Stat. 272; Pub. Law 107-56 § 411. Oct. 26, 2001.

Chapter 2

The War on Terror

We are at war. We are at war against Al-Qa'eda.

—Barack H. Obama

The War on Terror began for the United States on September 11, 2001, with coordinated suicide attacks using hijacked domestic airplanes by 19 members of a sophisticated international terrorist network known as al-Qa'eda. The simultaneous attacks occurred in New York, Washington, D.C., and Pennsylvania, incinerating 3,000 people and destroying billions of dollars in property. Prior to this attack, America responded to al-Qa'eda and al-Qa'eda-styled terrorism with traditional domestic criminal law tools rooted in the American Constitution. After 9/11 America determined that it would have to resort to the tools associated with the regulation of international armed conflict or law of war.

The question of how to best neutralize members of the al-Qa'eda terror network and associated forces is the central focus of the War on Terror. Prior to 9/11 the United States dealt with al-Qa'eda members in the same fashion as other radical Islamic terrorists—when individuals were taken into custody the United States used domestic criminal law to punish them for various terror related crimes. After 9/11, the United States added the more robust rule of law associated with the law of war to address al-Qa'eda enemy combatants. It is the application of the provisions of the law of war to al-Qa'eda enemy combatants that is most often challenged as "illegal" by critics.

In essence, the central issue in the War on Terror pivots around the question of whether or not the War on Terror is a real war or simply a metaphor, like the "war on drugs" or the "war on poverty." Simply put, if the War on Terror is a real war, or international armed conflict, then the United States is perfectly at liberty to apply the law of war to kill, capture, or detain enemy combatants (belligerents). For instance, under the law of war the United States has a wide variety of powerful legal tools at its disposal that would otherwise be unavailable. In accordance with the law of war the United States has the right to: (1) kill al-Qa'eda, Taliban, and associated enemy belligerent forces in armed conflict wherever they are found; (2) detain said enemy belligerents indefinitely until the war is over; and (3) try by military commissions certain enemy belligerents that have violated the law of war. On the other hand, if the War on Terror against al-Qa'eda is not a real war, then by taking such actions the United States is most certainly engaging in gross violations of both international and domestic law.

While various ideologues are quick to condemn the actions of the United States in the War on Terror at almost every turn, our representative democracy mandates that the answer to the question can only be found in the official pronouncements emanating from the three branches of government. Of course, the primary dilemma for our government rests in the fact that the law of war was written to address an armed conflict between nation-states, not an armed conflict between a nation-state and a non-state actor such as al-Qa'eda.

As this chapter will demonstrate, all three branches of the United States government have strongly signaled that the United States is acting lawfully in applying the law of war to the conflict with al-Qa'eda and associated forces. From September 11, 2001, when al-Qa'eda foot soldiers killed 3,000 people, President Bush remained unequivocal in his contention that, acting under his authority as the Commander in Chief, the law of war applied. To date, although he has not been as forceful or pronounced as President Bush in his public declarations that the nation is engaged in a real war with al-Qa'eda, President Obama has, by and large, adopted the policies of the Bush Administration by continuing to label enemy combatants, kill them, detain them, and prosecute them in military commissions. In a speech on January 7, 2010, Obama reminded the nation: "We are at war. We are at war against al-Qa'eda, a far-reaching network of violence and hatred that attacked us on 9/11, that killed nearly 3,000 innocent people, and that is plotting to strike us again. And we will do whatever it takes to defeat them." In tandem, the Congress of the United States has not formally "declared war" against al-Qa'eda, but there can be no doubt that it has "authorized" this War on Terror. Among the indicators of this fact are the 2001 Congressional Authorization for the Use of Military Force and the striking "war" language first set out in the 2006 Military Commissions Act and subsequently followed by the 2009 Military Commissions Act.

Finally, the Supreme Court has generally followed suit and continues to allow Congress and the President to conduct this conflict under the law of war with some restrictions. In a nutshell, the Court has clearly signaled that the United States has the legal power to designate enemy combatants and detain them until the war is over, subject to additional safeguards, e.g., habeas rights (if detained at Guantanamo Bay, Cuba), due to the nature of the non-State actor enemy. What makes the Supreme Court cases a source of contention is the fact that they are slowly, and quite painfully, developing a new rule of law that will bridge the gap between traditional law of war concepts and domestic criminal law concepts. Given the new threat of al-Qa'eda-styled mega terrorism, it is perfectly understandable that the new body of law will come in bits and pieces. Thus, the Court has signaled some confusion along the way with opinions that are bitterly divided, and broadly presented. Nevertheless, the judicial phrase that best exemplifies the evolving legal theme was rendered in 2004 in *Hamdi v. Rumsfeld*, where Justice O'Connor "made it clear that a *state of war* is not a blank check for the president [emphasis added]...."

Another problem facing the United States in its characterization of the War on Terror as an international armed conflict comes from the international community. Out of the 192 member nations of the United Nations, the United States is the only nation that uses the law of war against al-Qa'eda. Other nations plagued by radical Islamic terrorism have elected to amend their domestic criminal laws to, for example, detain suspected terrorists for extended periods of time, e.g., 28 days in the United Kingdom, without charging the terror suspect with a crime.

In short, the legal and policy frustrations stem from the fact that the United States is looking at a square block called the law of war and trying to fit it into a round peg called the al-Qa'eda virtual State. Obviously, it would be helpful if the international community would come together to develop a new set of rules to deal with the new phenomenon of al-Qa'eda-styled terrorism. Such is not likely, given the fact that the Untied Nations can't even agree on a definition of the term "terrorism." Nevertheless, al-Qa'eda exhibits many of the attributes of a nation-state; their goal is the goal of a nation at war in contrast to the goal of a criminal organization. Because they hide in the shadows and use the freedoms of open societies to shield themselves, it is imperative that the world community employ the full range of lawful tools to engage and defeat them.

2.1 September 11, 2001

Just as the term "World War II" did not describe who the United States was at war with in 1941-1945, the term War on Terror is a poor description of the current enemy. Terrorism is not an enemy, it is simply a method employed by a specific enemy—a method that intentionally targets innocent civilians. In turn, the War on Terror is not a war against a method, but a war against an identifiable enemy—al-Qa'eda terrorists who murder in the name of militant Islamic rhetoric. To be sure, the War on Terror is not against all militant Islamic groups in the world, but only against those militant Islamic groups that have targeted the United States with open-ended violence. This would include al-Qa'eda and all associated forces who adopt their goal of making "war" on the United States. While President Obama's January 2010 description of the "War Against Al-Qa'eda" is far superior in terms of clarity, the term War on Terror still remains as the most popular for the conflict.

In 1996, Osama bin Laden issued his first declaration that he was at war with the United States. After listing a rambling series of so-called grievances against the "Zionist-Crusaders," he stated:

> The walls of oppression and humiliation cannot be demolished except in a rain of bullets. The freeman does not surrender leadership to infidels and sinners. My Muslim Brothers of the World: Your brothers in Palestine and in the land of the two Holy Places are calling upon your help and asking you to take part in fighting against the enemy—your enemy and their enemy—the Americans and the Israelis.

On May 10, 1997, CNN aired a March 22, 1997, interview with Osama bin Laden by Peter Arnett. Bin Laden stated, "We declared jihad against the U.S. government, because the U.S. government is unjust, criminal and tyrannical." On February 22, 1998, Osama bin Laden and his so-called "World Islamic Front" again declared a religious *fatwa* (a formal statement backed by a religious declaration) urging in the strongest terms that all Muslims should engage in violence against "Jews and Crusaders." Rooting his hatred in his interpretation of Islam, he proclaimed:

> All these crimes and sins committed by the Americans are a clear declaration of war on Allah, his messenger, and Muslims. And *ulema* (clerics) have throughout Islamic history unanimously agreed that the jihad is an individual duty if the enemy destroys Muslim countries. On that basis, and in compliance with Allah's order, we issue the following fatwa to all Muslims: The ruling to kill the Americans and their allies—civilians and military—is an individual duty for every Muslim who can do it in any country in which it is possible to do it, in order to liberate the al-Aqsa Mosque [in Jerusalem] and the holy mosque [in Mecca] from their grip.

Any reasonable doubts as to the involvement of Osama bin Laden's terrorist network in the attacks of September 11, 2001, were dispelled by the December 13, 2001, public release of the so-called "bin Laden videotape." The tape established that bin Laden: (1) knew when the hijackers would strike; (2) knew that the hijackers understood that they were on a "martyrdom operation," but had no details until shortly before the attacks; (3) was pleasantly surprised by the total collapse of the two towers of the World Trade Center in New York; (4) listened with anticipation to radio broadcasts to confirm the terror attacks; and (5) expressed joy and amusement as he detailed the story of the attacks. The most damning segment of the thirty-nine-minute tape occurred when bin Laden stated:

> We calculated in advance the number of casualties from the enemy who would be killed based on the position of the tower. We calculated that the floors that would be hit would be three or four floors. I was the most optimistic of them all. Due to my experience in this field, I was thinking that the fire from the gas in the plane would melt the iron structure of the building and collapse the area where the plane hit and all the floors above it only. This is all that we had hoped for.

Almost a year to the day after the attack of September 11, 2001, the al-Qa'eda terrorist organization released another videotape claiming full credit for the attacks. The video specifically mentioned the World Trade Center attack, the Pentagon attack, and the attempted attack on the United States Capitol.

2.2 An Act of War-The War on Terror

"America is at war." So stated President Bush's letter of introduction to the March 2006, National Security Strategy of the United States of America. The phrase "War on Terror" was first used by President Bush on September 11, 2001, aboard Air Force One. His first major public address the next day also declared the terrorist attacks as "acts of war." In fact, the Bush Administration never departed from the position that the fight against al-Qa'eda and the Taliban constituted a global war. Although the term War on Terror is not descriptive, for the government of the United States the War on Terror is not a metaphor similar to the "war on poverty" or the "war on drugs." With the passage of the first Military Commissions Act of 2006, followed by the Military Commissions Act of 2009, there can be no question that both the executive and the legislative branches of the United States clearly view the War on Terror as real war or, in the vernacular of modern usage, a real international armed conflict between the United States and the Taliban, al-Qa'eda, and associated forces. In turn, as the federal courts continue to rule on various legal aspects of the conflict, it is apparent that they too are willing to accept the fact that the powers used by the United States are more associated with international armed conflict than not.

In a speech delivered in 1984, Ambassador Jeanne J. Kirkpatrick spoke of a coming "terrorist war [against the United States], [that] is part of a total war which sees the whole society as an enemy, and all members of a society as appropriate objects for violent actions." Her words became reality on September 11, 2001, and the world community came to understand terrorism as "an act of war." Viewing al-Qa'eda-styled terrorism as an act of war is a new manifestation of the changing nature of armed conflict. As such, it poses a new challenge for the historically fixed international rules relating to international armed conflict.

Apart from the enormity of the al-Qa'eda attack, what made the events of September 11, 2001, so vastly different from all previous incidents of terror was that the United States and the North Atlantic Treaty Organization (NATO) both specifically characterized the attack as an "armed attack" on the

United States. The unprecedented armed attack determination was significant because it, in turn, immediately signaled that the United States intended to frame the terror attack as an event equivalent to an "act of war" under international law, and not simply a criminal affair to be dealt with by means of traditional law enforcement tools.

Under the law of war, the use of the terms "war" or "act of war" refer to the use of aggressive force against a sovereign State by another State in violation of the United Nations Charter and customary international law. Historically, such illegal acts most often occur without a formal declaration of war; the aggressive act itself triggers the ensuing international armed conflict. Similarly, the term "self-defense" refers to the right of a State to respond with proportionate force to the initial armed attack.

Following September 11, 2001, the United States, NATO, and the U.N. Security Council elected to expand the legal framework concerning the use of force in self-defense to encompass not only any State that had actively participated in the attacks, but any organization or person that was responsible. Accordingly, an authorization for the "use of force" was passed by the United States Congress; the President labeled the attack "an act of war;" NATO invoked its collective self-defense clause, should a NATO member suffer an armed attack; and the U.N. Security Council passed a resolution that employed self-defense terminology associated with those responsible for the attacks. Thus, from its inception, the War on Terror was legally couched by the United States in terms of traditional international law of war terminology, even though the actual attack was carried out, strictly speaking, by a non-State actor.

2.3 The Rule of Law—Use of Force

Understanding the need for international approval for prosecuting the War on Terror under the rule of law, the United States turned to the U.N. Security Council on the day after the attack in hopes of obtaining a strong use of force resolution to address the attacks. The United States received something very close to that in U.N. Security Council Resolution 1368:

> The Security Council,
> Reaffirming the principles and purposes of the Charter of Nations,
> Determined to combat by all means threats to international peace and security caused by terrorist acts,
> *Recognizing the inherent right of the individual or collective self-defense in accordance with the Charter* [emphasis added],
> 1. Unequivocally condemns in the strongest terms the horrifying terrorist attacks which took place on 11 September 2001 in New York, Washington, D.C. and Pennsylvania and regards such acts, like any act of international terrorism, as a threat to international peace and security;...
> 3. Calls on all States to work together urgently to bring to justice the perpetrators, organizers and sponsors of these terrorist attacks and stresses that those responsible for aiding, supporting or harboring the perpetrators, organizers and sponsors of these acts will be held accountable;
> 4. Calls also on the international community to redouble their efforts to prevent and suppress terrorist acts by increased cooperation and full implementation of the relevant international anti-terrorist conventions and Security Council resolutions, in particular resolution 1269 (1999) of 19 October 1999;

5. Expresses its readiness to take all necessary steps to respond to the terrorist attacks of 11 September 2001, and to combat all forms of terrorism, in accordance with its responsibilities under the Charter of Nations;....

Because of the structured magnitude of the terrorist attack, Resolution 1368 specifically recognized America's "inherent right of individual and collective self-defense in accordance with the Charter" and specifically called on "all States to work together urgently to bring to justice the perpetrators, organizers and sponsors of these terrorist attacks." Resolution 1368 further addressed the issue of responsibility for those States who supported or sponsored the terrorist attacks by "stressing that those responsible for aiding, supporting or harboring the perpetrators, organizers and sponsors of these acts will be held accountable." Taken as a whole, it can be argued that Resolution 1368 provided the United States and its allies with the international legal authority necessary to respond to the terrorist attacks through the use of military force in self-defense not only against a State who supported, sponsored, or harbored the terrorists, but also against individual terrorists themselves. The rule of law would be the law of war.

If the mark of a civilized State is measured by how well it follows the rule of law, it is necessary to understand what that term means, particularly in the realm of waging war. The concept "rule of law" was first coined by Western legal scholars in the late sixteenth century. The term was initially used to refer to the common law system of jurisprudence with particular emphasis on equality before the courts. However, the more modern and common meaning is directly associated with all of those rules and legal standards of behavior recognized and practiced between civilized States in the context of the community of nations.

In this setting, one can logically trace the origins of the rule of law back to the 1648 Peace of Westphalia, which concluded the Thirty Years War in Europe. At that time a number of Christian European States officially recognized themselves as being in a community of sovereign nation-states and guided by certain rules of international and social intercourse. The utility of the nation-state concept soon spread throughout Europe, typified by the colonial powers of Europe holding themselves out as the "self-appointed executive committee of the family of nations." With the Treaty of Paris in 1856, non-Christian nations were also admitted and periodic international conferences were held in such cosmopolitan cities as Vienna and Geneva.

In early days, this community of nations was not deemed to be anything other than a loose association bound together by only a few international agreements and the thinnest of diplomatic threads. Although the primary purpose of this association was to promote world peace and to mitigate, when necessary, "the miseries of war," independent sovereignty reigned supreme because the association lacked any legal character or corporate personality. Thus, the rule of law remained a concept with little viability behind it.

After World War I reflected the total impotence of the association to deter those nations bent on aggression, the victorious European nations created the first international organization with legal parameters, the League of Nations. Formed in large part with the direct assistance of President Woodrow Wilson, the much-heralded League of Nations was the first truly international organization specifically directed toward the curtailment of war. As laudable as that goal might be, the League of Nations' efforts to maintain the peace were totally ineffective. In fact, they were actually counterproductive.

First, accepting the false premise that World War I had somehow been caused by a combination of misunderstandings and entangling collective security alliances, the League of Nations naively adopted a series of procedural requirements focused on third-party dispute settlement processes. The framers assumed that wars, like all disputes, could be settled through negotiation and arbitration. This approach is best reflected in Article 12 of the Covenant of the League of Nations:

> The members of the League agree that if there should arise between them any dispute likely to lead to a rupture, they will submit the matter either to arbitration or to inquiry by the council, and they agree in no case to resort to war until three months after the award by the arbitrators or the report of the Council.

Second, the League of Nations concentrated almost solely on disarmament as the best guarantee of world peace. Somehow the founders of the League of Nations believed that there existed a direct correlation between the number of weapons in existence and the probability of armed conflict. In short, they naively believed that the threat of war could be reduced or eliminated if the League of Nations implemented international agreements which called for the destruction of weapons and the reduction of military forces. In the next two decades, disarmament treaties such as the London Naval Conferences (1930) saw England, France and the United States completely emasculate their military while Germany and her allies, Japan and Italy, embarked on a massive buildup of their armies, navies, and air forces.

During this rush to disarm, other international agreements relating to armed conflict were drafted and adopted by the world community, of which the Geneva Conventions of 1929 was the most prominent. The most controversial document that came out of the post-World War I era was the Kellogg-Briand Pact. Signed by almost all of the major world powers, the Pact wishfully prohibited war as the solution to international disputes or as an instrument of national policy.

Although the Kellogg-Briand Pact was viewed by many as an idealistic proscription against war, the abolition of war did not mean that States gave up the inherent right of self-defense; all signatories strongly asserted that the defensive use of military force was absolutely legitimate under the Pact. Paradoxically, the Pact, spawned by a sincere desire to rid mankind of the scourge of war, was actually a dramatic and positive shift in the focus of the rule of law pertaining to war.

The Kellogg-Briand Pact shifted the emphasis from procedural and moral issues related to the legitimacy of war to simply prohibiting all *aggression* under "any circumstances." In effect, a red line of distinction was made between the aggressive use of force, which was always prohibited, and the defensive use of force in response to aggression, which was always lawful. Unfortunately, the Pact did not specifically spell out what it so strongly implied concerning permissive self-defense. The Kellogg-Briand Pact did not devote a single word to the traditional and inherent right of self-defense.

In summation, most of the League of Nations' activities were rooted in the sincere but naive assumption that war was intrinsically irrational and that rational Man could solve his differences simply through negotiation and reason. Incredibly, many nations thought this philosophy of negotiating, coupled with a massive disarming effort, would lead to the abolition of war.

In the first major application of this philosophy of negotiation, Neville Chamberlain, Prime Minister of England, tried to appease the Nazi dictator, Adolf Hitler, by traveling to Munich, Germany, in October of 1938. The resulting Munich Agreement prompted Chamberlain to foolishly remark, "I believe it is peace for our time…peace with honor." Of course, the fruits of appeasement produced the exact opposite. The clear signal given to the aggressor—peace at any price—prompted the Axis powers to launch the most destructive war in the history of mankind. A similar pattern has developed with how some nations have chosen to deal with the forces of Islamic terrorism. Many countries have simply decided that they will not engage in the War on Terror. Prior to the events of September 11, 2001, this attitude was also widely held in the United States.

When World War II ended in 1945, the international community once again sought to create a new methodology to reduce or to eliminate armed international conflict. Just as they had done following World War I, work quickly began on a series of international agreements and instruments designed to accomplish this ideal. Many of the efforts, ranging from the creation of the United Nations in 1945 to the 1949 Geneva Conventions, produced widespread and immediate acceptance throughout the world. In this regard, the civilized world recognized the necessity of anchoring its desire for world peace on ideas that would inhibit both the external and, to a lesser degree, the internal dimensions of State sovereignty. The unfettered power of member States to pursue activities and policies that threatened international peace and security had to be squarely addressed. In addition, great concern was voiced about the acts of States in regard to the treatment of their own citizens.

Since the sovereignty of each State would serve as the basis for the new world organization, internationally recognized legal constraints and attendant enforcement mechanisms had to be placed on those nations that threatened the peace. In leading the effort to create such an organization, the United States held out to the world community the vision of a world order based on four essential human freedoms. These four freedoms were first articulated in President Franklin Roosevelt's major speech before Congress on January 6, 1941: freedom of speech, freedom of religion, freedom from want, and freedom from fear. Echoing these ideals, the victorious powers of World War II formed the United Nations.

With the emergence of the United Nations and the principles of international behavior embodied in the Charter of the United Nations, the deficiencies in the Kellogg-Briand Pact were largely corrected. Prohibiting all forms of armed aggression, the U.N. Charter also specifically recognized a nation-state's inherent right of self-defense if attacked. Today, in the search for a workable model to address conflict management, the U.N. Charter is considered by many to be synonymous with the international rule of law.

As embodied in Articles 2(3) and 2(4) of the U.N. Charter, the maintenance of "international peace and security" is, in fact, the very purpose of the United Nations. Since all members of the United Nations are recognized as sovereign equals, no nation may resort to "threat or [the] use of force against the territorial integrity or political independence of any State" to settle any form of dispute. This, as well as the clear prohibition in Article 1 against any nation committing "acts of aggression or other breaches of the peace," resulted in a workable, legal framework dedicated to curtailing unlawful aggression. It established a concrete legal framework by which behavior could be gauged.

Recognizing that even the most brilliantly crafted legal framework is useless without an enforcement mechanism, the drafters of the U.N. Charter also established an extensive and flexible international framework for responding to those rogue nations which might choose to violate the provisions of the U.N. Charter and engage in unlawful aggression. Chapter VI of the U.N. Charter authorizes the Security Council to investigate any situation that might endanger the maintenance of international peace and security and to make recommendations for the peaceful resolution of such disputes. Chapter VII of the U.N. Charter authorizes the Security Council to determine the existence of a threat, a breach of peace, or act of aggression, and to take appropriate measures in response. Even though Article 43 provides for the mechanism for member nations to make troops available on the call of the Security Council, no such agreements have ever been concluded. Instead, to enforce the peace, the Security Council relies on the forces of member nations, contributed and organized on an ad hoc basis for each situation.

Finally, recognizing the utopian absurdity of outlawing war, but building upon the framework of the Kellogg-Briand Pact, the U.N. Charter does not restrict all uses of force; it only restricts the unlawful use of force: aggression. Thus, the final element in this legal structure, and the one that is of immeasurable value in the real world, rests upon the U.N. Charter's recognition of the lawful use of force to deter unlawful armed aggression.

Explicitly acknowledging the long-standing customary right of self-defense, Article 51 states that "nothing in the present Charter shall impair the inherent right of individual or collective self-defense if an armed attack occurs against a Member of the United Nations...." While there still exists lingering controversy over such matters as to what constitutes an armed attack and the utility of the term inherent, the modern rule of law specifically recognizes the fundamental distinction between unlawful aggression and lawful self-defense. In the overall picture, the rule of law has evolved from a vision of an "ideal aspiration towards universal values of law," to the reality of a world that acknowledges the existence and validity of established legal norms. If a nation operates in accordance with this rule of law, it can rightly claim the legal and moral high ground in any conflict.

In summary, there are four primary provisions of the U.N. Charter under which the use of force is analyzed. The starting point, of course, requires a firm understanding that the U.N. Charter does not outlaw the use of force; it only outlaws the use of *aggressive* force.

First, Articles 2(3) and 2(4) set out the general obligations of member States to settle disputes in a peaceful manner and to refrain from "the threat or use of force." U.N. Charter Article 2(3) requires that, "[a]ll Members shall settle their international disputes by peaceful means in such a manner that international peace and security, and justice are not endangered." U.N. Charter Article 2(4) states, "[a]ll Members shall refrain in their international relations from the threat or use of force against the territorial integrity or political independence of any State, or in any other manner inconsistent with the purposes of the United Nations."

Second, if a State engages in the use of aggressive force, Article 24 of the U.N. Charter actually gives the Security Council the "primary responsibility for the maintenance of international peace and security." Then, Article 27 requires that all permanent members of the U.N. Security Council must agree on enforcement provisions, e.g., the use of armed force. These five permanent members are listed in Article 23 of the U.N. Charter. They are China, France, Russia, Britain, and the United States. Still, even if the Security Council issues an enforcement ruling, there is no standing U.N. military force to enforce it. Historically, the United States has provided the lion's share of military muscle to back up the Security Council.

The third element of the analytical framework is Article 51 of the U.N. Charter, which sets out the codification of the "inherent right of self-defense." The inherent right of self-defense refers to the right of a country to unilaterally engage in acts of self-defense, regardless of what any other nation or organization, to include the United Nations, may or may not do. This is a well-known and ancient component of international law, a concept specifically recognized in U.N. Security Council Resolution 1368.

Article 51 of the U.N. Charter states:

Nothing in the present Charter shall impair the inherent right of individual or collective self-defense if an armed attack occurs against a Member of the United Nations, until the Security Council has taken measures to maintain international peace and security. Measures taken by Members in the exercise of the right of self-defense shall be immediately reported to the Security Council and shall not in any way affect the authority and responsibility of the Security

Council under the present Charter to take at any time such action as it deems necessary in order to maintain or restore international peace and security.

Finally, to complete the analysis, one must determine what is meant by the term "armed attack." In order to clearly define when an unlawful use of force in violation of Articles 2(3) and (4) occurs, international law looks primarily at the non-binding, but often cited, definition of aggression as adopted by resolution of the U.N. General Assembly. A State engages in aggression in the following ways according to U.N. Definition of Aggression, U.N. General Assembly Resolution 3314 (XXIX), Dec. 14, 1975:

Article 1
Aggression is the use of armed force by a State against the sovereignty, territorial integrity, or political independence of another State, or in any manner inconsistent with the Charter of the United Nations....
Article 2
The first use of armed force by a State in contravention of the Charter shall constitute prima facie evidence of an act of aggression....
Article 3
Any of the following acts, regardless of a declaration of war, shall...qualify as an act of aggression:
(a) The invasion or attack by the armed forces of a State...of another State or part thereof;
(b) Bombardment by the armed forces of a State against the territory of another State...
(c) The blockade of the ports or coasts of a State by the armed forces of another State;
(d) An attack by the armed forces of a State on the land, sea, or air forces, or marine and air fleets of another State;
(e) The use of armed forces of one State...in contravention of the conditions provided for in the agreement or any extension of their presence in such territory beyond the termination of the agreement;
(f) The action of a State in allowing its territory, which it has placed at the disposal of another State, to be used by that other State for perpetrating an act of aggression against a third State;
(g) The sending by or on behalf of a State of armed bands, groups, irregulars, or mercenaries, which carry out acts of armed force against another State of such gravity as to amount to the acts listed above, or its substantial involvement therein.

2.4 NATO

NATO, of which the United States is a full member, also viewed the attacks of September 11, 2001, as an "armed attack" under international law. For the first time in its history, NATO invoked its collective self-defense clause under Article 5 of the NATO Charter where "an armed attack on one or more of [its members] shall be considered an attack on all," and that the members may exercise the right of self-defense which includes the "use of armed force, to restore and maintain the security of the North Atlantic area." The real significance of invoking Article 5, of course, rested more in the European recognition that the terrorist attacks were, in fact, tantamount to an armed attack or act of war against the United States, and not just criminal acts of terrorism by a non-State actor.

2.5 Congressional War-Making Power

Congress was also quick to address the attacks in a manner that clearly established the premise that America was engaged in a real "war." Although Congress elected not to exercise its power to "declare war" under Article I, Section 8, of the Constitution (it has enacted eleven formal declarations of war relating to only five different conflicts of the 200+ times that the United States has introduced military forces into hostilities), it did provide the President with an expansive grant of power to conduct war against al-Qa'eda. Congress clearly authorized the Executive to conduct war. From its very title to its content, the Authorization for the Use of Military Force demonstrated the Congressional desire to frame the use of force as a military action. Specifically, Congress authorized the President to use military force, if necessary, to respond to the attacks with "all necessary and appropriate force against those nations, *organizations*, or *persons* he determines [emphasis added]" were associated with the terror attacks of September 11, 2001. In addition, the resolution also authorized the executive to take action to "prevent any future acts of international terrorism against the United States." Since the War on Terror is a global conflict, Congress placed no limit on where the President could use military force or for how long. In fact, nothing prohibits the President from applying the law of war within the continental United States. Finally, by inserting language regarding the satisfaction of the War Powers Resolution, Congress further provided the President with solid authority to introduce America's armed forces into hostilities as he saw fit. Passed only three days after 9/11 in an unprecedented show of unity, this resolution was passed by the Senate (98-0) and the House of Representatives (420-1) by an overwhelming majority, save one member from California.

AUTHORIZATION FOR THE USE OF MILITARY FORCE
Public Law 107-40, 107th Congress
Joint Resolution

To authorize the use of United States Armed Forces against those responsible for the recent attacks launched against the United States. NOTE: Sept. 18, 2001—[S.J. Res. 23]

Whereas, on September 11, 2001, acts of treacherous violence were committed against the United States and its citizens; and

Whereas, such acts render it both necessary and appropriate that the United States exercise its rights to self-defense and to protect United States citizens both at home and abroad; and

Whereas, in light of the threat to the national security and foreign policy of the United States posed by these grave acts of violence; and

Whereas, such acts continue to pose an unusual and extraordinary threat to the national security and foreign policy of the United States; and

Whereas, the President has authority under the Constitution to take action to deter and prevent acts of international terrorism against the United States: Now, therefore, be it Resolved by the Senate and House of Representatives of the United States of America in Congress assembled, NOTE: Authorization for Use of Military Force.

SECTION 1. SHORT TITLE.
This joint resolution may be cited as the "Authorization for Use of Military Force."

SEC. 2. AUTHORIZATION FOR USE OF UNITED STATES ARMED FORCES.

(a) In General.—That the President is authorized to use all necessary and appropriate force against those nations, organizations, or persons he determines planned, authorized, committed, or aided the terrorist attacks that occurred on September 11, 2001, or harbored such organizations or persons, in order to prevent any future acts of international terrorism against the United States by such nations, organizations or persons.

(b) War Powers Resolution Requirements—

(1) Specific statutory authorization—Consistent with section 8(a)(1) of the War Powers Resolution, the Congress declares that this section is intended to constitute specific statutory authorization within the meaning of section 5(b) of the War Powers Resolution.

(2) Applicability of other requirements—Nothing in this resolution supercedes any requirement of the War Powers Resolution.

Approved September 18, 2001.

Perhaps the most vivid recognition by Congress that the United States was using the law of war in a real global war came by way of the Military Commissions Act of 2006, where Congress specifically authorized the establishment of military commissions to try those illegal enemy combatants for war crimes. Understanding that military commissions can only be used in the wake of a lawful war, Congress most certainly understood this war to be a real war. Indeed, Congress spelled out exactly who the enemy combatants were in the 2006 Act:

(i) a person who has engaged in hostilities or who has purposefully and materially supported hostilities against the United States or its co-belligerents who is not a lawful enemy combatant (including a person who is part of the *Taliban, al Qaeda, or associated forces*); or

(ii) a person who, before, on, or after the date of the enactment of the Military Commissions Act of 2006, has been determined to be an unlawful enemy combatant by a Combatant Status Review Tribunal or another competent tribunal established under the authority of the President or the Secretary of Defense [emphasis added].

In 2009, a Democrat-controlled Congress passed the Military Commissions Act of 2009. In that legislation, Congress changed the term "unlawful enemy combatant" to "unprivileged enemy belligerent," but still specifically identified anyone who was a part of al-Qa'eda as the enemy. The 2009 Act states:

The term 'unprivileged enemy belligerent' means an individual (other than a privileged belligerent) who:

(A) has engaged in hostilities against the United States or its coalition partners;

(B) has purposefully and materially supported hostilities against the United States or its coalition partners; or

(C) was a part of al Qaeda at the time of the alleged offense under this chapter.

While Congress continues to pass legislation consistent with the idea that the War on Terror is a real armed conflict against al-Qa'eda, one power that Congress clearly has in war-making is over "the purse." Ultimately, Congress has the power to cut off funding to any protracted use of military forces. As a practical matter, the ongoing military operations in Iraq or Afghanistan could not continue without Congressional approval.

2.6 Presidential War-Making Power

Armed with the Congressional Joint Resolution, U.N. Resolution 1368, and the NATO Resolution, President George W. Bush exercised his authority as the Commander in Chief, under Article II, Section 3, of the Constitution, and quickly set about gathering the necessary evidence to find those who committed the attacks and to establish linkage to the State or States that may have provided material support to the terrorists. President Bush consistently held that the United States was in a state of armed conflict with al-Qa'eda. President Obama has agreed, but not as loudly or consistently.

Even without a Congressional resolution authorizing the use of military force, the President is the Commander in Chief and has independent Constitutional authority to order the military into action. In fact, there is a long history of American presidents utilizing military forces abroad in situations of armed conflict or potential armed conflict to protect United States citizens or promote United States interests. The number of instances where the executive has used military forces abroad without, for example, a Congressional declaration of War, well exceeds 200 in number. Selected instances include: 1798–1800, undeclared naval war with France; 1801–1805, the First Barbary War (Tripoli declared war but not the United States); 1806, Mexico Incursion; 1806–1810, Gulf of Mexico Incursion; 1810, West Florida Incursion; 1812, Amelia Island in Florida; 1813, West Florida; 1813–1814, Marquesas Islands; 1814–1825, Caribbean (engagements between pirates and American war ships in response to over 3,000 pirate attacks on merchantmen between 1815–1823); 1815, Second Barbary War; 1950–1953, Korean War; 1958, Lebanon; 1962, Cuba; 1962, Thailand; 1964, Congo; 1964–1973, Vietnam War; 1965, Dominican Republic; 1980, Iran; 1981, El Salvador; 1982, Lebanon; 1983, Honduras; 1983, Chad; 1983, Grenada; 1986, Libya; 1989, Panama; 1989, Andean Region; 1991, Persian Gulf War; 1993, Bosnia; 1993–1995, Somalia; 1993–1995, Haiti; 1997, Serbia; 2001, Afghanistan; and 2003, Iraq. In fact, the last time Congress "declared" war was in December 1941. In the vast majority of cases, Congress simply authorizes the conflict.

Nevertheless, the President's authority to use the armed forces and the authority of Congress to declare war or to otherwise share in the process of war-making has been the source of much debate over the life of the Republic. Clearly the framers gave each branch of government war-making powers in furtherance of their vision of a government of "checks and balances." This system of checks also ensured a built-in source of friction between the two branches.

The most well known source of contention between Congress and the executive branch is the 1973 War Powers Resolution, enacted over President Richard Nixon's veto. The War Powers Resolution seeks to curtail or limit the power of the executive in the employment of American forces abroad. It requires the President to consult with Congress if American forces are introduced into hostilities or into situations where hostilities are imminent and, after a time set at a maximum of ninety days, either obtain Congressional approval of any continued military action or withdraw. Needless to say, the War Powers Resolution raises serious separation of powers issues under the Constitution which, to date, the United States Supreme Court has not squarely addressed. In any event, no American president from either political party has directly complied with the War Powers Resolution. At most, when presidents have employed United States armed forces in hostile situations or in places where conflict was imminent, Congress has simply been notified in writing "consistent with the War Powers Resolution."

Finally, although the Bush Administration was steadfast in its view that it had the right to use the law of war against al-Qa'eda forces, it sometimes failed to apply this contention across the board. For example, while proclaiming that the law of war allowed the government to try by military commissions those al-Qa'eda members who committed serious crimes in violation of the law of war, the Bush Administration elected to prosecute at least two high-profile al-Qa'eda members in federal district court—Zacarias Moussaoui (the so-called twentieth terror plot member of 9/11) and Richard Reid (the al-Qa'eda shoe bomber). At the very least, these actions sent out some very confusing signals—some al-Qa'eda members went to federal court for trial where they enjoyed the full due process rights associated with criminal defendants while others went to military commissions for trial under less rigid due process protections. If we are in a state of war then by deed and action, the law of war tools must be applied to all al-Qa'eda members. Even though supporters of the Bush Administration point out that these two al-Qa'eda members were never labeled as "enemy combatants" by the President and thus not qualified to go to a military commissions process, the fact that the Bush Administration desired to demonstrate in the short term a "win" by prosecuting Moussaoui and Reid actually did great harm in the long term. In other words, if the government is serious about categorizing the War on Terror as a real war, then domestic politics should play no part in the process. Unfortunately, as set out in Chapter 3, President Obama has likewise demonstrated extremely confusing signals in terms of dealing with issues of detention and prosecution of enemy combatants.

In summary, the battlefield in the War on Terror is the entire globe and the President's inherent Constitutional authority, coupled with the Authorization for Use of Military Force, allows him to make war anywhere, even within the borders of the United States.

2.7 Article III Courts

The War on Terror has created much tension in American society concerning civil liberties. Recognizing that the struggle between civil liberties and increased security faces every democracy in time of conflict, courts have traditionally avoided involvement in national security concerns, leaving the matter to the legislature and executive, which are accountable to the people. Courts realize that bad decisions will become entrenched in the case law of the nation and can serve as a magnet for the development of even more problematic decisions in the future. Nevertheless, because the enemy in the War on Terror falls outside of the traditional definitions associated with armed conflict, not the least being that they are non-State actors, the federal courts have issued a variety of rulings in the years since 2001, the most important ones, of course, coming in 2004, 2006, and 2008 from the United States Supreme Court (all discussed in greater detail in Chapter 4).

In 2004, both critics and supporters of the United States government waited with great anticipation to see whether or not the Supreme Court would insert itself in the conflict. On June 28, 2004, a sometimes badly fractured Supreme Court issued three decisions—*Hamdi v. Rumsfeld*, *Rumsfeld v. Padilla*, and *Rasul v. Bush*. A fair reading of the cases indicate that the Court did not assert a co-equal role in the War on Terror, but rather reminded the other two branches that some due process concerns needed to be better addressed. More importantly, the Court recognized that, as a matter of law, the nation was involved in an armed conflict, or war, with al-Qa'eda and its affiliates.

In *Hamdi*, a plurality opinion (8–1) by Justice O'Connor, the Court acquiesced to the notion that a state of "war" existed and could extend even to U.S. citizens as enemy combatants. In fact, the Court noted that "there is no bar to this Nation's holding one of its own citizens as an enemy combatant." However, the Court remanded the case to give United States citizen Hamdi a "fair opportunity to rebut the Government's factual assertions [that he was an enemy combatant] before a neutral and detached decision maker." In October 2004, without charging him with any crimes, the United States released Hamdi from military detention and sent him back to Saudi Arabia (he denounced his U.S. citizenship). In *Padilla* (5–4), dealing with another U.S. citizen enemy combatant, the Court sidestepped the legal issues and dismissed Padilla's habeas petition without prejudice since, they concluded, he had filed in the wrong federal district court. In *Rasul*, the Court reversed the D.C. Circuit Court in *Al Odah v. United States*, and ruled (6–3) that U.S. courts possessed jurisdiction to consider habeas challenges of suspected al-Qa'eda and Taliban enemy combatants held at Guantanamo Bay, Cuba. The Court found that "aliens held at the base [Guantanamo Bay], no less than American citizens, are entitled to invoke the federal court's authority ... to determine the legality of the Executive's potentially indefinite detention of individuals who claim to be innocent of wrongdoing."

In the much anticipated 2006 decision of *Hamdan v. Rumsfeld*, a deeply divided Court again provided much needed guidance when it ruled that military commissions to try illegal enemy combatants had to be created by Congress, not the President. Seemingly concerned that Congress was not fully addressing the matter of military commissions, *Hamdan* struck down the President's ability to authorize military commissions under his Article II powers. In so doing, the Court also held that Common Article 3 of the Geneva Conventions applied to the detainees because the U.S. was in an "armed conflict." The Court acknowledged that the United States was at war and "that the AUMF [the 2001 Authorization for Use of Military Force] activated the President's war powers...." As covered in Chapter 4, in quick step the United States Congress responded to the *Hamdan* decision by passing the Military Commissions Act of 2006 where it specifically authorized the creation of military commissions to try unlawful enemy combatants with a variety of criminal offenses to include war crimes.

The bitterly divided (5-4 decision with the Chief Justice Roberts joining the minority) 2008 Supreme Court ruling in *Boumediene v. Bush* represents the third set of decisions that the Supreme Court has rendered regarding various issues associated with the War on Terror. In simple terms, *Boumediene* ruled that the detainees held as enemy combatants under the law of war at Guantanamo Bay had the right to contest their status by means of filing a habeas corpus petition to a federal judge. The ruling had nothing to do with the constitutionality of the congressionally mandated military commissions process then underway for those charged with various "war crimes," nor did it strike down the use of the law of war to kill or detain al-Qa'eda.

In summary, a fair understanding of the cases rendered to date by the Supreme Court support the view that the War on Terror is a real war and not a metaphor. Nevertheless, the Court has exhibited the fact that it too is struggling to find the line where traditional criminal law jurisprudence ends and law of war jurisprudence begins. As evidenced in *Boumediene*, this analytical process is further aggravated by ideological differences that exist on the Court. The liberal wing of the Court tends to employ concepts more associated with criminal law jurisprudence while the conservative wing employs traditional law of war factors. Again, in *Hamdi*, Justice O'Connor "made it clear that a *state of war* is not a blank check for the president [emphasis added]." Still, the decisions to date certainly uphold the right of the government to do what it has traditionally done in previous wars—detain indefinitely without criminal charge, enemy combatants outside the regular parameters of the domestic judicial system.

2.8 The Employment of Lawful Violence

In the days immediately following the attacks of September 11, 2001, a conclusive body of evidence pointed directly to the al-Qa'eda terrorist organization as the perpetrators of the attacks, and to Afghanistan's Taliban as the State-supporter of the terrorist al-Qa'eda organization. Determined to respond if necessary under the inherent right of self-defense, the Bush Administration offered the Taliban government a time certain ultimatum to turn over the al-Qa'eda leaders and to shut down all terrorist camps in Afghanistan. President Bush issued the ultimatum in a solemn speech given to a joint session of Congress on September 20, 2001. The pertinent part reads:

> And tonight, the United States of America makes the following demands on the Taliban: Deliver to the United States authorities all the leaders of al-Qa'eda who hide in your land…[c]lose immediately and permanently every terrorist training camp in Afghanistan, and hand over every terrorist, and every person in their support structure, to appropriate authorities. Give the United States full access to terrorist training camps, so we can make sure they are no longer operating. These demands are not open to negotiation or discussion. The Taliban must act, and act immediately. They will hand over the terrorist, or they will suffer their fate.

When the Taliban leadership refused to comply with any aspect of the demand, the United States exercised, in conjunction with NATO and its other allies, the lawful use of military force to accomplish those aims. Numerous nations contributed assistance to the American led effort including Pakistan, Saudi Arabia, Britain, Russia, Germany, Australia, France, Canada, Japan, and so on. In addition, much of the actual ground combat was borne by indigenous Afghan tribal fighters, primarily the so-called Northern Alliance, under the guidance and support of United States Army Special Forces and other United States Special Operations Forces conducting direct action and unconventional warfare missions. The military campaign to dislodge the Taliban and al-Qa'eda took approximately three months, from October 7 to December 23, 2001. Approximately 6,500 air combat missions were flown which attacked over 120 fixed targets. Four hundred vehicles were destroyed and an undetermined number of combatants were killed (some have put the figure as high as 10,000).

In tandem with the removal of the Taliban regime from power, the United States and its allies were able to destroy the al-Qa'eda camps and dismantle much of the infrastructure of the terrorist group in Afghanistan by the end of December 2001. By any account, the Bush strategy of using American air power, American Special Operations Forces, and the ground forces of various Afghan resistance groups worked brilliantly in terms of mitigating the loss of life to American forces and reducing civilian suffering. Early critics of the Bush approach incorrectly predicted that the United States could not achieve victory without the use of massive American ground forces and an attendant heavy loss of life. This same pessimism was seen in exaggerated predictions of American lives that would be lost in the 1991 Gulf War should the United States attempt to expel Iraq from Kuwait in accordance with U.N. Resolution 678.

Since the fall of the Taliban government, al-Qa'eda no longer operates with the open support of a State, but has been forced to revert to clandestine operations primarily as a sub-State terror group. In large part, they have reconstituted in the tribal regions of Western Pakistan. As of early 2011, States throughout the world have arrested or detained well over 8,000 members of the al-Qa'eda network on a variety of terror related charges. The number of terrorists that have been killed is unknown. American drone attacks alone in the last two years have killed over 500 according to the CIA. Of the top 37 al-Qa'eda leaders identified after 9/11, over half have been captured or killed to include Mohammad Atef (killed in Afghanistan), Khalid Shaikh Mohammed (in custody), Abu Zubaydah (in custody), and Ramzi bin al-Shibh (in custody). Bin Laden and his number two confederate Ayman al-Zawahiri still remain at large as of this writing.

When President Obama took office in 2009, there were approximately 34,000 coalition troops on the ground in Afghanistan, with the vast majority coming from the United States. The coalition troops are under the command of NATO's ISAF (International Security Assistance Force) and are drawn from approximately 30 nations. With President Obama's November 2009 decision to increase American forces, over 100,000 troops were on the ground by early 2011. The number of American casualties passed the 1,000 mark in the spring of 2010. The coalition soldiers are assisting in improving security, tracking down al-Qa'eda and Taliban holdouts, and most hopefully, assisting in building a new Afghan army and civilian government. They are supported in the rebuilding effort by tens of thousands of civilian contractors. If the efforts in Afghanistan are successful over the long term, it will be a rare example of a foreign power accomplishing nation building that remained viable into the future. On the other hand, the definition of Obama's "victory" in Afghanistan remains confused, particularly when the main infrastructure of al-Qa'eda is no longer located in Afghanistan. Critics allege that President Obama's "surge" strategy is simply a recipe for a Viet Nam-type disaster where American soldiers are asked to take and hold ground but are never allowed to take the battle to the heart of the enemy—al-Qa'eda in Western Pakistan.

2.9 Questions for Discussion

1. *War or simply a metaphor*? Is the War on Terror a real war or just political rhetoric? Can "war" be made against a group? In *Montoya v. United States* 180 U.S. 261 (1901), the Court considered whether or not a band of Indians that had broken away from the Mescalero Apache Indian reservation in Arizona to commit a series of hostile and murderous acts would activate the Indians Depredation Act, holding the tribe and the United States government liable for civil damages. The Court held that the tribe could not be held liable for the terrorist acts of the group that "was carrying on a war against the Government as an independent organization." Why is determining whether the War on Terror is a real war the central premise from which all legal issues should be viewed?

2. *Does al-Qa'eda qualify as a virtual-State*? The so-called *Al Qa'eda Training Manual,* captured by British authorities in a 2000 raid on the home of Nahihal Wadih Rashie (available at www.fas.org/irp/world/para/aqmanual.pdf) is considered by some to be irrefutable evidence of al-Qa'eda's ability to wage global war.

3. *Realistic expectations.* Is it realistic to expect nations to adhere to international law when pursuing a "war" on terrorists? Article 2(4) of the United Nations Charter states: "All Members shall refrain in their international relations from the threat or use of force against the territorial integrity or political independence of any state, or in any other manner inconsistent with the purposes of the United Nations." What roadblocks exist to international conformity on a use of force doctrine aimed specifically against terrorism?

4. *Congressional resolutions.* Following the attacks of September 11, 2001, Congress authorized the President "to use all necessary and appropriate force against those nations, organizations, or persons he determines planned, authorized, committed, or aided the terrorist attacks that occurred on September 11, 2001, or harbored such organizations or persons." *See* Autho-

rization for Use of Military Force, P.L. 107-40 (Sept. 18, 2001). How does such a resolution conflict with the United Nations Charter, if at all? Does such a resolution violate international law?

5. *American Civil Liberties Union.* If all three branches of the government proclaim that this is a real war, why does the ACLU still criticize the United States as acting illegally?

Selected Bibliography

Cordesman, Anthony H. TRANSNATIONAL THREATS FROM THE MIDDLE EAST: CRYING WOLF OR CRYING HAVOC? 1999.

Fenwick, Charles G. INTERNATIONAL LAW, 1965.

Grotius, Hugo. PROLEGOMENA TO THE LAW OF WAR AND PEACE, 1957.

Guiora, Amos N. FUNDAMENTALS OF COUNTERTERRORISM, 2008.

Kellogg-Briand Pact of Aug. 27, 1928, 2 U.S.B.S. 732 (1930).

Kirkpatrick, Jeanne J. Speech at the Jonathan Institute's Conference on International Terrorism. Washington, D.C. June 25, 1984.

League of Nations Covenant, Treaty of Versailles, 2 U.S.B.S. 43.

Lord Lloyd of Hampstead and M. D. A. Freeman. LLOYD'S INTRODUCTION TO JURISPRUDENCE, 1985.

McNeill, William H. THE PURSUIT OF POWER, 1982.

Petrochilos, George. *The Relevance of the Concepts of War and Armed Conflict to the Law of Neutrality*, 31 VAND. J. TRANSNAT'L L. 575 (1998).

President George W. Bush, State of the Union Address. Jan. 23, 2002.

Chapter 3

Expanding the War on Terror

The United States of America will not permit the world's most dangerous regimes to threaten us with the world's most destructive weapons.

—George W. Bush

The Iraq War, named Operation Iraqi Freedom, began on March 19, 2003, with a coordinated air attack by coalition forces against Iraqi military targets in Baghdad. Forming a "coalition of the willing" made up of like-minded democracies, President Bush acted under his Article II authority as the Commander in Chief and a Congressional use of force resolution passed by a healthy majority of both houses of Congress. Although the war occurred without specific approval for the "use of force" from the United Nations Security Council, the Security Council did pass Resolution 1441 just prior to the Iraq War. Resolution 1441 sternly warned Saddam Hussein's regime of "serious consequences" if Iraq failed to comply with full inspections by United Nations personnel regarding the regime's suspected possession of illegal biological and chemical weapons in violation of U.N. Security Council Resolution 687. Exactly what those "serious consequences" would be was left open, although the United States certainly interpreted the term to include military action.

With the establishment of an elected government headed by prime minister Nuri al-Maliki and the success of the 2006-2008 "surge," the United States and its coalition partners have now withdrawn the vast majority of combat forces from Iraq. Although President Bush declared an end to major combat operations in Iraq in May 2003, Iraq was plagued with extremely high levels of violence prior to the success of the surge. From a foreign policy stance, the United States has attempted to parlay the resounding success it achieved in removing two renegade regimes from power into a deterrence signal to other States who either support or sponsor terrorism. But was the expansion of the War on Terror to Iraq necessary and/or legal? Further, how has the Obama Administration differed, if at all, from the War on Terror policies developed during the Bush era?

3.1 The Bush Doctrine

The possible expansion of the War on Terror from Afghanistan to other targeted regimes was first announced by President Bush in his State of the Union Address on January 29, 2002, when the President cautioned the American people that even though Afghanistan was no longer a supporter of terrorist organizations, the War on Terror was not over. Apart from the fact that the United States would surely use its armed forces against any State that openly harbored al-Qa'eda, the President clearly alerted the nation that he intended to embark on a policy that was certain to expand the War on Terror in a way that might include military action against other States for other emerging threats.

In a bold shift of direction, President Bush signaled that renegade regimes that either possessed or were seeking to acquire weapons of mass destruction posed "a grave and growing danger" to world peace that could no longer be ignored. President Bush specifically labeled those rogue regimes—Saddam Hussein's Iraq, Iran, and North Korea—as an "axis of evil" because of their continuing support and sponsorship of terrorist groups and their desire to acquire, or their possession of, weapons of mass destruction. Bush's key point in the message to the nation was to demonstrate his resolve that the "United States of America will not permit the world's most dangerous regimes to threaten us with the world's most destructive weapons."

In short order, President Bush's remarks led to the formulation of the so-called Bush Doctrine for the preemptive use of armed force against certain rogue nations. In September 2002, the White House issued its National Security Strategy of the United States where it spelled out both the emerging threat posed by al-Qa'eda-styled terrorism and the criteria for the preemptive use of force. The 49-page March 2006 National Security Strategy continued the preemptive theme under a section entitled, Summary of National Security Strategy of 2002:

> The security environment confronting the United States today is radically different from what we have faced before. Yet the first duty of the United States Government remains what it always has been: to protect the American people and American interests. It is an enduring American principle that this duty obligates the government to anticipate and counter threats, using all elements of national power, before the threats can do grave damage. The greater the threat, the greater is the risk of inaction—and the more compelling the case for taking anticipatory action to defend ourselves, even if uncertainty remains as to the time and place of the enemy's attack. There are few greater threats than a terrorist attack with WMD.
>
> To forestall or prevent such hostile acts by our adversaries, the United States will, if necessary, act preemptively in exercising our inherent right of self-defense. The United States will not resort to force in all cases to preempt emerging threats. Our preference is that nonmilitary actions succeed. And no country should ever use preemption as a pretext for aggression.

Within a year of the 2002 National Security Strategy, the application of the Bush Doctrine would see the United States and its allies topple the totalitarian regime of Saddam Hussein and cause the once terrorist State of Libya to abandon its weapons of mass destruction program and embark upon limited democratic reforms. In 2008, Libya settled with the United States all outstanding lawsuits associated with the Libya bombing of Pan Am Flight 103 over Lockerbie, Scotland. This move was certainly a byproduct of the deterrence signal related to the American combat victory over Saddam Hussein in Iraq.

The Bush Doctrine raised much debate—both as a policy matter and as a legal matter. Considering that the use of armed force can only be justified under international law when used in "self-defense," was it lawful for the United States to go beyond the rhetoric and actually carry the War on Terror to those rogue nations identified as supporters and sponsors of terrorist activities, but who had not physically engaged in a specific act of aggression against the United States? Furthermore, even if the United States had legal justification to employ its military force against, for example, Iran, practical matters would have to be carefully considered. At a minimum, the United States would have to certainly demonstrate from the particular circumstances that the use of armed force would not create an even greater danger to international peace and security. Accordingly, in the months leading up to the 2003 war in Iraq, Vice President Cheney repeatedly argued that "[d]eliverable weapons of mass destruction in the hands of a terror network or a murderous dictator, or the two working together, constitutes as grave a threat as can be imagined. The risks of inaction are far greater than the risk of action." Clearly, the two justifications for the Iraq War were the issues of weapons of mass destruction and support for terrorist networks as reflected in the Congressional authorization for the use of force against Iraq, set out herein.

107th CONGRESS
2d Session
H. J. RES. 114
To authorize the use of United States Armed Forces against Iraq.
IN THE HOUSE OF REPRESENTATIVES
October 2, 2002
JOINT RESOLUTION

To authorize the use of United States Armed Forces against Iraq.

Whereas in 1990 in response to Iraq's war of aggression against an illegal occupation of Kuwait, the United States forged a coalition of nations to liberate Kuwait and its people in order to defend the national security of the United States and enforce United Nations Security Council resolutions relating to Iraq;

Whereas after the liberation of Kuwait in 1991, Iraq entered into a United Nations sponsored cease-fire agreement pursuant to which Iraq unequivocally agreed, among other things, to eliminate its nuclear, biological, and chemical weapons programs and the means to deliver and develop them, and to end its support for international terrorism;

Whereas the efforts of international weapons inspectors, United States intelligence agencies, and Iraqi defectors led to the discovery that Iraq had large stockpiles of chemical weapons and a large scale biological weapons program, and that Iraq had an advanced nuclear weapons development program that was much closer to producing a nuclear weapon than intelligence reporting had previously indicated;

Whereas Iraq, in direct and flagrant violation of the cease-fire, attempted to thwart the efforts of weapons inspectors to identify and destroy Iraq's weapons of mass destruction stockpiles and development capabilities, which finally resulted in the withdrawal of inspectors from Iraq on October 31, 1998;

Whereas in Public Law 105-235 (August 14, 1998), Congress concluded that Iraq's continuing weapons of mass destruction programs threatened vital United States interests and international peace and security, declared Iraq to be in 'material and unacceptable breach of its international obligations' and urged the President 'to take appropriate action, in accordance with the Constitution and relevant laws of the United States, to bring Iraq into compliance with its international obligations';

Whereas Iraq both poses a continuing threat to the national security of the United States and international peace and security in the Persian Gulf region and remains in material and unacceptable breach of its international obligations by, among other things, continuing to possess and develop a significant chemical and biological weapons capability, actively seeking a nuclear weapons capability, and supporting and harboring terrorist organizations;

Whereas Iraq persists in violating resolution of the United Nations Security Council by continuing to engage in brutal repression of its civilian population thereby threatening international peace and security in the region, by refusing to release, repatriate, or account for non-Iraqi citizens wrongfully detained by Iraq, including an American serviceman, and by failing to return property wrongfully seized by Iraq from Kuwait;

Whereas the current Iraqi regime has demonstrated its capability and willingness to use weapons of mass destruction against other nations and its own people;

Whereas the current Iraqi regime has demonstrated its continuing hostility toward, and willingness to attack, the United States, including by attempting in 1993 to assassinate former President Bush and by firing on many thousands of occasions on United States and Coalition Armed Forces engaged in enforcing the resolutions of the United Nations Security Council;

Whereas members of al Qaida, an organization bearing responsibility for attacks on the United States, its citizens, and interests, including the attacks that occurred on September 11, 2001, are known to be in Iraq;

Whereas Iraq continues to aid and harbor other international terrorist organizations, including organizations that threaten the lives and safety of United States citizens;

Whereas the attacks on the United States of September 11, 2001, underscored the gravity of the threat posed by the acquisition of weapons of mass destruction by international terrorist organizations;

Whereas Iraq's demonstrated capability and willingness to use weapons of mass destruction, the risk that the current Iraqi regime will either employ those weapons to launch a surprise attack against the United States or its Armed Forces or provide them to international terrorists who would do so, and the extreme magnitude of harm that would result to the United States and its citizens from such an attack, combine to justify action by the United States to defend itself;

Whereas United Nations Security Council Resolution 678 (1990) authorizes the use of all necessary means to enforce United Nations Security Council Resolution 660 (1990) and subsequent relevant resolutions and to compel Iraq to cease certain activities that threaten international peace and security, including the development of weapons of mass destruction and refusal or obstruction of United Nations weapons inspections in violation of United Nations Security Council Resolution 687 (1991), repression of its civilian population in violation of United Nations Security Council Resolution 688 (1991), and threatening its neighbors or United Nations operations in Iraq in violation of United Nations Security Council Resolution 949 (1994);

Whereas in the Authorization for Use of Military Force Against Iraq Resolution (Public Law 102-1), Congress has authorized the President 'to use United States Armed Forces pursuant to United Nations Security Council Resolution 678 (1990) in order to achieve implementation of Security Council Resolution 660, 661, 662, 664, 665, 666, 667, 669, 670, 674, and 677';

Whereas in December 1991, Congress expressed its sense that it 'supports the use of all necessary means to achieve the goals of United Nations Security Council Resolution 687 as being consistent with the Authorization of Use of Military Force Against Iraq Resolution (Public Law 102-1)', that Iraq's repression of its civilian population violates United Nations Security Council Resolution 688 and 'constitutes a continuing threat to the peace, security, and stability of the Persian Gulf region,' and that Congress, 'supports the use of all necessary means to achieve the goals of United Nations Security Council Resolution 688';

Whereas the Iraq Liberation Act of 1998 (Public Law 105-338) expressed the sense of Congress that it should be the policy of the United States to support efforts to remove from power the current Iraqi regime and promote the emergence of a democratic government to replace that regime;

Whereas on September 12, 2002, President Bush committed the United States to 'work with the United Nations Security Council to meet our common challenge' posed by Iraq and to 'work for the necessary resolutions,' while also making clear that 'the Security Council resolutions will be enforced, and the just demands of peace and security will be met, or action will be unavoidable';

Whereas the United States is determined to prosecute the war on terrorism and Iraq's ongoing support for international terrorist groups combined with its development of weapons of mass destruction in direct violation of its obligations under the 1991 cease-fire and other United Nations Security Council resolutions make clear that it is in the national security interests of the United States and in furtherance of the war on terrorism that all relevant United Nations Security Council resolutions be enforced, including through the use of force if necessary;

Whereas Congress has taken steps to pursue vigorously the war on terrorism through the provision of authorities and funding requested by the President to take the necessary actions against international terrorists and terrorist organizations, including those nations, organizations, or persons who planned, authorized, committed, or aided the terrorist attacks that occurred on September 11, 2001, or harbored such persons or organizations;

Whereas the President and Congress are determined to continue to take all appropriate actions against international terrorists and terrorist organizations, including those nations, organizations, or persons who planned, authorized, committed, or aided the terrorist attacks that occurred on September 11, 2001, or harbored such persons or organizations;

Whereas the President has authority under the Constitution to take action in order to deter and prevent acts of international terrorism against the United States, as Congress recognized in the joint resolution on Authorization for Use of Military Force (Public Law 107-40); and

Whereas it is in the national security interests of the United States to restore international peace and security to the Persian Gulf region: Now, therefore, be it

Resolved by the Senate and House of Representatives of the United States of America in Congress assembled,

SECTION 1. SHORT TITLE.
This joint resolution may be cited as the 'Authorization for Use of Military Force Against Iraq Resolution of 2002.'

SEC. 2. SUPPORT FOR UNITED STATES DIPLOMATIC EFFORTS.
The Congress of the United States supports the efforts by the President to—
   (1) strictly enforce through the United Nations Security Council all relevant Security Council resolutions regarding Iraq and encourages him in those efforts; and
   (2) obtain prompt and decisive action by the Security Council to ensure that Iraq abandons its strategy of delay, evasion and noncompliance and promptly and strictly complies with all relevant Security Council resolutions regarding Iraq.

SEC. 3. AUTHORIZATION FOR USE OF UNITED STATES ARMED FORCES.
(a) AUTHORIZATION—The President is authorized to use the Armed Forces of the United States as he determines to be necessary and appropriate in order to—
   (1) defend the national security of the United States against the continuing threat posed by Iraq; and
   (2) enforce all relevant United Nations Security Council resolutions regarding Iraq.
(b) PRESIDENTIAL DETERMINATION—In connection with the exercise of the authority granted in subsection (a) to use force the President shall, prior to such exercise or as soon thereafter as may be feasible, but no later than 48 hours after exercising such authority, make available to the Speaker of the House of Representatives and the President pro tempore of the Senate his determination that—
   (1) reliance by the United States on further diplomatic or other peaceful means alone either (A) will not adequately protect the national security of the United States against the continuing threat posed by Iraq or (B) is not likely to lead to enforcement of all relevant United Nations Security Council resolutions regarding Iraq; and
   (2) acting pursuant to this joint resolution is consistent with the United States and other countries continuing to take the necessary actions against international terrorist and terrorist organizations, including those nations, organizations, or persons who planned, authorized, committed or aided the terrorist attacks that occurred on September 11, 2001.
(c) WAR POWERS RESOLUTION REQUIREMENTS
   (1) SPECIFIC STATUTORY AUTHORIZATION—Consistent with section 8(a)(1) of the War Powers Resolution, the Congress declares that this section is intended to constitute specific statutory authorization within the meaning of section 5(b) of the War Powers Resolution.
   (2) APPLICABILITY OF OTHER REQUIREMENTS—Nothing in this joint resolution supersedes any requirement of the War Powers Resolution.

....

Accompanying the 2003 military defeat of Saddam Hussein's dictatorship in Iraq was a failure to discover significant stocks of weapons of mass destruction and only some evidence of a collaborative relationship with al-Qa'eda (the 9/11 Commission Report found "extensive" and "troubling" contacts between Hussein and al-Qa'eda, but no "collaborative operational relationship"). These two revelations caused much consternation by some about whether the War on Terror should have been expanded to Iraq. Nevertheless, it seems clear that the United States—both the Executive and the Congress—acted appropriately given the basis of the information it had at the time. Indeed, considering the track record of the Hussein regime, the argument that he would acquire (if he did not still have them) and then pass on weapons of mass destruction to terrorists in the post-9/11 world remains convincing. When President Bush provided a final ultimatum to Saddam Hussein to relinquish power and avoid war, his actions were certainly colored by the realities of the post-9/11 environment in light of the following factual information:

- Saddam Hussein aggressively attacked two other nations—Iran and Kuwait—in direct violation of the principles of the Charter of the United Nations.
- Saddam Hussein launched ballistic missiles at Israel and Saudi Arabia—acts of aggressive war.
- Saddam Hussein used poison gas (a weapon of mass destruction) against Kurdish civilians in Iraq and against Iranian soldiers. In addition, Saddam Hussein's regime murdered untold tens of thousands for political purposes.
- Saddam Hussein's final declaration to the Security Council in response to Security Council Resolution 1441 was patently false.
- Saddam Hussein failed to comply with 17 United Nations Security Council resolutions regarding inspection of weapons of mass destruction. On December 16, 1998, in response to Iraq's ejection of all U.N. inspectors, the United States and Britain conducted four days of air strikes with aircraft and cruise missiles against Iraqi targets (Operation Desert Fox).
- In 1998, Congress passed a resolution that President William Clinton signed entitled the "Iraq Liberation Act," indicating that it should be the policy of the United States to support efforts to remove from power the regime of Saddam Hussein and to promote the emergence of a democratic government in Iraq.
- Saddam Hussein continued aggressive military attacks against the United States and Britain after the formal cessation of hostilities in 1991 by firing thousands of times on coalition aircraft patrolling the United Nations imposed "no fly zones" created in accordance with the cease fire of 1991. These attacks on American and British aircraft continued even after U.N. Resolution 1441 was passed and constituted an ongoing state of war under international law. This legal basis was clearly the strongest argument for the use of force by the United States.

While the end to major combat operations in Iraq was declared by President Bush in mid-2003, a new and deadly chapter in the Iraq War quickly took hold—coalition forces and Iraqi civilians were targeted for murder by various groups of guerrilla fighters, common criminals, and terrorists. Even the capture of Saddam Hussein on December 13, 2003, did not significantly stem the growing volume of unconventional warfare. Only the dramatic Bush surge in combat troop strength spearheaded by General David Petraeus in 2007-2008 was able to put a halt to the cycle of violence.

The continued sectarian fighting between Shia and Sunni Muslims, as well as the al-Qa'eda terrorist attacks in Iraq, required the United States to alter its occupation strategy. Instead of reducing the number of troops on the ground in Iraq as hoped for in the occupation phase of the campaign, the United States was obliged to place about 150,000 military and 100,000 civilian personnel in Iraq (the exact number of civilian contractors was unknown, to include large number of security contractors). In turn, because of the associated strain on its active duty military forces, the United States found that it had to utilize a great number of its reserve personnel to maintain the troop strength. With a death toll that exceeds 4,000 American soldiers (slightly less than 1/5 of the casualties are from non-combat related accidents), the Obama Administration is now in the process of disengaging from a stabilized Iraq. Understanding the fact that there is no substitute for military victory, the United States is able to depart victorious. No enemy or critic can advance the false narrative that America lost the war or was driven out of the country. If Iraq falls apart in the coming years, the fault will rest with the Iraqi government and military, not the Americans. The Obama Administration has wisely adopted a reasonable timeline for withdrawal that involves a continued emphasis on training a dependable Iraqi military and police force to better quell the violence that has claimed thousands of Iraqi lives.

In any event, 25 million Iraqi people were liberated from the brutal regime of Saddam Hussein and the new government of Iraq processed him and other top leaders in their criminal justice system for their crimes. Perhaps more importantly, the war in Iraq sent a clear message to other totalitarian regimes that the United States might very well take action to remove those governments supporting and harboring al-Qa'eda-styled terrorists. Governments which had traditionally been sympathetic to radical terror groups in the past certainly took notice of the United States' position. As stated, the most immediate example was seen in the once terrorist State of Libya which took significant steps to destroy its weapons of mass destruction and embark upon limited democratic reforms. In fact, President Bush removed Libya from the State Department's State-sponsor terrorist list.

With the end of the international armed conflict in Iraq, the War on Terror settled down to its more limited meaning, to serve as a description of the ongoing global conflict between the United States and al-Qa'eda. Still, the Bush Doctrine may be revisited in the future and as such merits further discussion. First, the Bush Doctrine clearly departed from the policies of all previous administrations, from Reagan to Clinton, which, when it came to dealing with terrorist attacks on the United States, were content to "swat the mosquito." For example, the terror attacks on the United States embassies in Kenya and Tanzania in August 1998, which resulted in over 250 deaths, prompted only ineffectual cruise missile attacks against suspected al-Qa'eda targets in Afghanistan and Sudan. Limited responses were also taken in regards to the 1996 Khobar Towers barracks attack in Saudi Arabia, which killed nineteen American airmen, and the attack on the *U.S.S. Cole* in 2000, which killed seventeen American naval personnel.

In contrast, the Bush Doctrine was certainly focused on an ambitious campaign to "drain the swamps"—to eliminate those regimes that actively sponsored large scale terrorism. Because of the murderous nature of some branches of militant Islam, the Bush Doctrine declared that it was not enough to look for the needle in the haystack; the haystack must be destroyed. The premise upon which the Bush Doctrine rested involved two disturbing trends which in and of themselves posed a direct challenge to the peace and stability of the world and stood at odds with the central goals of the U.N. Charter to "maintain international peace and security" (Article 1(1)) and to "promot[e] and encourag[e] respect for human rights and for fundamental freedoms for all without distinction as to race, sex, language, or religion" (Article 1(3)). The first aspect related to the radical ideological beliefs of the suicide terrorists and the totalitarian States which either harbor them or, as the Bush Doctrine related, provides "arms to terrorists, giving them the means to match their hatred." The second aspect related to the willingness of these al-Qa'eda-styled terrorists to use weapons of mass destruction in their quest to carry out grandiose schemes to kill multitudes of civilians. Taken together, the mix remains lethal and a clear and present danger to the international peace and security of the United States and the global community.

The Bush Doctrine also embraced the concept of promoting the spread of democracy as the best long-term solution to defeating the terrorists. The 2006 National Security Strategy reaffirmed that "[i]n the long run, winning the war on terror means winning the battle of ideas, for it is ideas that can turn the disenchanted into murderers willing to kill innocent victims."

At its heart, the Bush Doctrine was created due to the threat of a weapon of mass destruction passing into the hands of a terrorist through a radical State such as Iran. The Obama Administration may have discarded the Bush Doctrine, but it must understand this clear and present threat. Judging by its policy with Iran, however, the Obama White House has clearly concentrated on diplomacy and partnership building as the primary means of response, a policy sure to invite disastrous historical consequences.

3.2 Weapons of Mass Murder

In London in 1605, a terror plot was uncovered to use barrels of gunpowder—the weapon of mass destruction of the day—to blow up the English House of Lords and kill King James I. The terrorists were a group of Catholic radicals wishing to eliminate Protestant rule in England. Guy Fawkes, the leader of the plot was convicted and executed. Four hundred years later the United Nation's chief nuclear watchdog, El Baradei, warned that the most imminent threat facing the world is deadly nuclear material falling into the hands of extremists.

The world must wake from its millenary sleep and recognize the real possibility that weapons of mass destruction will be used against large civilian population centers. Clearly, the terror attacks of September 11, 2001, demonstrated that international terrorism has now "broke us across the threshold" of creating mass casualties far in excess of anything Guy Fawkes could have imagined. The al-Qa'eda-styled terrorist is not content to kill in the tens or twenties: he aggressively seeks access to weapons of mass destruction in order to murder in the thousands and tens of thousands. Al-Qa'eda has openly boasted that it seeks nuclear weapons. While nuclear weapons may be beyond the reach of international terrorists at this time, biological weapons, chemical weapons, and "dirty bombs" are not. Biological and chemical agents are inexpensive, easy to obtain, hard to trace, and capable of killing thousands upon thousands. Dirty bombs are devices which use conventional explosives in conjunction with nuclear, chemical, or biological byproducts. In addition, terrorists may strike "live" nuclear facilities as the arrest of the "Toronto 19" terror cell in August 2003 exemplified (reports of the alleged plot by 19 radical Muslim males included crashing a plane into the Seabrook Nuclear Reactor in Massachusetts).

Finally, as terrorists become more sophisticated in the cyber world, they will soon engage in significant cyberterrorism attacks to disrupt entire networks that control vital infrastructure systems. Even now, al-Qa'eda terror cells routinely depend on the Internet for training and tactical support to, for example, provide instructions on how to make a bomb from commercial materials. According to terror expert Gabriel Weimann, the number of terror-related websites has risen from 12 in 1996, to more than 4,500 as of 2005. Militant Islam's goal of global war fits perfectly with the Internet's anonymity and ability to reach millions. The terror groups need not even use fixed Internet sites that can be monitored, since discussion boards and encrypted messages are nearly impossible to break.

Add into the equation the fact that al-Qa'eda terrorists have demonstrated a clear desire to use weapons of mass murder, if possible, and President Bush's call for expanding the War on Terror to any

State that exhibits a willingness to support terror makes fundamental sense. Even without a renegade State to supply them with weapons of mass murder, terrorists can acquire them in the following ways. According to a *Public Agenda Special Report: Terrorism*, there are four general scenarios regarding the terrorist use of nuclear devices: (1) the terrorist makes a crude nuclear bomb using smuggled uranium or fissile material; (2) an unstable nation falls into the hands of terrorists (e.g., Pakistan is said to have dozens of nuclear weapons); (3) a conventional bomb is employed to explode radioactive materials (so-called dirty bomb); or (4) a nuclear power plant is attacked. Accordingly, a doomsday scenario becomes a central consideration of whether or not the War on Terror should be expanded. Researchers at Stanford University have compiled a "database of lost, stolen and misplaced nuclear material depicting a world awash in weapons grade uranium and plutonium that is not publicly accounted for." Again, even one or two dedicated suicide bombers armed with a chemical, biological, or nuclear weapon could inflict catastrophic death and destruction in an urban environment.

The problem, of course, is how does one deal with an ideology steeped in pseudo-religious fanaticism which compels its foot soldiers of terror to gladly commit suicide in order to kill innocent civilians? As discussed in Chapter 1, the phenomenon of martyrdom in the name of God is known as *Istishad* and it represents a chilling development in four aspects:

- Suicide bombings can result in massive casualties and infrastructure damage.
- Suicide bombings attract wide media attention and vividly portray the determination of the suicide bomber to the "cause."
- Because there is no exit strategy for the suicide bomber to save himself, the suicide attack can be executed at the optimum time and place to ensure success.
- Since the suicide bomber is killed in the attack, there is no possibility to interrogate the attacker for information.

If it seems obvious that third party dispute mechanisms will bear no fruit with terrorists who are filled with such hate, one is left with the stark truism voiced by the ancient Romans—*oderint dum metuatant* ("let them hate us as long as they respect us"). In the short term, the United States was not able to reason with either the Taliban regime or Saddam Hussein. Neither of them wished to comply with the principles of peace embodied in the U.N. Charter. Fortunately, America was able to employ the proper application of force under the rule of law to, as President Bush pledged in his first major speech following the September 11, 2001, attack, "bring them to justice or bring justice to them."

In addition, America was extremely fortunate that the War on Terror began prior to al-Qa'eda gaining access to a stockpile of weapons of mass murder. September 11, 2001, could have happened at any time, but at least now the United States has embarked on a worldwide War on Terror without having suffered the devastation of a true weapons of mass destruction event. The use of the military arm of the United States must not be put aside until the States that support al-Qa'eda-styled terrorism have been neutralized and the al-Qa'eda network itself is destroyed.

On the other hand, particularly in Europe where the Muslim population is large (the Muslim population in France is 10 percent; Britain is 3 percent; and America is 1 percent, with seven million Muslims and 2,000 Mosques), the task for law enforcement is to weed out the radical clerics and terrorists without creating a climate of fear and intimidation in the Muslim community. In addition, the 2005 London bombings clearly demonstrate that one cannot simply blame "outsiders" for the attacks. The Muslim terrorists that packed acetone peroxide (the bomb of choice which is known as the Mother of Satan) into four rucksacks and then murdered 52 innocent people on July 7, 2005, were all members of British society. Likewise, the 24 arrests made in the August 2006 London raids that disrupted the bombing of up to ten transatlantic airliners were British Muslims as were the dozen Canadian Muslim terrorists arrested in Canada in 2006 who had about three tons of ammonium nitrate in their possession and planned to behead the prime minister.

3.3 Anticipatory Self-Defense and the Rule of Law

Currently, only the United States has chosen to employ the law of war against al-Qa'eda and associated forces. Other nations have chosen to modify their existing criminal law framework to allow, for example, increased detention periods pending the investigation of a terrorist-related offense. In 2006, the British passed the Terrorism Act of 2006 that allowed for a 28 day detention of a suspected terrorist. In the larger picture, the challenging question for the United States and the entire civilized world is how to legally frame a rule of law that speaks to preventing future attacks by sophisticated virtual-State terrorist groups, particularly in light of their potential use of weapons of mass destruction and the existence of renegade States to support them. If the employment of a weapon of mass murder is on the near horizon, do the current international rules relating to the use of force (i.e., only used in self-defense) actually work in the post-9/11 world? In other words, must a State wait for a catastrophic State-sponsored or State-supported terrorist attack before it can respond, or does a threatened State have the right to engage in anticipatory self-defense, or perhaps even in a controversial legal theory known as "counter proliferation self-help," against a regime or sub-State terror group it believes capable of such acts?

The concept of anticipatory self-defense is also termed alternatively as "preemption self-defense" or "preventative self-defense," and has been used by the Israelis, as illustrated by Israel's preemptive air strike on Arab airfields in the 1967 War and against individual Palestinian terrorists like HAMAS in the ongoing Palestinian conflict.

The United States has long recognized the right of anticipatory self-defense to counter threats to its national security. American scholars regularly cite the famous Caroline Doctrine, which domestically defines the circumstances permitting forcible self-help or self-defense. The Caroline Doctrine grew out of an 1837 raid by Canadian troops to burn a ship harbored in New York. Responding to the Canadian military attack on the ship (which was being used by Canadian rebels) under the concept of self-defense or, more precisely, anticipatory self-defense, the United States Secretary of State, Daniel Webster, penned the Caroline Doctrine. Under the Caroline Doctrine a nation may resort to necessary and proportional acts of self-defense if such acts arise out of an instant and overwhelming necessity, leaving no choice of means and no moment of deliberation.

The problem, of course, is that a State may claim the right of anticipatory self-defense as a pretext for aggression. To weigh the validity of the concept of anticipatory self-defense, international law views the employment of this doctrine in the context of an "imminent" armed attack and most often as a part of the inherent right of self-defense found in Article 51 of the U.N. Charter. Traditionally, the analysis was fairly clear cut; imminent was viewed in terms of the actual mobilization by the aggressor State of its conventional military forces in preparation for an armed attack. In the War on Terror, however, the enemy is not a nation-state and does not rely on conventional forces. Al-Qa'eda-styled suicide terrorists may rely on the use of weapons of mass murder targeted at civilians which, in their hands, may very well satisfy the rule of law requirement of "imminent." Regardless, the use of force in preemption must be reasonably proportionate to the specific danger that is to be averted.

Former United States Deputy Secretary of Defense Paul Wolfowitz was an early and vocal proponent of anticipatory self-defense, speaking with approval for the Israeli military's use of preemptive force in regard to the killing of known Palestinian terrorists and embracing the idea as a necessary instrument of United States policy in the War on Terror. According to Wolfowitz: "Our approach has been to aim at prevention and not merely punishment. We are at war. Self-defense requires prevention and sometimes preemption." The White House's 2002 National Security Strategy of the United States spelled out America's intention to employ the concept of preemption. As noted, this strategy is also known as the Bush Doctrine:

The United States has long maintained the option of preemptive actions to counter a sufficient threat to our national security. The greater the threat, the greater the risk of inaction—and the more compelling the case for taking anticipatory action to defend ourselves, even if uncertainty remains as to the time and place of the enemy's attack. To forestall or prevent such hostile acts by our adversaries, the United States will, if necessary, act preemptively.

The 2002 National Security Strategy (retained in the 2006 National Security Strategy) document spelled out a three-part approach to weigh the use of preemption.

We will always proceed deliberately, weighing the consequences of our actions. To support preemptive options, we will:
- build better, more integrated intelligence capabilities to provide timely, accurate information on threats, wherever they may emerge;
- coordinate closely with allies to form a common assessment of the most dangerous threats; and
- continue to transform our military forces to ensure our ability to conduct rapid and precise operations to achieve decisive results.

The concept of counter proliferation self-help takes the matter of anticipatory self-defense to the next level, although in the 2002 National Security Strategy, the distinction was essentially swallowed under preemption. Counter proliferation self-help is focused specifically on rogue totalitarian States that seek to acquire weapons of mass destruction. The concept argues that when the threat of a totalitarian State or terrorist group using a weapon of mass destruction directly threatens the national survival of another State, a new international legal regimen should allow for the threatened State to engage in, as international law expert Guy Roberts argues, "preventive or preemptive use of force to either deter acquisition plans, eliminate acquisition programs, or destroy illicit weapons of mass destruction sites at any stage in the proliferators acquisition efforts."

The 1981 Israeli air attack on Iraq's Osiraq nuclear reactor is the best illustration of this emerging and much-needed doctrine. Although the international community condemned the Israelis for violating the rule of law regarding the use of force in self-defense, both history and common sense prove their actions were entirely justified. In contrast, the 2008 Israeli air attack on an alleged Syrian proto nuclear facility was greeted by silence from the international community.

Tragically, the totalitarian Iranian regime under Mahmoud Ahmadinejad (the real power is held by the supreme religious leader Ayatollah Ali Khamenei) is now approaching the same level of development for its own nuclear program. Some experts believe that Iran will have nuclear capability by 2012. Not only does Iran support and sponsor terrorist organizations like Hizballah, but the findings of the 9/11 Commission Report amplify the danger of a nuclear Iran, recognizing that Iran provided al-Qa'eda operatives pass-through rights without border stamps. In fact, eight to ten of the 9/11 hijackers passed through Iran between October 2000 and February 2001.

Although Iran continues to act in direct defiance of the U.N. Security Council by refusing to cooperate with the International Atomic Energy Agency (IAEA) and is violating its own treaty obligations, it remains to be seen if free nations will simply do nothing or engage in preemptive force to shut down the Iranian program before Iran either uses the nuclear weapons it is developing or passes them on to terrorists for use against the United States or other free nations. The U.N. Security Council has taken some limited action, but few anticipate that the use of force will ever be authorized. In many respects, Iran represents a greater danger than Saddam Hussein. With Iran's 18 to 30 nuclear-related facilities dispersed around the country, the West may have to focus its efforts on the slim hope that Cold War deterrence strategies will keep Iran at bay.

The Bush argument that the War on Terror had to be enlarged rested on the overwhelming danger to the global community in an era of Islamic militant terrorism and weapons of mass destruction. In the mind of the Bush Administration, the reason that Iraq was targeted for a preemptive military strike was not because Saddam Hussein could not be deterred. It was because Saddam was likely to provide weapons of mass murder to an al-Qa'eda-styled terrorist organization which could not be deterred. Again, the delivery system for a weapon of mass destruction is a terrorist seeking martyrdom. It is hard to argue against the logic that in the post-9/11 world, any rogue nation that exhibits the potential to pass on weapons and support to al-Qa'eda-styled terrorists threatens the world and should be a candidate for swift military action.

Finally, a less-discussed legal basis for military intervention against a rogue nation falls under the evolving legal theory known as humanitarian intervention. For example, although conducted with the specific approval of the United Nations, the December 1992 United States military intervention in Somalia was motivated purely on humanitarian grounds to alleviate human suffering and, even without United Nations sanction, would appear on its face to be a proper exercise of the developing customary legal theory of humanitarian intervention. This theory was also advanced when President Clinton directed a military bombing campaign against Serbia in 1999.

The theory of humanitarian intervention, recognized by many modern international scholars, holds that when the government and infrastructure of a country have disintegrated to the point that its people are being subjected to a widespread pattern of gross human rights violations over a prolonged period of time, another nation may intervene to stop the loss of life and to assist in the restoration of law and order. The caveat to the theory, of course, is that once the loss of life has stopped and law and order have been restored, the intervening force must immediately depart.

3.4 Power versus Words—the Rule of Law

The argument is sometimes made, rather cynically, that what really matters in achieving a particular goal is the possession of the necessary power to influence the desired outcome. Since the overriding goal of the War on Terror is the protection of American interests and the maintenance of global stability through prevention of terrorism and unlawful aggression, the United States should depend upon dispositions of effective power without concern for the rearrangement of authoritative words to color that power. In other words, in weighing the use of force in the War on Terror, some argue that concentration should simply rest on the use of power, downplaying the necessity or impact of words. This approach might be termed a power over words argument, a phenomenon which rests particularly well with totalitarian regimes, but is also periodically raised by members of democratic societies facing peril.

Thus, when Iraq invaded and conquered the sovereign nation of Kuwait in 1990, no amount of words, treaty obligations or diplomacy halted their exercise of total and brutal aggression against the territory, people, and environment of Kuwait. Exercising what is termed the law of the jungle, Iraq simply took what it wanted. The fact that Iraq was a member of the United Nations and bound by the principles relating to dispute settlement through means other than the use of force had no effect whatsoever on its activities. In this regard, the words and ideas contained in the U.N Charter deterred neither Iraq's open and brutal aggression of Kuwait, nor Saddam Hussein's lust for power and territory.

In fact, throughout the entire Gulf crisis, Iraq made no real attempt to conceal, let alone justify, its violations of the U.N. Charter, the Geneva Conventions, or other applicable treaties. In the end, it was only the application of power through the superior military might of the allied coalition headed in chief by the United States which succeeded in halting Iraq's aggression.

Other examples of the apparent disconnect of power *vis-à-vis* words can be found in the arena of human rights. The willingness of many States to eagerly endorse numerous human rights covenants that are never put into practice shows that this cynical model finds some basis in fact. If power is all that ultimately counts, then what use do words have in the real world of dealing with international conflict?

On the other hand, casting the use of power as the dominant factor in the use of force captures only a portion of the issue at hand. While it is true that words without corresponding force have little effect in the deterrence of unlawful activities, such a model incorrectly dismisses the positive role of words in the process. Of course, aggression can never be halted by words alone, no matter how much those words reflect accepted norms. However, the deficiency of this reasoning ultimately rests on misunderstanding the critical role which universally defined norms play in the process of deterrence. Clearly defined norms actually provide stimulus and sinew for subsequent action. Such norms are the very building blocks necessary for a democracy to generate the homefront support to defeat unlawful activities by the use of force.

If words are the basis for viable action, words must impart unambiguous understanding. A basic tenet of providing instruction is simplicity, appropriately known in the vernacular of the military as KISS (keep it simple stupid). To be efficacious to a wide audience, concepts should be kept as simple as possible. Additionally, since each discipline of study has its own unique system of terminology, effective communication mandates that the more complex the body of material to be learned, the greater one must rely on shorter concepts which take the place of longer chains of thought. Hence, although the proper designation for the War on Terror should be the "War Against Taliban, al-Qa'eda, and Associated Forces," that concept is far too long to be effective.

Along with simplicity, concepts must be thoroughly inculcated to be retained. Repetition is also key to all learning; it alone can ensure comprehension and, hence, meaningful communication. Thus, the more complex the body of learning, the greater the need for repetition.

In the War on Terror the Bush Administration made mistakes, but it actually demonstrated a high level of sophistication concerning the need to couch actions in simple, yet meaningful terminology. And, more importantly, the terminology employed was largely cemented in the rule of law as it pertained to the use of force.

One of the lessons contemporary science has taught us about human behavior is that it helps in creating the conditions necessary for the achievement of a goal to have the goal more sharply delineated. The clarification in detail of distinctions between lawful and unlawful coercion will not, of course, by itself establish all the necessary conditions for restraint of unlawful coercion. Nevertheless, it may perform the very necessary task of outlining the major contours of the effects sought in terms of which alternative choices in the rearrangement of effective power and in the adoption of new modalities in practice that must be appraised.

As previously outlined, when President Bush formed the allied coalition against the Taliban, he firmly rooted the campaign in the norms of the U.N. Charter and under the domestic law of the United States. The subsequent force applied by the United States and its allies had the full backing of a universally recognized set of lawful standards contained in Article 51 of the U.N. Charter. Similarly, the primary Security Council resolution dealing with the attack on America was based upon the lawful authority of the U.N. Charter. Conversely, the Taliban regime had no legal basis in which to frame its aggression and, apart from a few non-democratic States, almost no supporters within the community of nations.

As the decade worth of U.N. Security Council resolutions over weapons inspections in Iraq also demonstrated, words issued without the necessary power to enforce them are almost as counterproductive as power applied without the framework of words. Unfortunately, the same pattern of behavior is unfolding in the context of Iran's nuclear ambitions. Still, to emphasize power in the power-versus-words analysis fails completely in the long run because words are the very basis for establishing acceptable norms of agreed behavior which, in turn, distinguish lawful actions from those that are unlawful.

Furthermore, most of the world can quickly grasp the idea of following the democratically based rule of law in halting an aggressor who has broken the law, or who threatens the employment of weapons of mass murder. In this light, America is only defending itself against rogue nations; *they* have been at war with the United States for a long time.

The rule of law has its problems, but those problems are more in the context of application rather than definition; the meaning is simply framed, the application is not. In its strict meaning, the rule of law has immediate association. The meaning of the rule of law will always refer to that body of well-recognized principles of international law accepted by democratic nations, the most critical being in the context of the use of force. It is safe to say, in terms of international behavior, that the phrase rule of law will always bring to mind the illegality of the use of aggressive force. The struggle is not so much in meaning, it is whether the rule of law will prevail as the means of justification in a given situation.

If respect for the rule of law is to survive as the measure of civilized behavior, it does not contribute to the discussion to advocate the use of force apart from legal parameters. At a minimum, the United States must abide by the international principles as they now exist. While it is certainly prudent to sternly warn States that support or sponsor terrorism that they will be held absolutely accountable for any acts of aggression, anticipatory self-defense can only be used if the United States reasonably makes the case to the nation that a significant attack by terrorists using weapons of mass murder is imminent.

Thus, even if the attacks of September 11, 2001, are considered an act of war by al-Qa'eda and the Taliban, the United States cannot unilaterally expand the War on Terror to nations not directly linked to 9/11, unless it articulates a credible self-defense argument. As noted previously, in considering whether the war should have been expanded to Saddam's Iraq, for example, there was at least evidence that Iraq had plans to develop weapons of mass destruction in violation of U.N. Security Council resolutions as well as a disposition to support international terrorism. Both Congress and the Bush Administration presented their case to the American people and the rest of the civilized world. Under domestic American law, the war was legal; both Congress and the Executive approved. While one can argue that the intelligence part was terribly flawed, the war was certainly not based on a "lie" in light of the applicable U.N. resolutions and the history of the Iraqi regime for duplicity. On the contrary, the U.N. Security Council has never condemned the United States for the war in Iraq (as a practical matter the United States would simply veto any such resolution), but it has passed resolutions supporting the reconstruction of the country under the U.S. led coalition. Interestingly, despite the fact that the U.N. did not pass a use of force resolution, the United Nations Security Council voted unanimously (14–0) in May of 2003 to grant the United States and the United Kingdom effective legal control over all aspects of the Iraqi economy and political process pending the creation of an internationally recognized interim government. This action was tantamount to recognizing that the use of force against Saddam Hussein was acceptable to the international community. Similarly, in June 2004, the Security Council again voted unanimously (14–0) to fully recognize the legitimacy of the interim Iraqi government which took power on June 28, 2004.

Historically, the United Nations has only authorized armed force on two occasions; both instances related to stopping clearly defined acts of aggression. In a stunning show of world solidarity immediately following the Cold War era, President George H. Bush was able to obtain a clear "use of force" resolution from the U.N. Security Council prior to using lawful violence to expel the 1990 illegal Iraqi invasion and occupation of Kuwait. Resolution 678 reads in relevant part:

> The Security Council…
> Authorizes member States cooperating with the government of Kuwait, unless Iraq on or before January 15, 1991 fully implements…the foregoing Resolutions, to use all necessary means to uphold and implement the Security Council Resolution 660 and all subsequent relevant Resolutions and to restore international peace and security in the area.…

The only parallel to the Security Council's authorization for the use of force in the 1991 Gulf War was in the Korean War. On July 7, 1950, responding to North Korea's armed aggression into South Korea, the Security Council authorized the creation of a unified command under the authority of the United States. The resolution was passed, however, only due to the temporary absence of the Soviet Union's ambassador.

Considering the new threats which the War on Terror presents in terms of rogue terrorist States and large militant al-Qa'eda-styled terrorist organizations, American policy makers can and must develop an active global-based strategy designed to deter and defeat future terror attacks both in areas where American forces are located overseas and on the homeland. At a minimum this means new thinking in four areas.

First, the United Nations must be energized to immediately address the issue of reaching a consensus on a universal definition for terrorism. This effort should also include language regarding when a particular act of terrorism may be considered as an act of war. If this is not achieved the United States must denounce the United Nations for its impotence and press forward with the creation of a new international organization made up of like-minded democracies.

Second, the United States must insist that the concept of counter proliferation self-help be placed on the table as a viable addition to the international rule of law regarding the use of force against a radical State seeking access to weapons of mass destruction. Most certainly, the United States will do well to obtain the direct assistance and input of the major powers, particularly the Russians. In fact, the Russians have suffered devastating terror attacks at the hands of radical Islam to include the black year of 2004 where two metros were bombed, two commercial aircraft blown out of the sky, and school children in Beslan were slaughtered. In 2010, two separate metro attacks killed over 40 people. The Russians are ripe for engagement.

Third, juxtaposed to pressing the international community for concrete definitions and new legal approaches on how to fight terrorism in the post-9/11 world, the United States should continue to earnestly endorse the spread of democratic values as the absolute best avenue to promote terrorism avoidance over the long term. Democracy is not an American value; democracy and human rights are normative world values. Unfortunately, the world community has not made assistance to the new Afghan government to build roads, schools, factories, homes, and so forth, contingent on its movement towards the adoption of democratic values; more must be done in this region of the world. When the Afghan government is able to sentence a person to death, as it did in 2007, for converting from Islam to Christianity, there is no reason to hope that the concepts of freedom will soon take hold. At the end of the day, the totalitarian ponds that foster terrorism must be drained. The goal is extremely ambitious, particularly with the reemergence of the Taliban and al-Qa'eda in Afghanistan, but the cost of inaction is too great. As long as there is a reasonable chance for some level of measured success, the United States cannot precipitously pull out of Afghanistan. With President Obama's 2010 increase of American military forces in Afghanistan to 100,000 coalition forces, the stakes could not be greater. Again, as the U.S. pulls its remaining forces out of a stabilized Iraq, none can claim that America was driven out or defeated. Taking effect on September 1, 2010, the military operation name changed from Operation Iraqi Freedom to Operation New Dawn. Unfortunately, the same may not be true in Afghanistan, which will surely descend into an orgy of bloodshed once America departs. More importantly, the perceived "defeat" of the United States will be a narrative that will resonate with our enemies and advance the cause of radical Islamic terror ten-fold. President Obama has raised the stakes in Afghanistan and America must be perceived as victorious.

Finally, whatever the future may hold, the United States must continue to reinforce the basic truism that a democracy never answers terror with terror in the context of the employment of military force in self-defense. The United States is absolutely obligated under international law to follow the law of war as well as all applicable international and customary laws. By all level headed assessments, the American military has done an outstanding job in the combat activities in Afghanistan and Iraq in abiding by the law of armed conflict, while caring for basic humanitarian needs of civilians caught up in the conflict. As the world's leading democracy, it is imperative that the United States continues to exercise the lawful use of military force in accordance with the letter and spirit of the rule of law or face the possibility that it will be battling the children of hate and terrorism in the next generation.

The twenty-first century is still young, but it does not appear that the road to promoting human rights and democracy in the Islamic world will be an easy task. Accordingly, deterrence must always stand as the central pillar of national security. In turn, understanding that totalitarian regimes will respond to the rattle of the saber means that the United States must always maintain a saber that can be rattled, and used, if necessary.

3.5 The Obama Approach to the War on Terror

When Senator Barack Obama ran for President of the United States in the 2008 election against Senator John McCain, his major campaign slogan was based on a cry for "change." Of course, even the novice student of political science knows that the promise of change crops up during practically every presidential campaign in American history and then quickly fades into oblivion once the winner takes office. In short, there really has been no significant changes from the Bush policies to the Obama policies. Indeed, in terms of dealing with the threat of militant Islam posed by al-Qa'eda, the Taliban, and associated forces, there can be little question that during his presidency, Obama actually retained many key

Bush Administration policies. Although his efforts in the beginning to portray his ideas as somehow different played well with the mainstream media headlines of the day, Obama was largely ineffective in setting a clear departure from the policies of the Bush Administration. If anything, Obama sowed more confusion than Bush. For instance, President Obama's promised change to provide a so-called "new and comprehensive strategy for Afghanistan and Pakistan" to address the threat of militant Islam took over ten months to hatch and resulted in the adoption of a Bush-styled "surge" (used in the Iraq War) to simply deploy an additional 40,000 troops on the ground in Afghanistan. His campaign-era thoughts to send American troops to Western Pakistan where the main al-Qa'eda structure has reconstituted never materialized. Instead, President Obama sought a stabilized Afghanistan.

President Obama's expressed desire to dismantle key elements of the Bush policies *vis-à-vis* al-Qa'eda, the Taliban, and associated forces began only days after taking the oath of office. Instead of creating an interagency task force to conduct a detailed study of all viable options and recommendations on how best to proceed in the War on Terror, the President issued haphazard executive orders mandating what were billed as sweeping changes in policy, and then established an interagency task force to study the consequences of his directives. In three executive orders (EO) issued on January 22, 2009, the President ordered: (1) EO 13492, the closure of Guantanamo Bay within one year; (2) EO 13492, the immediate halt of all ongoing military commissions (even though Congress had specifically authorized them); and (3) EO 13440, the suspension of the CIA's enhanced interrogation program. Ironically, within one year of the announcement, the first and second executive orders would be, for all practical purposes, functionally nullified and the third a non-event.

Next, wishing to establish a new theme to describe the conflict with al-Qa'eda, the Taliban, and associated forces, President Obama took direct aim at the phrase most associated with President Bush's overall framework for dealing with the threat of al-Qa'eda-styled terrorism—the War on Terror. In quick step, Secretary of Homeland Security Janet Napolitano confirmed that the term War on Terror was not to be used because it "does not describe properly the nature of the terrorist threat to the US." The new phrase offered by the Obama Administration to describe the threat of al-Qa'eda transnational terrorism was the decidedly sterile "Overseas Contingency Operations."

Taken from the dictionary of military terminology, 10 U.S.C. §101 describes the phrase as follows:

> The term "contingency operation" means a military operation that—
> (A) is designated by the Secretary of Defense as an operation in which members of the armed forces are or may become involved in military actions, operations, or hostilities against an enemy of the United States or against an opposing military force; or
> (B) results in the call or order to, retention on, active duty of members of the uniformed services...during a war or during a national emergency declared by the President or Congress.

Overseas contingency operations were once called military operations other than war (MOOTW), and can encompass a wide range of actions to include: arms control, combating terrorism, Department of Defense support to counterdrug operations, enforcement of sanctions and maritime intercept operations, enforcement of exclusion zones, ensuring freedom of navigation and overflight, humanitarian assistance, military support to civilian authorities, nation assistance and support to counterinsurgencies, noncombat evacuation operations, peace operations, protection of shipping operations, recovery operations, show of force operations, strikes and raids, and support to insurgencies.

If Bush's War on Terror was considered to be non-descriptive by critics, Obama's Overseas Contingency Operations was both over-descriptive and non-descriptive at the same time. Predictably, the shelf life of the phrase Overseas Contingency Operations was measured in days and provided a lightning rod for those who believed that Obama was naive or disoriented to the reality of the threat posed by al-Qa'eda. More importantly, however, the phrase was an abject rule of law failure because it did not include the word "war," the most critical element of all. Indeed, the very rule of law tools that the Obama Administration uses—the use of deadly force by the military in combat (to include "drone" air strikes in Somalia, Yemen, Afghanistan, Pakistan, and Sudan), the labeling of enemy combatants, the detention of said combatants without criminal charges, etc.—can only be conducted in a time of war. As such, Secretary of Homeland Security Janet Napolitano's 2009 remarks that the phrase War on Terror was abandoned because "[i]n some respects 'war' is too limiting" were grossly inaccurate. Without question, the use of the law of war expands, not restricts, the available legal powers necessary to deal with al-Qa'eda terrorism.

Historically, all labels for all wars that America has fought have included the word "war." This is a fundamental ingredient that provides the clearest signal that the nation is using the law of war and not operating outside the rule of law. In addition, from a public relations standpoint, Obama signaled added consternation to the American people: parents are more likely to understand that their son died in a war, rather than in an overseas contingency operation. It was not until January 7, 2010, that President Obama pronounced a truly unequivocal statement that the U.S. was at "[W]ar against al-Qa'eda." Paradoxically, this statement was made only after the intense criticism of the Obama Administration following the arrest of al-Qa'eda member Umar Farouk Abdulmutallab for trying to detonate an explosive device on a U.S. aircraft over Detroit on Christmas Day 2009.

Over 800 detainees have resided at one time or another at Guantanamo Bay, coming from approximately 40 countries, with Saudi Arabia, Afghanistan, and Yemen the most represented. When President Bush left office in January 2009, less than 250 detainees remained. The individuals held there during President Obama's tenure were detained under the same legal theory used by President Bush: under the law of war they were detained as enemy combatants until either hostilities ceased or specific charges were levied against them in a military commission or, if they were U.S. citizens (like al-Qa'eda member Jose Padilla), in a federal court.

Strangely, while President Obama was unwilling for most of his first year in office to publicly and unequivocally call the conflict with al-Qa'eda a "war," his Administration early on vigorously argued before the federal district court in *Al Maqaleh v. Gates* that the conflict was in fact a war and that the Executive branch was entitled to detain indefinitely al-Qa'eda, Taliban, and associated enemy forces in Bagram Air Force Base, Afghanistan, under the 2001 Congressional Authorization for Use of Military Force.

Returning to his 2009 executive orders, President Obama's desire to close the detention facility at Guantanamo Bay within a year never happened. In part, Obama's desire to close the facility met with a firestorm of opposition from the American people, even from his own Democrat Party. Not only did the Democrat-controlled Congress refuse to provide the Obama Administration with the $80 million it requested to close the facility, but Congress also placed numerous caveats on when, where, and how the President could transfer detainees, particularly if he wished to send them to the United States.

On June 8, 2009, President Obama first indicated that he intended to reverse course from his January 2009 executive order halting military commissions and would restart the process for alleged al-Qa'eda enemy combatant war criminals. The first case tried was Ibrahim al Qosi convicted in August

2010 by military commission. Still, President Obama was quick to repeat and actually advance the Bush Administration's confusion regarding the appropriate judicial forum to prosecute al-Qa'eda enemy combatants for their crimes. Obama first did this by directing the June 2009 transfer from Guantanamo Bay of al-Qa'eda enemy combatant Ahmed Ghailani to New York federal district court to face murder charges for his role in al-Qa'eda terrorist bombings in Africa in 1998. Then, in November 2009, the Obama Administration made the strange decision to prosecute Khalid Sheikh Mohammed and four other senior al-Qa'eda leaders in federal court in New York City. While President Bush could somewhat mask his confused decision about applying the proper rule of law to enemy combatants by asserting that the al-Qa'eda members that he sent to federal district court—Zacarias Moussaoui and Richard Reid—had not been formally labeled as enemy combatants, President Obama could not. All five of the al-Qa'eda members slated for trial in New York had been detained for years as enemy combatants. In addition, to make matters even more confused, the announcement by the Obama Administration which disclosed that five enemy combatant (now termed "unprivileged enemy belligerent" by some members of the Obama Administration) al-Qa'eda members—including Khalid Sheikh Mohammed—would be tried in federal district court, came in tandem with the announcement that another five enemy combatant al-Qa'eda members held at Guantanamo Bay would be tried by military commissions.

President Obama also made great fanfare of his January 2009 executive order halting CIA interrogations. However, the CIA's high value al-Qa'eda detainees had long since been released and President Bush's 2007 EO 13440 had already halted interrogation techniques that violated Common Article 3 of the Geneva Conventions. President Obama's order was not a departure from the policy that was already in effect; DOD rules applied to all interrogations. The greatest impact of Obama's order was to strongly reinforce the requirement that DOD standards apply to all government agencies, no exceptions.

In reality, the most perplexing interrogation issue aired by the Obama Administration revolved around the waterboarding of three senior al-Qa'eda members in CIA custody under the first term of the Bush Administration. President Obama publicly asserted that waterboarding was torture but then refused to take any criminal action against those who authorized or carried out the technique. As discussed in Chapter 6, Obama placed his Administration and himself in violation of international law because he was required under Article 7 of the Torture Convention to either extradite the alleged torturer or "submit the case to…competent authorities for the purpose of prosecution." He refused to do either.

While other radical Islamic terrorists must be processed by domestic criminal law, the War on Terror is a real war against al-Qa'eda, the Taliban, and associated forces. It is imperative that President Obama, as the Commander in Chief, communicate this fact with clarity to the American people and the world. Only then will he be able to provide clear and decisive leadership by matching the correct rule of law words with the proper deeds. Acting in accordance with the new discipline of "lawfare," legal clarity mandates that the President voice fewer platitudes about "change," particularly given the fact that, like all wars, it is not solely a matter of putting "steel on target," i.e., killing the enemy; it is a propaganda effort as well.

Unfortunately, President Obama's Administration is rubricated by confusion and frustration in a desire to somehow change Bush Administration policies. For instance, the Obama Administration's refusal to irrevocably and sternly tell the public that the conflict with al-Qa'eda terrorist forces is a "war," contrasts sharply with his simultaneous argument in various federal courts that al-Qa'eda fighters are in fact illegal enemy combatants subject to the law of war. This lack of clarity only provides fuel for

America's enemies to perpetuate the false propaganda that the United States is acting illegally by, for example, detaining people without trial in Guantanamo Bay.

Leadership skills rooted in the panacea of dialogue and a "see where it takes us" approach in terms of national security are disastrous when confronting totalitarian fanatics. If the events of 9/11 have taught Americans anything, it is that the United States must operate under the law of war against those individual al-Qa'eda Islamic terrorists designated as enemy combatants. President Obama must put aside political partisanship and forcefully acknowledge the manifest fact that America is at war, and then institutionalize comprehensive policies that are fully rooted in the context of the law of war, not domestic criminal law. Many of these law of war foundational policies—detaining enemy combatants, military commissions, interrogation—were developed during the Bush years and require only slight refinement, not change. Congress has provided some leadership with the passage of the 2009 Military Commissions Act, but the Executive branch must assert greater leadership. If this means that President Obama must acknowledge successes in the previous Administration, then so be it. The nation is at war, the Commander in Chief must lead in accordance with that premise.

3.6 Questions for Discussion

1. *Roots of militant Islamic aggression.* The 9/11 Commission convened by Congress tried to explain the root of militant Islamic thought:

   They (Bin Laden and al Qaeda) say that America had attacked Islam; America is responsible for all conflicts involving Muslims. Thus Americans are blamed when Israelis fight with Palestinians, when Russians fight with Chechens, when Indians fight with Kashmiri Muslims, and when the Philippine government fights ethnic Muslims in its southern islands. America is also held responsible for the governments of Muslim countries, derided by al Qaeda as "your agents." Bin Laden has stated flatly, "Our fight against these governments is not separate from our fight against you." These charges found a ready audience among millions of Arabs and Muslims angry at the United States because of issues ranging from Iraq to Palestine to America's support for their countries' repressive rulers.

   How does the Obama approach to the War on Terror help or hinder victory? If the hatred is as pervasive as the 9/11 Commission found, are there any viable alternatives to the use of force?

2. *Preemptive self-defense.* Preemptive use of military force was a central tenet of the Bush Doctrine. Preemptive use of force is designed to prevent enemy attacks by attacking the enemy before they have a chance to strike. Do preemptive measures inherently violate international law? What if the attack is made against a sub-State terror group without the permission of the host nation? Could President Obama use this doctrine to attack Iran?

3. *Will cold-war deterrence work against al-Qa'eda?* *See* David Rising, *Iraq Terror Boss Seeks Nuke Experts*, SAN ANTONIO EXPRESS NEWS, Sept. 29, 2006, at A1 (Before his death in 2010, Al-Qa'eda's chief in Iraq, Abu Ayyub al-Masri, called for nuclear scientists to join his group's holy war against the West).

Selected Bibliography

Addicott, Jeffrey F. *U.S. Must Follow the Law of War or Battle Enemy's Children*, BIRMINGHAM NEWS, Oct. 28, 2001, at C5.

Lake, Anthony. Special Assistant to the President for National Security Affairs, Address to Johns Hopkins University, School of Advanced International Studies. Oct. 21, 1993.

Lesser, Ian O., et al. COUNTERING THE NEW TERRORISM, 1999.

Lillich, Richard. HUMANITARIAN INTERVENTION AND THE UNITED NATIONS, 1973.

Living with Faith and Hope After September 11, U.S. Conference of Catholic Bishops, Dec. 2001. Pub. No. 5-491 USCCB Pub. Wash. D.C.

McDougal, Myers S., and Florentino P. Feliciano. LAW AND MINIMUM WORLD PUBLIC ORDER, 1961.

McHugh, William. *Forcible Self-help in International Law*, NAVAL WAR COLLEGE REVIEW, No. 25 (1972).

National Defense Authorization Act for Fiscal Year 2010, Pug. L. No. 111-84, 12 Stat. 2190.

President George W. Bush, State of the Union Address. January 29, 2002.

Quinn, Andrew. *Loss of Nuclear Material Tabulated*, SAN JOSE MERCURY NEWS, Mar. 7, 2002, at A1.

Roberts, Guy B. *The Counterproliferation Self-Help Paradigm: A Legal Regime for Enforcing the Norm Prohibiting the Proliferation of Weapons of Mass Destruction*, DENVER JOURNAL OF INTERNATIONAL LAW & POLICY 485 (Summer 1999).

Rummel, R. J. DEATH BY GOVERNMENT: GENOCIDE AND MASS MURDER IN THE TWENTIETH CENTURY, 1994.

Stone, Andrea. *In Poll, Islamic World Says Arabs Not Involved in 9/11*, USA TODAY, Feb. 27, 2002 at A1.

The 9/11 Commission Report: The National Commission on Terrorist Attacks Upon the United States, 107th Cong. 51. 2004.

Von Glahn, Gerhard. LAW AMONG NATIONS, SIXTH EDITION. 1992.

Zakaria, Fareed. *Why Do They Hate Us?* NEWSWEEK, Oct. 22, 2001, at 24.

Chapter 4

Civil Liberties and the War on Terror

The boisterous sea of liberty is never without a wave.

—Thomas Jefferson

The probability that terrorist organizations like al-Qa'eda may employ chemical, nuclear, or biological weapons of mass destruction in suicide attacks poses not only a direct threat to the well-being of tens of thousands of innocent people, but also raises new controversies regarding the possible curtailment of long recognized civil liberties. In creating greater domestic security from future terrorist attacks, the United States government must not trample on American liberties in the name of preserving them. This concern speaks to the matter of "due process." The term due process is most commonly used to describe the rights that Americans enjoy as spelled out in the Fourteenth Amendment of the United States Constitution:

> All persons born or naturalized in the United States, and subject to the jurisdiction thereof, are citizens of the United States and of the State wherein they reside. No State shall make or enforce any law which shall abridge the privileges or immunities of citizens of the United States; nor shall any State deprive any person of life, liberty, or property, without due process of law; nor deny to any person within its jurisdiction the equal protection of the laws.

The term has also come to be associated with American values of fairness and reasonableness in the treatment of others.

By definition, the traditional approach to combating terrorism is encompassed in two terms—antiterrorism and counterterrorism. Although most associate the term *counterterrorism* to cover both

59

concepts, strictly speaking, antiterrorism involves all those steps and actions taken by authorities to decrease the probability of a terrorist act from occurring. Antiterrorism, the proactive, preventative stage of stopping terrorism, includes techniques designed to harden potential high profile targets (e.g., government buildings or military installations), as well as actions taken to detect a planned terrorist attack before it occurs. For example, to prevent future terrorist attacks, both the Pentagon and private industry are experimenting with video surveillance, modeling techniques, and commercial technologies such as those used to identify automatic teller machine customers by scanning their faces.

One of the facets of the War on Terror is the realization that antiterrorism relies heavily on the efforts of ordinary citizens who, when observing suspicious behavior, are willing to notify law enforcement. The Department of Homeland Security regularly reminds the public that the "most effective weapon against terrorism is you." Suspicious activity is the key and can involve reporting on witnessing activity in any of the five basic elements related to conducting a terror attack: (1) target identification, (2) intelligence gathering and planning, (3) logistics and training, (4) conducting rehearsals or dry runs, and (5) the attack itself. Sometimes the suspicions prove profitable, as with the September 2002 arrest of six members of the Lackawanna radical Islamic sleeper terrorist cell in New York (based on a tip by an Arab American), the August 2006 arrest of 24 al-Qa'eda-styled radicals in the failed plot to detonate liquid bombs on ten planes bound to the United States from Britain (based also on a tip from the British Muslim community), or the failed plot by Faisal Shahzad in May 2010 to car bomb New York's Times Square. However, sometimes the suspicions prove incorrect, as in the 2003 case of three men of Middle Eastern descent who were overheard "joking" at a Georgia restaurant about a terrorist plot to be conducted in Miami, Florida (the three were subsequently stopped in Florida and, after a day-long investigation, were released). Therefore, antiterrorism is very much a bottom-up approach which must include ordinary citizens as a first line of defense.

America allows free speech in most circumstances, but never allows illegal violence. Another innovative antiterrorism program is designed to ease tensions between the government and a variety of antigovernment organizations. Following the 1995 Oklahoma terror bombing, for instance, this approach saw Federal Bureau of Investigation (FBI) agents talking directly to various so-called militia leaders. From Montana to Indiana, federal agents opened dialogues with leaders of several militia organizations to provide a forum for discussion in the hope that channels of communication would help prevent acts of violence. While this approach will bear little fruit with al-Qa'eda-styled terrorists, it is still wise to explore all avenues of prevention measures—informants can be recruited to work against the terror group.

Counterterrorism measures are those tactical actions taken by authorities in response to an actual terrorist incident. In this vein, planning and training will have a great impact on the success or failure of real world counterterrorist measures. While National Security Presidential Directive 5 and Presidential Decision Directive 39 designate the Department of Justice (DOJ), through the FBI, as the lead agency in the event of a terrorist attack on the homeland, the expected mass casualties, physical damage, and potential for civil disorder resulting from a weapon of mass destruction attack would undoubtedly see a shift to the Department of Defense (DOD) as the *de facto* lead federal agency for many counterterrorism issues.

Currently, there are seven main areas of concern that have been voiced in the public square as the government struggles to develop durable legal and policy underpinings to what promises to be a long conflict with al-Qa'eda-styled terrorism. They involve: (1) the use of military commissions; (2) the power of the United States to investigate, detain, and question terrorist suspects; (3) the expansion of the use of the United States military to enforce domestic law; (4) immigration; (5) the use of new information-gathering technologies; (6) the issue of "assassination"; and (7) the protection of Constitutional rights.

4.1 Past Efforts to Address Terrorism

As the world watched helplessly while hijacked planes smashed into the World Trade Center and the Pentagon, the attack exposed gaping vulnerabilities in both United States military and law enforcement strategies to guard the nation against a full-fledged terrorist assault by suicidal murderers. Although the threat of a significant terrorist attack on American soil was not an unknown topic of discussion prior to the events of September 11, 2001, very little was done by the federal government in the area of antiterrorism. In 2004, the 567 page 9/11 Commission Report, not only traced the movements of the nineteen hijackers as they circumvented various law enforcement and administrative barriers without detection, but also pointed out in detail how the entire intelligence community failed to stop the attacks.

Prior to 9/11, the actions to address the threat of organized terrorism, particularly militant Islamic groups that targeted American interests, were piecemeal and misguided. Methods were long on rhetoric but short on action. After the dual bombings of two American embassies in Africa in the summer of 1998 left more than 300 people dead, President Clinton vowed that "[n]o matter how long it takes, or where it takes us, we will pursue terrorists until the cases are solved and justice is done." Militarily, President Clinton launched seventy-five cruise missiles at some al-Qa'eda terrorist training camps in Afghanistan and a suspected VX nerve gas production facility at the Shifa Pharmaceuticals plant in Khartoum, Sudan. Nancy Soderberg, a former National Security Council senior aide in the Clinton administration later admitted: "In hindsight, it wasn't enough, and anyone involved in policy would have to admit that." In the kindest light to all administrations (including Ronald Reagan) before September 11, 2001, action by the government was ineffectual because the United States had no frame of reference in which to gauge the magnitude of the threat. The government was mired in old thinking and, as the 9/11 Commission Report related, a "lack of imagination" by our intelligence community.

In the international sphere, a brief survey of the American approach to global terrorism prior to September 11, 2001, reveals that America was content to enter into a handful of specific international conventions aimed at encouraging multilateral cooperation in punishing certain narrowly defined acts of terrorism such as hostage taking and hijacking of aircraft. Some examples of specific antiterrorist conventions include: The Convention on Offenses and Certain Other Acts Committed on Board Aircraft (Tokyo Convention, 1963); Convention for the Suppression of Unlawful Seizure of Aircraft (Hague Convention, 1971); Convention for the Suppression of Unlawful Acts Against the Safety of Civil Aviation (Montreal Convention, 1973); Convention on the Prevention and Punishment of Crimes Against Internationally Protected Persons, Including Diplomatic Agents (New York Convention, 1976-1977); and the International Convention Against the Taking of Hostages (Hostages Convention, 1979). As impressive as the titles sound for these ad hoc conventions, the general position of the United States was simply a mirror of the world community's ineffective approach to the emerging problem of global Islamic terrorism. Washington seemed content to react to terrorism incidents, using the criminal justice system when it could.

In the domestic arena, apart from various criminal reforms making terrorist acts abroad a crime under United States domestic law, most of the attention of the executive and legislative branches of government were focused on passing various pieces of domestic counterterrorism legislation, such as the 1996 Defense Against Weapons of Mass Destruction Act, commonly referred to as the NLD Act after its sponsors' names, Senators Nunn, Lugar, and Domenici. This legislation was limited in scope and designed primarily to assist in planning and training efforts for the use of emergency personnel responding to a major terrorist incident involving a weapon of mass destruction. Early on, these initiatives received much deserved criticism as a band-aid approach to the real world problem of a major terrorist attack.

In most areas of management, meaningful reorganizations of large bureaucracies only occur in response to crisis. Counterterrorism initiatives are no exception. Since the 1980s, there have been numerous legislative initiatives that address terrorist activities, most enacted on the heels of some type of terrorist attack. The central focus of any umbrella security program must involve the coordinated efforts of key federal and State agencies designed to protect United States personnel and property.

4.2 Addressing Terrorism Since 9/11

As is often the case in addressing new threats, the exact scope of the danger posed by al-Qa'eda-styled terrorism is often very difficult to assess. Speculation concerning asymmetric tactics can run from biological terrorism to nuclear terrorism to cyberterrorism, but only probabilities serve to gauge the scenarios. Mega-terrorism is the great known unknown. We know it can happen, but we do not know when, where, or in what form it will next come. In turn, any new security measure is going to threaten, to some degree, the lifestyle and perhaps some basic rights that Americans have long enjoyed. The Obama Administration's employment of almost 1,000 new body scanners at airports, following the Christmas Day 2009 attempted Detroit airplane bombing by al-Qa'eda recruit Abdulmutallab, caused a renewed debate about privacy violations. Proclaiming that any changes in the name of national security will entail a "slippery slope" that will see the nation slide into a draconian police state, some so-called civil libertarians prefer to remain frozen in place, vehemently opposed to all changes. The proper approach, of course, is for one to identify specific notches in the slope—bright and clearly defined lines—where the new rule of law will be established for a particular security measure.

The government has taken two major steps to fulfill its obligation to protect the American people from future attacks by al-Qa'eda-styled terrorists. The first was the creation of a new cabinet-level department entitled the Office of Homeland Security and the second was the passage of an exhaustive piece of anti-terror legislation known by short title as the USA PATRIOT Act and amended in 2006 by the 2005 USA PATRIOT Improvement and Reauthorization Act (USA PATRIOT Act II) and again in 2009. The 2001 USA PATRIOT Act passed in the Senate by a vote of 98–1. The House of Representatives passed their version by a vote of 377-56. Although a number of provisions of the USA PATRIOT Act were scheduled to expire on December 31, 2005, Congress passed new legislation in 2006 and 2009 that, for all practical purposes, extends the majority of the provisions on a permanent basis.

The Homeland Security Act (HSA) of 2002 consolidated the federal government's emergency response capabilities under the Department of Homeland Security (DHS). The Act directs the Secretary of DHS to oversee the personnel and assets of the Federal Emergency Management Agency (FEMA) and other related agencies. The DHS (through FEMA) is the lead federal agency for consequence management and support to law enforcement and has the authority to coordinate the federal government's response to both natural and man-made disasters, including terrorist attacks, on American soil. DHS houses over 170,000 employees from 22 agencies. DHS is divided into four separate entities: (1) Information and Infrastructure Protection; (2) Border and Transportation Security; (3) Science and Technology; and (4) Emergency Response. The most notable agencies under the DHS umbrella include the U.S. Coast Guard, Customs Service, Immigration and Naturalization Service (now abolished and divided into three agencies), Border Patrol, Secret Service, Transportation Security Administration and Federal Management Agency.

The HSA provides for a number of new legal standards regarding security issues. For instance, fearing that terrorists may target any number of the nation's critical infrastructures such as power plants, financial networks, airlines, etc., the HSA included rather broad exceptions to the Freedom of Information Act (FOIA) protecting private entities that voluntarily submit "critical infrastructure information" (CII) to the government. The law also provides that any government employee that willfully discloses CII information to the public shall be held criminally liable.

Another HSA provision that provides a legal liability shield to anti-terrorism technologies is the Support Anti-Terrorism by Fostering Effective Technologies Act (SAFETY Act). The Act provides that the DHS Secretary may exempt "sellers" of anti-terrorism technology from tort liability for injuries sustained by third parties resulting from a terrorist attack. Thus, sellers of "any product, equipment, service, device, or technology designed, developed, modified, or procured for the specific purpose of preventing, detecting, identifying, or deterring acts of terrorism" can apply for government certification from DHS. Once the Secretary has certified that the proposed "goods" conform to the seller's specifications, a rebuttable presumption is established that can "only be overcome by evidence showing that the seller acted fraudulently or with willful misconduct in submitting information to the Secretary during the course of the Secretary's consideration of such technology." The SAFETY Act approach departs from the government contractors defense set out in *Boyle v. United Technologies Corp*, where the private party contractor obtained immunity only if he conformed to the government's specifications.

In tandem with domestic strategies to address terrorism, the 9/11 Commission Report correctly recommended that the United States had to more sharply define a strategy that would ensure that terror groups would not find sanctuary in what it called "the least governed, most lawless places in the world." The Commission listed western Pakistan, Afghanistan, Saudi Arabia, Yemen, West Africa, and Southeast Asia as among the most troubled. Other trouble spots which bear note include places like Morocco, a known sanctuary for al-Qa'eda adherents and the home of most of the seventeen suspects jailed in the March 11, 2004, bombings which killed over 200 people in Spain.

4.3 Detainee Status

After the 2002 military campaign in Afghanistan overthrew the Taliban government, the vast majority of the Taliban fighters were processed and released in Afghanistan. Nevertheless, a large detention facility was created by the United States military at Bagram Air Force Base in Afghanistan to detain those al-Qa'eda and Taliban fighters deemed to be either too dangerous to parole or who were suspected of committing war crimes. Over the years, with the continuing war in Afghanistan, the population at Bagram grew to well over 800 by 2010. While the detention facility at Bagram Air Force Base never received much international attention, its sister detention facility created in 2002 at the U.S. Navy Base in Guantanamo Bay, Cuba, quickly became the epicenter of a relentless propaganda campaign by those opposed to the War on Terror. At its peak, the al-Qa'eda and Taliban enemy combatants sent to Guantanamo Bay, Cuba, numbered up to 800 detainees representing approximately 40 countries, with Saudi Arabia, Afghanistan, and Yemen the most represented. Under a "rehabilitation" policy, the Bush Administration released over 500 of those detained at Guantanamo Bay. Countries to which detainees have been released include Albania, Afghanistan, Australia, Bangladesh, Bahrain, Belgium, Britain, Denmark, Egypt, France, Germany, Iran, Iraq, Jordan, Kuwait, Libya, Maldives, Mauritania, Morocco, Pakistan, Russia, Saudi Arabia, Spain, Sweden, Sudan, Tajikistan, Turkey, Uganda, and Yemen. By early 2011, around 150 were still being held at Guantanamo Bay, to include 14 high-level al-Qa'eda operatives who had been previously kept in undisclosed locations. Although President Obama sternly vowed in January 2009 to close the Guantanamo detention facility by January 2010, he failed to do so. Nevertheless, the legal theory employed by the Obama Administration to detain these individuals without criminal charges is the same as the Bush Administration—they are detained under the law of war as enemy combatants and will be detained until either hostilities cease or, in the cases of many, specific charges are levied against them in a military commission or other legal forum for associated crimes.

Early on, two questions arose regarding due process concerns for these individuals. First, were they entitled to treatment as prisoners of war or as "other detainees" under the Geneva Conventions? Second, if the United States opted to try these individuals criminally, should they be tried in a United States federal district court or by means of the military commissions process?

An analysis of the first question regarding the status of al-Qa'eda and Taliban fighters under international law begins with the fact that the United States has long incorporated in its laws the international law of war (the term "laws of war" is also used), both customary and codified (*Paquete Habana*, 175 U.S. 667). In a confusing 2002 determination, the Bush Administration unilaterally determined that the captured al-Qa'eda and Taliban fighters were not eligible for prisoner of war status nor were they entitled to protections contained in Common Article 3 of the 1949 Geneva Conventions, which sets out the minimum standards of treatment for all detainees in armed conflict. Acting under this line of reasoning the Bush Administration blocked the military from using the "Article 5 tribunal" provisions of the Third Geneva Convention to determine whether a particular detainee should be accorded prisoner of war (POW) status or not.

The Bush Administration reasoned that since the al-Qa'eda fighters belonged to a terrorist organization and were not recognized members of an armed force, they are unlawful belligerents under the law of war. *Army Field Manual* (FM) 27-10, The Law of Land Warfare, codifies the law of land warfare. Paragraph 60(b) of FM 27-10 indicates that "[p]ersons who are not members of the armed forces as defined in [the Geneva Conventions], who bear arms or engage in other conduct hostile to the enemy thereby deprive themselves of many of the privileges attaching to the members of the civilian population." As set out in more detail in Chapter 6, this means that they are responsible for breaches of the law of war, but are not entitled to the status of POW. In the view of the Bush Administration, al-Qa'eda engaged in acts of war both in the September 11, 2001, attacks and in fighting alongside the Taliban forces in the internationally recognized armed conflict in Afghanistan. Actually, it can be argued that al-Qa'eda has been engaged in acts of war against the United States government since 1996, due to their direct connections with the 1996 bombing of the United States military barracks at Khobar Towers, Saudi Arabia, followed by the 1998 United States Embassy bombings in Kenya and Tanzania and the 2000 suicide boat attack on the *U.S.S. Cole* in Yemen.

As to the captured Taliban fighters, the Bush Administration determined that they were likewise not entitled to POW status under the Geneva Conventions because of their failure to comply with the Conventions' criterion which requires lawful combatants to wear distinctive military insignia, i.e., uniforms which would make them distinguishable from the civilian population at a distance. In finding that the Taliban "have not effectively distinguished themselves from the civilian population," the United States also added that the Taliban fighters had further forfeited any special status because they had "adopted and provided support to the unlawful terrorist objectives of the al-Qa'eda." While the latter finding would not necessarily indicate that the Taliban fighters would not be entitled to POW status, the former finding would. In short, POW status is conferred solely on those persons who are "[m]embers of armed forces of a Party to the conflict or members of militias and members of other volunteer corps, including those of organized resistance movements, belonging to a Party…provided that such…fulfill[s]" four specific conditions:

a) That of being commanded by a person responsible for his subordinates;
b) That of having a fixed distinctive sign recognizable at a distance;
c) That of carrying arms openly; and
d) That of conducting their operations in accordance with the laws and customs of war.

The Bush Administration also determined that the additional protections of the Geneva Conventions, i.e., Common Article 3, did not apply, although the Administration repeatedly indicated that all detainees were to be treated in accordance with the humanitarian concerns set out in the Geneva Conventions.

The Bush Administration's rejection of the long standing rules associated with detaining, classifying, and treating combatants under the law of war as codified in various Army documents to include Army Regulation 190-8, Enemy Prisoners of War, Retained Personnel, Civilian Internees and Other Detainees (Oct. 1997), was finally rejected by the June 2006 Supreme Court decision in *Hamdan v. Rumsfeld*. The Court found that even though the detainees were not entitled to the status of POW, Common Article 3 of the Geneva Conventions did apply and did in fact protect the detainees from being subjected to violence, outrages on personal dignity, torture, and cruel, humiliating, or degrading treatment. Although existing Department of Defense directives, orders, policies and doctrine conformed already with the standards of Common Article 3, the DOD quickly issued new treatment guidelines for detainees that incorporated the basic standards set out in Common Article 3.

As to the 2003 Iraq War, the Bush Administration went to war applying the Geneva Conventions in full. With the end of major combat operations against the Iraqi military in May 2003, however, the picture became far less clear. Like the Afghanistan theater of war, the Iraq War also mandated that the large number of detainees apprehended had to be categorized and housed. Accordingly, the United States grouped the Iraqi detainees into one of three categories: (1) Iraqi soldiers who qualified as POWs under the Geneva Conventions; (2) those suspected of having links to terrorist groups (to include sectarian militias such as Muatada al-Sadr's Mahdi Army and Saddam loyalists), called "security detainees;" and (3) common criminals.

Those in the first category were mostly captured during the major combat phase of the Iraq War and were quickly processed and released back into Iraqi society within a few months. While most of the prisoners were treated in accordance with the protections of the Geneva Conventions, the U.S. military self-reported several separate incidents of physical abuse by American guards, most often physical assaults during the first few hours of the detention. As POWs, this particular class of detainees was not required to give any further information upon additional questioning by American forces. To ensure that all parties to the conflict understood this rule of law, Article 17 of the Third Geneva Convention provides the following:

No physical or mental torture, *nor any other form of coercion*, may be inflicted on prisoners of war to secure from them information of any kind whatever. Prisoners of war who refuse to answer may not be *threatened, insulted, or exposed to any unpleasant or disadvantageous treatment of any kind* [emphasis added].

Those in the second category were held for indefinite periods of time pending interrogation and then either released or transferred to the new Iraqi justice system. The number of detainees in United States custody in Iraq peaked in 2007 at 26,000. The security detainees were held in two camps, one in Baghdad and the other in southern Iraq (Abu Ghraib was closed in 2006). In 2008 the numbers fell below 20,000 and continued to dramatically decline in 2009 until all were turned over to Iraqi control by 2010. Currently, the Iraqi government now has control over all detention operations.

4.4 Case Law on Detainee Issues

This section contains the most prominent federal court cases associated with the War on Terror with the exception of the 2006 Supreme Court case of *Hamdan v. Rumsfeld*. While *Hamdan* is significant because it mandated that Common Article 3 of the Geneva Conventions applied to all detainees, its primary impact rests on the issue of military commissions and will be addressed in the next section of this chapter.

On June 28, 2004, the same day that the United States transferred power to the interim government in Iraq, the United States Supreme Court handed down a series of opinions regarding the Bush Administration's authority to designate suspected terrorists as "enemy combatants" and to hold such individuals and others without trial, without access to the courts, without charges, and incommunicado. Disregarding the Supreme Court's 1950 decision in *Johnson v. Eisentrager*, which held that the right of habeas did not attach to an "enemy alien who, at no relevant time and in no stage of his captivity, has been within the territorial jurisdiction" of the United States, the Court held in *Rasul v. Bush*, that the federal court considered Guantanamo Bay, Cuba, to be within the court's jurisdiction. In *Hamdi v. Rumsfeld*, an 8-1 plurality opinion provided that even in "a state of war" the President's decision to designate an individual, in this case a U.S. citizen, as an enemy combatant would still allow that individual a "fair opportunity to rebut the government's factual assertions before a neutral decisionmaker." Despite sensationalized news media headlines that the Bush Administration had been chastised by the Supreme Court, the Court actually upheld the major thrust of the executive's war-making power to designate an individual (even a United States citizen) as an enemy combatant and to hold that person indefinitely without criminal charges. In other words, *Hamdi* held that the President did have the authority to designate a suspected al-Qa'eda terrorist as an "enemy combatant," which means that the individual could be held without charges, but the individual so designated had the right to contest that designation before a neutral decisionmaker. Hamdi, who was apprehended in Afghanistan, was released subsequent to the 2004 Supreme Court ruling under the terms of an agreement between the government and Hamdi.

In a clear effort to get Congress to pass legislation authorizing the establishment of a judicial panel to make those determinations for all detainees held in Guantanamo Bay and for United States citizen Hamdi, the Court did not define what it meant by a neutral decisionmaker. Amazingly, leaving it up to the lower courts, Congress, or the Bush Administration to work out the exact standards, the Court did signal that the hearings might not be very extensive in nature, the burden could be shifted to the detainee, and that a reviewing judge could relax the standards for admissibility of evidence. Speaking for four members of the majority, Justice O'Connor (her husband was a former Army officer in the Army's Judge Advocate General Corps) even went so far as to observe that "[t]here remains the possibility that the standards we have articulated could be met by...[a] military tribunal."

One immediate by-product of the Supreme Court decisions was the creation of a Combatant Status Review Tribunal (CSRT) in July of 2004. The CSRT was established by the Secretary of Defense to make independent determinations about whether the detainees held at Guantanamo Bay were properly classified as enemy combatants. The term enemy combatant is "an individual who was part of or supporting the Taliban or al-Qa'eda forces, or associated forces that are engaged in hostilities against the United States or its coalition partners...." The panel, made up of three senior military officers, held an administrative hearing where each detainee had the opportunity to present reasonably available evidence and witnesses. As an administrative hearing, the CSRT was not bound by the rules of evidence that would apply in a court but was bound to assess, "to the extent practicable, whether any statement derived from or relating to such detainee was obtained as a result of coercion and the probative values, if any, of such statement." The detainee was represented by a military officer and the detainee's personal representative could view classified information. The CSRT standard for its determination was a "preponderance of the evidence," but a detainee could request a new CSRT at least once a year to present evidence that the detainee was no longer a threat and should be released. The CSRT reviewed the cases of all individual detainees in Guantanamo Bay who wished to appear. In fact, as a consequence of this process, over 500 detainees were deemed not likely to engage in future hostilities against the United States and released from Guantanamo Bay. Nevertheless, reports show that in many cases the CSRT was wrong—scores of released detainees have actively rejoined hostilities and engaged in additional acts of terrorism. Some estimates are that over 30 percent of those released have rejoined the ranks of radical Islam. Currently, the Obama Administration conducts these assessments of detainee status via an interagency Guantanamo Review Task Force. The Task Force must approve release by unanimous consent and in accordance with new Congressionally-mandated rules, the Obama Administration must inform Congress of its intent to transfer/release a detainee at least 15 days before their transfer.

HAMDI v. RUMSFELD
Supreme Court of the United States
542 U.S. 507; 124 S. Ct. 2633 (2004)

Justice O'CONNOR announced the judgment of the Court and delivered an opinion, in which the Chief Justice, Justice KENNEDY, and Justice BREYER join.

At this difficult time in our Nation's history, we are called upon to consider the legality of the Government's detention of a United States citizen on United States soil as an "enemy combatant" and to address the process that is constitutionally owed to one who seeks to challenge his classification as such. The United States Court of Appeals for the Fourth Circuit held that petitioner's detention was legally authorized and that he was entitled to no further opportunity to challenge his enemy-combatant label. We now vacate and remand. We hold that although Congress authorized the detention of combatants in the narrow circumstances alleged here, due process demands that a citizen held in the United States as an enemy combatant be given a meaningful opportunity to contest the factual basis for that detention before a neutral decision-maker.

I

On September 11, 2001, the al Qaeda terrorist network used hijacked commercial airliners to attack prominent targets in the United States. Approximately 3,000 people were killed in those attacks. One week later, in response to these "acts of treacherous violence," Congress passed a resolution authorizing the President to "use all necessary and appropriate force against those nations, organizations, or persons he determines planned, authorized, committed, or aided the terrorist attacks" or "harbored such organizations or persons, in order to prevent any future acts of international terrorism against the United States by such nations, organizations or persons." Authorization for Use of Military Force ("the AUMF"), 115 Stat 224. Soon thereafter, the President ordered United States Armed Forces to Afghanistan, with a mission to subdue al Qaeda and quell the Taliban regime that was known to support it.

This case arises out of the detention of a man whom the Government alleges took up arms with the Taliban during this conflict. His name is Yaser Esam Hamdi. Born an American citizen in Louisiana in 1980, Hamdi moved with his family to Saudi Arabia as a child. By 2001, the parties agree, he resided in Afghanistan. At some point that year, he was seized by members of the Northern Alliance, a coalition of military groups opposed to the Taliban government, and eventually was turned over to the United States military. The Government asserts that it initially detained and interrogated Hamdi in Afghanistan before transferring him to the United States Naval Base in Guantanamo Bay in January 2002. In April 2002, upon learning that Hamdi is an American citizen, authorities transferred him to a naval brig in Norfolk, Virginia, where he remained until a recent transfer to a brig in Charleston, South Carolina. The Government contends that Hamdi is an "enemy combatant," and that this status justifies holding him in the United States indefinitely—without formal charges or proceedings—unless and until it makes the determination that access to counsel or further process is warranted.

…

II

The threshold question before us is whether the Executive has the authority to detain citizens who qualify as "enemy combatants." There is some debate as to the proper scope of this term, and the Government has never provided any court with the full criteria that it uses in classifying individuals as such. It has made clear, however, that, for purposes of this case, the "enemy combatant" that it is seeking to detain is an individual who, it alleges, was "part of or supporting forces hostile to the United States or coalition partners" in Afghanistan and who "engaged in an armed conflict against the United States" there. We therefore answer only the narrow question before us: whether the detention of citizens falling within that definition is authorized.

The Government maintains that no explicit congressional authorization is required, because the Executive possesses plenary authority to detain pursuant to Article II of the Constitution. We do not reach the question whether Article II provides such authority, however, because we agree with the Government's alternative position, that Congress has in fact authorized Hamdi's detention, through the AUMF.

Our analysis on that point, set forth below, substantially overlaps with our analysis of Hamdi's principal argument for the illegality of his detention. He posits that his detention is forbidden by *18 U.S.C. § 4001(a) [18 USCS § 4001(a)]*. *Section 4001(a)* states that "[n]o citizen shall be imprisoned or otherwise detained by the United States except pursuant to an Act of Congress." Congress passed *§ 4001(a)* in 1971 as part of a bill to repeal the Emergency Detention Act of 1950, *50 U.S.C. § 811 et seq [50 USCS § 811 et seq.]*, which provided procedures for executive detention, during times of emergency, of individuals deemed likely to engage in espionage or sabotage. Congress was particularly concerned about the possibility that the Act could be used to reprise the Japanese internment camps of World War II. H. R. Rep. No. 92-116 (1971); ("The concentration camp implications of the legislation render it abhorrent").

The Government again presses two alternative positions. First, it argues that *§ 4001(a)*, in light of its legislative history and its location in Title 18, applies only to "the control of civilian prisons and related detentions," not to military detentions. Second, it maintains that *§ 4001(a)* is satisfied, because Hamdi is being detained "pursuant to an Act of Congress"—the AUMF. Again, because we conclude that the Government's second assertion is correct, we do not address the first. In other words, for the reasons that follow, we conclude that the AUMF is explicit congressional authorization for the detention of individuals in the narrow category we describe (assuming, without deciding, that such authorization is required), and that the AUMF satisfied *§ 4001(a)*'s requirement that a detention be "pursuant to an Act of Congress" (assuming, without deciding, that *§ 4001(a)* applies to military detentions).

The AUMF authorizes the President to use "all necessary and appropriate force" against "nations, organizations, or persons" associated with the September 11, 2001, terrorist attacks. There can be no doubt that individuals who fought against the United States in Afghanistan as part of the Taliban, an organization known to have supported the al Qaeda terrorist network responsible for those attacks, are individuals Congress sought to target in passing the AUMF. We conclude that detention of individuals falling into the limited category we are considering, for the duration of the particular conflict in which they were captured, is so fundamental and accepted an incident to war as to be an exercise of the "necessary and appropriate force" Congress has authorized the President to use.

The capture and detention of lawful combatants and the capture, detention, and trial of unlawful combatants, by "universal agreement and practice," are "important incident[s] of war." *Ex parte Quirin*, 317 U.S., at 28, 87 L. Ed. 3, 63 S. Ct. 2. The purpose of detention is to prevent captured individuals from returning to the field of battle and taking up arms once again. Naqvi, Doubtful Prisoner-of-War Status, 84 Int'l Rev. Red Cross 571, 572 (2002) ("[C]aptivity in war is 'neither revenge, nor punishment, but solely protective custody, the only purpose of which is to prevent the prisoners of war from further participation in the war'" (quoting decision of Nuremberg Military Tribunal, reprinted in *41 Am. J. Int'l L. 172, 229 (1947)*)); W. Winthrop, Military Law and Precedents 788 (rev. 2d ed. 1920) ("The time has long passed when 'no quarter' was the rule on the battlefield....It is now recognized that 'Captivity is neither a punishment nor an act of vengeance,' but 'merely a temporary detention which is devoid of all penal character.'...'A prisoner of war is no convict; his imprisonment is a simple war measure.'"

...

There is no bar to this Nation's holding one of its own citizens as an enemy combatant. In *Quirin*, one of the detainees, Haupt, alleged that he was a naturalized United States citizen. *317 U.S., at 20, 87 L. Ed. 3, 63 S. Ct. 2.* We held that "[c]itizens who associate themselves with the military arm of the enemy government, and with its aid, guidance and direction enter this country bent on hostile acts, are enemy belligerents within the meaning of...the law of war." While Haupt was tried for violations of the law of war, nothing in *Quirin* suggests that his citizenship would have precluded his mere detention for the duration of the relevant hostilities. Nor can we see any reason for drawing such a line here. A citizen, no less than an alien, can be "part of or supporting forces hostile to the United States or coalition partners" and "engaged in an armed conflict against the United States," such a citizen, if released, would pose the same threat of returning to the front during the ongoing conflict.

In light of these principles, it is of no moment that the AUMF does not use specific language of detention. Because detention to prevent a combatant's return to the battlefield is a fundamental incident of waging war, in permitting the use of "necessary and appropriate force," Congress has clearly and unmistakably authorized detention in the narrow circumstances considered here.

Hamdi objects, nevertheless, that Congress has not authorized the *indefinite* detention to which he is now subject. The Government responds that "the detention of enemy combatants during World War II was just as 'indefinite' while that war was being fought." We take Hamdi's objection to be not to the lack of certainty regarding the date on which the conflict will end, but to the substantial prospect of perpetual detention. We recognize that the national security underpinnings of the "war on terror," although crucially important, are broad and malleable. As the Government concedes, "given its unconventional nature, the current conflict is unlikely to end with a formal cease-fire agreement." The prospect Hamdi raises is therefore not far-fetched. If the Government does not consider this unconventional war won for two generations, and if it maintains during that time that Hamdi might, if released, rejoin forces fighting against the United States, then the position it has taken throughout the litigation of this case suggests that Hamdi's detention could last for the rest of his life.

It is a clearly established principle of the law of war that detention may last no longer than active hostilities. See Article 118 of the Geneva Convention (III) Relative to the Treatment of Prisoners of War, Aug. 12, 1949, [1955] *6 U. S. T. 3316, 3406*, T. I. A. S. No. 3364 ("Prisoners of war shall be released and repatriated without delay after the cessation of active hostilities"). See also Article 20 of the Hague Convention (II) on Laws and Customs of War on Land, July 29, 1899, 32 Stat 1817 (as soon as possible after "conclusion of peace"); Hague Convention (IV), *supra*, Oct. 18, 1907, 36 Stat 2301 ("conclusion of peace" (Art. 20)); Geneva Convention, *supra*, July 27, 1929, 47 Stat 2055 (repatriation should be accomplished with the least possible delay after conclusion of peace (Art. 75)); Praust, Judicial Power to Determine the Status and Rights of Persons Detained without Trial, *44 Harv. Int'l L. J. 503, 510–511 (2003)* (prisoners of war "can be detained during an armed conflict, but the detaining country must release and repatriate them 'without delay after the cessation of active hostilities,' unless they are being lawfully prosecuted or have been lawfully convicted of crimes and are serving sentences" (citing Arts. 118, 85, 99, 119, 129, Geneva Convention (III), 6 T. I. A. S., at 3384, 3392, 3406, 3418)).

Hamdi contends that the AUMF does not authorize indefinite or perpetual detention. Certainly, we agree that indefinite detention for the purpose of interrogation is not authorized. Further, we understand Congress' grant of authority for the use of "necessary and appropriate force" to include the authority to detain for the duration of the relevant conflict, and our understanding is based on longstanding law-of-war principles. If the practical circumstances of a given conflict are entirely unlike those of the conflicts that informed the development of the law of war, that understanding may unravel. But that is not the situation we face as of this date. Active combat operations against Taliban fighters apparently are ongoing in Afghanistan. See, e.g., Constable, U. S. Launches New Operation in Afghanistan, Washington Post, Mar. 14, 2004, p A22 (reporting that 13,500 United States troops remain in Afghanistan, including several thousand new arrivals); J. Abizaid, Dept. of Defense, Gen. Abizaid Central Command Operations

Update Briefing, Apr. 30, 2004, http://www.defenselink.mil/transcripts/2004/tr20040430-1402. html (as visited June 8, 2004, and available in the Clerk of Court's case file) (media briefing describing ongoing operations in Afghanistan involving 20,000 United States troops). The United States may detain, for the duration of these hostilities, individuals legitimately determined to be Taliban combatants who "engaged in an armed conflict against the United States." If the record establishes that United States troops are still involved in active combat in Afghanistan, those detentions are part of the exercise of "necessary and appropriate force," and therefore are authorized by the AUMF.

> *Ex parte Milligan*, 71 U.S. 2, 4 Wall. 2, 125, 18 L. Ed. 281 (1866), does not undermine our holding about the Government's authority to seize enemy combatants, as we define that term today. In that case, the Court made repeated reference to the fact that its inquiry into whether the military tribunal had jurisdiction to try and punish Milligan turned in large part on the fact that Milligan was not a prisoner of war, but a resident of Indiana arrested while at home there. *Id., at 118, 131, 7 U.S. 2, 18 L. Ed. 281.* That fact was central to its conclusion. Had Milligan been captured while he was assisting Confederate soldiers by carrying a rifle against Union troops on a Confederate battlefield, the holding of the Court might well have been different. The Court's repeated explanations that Milligan was not a prisoner of war suggest that had these different circumstances been present he could have been detained under military authority for the duration of the conflict, whether or not he was a citizen.

...

Quirin was a unanimous opinion. It both postdates and clarifies *Milligan*, providing us with the most apposite precedent that we have on the question of whether citizens may be detained in such circumstances. Brushing aside such precedent—particularly when doing so gives rise to a host of new questions never dealt with by this Court—is unjustified and unwise.

III

...

Even in cases in which the detention of enemy combatants is legally authorized, there remains the question of what process is constitutionally due to a citizen who disputes his enemy-combatant status. Hamdi argues that he is owed a meaningful and timely hearing and that "extrajudicial detention [that] begins and ends with the submission of an affidavit based on third-hand hearsay" does not comport with the *Fifth* and *Fourteenth Amendments*. The Government counters that any more process than was provided below would be both unworkable and "constitutionally intolerable." Our resolution of this dispute requires a careful examination both of the writ of habeas corpus, which Hamdi now seeks to employ as a mechanism of judicial review, and of the *Due Process Clause*, which informs the procedural contours of that mechanism in this instance.

...

B

First, the Government urges the adoption of the Fourth Circuit's holding below—that because it is "undisputed" that Hamdi's seizure took place in a combat zone, the habeas determination can be made purely as a matter of law, with no further hearing or factfinding necessary. This argument is easily rejected. As the dissenters from the denial of rehearing en banc noted, the circumstances surrounding Hamdi's seizure cannot in any way be characterized as "undisputed," as "those circumstances are neither conceded in fact, nor susceptible to concession in law, because Hamdi has not been permitted to speak for himself or even through counsel as to those circumstances." *337 F.3d 335, 357 (CA4 2003)* (Luttig, J., dissenting from denial of rehearing en banc); see also *id., at 371–372* (Motz, J., dissenting from denial of rehearing en banc). Further, the "facts" that constitute the alleged concession are insufficient to support Hamdi's detention. Under the definition of enemy combatant that we accept today as falling within the scope of Congress' authorization, Hamdi would need to be "part of or supporting forces hostile to the United States or coalition partners" and "engaged in an armed conflict against the United States" to justify his detention in the United States for the duration of the relevant conflict. The habeas petition states only that "[w]hen seized by the United States Government, Mr. Hamdi resided in Afghanistan." An assertion that one resided in a country in which combat operations are taking place is not a concession that one was "captured in a zone of active combat operations in a foreign theater of war," *316 F.3d at 459* (emphasis added), and certainly is not a concession that one was "part of or supporting forces hostile to the United States or coalition partners" and "engaged in an armed conflict against the United States." Accordingly, we reject any argument that Hamdi has made concessions that eliminate any right to further process.

C

The Government's second argument requires closer consideration. This is the argument that further factual exploration is unwarranted and inappropriate in light of the extraordinary constitutional interests at stake. Under the Government's most extreme rendition of this argument, "[r]espect for separation of powers and the limited institutional capabilities of courts in matters of military decision-making in connection with an ongoing conflict" ought to eliminate entirely any individual process, restricting the courts to investigating only whether legal authorization exists for the broader detention scheme. At most, the Government argues, courts should review its determination that a citizen is an enemy combatant under a very deferential "some evidence" standard. ("Under the some evidence standard, the focus is exclusively on the factual basis supplied by the Executive to support its own determination" (citing *Superintendent, Mass. Correctional Institution at Walpole v. Hill, 472 U.S. 445, 455-457, 86 L. Ed. 2d 356, 105 S. Ct. 2768 (1985)* (explaining that the some evidence standard "does not require" a "weighing of the evidence," but rather calls for assessing "whether there is any evidence in the record that could support the conclusion")). Under this review, a court would assume the accuracy of the Government's articulated basis for Hamdi's detention, as set forth in the Mobbs Declaration, and assess only whether that articulated basis was a legitimate one. Brief for Respondents 36; see also *316 F.3d at 473–474* (declining to address whether the "some evidence" standard should govern the adjudication of such claims, but noting that "[t]he factual averments in the [Mobbs] affidavit, if accurate, are sufficient to confirm" the legality of Hamdi's detention).

In response, Hamdi emphasizes that this Court consistently has recognized that an individual challenging his detention may not be held at the will of the Executive without recourse to some proceeding before a neutral tribunal to determine whether the Executive's asserted justifications for that detention have basis in fact and warrant in law. He argues that the Fourth Circuit inappropriately "ceded power to the Executive during wartime to define the conduct for which a citizen may be detained, judge whether that citizen has engaged in the proscribed conduct, and imprison that citizen indefinitely," and that due process demands that he receive a hearing in which he may challenge the Mobbs Declaration and adduce his own counter evidence. The District Court, agreeing with Hamdi, apparently believed that the appropriate process would approach the process that accompanies a criminal trial. It therefore disapproved of the hearsay nature of the Mobbs Declaration and anticipated quite extensive discovery of various military affairs. Anything less, it concluded, would not be "meaningful judicial review."

Both of these positions highlight legitimate concerns. And both emphasize the tension that often exists between the autonomy that the Government asserts is necessary in order to pursue effectively a particular goal and the process that a citizen contends he is due before he is deprived of a constitutional right. The ordinary mechanism that we use for balancing such serious competing interests, and for determining the procedures that are necessary to ensure that a citizen is not "deprived of life, liberty, or property, without due process of law," *U.S. Const., Amdt. 5*, is the test that we articulated in *Mathews v. Eldridge, 424 U.S. 319, 47 L. Ed. 2d 18, 96 S. Ct. 893 (1976)*. *Mathews* dictates that the process due in any given instance is determined by weighing "the private interest that will be affected by the official action" against the Government's asserted interest, "including the function involved" and the burdens the Government would face in providing greater process. *424 U.S., at 335, 47 L. Ed. 2d 18, 96 S. Ct. 893*. The *Mathews* calculus then contemplates a judicious balancing of these concerns, through an analysis of "the risk of an erroneous deprivation" of the private interest if the process were reduced and the "probable value, if any, of additional or substitute safeguards." We take each of these steps in turn.

1

It is beyond question that substantial interests lie on both sides of the scale in this case. Hamdi's "private interest…affected by the official action," is the most elemental of liberty interests—the interest in being free from physical detention by one's own government. *Foucha v. Louisiana, 504 U.S. 71, 80, 118 L. Ed. 2d 437, 112 S. Ct. 1780 (1992)* ("Freedom from bodily restraint has always been at the core of the liberty protected by the *Due Process Clause* from arbitrary governmental action"); see also *Parham v. J. R., 442 U.S. 584, 600, 61 L. Ed. 2d 101, 99 S. Ct. 2493 (1979)* (noting the "substantial liberty interest in not being confined unnecessarily"). "In our society liberty is the norm," and detention without trial "is the carefully limited exception." *Salerno, supra, at 755, 95 L. Ed. 2d 697, 107 S. Ct. 2095*. "We have always been careful not to 'minimize the importance and fundamental nature' of the individual's right to liberty," *Foucha, supra, at 80, 118 L. Ed. 2d 437, 112 S. Ct. 1780* (quoting *Salerno, supra, at 750, 95 L. Ed. 2d 697, 107 S. Ct. 2095*), and we will not do so today.

Nor is the weight on this side of the *Mathews* scale offset by the circumstances of war or the accusation of treasonous behavior, for "[i]t is clear that commitment for any purpose constitutes a significant deprivation of liberty that requires due process protection," *Jones v. United States, 463 U.S. 354, 361, 77 L. Ed. 2d 694, 103 S. Ct. 3043 (1983)* (emphasis added; internal quotation marks omitted), and at this stage in the *Mathews* calculus, we consider the interest of the *erroneously* detained individual. *Carey v. Piphus, 435 U.S. 247, 259, 55 L. Ed. 2d 252, 98 S. Ct. 1042 (1978)* ("Procedural due process rules are meant to protect persons not from the deprivation, but from the mistaken or unjustified deprivation of life, liberty, or property"); see also *id., at 266, 55 L. Ed. 2d 252, 98 S. Ct. 1042* (noting "the importance to organized society that procedural due process be observed," and emphasizing that "the right to procedural due process is 'absolute' in the sense that it does not depend upon the merits of a claimant's substantive assertions"). Indeed, as *amicus* briefs from media and relief organizations emphasize, the risk of erroneous deprivation of a citizen's liberty in the absence of sufficient process here is very real....Moreover, as critical as the Government's interest may be in detaining those who actually pose an immediate threat to the national security of the United States during ongoing international conflict, history and common sense teach us that an unchecked system of detention carries the potential to become a means for oppression and abuse of others who do not present that sort of threat. See *Ex parte Milligan, 4 Wall., at 125, 71 U.S. 2, 18 L. Ed. 281* ("[The Founders] knew—the history of the world told them—the nation they were founding, be its existence short or long, would be involved in war; how often or how long continued, human foresight could not tell; and that unlimited power, wherever lodged at such a time, was especially hazardous to freemen"). Because we live in a society in which "[m]ere public intolerance or animosity cannot constitutionally justify the deprivation of a person's physical liberty," *O'Connor v. Donaldson, 422 U.S. 563, 575, 45 L. Ed. 2d 396, 95 S. Ct. 2486 (1975)*, our starting point for the *Mathews v. Eldridge* analysis is unaltered by the allegations surrounding the particular detainee or the organizations with which he is alleged to have associated. We reaffirm today the fundamental nature of a citizen's right to be free from involuntary confinement by his own government without due process of law, and we weigh the opposing governmental interests against the curtailment of liberty that such confinement entails.

2

On the other side of the scale are the weighty and sensitive governmental interests in ensuring that those who have in fact fought with the enemy during a war do not return to battle against the United States. As discussed above, *supra*, at ____, *159 L. Ed. 2d, at 592*, the law of war and the realities of combat may render such detentions both necessary and appropriate, and our due process analysis need not blink at those realities. Without doubt, our Constitution recognizes that core strategic matters of warmaking belong in the hands of those who are best positioned and most politically accountable for making them. *Dep't of the Navy v. Egan, 484 U.S. 518, 530, 98 L. Ed. 2d 918, 108 S. Ct. 818 (1988)* (noting the reluctance of the courts "to intrude upon the authority of the Executive in military and national security affairs"); *Youngstown Sheet & Tube Co. v. Sawyer, 343 U.S. 579, 587, 96 L. Ed. 1153, 72 S. Ct. 863, 62 Ohio Law Abs. 417 (1952)* (acknowledging "broad powers in military commanders engaged in day-to-day fighting in a theater of war").

The Government also argues at some length that its interests in reducing the process available to alleged enemy combatants are heightened by the practical difficulties that would accompany a system of trial-like process. In its view, military officers who are engaged in the serious work of waging battle would be unnecessarily and dangerously distracted by litigation half a world away, and discovery into military operations would both intrude on the sensitive secrets of national defense and result in a futile search for evidence buried under the rubble of war. To the extent that these burdens are triggered by heightened procedures, they are properly taken into account in our due process analysis.

3

Striking the proper constitutional balance here is of great importance to the Nation during this period of ongoing combat. But it is equally vital that our calculus not give short shrift to the values that this country holds dear or to the privilege that is American citizenship. It is during our most challenging and uncertain moments that our Nation's commitment to due process is most severely tested; and it is in those times that we must preserve our commitment at home to the principles for which we fight abroad. See *Kennedy v. Mendoza-Martinez, 372 U.S. 144, 164-165, 9 L. Ed. 2d 644, 83 S. Ct. 554 (1963)* ("The imperative necessity for safeguarding these rights to procedural due process under the gravest of emergencies has existed throughout our constitutional history, for it is then, under the pressing exigencies of crisis, that there is the greatest temptation to dispense with guarantees which, it is feared, will inhibit government action"); see also *United States v. Robel, 389 U.S. 258, 264, 19 L. Ed. 2d 508, 88 S. Ct. 419 (1967)* ("It would indeed be ironic if, in the name of national defense, we would sanction the subversion of one of those liberties…which makes the defense of the Nation worthwhile").

With due recognition of these competing concerns, we believe that neither the process proposed by the Government nor the process apparently envisioned by the District Court below strikes the proper constitutional balance when a United States citizen is detained in the United States as an enemy combatant. That is, "the risk of erroneous deprivation" of a detainee's liberty interest is unacceptably high under the Government's proposed rule, while some of the "additional or substitute procedural safeguards" suggested by the District Court are unwarranted in light of their limited "probable value" and the burdens they may impose on the military in such cases.

We therefore hold that a citizen-detainee seeking to challenge his classification as an enemy combatant must receive notice of the factual basis for his classification, and a fair opportunity to rebut the Government's factual assertions before a neutral decisionmaker….These essential constitutional promises may not be eroded. At the same time, the exigencies of the circumstances may demand that, aside from these core elements, enemy combatant proceedings may be tailored to alleviate their uncommon potential to burden the Executive at a time of ongoing military conflict. Hearsay, for example, may need to be accepted as the most reliable available evidence from the Government in such a proceeding. Likewise, the Constitution would not be offended by a presumption in favor of the Government's evidence, so long as that presumption remained a rebuttable one and fair opportunity for rebuttal were provided. Thus, once the Government puts forth credible evidence that the habeas petitioner meets the enemy-combatant criteria, the onus could shift to the petitioner to rebut that evidence with more persuasive evidence that he falls outside the criteria. A burden-shifting scheme of this sort would meet the goal of ensuring that the errant tourist, embedded journalist, or local aid worker has a chance to prove military error while giving due regard to the Executive once it has put forth meaningful support for its conclusion that the detainee is in fact an enemy combatant.

…

We think it unlikely that this basic process will have the dire impact on the central functions of warmaking that the Government forecasts. The parties agree that initial captures on the battle-field need not receive the process we have discussed here; that process is due only when the determination is made to *continue* to hold those who have been seized. The Government has made clear in its briefing that documentation regarding battlefield detainees already is kept in the ordinary course of military affairs. Any factfinding imposition created by requiring a knowledgeable affiant to summarize these records to an independent tribunal is a minimal one. Likewise, arguments that military officers ought not have to wage war under the threat of litigation lose much of their steam when factual disputes at enemy-combatant hearings are limited to the alleged combatant's acts. This focus meddles little, if at all, in the strategy or conduct of war, inquiring only into the appropriateness of continuing to detain an individual claimed to have taken up arms against the United States. While we accord the greatest respect and consideration to the judgments of military authorities in matters relating to the actual prosecution of a war, and recognize that the scope of that discretion necessarily is wide, it does not infringe on the core role of the military for the courts to exercise their own time-honored and constitutionally mandated roles of reviewing and resolving claims like those presented here. Cf. *Korematsu v. United States, 323 U.S. 214, 233-234, 89 L. Ed. 194, 65 S. Ct. 193 (1944)* (Murphy, J., dissenting) ("[L]ike other claims conflicting with the asserted constitutional rights of the individual, the military claim must subject itself to the judicial process of having its reasonableness determined and its conflicts with other interests reconciled"); *Sterling v. Constantin, 287 U.S. 378, 401, 77 L. Ed. 375, 53 S. Ct. 190 (1932)* ("What are the allowable limits of military discretion, and whether or not they have been overstepped in a particular case, are judicial questions").

In sum, while the full protections that accompany challenges to detentions in other settings may prove unworkable and inappropriate in the enemy-combatant setting, the threats to military operations posed by a basic system of independent review are not so weighty as to trump a citizen's core rights to challenge meaningfully the Government's case and to be heard by an impartial adjudicator.

…

There remains the possibility that the standards we have articulated could be met by an appropriately authorized and properly constituted military tribunal. Indeed, it is notable that military regulations already provide for such process in related instances, dictating that tribunals be made available to determine the status of enemy detainees who assert prisoner-of-war status under the Geneva Convention. See Enemy Prisoners of War, Retained Personnel, Civilian Internees and Other Detainees, Army Regulation 190-8, § 1-6 (1997). In the absence of such process, however, a court that receives a petition for a writ of habeas corpus from an alleged enemy combatant must itself ensure that the minimum requirements of due process are achieved. Both courts below recognized as much, focusing their energies on the question of whether Hamdi was due an opportunity to rebut the Government's case against him. The Government, too, proceeded on this assumption, presenting its affidavit and then seeking that it be evaluated under a deferential standard of review based on burdens that it alleged would accompany any greater process. As we have discussed, a habeas court in a case such as this may accept affidavit evidence like that contained in the Mobbs Declaration, so long as it also permits the alleged combatant to present his own factual case to rebut the Government's return. We anticipate that a District Court would proceed with the caution that we have indicated is necessary in this setting, engaging in a factfinding process that is both prudent and incremental. We have no reason to doubt that courts faced with these sensitive matters will pay proper heed both to the matters of national security that might arise in an individual case and to the constitutional limitations safeguarding essential liberties that remain vibrant even in times of security concerns.

IV

Hamdi asks us to hold that the Fourth Circuit also erred by denying him immediate access to counsel upon his detention and by disposing of the case without permitting him to meet with an attorney. Since our grant of certiorari in this case, Hamdi has been appointed counsel, with whom he has met for consultation purposes on several occasions, and with whom he is now being granted unmonitored meetings. He unquestionably has the right to access to counsel in connection with the proceedings on remand. No further consideration of this issue is necessary at this stage of the case.

…

The judgment of the United States Court of Appeals for the Fourth Circuit is vacated, and the case is remanded for further proceedings. It is so ordered.

Besides Hamdi, President Bush exercised his authority as the Commander in Chief to designate certain other individuals as "enemy combatants," to include another U.S. citizen named Jose Padilla, and to detain said individuals in military custody without criminal charge. On May 8, 2002, Padilla was apprehended at the Chicago airport by federal agents executing a material witness warrant issued by the United States District Court for the Southern District of New York in connection with its grand jury investigation of the 9/11 terrorist attacks. On June 9, 2002, President Bush issued an order to Secretary of Defense Donald H. Rumsfeld designating Padilla as an "enemy combatant." Padilla was transferred to military custody at the Consolidated Naval Brig in Charleston, South Carolina. In 2005, the U.S. Court of Appeals for the Fourth Circuit affirmed the President's power under the 2001 Authorization for Use of Military Force to label a U.S. citizen as an enemy combatant and detain said citizen. Then, in late 2005 Padilla was transferred back to federal jurisdiction—no longer designated as an illegal enemy combatant—and charged with a variety of federal crimes related to terrorist activity, since the U.S. self-imposed the legal rule that U.S. citizens cannot be tried by military commissions. In early 2008, Padilla was convicted in a federal criminal court in Florida and sentenced to 17 years confinement.

PADILLA v. HANFT
United States Court of Appeals for the Fourth Circuit
No. 05-6396 (Sept. 9, 2005)

LUTTIG, Circuit Judge:

Appellee Jose Padilla, a United States citizen, associated with forces hostile to the United States in Afghanistan and took up arms against United States forces in that country in our war against al Qaeda. Upon his escape to Pakistan from the battlefield in Afghanistan, Padilla was recruited, trained, funded, and equipped by al Qaeda leaders to continue prosecution of the war in the United States by blowing up apartment buildings in this country. Padilla flew to the United

States on May 8, 2002, to begin carrying out his assignment, but was arrested by civilian law enforcement authorities upon his arrival at O'Hare International Airport in Chicago.

Thereafter, in a letter to the Secretary of Defense, the President of the United States personally designated Padilla an "enemy combatant" against this country, stating that the United States is "at war" with al Qaeda, that "Mr. Padilla engaged in conduct that constituted hostile and war-like acts, including conduct in preparation for acts of international terrorism that had the aim to cause injury to or adverse effects on the United States," and that "Mr. Padilla represents a continuing, present and grave danger to the national security of the United States." Having determined that "detention of Mr. Padilla is necessary to prevent him from aiding al Qaeda in its efforts to attack the United States or its armed forces, other governmental personnel, or citizens," the President directed the Secretary of Defense to take Padilla into military custody, in which custody Padilla has remained ever since. The full text of the President's memorandum to the Secretary of Defense reads as follows:

THE WHITE HOUSE
WASHINGTON
FOR OFFICIAL USE ONLY

TO THE SECRETARY OF DEFENSE:
Based on the information available to me from all sources,
REDACTED
In accordance with the Constitution and consistent with the laws of the United States, including the Authorization for Use of Military Force Joint Resolution (Public Law 107-40);
I, GEORGE W. BUSH, as President of the United States and Commander in Chief of the U.S. armed forces, hereby DETERMINE for the United States of America that:
(1) Jose Padilla, who is under the control of the Department of Justice and who is a U.S. citizen, is, and at the time he entered the United States in May 2002 was, an enemy combatant;
(2) Mr. Padilla is closely associated with al Qaeda, an international terrorist organization with which the United States is at war;
(3) Mr. Padilla engaged in conduct that constituted hostile and war-like acts, including conduct in preparation for acts of international terrorism that had the aim to cause injury to or adverse effects on the United States;
(4) Mr. Padilla possesses intelligence, including intelligence about personnel and activities of al Qaeda, that, if communicated to the U.S., would aid U.S. efforts to prevent attacks by al Qaeda on the United States or its armed forces, other governmental personnel, or citizens;
(5) Mr. Padilla represents a continuing, present and grave danger to the national security of the United States, and detention of Mr. Padilla is necessary to prevent him from aiding al Qaeda in its efforts to attack the United States or its armed forces, other governmental personnel, or citizens;
(6) it is in the interest of the United States that the Secretary of Defense detain Mr. Padilla as an enemy combatant; and

(7) it is REDACTED consistent with U.S. law and the laws of war for the Secretary of Defense to detain Mr. Padilla as an enemy combatant.
Accordingly, you are directed to receive Mr. Padilla from the Department of Justice and to detain him as an enemy combatant.
DATE: June 9, 2002   Signature /George Bush/

The exceedingly important question before us is whether the President of the United States possesses the authority to detain militarily a citizen of this country who is closely associated with al Qaeda, an entity with which the United States is at war; who took up arms on behalf of that enemy and against our country in a foreign combat zone of that war; and who thereafter traveled to the United States for the avowed purpose of further prosecuting that war on American soil, against American citizens and targets.

We conclude that the President does possess such authority pursuant to the Authorization for Use of Military Force Joint Resolution enacted by Congress in the wake of the attacks on the United States of September 11, 2001. Accordingly, the judgment of the district court is reversed.

…

B

Padilla marshals essentially four arguments for the conclusion that his detention is unlawful. None of them ultimately is persuasive.

1

Recognizing the hurdle to his position represented by the Supreme Court's decision in Hamdi, Padilla principally argues that his case does not fall within the "narrow circumstances" considered by the Court in that case because, although he too stood alongside Taliban forces in Afghanistan, he was seized on American soil, whereas Hamdi was captured on a foreign battlefield. In other words, Padilla maintains that capture on a foreign battlefield was one of the "narrow circumstances" to which the plurality in Hamdi confined its opinion. We disagree. When the plurality articulated the "narrow question" before it, it referred simply to the permissibility of detaining "an individual who…was '"part of or supporting forces hostile to the United States or coalition partners"' in Afghanistan and who '"engaged in an armed conflict against the United States"' there." Nowhere in its framing of the "narrow question" presented did the plurality even mention the locus of capture.

The actual reasoning that the plurality thereafter employed is consistent with the question having been framed so as to render locus of capture irrelevant. That reasoning was that Hamdi's detention was an exercise of "necessary and appropriate force" within the meaning of the AUMF because "detention to prevent a combatant's return to the battlefield is a fundamental incident of waging war." This reasoning simply does not admit of a distinction between an enemy combatant captured abroad and detained in the United States, such as Hamdi, and an enemy combatant who escaped capture abroad but was ultimately captured domestically and detained in the United States, such as Padilla. As we previously explained, Padilla poses the same threat of returning to the battlefield as Hamdi posed at the time of the Supreme Court's adjudication of Hamdi's petition. Padilla's detention is thus "necessary and appropriate" to the same extent as was Hamdi's.

Padilla directs us to a passage from the plurality's opinion in Hamdi in which, when responding to the dissent, the plurality charged that the dissent "ignore[d] the context of th[e] case: a United States citizen captured in a foreign combat zone." Padilla argues that this passage proves that capture on a foreign battlefield was one of the factual circumstances by which the Court's opinion was limited. If this language stood alone, Padilla's argument as to the limitation of Hamdi at least would have more force, though to acknowledge that foreign battlefield capture was part of the context of the case still is not to say (at least not necessarily) that the locus of capture was essential to the Court's reasoning. However, this language simply cannot bear the weight that Padilla would have it bear when it is considered against the backdrop of both the quite different limitations that were expressly imposed by the Court through its framing of the question presented, and the actual reasoning that was employed by the Court in reaching its conclusion, which reasoning was consistent with the question having been framed so as to render an enemy combatant's point of capture irrelevant to the President's power to detain. In short, the plurality carefully limited its opinion, but not in a way that leaves room for argument that the President's power to detain one who has associated with the enemy and taken up arms against the United States in a foreign combat zone varies depending upon the geographic location where that enemy combatant happens to be captured.

Our conclusion that the reasoning in *Hamdi* does not support a distinction based on the locus of capture is buttressed by the plurality's analysis of *Quirin*. Although at issue in *Quirin* was the authority of the President to subject a United States citizen who was also an enemy combatant to military trial, the plurality in *Hamdi* went to lengths to observe that Haupt, who had been captured domestically, could instead have been permissibly detained for the duration of hostilities. That analysis strongly suggests, if it does not confirm, that the plurality did not regard the locus of capture (within or without the United States) as relevant to the President's authority to detain an enemy combatant who is also a citizen, and that it believed that the detention of such a combatant is not more or less a necessary incident of the President's power to wage war depending upon the locus of eventual capture.

Given the lack of any reference to locus of capture in the plurality's articulation of the "narrow question" before it, the absence of any basis in Hamdi's reasoning for a distinction between foreign and domestic capture of one who has both associated with the enemy and taken up arms against the United States on behalf of that enemy in a foreign combat zone, and the plurality's understanding of and reliance upon *Quirin* as a precedent that would permit the detention of an enemy combatant who had been captured domestically, we simply cannot ascribe to the rejoinder to Justice Scalia the significance, much less the dispositive significance, that Padilla urges.

2

Padilla also argues, and the district court held, that Padilla's military detention is "neither necessary nor appropriate" because he is amenable to criminal prosecution. Related to this argument, Padilla attempts to distinguish *Quirin* from his case on the grounds that he has simply been detained, unlike Haupt who was charged and tried in *Quirin*. Neither the argument nor the attempted distinction is convincing.

As to the fact that Padilla can be prosecuted, the availability of criminal process does not distinguish him from Hamdi. If the mere availability of criminal prosecution rendered detention unnecessary within the meaning of the AUMF, then Hamdi's detention would have been unnecessary and therefore unauthorized, since he too was detained in the United States and amenable to criminal prosecution. We are convinced, in any event, that the availability of criminal process cannot be determinative of the power to detain, if for no other reason than that criminal prosecution may well not achieve the very purpose for which detention is authorized in the first place—the prevention of return to the field of battle. Equally important, in many instances criminal prosecution would impede the Executive in its efforts to gather intelligence from the detainee and to restrict the detainee's communication with confederates so as to ensure that the detainee does not pose a continuing threat to national security even as he is confined—impediments that would render military detention not only an appropriate, but also the necessary, course of action to be taken in the interest of national security.

The district court acknowledged the need to defer to the President's determination that Padilla's detention is necessary and appropriate in the interest of national security. However, we believe that the district court ultimately accorded insufficient deference to that determination, effectively imposing upon the President the equivalent of a least-restrictive-means test. To subject to such exacting scrutiny the President's determination that criminal prosecution would not adequately protect the Nation's security at a very minimum fails to accord the President the deference that is his when he acts pursuant to a broad delegation of authority from Congress, such as the AUMF.

As for Padilla's attempted distinction of *Quirin* on the grounds that, unlike Haupt, he has never been charged and tried by the military, the plurality in Hamdi rejected as immaterial the distinction between detention and trial (apparently regarding the former as a lesser imposition than the latter), noting that "nothing in *Quirin* suggests that [Haupt's United States] citizenship would have precluded his mere detention for the duration of the relevant hostilities." *Hamdi*, 124 S. Ct. at 2640 (emphasis added).

3

Padilla, citing *Ex parte Endo*, 323 U.S. 283 (1944), and relying upon *Quirin*, next argues that only a clear statement from Congress can authorize his detention, and that the AUMF is not itself, and does not contain, such a clear statement.

In *Endo*, the Court did state that, when asked to find implied powers in a wartime statute, it must assume that "the law makers intended to place no greater restraint on the citizen than was clearly and unmistakably indicated by the language [the law makers] used." The Court almost immediately thereafter observed, however, that the "fact that the Act" at issue was "silent on detention [did] not of course mean that any power to detain [was] lacking," an observation that proves that the Court did not adopt or even apply in that case a "clear statement" rule of the kind for which Padilla argues.

Padilla contends that *Quirin* also supports the existence of a clear statement rule. However, in no place in *Quirin* did the Court even purport to establish a clear statement rule. In its opinion, the Court did note that Congress had "explicitly" authorized Haupt's military trial. See 317 U.S. at 28. But to conclude from this passing note that the Court required a clear statement as a matter of law would be unwarranted. In fact, to the extent that *Quirin* can be understood to have addressed the need for a clear statement of authority from Congress at all, the rule would appear the opposite:

> [T]he detention and trial of petitioners—ordered by the President in the declared exercise of his powers as Commander in Chief of the Army in time of war and of grave public danger—are not to be set aside by the courts without the clear conviction that they are in conflict with the Constitution or laws of Congress constitutionally enacted.

Of course, even were a clear statement by Congress required, the AUMF constitutes such a clear statement according to the Supreme Court. In *Hamdi*, stating that "it [was] of no moment that the AUMF does not use specific language of detention," 124 S. Ct. at 2641, the plurality held that the AUMF "clearly and unmistakably authorized" Hamdi's detention. Nothing in the AUMF permits us to conclude that the Joint Resolution clearly and unmistakably authorized Hamdi's detention but not Padilla's. To the contrary, read in light of its purpose clause ("in order to prevent any future acts of international terrorism against the United States") and its preamble (stating that the acts of 9/11 "render it both necessary and appropriate…to protect United States citizens both at home and abroad"), the AUMF applies even more clearly and unmistakably to Padilla than to Hamdi. Padilla, after all, in addition to supporting hostile forces in Afghanistan and taking up arms against our troops on a battlefield in that country like Hamdi, *also* came to the United States in order to commit future acts of terrorism against American citizens and targets.

These facts unquestionably establish that Padilla poses the requisite threat of return to battle in the ongoing armed conflict between the United States and al Qaeda in Afghanistan, and that his detention is authorized as a "fundamental incident of waging war," in order "to prevent a combatant's return to the battlefield," *id.* Congress "clearly and unmistakably," authorized such detention when, in the AUMF, it "permitt[ed] the use of 'necessary and appropriate force,'" to prevent other attacks like those of September 11, 2001.

4

Finally, Padilla argues that, even if his detention is authorized by the AUMF, it is unlawful under *Ex parte Milligan*, 71 U.S. (4 Wall.) 2 (1866). In *Milligan*, the Supreme Court held that a United States citizen associated with an anti-Union secret society but unaffiliated with the Confederate army could not be tried by a military tribunal while access to civilian courts was open and unobstructed. *Milligan* purported to restrict the power of Congress as well as the power of the President. ("[N]o usage of war could sanction a military trial…for any offence whatever of a citizen in civil life, in nowise connected with the military service. Congress could grant no such power…"). *Quirin*, however, confirmed that *Milligan* does not extend to enemy combatants. As the Court in *Quirin* explained, the *Milligan* Court's reasoning had "particular reference to the facts before it," namely, that Milligan was not "a part of or associated with the armed forces of the enemy." The *Hamdi* plurality in turn reaffirmed this limitation on the reach of *Milligan*, emphasizing that *Quirin*, a unanimous opinion, "both postdates and clarifies *Milligan*." 124 S. Ct. at 2643. Thus confined, *Milligan* is inapposite here because Padilla, unlike Milligan, associated with, and has taken up arms against the forces of the United States on behalf of, an enemy of the United States.

III

The Congress of the United States, in the Authorization for Use of Military Force Joint Resolution, provided the President all powers necessary and appropriate to protect American citizens from terrorist acts by those who attacked the United States on September 11, 2001. As would be expected, and as the Supreme Court has held, those powers include the power to detain identified and committed enemies such as Padilla, who associated with al Qaeda and the Taliban regime, who took up arms against this Nation in its war against these enemies, and who entered the United States for the avowed purpose of further prosecuting that war by attacking American citizens and targets on our own soil—a power without which, Congress understood, the President could well be unable to protect American citizens from the very kind of savage attack that occurred four years ago almost to the day.

The detention of petitioner being fully authorized by Act of Congress, the judgment of the district court that the detention of petitioner by the President of the United States is without support in law is hereby reversed.

As previously discussed, *Hamdi* resulted in the creation of the CSRT in July 2004. Interestingly, the CSRT process was deemed to be an entirely sufficient mechanism by Congress—the Detainee Treatment Act of 2005 (DTA) and the Military Commissions Act of 2006 (MCA)—for alien enemy combatants to challenge the legality of their designation. In fact, in the 2006 MCA, Congress specifically recognized the CSRT as the only recourse that detainees had for contesting their designation as "illegal enemy combatants." Although the U.S. Court of Appeals for the D.C. Circuit issued an order in 2007 dismissing detainee cases based on the MCA provisions, in the 2008 consolidated cases of *Boumediene v. Bush* and *Al Odah v. United States*, a narrow majority (5-4) ruling by the Supreme Court struck down Section 7 of the 2006 MCA, which applied DTA review procedures to detainee challenges to detention, and found that aliens designated as enemy combatants detained at Guantanamo Bay had the constitutional privilege of habeas corpus review before a federal court.

BOUMEDIENE v. BUSH
Supreme Court of the United States
128 S. Ct. 2229 (2008)

Justice Kennedy delivered the opinion of the Court, in which Stevens, Souter, Ginsburg, and Breyer, JJ., joined.

Petitioners are aliens designated as enemy combatants and detained at the United States Naval Station at Guantanamo Bay, Cuba. There are others detained there, also aliens, who are not parties to this suit.

Petitioners present a question not resolved by our earlier cases relating to the detention of aliens at Guantanamo: whether they have the constitutional privilege of habeas corpus, a privilege not to be withdrawn except in conformance with the Suspension Clause, Art. I, § 9, cl. 2. We hold these petitioners do have the habeas corpus privilege. Congress has enacted a statute, the Detainee Treatment Act of 2005(DTA), 119 Stat. 2739, that provides certain procedures for review of the detainees' status. We hold that those procedures are not an adequate and effective substitute for habeas corpus. Therefore § 7 of the Military Commissions Act of 2006 (MCA), 28 U.S.C.A. § 2241(e) (Supp.2007), operates as an unconstitutional suspension of the writ. We do not address whether the President has authority to detain these petitioners nor do we hold that the writ must issue. These and other questions regarding the legality of the detention are to be resolved in the first instance by the District Court.

I

Under the Authorization for Use of Military Force (AUMF), § 2(a), 115 Stat. 224, note following 50 U.S.C. § 1541 (2000 ed., Supp. V), the President is authorized "to use all necessary and appropriate force against those nations, organizations, or persons he determines planned, authorized, committed, or aided the terrorist attacks that occurred on September 11, 2001, or harbored such organizations or persons, in order to prevent any future acts of international terrorism against the United States by such nations, organizations or persons."

In *Hamdi v. Rumsfeld*, 542 U.S. 507 (2004), five Members of the Court recognized that detention of individuals who fought against the United States in Afghanistan "for the duration of the particular conflict in which they were captured, is so fundamental and accepted an incident to war as to be an exercise of the 'necessary and appropriate force' Congress has authorized the President to use." *Id.*, at 518, 124 S.Ct. 2633 (plurality opinion of O'Connor, J.), *id.*, at 588-589, 124 S.Ct. 2633 (Thomas, J., dissenting). After *Hamdi*, the Deputy Secretary of Defense established Combatant Status Review Tribunals (CSRTs) to determine whether individuals detained at Guantanamo were "enemy combatants," as the Department defines that term. See App. to Pet. for Cert. in No. 06-1195, p. 81a. A later memorandum established procedures to implement the CSRTs. See App. to Pet. for Cert. in No. 06-1196, p. 147. The Government maintains these procedures were designed to comply with the due process requirements identified by the plurality in *Hamdi*.

Interpreting the AUMF, the Department of Defense ordered the detention of these petitioners, and they were transferred to Guantanamo. Some of these individuals were apprehended on the battlefield in Afghanistan, others in places as far away from there as Bosnia and Gambia. All are foreign nationals, but none is a citizen of a nation now at war with the United States. Each denies he is a member of the al Qaeda terrorist network that carried out the September 11 attacks or of the Taliban regime that provided sanctuary for al Qaeda. Each petitioner appeared before a separate CSRT; was determined to be an enemy combatant; and has sought a writ of habeas corpus in the United States District Court for the District of Columbia.

…

The Court of Appeals concluded that MCA § 7 must be read to strip from it, and all federal courts, jurisdiction to consider petitioners' habeas corpus applications, *id.*, at 987; that petitioners are not entitled to the privilege of the writ or the protections of the Suspension Clause, *id.*, at 990-991; and, as a result, that it was unnecessary to consider whether Congress provided an adequate and effective substitute for habeas corpus in the DTA.

We granted certiorari.…

II

As a threshold matter, we must decide whether MCA § 7 denies the federal courts jurisdiction to hear habeas corpus actions pending at the time of its enactment. We hold the statute does deny that jurisdiction, so that, if the statute is valid, petitioners' cases must be dismissed.:

...

We acknowledge...the litigation history that prompted Congress to enact the MCA. In *Hamdan* the Court found it unnecessary to address the petitioner's Suspension Clause arguments but noted the relevance of the clear statement rule in deciding whether Congress intended to reach pending habeas corpus cases....If the Court invokes a clear statement rule to advise that certain statutory interpretations are favored in order to avoid constitutional difficulties, Congress can make an informed legislative choice either to amend the statute or to retain its existing text. If Congress amends, its intent must be respected even if a difficult constitutional question is presented. The usual presumption is that Members of Congress, in accord with their oath of office, considered the constitutional issue and determined the amended statute to be a lawful one; and the Judiciary, in light of that determination, proceeds to its own independent judgment on the constitutional question when required to do so in a proper case.

...

III

...

That the Framers considered the writ a vital instrument for the protection of individual liberty is evident from the care taken to specify the limited grounds for its suspension....

In our own system the Suspension Clause is designed to protect against these cyclical abuses. The Clause protects the rights of the detained by a means consistent with the essential design of the Constitution. It ensures that, except during periods of formal suspension, the Judiciary will have a time-tested device, the writ, to maintain the "delicate balance of governance" that is itself the surest safeguard of liberty. See *Hamdi,* 542 U.S., at 536 (plurality opinion). The Clause protects the rights of the detained by affirming the duty and authority of the Judiciary to call the jailer to account....The separation-of-powers doctrine, and the history that influenced its design, therefore must inform the reach and purpose of the Suspension Clause.

...

These considerations resulted in the doctrine of territorial incorporation, under which the Constitution applies in full in incorporated Territories surely destined for statehood but only in part in unincorporated Territories.

...

Second, because the United States lacked both *de jure* sovereignty and plenary control over Landsberg Prison,...it is far from clear that the *Eisentrager* Court used the term sovereignty only in the narrow technical sense and not to connote the degree of control the military asserted over the facility.

...

Our basic charter cannot be contracted away like this. The Constitution grants Congress and the President the power to acquire, dispose of, and govern territory, not the power to decide when and where its terms apply. Even when the United States acts outside its borders, its powers are not "absolute and unlimited" but are subject "to such restrictions as are expressed in the

Constitution." *Murphy v. Ramsey*, 114 U.S. 15, 44, 5 S.Ct. 747, 29 L.Ed. 47 (1885). Abstaining from questions involving formal sovereignty and territorial governance is one thing. To hold the political branches have the power to switch the Constitution on or off at will is quite another. The former position reflects this Court's recognition that certain matters requiring political judgments are best left to the political branches. The latter would permit a striking anomaly in our tripartite system of government, leading to a regime in which Congress and the President, not this Court, say "what the law is." *Marbury v. Madison*, 1 Cranch 137, 177, 2 L.Ed. 60 (1803).

These concerns have particular bearing upon the Suspension Clause question in the cases now before us, for the writ of habeas corpus is itself an indispensable mechanism for monitoring the separation of powers. The test for determining the scope of this provision must not be subject to manipulation by those whose power it is designed to restrain.

C

As we recognized in *Rasul*, 542 U.S., at 476 (Kennedy, J., concurring in judgment), the outlines of a framework for determining the reach of the Suspension Clause are suggested by the factors the Court relied upon in *Eisentrager*. In addition to the practical concerns discussed above, the *Eisentrager* Court found relevant that each petitioner:

> "(a) is an enemy alien; (b) has never been or resided in the United States; (c) was cap-
> tured outside of our territory and there held in military custody as a prisoner of war; (d)
> was tried and convicted by a Military Commission sitting outside the United States; (e)
> for offenses against laws of war committed outside the United States; (f) and is at all
> times imprisoned outside the United States." 339 U.S., at 777.

Based on this language from *Eisentrager*, and the reasoning in our other extraterritoriality opinions, we conclude that at least three factors are relevant in determining the reach of the Suspension Clause: (1) the citizenship and status of the detainee and the adequacy of the process through which that status determination was made; (2) the nature of the sites where apprehension and then detention took place; and (3) the practical obstacles inherent in resolving the prisoner's entitlement to the writ....

In comparison the procedural protections afforded to the detainees in the CSRT hearings are far more limited, and, we conclude, fall well short of the procedures and adversarial mechanisms that would eliminate the need for habeas corpus review. Although the detainee is assigned a "Personal Representative" to assist him during CSRT proceedings, the Secretary of the Navy's memorandum makes clear that person is not the detainee's lawyer or even his "advocate." The Government's evidence is accorded a presumption of validity. The detainee is allowed to present "reasonably available" evidence, but his ability to rebut the Government's evidence against him is limited by the circumstances of his confinement and his lack of counsel at this stage. And although the detainee can seek review of his status determination in the Court of Appeals, that review process cannot cure all defects in the earlier proceedings.

As to the second factor relevant to this analysis, the detainees here are similarly situated to the *Eisentrager* petitioners in that the sites of their apprehension and detention are technically outside the sovereign territory of the United States. As noted earlier, this is a factor that weighs against finding they have rights under the Suspension Clause. But there are critical differences between Landsberg Prison, circa 1950, and the United States Naval Station at Guantanamo Bay in 2008. Unlike its present control over the naval station, the United States' control over the prison in Germany was neither absolute nor indefinite. Like all parts of occupied Germany, the prison was under the jurisdiction of the combined Allied Forces....The Allies had not planned a long-term occupation of Germany, nor did they intend to displace all German institutions even during the period of occupation....Guantanamo Bay, on the other hand, is no transient possession. In every practical sense Guantanamo is not abroad; it is within the constant jurisdiction of the United States....

We hold that Art. I, § 9, cl. 2, of the Constitution has full effect at Guantanamo Bay. If the privilege of habeas corpus is to be denied to the detainees now before us, Congress must act in accordance with the requirements of the Suspension Clause. Cf. *Hamdi,* 542 U.S., at 564 (Scalia, J., dissenting) ("[I]ndefinite imprisonment on reasonable suspicion is not an available option of treatment for those accused of aiding the enemy, absent a suspension of the writ"). This Court may not impose a *de facto* suspension by abstaining from these controversies....The MCA does not purport to be a formal suspension of the writ; and the Government, in its submissions to us, has not argued that it is. Petitioners, therefore, are entitled to the privilege of habeas corpus to challenge the legality of their detention.

V

...

The Court of Appeals, having decided that the writ does not run to the detainees in any event, found it unnecessary to consider whether an adequate substitute has been provided. In the ordinary course we would remand to the Court of Appeals to consider this question in the first instance....Departure from the rule is appropriate in "exceptional" circumstances.

...

B

We do not endeavor to offer a comprehensive summary of the requisites for an adequate substitute for habeas corpus. We do consider it uncontroversial, however, that the privilege of habeas corpus entitles the prisoner to a meaningful opportunity to demonstrate that he is being held pursuant to "the erroneous application or interpretation" of relevant law. *St. Cyr,* 533 U.S., at 302, 121 S.Ct. 2271. And the habeas court must have the power to order the conditional release of an individual unlawfully detained-though release need not be the exclusive remedy and is not the appropriate one in every case in which the writ is granted....These are the easily identified attributes of any constitutionally adequate habeas corpus proceeding. But, depending on the circumstances, more may be required.

...

Accordingly, where relief is sought from a sentence that resulted from the judgment of a court of record, as was the case in *Watkins* and indeed in most federal habeas cases, considerable deference is owed to the court that ordered confinement....Likewise in those cases the prisoner should exhaust adequate alternative remedies before filing for the writ in federal court.

...

Where a person is detained by executive order, rather than, say, after being tried and convicted in a court, the need for collateral review is most pressing. A criminal conviction in the usual course occurs after a judicial hearing before a tribunal disinterested in the outcome and committed to procedures designed to ensure its own independence. These dynamics are not inherent in executive detention orders or executive review procedures. In this context the need for habeas corpus is more urgent. The intended duration of the detention and the reasons for it bear upon the precise scope of the inquiry. Habeas corpus proceedings need not resemble a criminal trial, even when the detention is by executive order. But the writ must be effective. The habeas court must have sufficient authority to conduct a meaningful review of both the cause for detention and the Executive's power to detain.

...

Even if we were to assume that the CSRTs satisfy due process standards, it would not end our inquiry. Habeas corpus is a collateral process that exists, in Justice Holmes' words, to "cu[t] through all forms and g[o] to the very tissue of the structure. It comes in from the outside, not in subordination to the proceedings, and although every form may have been preserved opens the inquiry whether they have been more than an empty shell." *Frank v. Mangum,* 237 U.S. 309, 346 (1915) (dissenting opinion). Even when the procedures authorizing detention are structurally sound, the Suspension Clause remains applicable and the writ relevant....

The extent of the showing required of the Government in these cases is a matter to be determined. We need not explore it further at this stage. We do hold that when the judicial power to issue habeas corpus properly is invoked the judicial officer must have adequate authority to make a determination in light of the relevant law and facts and to formulate and issue appropriate orders for relief, including, if necessary, an order directing the prisoner's release.

...

VI

...

The Government argues petitioners must seek review of their CSRT determinations in the Court of Appeals before they can proceed with their habeas corpus actions in the District Court. As noted earlier, in other contexts and for prudential reasons this Court has required exhaustion of alternative remedies before a prisoner can seek federal habeas relief....

The real risks, the real threats, of terrorist attacks are constant and not likely soon to abate. The ways to disrupt our life and laws are so many and unforeseen that the Court should not attempt even some general catalogue of crises that might occur. Certain principles are apparent, however. Practical considerations and exigent circumstances inform the definition and reach of the law's writs, including habeas corpus. The cases and our tradition reflect this precept.

In cases involving foreign citizens detained abroad by the Executive, it likely would be both an impractical and unprecedented extension of judicial power to assume that habeas corpus would be available at the moment the prisoner is taken into custody. If and when habeas corpus jurisdiction applies, as it does in these cases, then proper deference can be accorded to reasonable procedures for screening and initial detention under lawful and proper conditions of confinement and treatment for a reasonable period of time. Domestic exigencies, furthermore, might also impose such onerous burdens on the Government that here, too, the Judicial Branch would be required to devise sensible rules for staying habeas corpus proceedings until the Government can comply with its requirements in a responsible way. Cf. *Ex parte Milligan,* 4 Wall., at 127 ("If, in foreign invasion or civil war, the courts are actually closed, and it is impossible to administer criminal justice according to law, *then,* on the theatre of active military operations, where war really prevails, there is a necessity to furnish a substitute for the civil authority, thus overthrown, to preserve the safety of the army and society; and as no power is left but the military, it is allowed to govern by martial rule until the laws can have their free course").

…

Our decision today holds only that the petitioners before us are entitled to seek the writ; that the DTA review procedures are an inadequate substitute for habeas corpus; and that the petitioners in these cases need not exhaust the review procedures in the Court of Appeals before proceeding with their habeas actions in the District Court. The only law we identify as unconstitutional is MCA § 7, 28 U.S.C.A. § 2241(e) (Supp.2007). Accordingly, both the DTA and the CSRT process remain intact. Our holding with regard to exhaustion should not be read to imply that a habeas court should intervene the moment an enemy combatant steps foot in a territory where the writ runs. The Executive is entitled to a reasonable period of time to determine a detainee's status before a court entertains that detainee's habeas corpus petition. The CSRT process is the mechanism Congress and the President set up to deal with these issues. Except in cases of undue delay, federal courts should refrain from entertaining an enemy combatant's habeas corpus petition at least until after the Department, acting via the CSRT, has had a chance to review his status.

B

Although we hold that the DTA is not an adequate and effective substitute for habeas corpus, it does not follow that a habeas corpus court may disregard the dangers the detention in these cases was intended to prevent….Certain accommodations can be made to reduce the burden habeas corpus proceedings will place on the military without impermissibly diluting the protections of the writ.

…

In considering both the procedural and substantive standards used to impose detention to prevent acts of terrorism, proper deference must be accorded to the political branches. See *United States v. Curtiss-Wright Export Corp.,* 299 U.S. 304, 320 (1936). Unlike the President and some designated Members of Congress, neither the Members of this Court nor most federal judges begin the day with briefings that may describe new and serious threats to our Nation and its people. The law must accord the Executive substantial authority to apprehend and detain those who pose a real danger to our security.

Officials charged with daily operational responsibility for our security may consider a judicial discourse on the history of the Habeas Corpus Act of 1679 and like matters to be far removed from the Nation's present, urgent concerns. Established legal doctrine, however, must be consulted for its teaching. Remote in time it may be; irrelevant to the present it is not. Security depends upon a sophisticated intelligence apparatus and the ability of our Armed Forces to act and to interdict. There are further considerations, however. Security subsists, too, in fidelity to freedom's first principles. Chief among these are freedom from arbitrary and unlawful restraint and the personal liberty that is secured by adherence to the separation of powers. It is from these principles that the judicial authority to consider petitions for habeas corpus relief derives.

Our opinion does not undermine the Executive's powers as Commander in Chief. On the contrary, the exercise of those powers is vindicated, not eroded, when confirmed by the Judicial Branch. Within the Constitution's separation-of-powers structure, few exercises of judicial power are as legitimate or as necessary as the responsibility to hear challenges to the authority of the Executive to imprison a person. Some of these petitioners have been in custody for six years with no definitive judicial determination as to the legality of their detention. Their access to the writ is a necessity to determine the lawfulness of their status, even if, in the end, they do not obtain the relief they seek.

Because our Nation's past military conflicts have been of limited duration, it has been possible to leave the outer boundaries of war powers undefined. If, as some fear, terrorism continues to pose dangerous threats to us for years to come, the Court might not have this luxury. This result is not inevitable, however. The political branches, consistent with their independent obligations to interpret and uphold the Constitution, can engage in a genuine debate about how best to preserve constitutional values while protecting the Nation from terrorism. Cf. *Hamdan,* 548 U.S., at 636 (Breyer, J., concurring) ("[J]udicial insistence upon that consultation does not weaken our Nation's ability to deal with danger. To the contrary, that insistence strengthens the Nation's ability to determine-through democratic means-how best to do so").

It bears repeating that our opinion does not address the content of the law that governs petitioners' detention. That is a matter yet to be determined. We hold that petitioners may invoke the fundamental procedural protections of habeas corpus. The laws and Constitution are designed to survive, and remain in force, in extraordinary times. Liberty and security can be reconciled; and in our system they are reconciled within the framework of the law. The Framers decided that habeas corpus, a right of first importance, must be a part of that framework, a part of that law.

The determination by the Court of Appeals that the Suspension Clause and its protections are inapplicable to petitioners was in error. The judgment of the Court of Appeals is reversed. The cases are remanded to the Court of Appeals with instructions that it remand the cases to the District Court for proceedings consistent with this opinion.

It is so ordered.

...

Chief Justice ROBERTS, with whom Justice SCALIA, Justice THOMAS, and Justice ALITO join, dissenting.

Today the Court strikes down as inadequate the most generous set of procedural protections ever afforded aliens detained by this country as enemy combatants. The political branches crafted these procedures amidst an ongoing military conflict, after much careful investigation and thorough debate. The Court rejects them today out of hand, without bothering to say what due process rights the detainees possess, without explaining how the statute fails to vindicate those rights, and before a single petitioner has even attempted to avail himself of the law's operation. And to what effect? The majority merely replaces a review system designed by the people's representatives with a set of shapeless procedures to be defined by federal courts at some future date. One cannot help but think, after surveying the modest practical results of the majority's ambitious opinion, that this decision is not really about the detainees at all, but about control of federal policy regarding enemy combatants.

The majority is adamant that the Guantanamo detainees are entitled to the protections of habeas corpus-its opinion begins by deciding that question. I regard the issue as a difficult one, primarily because of the unique and unusual jurisdictional status of Guantanamo Bay. I nonetheless agree with Justice Scalia's analysis of our precedents and the pertinent history of the writ, and accordingly join his dissent. The important point for me, however, is that the Court should have resolved these cases on other grounds. Habeas is most fundamentally a procedural right, a mechanism for contesting the legality of executive detention. The critical threshold question in these cases, prior to any inquiry about the writ's scope, is whether the system the political branches designed protects whatever rights the detainees may possess. If so, there is no need for any additional process, whether called "habeas" or something else.

Congress entrusted that threshold question in the first instance to the Court of Appeals for the District of Columbia Circuit, as the Constitution surely allows Congress to do. See Detainee Treatment Act of 2005(DTA), § 1005(e)(2)(A). But before the D.C. Circuit has addressed the issue, the Court cashiers the statute, and without answering this critical threshold question itself. The Court does eventually get around to asking whether review under the DTA is, as the Court frames it, an "adequate substitute" for habeas, *ante,* at 2262, but even then its opinion fails to determine what rights the detainees possess and whether the DTA system satisfies them. The majority instead compares the undefined DTA process to an equally undefined habeas right-one that is to be given shape only in the future by district courts on a case-by-case basis. This whole approach is misguided.

It is also fruitless. How the detainees' claims will be decided now that the DTA is gone is anybody's guess. But the habeas process the Court mandates will most likely end up looking a lot like the DTA system it replaces, as the district court judges shaping it will have to reconcile review of the prisoners' detention with the undoubted need to protect the American people from the terrorist threat-precisely the challenge Congress undertook in drafting the DTA. All that today's opinion has done is shift responsibility for those sensitive foreign policy and national security decisions from the elected branches to the Federal Judiciary.

I believe the system the political branches constructed adequately protects any constitutional rights aliens captured abroad and detained as enemy combatants may enjoy. I therefore would dismiss these cases on that ground. With all respect for the contrary views of the majority, I must dissent.

…

III

For all its eloquence about the detainees' right to the writ, the Court makes no effort to elaborate how exactly the remedy it prescribes will differ from the procedural protections detainees enjoy under the DTA. The Court objects to the detainees' limited access to witnesses and classified material, but proposes no alternatives of its own. Indeed, it simply ignores the many difficult questions its holding presents. What, for example, will become of the CSRT process? The majority says federal courts should *generally* refrain from entertaining detainee challenges until after the petitioner's CSRT proceeding has finished. See *ante,* at 2275-2276 ("[e]xcept in cases of undue delay"). But to what deference, if any, is that CSRT determination entitled?

There are other problems. Take witness availability. What makes the majority think witnesses will become magically available when the review procedure is labeled "habeas"? Will the location of most of these witnesses change-will they suddenly become easily susceptible to service of process? Or will subpoenas issued by American habeas courts run to Basra? And if they did, how would they be enforced? Speaking of witnesses, will detainees be able to call active-duty military officers as witnesses? If not, why not?

...

The majority rests its decision on abstract and hypothetical concerns. Step back and consider what, in the real world, Congress and the Executive have actually granted aliens captured by our Armed Forces overseas and found to be enemy combatants:

- The right to hear the bases of the charges against them, including a summary of any classified evidence.
- The ability to challenge the bases of their detention before military tribunals modeled after Geneva Convention procedures. Some 38 detainees have been released as a result of this process. Brief for Federal Respondents 57, 60.
- The right, before the CSRT, to testify, introduce evidence, call witnesses, question those the Government calls, and secure release, if and when appropriate.
- The right to the aid of a personal representative in arranging and presenting their cases before a CSRT.
- Before the D.C. Circuit, the right to employ counsel, challenge the factual record, contest the lower tribunal's legal determinations, ensure compliance with the Constitution and laws, and secure release, if any errors below establish their entitlement to such relief.

In sum, the DTA satisfies the majority's own criteria for assessing adequacy. This statutory scheme provides the combatants held at Guantanamo greater procedural protections than have ever been afforded alleged enemy detainees-whether citizens or aliens-in our national history.

So who has won? Not the detainees. The Court's analysis leaves them with only the prospect of further litigation to determine the content of their new habeas right, followed by further litigation to resolve their particular cases, followed by further litigation before the D.C. Circuit-where they could have started had they invoked the DTA procedure. Not Congress, whose attempt to "determine-through democratic means-how best" to balance the security of the American people with the detainees' liberty interests, see *Hamdan v. Rumsfeld,* 548 U.S. 557 (2006) (Breyer, J., concurring), has been unceremoniously brushed aside. Not the Great Writ, whose majesty is hardly enhanced by its extension to a jurisdictionally quirky outpost, with no tangible benefit to anyone. Not the rule of law, unless by that is meant the rule of lawyers, who will now arguably have a greater role than military and intelligence officials in shaping policy for alien enemy combatants. And certainly not the American people, who today lose a bit more control over the conduct of this Nation's foreign policy to unelected, politically unaccountable judges.

I respectfully dissent.

Justice SCALIA, with whom THE CHIEF JUSTICE, Justice THOMAS, and Justice ALITO join, dissenting.
Today, for the first time in our Nation's history, the Court confers a constitutional right to habeas corpus on alien enemies detained abroad by our military forces in the course of an ongoing war.

THE CHIEF JUSTICE's dissent, which I join, shows that the procedures prescribed by Congress in the Detainee Treatment Act provide the essential protections that habeas corpus guarantees; there has thus been no suspension of the writ, and no basis exists for judicial intervention beyond what the Act allows. My problem with today's opinion is more fundamental still: The writ of habeas corpus does not, and never has, run in favor of aliens abroad; the Suspension Clause thus has no application, and the Court's intervention in this military matter is entirely *ultra vires.*

I shall devote most of what will be a lengthy opinion to the legal errors contained in the opinion of the Court. Contrary to my usual practice, however, I think it appropriate to begin with a description of the disastrous consequences of what the Court has done today.

I

America is at war with radical Islamists....

The game of bait-and-switch that today's opinion plays upon the Nation's Commander in Chief will make the war harder on us. It will almost certainly cause more Americans to be killed. That consequence would be tolerable if necessary to preserve a time-honored legal principle vital to our constitutional Republic. But it is this Court's blatant *abandonment* of such a principle that produces the decision today. The President relied on our settled precedent in *Johnson v. Eisentrager,* 339 U.S. 763 (1950), when he established the prison at Guantanamo Bay for enemy aliens. Citing that case, the President's Office of Legal Counsel advised him "that the great weight of legal authority indicates that a federal district court could not properly exercise habeas jurisdiction over an alien detained at [Guantanamo Bay]." Memorandum from Patrick F. Philbin and John C. Yoo, Deputy Assistant Attorneys General, Office of Legal Counsel, to William J. Haynes II, General Counsel, Dept. of Defense (Dec. 28, 2001). Had the law been otherwise, the military surely would not have transported prisoners there, but would have kept them in Afghanistan, transferred them to another of our foreign military bases, or turned them over to allies for detention. Those other facilities might well have been worse for the detainees themselves.

In the long term, then, the Court's decision today accomplishes little, except perhaps to reduce the well-being of enemy combatants that the Court ostensibly seeks to protect. In the short term, however, the decision is devastating. At least 30 of those prisoners hitherto released from Guantanamo Bay have returned to the battlefield. See S.Rep. No. 110-90, pt. 7, p. 13 (2007) (Minority Views of Sens. Kyl, Sessions, Graham, Cornyn, and Coburn) (hereinafter Minority Report). Some have been captured or killed. See *ibid.;* see also Mintz, Released Detainees Rejoining the Fight, Washington Post, Oct. 22, 2004, pp. A1, A12. But others have succeeded in carrying on their atrocities against innocent civilians. In one case, a detainee released from Guantanamo Bay masterminded the kidnapping of two Chinese dam workers, one of whom was later shot to death when used as a human shield against Pakistani commandoes. See Khan & Lancaster, Pakistanis Rescue Hostage; 2nd Dies, Washington Post, Oct. 15, 2004, p. A18. Another former detainee promptly resumed his post as a senior Taliban commander and murdered a United Nations engineer and three Afghan soldiers. Mintz, *supra.* Still another murdered an Afghan judge. See Minority Report 13. It was reported only last month that a released detainee carried out a suicide bombing against Iraqi soldiers in Mosul, Iraq. See White, Ex-Guantanamo Detainee Joined Iraq Suicide Attack, Washington Post, May 8, 2008, p. A18.

These, mind you, were detainees whom *the military* had concluded were not enemy combatants. Their return to the kill illustrates the incredible difficulty of assessing who is and who is not an enemy combatant in a foreign theater of operations where the environment does not lend itself to rigorous evidence collection. Astoundingly, the Court today raises the bar, requiring military officials to appear before civilian courts and defend their decisions under procedural and evidentiary rules that go beyond what Congress has specified. As The Chief Justice's dissent makes clear, we have no idea what those procedural and evidentiary rules are, but they will be determined by civil courts and (in the Court's contemplation at least) will be more detainee-friendly than those now applied, since otherwise there would no reason to hold the congressionally prescribed procedures unconstitutional. If they impose a higher standard of proof (from foreign battlefields) than the current procedures require, the number of the enemy returned to combat will obviously increase.

But even when the military has evidence that it can bring forward, it is often foolhardy to release that evidence to the attorneys representing our enemies. And one escalation of procedures that the Court *is* clear about is affording the detainees increased access to witnesses (perhaps troops serving in Afghanistan?) and to classified information. See *ante,* at 2269-2270. During the 1995 prosecution of Omar Abdel Rahman, federal prosecutors gave the names of 200 unindicted co-conspirators to the "Blind Sheik's" defense lawyers; that information was in the hands of Osama Bin Laden within two weeks. See Minority Report 14-15. In another case, trial testimony revealed to the enemy that the United States had been monitoring their cellular network, whereupon they promptly stopped using it, enabling more of them to evade capture and continue their atrocities. See *id.,* at 15.

And today it is not just the military that the Court elbows aside. A mere two Terms ago in *Hamdan v. Rumsfeld,* 548 U.S. 557 (2006), when the Court held (quite amazingly) that the Detainee Treatment Act of 2005 had not stripped habeas jurisdiction over Guantanamo petitioners' claims, four Members of today's five-Justice majority joined an opinion saying the following:

> "Nothing prevents the President from returning to Congress to seek the authority [for trial by military commission] he believes necessary."

...

The category of prisoner comparable to these detainees are not the *Eisentrager* criminal defendants, but the more than 400,000 prisoners of war detained in the United States alone during World War II. Not a single one was accorded the right to have his detention validated by a habeas corpus action in federal court-and that despite the fact that they were present on U.S. soil. See Bradley, The Military Commissions Act, Habeas Corpus, and the Geneva Conventions, 101 Am. J. Int'l L. 322, 338 (2007). The Court's analysis produces a crazy result: Whereas those convicted and sentenced to death for war crimes are without judicial remedy, all enemy combatants detained during a war, at least insofar as they are confined in an area away from the battlefield over which the United States exercises "absolute and indefinite" control, may seek a writ of habeas corpus in federal court. And, as an even more bizarre implication from the Court's reasoning, those prisoners whom the military plans to try by full-dress Commission at a future date may file habeas petitions and secure release before their trials take place.

...

Today the Court warps our Constitution in a way that goes beyond the narrow issue of the reach of the Suspension Clause, invoking judicially brainstormed separation-of-powers principles to establish a manipulable "functional" test for the extraterritorial reach of habeas corpus (and, no doubt, for the extraterritorial reach of other constitutional protections as well). It blatantly misdescribes important precedents, most conspicuously Justice Jackson's opinion for the Court in *Johnson v. Eisentrager*. It breaks a chain of precedent as old as the common law that prohibits judicial inquiry into detentions of aliens abroad absent statutory authorization. And, most tragically, it sets our military commanders the impossible task of proving to a civilian court, under whatever standards this Court devises in the future, that evidence supports the confinement of each and every enemy prisoner.

The Nation will live to regret what the Court has done today. I dissent.

While *Boumediene* did not specifically decide whether the CSRT process satisfied the due process requirements of *Hamdi*, the ruling allowed detainees at Guantanamo Bay access to the habeas corpus constitutional protections that no other enemy combatant has ever enjoyed—access to the federal courts to review the legality and possibly the circumstances of their detention. Taken to its logical conclusion some have asked whether this decision would mean that the over 450,000 detainees in the United States during World War II would have access to federal courts to determine their status?

In any event, as the D.C. federal district courts continue to entertain habeas petitions from Guantanamo Bay detainees, they have developed applicable standards for the review process in keeping with the *Boumediene* mandate that detainees are entitled to the "fundamental procedural protections of habeas corpus." The 2010 case of *Al-Bihani v Obama* explores a variety of issues associated with the President's authority to designate enemy combatants as well as identifying the list of procedures that are fundamental in habeas review for Guantanamo Bay detainees.

AL-BIHANI v. OBAMA
United States Court of Appeals for the District of Columbia Circuit
No. 09-5051 (Jan. 5, 2010)

BROWN, *Circuit Judge*:

Ghaleb Nassar Al-Bihani appeals the denial of his petition for a writ of habeas corpus and seeks reversal or remand. He claims his detention is unauthorized by statute and the procedures of his habeas proceeding were constitutionally infirm. We reject these claims and affirm the denial of his petition.

I

Al-Bihani, a Yemeni citizen, has been held at the U.S. naval base detention facility in Guantanamo Bay, Cuba since 2002. He came to Guantanamo by a circuitous route. It began in Saudi Arabia in the first half of 2001 when a local sheikh issued a religious challenge to Al-Bihani. In response, Al-Bihani traveled through Pakistan to Afghanistan eager to defend the Taliban's Islamic state against the Northern Alliance. Along the way, he stayed at what the government alleges were Al Qaeda-affiliated guesthouses; Al-Bihani only concedes they were affiliated with the Taliban. During this transit period, he may also have received instruction at two Al Qaeda terrorist training camps, though Al-Bihani disputes this. What he does not dispute is that he eventually accompanied and served a paramilitary group allied with the Taliban, known as the 55th Arab Brigade, which included Al Qaeda members within its command structure and which fought on the front lines against the Northern Alliance. He worked as the brigade's cook and carried a brigade-issued weapon, but never fired it in combat. Combat, however—in the form of bombing by the U.S.-led Coalition that invaded Afghanistan in response to the attacks of September 11, 2001—forced the 55th to retreat from the front lines in October 2001. At the end of this protracted retreat, Al-Bihani and the rest of the brigade surrendered, under orders, to Northern Alliance forces, and they kept him in custody until his handover to U.S. Coalition forces in early 2002. The U.S. military sent Al-Bihani to Guantanamo for detention and interrogation.

After the Supreme Court held in *Rasul v. Bush*, 542 U.S. 466, 483-84 (2004), that the statutory habeas jurisdiction of federal courts extended to Guantanamo Bay, Al-Bihani filed a habeas petition with the U.S. District Court for the District of Columbia, challenging his detention under 28 U.S.C. § 2241(a). The district court stayed the petition until the Supreme Court in *Boumediene v. Bush*, 128 S. Ct. 2229 (2008), held that the section of the Military Commissions Act of 2006 (2006 MCA), Pub. L. No. 109-366, 120 Stat. 2600 (codified in part at 28 U.S.C. § 2241 & note), that withdrew jurisdiction from the courts to entertain habeas petitions filed by Guantanamo detainees was an unconstitutional suspension of the writ. 128 S. Ct. at 2274. *Boumediene* held that detainees were entitled to proceed with habeas challenges under procedures crafted to account for the special circumstances of wartime detention. *Id.* at 2276.

Soon after the *Boumediene* decision, the district court, acting with admirable dispatch, revived Al-Bihani's petition and convened counsel to discuss the process to be used. The district court finalized the procedure in a published case management order. *See Al-Bihani v. Bush* (CMO), 588 F. Supp.2d 19 (D.D.C. 2008) (case management order). The order established that the government had the burden of proving the legality of Al-Bihani's detention by a preponderance of the evidence; it obligated the government to explain the legal basis for Al-Bihani's detention, to share all documents used in its factual return, and to turn over any exculpatory evidence found in preparation of its case. To Al-Bihani, the order afforded the opportunity to file a traverse and supplements to the traverse rebutting the government's factual return, to introduce new evidence, and to move for discovery upon a showing of good cause and the absence of undue burden on the government. The order reserved the district court's discretion, when appropriate, to adopt a rebuttable presumption in favor of the accuracy of the government's evidence and to admit relevant and material hearsay, the credibility and weight of which the opposing party could challenge. The order also scheduled status conferences to clarify any discovery and evidentiary issues with the government's factual return and to identify issues of law and fact prior to the habeas hearing where such issues would be contested. *See id.* at 20-21.

After the parties filed their cases in accordance with the case management order and the district court held a day and a half of hearings, the district court denied Al-Bihani's petition. Adopting a definition that allowed the government to detain anyone "who was part of or supporting Taliban or al Qaeda forces, or associated forces that are engaged in hostilities against the United States or its coalition partners,"[1] the district court found Al-Bihani's actions met

---

1. This was the initial definition offered by the government as the controlling standard. In its filings before this court, the government modified the definition in its initial habeas return to replace the term "support" with "substantially supported." *See* Brief for Appellees at 21-22. The district court adopted the initial definition. *See* Mem. Op. at 38.

the standard. *See Al-Bihani v. Obama* (Mem. Op.), 594 F. Supp.2d 35, 38, 40 (D.D.C. 2009) (memorandum opinion). It cited as sufficiently credible the evidence—primarily drawn from Al-Bihani's own admissions during interrogation—that Al-Bihani stayed at Al Qaeda-affiliated guesthouses and that he served in and retreated with the 55th Arab Brigade. *See id.* at 39-40. The district court declined to rely on evidence drawn from admissions—later recanted by Al-Bihani—that he attended Al Qaeda training camps on his way to the front lines. *See id.* at 39.

Al-Bihani appealed the district court's denial to this court under 28 U.S.C. § 2253(a), alleging numerous substantive and procedural defects with the order. We review the district court's findings of fact for clear error, *DeBerry v. Portuondo*, 403 F.3d 57, 66 (2d Cir. 2005), its habeas determination *de novo*, *id.*, and any challenged evidentiary rulings for abuse of discretion, *Al Odah v. United States*, 559 F.3d 539, 544 (D.C. Cir. 2009).

II

Al-Bihani's many arguments present this court with two overarching questions regarding the detainees at the Guantanamo Bay naval base. The first concerns whom the President can lawfully detain pursuant to statutes passed by Congress. The second asks what procedure is due to detainees challenging their detention in habeas corpus proceedings. The Supreme Court has provided scant guidance on these questions, consciously leaving the contours of the substantive and procedural law of detention open for lower courts to shape in a common law fashion. *See Hamdi v. Rumsfeld*, 542 U.S. 507, 522 n.1 (2004) (plurality opinion of O'Connor, J.) ("The permissible bounds of the [enemy combatant] category will be defined by the lower courts as subsequent cases are presented to them."); *Boumediene*, 128 S. Ct. at 2276 ("We make no attempt to anticipate all of the evidentiary and access-to-counsel issues…and the other remaining questions [that] are within the expertise and competence of the District Court to address in the first instance."). In this decision, we aim to narrow the legal uncertainty that clouds military detention.

A

Al-Bihani challenges the statutory legitimacy of his detention by advancing a number of arguments based upon the international laws of war. He first argues that relying on "support," or even "substantial support" of Al Qaeda or the Taliban as an independent basis for detention violates international law. As a result, such a standard should not be read into the ambiguous provisions of the Authorization for Use of Military Force (AUMF), Pub. L. No. 107-40, § 2(a), 115 Stat. 224, 224 (2001) (reprinted at 50 U.S.C. § 1541 note), the Act empowering the President to respond to the attacks of September 11, 2001. Al-Bihani interprets international law to mean anyone not belonging to an official state military is a civilian, and civilians, he says, must commit a direct hostile act, such as firing a weapon in combat, before they can be lawfully detained. Because Al-Bihani did not commit such an act, he reasons his detention is unlawful. Next, he argues the members of the 55th Arab Brigade were not subject to attack or detention by U.S. Coalition forces under the laws of co-belligerency because the 55th, although allied with the Taliban against the Northern Alliance, did not have the required opportunity to declare its neutrality in the fight against the United States. His third argument is that the conflict in which he was detained, an international war between the United States and Taliban-controlled Afghanistan, officially ended when the Taliban lost control of the Afghan government. Thus, absent a determination of future dangerousness, he must be released. *See* Geneva Convention Relative to the Treatment of Prisoners of War (Third Geneva Convention) art. 118, Aug. 12, 1949, 6 U.S.T. 3316, 75 U.N.T.S. 135. Lastly, Al-Bihani posits a type of "clean hands" theory by which any authority the government has to detain him is undermined by its failure to accord him the prisoner-of-war status to which he believes he is entitled by international law.

Before considering these arguments in detail, we note that all of them rely heavily on the premise that the war powers granted by the AUMF and other statutes are limited by the international laws of war. This premise is mistaken. There is no indication in the AUMF, the Detainee Treatment Act of 2005, Pub. L. No. 109-148, div. A, tit. X, 119 Stat. 2739, 2741-43, or the MCA of 2006 or 2009, that Congress intended the international laws of war to act as extra-textual limiting principles for the President's war powers under the AUMF. The international laws of war as a whole have not been implemented domestically by Congress and are therefore not a source of authority for U.S. courts. *See* RESTATEMENT (THIRD) OF FOREIGN RELATIONS LAW OF THE UNITED STATES § 111(3)-(4) (1987). Even assuming Congress had at some earlier point implemented the laws of war as domestic law through appropriate legislation, Congress had the power to authorize the President in the AUMF and other later statutes to exceed those bounds. *See id.* § 115(1)(a). Further weakening their relevance to this case, the international laws of war are not a fixed code. Their dictates and application to actual events are by nature contestable and fluid. *See id.* § 102 cmts. b & c (stating there is "no precise formula" to identify a practice as custom and that "[i]t is often difficult to determine when [a custom's] transformation into law has taken place"). Therefore, while the international laws of war are helpful to courts when identifying the general set of war powers to which the AUMF speaks, *see Hamdi*, 542 U.S. at 520, their lack of controlling legal force and firm definition render their use both inapposite and inadvisable when courts seek to determine the limits of the President's war powers.

Therefore, putting aside that we find Al-Bihani's reading of international law to be unpersuasive, we have no occasion here to quibble over the intricate application of vague treaty provisions and amorphous customary principles. The sources we look to for resolution of Al-Bihani's case are the sources courts always look to: the text of relevant statutes and controlling domestic caselaw.

Under those sources, Al-Bihani is lawfully detained whether the definition of a detainable person is, as the district court articulated it, "an individual who was part of or supporting Taliban or al Qaeda forces, or associated forces that are engaged in hostilities against the United States or its coalition partners," or the modified definition offered by the government that requires that an individual "substantially support" enemy forces. The statutes authorizing the use of force and detention not only grant the government the power to craft a workable legal standard to identify individuals it can detain, but also cabin the application of these definitions. The AUMF authorizes the President to "use all necessary and appropriate force against those nations, organizations, or persons he determines planned, authorized, committed, or aided the terrorist attacks that occurred on September 11, 2001, or harbored such organizations or persons." AUMF § 2(a). The Supreme Court in *Hamdi* ruled that "necessary and appropriate force" includes the power to detain combatants subject to such force. 542 U.S. at 519. Congress, in the 2006 MCA, provided guidance on the class of persons subject to detention under the AUMF by defining "unlawful enemy combatants" who can be tried by military commission. 2006 MCA sec. 3, § 948a(1). The 2006 MCA authorized the trial of an individual who "engaged in hostilities or who has purposefully and materially supported hostilities against the United States or its co-belligerents who is not a lawful enemy combatant (including a person who is part of the Taliban, al Qaeda, or associated forces)." *Id.* § 948a(1)(A)(i). In 2009, Congress enacted a new version of the MCA with a new definition that authorized the trial of "unprivileged enemy belligerents," a class of persons that includes those who "purposefully and materially supported hostilities against the United States or its coalition partners." Military Commissions Act of 2009 (2009 MCA) sec. 1802, §§ 948a(7), 948b(a), 948c, Pub. L. No. 111-84, tit. XVIII, 123 Stat. 2190, 2575-76. The provisions of the 2006 and 2009 MCAs are illuminating in this case because the government's detention authority logically covers a category of persons no narrower than is covered by its military commission authority. Detention authority in fact sweeps wider, also extending at least to traditional P.O.W.s, *see id.* § 948a(6), and arguably to other categories of persons. But for this case, it is enough to recognize that any person subject to a military commission trial is also subject to detention, and that category of persons includes those who are part of forces associated with Al Qaeda or the Taliban or those who purposefully and materially support such forces in hostilities against U.S. Coalition partners.

Within these provisions of the 2006 and 2009 MCAs, the facts that were both found by the district court and offered by Al-Bihani in his traverse place Al-Bihani within the "part of" and "support" prongs of the relevant statutory definition. The district court found Al Qaeda members participated in the command structure of the 55th Arab Brigade, *see* Mem. Op. at 40, making the brigade an Al Qaeda-affiliated outfit, and it is unquestioned that the 55th fought alongside the Taliban while the Taliban was harboring Al Qaeda. Al-Bihani's evidence confirmed these points, establishing that the 55th "supported the Taliban against the Northern Alliance," a Coalition partner, and that the 55th was "aided, or even, at times, commanded, by al-Qaeda members." Brief for Petitioner-Appellant at 33. Al-Bihani's connections with the 55th therefore render him detainable. His acknowledged actions—accompanying the brigade on the battlefield, carrying a brigade-issued weapon, cooking for the unit, and retreating and surrendering under brigade orders—strongly suggest, in the absence of an official membership card, that he was part of the 55th. Even assuming, as he argues, that he was a civilian "contractor" rendering services, *see id.* at 32, those services render Al-Bihani detainable under the "purposefully and materially supported" language of both versions of the MCA. That language constitutes a standard whose outer bounds are not readily identifiable. But wherever the outer bounds may lie, they clearly include traditional food operations essential to a fighting force and the carrying of arms. Viewed in full, the facts show Al-Bihani was part of and supported a group—prior to and after September 11—that was affiliated with Al Qaeda and Taliban forces and engaged in hostilities against a U.S. Coalition partner. Al-Bihani, therefore, falls squarely[2] within the scope of the President's statutory detention powers.

2. In reaching this conclusion, we need not rely on the evidence suggesting that Al-Bihani attended Al Qaeda training camps in Afghanistan and visited Al Qaeda guesthouses. We do note, however, that evidence supporting the military's reasonable belief of either of those two facts with respect to a non-citizen seized abroad during the ongoing war on terror would seem to overwhelmingly, if not definitively, justify the government's detention of such a non-citizen. *Cf.* NAT'L COMM'N ON TERRORIST ATTACKS UPON THE UNITED STATES, THE 9/11 COMMISSION REPORT 66-67.

The government can also draw statutory authority to detain Al-Bihani directly from the language of the AUMF. The AUMF authorizes force against those who "harbored...organizations or persons" the President determines "planned, authorized, committed, or aided the terrorist attacks of September 11, 2001." AUMF § 2(a). It is not in dispute that Al Qaeda is the organization responsible for September 11 or that it was harbored by the Taliban in Afghanistan. It is also not in dispute that the 55th Arab Brigade defended the Taliban against the Northern Alliance's efforts to oust the regime from power. Drawing from these facts, it cannot be disputed that the actual and foreseeable result of the 55th's defense of the Taliban was the maintenance of Al Qaeda's safe haven in Afghanistan. This result places the 55th within the AUMF's wide ambit as an organization that harbored Al Qaeda, making it subject to U.S. military force and its members and supporters—including Al-Bihani—eligible for detention.

Al-Bihani disagrees with this conclusion, arguing that the 55th Arab Brigade was not lawfully subject to attack and detention. He points to the international laws of co-belligerency to demonstrate that the brigade should have been allowed the opportunity to remain neutral upon notice of a conflict between the United States and the Taliban. We reiterate that international law, including the customary rules of co-belligerency, do not limit the President's detention power in this instance. But even if Al-Bihani's argument were relevant to his detention and putting aside all the questions that applying such elaborate rules to this situation would raise, the laws of co-belligerency affording notice of war and the choice to remain neutral have only applied to nation states. *See* 2 L. OPPENHEIM, INTERNATIONAL LAW: A TREATISE § 74 (1906). The 55th clearly was not a state, but rather an irregular fighting force present within the borders of Afghanistan at the sanction of the Taliban. Any attempt to apply the rules of co-belligerency to such a force would be folly, akin to this court ascribing powers of national sovereignty to a local chapter of the Freemasons.

While we think the facts of this case show Al-Bihani was both part of and substantially supported enemy forces, we realize the picture may be less clear in other cases where facts may indicate only support, only membership, or neither. We have no occasion here to explore the outer bounds of what constitutes sufficient support or indicia of membership to meet the detention standard. We merely recognize that both prongs are valid criteria that are independently sufficient to satisfy the standard.

With the government's detention authority established as an initial matter, we turn to the argument that Al-Bihani must now be released according to longstanding law of war principles because the conflict with the Taliban has allegedly ended. *See Hamdi*, 542 U.S. at 521. Al-Bihani offers the court a choice of numerous event dates—the day Afghans established a post-Taliban interim authority, the day the United States recognized that authority, the day Hamid Karzai was elected President—to mark the official end of the conflict. No matter which is chosen, each would dictate the release of Al-Bihani if we follow his reasoning. His argument fails on factual and practical grounds. First, it is not clear if Al-Bihani was captured in the conflict with the Taliban or with Al Qaeda; he does not argue that the conflict with Al Qaeda is over. Second, there are currently 34,800 U.S. troops and a total of 71,030 Coalition troops in Afghanistan, *see* N. Atl. Treaty Org. [NATO], *International Security Assistance Force and Afghan National Army Strength & Laydown*, at 2, Oct. 22, 2009, *available at* http://www.nato.int/ISAF/docu/epub/pdf/isaf_ placemat.pdf, with tens of thousands more to be added soon. The principle Al-Bihani espouses—were it accurate—would make each successful campaign of a long war but a Pyrrhic prelude to defeat. The initial success of the United States and its Coalition partners in ousting the Taliban from the seat of government and establishing a young democracy would trigger an obligation to release Taliban fighters captured in earlier clashes. Thus, the victors would be commanded to constantly refresh the ranks of the fledgling democracy's most likely saboteurs.

In response to this commonsense observation, Al-Bihani contends the current hostilities are a different conflict, one against the Taliban reconstituted in a non-governmental form, and the government must prove that Al-Bihani would join this insurgency in order to continue to hold him. But even the laws of war upon which he relies do not draw such fine distinctions. The Geneva Conventions require release and repatriation only at the "cessation of active hostilities." Third Geneva Convention art. 118. That the Conventions use the term "active hostilities" instead of the terms "conflict" or "state of war" found elsewhere in the document is significant. It serves to distinguish the physical violence of war from the official beginning and end of a conflict, because fighting does not necessarily track formal timelines. *See id.* art. 2 (provisions apply "even if the state of war is not recognized"), art. 118 (discussing the possibility of the cessation of active hostilities even in the absence of an agreement to cease hostilities). The Conventions, in short, codify what common sense tells us must be true: release is only required when the fighting stops.

Even so, we do not rest our resolution of this issue on international law or mere common sense. The determination of when hostilities have ceased is a political decision, and we defer to the Executive's opinion on the matter, at least in the absence of an authoritative congressional declaration purporting to terminate the war. *See Ludecke v. Watkins*, 335 U.S. 160, 168-70 & n.13 (1948) ("[T]ermination [of a state of war] is a political act."). Al-Bihani urges the court to ignore *Ludecke*'s controlling precedent because the President in that case had pronounced that a war was ongoing, whereas in this case the President has made no such pronouncement. We reject Al-Bihani's entreaty. A clear statement requirement is at odds with the wide deference the judiciary is obliged to give to the democratic branches with regard to questions concerning national security. In the absence of a determination by the political branches that hostilities in Afghanistan have ceased, Al-Bihani's continued detention is justified.

Al-Bihani also argues he should be released because the government's failure to accord him P.O.W. status violated international law and undermined its otherwise lawful authority to detain him. Even assuming Al-Bihani is entitled to P.O.W. status, we find no controlling authority for this "clean hands" theory in statute or in caselaw. The AUMF, DTA, and MCA of 2006 and 2009 do not hinge the government's detention authority on proper identification of P.O.W.s or compliance with international law in general. In fact, the MCA of 2006, in a provision not altered by the MCA of 2009, explicitly precludes detainees from claiming the Geneva conventions—which include criteria to determine who is entitled to P.O.W. status—as a source of rights. *See* 2006 MCA sec. 5(a). And the citation Al-Bihani gives to support his theory is not controlling. The section of Justice Souter's separate opinion in *Hamdi* in which he discusses a clean hands theory was part of his dissent in that case. *See* 542 U.S. at 553 (Souter, J., concurring in part, dissenting in part, and concurring in the judgment) ("For me, it suffices that the Government has failed to justify [detention] in the absence of…a showing that the detention conforms to the laws of war….[T]his disposition does not command a majority of the Court."). Moreover, Justice Souter's opinion fails to identify any other controlling authority that establishes or discusses this theory in any way. This leaves no foundation for Al-Bihani's clean hands argument, and it fails to persuade.

B

We now turn to Al-Bihani's procedural challenge. He claims the habeas process afforded him by the district court fell short of the requirements of the Suspension Clause and that his case should be remanded for rehearing in line with new, more protective procedures. The Supreme Court in *Boumediene* held detainees are entitled to the "fundamental procedural protections of habeas corpus." 128 S. Ct. at 2277. The *Boumediene* Court refrained from identifying the full list of procedures that are fundamental, but it did say that a petitioner is entitled to "a meaningful opportunity to demonstrate that he is being held pursuant to the erroneous application or interpretation of relevant law," and that "the habeas court must have the power to order the conditional release" of the petitioner. *Id.* at 2266. Meaningful review in this context requires that a court have "some authority to assess the sufficiency of the Government's evidence against the detainee" and to "admit and consider relevant exculpatory evidence" that may be added to the record by petitioners during review. *Id.* at 2270.

Drawing upon *Boumediene*'s holding, Al-Bihani challenges numerous aspects of the habeas procedure devised by the district court. He claims the district court erred by: (1) adopting a preponderance of the evidence standard of proof; (2) shifting the burden to him to prove the unlawfulness of his detention; (3) neglecting to hold a separate evidentiary hearing; (4) admitting hearsay evidence; (5) presuming the accuracy of the government's evidence; (6) requiring him to explain why his discovery request would not unduly burden the government; and (7) denying all but one of his discovery requests. In support of these claims, Al-Bihani cites statutes prescribing habeas procedure for review of federal and state court convictions and analogizes to a number of cases concerning review of detentions related to criminal prosecutions. Brief for Petitioner-Appellant at 48-49. By referencing these sources, Al-Bihani traces the district court's supposed errors to its failure to accord him procedural parity with safeguards found in review of criminal proceedings.

Al-Bihani's argument clearly demonstrates error, but that error is his own. Habeas review for Guantanamo detainees need not match the procedures developed by Congress and the courts specifically for habeas challenges to criminal convictions. *Boumediene*'s holding explicitly stated that habeas procedures for detainees "need not resemble a criminal trial," 128 S. Ct. at 2269. It instead invited "innovation" of habeas procedure by lower courts, granting leeway for "[c]ertain accommodations [to] be made to reduce the burden habeas corpus proceedings will place on the military." *Id.* at 2276. *Boumediene*'s holding therefore places Al-Bihani's procedural argument on shaky ground. The Suspension Clause protects only the fundamental character of habeas proceedings, and any argument equating that fundamental character with all the accoutrements of habeas for domestic criminal defendants is highly suspect.

In considering Al-Bihani's argument, we recognize that the Great Writ is not a static institution and it did not begin its life looking like it does today. Rather, like a tree extending its branches, habeas has grown over a long history to develop various procedures applicable to various circumstances of detention. *See id.* ("[Past cases] stand for the proposition that the Suspension Clause does not resist innovation in the field of habeas corpus."); *Developments in the Law—Federal Habeas Corpus*, 83 HARV. L. REV. 1038, 1269 (1970) ("It is then the nature of the writ that it grow and adapt to new conditions…through a combination of statutory and judicial innovation."). For example, federal habeas review of criminal prosecutions at common law began as a cursory review of the legitimacy of a court's jurisdiction. *See United States v. Hayman*, 342 U.S. 205, 211 (1952). Congress expanded this review authority in 1867 to reach a determination of actual facts, *id.*, likely motivated by a desire to rein in what it viewed as recalcitrant law enforcement in the former Confederate states during Reconstruction. *See* Evan Tsen Lee, *The Theories of Federal Habeas Corpus*, 72 WASH. U. L.Q. 151, 182 (1994). As the twentieth century progressed, the protections and rules of criminal habeas expanded further to account for a growing number of recognized constitutional and statutory rights and to manage the sheer number of petitions coursing through the federal courts. *See, e.g.*, 28 U.S.C. § 2246 (prescribing a right for petitioner to propound interrogatories or file answering affidavits); 18 U.S.C. § 3771(b)(2) (guaranteeing certain rights to crime victims in habeas proceedings); 28 U.S.C. § 2255 (providing alternate forum to streamline habeas petition review); Act of Sept. 28, 1976, Pub. L. No. 94-426, 90 Stat. 1334 (adopting rules governing § 2254 and § 2255 proceedings); *Jackson v. Virginia*, 443 U.S. 307, 321-24 (1979) (holding that federal court reviewing state court conviction must determine whether sufficient evidence existed to justify conviction beyond a reasonable doubt); *Holiday v. Johnston*, 313 U.S. 342, 352-54 (1941) (requiring review of habeas petitions be conducted by judges). Rules governing habeas petitions apart from the criminal sphere—such as those challenging post-removal-period detention in the immigration context, *see, e.g.*, *Zadvydas v. Davis*, 533 U.S. 678, 701 (2001) (establishing scheme of presumptions and burden shifting), and those filed pursuant to the Force Act of 1833, ch. 57, § 7, 4 Stat. 632, 634-35 (creating additional penalties for defying court's jurisdiction to review such petitions)—developed separately. This brief account of habeas' evolving nature serves to make clear that, in the shadow of *Boumediene*, courts are neither bound by the procedural limits created for other detention contexts nor obliged to use them as baselines from which any departures must be justified. Detention of aliens outside the sovereign territory of the United States during wartime is a different and peculiar circumstance, and the appropriate habeas procedures cannot be conceived of as mere extensions of an existing doctrine. Rather, those procedures are a whole new branch of the tree.

Al-Bihani, however, argues his case does not rest on that branch. He points to one of the seven concurring opinions in *Al-Marri v. Pucciarelli*, 534 F.3d 213, 269 (4th Cir. 2008) (Traxler, J., concurring in the judgment), to support his contention that the Supreme Court did not authorize less demanding procedures for a case like his. *See* Brief for Petitioner-Appellant at 50. Judge Traxler's opinion reasoned the *Hamdi* Court blessed lower procedural standards only upon a showing of undue hardship by the government, but such hardship was especially clear when a petitioner was seized on a foreign battlefield where the prospect of high evidentiary standards might interfere with military operations. *See Al-Marri*, 534 F.3d at 270-71. Because the petitioner in *Al-Marri* was seized by federal law enforcement in Illinois, Judge Traxler concluded that as a general rule he was "entitled to the normal due process protections available to all within this country," absent a satisfactory showing by the government. *Id.* at 273. We do not express an opinion on whether or when different habeas procedures are appropriate for petitioners seized domestically pursuant to the AUMF; those questions are for another case. It is enough for us to point out that Judge Traxler's opinion is of no help to Al-Bihani; he falls squarely in the category of petitioners that Judge Traxler and the Supreme Court in *Hamdi* deemed deserving of leaner procedures.[3]

Unlike either Hamdi or Al-Marri, Al-Bihani is a non-citizen who was seized in a foreign country. Requiring highly protective procedures at the tail end of the detention process for detainees like Al-Bihani would have systemic effects on the military's entire approach to war. From the moment a shot is fired, to battlefield capture, up to a detainee's day in court, military operations would be compromised as the government strove to satisfy evidentiary standards in anticipation of habeas litigation. Al-Bihani suggests no such danger is posed in his case because the evidence presented in the government's return consisted mainly of records of interrogations that took place at Guantanamo and not of evidence procured from the battlefield. *See* Brief for Petitioner-Appellant at 49-50. Logically, however, had the district court imposed stringent standards of evidence in the first instance, the government may well have been obligated to go beyond Al-Bihani's interrogation records and into the battlefield to present a case that met its burden. That the district court's tailored procedure prevented such a scenario cannot possibly make the procedure constitutionally infirm.

With Al-Bihani's limited procedural entitlement established as a general matter, we turn to the specific procedural claims warranting serious consideration. The question of what standard of proof is due in a habeas proceeding like Al-Bihani's has not been answered by the Supreme Court. *See Boumediene*, 128 S. Ct. at 2271 ("The extent of the showing required of the Government in these cases is a matter to be determined."). Attempting to fill this void, Al-Bihani argues the prospect of indefinite detention in this unconventional war augurs for a reasonable doubt standard or, in the alternative, at least a clear and convincing standard. Brief for Petitioner-Appellant at 48. The government disagrees, arguing that *Hamdi*'s plurality opinion indirectly endorsed a preponderance standard when it suggested due process requirements may have been satisfied by a military tribunal, the regulations of which adopt a preponderance standard. Brief for Appellees at 55-56, *citing* U.S. Dep'ts of the Army, the Navy, the Air Force, and the Marine Corps, Army Regulation 190-8, Enemy Prisoners of War, Retained Personnel, Civilian Internees and Other Detainees § 1-6(e)(9) (Oct. 1, 1997), *available at* http://www.au.af.mil/au/awc/awcgate/law/ar190-8.pdf.

We believe the government's argument stands on more solid ground. In addition to the *Hamdi* plurality's approving treatment of military tribunal procedure, it also described as constitutionally adequate—even for the detention of U.S. citizens—a "burden-shifting scheme" in which the government need only present "credible evidence that the habeas petitioner meets the enemy-combatant criteria" before "the onus could shift to the petitioner to rebut that evidence with more persuasive evidence that he falls outside the criteria." *Hamdi*, 542 U.S. at 533-34. That description mirrors a preponderance standard. We emphasize our opinion does not endeavor to identify what standard would represent the minimum required by the Constitution.[4] Our narrow charge is to determine whether a preponderance standard is unconstitutional. Absent more specific and relevant guidance, we find no indication that it is.

---

3. Both *Hamdi* and *Al-Marri* involved American citizens or legal residents; the procedures to which Americans are entitled are likely greater than the procedures to which non-citizens seized abroad during the war on terror are entitled.

4. In particular, we need not address whether a some evidence, reasonable suspicion, or probable cause standard of proof could constitutionally suffice for preventative detention of non-citizens seized abroad who are suspected of being terrorist threats to the United States. *See Zadvydas*, 533 U.S. at 696; *cf.* Anti-terrorism, Crime and Security Act, 2001, c. 24, §§ 21, 23 (Eng.) (adopting a reasonable suspicion standard in Britain; later overturned as inconsistent with European Union law).

As already discussed, traditional habeas review did not entail review of factual findings, particularly in the military context. *See In re Yamashita*, 327 U.S. 1, 8 (1946) ("If the military tribunals have lawful authority to hear, decide and condemn, their action is not subject to judicial review merely because they have made a wrong decision on disputed facts."). Where factual review has been authorized, the burden in some domestic circumstances has been placed *on the petitioner* to prove his case under a clear and convincing standard. *See* 28 U.S.C. § 2254(e)(1) (regulating federal review of state court factual findings). If it is constitutionally permissible to place that higher burden on a citizen petitioner in a routine case, it follows a priori that placing a lower burden on the government defending a wartime detention—where national security interests are at their zenith and the rights of the alien petitioner at their nadir—is also permissible.

We find Al-Bihani's hearsay challenges to be similarly unavailing. Al-Bihani claims that government reports of his interrogation answers—which made up the majority, if not all, of the evidence on which the district court relied—and other informational documents were hearsay improperly admitted absent an examination of reliability and necessity. Brief for Petitioner-Appellant at 47, 50-52. He contends, in fact, that government reports of his interrogation answers were "*double* hearsay" because his answers were first translated by an interpreter and then written down by an interrogator. Petitioner-Appellant Rule 28(j) Letter, Sept. 28, 2009. We first note that Al-Bihani's interrogation answers themselves were not hearsay; they were instead party-opponent admissions that would have been admitted in any U.S. court. *See* FED. R. EVID. 801(d)(2)(A). That they were translated does not affect their status. *See United States v. Da Silva*, 725 F.2d 828, 831-32 (2d Cir. 1983) (holding that government employee translation of defendant's statement was not hearsay). However, that the otherwise admissible answers were relayed through an interrogator's account does introduce a level of technical hearsay because the interrogator is a third party unavailable for cross examination. Other information, such as a diagram of Al Qaeda's leadership structure, was also hearsay.

But that such evidence was hearsay does not automatically invalidate its admission—it only begins our inquiry. We observe Al-Bihani cannot make the traditional objection based on the Confrontation Clause of the Sixth Amendment. This is so because the Confrontation Clause applies only in criminal prosecutions, *see* U.S. CONST. amend. VI, and is not directly relevant to the habeas setting, *cf.* 28 U.S.C. § 2246 (granting discretion to habeas judge to admit affidavits into evidence). The Confrontation Clause seeks to ensure the reliability of evidence, but it also seeks to eliminate the ephemeral perception of unfairness associated with the use of hearsay evidence. *See Coy v. Iowa*, 487 U.S. 1012, 1017-19 (1988) ("The Sixth Amendment's guarantee of face-to-face encounter…serves ends related both to appearances and to reality…[and] contributes to…the perception as well as the reality of fairness."). Al-Bihani, however, does not enjoy a right to the psychic value of excluding hearsay and whatever right he has is not an independent procedural entitlement. Rather, it operates only to the extent that it provides the baseline level of evidentiary reliability necessary for the "meaningful" habeas proceeding *Boumediene* requires under the Suspension Clause. *See* 128 S. Ct. at 2266.

Therefore, the question a habeas court must ask when presented with hearsay is not whether it is admissible—it is always admissible—but what probative weight to ascribe to whatever indicia of reliability it exhibits. This approach is evident in the relevant caselaw. *Boumediene* did not say exactly how a habeas court should treat hearsay, but it broadly required that a court be able to "assess the sufficiency of the Government's evidence." *Id.* at 2270. In *Hamdi*, the

Supreme Court said hearsay "may need to be accepted as the most reliable available evidence" as long as the petitioner is given the opportunity to rebut that evidence. *See* 542 U.S. at 533-34. *Hamdi* pointed to a declaration from a government official describing his expertise regarding the facts of the case as an example of reliable hearsay. *Id.* at 538. And a panel of this court in the related context of DTA review did not reject hearsay evidence as inadmissible, but rather considered it and deemed it insufficient to support detention because the panel could not "assess the reliability" of its "bare assertions" in the absence of contextual information. *Parhat v. Gates*, 532 F.3d 834, 847 (D.C. Cir. 2008).

A procedure that seeks to determine hearsay's reliability instead of its mere admissibility comports not only with the requirements of this novel circumstance, but also with the reality that district judges are experienced and sophisticated fact finders. Their eyes need not be protected from unreliable information in the manner the Federal Rules of Evidence aim to shield the eyes of impressionable juries. *See* FED. R. EVID. 103(c) (requiring courts to "prevent inadmissible evidence from being suggested to the jury by any means"); JAMES BRADLEY THAYER, A PRELIMINARY TREATISE ON EVIDENCE AT THE COMMON LAW 266 (1898) (describing the law of evidence as "the child of the jury system" that excludes probative evidence because of possible adverse effects on a lay jury). Where the touchstone of a proceeding is "meaningfulness," empowering a district court to review and assess all evidence from both sides is a logical process. It is one that bolsters the traditional power of the habeas court to "cut[] through all forms and go[] to the very tissue of the structure" of a proceeding and "look facts in the face." *Frank v. Mangum*, 237 U.S. 309, 346, 349 (1915) (Holmes, J., dissenting). The habeas judge is not asked, as he would be in a trial, to administrate a complicated clash of adversarial viewpoints to synthesize a process-dependent form of Hegelian legal truth. *See Blakely v. Washington*, 542 U.S. 296, 313 (2004) ("[T]he Framers' paradigm for criminal justice [was] not the civil-law ideal of administrative perfection, but the common-law ideal of limited state power accomplished by strict division of authority between judge and jury."). Rather, in a detainee case, the judge acts as a neutral decisionmaker charged with seizing the actual truth of a simple, binary question: is detention lawful? This is why the one constant in the history of habeas has never been a certain set of procedures, but rather the independent power of a judge to assess the actions of the Executive. This primacy of independence over process is at the center of the *Boumediene* opinion, which eschews prescribing a detailed procedural regime in favor of issuing a spare but momentous guarantee that a "judicial officer must have adequate authority to make a determination in light of the relevant law and facts." *Boumediene*, 128 S. Ct. at 2271; *cf. id.* at 2270 ("Even when the procedures authorizing detention are structurally sound, the Suspension Clause remains applicable and the writ relevant.").

In Al-Bihani's case, the district court clearly reserved that authority in its process and assessed the hearsay evidence's reliability as required by the Supreme Court. First, the district court retained the authority to assess the weight of the evidence. *See* CMO at 21 ("The Government bears the ultimate burden of persuasion…[and t]he Court will determine, as to any evidence introduced by the Government, whether a presumption of accuracy and/or authenticity should be accorded."); Mem. Op. at 39 (judging admissions presented by government to be "credible and consistent"). Second, the district court had ample contextual information about evidence in the government's factual return to determine what weight to give various pieces of evidence. *See* Government's Classified Factual Return (Nov. 21, 2008). Third, the district court afforded Al-Bihani the opportunity in a traverse to rebut the evidence and to attack its credibility. *See* CMO at 21. Further, Al-Bihani did not contest the truth of the majority of his admissions upon which the district court relied, enhancing the reliability of those reports. We therefore find that the district court did not improperly admit hearsay evidence.

The rest of Al-Bihani's procedural claims can be disposed of without extended discussion. His claim that the burden of proof was placed on him is based on a strained reading of the hearing transcript that twists and magnifies questions asked by the judge. This claim has no merit and we need not consider it further. Likewise, Al-Bihani's claim that an evidentiary hearing was denied to him in violation of his right to a hearing is groundless. First, while courts reviewing state or federal court decisions have the discretion to grant fact hearings upon a proper showing by a petitioner, *see* 28 U.S.C. § 2254(e)(2); *Newfield v. United States*, 565 F.2d 203, 207 (2d Cir. 1977) (explaining that courts retain discretion under 28 U.S.C. § 2255 to grant fact hearings), Al-Bihani cites no authority that a petitioner in his position is entitled to such a hearing as of right. Second, it is clear from the CMO and the transcript of the full habeas hearing that the district court did hear the facts of Al-Bihani's case and provided ample opportunity in conference and in a hearing for the parties to air concerns over evidence. *See* CMO at 20-21; Classified Hearing Transcript, P.M. Session (Jan. 15, 2009). To the extent that Al-Bihani possesses any right to a hearing to develop facts or argue evidentiary issues, it was satisfied by the district court's procedure.

Finally, regarding Al-Bihani's challenge to the discovery procedures adopted by the district court and to the denial of most of his discovery requests, we are inclined to find the procedures were permissible and the court's denial was not an abuse of discretion. However, we need not reach these issues. Even assuming error, the errors were harmless because discovery would not have changed the outcome of the case. None of the discovery requests that were denied would have had any impact on the factual basis on which the district court found Al-Bihani to be properly detained. All of the discovery requests pertained to the disputed facts surrounding whether Al-Bihani attended Al Qaeda training camps. The district court assiduously avoided those facts in its decision.

III

Al-Bihani's detention is authorized by statute and there was no constitutional defect in the district court's habeas procedure that would have affected the outcome of the proceeding. For these reasons, the order of the district court denying Al-Bihani's petition for a writ of habeas corpus is
Affirmed.

...

Predictably, although the 2008 *Boumediene* ruling only addressed the habeas rights of Guantanamo Bay detainees, another group of detainees quickly filed suit in federal court in Washington seeking habeas review for their cases—detainees designated as enemy combatants and held at Bagram Air Force Base, Afghanistan. Despite the Obama Administration's heated efforts to argue that these individuals should not receive federal court habeas review of their status determination, the D.C. District Court in the consolidated cases entitled *Al Maqaleh v. Gates* ruled that those who were not Afghan citizens and not captured in Afghanistan were entitled to habeas review. The government immediately sought review of this determination to the D.C. Circuit Court of Appeals and won.

AL MAQALEH v. GATES
United States Court of Appeals for the District of Columbia Circuit
No. 09-5265 (May 21, 2010)

Sentelle, Tatel, and Edwards, Circuit Judges

I. Background

A. The Petitioners

All three petitioners are being held as unlawful enemy combatants at the Bagram Theater Internment Facility on the Bagram Airfield Military Base in Afghanistan. Petitioner Fadi Al-Maqaleh is a Yemeni citizen who alleges he was taken into custody in 2003. While Al-Maqaleh's petition asserts "on information and belief" that he was captured beyond Afghan borders, a sworn declaration from Colonel James W. Gray, Commander of Detention Operations, states that Al-Maqaleh was captured in Zabul, Afghanistan. Redha Al-Najar is a Tunisian citizen who alleges he was captured in Pakistan in 2002. Amin Al-Bakri is a Yemeni citizen who alleges he was captured in Thailand in 2002. Both Al-Najar and Al-Bakri allege they were first held in some other unknown location before being moved to Bagram.

B. The Place of Confinement

Bagram Airfield Military Base is the largest military facility in Afghanistan occupied by United States and coalition forces. The United States entered into an "Accommodation Consignment Agreement for Lands and Facilities at Bagram Airfield" with the Islamic Republic of Afghanistan in 2006, which "consigns all facilities and land located at Bagram Airfield...owned by [Afghanistan,] or Parwan Province, or private individuals, or others, for use by the United States and coalition forces for military purposes." (Accommodation and Consignment Agreement for Lands and Facilities at Bagram Airfield Between the Islamic Republic of Afghanistan and the United States of America) (internal capitalization altered). The Agreement refers to Afghanistan as the "host nation" and the United States "as the lessee." The leasehold created by the agreement is to continue "until the United States or its successors determine that the premises are no longer required for its use." *Id.* (internal capitalization altered).

Afghanistan remains a theater of active military combat. The United States and coalition forces conduct "an ongoing military campaign against al Qaeda, the Taliban regime, and their affiliates and supporters in Afghanistan." These operations are conducted in part from Bagram Airfield. Bagram has been subject to repeated attacks from the Taliban and al Qaeda, including a March 2009 suicide bombing striking the gates of the facility, and Taliban rocket attacks in June of 2009 resulting in death and injury to United States service members and other personnel.

While the United States provides overall security to Bagram, numerous other nations have compounds on the base. Some of the other nations control access to their respective compounds.

The troops of the other nations are present at Bagram both as part of the American-led military coalition in Afghanistan and as members of the International Security Assistance Force (ISAF) of the North Atlantic Treaty Organization. The mission of the ISAF is to support the Afghan government in the maintenance of security in Afghanistan. *See* S.C. Res. 1386, U.N. Doc. S/RES/1386 (Dec. 20, 2001); S.C. Res. 1510, U.N. Doc. S/RES/1510 (Oct. 13, 2003); S.C. Res. 1833, U.N. Doc. S/RES/1833 (Sept. 22, 2008). According to the United States, as of February 1, 2010, approximately 38,000 non-United States troops were serving in Afghanistan as part of the ISAF, representing 42 other countries. *See* International Security Assistance Force, *International Security Assistance Force and Afghan National Army Strength & Laydown*, http://www.nato.int/isaf/docu/epub/pdf/placemat.pdf.

C. The Litigation

Appellees in this action, three detainees at Bagram, filed habeas petitions against the President of the United States and the Secretary of Defense in the district court. The government moved to dismiss for lack of jurisdiction, relying principally upon § 7(a) of the Military Commissions Act of 2006. The district court consolidated these three cases and a fourth case, not a part of these proceedings, for argument. After the change in presidential administrations on January 22, 2009, the court invited the government to express any change in its position on the jurisdictional question. The government informed the district court that it "adheres to its previously articulated position."

…

II. Analysis

…

B. Application to the Bagram Petitioners

Our duty, as explained above, is to determine the reach of the right to habeas corpus and therefore of the Suspension Clause to the factual context underlying the petitions we consider in the present appeal. In doing so, we are controlled by the Supreme Court's interpretation of the Constitution in *Eisentrager* as construed and explained in the Court's more recent opinion in *Boumediene*….

At the outset, we note that each of the parties has asserted both an extreme understanding of the law after *Boumediene* and a more nuanced set of arguments upon which each relies in anticipation of the possible rejection of the bright-line arguments. The United States would like us to hold that the *Boumediene* analysis has no application beyond territories that are, like Guantanamo, outside the *de jure* sovereignty of the United States but are subject to its *de facto* sovereignty. As the government puts it in its reply brief, "[t]he real question before this Court, therefore, is whether Bagram may be considered effectively part of the United States in light of the nature and history of the U.S. presence there." Reply Br. of the United States at 7. We disagree.

…

The status of the Bagram detainees is determined not by a Combatant Status Review Tribunal but by an "Unlawful Enemy Combatant Review Board" (UECRB). As the district court correctly noted, proceedings before the UECRB afford even less protection to the rights of detainees in the determination of status than was the case with the CSRT. Therefore, as the district court noted, "while the important adequacy of process factor strongly supported the extension of the Suspension Clause and habeas rights in *Boumediene*, it even more strongly favors petitioners here." *Al Maqaleh*, 604 F. Supp. 2d at 227. Therefore, examining only the first of the Supreme Court's three enumerated factors, petitioners have made a strong argument that the right to habeas relief and the Suspension Clause apply in Bagram as in Guantanamo. However, we do not stop with the first factor.

The second factor, "the nature of the sites where apprehension and then detention took place," weighs heavily in favor of the United States. Like all petitioners in both *Eisentrager* and *Boumediene*, the petitioners here were apprehended abroad. While this in itself would appear to weigh against the extension of the writ, it obviously would not be sufficient, otherwise *Boumediene* would not have been decided as it was. However, the nature of the place where the detention takes place weighs more strongly in favor of the position argued by the United States and against the extension of habeas jurisdiction than was the case in either *Boumediene* or *Eisentrager*. In the first place, while *de facto* sovereignty is not determinative, for the reasons discussed above, the very fact that it was the subject of much discussion in *Boumediene* makes it obvious that it is not without relevance. As the Supreme Court set forth, Guantanamo Bay is "a territory that, while technically not part of the United States, is under the complete and total control of our Government." 128 S. Ct. at 2262. While it is true that the United States holds a leasehold interest in Bagram, and held a leasehold interest in Guantanamo, the surrounding circumstances are hardly the same. The United States has maintained its total control of Guantanamo Bay for over a century, even in the face of a hostile government maintaining *de jure* sovereignty over the property. In Bagram, while the United States has options as to duration of the lease agreement, there is no indication of any intent to occupy the base with permanence, nor is there hostility on the part of the "host" country. Therefore, the notion that *de facto* sovereignty extends to Bagram is no more real than would have been the same claim with respect to Landsberg in the *Eisentrager* case. While it is certainly realistic to assert that the United States has *de facto* sovereignty over Guantanamo, the same simply is not true with respect to Bagram. Though the site of detention analysis weighs in favor of the United States and against the petitioners, it is not determinative.

But we hold that the third factor, that is "the practical obstacles inherent in resolving the prisoner's entitlement to the writ," particularly when considered along with the second factor, weighs overwhelmingly in favor of the position of the United States. It is undisputed that Bagram, indeed the entire nation of Afghanistan, remains a theater of war. Not only does this suggest that the detention at Bagram is more like the detention at Landsberg than Guantanamo, the position of the United States is even stronger in this case than it was in *Eisentrager*. As the Supreme Court recognized in *Boumediene*, even though the active hostilities in the European theater had "c[o]me to an end," 23 at the time of the *Eisentrager* decision, many of the problems of a theater of war remained: In addition to supervising massive reconstruction and aid efforts the American forces stationed in Germany faced potential security threats from a defeated enemy. In retrospect the post-War occupation may seem uneventful. But at the time *Eisentrager* was decided, the Court was right to be concerned about judicial interference with the military's efforts to contain "enemy elements, guerilla fighters, and 'were-wolves.'" 128 S. Ct. at 2261 (quoting *Eisentrager*, 339 U.S. at 784).

In ruling for the extension of the writ to Guantanamo, the Supreme Court expressly noted that "[s]imilar threats are not apparent here." 128 S. Ct. at 2261. In the case before us, similar, if not greater, threats are indeed apparent. The United States asserts, and petitioners cannot credibly dispute, that all of the attributes of a facility exposed to the vagaries of war are present in Bagram. The Supreme Court expressly stated in *Boumediene* that at Guantanamo, "[w]hile obligated to abide by the terms of the lease, the United States is, for all practical purposes, answerable to no other sovereign for its acts on the base. Were that not the case, *or if the detention facility were located in an active theater of war*, arguments that issuing the writ would be 'impractical or anomalous' would have more weight." *Id.* at 2261-62 (emphasis added). Indeed, the Supreme Court supported this proposition with reference to the separate opinion of Justice Harlan in *Reid*, where the Justice expressed his doubts that "every provision of the Constitution must always be deemed automatically applicable to United States citizens in every part of the world." *See* 354 U.S. at 74 (Harlan, J., concurring in the result). We therefore conclude that under both *Eisentrager* and *Boumediene*, the writ does not extend to the Bagram confinement in an active theater of war in a territory under neither the *de facto* nor *de jure* sovereignty of the United States and within the territory of another *de jure* sovereign.

We are supported in this conclusion by the rationale of *Eisentrager*, which was not only not overruled, but reinforced by the language and reasoning just referenced from *Boumediene*. As we referenced in the background discussion of this opinion, we set forth more fully now concerns expressed by the Supreme Court in reaching its decision in *Eisentrager*:

Such trials would hamper the war effort and bring aid and comfort to the enemy. They would diminish the prestige of our commanders, not only with enemies but with wavering neutrals. It would be difficult to devise more effective fettering of a field commander than to allow the very enemies he is ordered to reduce to submission to call him to account in his own civil courts and divert his efforts and attention from the military offensive abroad to the legal defensive at home. Nor is it unlikely that the result of such enemy litigiousness would be a conflict between judicial and military opinion highly comforting to enemies of the United States.

Eisentrager, 339 U.S. at 779. Those factors are more relevant to the situation at Bagram than they were at Landsberg. While it is true, as the Supreme Court noted in *Boumediene*, that the United States forces in Germany in 1950 faced the possibility of unrest and guerilla warfare, operations in the European theater had ended with the surrender of Germany and Italy years earlier. Bagram remains in a theater of war. We cannot, consistent with *Eisentrager* as elucidated by *Boumediene*, hold that the right to the writ of habeas corpus and the constitutional protections of the Suspension Clause extend to Bagram detention facility in Afghanistan, and we therefore must reverse the decision of the district court denying the motion of the United States to dismiss the petitions.

We do not ignore the arguments of the detainees that the United States chose the place of detention and might be able "to evade judicial review of Executive detention decisions by transferring detainees into active conflict zones, thereby granting the Executive the power to switch the Constitution on or off at will." Brief of Appellees at 34 (quotation marks and citation omitted). However, that is not what happened here. Indeed, without dismissing the legitimacy or sincerity of appellees' concerns, we doubt that this fact goes to either the second or third of the Supreme Court's enumerated factors. We need make no determination on the importance of this possibility, given that it remains only a possibility; its resolution can await a case in which the claim is a reality rather than a speculation. In so stating, we note that the Supreme Court did not dictate that the three enumerated factors are exhaustive. It only told us that "*at least* three factors" are relevant. *Boumediene*, 128 S. Ct. at 2259 (emphasis added). Perhaps such manipulation by the Executive might constitute an additional factor in some case in which it is in fact present. However, the notion that the United States deliberately confined the detainees in the theater of war rather than at, for example, Guantanamo, is not only unsupported by the evidence, it is not supported by reason. To have made such a deliberate decision to "turn off the Constitution" would have required the military commanders or other Executive officials making the situs determination to anticipate the complex litigation history set forth above and predict the *Boumediene* decision long before it came down.

Also supportive of our decision that the third factor weighs heavily in favor of the United States, as the district court recognized, is the fact that the detention is within the sovereign territory of another nation, which itself creates practical difficulties. Indeed, it was on this factor that the district court relied in dismissing the fourth petition, which was filed by an Afghan citizen detainee. *Al Maqaleh*, 604 F. Supp. 2d at 229-30, 235. While that factor certainly weighed more heavily with respect to an Afghan citizen, it is not without force with respect to detainees who are alien to both the United States and Afghanistan. The United States holds the detainees pursuant to a cooperative arrangement with Afghanistan on territory as to which Afghanistan is sovereign. While we cannot say that extending our constitutional protections to the detainees would be in any way disruptive of that relationship, neither can we say with certainty what the reaction of the Afghan government would be.

In sum, taken together, the second and especially the third factors compel us to hold that the petitions should have been dismissed.

Conclusion

For the reasons set forth above, we hold that the jurisdiction of the courts to afford the right to habeas relief and the protection of the Suspension Clause does not extend to aliens held in Executive detention in the Bagram detention facility in the Afghan theater of war. We therefore reverse the order of the district court denying the motion for dismissal of the United States and order that the petitions be dismissed for lack of jurisdiction. So ordered.

4.5 Military Commissions

Ostensibly, if the detainees are correctly designated as enemy combatants, the United States has six options which it may pursue against the detainees: (1) release the detainee to his country of origin (or any other country that will take him); (2) turn the accused over to an appropriate foreign criminal jurisdiction (e.g., the new government in Afghanistan); (3) turn the accused over to an International Tribunal; (4) try the accused in a United States federal district court; (5) try the accused in a United States military commission; or (6) detain him indefinitely as an enemy combatant until the war is over. If one is only concerned with expediency, the first option is probably the most attractive and needs little discussion. Likewise, the use of an International Tribunal is attractive but probably not workable due to concerns over such issues as the absence of a death penalty and possible security compromises of "sources and techniques" the United States employs for gathering intelligence.

The final forum available to prosecute those individuals taken from Afghanistan (or any other location, e.g., Iraq) who are suspected of committing war crimes is the military commission. On November 13, 2001, President Bush signed an executive (military) order which authorized the creation of military commissions to try certain "non-citizens" for engaging in terrorist acts against the United States or aiding or abetting in terrorist acts against the United States. The Supreme Court in *Hamdan v. Rumsfeld* found that the military commissions were not consistent with the standards of Common Article 3 which required that the "passing of sentences" had to be "pronounced by a regularly constituted court affording all the judicial guarantees which are recognized as indispensable by civilized peoples." Further, the Court rejected the idea that the 2001 Congressional Authorization for Use of Military Force allowed the President to authorize military commissions. In fact, the majority decided that the President's military commissions order was not lawful because it was "not regularly constituted" as required by Common Article 3. In short, the Court seemed willing to accept a military commission to try enemy combatants, but only if it was authorized by Congress, not the President.

Because military commissions have not been used since the end of World War II, the efficacy of using this forum to prosecute the al-Qa'eda and Taliban fighters for war crimes mandates analysis from both legal and historical perspectives. Probably 50 or more detainees at Guantanamo Bay are now standing or pending trial by military commission.

Military commissions are non-Article III courts. They derive their basic grant of authority from Articles I and II of the United States Constitution. Respectively, Congress has the power to "define and punish...offenses against the Law of Nations," and the President is the "Commander in Chief of the Army and Navy."

Historically, military commissions (and military tribunals) have been used in a variety of situations associated with urgent government needs related to war. In *Madsen v. Kinsella*, the Supreme Court spoke at some length on the history of military commissions and tribunals, stating: "Since our nation's earliest days, such commissions have been constitutionally recognized agencies for meeting many urgent governmental responsibilities relating to war." In addition, the Court has recognized the fact that military commissions have been used without Congress specifically "declaring war" (*Talbot v. Seeman*). For example, military tribunals were used in the War with Mexico, even though Congress never formally declared war. The War with Mexico lasted from 1846–1848, and broke out when Texas, an American settled province of Mexico that had broken away in 1836, was annexed as a State by the United States in 1845. Congress passed the Act of Congress of May 13, 1846, which did not declare war, but recognized "a state of war as existing by the act of the Republic of Mexico" (*Prize Cases*, 67 U.S. 365).

A military commission consists of a panel of military officers who are authorized to render a verdict and sentence. The historical concern in this instance is not whether military commissions can be used to prosecute United States citizens who may or may not be belligerents, but whether commissions are constitutionally able to prosecute non-citizen belligerents for offenses in violation of the law of war. Regarding the use of military tribunals to try United States citizens who are not belligerents, the Supreme Court rendered its opinion in 1866 in *Ex Parte Milligan*, where it held that as long as the civilian courts were operating, the use of military tribunals to try United States citizens who were not actual belligerents was unconstitutional. In December of 1866, the United States Supreme Court granted a writ of habeas corpus to a civilian noncombatant named Lambdin P. Milligan, a pro-Confederate Indiana resident who was convicted in October 1864 by a military tribunal convened in Indianapolis, Indiana. Milligan was convicted of treason and sentenced to be hanged. The lower federal court denied his petition for habeas corpus. In granting the writ for review, the Supreme Court held that although the American Civil War was still in progress at the time of the trial, the circumstances in Indiana, a Union State not in control by Confederate forces, did not justify the use of a military tribunal to prosecute a United States citizen because the civil courts were open and free to function. As to the use of military commissions to prosecute noncitizen and citizen belligerents for offenses in violation of the law of war, the standard is set out in the World War II case of *Ex Parte Quirin*.

In *Ex Parte Quirin*, the United States Supreme Court upheld the convictions of eight German saboteurs who had been captured in the United States and tried by a military commission ordered by President Franklin Roosevelt. The Germans had been sent to attack public and government facilities. At least one of the Germans claimed American citizenship. The Court upheld the jurisdiction of military commissions against all of the Germans, stating: "By the Articles of War, and especially Article 15, Congress has explicitly provided, so far as it may constitutionally do so, that military tribunals shall have jurisdiction to try offenders or offenses against the law of war in appropriate cases." The Court easily distinguished the case from *Ex Parte Milligan*, holding that offenses against the law of war by actual belligerents were constitutionally authorized to be tried by military commissions. Besides the trials of the German saboteurs during World War II, subsequent military commissions were used to prosecute approximately 2,600 members of the Axis for violations of the law of war, including the murder of captured American soldiers at the Battle of the Bulge. The surviving high-ranking war criminals in the German military and government were tried by a special international tribunal in Nuremberg, Germany, at the Nuremberg Trials. The senior Japanese leaders were tried at the International Military Tribunal for the Far East.

Although the Supreme Court has long held that the Constitution's Fifth and Sixth Amendment protections apply to non-United States citizens (*Wong Wing v. United States*, 163 U.S. 228), such protections do not extend to belligerents subject to trial in military commissions for war crimes. Seemingly, the use of military commissions has deeply seated historical and legal precedent as long as the accused are actual combatants charged with violations of the law of war. In *Application of Yamashita*, the Court traced the history of military commissions and concluded: "By thus recognizing military commissions in order to preserve their traditional jurisdiction over enemy combatants…Congress gave sanction, as we held in *Ex Parte Quirin* to any use of military commissions contemplated by the common law of war." In its January 2002 report on the lawfulness of using military commissions, the American Bar Association Task Force on Terrorism and Law found that the terror attacks of September 11, 2001, were arguably violations of the law of war that would justify the use of military commissions to prosecute accused terrorists.

Among the detainees who have been convicted by military commissions is Salim Ahmed Hamdan, of Yemen. Hamdan, who acknowledged that he was a former driver for Osama bin Laden, was charged with a variety of offenses including conspiracy to attack civilians. Although the military commissions process was halted by a district court ruling in 2004, the D.C. Circuit in July 2005 reversed, upholding the legality of the military commissions set up by Executive Order. Then, on June 29, 2006, a sharply divided Court in *Hamdan v. Rumsfeld* reversed the Court of Appeals ruling that the Military Commissions process established by President Bush violated Common Article 3 of the Geneva Conventions as well as the military Uniform Code of Military Justice.

HAMDAN v. RUMSFELD
Supreme Court of the United States
126 S. Ct. 2749 (2006)

Justice STEVENS announced the judgment of the Court and delivered the opinion of the Court with respect to Parts I through IV, Parts VI through VI-D-iii, Part VI-D-v, and Part VII, and an opinion with respect to Parts V and VI-D-iv, in which Justice SOUTER, Justice GINSBURG, and Justice BREYER join.

Petitioner Salim Ahmed Hamdan, a Yemeni national, is in custody at an American prison in Guantánamo Bay, Cuba. In November 2001, during hostilities between the United States and the Taliban (which then governed Afghanistan), Hamdan was captured by militia forces and turned over to the U.S. military. In June 2002, he was transported to Guantánamo Bay. Over a year later, the President deemed him eligible for trial by military commission for then-unspecified crimes. After another year had passed, Hamdan was charged with one count of conspiracy "to commit...offenses triable by military commission."

Hamdan filed petitions for writs of habeas corpus and mandamus to challenge the Executive Branch's intended means of prosecuting this charge. He concedes that a court-martial constituted in accordance with the Uniform Code of Military Justice (UCMJ) would have authority to try him. His objection is that the military commission the President has convened lacks such authority, for two principal reasons: First, neither congressional Act nor the common law of war supports trial by this commission for the crime of conspiracy—an offense that, Hamdan says, is not a violation of the law of war. Second, Hamdan contends, the procedures that the President has adopted to try him violate the most basic tenets of military and international law, including the principle that a defendant must be permitted to see and hear the evidence against him.

The District Court granted Hamdan's request for a writ of habeas corpus. The Court of Appeals for the District of Columbia Circuit reversed. Recognizing, as we did over a half-century ago, that trial by military commission is an extraordinary measure raising important questions about the balance of powers in our constitutional structure, *Ex parte Quirin,* 317 U.S. 1, 19 (1942), we granted certiorari.

For the reasons that follow, we conclude that the military commission convened to try Hamdan lacks power to proceed because its structure and procedures violate both the UCMJ and the Geneva Conventions. Four of us also conclude, *See* Part V, *infra,* that the offense with which Hamdan has been charged is not an "offens[e] that by...the law of war may be tried by military commissions." 10 U.S.C. § 821.

...

IV

The military commission, a tribunal neither mentioned in the Constitution nor created by statute, was born of military necessity. *See* W. Winthrop, Military Law and Precedents 831 (rev.2d ed.1920) (hereinafter Winthrop). Though foreshadowed in some respects by earlier tribunals like the Board of General Officers that General Washington convened to try British Major John

Andre for spying during the Revolutionary War, the commission "as such" was inaugurated in 1847. *Id.* at 832; G. Davis, A Treatise on the Military Law of the United States 308 (2d ed.1909) (hereinafter Davis). As commander of occupied Mexican territory, and having available to him no other tribunal, General Winfield Scott that year ordered the establishment of both "'*military commissions*'" to try ordinary crimes committed in the occupied territory and a "*council of war*" to try offenses against the law of war.

When the exigencies of war next gave rise to a need for use of military commissions, during the Civil War, the dual system favored by General Scott was not adopted. Instead, a single tribunal often took jurisdiction over ordinary crimes, war crimes, and breaches of military orders alike. As further discussed below, each aspect of that seemingly broad jurisdiction was in fact supported by a separate military exigency. Generally, though, the need for military commissions during this period—as during the Mexican War—was driven largely by the then very limited jurisdiction of courts-martial: "The *occasion* for the military commission arises principally from the fact that the jurisdiction of the court-martial proper, in our law, is restricted by statute almost exclusively to members of the military force and to certain specific offences defined in a written code."

Exigency alone, of course, will not justify the establishment and use of penal tribunals not contemplated by Article I, § 8 and Article III, § 1 of the Constitution unless some other part of that document authorizes a response to the felt need. And that authority, if it exists, can derive only from the powers granted jointly to the President and Congress in time of war. *See In re Yamashita,* 327 U.S. 1, 11 (1946).

The Constitution makes the President the "Commander in Chief" of the Armed Forces, Art. II, § 2, cl. 1, but vests in Congress the powers to "declare War...and make Rules concerning Captures on Land and Water," Art. I, § 8, cl. 11, to "raise and support Armies," *id.,* cl. 12, to "define and punish...Offences against the Law of Nations," *id.,* cl. 10, and "To make Rules for the Government and Regulation of the land and naval Forces," *id.,* cl. 14. The interplay between these powers was described by Chief Justice

Chase in the seminal case of *Ex parte Milligan,* 4 Wall. 2, 139-40 (1866):

The power to make the necessary laws is in Congress; the power to execute in the President. Both powers imply many subordinate and auxiliary powers. Each includes all authorities essential to its due exercise. But neither can the President, in war more than in peace, intrude upon the proper authority of Congress, nor Congress upon the proper authority of the President....Congress cannot direct the conduct of campaigns, nor can the President, or any commander under him, without the sanction of Congress, institute tribunals for the trial and punishment of offences, either of soldiers or civilians, unless in cases of a controlling necessity, which justifies what it compels, or at least insures acts of indemnity from the justice of the legislature.

Whether Chief Justice Chase was correct in suggesting that the President may constitutionally convene military commissions "without the sanction of Congress" in cases of "controlling necessity" is a question this Court has not answered definitively, and need not answer today. For we held in *Quirin* that Congress had, through Article of War 15, sanctioned the use of military commissions in such circumstances. Article 21 of the UCMJ, the language of which is substantially identical to the old Article 15 and was preserved by Congress after World War II, reads as follows:

> Jurisdiction of courts-martial not exclusive. The provisions of this code conferring jurisdiction upon courts-martial shall not be construed as depriving military commissions, provost courts, or other military tribunals of concurrent jurisdiction in respect of offenders or offenses that by statute or by the law of war may be tried by such military commissions, provost courts, or other military tribunals.

...

C

In part because the difference between military commissions and courts-martial originally was a difference of jurisdiction alone, and in part to protect against abuse and ensure evenhandedness under the pressures of war, the procedures governing trials by military commission historically have been the same as those governing courts-martial. Accounts of commentators from Winthrop through General Crowder—who drafted Article of War 15 and whose views have been deemed "authoritative" by this Court, *Madsen v. Kinsella,* 343 U.S. 341, 353 (1952)—confirm as much. As recently as the Korean and Vietnam wars, during which use of military commissions was contemplated but never made, the principle of procedural parity was espoused as a background assumption.

There is a glaring historical exception to this general rule. The procedures and evidentiary rules used to try General Yamashita near the end of World War II deviated in significant respects from those then governing courts-martial. *See* 327 U.S. 1. The force of that precedent, however, has been seriously undermined by post-World War II developments.

Yamashita, from late 1944 until September 1945, was Commanding General of the Fourteenth Army Group of the Imperial Japanese Army, which had exercised control over the Philippine Islands. On September 3, 1945, after American forces regained control of the Philippines, Yamashita surrendered. Three weeks later, he was charged with violations of the law of war. A few weeks after that, he was arraigned before a military commission convened in the Philippines. He pleaded not guilty, and his trial lasted for two months. On December 7, 1945, Yamashita was convicted and sentenced to hang. *See id*. at 5; *id*. at 31-34 (Murphy, J., dissenting). This Court upheld the denial of his petition for a writ of habeas corpus.

The procedures and rules of evidence employed during Yamashita's trial departed so far from those used in courts-martial that they generated an unusually long and vociferous critique from two Members of this Court. *See id*. at 41-81 (Rutledge, J., joined by Murphy, J., dissenting). Among the dissenters' primary concerns was that the commission had free rein to consider all evidence "which in the commission's opinion 'would be of assistance in proving or disproving the charge,' without any of the usual modes of authentication." *Id*. at 49 (Rutledge, J.).

The majority, however, did not pass on the merits of Yamashita's procedural challenges because it concluded that his status disentitled him to any protection under the Articles of War (specifically, those set forth in Article 38, which would become Article 36 of the UCMJ) or the Geneva Convention of 1929, 47 Stat.2021 (1929 Geneva Convention). The Court explained that Yamashita was neither a "person made subject to the Articles of War by Article 2" thereof,

327 U.S. at 20, nor a protected prisoner of war being tried for crimes committed during his detention, *id.* at 21.

At least partially in response to subsequent criticism of General Yamashita's trial, the UCMJ's codification of the Articles of War after World War II expanded the category of persons subject thereto to include defendants in Yamashita's (and Hamdan's) position, and the Third Geneva Convention of 1949 extended prisoner-of-war protections to individuals tried for crimes committed before their capture. The most notorious exception to the principle of uniformity, then, has been stripped of its precedential value.

The uniformity principle is not an inflexible one; it does not preclude all departures from the procedures dictated for use by courts-martial. But any departure must be tailored to the exigency that necessitates it. That understanding is reflected in Article 36 of the UCMJ, which provides:

> (a) The procedure, including modes of proof, in cases before courts-martial, courts of inquiry, military commissions, and other military tribunals may be prescribed by the President by regulations which shall, so far as he considers practicable, apply the principles of law and the rules of evidence generally recognized in the trial of criminal cases in the United States district courts, but which may not be contrary to or inconsistent with this chapter.
>
> (b) All rules and regulations made under this article shall be uniform insofar as practicable and shall be reported to Congress.

Article 36 places two restrictions on the President's power to promulgate rules of procedure for courts-martial and military commissions alike. First, no procedural rule he adopts may be "contrary to or inconsistent with" the UCMJ—however practical it may seem. Second, the rules adopted must be "uniform insofar as practicable." That is, the rules applied to military commissions must be the same as those applied to courts-martial unless such uniformity proves impracticable.

Hamdan argues that Commission Order No. 1 violates both of these restrictions; he maintains that the procedures described in the Commission Order are inconsistent with the UCMJ and that the Government has offered no explanation for their deviation from the procedures governing courts-martial, which are set forth in the Manual for Courts-Martial, United States (2005 ed.) (Manual for Courts-Martial). Among the inconsistencies Hamdan identifies is that between § 6 of the Commission Order, which permits exclusion of the accused from proceedings and denial of his access to evidence in certain circumstances, and the UCMJ's requirement that "[a]ll...proceedings" other than votes and deliberations by courts-martial "shall be made a part of the record and shall be in the presence of the accused." Hamdan also observes that the Commission Order dispenses with virtually all evidentiary rules applicable in courts-martial.

The Government has three responses. First, it argues, only 9 of the UCMJ's 158 Articles—the ones that expressly mention "military commissions"—actually apply to commissions, and Commission Order No. 1 sets forth no procedure that is "contrary to or inconsistent with" those 9 provisions. Second, the Government contends, military commissions would be of no use if the President were hamstrung by those provisions of the UCMJ that govern courts-martial. Finally, the President's determination that "the danger to the safety of the United States and the nature of international terrorism" renders it impracticable "to apply in military commissions…the principles of law and rules of evidence generally recognized in the trial of criminal cases in the United States district courts," November 13 Order § 1(f), is, in the Government's view, explanation enough for any deviation from court-martial procedures.

Hamdan has the better of this argument. Without reaching the question whether any provision of Commission Order No. 1 is strictly "contrary to or inconsistent with" other provisions of the UCMJ, we conclude that the "practicability" determination the President has made is insufficient to justify variances from the procedures governing courts-martial. Subsection (b) of Article 36 was added after World War II, and requires a different showing of impracticability from the one required by subsection (a). Subsection (a) requires that the rules the President promulgates for courts-martial, provost courts, and military commissions alike conform to those that govern procedures in *Article III courts,* "so far as *he considers* practicable." Subsection (b), by contrast, demands that the rules applied in courts-martial, provost courts, and military commissions—whether or not they conform with the Federal Rules of Evidence—be "uniform *insofar as practicable.*" Under the latter provision, then, the rules set forth in the Manual for Courts-Martial must apply to military commissions unless impracticable.

The President here has determined, pursuant to subsection (a), that it is impracticable to apply the rules and principles of law that govern "the trial of criminal cases in the United States district courts," to Hamdan's commission. We assume that complete deference is owed that determination. The President has not, however, made a similar official determination that it is impracticable to apply the rules for courts-martial. And even if subsection (b)'s requirements may be satisfied without such an official determination, the requirements of that subsection are not satisfied here.

…

D

The procedures adopted to try Hamdan also violate the Geneva Conventions. The Court of Appeals dismissed Hamdan's Geneva Convention challenge on three independent grounds: (1) the Geneva Conventions are not judicially enforceable; (2) Hamdan in any event is not entitled to their protections; and (3) even if he is entitled to their protections, *Councilman* abstention is appropriate. Judge Williams, concurring, rejected the second ground but agreed with the majority respecting the first and the last. As we explained in Part III, *supra,* the abstention rule applied in *Councilman,* 420 U.S. 738, is not applicable here. And for the reasons that follow, we hold that neither of the other grounds the Court of Appeals gave for its decision is persuasive.

…

i

The Court of Appeals relied on *Johnson v. Eisentrager,* 339 U.S. 763 (1950), to hold that Hamdan could not invoke the Geneva Conventions to challenge the Government's plan to prosecute him in accordance with Commission Order No. 1. *Eisentrager* involved a challenge by 21 German nationals to their 1945 convictions for war crimes by a military tribunal convened in Nanking, China, and to their subsequent imprisonment in occupied Germany. The petitioners argued, *inter alia,* that the 1929 Geneva Convention rendered illegal some of the procedures employed during their trials, which they said deviated impermissibly from the procedures used by courts-martial to try American soldiers. *See id.* at 789. We rejected that claim on the merits because the petitioners (unlike Hamdan here) had failed to identify any prejudicial disparity "between the Commission that tried [them] and those that would try an offending soldier of the American forces of like rank," and in any event could claim no protection, under the 1929 Convention, during trials for crimes that occurred before their confinement as prisoners of war.

Buried in a footnote of the opinion, however, is this curious statement suggesting that the Court lacked power even to consider the merits of the Geneva Convention argument:

> We are not holding that these prisoners have no right which the military authorities are bound to respect. The United States, by the Geneva Convention of July 27, 1929, 47 Stat.2021, concluded with forty-six other countries, including the German Reich, an agreement upon the treatment to be accorded captives. These prisoners claim to be and are entitled to its protection. It is, however, the obvious scheme of the Agreement that responsibility for observance and enforcement of these rights is upon political and military authorities. Rights of alien enemies are vindicated under it only through protests and intervention of protecting powers as the rights of our citizens against foreign governments are vindicated only by Presidential intervention.

The Court of Appeals, on the strength of this footnote, held that "the 1949 Geneva Convention does not confer upon Hamdan a right to enforce its provisions in court."

Whatever else might be said about the *Eisentrager* footnote, it does not control this case. We may assume that "the obvious scheme" of the 1949 Conventions is identical in all relevant respects to that of the 1929 Convention, and even that that scheme would, absent some other provision of law, preclude Hamdan's invocation of the Convention's provisions as an independent source of law binding the Government's actions and furnishing petitioner with any enforceable right. For, regardless of the nature of the rights conferred on Hamdan, they are, as the Government does not dispute, part of the law of war. *See Hamdi,* 542 U.S. at 520-521 (plurality opinion). And compliance with the law of war is the condition upon which the authority set forth in Article 21 is granted.

ii

For the Court of Appeals, acknowledgment of that condition was no bar to Hamdan's trial by commission. As an alternative to its holding that Hamdan could not invoke the Geneva Conventions at all, the Court of Appeals concluded that the Conventions did not in any event apply to the armed conflict during which Hamdan was captured. The court accepted the Executive's assertions that Hamdan was captured in connection with the United States' war with al Qaeda and that that war is distinct from the war with the Taliban in Afghanistan. It further reasoned that the war with al Qaeda evades the reach of the Geneva Conventions. We, like Judge Williams, disagree with the latter conclusion.

The conflict with al Qaeda is not, according to the Government, a conflict to which the full protections afforded detainees under the 1949 Geneva Conventions apply because Article 2 of those Conventions (which appears in all four Conventions) renders the full protections applicable only to "all cases of declared war or of any other armed conflict which may arise between two or more of the High Contracting Parties." Since Hamdan was captured and detained incident to the conflict with al Qaeda and not the conflict with the Taliban, and since al Qaeda, unlike Afghanistan, is not a "High Contracting Party"—*i.e.*, a signatory of the Conventions, the protections of those Conventions are not, it is argued, applicable to Hamdan.

We need not decide the merits of this argument because there is at least one provision of the Geneva Conventions that applies here even if the relevant conflict is not one between signatories. Article 3, often referred to as Common Article 3 because, like Article 2, it appears in all four Geneva Conventions, provides that in a "conflict not of an international character occurring in the territory of one of the High Contracting Parties, each Party to the conflict shall be bound to apply, as a minimum," certain provisions protecting "[p]ersons taking no active part in the hostilities, including members of armed forces who have laid down their arms and those placed *hors de combat* by…detention." One such provision prohibits "the passing of sentences and the carrying out of executions without previous judgment pronounced by a regularly constituted court affording all the judicial guarantees which are recognized as indispensable by civilized peoples."

The Court of Appeals thought, and the Government asserts, that Common Article 3 does not apply to Hamdan because the conflict with al Qaeda, being "'international in scope,'" does not qualify as a "'conflict not of an international character.'" That reasoning is erroneous. The term "conflict not of an international character" is used here in contradistinction to a conflict between nations. So much is demonstrated by the "fundamental logic [of] the Convention's provisions on its application." Common Article 2 provides that "the present Convention shall apply to all cases of declared war or of any other armed conflict which may arise between two or more of the High Contracting Parties." High Contracting Parties (signatories) also must abide by all terms of the Conventions *vis-à-vis* one another even if one party to the conflict is a nonsignatory "Power," and must so abide *vis-à-vis* the nonsignatory if "the latter accepts and applies" those terms. Common Article 3, by contrast, affords some minimal protection, falling short of full protection under the Conventions, to individuals associated with neither a signatory nor even a nonsignatory "Power" who are involved in a conflict "in the territory of" a signatory. The latter kind of conflict is distinguishable from the conflict described in Common Article 2 chiefly because it does not involve a clash between nations (whether signatories or not). In context, then, the phrase "not of an international character" bears its literal meaning.

Although the official commentaries accompanying Common Article 3 indicate that an important purpose of the provision was to furnish minimal protection to rebels involved in one kind of "conflict not of an international character," *i.e.*, a civil war, the commentaries also make clear "that the scope of the Article must be as wide as possible." In fact, limiting language that would have rendered Common Article 3 applicable "especially [to] cases of civil war, colonial conflicts, or wars of religion," was omitted from the final version of the Article, which coupled broader scope of application with a narrower range of rights than did earlier proposed iterations.

iii

Common Article 3, then, is applicable here and, as indicated above, requires that Hamdan be tried by a "regularly constituted court affording all the judicial guarantees which are recognized as indispensable by civilized peoples." While the term "regularly constituted court" is not specifically defined in either Common Article 3 or its accompanying commentary, other sources disclose its core meaning. The commentary accompanying a provision of the Fourth Geneva Convention, for example, defines "'regularly constituted'" tribunals to include "ordinary military courts" and "definitely exclud[e] all special tribunals." And one of the Red Cross' own treatises defines "regularly constituted court" as used in Common Article 3 to mean "established and organized in accordance with the laws and procedures already in force in a country."

The Government offers only a cursory defense of Hamdan's military commission in light of Common Article 3. As JUSTICE KENNEDY explains, that defense fails because "[t]he regular military courts in our system are the courts-martial established by congressional statutes." *Post* (opinion concurring in part). At a minimum, a military commission "can be 'regularly constituted' by the standards of our military justice system only if some practical need explains deviations from court-martial practice." As we have explained, *see* Part VI-C, *supra,* no such need has been demonstrated here.

iv

Inextricably intertwined with the question of regular constitution is the evaluation of the procedures governing the tribunal and whether they afford "all the judicial guarantees which are recognized as indispensable by civilized peoples." Like the phrase "regularly constituted court," this phrase is not defined in the text of the Geneva Conventions. But it must be understood to incorporate at least the barest of those trial protections that have been recognized by customary international law. Many of these are described in Article 75 of Protocol I to the Geneva Conventions of 1949, adopted in 1977 (Protocol I). Although the United States declined to ratify Protocol I, its objections were not to Article 75 thereof. Indeed, it appears that the Government "regard[s] the provisions of Article 75 as an articulation of safeguards to which all persons in the hands of an enemy are entitled." Among the rights set forth in Article 75 is the "right to be tried in [one's] presence." Protocol I, Art. 75(4)(e).

We agree with JUSTICE KENNEDY that the procedures adopted to try Hamdan deviate from those governing courts-martial in ways not justified by any "evident practical need," *post,* and for that reason, at least, fail to afford the requisite guarantees. We add only that, as noted in Part VI-A, *supra,* various provisions of Commission Order No. 1 dispense with the principles, articulated in Article 75 and indisputably part of the customary international law, that an accused must, absent disruptive conduct or consent, be present for his trial and must be privy to the evidence against him. That the Government has a compelling interest in denying Hamdan access to certain sensitive information is not doubted. But, at least absent express statutory provision to the contrary, information used to convict a person of a crime must be disclosed to him.

V

Common Article 3 obviously tolerates a great degree of flexibility in trying individuals captured during armed conflict; its requirements are general ones, crafted to accommodate a wide variety of legal systems. But *requirements* they are nonetheless. The commission that the President has convened to try Hamdan does not meet those requirements.

VII

We have assumed, as we must, that the allegations made in the Government's charge against Hamdan are true. We have assumed, moreover, the truth of the message implicit in that charge—viz., that Hamdan is a dangerous individual whose beliefs, if acted upon, would cause great harm and even death to innocent civilians, and who would act upon those beliefs if given the opportunity. It bears emphasizing that Hamdan does not challenge, and we do not today address, the Government's power to detain him for the duration of active hostilities in order to prevent such harm. But in undertaking to try Hamdan and subject him to criminal punishment, the Executive is bound to comply with the Rule of Law that prevails in this jurisdiction.

The judgment of the Court of Appeals is reversed, and the case is remanded for further proceedings.

It is so ordered.

THE CHIEF JUSTICE took no part in the consideration or decision of this case.
Justice BREYER, with whom Justice KENNEDY, Justice SOUTER, and Justice GINSBURG join, concurring.
…

Justice SCALIA, with whom Justice THOMAS and Justice ALITO join, dissenting.

On December 30, 2005, Congress enacted the Detainee Treatment Act (DTA). It unambiguously provides that, as of that date, "no court, justice, or judge" shall have jurisdiction to consider the habeas application of a Guantánamo Bay detainee. Notwithstanding this plain directive, the Court today concludes that, on what it calls the statute's *most natural* reading, *every* "court, justice, or judge" before whom such a habeas application was pending on December 30 has jurisdiction to hear, consider, and render judgment on it. This conclusion is patently erroneous. And even if it were not, the jurisdiction supposedly retained should, in an exercise of sound equitable discretion, not be exercised.
…
For the foregoing reasons, I dissent.

Justice THOMAS, with whom Justice SCALIA joins, and with whom Justice ALITO joins in all but Parts I, II-C-1, and III-B-2, dissenting.

For the reasons set forth in JUSTICE SCALIA's dissent, it is clear that this Court lacks jurisdiction to entertain petitioner's claims. The Court having concluded otherwise, it is appropriate to respond to the Court's resolution of the merits of petitioner's claims because its opinion openly flouts our well-established duty to respect the Executive's judgment in matters of military operations and foreign affairs. The Court's evident belief that *it* is qualified to pass on the "[m]ilitary necessity," of the Commander in Chief's decision to employ a particular form of force against our enemies is so antithetical to our constitutional structure that it simply cannot go unanswered. I respectfully dissent.

...

Prompted by the Supreme Court's holding in *Hamdan*, an energized Congress understood that they could no longer remain on the sidelines in the War on Terror. In late 2006, Congress established the creation of military commissions, affirming quite satisfactorily that the Military Commissions Act (MCA) of 2006 was consistent with the requirements of Common Article 3 of the Geneva Conventions—the military commissions so established constituted a "regularly constituted court," affording all the necessary "judicial guarantees which are recognized as indispensable by civilized peoples." Indeed, with the passage of the 2006 MCA, Congress firmly committed itself to the view that the nation was at war and that the legislative branch of government had a significant role to play in a variety of legal issues associated with the "enemy combatants"—both legal and illegal—that seek to do great physical harm to the United States and its allies. While the Detainee Treatment Act of 2005 provided an advanced signal that Congress was at last willing to get involved in a limited manner in some of the thorny legal aspects of the War on Terror, the 2006 MCA represented a major Congressional shift in scope. In short, the 2006 MCA was a resounding statutory broadside that impacted forcefully and with great effect across the entire legal landscape.

Without question, the 2006 MCA certainly washed away all doubt regarding Congress' willingness to characterize the War on Terror as a real global war against real enemies who desire to murder and terrorize. Accordingly, Congress demonstrated that it was more than willing to employ the full weight of the rule of law pertaining to armed conflict against the enemies of the United States. In fact, the Democrat controlled Congress followed suit by amending portions of the MCA in its 2009 Military Commissions Act.

Not only did the 2006 MCA provide crystal clear guidance in the context of the establishment and operation of military commissions to try "any alien unlawful enemy combatant" (al-Qa'eda and al-Qa'eda-styled Islamic terrorists) it provided concrete statutory definitions concerning a wide variety of terms that had been previously hotly debated. The 2006 MCA also clearly placed a large legal "seal of approval" on many of the initiatives taken by the Bush Administration in the War on Terror. For instance, the 2006 MCA defined "unlawful enemy combatants" in precise language:

(i) a person who has engaged in hostilities or who has purposefully and materially supported hostilities against the United States or its co-belligerents who is not a lawful enemy combatant (including a person who is part of the Taliban, al Qaeda, or associated forces); or

(ii) a person who, before, on, or after the date of the enactment of the Military Commissions Act of 2006, has been determined to be an unlawful enemy combatant by a Combatant Status Review Tribunal or another competent tribunal established under the authority of the President or the Secretary of Defense.

While the 2009 MCA changed the 2006 MCA term "unlawful enemy combatant" to "unprivileged enemy belligerent" it still provided a similar detailed description of who qualified as the enemy in the War on Terror: "An individual (other than a privileged belligerent) who has engaged in hostilities against the United States or its coalition partners; or has purposefully and materially supported hostilities against the United States or its coalition partners; or an individual who was a member of al-Qaeda at the time the offense occurred."

In accordance with its constitutional power to "define and punish...offenses against the Law of Nations," the MCA also lists in detail the criminal offenses that fall within the jurisdiction of the military commissions. Apart from the traditional list of war crimes that one would expect to encounter, the MCA appropriately includes "conspiracy" and "providing material support for terrorism," drawing definitional language from the Material Support Act provisions at Section 2339A. While *Boumediene* struck down the 2006 MCA provisions restricting habeas corpus, the major thrust of the 2009 MCA serves as the centerpiece for an emerging rule of law in the War on Terror.

In the sphere of authorizing trial by military commissions, Congress wisely allows for military commissions to operate in the traditional manner of all previous military commissions (hundreds were tried by military commissions in World War II, some were even U.S. citizens) and consider, for example, hearsay evidence and information gathered without a search warrant. In terms of hearsay evidence, the 2009 MCA holds that evidence not otherwise admissible under the rules of evidence applicable in trial by general-courts-martial may still be admitted under certain circumstances should the military judge determine that the evidence would have probative value and the proponent provides advanced notice. However, the burden of persuasion to demonstrate unreliability or lack of probative value rests on the profferer of the evidence. Physical evidence seized outside the United States shall not be excluded on the grounds that it was seized without a search warrant or other authorization. The 2009 MCA also allows verbal and written statements from the accused so long as the statement was not obtained by the use of torture or by cruel, inhuman, or degrading treatment.

Ironically, some still view the common sense evidentiary provisions in the 2009 MCA as a violation of Common Article 3's requirement that the accused be afforded all the necessary "guarantees...recognized as indispensable by civilized peoples." Such ethnocentric views are quickly dispelled when one considers the day-to-day activity of most modern European criminal courts where hearsay is regularly considered and far different legal avenues regarding the introduction of evidence are regularly employed. Even the International Criminal Court, the icon of those who worship at the altar of internationalism, allows hearsay. In fact, earlier calls by some (including uniformed judge advocates who should have known better) that a military commission should include the same due process standards that American soldiers enjoy at a military courts-martial under the Uniform Code of Military Justice were wisely disregarded by Congress in 2006 and 2009. Obviously, these "relaxed" provisions in the MCA are necessary due to the exigencies of war—witnesses and victims may be dead, investigators are not able to get to the crime scene, etc. Nevertheless, the 2009 MCA provides more due process rights to the accused than any military commission in the history of military commissions in the history of war. In general frame, the 2009 MCA provides the following rights for the accused who is charged:

- a copy of the charges in English and a language he understands;
- right to a free military attorney or to hire a civilian attorney, may also have foreign consultants;
- a presumption of innocence for the accused;

- guilt must be proven by the government beyond a reasonable doubt;
- access to evidence that the prosecution plans to present at trial;
- access to evidence known or reasonably should be known to the prosecution tending to exculpate the accused;
- right to remain silent;
- no adverse inference for remaining silent;
- right to testify subject to cross-examination;
- right to obtain witnesses and documents for defense;
- right to present evidence and cross-examine witnesses;
- no statement obtained by torture or by cruel, inhuman, or degrading treatment is admissible;
- accused will see every piece of evidence that the panel sees (even classified);
- appointment of interpreters to assist defense;
- right to be present at every stage of trial (except when proceedings are closed for national security) unless disruptive;
- access to sentencing evidence;
- cannot be tried again by military commission once verdict is final;
- right to submit a plea agreement;
- a panel consists of at least five members (at least 12 members if death penalty case);
- challenges to members of the panel by the defense;
- two-thirds of the military officers on the panel must agree on findings of guilt;
- unanimous decision for death sentence;
- trial is open to the public (exceptions recognized for physical safety of participants);
- automatic appellate review by a Court of Military Commission Review (CMCR);
- further review by petition to the D.C. Court of Appeals and by writ of certiorari to the Supreme Court.

A final way to compare the procedures and rights of the accused is revealed in the following chart, which compares the current MCA with the processes used in current military courts-martial trials for American soldiers, federal district courts, and the International Criminal Courts. Clearly, the MCA process is well within the norm of other judicial forums.

Comparison Chart of Procedures and Rights for Persons Being Tried by Military Commissions, Courts-Martial, U.S. District Courts, and International Criminal Courts

Procedures and or Rights	Military Commissions Act 2009 Manual for Military Commissions	Uniform Code of Military Justice (UCMJ)	U.S. District Court	Nuremberg Trials (WWII)	International Criminal Courts
Presumption of Innocence	Defendant is presumed innocent	Same	Same	Not specified	Same
Burden of Proof	Burden of proof on government	Same	Same	Same	Same
Standard of Proof	Burden of proof is "beyond a reasonable doubt."	Same	Same	Not specified	Same
Right to Speedy Trial	Right to Speedy trial—arraignment in 30 days, assemble commission in 120; unknown for MCA	120 days after the earlier of preferral of charges, restraint or entry on active duty	Within 70 days of indictment	Expeditious	Without undue delay
Right to Be Informed of Charges	Defendant must be informed of charges as soon as practicable	As soon as practicable	After indictment	Reasonable time before trial	Promptly and to provide adequate time for defense
Assistance of Defense Counsel	Right to detailed defense counsel at no charge to accused	Detailed defense counsel, individual military counsel or civilian counsel	Public defender at no charge	Right to counsel	Choice of counsel from court list
Right to Be Present at Trial	Defendant entitled to be present at trial; may be removed for disruptive or dangerous conduct	Same	Same	Accused not entitled to be present at trial	Same
Right to Confront Witnesses	Right to cross-examine witnesses	Same	Same	Same	Same
Double Jeopardy	No double jeopardy	Same	Same	Not specified	Allowed
Right to Assistance of Interpreter	Right to interpreter	Same	Same	Same	Same
Right Against Self-Incrimination	Yes	Same	Same	No. Tribunal may interrogate any defendant	Same

Procedures and or Rights	Military Commissions Act 2009 Manual for Military Commissions	Uniform Code of Military Justice (UCMJ)	U.S. District Court	Nuremberg Trials (WWII)	International Criminal Courts
Judge/Jury Model; Panel of Judges	Military Judge and Members	Same	Judge and Jury	Panel of judges	Panel of judges
Pretrial Legal Review	Convening Authority reviews charges and decides whether to refer them to military commission for trial	Same	Grand Jury	Same	Same
Admissibility of Hearsay Evidence	Hearsay admissible if deemed probative	Hearsay not admissible unless a specific exception exists	Hearsay not admissible unless a specific exception exists	Hearsay admissible if deemed probative	Hearsay admissible if deemed probative, unless it is gathered in violation of ICC statute or internationally recognized human rights
Compulsory Process to Obtain Defense Witnesses	Defense has reasonable opportunity to obtain witnesses	Accused may obtain witnesses for defense	Accused may obtain witnesses for defense	Defense may apply for production of witnesses and will be granted, subject to certain requirements	Trial Chamber may require attendance and testimony of witness
Exclusionary Rules	Statements obtained through torture or ill treatment are not admissible. Fourth Amendment protections not available for evidence seized outside United States	Exclusionary rules apply	Exclusionary rules a apply	No exclusionary rule. Evidence of probative value admitted.	Exclusionary rules apply
Challenges to Court Members/Jury	Challenges to members of court permitted	Same	Same	Not permitted	Same
Public Trial	Public trial, subject to some exceptions	Same	Same	Not specified	Same
Votes Required to Convict	2/3 vote of members required to convict, 3/4 required for more than 10 years, unanimous for death	Same	Unanimous in all cases	3 of 4 members	Majority
Appellate Review	Four levels of appellate review, including review by Supreme Court	Three levels of appellate review, including review by Supreme Court	Two levels of appellate review, including Supreme Court	No appellate review	One level of appellate review

In 2008, the first contested military commission trial was completed for al-Qa'eda member Salim Hamdan (David Hicks was convicted in 2007 by military commission after a guilty plea). Clearly a rebuff to those that view the military commissions process a "rubber stamp" or "kangaroo court," Hamdan was convicted of only about half of the charges he was charged with:

Count 1: Conspiracy

Specification 1: conspiracy to commit a variety of offenses (attacks on civilians, etc.)—**acquitted**

Specification 2: conspiracy to commit murder in violation of the law of war by attacking US and coalition servicemen—**acquitted** (Judge Allred instructed the panel that the charge required proof that the conspiracy targeted "protected persons"—civilians or persons rendered hors de combat).

Count 2: Material Support

Specification 1: Providing himself as personnel to al Qaeda with knowledge or intent that this support would "be used for an act of terrorism" (a count analogous to 18 USC 2339A)—**acquitted**

Specification 2: Providing himself as personnel to al Qa'eda, period (a count analogous to 18 USC 2339B, which unlike 2339A does not require any linkage to another offense)—**CONVICTED**

Specification 3: Providing al Qa'eda with SA-7 surface-to-air missiles in November 2001, knowing they would be used for an act of terrorism (again along the lines of 2339A)—**acquitted**

Specification 4: Providing al Qa'eda with SA-7 surface-to-air missiles in November 2001, period (again along the lines of 2339B)—**acquitted**

Specification 5: Providing support to al Qa'eda through his service as a driver, knowing this would facilitate communications and planning for terrorist acts—**CONVICTED**

Specification 6: Similar to Specification 5—**CONVICTED**

Specification 7: Providing support to al Qa'eda through service as a bodyguard, knowing this would facilitate communications and planning for terrorist acts—**CONVICTED**

Specification 8: Similar to Specification 7—**CONVICTED**

As various legal challenges to portions of the 2009 MCA make their way through the lower courts, it is highly doubtful that the Supreme Court will strike down very much of the MCA as unconstitutional. Indeed, in time of war the Court has traditionally been most reluctant to intervene in matters of national security, particularly when the executive and legislative branches have joined together in such a seamless fashion.

With the exception of the 2005 Detainee Treatment Act legislation, that dealt with the treatment, interrogation, and trial of detainees, Congress at first seemed content to sit on the sidelines in the War on Terror. With the passage of the 2006 MCA and then the 2009 MCA, Congress has become properly energized in the War on Terror. While rational people understand that the unique threat of al-Qa'eda-styled terrorism against the United States can best be addressed by employing the laws established for armed conflict, it is equally true that the law of war needs to be updated to encompass the new paradigm. Since the international community will not act, this means that Congress must remain involved and informed.

4.6 Federal Courts

It is well settled that federal district courts of the United States have the legal authority under both domestic and international law to prosecute nonresident aliens for terrorist crimes committed on foreign soil as well as for war crimes. This power has been exercised many times against militant Islamic terrorists, both prior to and after 9/11. In contrast to military commissions, which can only try enemy combatants, federal courts can prosecute enemy combatants and Islamic terrorists who do not qualify as enemy combatants.

A widely cited precedent which amplifies just how far the jurisdictional reach extends in this regard is the case of *United States v. Yunis*. The *Yunis* case involved the federal criminal trial of Fawaz Yunis, an Arab terrorist who participated in the hijacking of a Royal Jordanian Airlines airplane at Beirut International Airport in June 1985. The only connection the act had with the United States was the fact that a handful of American citizens were on board the hijacked plane. After reviewing the pertinent international agreements relating to hostage taking and hijacking, the federal district court denied a defense motion to dismiss for lack of jurisdiction and Yunis was convicted of conspiracy, hostage taking and air piracy.

On appeal of his conviction, the Court of Appeals for the D.C. Circuit said the following about the concept of customary international law as it applied to certain criminal acts: "Nor is jurisdiction precluded by norms of customary international law. The district court [correctly] concluded that two jurisdictional theories of international law, the 'universal principle' and the 'passive personal principle,' (*United States v. Benitez*, 741 F.2d. 1312) supported assertion of United States jurisdiction to prosecute Yunis on hijacking and hostage-taking charges." According to the appellate court, the "universal principle" of jurisdiction allows States to prosecute those "offenses recognized by the community of nations as of universal concern, such as piracy, slave trade, attacks on or hijacking of aircraft, genocide, war crimes, and perhaps certain acts of terrorism." Under the "passive personal principle," a State may prosecute non-nationals for crimes committed against its nationals outside of its territory. Furthermore, the circuit court found that the conduct of the government in bringing Yunis (with some amount of violence to his person) into the United States would not be a bar to his prosecution. Under the Supreme Court's Ker-Frisbie rule, even the illegal arrest of a defendant is not sufficient to warrant a dismissal of charges. The illegal conduct must "shock the conscience of the court."

A constant problem for the government in dealing with the threat of al-Qa'eda-styled terrorism is expressed in the policy of "anticipatory prosecution," or "pre-emptive prosecution." Desiring to avoid another 9/11 attack on the United States, the government's policy in the first years after 9/11 was to arrest suspected terrorists at the earliest opportunity in a given investigation, as opposed to letting a particular terror plot mature. The down side to this policy was that the government was not able to prove the more serious terror offenses in a court of law, leaving the suspects charged with lesser offenses and sentenced to shorter terms. Responding to criticism that DOJ should wait longer before intervening with premature arrests in a terror investigation, a September 11, 2008 DOJ document entitled: Fact Sheet: Justice Department Counter-Terrorism Efforts Since 9/11 explains:

> In each of these cases, the Department has faced critical decisions on when to bring criminal charges, given that a decision to prosecute a suspect exposes the Government's interest in that person and effectively ends covert intelligence investigation. Such determinations require the careful balancing of competing interests, including the immediate incapacitation of a suspect and disruption of terrorist activities through prosecution, on the one hand; and the continuation of intelligence collection about the suspect's plans, capabilities, and confederates, on the other; as well as the inherent risk that a suspect could carry out a violent act while investigators and prosecutors attempt to perfect their evidence.
>
> While it might be easier to secure convictions after an attack has occurred and innocent lives are lost, in such circumstances, the Department would be failing in its fundamental mission to protect America and its citizens, despite a court victory. For these reasons, the Department continues to act against terror threats as soon as the law, evidence, and unique circumstances of each case permit, using any charge available. As Attorney General Mukasey has stated: "[W]hen it comes to deciding whether and when to bring charges against terrorists, I am comfortable knowing this: I would rather explain to the American people why we acted when we did, even if it is at a very early stage, than try to explain why we failed to act when we could have, and it is too late."

As the horror of 9/11 fades into history, the federal authorities have become more patient. For instance, the Fort Dix Six case where a cell of radical Islamic terrorists were planning to enter Fort Dix, New Jersey, and murder military personnel was allowed to mature for a year before the arrests were made. Also, in 2010, radical Islamic terrorists Mohamed Mahmood Alessa and Carlos Almonte were arrested for conspiracy to commit murder after over four years of surveillance by the FBI.

By law and custom federal prosecutors are authorized the discretion to decline cases brought to them by investigative agencies. According to a 2009 Syracuse University study by the Transactional Records Access Clearinghouse, from 2004 to 2008 various federal investigative agencies initially characterized nearly 8,900 individuals arrested as "international terrorists." Of that number, only 2,302 individuals were convicted in federal district courts on either criminal statutes penalizing terrorist activity or other criminal statutes dealing with more general offenses, e.g., immigration violations, identity theft, or false statement charges. In turn, only 1,245 of the 2,302 received prison confinement, and only 52 were sentenced to 20 years or more in confinement. Reflecting the policy of anticipatory prosecution, although the 2,302 convicted persons were designated as "international terrorists" by the DOJ, the actual crimes they were charged with often had no direct connection to what courts normally deem to be terrorist activity. In fact, the primary lead charge was 18 U.S.C. § 1001 (fraud/false statements, identity theft). In labeling an individual as a terrorist, Courts generally turn to a group of 14 federal statutes determined to be "terrorist" offenses, such as 18 U.S.C. § 2332 (terrorism transcending national borders) and 18 U.S.C. § 2339 (providing material support to terrorists).

Interestingly, only one American, Adam Gadahn (aka Azzam al-Amriki), has been charged with the crime of treason (seditious conspiracy charges were used against the terrorists who conducted the 1993 bombing on the World Trade Center). Gadahn converted to Islam in 1995 and later moved to Pakistan where he has since appeared in a series of videos, calling for terrorist attacks on Americans. Treason, the only crime spelled out in the Constitution, is codified at 18 U.S.C. § 2381. The indictment alleges that Gadahn, owing allegiance to the United States, knowingly adhered to al-Qa'eda and provided it aid-and-comfort, with intent to "betray the United States." The indictment then provides extensive quotations from five separate al-Qa'eda videos in which he appeared and urged others to attack the United States. He is also charged with providing material support in violation of 18 U.S.C. § 2339B.

The violation of immigration laws served as the primary authority for the FBI and immigration officials to detain approximately 1,000 individuals across the United States in the wake of the 9/11 terrorist attacks. Many were detained at the Metropolitan Detention Center (MDC) in Brooklyn, New York. Within four months, about two-thirds of those detained accepted voluntary departure orders and were deported; others were convicted of lesser crimes and deported. It is unclear how many of these deported illegal aliens were actually terrorists or had firm links to militant Islamic groups. Predictably, many of those detained made allegations of abuse by guards and harsh conditions based on their race, religion, or national origin. The Supreme Court in *Ashcroft v. Iqbal* (2009) rejected an effort by a Pakistani detainee at the MDC, who served a 16 month sentence before being deported, to sue former high-ranking Bush Administration officials. In the 5-4 decision, Justice Kennedy ruled that the detainees were not purposefully detained and housed based on race, religion, or national origin, but "in the aftermath of a devastating attack [the government] sought to keep suspected terrorists in the most secure conditions available until the suspects could be cleared of terrorist activity."

In the past ten years, the FBI has broken up numerous al-Qa'eda and radical Islamic cells in the United States. Fortunately, because of the hard work of law enforcement at all levels, the vast majority of the plots were unsuccessful, with the marked exception of the murder of 13 soldiers at Fort Hood, Texas, in 2009. These plots included attacks on military installations, subway systems, famous landmarks, shopping malls, airports, airplanes, tunnels, bridges, and schools. A list of the more notable Islamic terrorism prosecutions and charges are listed in Appendix J.

Charging considerations also raise unique issues, as do defenses of freedom of religion and privacy, as illustrated in the case of Sheik Omar Abdel Rahman, one of the most notorious Islamic militants prosecuted to date. The so-called blind Sheik was associated with the 1993 terror bombing of the World Trade Center.

UNITED STATES v. RAHMAN
United States Court of Appeals for the Second Circuit
189 F.3d 88 (2nd Cir. 1999)

NEWMAN, LEVAL, and PARKER, Circuit Judges.
PER CURIAM:

INTRODUCTION

These are appeals by ten defendants convicted of seditious conspiracy and other offenses arising out of a wide-ranging plot to conduct a campaign of urban terrorism. Among the activities of some or all of the defendants were rendering assistance to those who bombed the World Trade Center, planning to bomb bridges and tunnels in New York City, murdering Rabbi Meir

Kahane, and planning to murder the President of Egypt. We affirm the convictions of all the defendants. We also affirm all of the sentences, with the exception of the sentence of Ibrahim El-Gabrowny, which we remand for further consideration.

BACKGROUND

Defendants-Appellants Sheik Omar Abdel Rahman, El Sayyid Nosair, Ibrahim El-Gabrowny, Clement Hampton-El, Amir Abdelgani ("Amir"), Fares Khallafalla, Tarig Elhassan, Fadil Abdelgani ("Fadil"), Mohammed Saleh, and Victor Alvarez (collectively "defendants") appeal from judgments of conviction entered on January 17, 1996, following a nine-month jury trial in the United States District Court for the Southern District of New York (Michael B. Mukasey, District Judge).

The defendants were convicted of the following: seditious conspiracy (all defendants); soliciting the murder of Egyptian President Hosni Mubarak and soliciting an attack on American military installations (Rahman); conspiracy to murder Mubarak (Rahman); bombing conspiracy (all defendants found guilty except Nosair and El-Gabrowny); attempted bombing (Hampton-El, Amir, Fadil, Khallafalla, Elhassan, Saleh, and Alvarez); two counts of attempted murder and one count of murder in furtherance of a racketeering enterprise (Nosair); attempted murder of a federal officer (Nosair); three counts of use of a firearm in relation to a crime of violence (Nosair); possession of a firearm with an obliterated serial number (Nosair); facilitating the bombing conspiracy by shipping a firearm in interstate commerce and using and carrying a firearm in relation to a crime of violence (Alvarez); two counts of assault on a federal officer (El-Gabrowny); assault impeding the execution of a search warrant (El-Gabrowny); five counts of possession of a fraudulent foreign passport, and one count of possession with intent to transfer false identification documents (El-Gabrowny).

...

II. The Defense Case

The defendants presented their case for two months, calling 71 witnesses. Hampton-El, Elhassan, Alvarez, and Fadil Abdelgani each testified on his own behalf. The specific defenses put forth by the individual defendants will be set out below as they become relevant to particular claims on appeal. Siddig Ali, among others, was charged in the same indictment as the defendants but was not part of the trial because he pleaded guilty to all counts with which he was charged and cooperated, to a degree, with the Government.

III. Verdicts and Sentences

The jury trial in the case ran from January 9, 1995, to October 1, 1995. The jury returned verdicts finding defendants guilty on all submitted charges, except that Nosair and El-Gabrowny obtained not guilty verdicts on the Count Five bombing conspiracy charges. The defendants were sentenced as follows: Rahman and Nosair, life imprisonment; El-Gabrowny, 57 years; Alvarez, Hampton-El, Elhassan, and Saleh, 35 years; Amir Abdelgani and Khallafalla, 30 years; Fadil Abdelgani, 25 years. The sentences are more fully explained in Part IV(A), infra.

DISCUSSION
I. Constitutional Challenges
A. Seditious Conspiracy Statute and the Treason Clause

Defendant Nosair (joined by other defendants) contends that his conviction for seditious conspiracy, in violation of *18 U.S.C. § 2384*, was illegal because it failed to satisfy the requirements of the Treason Clause of the U.S. Constitution, Art. III, 3.

Article III, Section 3 provides, in relevant part:

> Treason against the United States, shall consist only in levying War against them, or in adhering to their Enemies, giving them Aid and Comfort. No Person shall be convicted of Treason unless on the Testimony of two Witnesses to the same overt Act, or on Confession in open Court.

The seditious conspiracy statute [18 U.S.C. *§ 2384]* provides:

> If two or more persons in any State or Territory, or in any place subject to the jurisdiction of the United States, conspire to overthrow, put down or to destroy by force the Government of the United States, or to levy war against them, or to oppose by force the authority thereof, or by force to prevent, hinder or delay the execution of any law of the United States, or by force to seize, take, or possess any property of the United States contrary to the authority thereof, they shall each be fined under this title or imprisoned not more than twenty years, or both.

...

Seditious conspiracy by levying war includes no requirement that the defendant owe allegiance to the United States, an element necessary to conviction of treason. See *18 U.S.C. § 2381* (defining "allegiance to United States" as an element of treason). Nosair nevertheless maintains that "the only distinction between the elements of seditious conspiracy under the levy war prong and treason by levying war is that the former requires proof of a conspiracy while the latter requires proof of the substantive crime." Noting that the requirement of allegiance appears explicitly in the treason statute, but not in the Treason Clause, Nosair suggests that allegiance to the United States is not an element of treason within the contemplation of the Constitution. He concludes that, for constitutional purposes, the elements constituting seditious conspiracy by levying war and treason by levying war are identical, and consequently that prosecutions for seditious conspiracy by levying war must conform to the requirements of the Treason Clause.

The argument rests on a false premise. The Treason Clause does not, as Nosair supposes, purport to specify the elements of the crime of treason. Instead, in addition to providing evidentiary safeguards, the Clause restricts the conduct that may be deemed treason to "levying war" against the United States and "adhering to their Enemies, giving them Aid and Comfort." It does not undertake to define the constituent elements of the substantive crime.

...

B. Seditious Conspiracy Statute and the First Amendment

Rahman, joined by the other appellants, contends that the seditious conspiracy statute, *18 U.S.C. § 2384*, is an unconstitutional burden on free speech and the free exercise of religion in violation of the First Amendment. First, Rahman argues that the statute is facially invalid because it criminalizes protected expression and that it is overbroad and unconstitutionally vague. Second, Rahman contends that his conviction violated the First Amendment because it rested solely on his political views and religious practices.

1. Facial Challenge

a. *Restraint on Speech. Section 2384 provides:* If two or more persons in any State or Territory, or in any place subject to the jurisdiction of the United States, conspire to overthrow, put down, or destroy by force the Government of the United States, or to levy war against them, or to oppose by force the authority thereof, or by force to prevent, hinder, or delay the execution of any law of the United States, or by force to seize, take, or possess any property of the United States contrary to the authority thereof, they shall be fined under this title or imprisoned not more than twenty years, or both.

18 U.S.C. § 2384.

As Section 2384 proscribes "speech" only when it constitutes an agreement to use force against the United States, Rahman's generalized First Amendment challenge to the statute is without merit. Our court has previously considered and rejected a First Amendment challenge to Section 2384.
…

2. Application of Section 2384 to Rahman's Case

Rahman also argues that he was convicted not for entering into any conspiratorial agreement that Congress may properly forbid, but "solely for his religious words and deeds" which, he contends, are protected by the First Amendment. In support of this claim, Rahman cites the Government's use in evidence of his speeches and writings.

There are two answers to Rahman's contention. The first is that freedoms of speech and of religion do not extend so far as to bar prosecution of one who uses a public speech or a religious ministry to commit crimes. Numerous crimes under the federal criminal code are, or can be, committed by speech alone. As examples: Section 2 makes it an offense to "counsel," "command," "induce" or "procure" the commission of an offense against the United States. *18 U.S.C. § 2(a)*. Section 371 makes it a crime to "conspire…to commit any offense against the United States." *18 U.S.C. § 371*. Section 373, with which Rahman was charged, makes it a crime to "solicit, command, induce, or otherwise endeavor to persuade" another person to commit a crime of violence. *18 U.S.C. § 373(a)*. Various other statutes, like Section 2384, criminalize conspiracies of specified objectives, see, e.g., *18 U.S.C. § 1751(d)* (conspiracy to kidnap); *18 U.S.C. § 1951* (conspiracy to interfere with commerce through robbery, extortion, or violence); *21 U.S.C. § 846* conspiracy to violate drug laws). All of these offenses are characteristically committed through speech. Notwithstanding that political speech and religious exercise are among the activities most jealously guarded by the First Amendment, one is not immunized from prosecution for such speech-based offenses merely because one commits them through the medium of political speech or religious preaching. Of course, courts must be vigilant to insure [sic] that prosecutions are not improperly based on the mere expression of unpopular ideas. But if the evidence shows that the speeches crossed the line into criminal solicitation, procurement of criminal activity, or conspiracy to violate the laws, the prosecution is permissible.

The evidence justifying Rahman's conviction for conspiracy and solicitation showed beyond a reasonable doubt that he crossed this line. His speeches were not simply the expression of ideas; in some instances they constituted the crime of conspiracy to wage war on the United States under Section 2384 and solicitation of attack on the United States military installations, as well as of the murder of Egyptian President Hosni Mubarak under Section 373.

For example:

Rahman told Salem he "should make up with God…by turning his rifle's barrel to President Mubarak's chest, and killing him."

On another occasion, speaking to Abdo Mohammed Haggag about murdering President Mubarak during his visit to the United States, Rahman told Haggag, "Depend on God. Carry out this operation. It does not require a fatwa.…You are ready in training, but do it. Go ahead."

The evidence further showed that Siddig Ali consulted with Rahman about the bombing of the United Nations Headquarters, and Rahman told him, "Yes, it's a must, it's a duty."

On another occasion, when Rahman was asked by Salem about bombing the United Nations, he counseled against it on the ground that it would be "bad for Muslims," but added that Salem should "find a plan to destroy or to bomb or to…inflict damage to the American Army."

Words of this nature—ones that instruct, solicit, or persuade others to commit crimes of violence—violate the law and may be properly prosecuted regardless of whether they are uttered in private, or in a public speech, or in administering the duties of a religious ministry. The fact that his speech or conduct was "religious" does not immunize him from prosecution under generally-applicable criminal statutes.

Rahman also protests the Government's use in evidence of his speeches, writings, and preachings that did not in themselves constitute the crimes of solicitation or conspiracy. He is correct that the Government placed in evidence many instances of Rahman's writings and speeches in which Rahman expressed his opinions within the protection of the First Amendment. However, while the First Amendment fully protects Rahman's right to express hostility against the United States, and he may not be prosecuted for so speaking, it does not prevent the use of such speeches or writings in evidence when relevant to prove a pertinent fact in a criminal prosecution. The Government was free to demonstrate Rahman's resentment and hostility toward the United States in order to show his motive for soliciting and procuring illegal attacks against the United States and against President Mubarak of Egypt. See *Mitchell, 508 U.S. at 487* ("The First Amendment…does not prohibit the evidentiary use of speech to establish the elements of a crime or to prove motive or intent."); *United States v. Hoffman, 806 F.2d 703, 708-09 (7th Cir. 1986)* (evidence of religious affiliation relevant to show defendant's motive to threaten President, because defendant leader of religious group was imprisoned by Government at time of threats).

Furthermore, Judge Mukasey properly protected against the danger that Rahman might be convicted because of his unpopular religious beliefs that were hostile to the United States. He explained to the jury the limited use it was entitled to make of the material received as evidence of motive. He instructed that a defendant could not be convicted on the basis of his beliefs or the expression of them—even if those beliefs favored violence. He properly instructed the jury that it could find a defendant guilty only if the evidence proved he committed a crime charged in the indictment.

We reject Rahman's claim that his conviction violated his rights under the First Amendment.

…

3. Rahman

Rahman argues that the evidence presented by the Government was insufficient to support a conviction for any of the counts with which he was charged. Rahman asserts that he had limited contact with most of the other defendants, that he was physically incapable, due to his blindness, of participating in the "operational" aspects of the conspiracies, and that there was little direct evidence of his knowledge of many of the events in question. We find Rahman's claims unavailing.

a. Seditious Conspiracy and Bombing Conspiracy. To support a conviction for seditious conspiracy under *18 U.S.C. § 2384*, the Government must demonstrate that: (1) in a State, or Territory, or place subject to the jurisdiction of the United States, (2) two or more persons conspired to "levy war against" or "oppose by force the authority of" the United States government, and (3) that the defendant was a member of the conspiracy. *18 U.S.C. § 2384.*

First, we find ample evidence in the record to support the jury's finding that there was indeed a conspiracy to "levy war" against the United States. Over the course of the trial, the jury was presented with considerable evidence of a conspiracy. The evidence included the fact that many of the defendants in this case, as well as many the World Trade Center defendants, participated in military training exercises the purpose of which was to train members to carry out jihad "operations." Appellant Nosair murdered Kahane in 1990, assisted by Salameh (who had been present at the training sessions). Among Nosair's possessions, the Government found notebooks describing "war" on the enemies of Islam and the manner of prosecuting such, including "exploding…their high world buildings," as well as manuals on guerilla warfare tactics and explosives.

…

As to the bombing conspiracy count, the Government must prove: (1) that Rahman was a member of a conspiracy to "destroy, by means of fire or explosives, any building, vehicle or other real or personal property" in interstate commerce, *18 U.S.C. §§ 371*, 844(i); and (2) that one or more of the conspirators did "any act to effect the object of the conspiracy." *18 U.S.C. §*

371. Even if we assume that this count is limited to the Spring 1993 plot, there is clear evidence to support a reasonable conclusion that there was a conspiracy of which Rahman was a member, and that the conspirators had taken overt acts "to effect the object" thereof. The conspirators had, among other things: (1) scouted the Lincoln and Holland Tunnels; (2) contributed rent for a place to make the bombs; (3) purchased fuel oil, fertilizer, and timers from which to make the bombs; and (4) begun mixing the fuel and fertilizer.

Particularly relevant to the finding of Rahman's membership are the statements of Siddig Ali to Salem that Rahman had issued a fatwa for the Spring 1993 bombing plot, and had called it a "must" and a "duty." Although Rahman wavered on the target of the bombing during his conversation with Salem, he nonetheless approved bombing as the method and suggested alternative targets. Rahman and Siddig Ali met together several times during the bombing preparations. On June 17, 1993, less than two weeks before the anticipated bombing, Rahman held a press conference (using Siddig Ali as his translator) during which he warned that the United States would pay a terrible price for supporting Mubarak.

This evidence, taken together, was sufficient to support a reasonable conclusion that Rahman was guilty of the bombing conspiracy.

…

Rahman submitted lengthy offers of proof on the subjects to be covered by the proposed testimony. These offers, from which we quote extensively below, were submitted in a letter from one of Rahman's lawyers. Counsel argued that this testimony would help the jury to understand Rahman's ministerial relationship with his co-defendants, and would show that his conversations with them amounted only to "legitimate and well-recognized religious practice" rather than a criminal conspiracy. The points to be covered by the proposed expert testimony fell into several different categories. Most of the material provided general information about Islam and suggested that Rahman's actions and statements were governed by Islamic law. These included the following statements:

"Islam" means submission to the will of God.

[A] strict monotheism is at the heart of Islamic theology.

Polytheism (shirk) is the concept of worshiping more than one god and is anathema to the strict monotheism of Moslems.

Muslim clerics' sermons are frequently combined with Quranic references….

The Arabic word "sharia" refers to the corpus of Islamic law which is derived from two main sources, the Quran and the sayings of the Prophet as well as analogical reasoning and the consensus of scholars….

Islam…started in the 7th Century A.D. and now claims one billion adherents in the world.

The five pillars or basic precepts of Islam [are] Faith, Prayer, Alms, Pilgrimage, and Fasting.

Muslim clerics and scholars have preached about…a Muslim's necessity to engage in jihad….

Jihad [had its] origins in Islam after Prophet Mohammed began preaching in the 7th Century....

Jihad is cast in the mold of a legal doctrine....

Jihad has come to mean...the combating of oppression....

The Muslim community as a whole has a collective duty or obligation to engage in armed struggle in the path of God [, which] must be organized and announced by a Caliph or Sultan. It is only when the enemy attacks Muslim territory that jihad becomes an individual duty....

It is an individual obligation for able-bodied Muslims from all over to come to the aid of their brethren [and] jihad is governed by a very clear set of rules such as an invitation to embrace Islam, treatment of prisoners and division of spoils.

[A] person who provides a fatwa is called a Mufti.

According to Islamic law a leadership cannot be conferred on a blind person.

An Imam...leads communal prayer and...a sheik is...an elder who is accorded respect and deference.

[A] sheik may also be a scholar in which case he has...certain duties [including] to lead the Muslims in prayer and deliver a Friday sermon,...provide lessons and religious instruction,...to provide advice, counsel and mediation in situations of dispute, and...where he is questioned on a matter involving the interpretation of Islamic law, to provide...a nonbinding advisory opinion....

When a scholar is being asked to render an opinion about a subject matter for which he knows the answer he may not simply dismiss the questioner and...to do so would erode his authority....

Letter from Abdeen Jabara, counsel for Rahman, to Andrew C. McCarthy, Asst. U.S. Atty. (July 7, 1995) (hereinafter "Jabara Letter").

We find no abuse of discretion in Judge Mukasey's rejection of this testimony. The vast majority of what was proffered was not relevant to the issues before the jury. If the evidence showed that Rahman conspired to levy war against the United States or solicited others to commit crimes of violence—including mass killing and destruction through the blowing up of buildings and tunnels—it would not constitute a defense that he was justified in doing so within a framework of Islamic law.

One of the issues stressed by defense counsel in the argument on the admissibility of the testimony was the fact that an Islamic scholar, when asked to render an opinion, "may not simply dismiss the questioner...[without] eroding his authority, stature and position as a scholar." We agree with the District Judge that such details of Islamic tradition were irrelevant to the issues before the jury. As a matter of United States law, the fact that a Mufti or scholar must render an opinion when asked would neither explain nor excuse solicitation to commit acts of terrorism and violence when rendering that opinion.

...

CONCLUSION

The ten defendants were accorded a full and fair jury trial lasting nine months. They were vigorously defended by able counsel. The prosecutors conducted themselves in the best traditions of the high standards of the Office of the United States Attorney for the Southern District of New York. The trial judge, the Honorable Michael B. Mukasey, presided with extraordinary skill and patience, assuring fairness to the prosecution and to each defendant and helpfulness to the jury. His was an outstanding achievement in the face of challenges far beyond those normally endured by a trial judge.

We have considered all of the other claims raised on appeal by all of the defendants, beyond those discussed in this opinion, and conclude that they are without merit. The convictions of all ten defendants are affirmed. With the exception of the sentence of defendant El-Gabrowny, which is remanded for further proceedings as set forth in this opinion, the sentences of all the other defendants are affirmed.

A cornerstone law enforcement tool for prosecuting those accused of engaging in domestic terrorism is the so-called Material Support Act which first appeared in the Antiterrorism and Effective Death Penalty Act of 1996. The Material Support Act provides an independent substantive offense used as a basis for early intervention where the alleged terrorist activity is "nipped in the bud." Embodied in two sections, the law makes it a criminal offense for anyone to provide *material support or resources* in aid of terrorist offenses or to provide *material support or resources* to a foreign terrorist group so designated by the Secretary of State. This means that it is a federal crime to provide almost anything of value, including training, money, or personnel to such terror groups. If no deaths are involved, the maximum penalty is fifteen years in jail. On the other hand, if the death of any person results from the support activities, the offender can be incarcerated for any term or for life. The impact of the Material Support Act on law enforcement is significant. According to Norman Abrams, it "may be the most significant doctrinal development in the federal criminal law since the enactment of RICO and the other organizational crime statutes, the money laundering statutes, and the criminal forfeiture laws [because] [t]hey show how each new federal criminal 'war'—from Prohibition through the wars on organized crime, on illegal drugs, and now on terror—has spawned new laws or legal doctrines designed to expand the [grasp] of the federal government's criminal enforcement arm."

Despite concerns regarding the expansiveness of the Material Support Act and its effect on civil liberties (the Material Support Act was amended in the Intelligence Reform and Terrorism Protection Act of 2004 in response to a number of judicial decisions interpreting the previous language), there is no doubt that the Act has become a vital weapon in addressing the breakup of domestic terror cells in the War on Terror. Because many of the dozens of cases have been resolved by guilty pleas, relatively few have produced lower court opinions interpreting the provisions.

Providing Material Support To Terrorists
18 U.S.C.A. § 2339A

(a) Offense—Whoever provides material support or resources or conceals or disguises the nature, location, source, or ownership of material support or resources, knowing or intending that they are to be used in preparation for, or in carrying out, a violation of section 32, 37, 81,

175, 229, 351, 831, 842(m) or (n), 844(f) or (i), 930(c), 956, 1114, 1116, 1203, 1361, 1362, 1363, 1366, 1751, 1992, 1993, 2155, 2156, 2280, 2281, 2332, 2332a, 2332b, 2332f, or 2340A of this title, section 236 of the Atomic Energy Act of 1954 (42 U.S.C. 2284), section 46502 or 60123(b) of title 49, or any offense listed in section 2332b(g)(5)(B) (except for sections 2339A and 2339B) or in preparation for, or in carrying out, the concealment of an escape from the commission of any such violation, or attempts or conspires to do such an act, shall be fined under this title, imprisoned not more than 15 years, or both, and, if the death of any person results, shall be imprisoned for any term of years or for life....

(b) Definitions—As used in this section
(1) the term "material support or resources" means any property, tangible or intangible, or service, including currency or monetary instruments or financial securities, financial services, lodging, training, expert advice or assistance, safehouses, false documentation or identification, communications equipment, facilities, weapons, lethal substances, explosives, personnel, transportation, and other physical assets, except medicine or religious materials;
(2) the term "training" means instruction or teaching designed to impart a specific skill, as opposed to general knowledge; and
(3) the term "expert advice or assistance" means advice or assistance derived from scientific, technical or other specialized knowledge.

Providing Material Support or Resources to Designated Foreign Terrorist Organizations
18 U.S.C.A. § 2339B

(a) Prohibited activities.
(1) Unlawful conduct. Whoever, within the United States or subject to the jurisdiction of the United States, knowingly provides material support or resources to a foreign terrorist organization, or attempts or conspires to do so, shall be fined under this title or imprisoned not more than 15 years, or both, and, if the death of any person results, shall be imprisoned for any term of years or for life....
(g) Definitions. As used in this section...
(4) the term "material support or resources" has the same meaning as in section 2339A;...
(6) the term "terrorist organization" means an organization designated as a terrorist organization under section 219 of the Immigration and Nationality Act.

The latest revisions to the Material Support Act provide the government with the ability to obtain convictions by proving a mens rea of "knowing or intending" for § 2339A violations, and "knowingly" for § 2339B violations. While the Clinton Administration era law does not penalize membership in a terror group, it does outlaw what is termed "material support." Thus, the government need only show that the individual knowingly provided the proscribed group with some material support, which in many of the cases so far adjudicated has involved attendance at a radical terror training camp in Afghanistan. To date, federal judges have largely upheld the legality of the statute and numerous members of terror sleeper cells have been convicted, including New York's Lackawanna Six.

Many have expressed concern that the Material Support Act, as it is currently enforced at § 2339B, grants the Secretary of State too much latitude in designating which organizations qualify as terrorist organizations. In contrast, some have argued that terrorist organizations savvy enough to compartmentalize themselves into different sub-organizations would still be able to receive contributions to assist their non-military activities. Nevertheless, the designation of a terrorist organization by the State Department under the statute remains subject to a rigorous administrative procedure which requires all conclusions to be supported with exhaustive fact finding, the opportunity for congressional members to object to the designation prior to its publication in the Federal Register, and the organization itself allowed to appeal its designation to the D.C. Circuit of the U.S. Court of Appeals. These facts alone demonstrate that the United States is determined to vigorously fight terror before it strikes without succumbing to a "Star Chamber" mentality that threatens the civil liberties of all in the name of security. The 2010 Supreme Court case of *Holder v. Humanitarian Law Project* (6-3) rejected the idea that the Material Support Act was unconstitutionally vague and that it required a mens rea element of specific intent as opposed to just knowledge of the identity of the terror organization. The Court also rejected the plaintiff's First Amendment argument and freedom of association argument.

HOLDER v. HUMANITARIAN LAW PROJECT
Supreme Court of the United States
561 U.S. ____ (2010)

CHIEF JUSTICE ROBERTS delivered the opinion of the Court.

Congress has prohibited the provision of "material support or resources" to certain foreign organizations that engage in terrorist activity. 18 U.S.C. §2339B(a)(1). That prohibition is based on a finding that the specified organizations "are so tainted by their criminal conduct that any contribution to such an organization facilitates that conduct." Antiterrorism and Effective Death Penalty Act of 1996 (AEDPA), §301(a)(7), 110 Stat. 1247, note following 18 U.S.C. §2339B (Findings and Purpose). The plaintiffs in this litigation seek to provide support to two such organizations. Plaintiffs claim that they seek to facilitate only the lawful, nonviolent purposes of those groups, and that applying the material-support law to prevent them from doing so violates the Constitution. In particular, they claim that the statute is too vague, in violation of the Fifth Amendment, and that it infringes their rights to freedom of speech and association, in violation of the First Amendment. We conclude that the material-support statute is constitutional as applied to the particular activities plaintiffs have told us they wish to pursue. We do not, however, address the resolution of more difficult cases that arise under the stature in the future.

I

This litigation concerns 18 U.S.C. §2339B, which makes it a federal crime to "knowingly provid[e] material support or resources to a foreign terrorist organization." Congress has amended the definition of "material support or resources" periodically, but at present it is defined as follows:

[T]he term 'material support or resources' means any property, tangible or intangible, or service, including currency or monetary instruments or financial securities, financial services, lodging, training, expert advice or assistance, safehouses, false documentation or identification, communications equipment, facilities, weapons, lethal substances, explosives, personnel (1 or more individuals who may be or include oneself), and transportation, except medicine or religious materials." §2339A(b)(1); see also §2339B(g)(4).

The authority to designate an entity a "foreign terrorist organization" rests with the Secretary of State. 8 U.S.C. §§1189(a)(1), (d)(4). She may, in consultation with the Secretary of the Treasury and the Attorney General, so designate an organization upon finding that it is foreign, engages in "terrorist activity" or "terrorism," and thereby "threatens the security of the United States nationals or the national security of the United States." §§1189(a)(1), (d)(4). "'[National security' means the national defense, foreign relations, or economic interests of the United States." An entity designated a foreign terrorist organization may seek review of that designation before the D.C. Circuit within 30 days of that designation. §1189(c)(1).

In 1997, the Secretary of State designated 30 groups as foreign terrorist organizations. See 62 Fed. Reg. 52650. Two of those groups are the Kurdistan Workers' Party (also known as the Partiya Karkeran Kurdistan, or PKK) and the Liberation Tigers of Tamil Eelam (LTTE).... The District Court in this action found that the PKK and the LTTE engage in political and humanitarian activities. See 9 F. Supp. 2d, at 1180-1182. The Government has presented evidence that both groups have also committed numerous terrorist attacks, some of which have harmed American citizens. See App. 128-133. The LTTE sought judicial review of its designation as a foreign terrorist organization; the D.C. Circuit upheld that designation. See *People's Mojaedin Organization of Iran v. Dept. of State*, 182 F. 3d 17, 18-19, 25 (1999). The PKK did not challenge its designation. 9 F. Supp. 2d, at 1180.

Plaintiffs in this litigation are two U.S. citizens and six domestic organizations: the Humanitarian Law Project (HLP) (a human rights organization with consultative status to the United Nations)....

As relevant here, plaintiffs claimed that the material-support statute was unconstitutional on two grounds: First, it violated their freedom of speech and freedom of association under the First Amendment, because it criminalized their provision of material support to the PKK and LTTE, without requiring the Government to prove that plaintiffs had a specific intent to further the unlawful ends of those organizations. *Id.*, 1184. Second, plaintiffs argued that the statute was unconstitutionally vague. *Id.*, at 1184-1185.

Meanwhile, in 2001, Congress amended the definition of "material support or resources" to add the term "expert advice or assistance." Uniting and Strengthening America by Providing Appropriate Tools Required to Intercept and Obstruct Terrorism Act of 2001 (Patriot Act), §805(a)(2)(B), 115 Stat. 377. In 2003, plaintiffs filed a second action challenging the constitutionality of that term as applied to them. 309 F. Supp. 2d 1185, 1192 (CD Cal. 2004).... Congress also added the term "service" to the definition of "material support or resources," §2339A(b)(1), and defined "training" to mean "instruction or teaching designed to impart a specific skill, as opposed to general knowledge," §2339A(b)(2). It also defined "expert advice or assistance" to mean "advice or assistance derived from scientific, technical or other specialized knowledge." §2339A(b)(3). Finally, IRTPA clarified the scope of the term "personnel" by providing:

> No person may be prosecuted under [§2339B] in connection with the term "personnel" unless that person has knowingly provided, attempted to provide, or conspired to provide a foreign terrorist organization with 1 or more individuals (who may be or include himself) to work under that terrorist organization's direction or control or to organize, manage, supervise, or otherwise direct the operation of that organization. Individuals who act entirely independently of the foreign terrorist organization to advance its goals or objectives shall not be considered to be working under the foreign terrorist organization's direction and control. §2339B(h).

…

II

Given the complicated 12-year history of this litigation, we pause to clarify the questions before us. Plaintiffs challenge §2339B's prohibition on four types of material support—"training," "expert advice or assistance," "service," and "personnel." They raise three constitutional claims. First, plaintiffs claim that §2339B violates the Due Process Clause of the Fifth Amendment because these four statutory terms are impermissibly vague. Second, plaintiffs claim that §2339B violates their freedom of speech under the First Amendment. Third, plaintiffs claim that §2339B violates their First Amendment freedom of association.

…

III

Plaintiffs claim, as a threshold matter, that we should affirm the Court of Appeals without reaching any issues of constitutional law. They contend that we should interpret the material-support statute, when applied to speech, to require proof that a defendant intended to further a foreign terrorist organization's illegal activities. That interpretation, they say, would end the litigation because plaintiffs' proposed activities consist of speech, but plaintiffs do not intend to further unlawful conduct by the PKK or the LTTE.

We reject the plaintiffs' interpretation of §2339B because it is inconsistent with the text of the statute. Section 2339B(a)(1) prohibits "knowingly" providing material support. It then specifically describes the type of knowledge that is required: "To violate this paragraph, a person must have knowledge that the organization is a designated terrorist organization…, that the organization has engaged or engages in terrorist activity…, or that the organization has engaged or engages in terrorism…" *Ibid.* Congress plainly spoke to the necessary mental state for a violation of §2339B, and it chose knowledge about the organization's connection to terrorism, not specific intent to further the organization's terrorist activities.

Plaintiff's interpretation is also untenable in light of the sections immediately surrounding §2339B, both of which do refer to intent to further terrorist activity. See §2339A(a) (establishing criminal penalties for one who "provides material support or resources…knowingly or intending that they are to be used in preparation for, or in carrying out, a violation of" statutes prohibiting violent terrorist acts); §2339C(a)(1) (setting criminal penalties for one who "unlawfully and willfully provides or collects funds with the intention that such funds be used, or with the knowledge that such funds are to be used, in full or in part, in order to carry out" other unlawful acts). Congress enacted §2339A in 1994 and §2339C in 2002. See §12005(a), 108 Stat. 2022 (§2339A); §202(a), 116 Stat. 724 (§2339C). Yet Congress did not import the intent language of those provisions into §2339B, either when it enacted §2339B in 1996, or when it clarified §2339B's knowledge requirement in 2004.

Finally, plaintiff's give the game away when they argue that a specific intent requirement should apply only when the material-support statute applies to speech. There is no basis whatsoever in the text of §2339B to read the same provisions in that statute as requiring intent in some circumstances but not others. It is therefore clear that plaintiffs are asking us not to interpret §2339B, but to revise it. "Although this Court will often strain to construe legislation so as to save it against constitutional attack, it must not and will not carry this to the point of perverting the purpose of a statute." *Scales v. United States*, 367 U.S. 203, 211 (1961).

Scales is the case on which plaintiff's most heavily rely, but it is readily distinguishable. That case involved the Smith Act, which prohibited membership in a group advocating the violent overthrow of the government. The Court held that a person could not be convicted under the statute unless he had knowledge of the group's illegal advocacy and a specific intent to bring about violent overthrow. *Id.*, at 220-222, 229. This action is different: Section 2339B does not criminalize mere membership in a designated foreign terrorist organization. It instead prohibits providing "material support" to such a group. See *infra*, at 20-21, 35.

…

IV

We turn to the question whether the material-support statute, as applied to the plaintiffs, is impermissibly vague under the Due Process Clause of the Fifth Amendment. "A conviction fails to comport with due process if the statute under which it is obtained fails to provide a person of ordinary intelligence fair notice of what is prohibited, or is so standardless that it authorizes or encourages seriously discriminatory enforcement." *United States* v. *Williams*, 553 U.S. 285, 304 (2008). We consider whether a statute is vague as applied to the particular facts at issue, for "[a] plaintiff who engages in some conduct that is clearly proscribed cannot complain of the vagueness of the law as applied to the conduct of others." *Hoffman Estates* v. *Flipside, Hoffman Estates, Inc.*, 455 U.S. 489, 495 (1982). We have said that when a statute "interferes with the right of free speech or of association, a more stringent vagueness test should apply." *Id.*, at 499. "But 'perfect clarity and precise guidance have never been required even of regulations that restrict expressive activity.'" *Williams, supra*, at 304 (quoting *Ward* v. *Rock Against Racism*, 491 U.S. 781, 794 (1989)).

The Court of Appeals did not adhere to these principles. Instead, the lower court merged plaintiffs' vagueness challenge with their First Amendment claims, holding that portions of the material-support statute were unconstitutionally vague because they applied to protected speech—regardless of whether those applications were clear. The court stated that, even if persons of ordinary intelligence understood the scope of the term "training," that term would "remai[n] impermissibly vague" because it could "be read to encompass speech and advocacy protected by the First Amendment." 552 F. 3d. at 929. It also found "service" and a portion of "expert advice or assistance" to be vague because those terms covered protected speech. *Id.*, at 929-930.

…

Under a proper analysis, plaintiff's claims of vagueness lack merit. Plaintiffs do not argue that the material-support statute grants too much enforcement discretion to the Government. We therefore address only whether the statute "provide[s] a person of ordinary intelligence fair notice of what is prohibited." *Williams*, 553 U.S., at 304.

As a general matter, the statutory terms at issue here are quite different from the sorts of terms that we have previously declared to be vague. We have in the past "struck down statutes that tied criminal culpability to whether the defendant's conduct was 'annoying' or 'indecent'—wholly subjective judgements without statutory definitions, narrowing context, or settled legal meanings." *Id.*, at 306; see also *Papachristou* v. *Jacksonville*, at 405 U.S. 156, n. 1 (1972) (holding vague an ordinance that punished "vagrants," defined to include "rogues and vagabonds," "persons who use juggling," and "common night walkers" (internal quotation marks omitted)). Applying the statutory terms in this action—"training," "expert advice or assistance," "service," and "personnel"—does not require similarly untethered, subjective judgments.

Congress also took care to add narrowing definitions to the material-support statute over time. These definitions increased the clarity of the statute's terms. See §2339A(b)(2) ("'training' means instruction or teaching designed to impart a specific skill, as opposed to general knowledge"); §2339A(b)(3) ("'expert advice or assistance' means advice or assistance derived from scientific, technical or other specialized knowledge"); §2339B(h) (clarifying the scope of "personnel"). And the knowledge requirement of the statute further reduces any potential for vagueness, as we have held with respect to other statutes containing a similar requirement. See *Hill* v. *Colorado*, 530 U.S. 703, 732 (2000); *Posters 'N Things, Ltd.* v. *United States*, 511 U.S. 513, 523, 526 (1994); see also *Hoffman Estates,* 455 U.S. at 499.

Of course, the scope of the material-support statute may not be clear in their application to plaintiffs' proposed conduct, which means that the plaintiffs' vagueness challenge must fail. Even assuming that a heightened standard applies because the material-support statute potentially implicates speech, the statutory terms are not vague as applied to plaintiffs. See *Grayned* v. *City of Rockford*, 408 U.S. 104, 114-115 (1972) (rejecting a vagueness challenge to a criminal law that implicated First Amendment activities); *Scales*, 367 U.S., at 223 (same).

Most of the activities in which plaintiffs seek to engage readily fall within the scope of the terms "training" and "expert advice or assistance." Plaintiffs want to "train members of [the] PKK on how to use humanitarian and international law to peacefully resolve disputes," and "teach PKK members how to petition various representative bodies such as the United Nations for relief." 552 F. 3d, at 921, n. 1. A person or ordinary intelligence would understand that instruction on resolving disputes through international law falls within the statute's definition of "training" because it imparts a "specific skill," not "general knowledge." §2339A(b)(2). Plaintiffs' activities also fall comfortably within the scope of "expert advice or assistance": A reasonable person would recognize that teaching the PKK how to petition for humanitarian relief before the United Nations involves advice derived from, as the statute puts it, "specialized knowledge." §2339A(b)(3). In fact, plaintiffs themselves have repeatedly used the terms "training" and "expert advice" throughout this litigation to describe their own proposed activities, demonstrating that these common terms readily and naturally cover plaintiffs' conduct. See, *e.g.*, Brief for Plaintiffs 10, 11; App. 56, 58, 59, 61, 62, 80, 81, 98, 99, 106, 107, 117.

. . .

V

A

We next consider whether the material-support statute, as applied to plaintiffs, violates the freedom of speech guaranteed by the First Amendment. Both plaintiffs and the Government take extreme positions on this question. Plaintiffs claim that Congress banned their "pure political speech." *E.g.*, Brief for Plaintiffs 2, 25, 43. It has not. Under the material-support statute, plaintiffs may say anything they wish on any topic. They may speak and write freely about the PKK and LTTE, the governments of Turkey and Sri Lanka, human rights, and international law. They may advocate before the United Nations. As the Government states: "The statute does not prohibit independent advocacy or expression of any kind." Brief for Government 13. Section 2339B also "does not prevent [plaintiffs] from becoming members of the PKK and LTTE or impose any sanction on them for doing so." *Id.*, at 60. Congress has not, therefore, sought to suppress ideas or opinions in the form of "pure political speech." Rather, Congress has prohibited "material support," which most often does not take the form of speech at all. And when it does, the statute is carefully drawn to cover only a narrow category of speech to, under the direction of, or in coordination with foreign groups that the speaker knows to be terrorist organizations.

…

B

The First Amendment issue before us is more refined than either plaintiffs or the Government would have it. It is not whether the Government may prohibit pure political speech, or may prohibit material support in the form of conduct. It is instead whether the Government may prohibit what the plaintiffs want to do—provide material support to the PKK and LTTE in the form of speech.

Every one agrees the Government's interest in combating terrorism is an urgent objective of the highest order. See Brief for Plaintiffs 51. Plaintiffs' complaint is that the ban on material support, applied to what they wish to do, is not "necessary to further that interest." *Ibid*. The objective of combating terrorism does not justify prohibiting their speech, plaintiffs argue, because their support will advance only the legitimate activities of the designated terrorist organizations, not their terrorism. *Id.*, at 51-52.

Whether foreign terrorist organizations meaningfully segregate support of their legitimate activities from support of terrorism is an empirical question. When it enacted §2339B in 1996, Congress made specific findings regarding the serious threat posed by international terrorism. See AEDPA §§301(a)(1)-(7), 110 Stat. 1247, note following 18 U.S.C. §2339B (Findings and Purpose). One of those findings explicitly rejects plaintiffs' contention that their support would not further the terrorist activities of the PKK and the LTTE: "[F]oreign organizations that engage in terrorist activity are so tainted by their criminal conduct that *any contribution to such an organization* facilitates that conduct." §301(a)(7) (emphasis added).

Plaintiffs argue that the reference to "any contribution" in this finding meant only monetary support. There is no reason to read the finding to be so limited, particularly because Congress expressly prohibited so much more than monetary support in §2339B. Congress's use of the term "contribution" is best read to reflect a determination that any form of material support furnished "to" a foreign terrorist organization should be barred, which is precisely what the material-support statute does. Indeed, when Congress enacted §2339B, Congress simultaneously removed an exception that had existed in §2339A(a) (1994 ed.) for the provision of material support in the form of "humanitarian assistance to persons not directly involved in" terrorist activity. AEDPA §323, 110 Stat. 1225; 205 F 3d, at 1136. That repeal demonstrates that Congress considered and rejected the view that ostensibly peaceful aid would have no harmful effects.

We are convinced that Congress was justified in rejecting that view. The PKK and the LTTE are deadly groups....

Money is fungible, and "[w]hen foreign terrorist organizations that have a dual structure raise funds, they highlight the civilian and humanitarian ends to which such moneys could be put." McKune Affidavit, App. 134, ¶9. But "there is reason to believe that foreign terrorist organizations do not maintain legitimate *financial* firewalls between those funds raised for civil, nonviolent activities, and those ultimately used to support violent, terrorist operations." *Id.*, at 135, ¶12. Thus, "[f]unds raised ostensibly for charitable purposes have in the past been redirected by some terrorist groups to fund the purchase of arms and explosives." *Id.* at 134, ¶10. See also Brief for Anti-Defamation League as *Amicus Curiae* 19-29 (describing fundraising activities by the PKK, LTTE, and HAMAS); *Regan* v. *Wald*, 468 U.S. 222, 243 (1984) (upholding President's decision to impose travel ban to Cuba "to curtail the flow of hard currency to Cuba—currency that could then be used in support of Cuban adventurism"). There is evidence that the PKK and the LTTE, in particular, have not "respected the line between humanitarian and violent activities." McKune Affidavit, App. 135, ¶13 (discussing PKK); see *id.*, at 134 (LTTE).

The dissent argues that there is "no natural stopping place" for the proposition that aiding a foreign terrorist organization's lawful activity promotes the terrorist organization as a whole. *Post*, at 10. But Congress has settled on just a natural stopping place: The statute reaches only material support coordinated with or under the direction of a designated foreign terrorist organization. Independent advocacy that might be viewed as promoting the group's legitimacy is not covered. See *supra*, at 18-21.

Providing foreign terrorist groups with material support in any form also furthers terrorism by straining the United States' relationships with its allies and undermining cooperative efforts between nations to prevent terrorist attacks. We see no reason to question Congress's finding that "international cooperation is required for an effective response to terrorism, as demonstrated by the numerous multilateral conventions in force providing universal prosecutive jurisdiction over persons involved in a variety of terrorist acts, including hostage taking, murder of an internationally protected person, and aircraft piracy and sabotage." AEDPA §301(a)(5), 110 Stat. 1247, note following 18 U.S.C. §2339B (Findings and Purpose). The material-support statute furthers this international effort by prohibiting aid for foreign terrorist groups that harm the United States' partners abroad: "A number of designated foreign terrorist organizations have attacked moderate governments with which the United States has vigorously endeavored to maintain close and friendly relations," and those attacks "threaten [the] social, economic and political stability" of such governments. McKune Affidavit, App. 137, ¶16. "[O]ther foreign terrorist organizations attack our NATO allies, thereby implicating important and sensitive multilateral security arrangements." *Ibid.*

...

C

In analyzing whether it is possible in practice to distinguish material support for a foreign terrorist group's violent activities and its nonviolent activities, we do not rely exclusively on our own inferences drawn from the record evidence. We have before us an affidavit stating the Executive Branch's conclusion on that question. The State Department informs us that "[t]he experience and analysis of the U.S. government agencies charged with combating terrorism strongly suppor[t]" Congress's finding that all contributions to foreign terrorist organizations further their terrorism. McKune Affidavit, App. 133, ¶8. See *Winter* v. *Natural Resources Defense Council, Inc.,* 555 U.S. ____, ____ (2008) (slip op., at 14-15) (looking to similar affidavits to support according weight to national security claims). In the Executive's view: "Given the purposes, organizational structure, and clandestine nature of foreign terrorist organizations, it is highly likely that any material support to these organizations will ultimately inure to the benefit of their criminal, terrorist functions — regardless of whether such support was ostensibly intended to support non-violent, non-terrorist activities." McKune Affidavit, App. 133, ¶8.

That elevation of facts by the Executive, like Congress's assessment, is entitled to deference. This litigation implicates sensitive and weighty interests of national security and foreign affairs. The PKK and the LTTE have committed terrorist acts against American citizens abroad, and the material-support statute addresses acute foreign policy concerns involving relationships with our Nation's allies.

...

VI

Plaintiffs' final claim is that the material-support statute violates their freedom of association under the First Amendment. Plaintiffs argue that the statute criminalizes the mere fact of their associating with the PKK and the LTTE, thereby running afoul of decisions like *De Jonge* v. *Oregon,* 299 U.S. 353 (1937), and cases in which we have overturned sanctions for joining the Communist Party, see, *e.g., Keyishian* v. *Board of Regents of Univ. of State of N.Y.,* 385 U.S. 589 (1967); *United States* v. *Robel,* 389 U.S. 258 (1967).

The Court of Appeals correctly rejected this claim because the statute does not penalize mere association with a foreign terrorist organization. As the Ninth Circuit put it: "The statute does not prohibit being a member of one of the designated groups or vigorously promoting and supporting the political goals of the group... What [§2339B] prohibits is the act of giving material support..." 205 F. 3d, at 1133. Plaintiffs want to do the latter.

...

***

The Preamble to the Constitution proclaims that the people of the United States ordained and established that charter of the government in part to "provide for the common defence." As Madison explained, "[s]ecurity against foreign danger is... an avowed and essential object of the American Union." The Federalist No. 41 p. 269 (J. Cooke ed. 1961). We hold that, in regulating the particular forms of support that plaintiffs seek to provide to foreign terrorist organizations, Congress has pursued that objective consistent with the limitations of the First and Fifth Amendments.

The judgment of the United States of Appeals for the Ninth Circuit is affirmed in part and reversed in part, and the cases are remanded for further proceedings consistent with this opinion.

It is so ordered.

In summary, United States federal district courts have jurisdiction to try individuals for terrorist-related offenses under a variety of statutes. However, instead of charging suspected al-Qa'eda war criminals with violations of the law of war, the federal courts apply parallel statutes related to the *malum in se* crime or apply the appropriate terrorist statute. Some of the al-Qa'eda members that were not designated as enemy combatants have been sent to federal court, such as Richard Reid and Zacarias Moussaoui, while other members that were designated as enemy combatants faced trial by military commissions. Confusion has occurred when a designated enemy combatant is sent to federal court for trial and not to a military commission, as was the ill-informed desire of the Obama Administration in November 2009 to send five al-Qa'eda enemy combatants to stand trial in New York City. Obviously, this disjointed policy allows a great amount of flexibility for the government, but also causes massive confusion to the public. Again, the vast majority of Islamic terrorists jailed in this nation had to be tried in federal court (over 350 since 9/11) because they were never labeled as enemy combatants by the President. These terrorists were clearly influenced and "infected" with the virus of radical Islam but they did not qualify as enemy combatants and therefore could not be tried by means of the military commissions process.

4.7 Investigating Terrorist Suspects

One of the first issues of concern that captured the attention of the public following the terrorist attacks of September 11, 2001, was the possibility that other al-Qa'eda terrorist cells were at large on American soil. Federal, State, and local law enforcement personnel were put on the highest alert and an immediate search for suspected terrorists associated with the attacks on America began under the direction of the DOJ.

If you are trying to stop terrorists at the airport, you are too late. If the most important weapon in the War on Terror is intelligence, then it is certain that America's first line of defense must be anchored on reliable intelligence. America's ability to gather and analyze intelligence is much greater than that of al-Qa'eda-styled terrorists and this advantage must be maintained. To better assist law enforcement to prevent future acts of terrorism against the United States, Congress passed the USA PATRIOT Act which contains a variety of criminal procedure provisions. Many of the revisions are related to the Foreign Intelligence and Surveillance Act (FISA) and the anonymous judges of the FISA court.

FISA codifies in federal law the procedures associated with how the intelligence community conducts electronic surveillance and physical searches for the acquisition of foreign intelligence for reasons of national security. Since its passage in 1978, FISA has withstood a variety of legal challenges, most related to concerns regarding violation of the Fourth Amendment to the Constitution.

In passing FISA, the intent of Congress was to strike an appropriate balance between the need to protect national security with the need to protect civil liberty rights of Americans. FISA was certainly never intended to impact adversely on American government intelligence community activities directed at places or people outside of the United States.

FISA created two layers of special courts: one to issue orders and the other to provide review. The Foreign Intelligence Surveillance Court (FISC) is a "secret" court comprised of eleven non-disclosed federal district court judges appointed by the Chief Justice of the Supreme Court. Since these appointed judges are federal district court judges the FISC court is a proper Article III court. A FISC judge rules on the submitted intelligence community applications for court orders authorizing or denying electronic surveillance and physical searches. The Foreign Intelligence Surveillance Court of Review (FISCR) is also a "secret" court and consists of three non-disclosed federal district or federal appellate judges with the power to review FISC actions.

The basic mechanics for how the FISC court order process works reveals a stringent system of agency checks and cross checks prior to submission to the FISC judge. An application to conduct an electronic surveillance is initiated by a federal intelligence community officer. After going through a variety of internal agency bureaucratic procedures and rules, culminating with the approval of the Attorney General, the application is then presented under oath to a FISC judge. The central language in the application must clearly address a number of issues to include the following: (1) the target of the electronic surveillance must be identified as well as the information relied on by the government to demonstrate that the target is either a "foreign power" or an "agent of a foreign power;" (2) the type of surveillance which will be used; (3) the minimization procedures to be employed; and (4) certification by a high-ranking Executive Branch official that he specially determines that the information sought is "foreign intelligence information" and that "a significant purpose" of the electronic surveillance or search is to obtain foreign intelligence information.

In order to issue a court order authorizing the surveillance, the FISC judge reviewing the application must specifically determine that there is probable cause to believe that the target of the surveillance or search is a foreign power or agent of a foreign power and that a significant purpose of the electronic surveillance or search is to collect foreign intelligence. Nevertheless, the representations in the application must be accepted unless he finds that they are "clearly erroneous." In the case of a United States person, the FISC judge must also determine that the target of the surveillance is not being considered an agent of a foreign power based on activities protected by the First Amendment.

In 2006 and 2009, Congress extended most all of the provisions in the original USA PATRIOT Act. Because almost all of the provisions in the USA PATRIOT Act amend or add language to existing federal statutes, it will be some time before the meaning and impact of many of the provisions can be fully evaluated in terms of constitutionality. For example, Section 203 of the Act amends the *Federal Rules of Criminal Procedure* (FRCP) to allow the sharing of grand jury information with other interested federal agencies if it relates to foreign intelligence. Section 203 also allows law enforcement and intelligence officers to break down the so-called "wall" that once prohibited the two agencies from sharing information in cases associated with national security. Amazingly, the ability to exchange terrorist-related information did not exist prior to the USA PATRIOT Act. Currently, federal law enforcement and federal intelligence officers share a wide variety of information associated with criminal investigations and foreign intelligence.

Similarly, Section 218 allows FISA court orders in cases where "a significant purpose" of the investigation is obtaining foreign intelligence. This provision also breaks down the wall between law enforcement and intelligence officers. In fact, Section 218 authority was instrumental in the disruption of the 2002 terror sleeper cell known as the Portland Seven out of Portland, Oregon. Six of these militant Islamic terrorists were convicted and sentenced to terms in prison ranging from three to 18 years; the remaining terror suspect was killed in a gun battle with Pakistani authorities in 2003.

Section 219 amends the FRCP to authorize nationwide search warrants for terrorism cases. Section 209 permits stored voicemail to be obtained by a search warrant and not a wiretap court order. Section 214 provides for FISA courts to issue pen-register and trap-and-trace orders in terrorist cases similar to the process used in the context of criminal investigations. Previously, the order could not be issued unless the subject was contacting a foreign power.

Section 215 amends the old "business records" authority of the FISA. At one time, Section 215 was perhaps the most controversial provision of the USA PATRIOT Act, which authorizes investigators to seek a court order compelling the production of any "tangible item" no matter who held it, relevant to certain counterintelligence and counterterrorism investigations. Despite the fact that the Justice Department indicated that, as of March 2005, the Section 215 authority had been used on only 35 occasions, some continued to raise a variety of civil rights concerns, e.g., it could be used to look at library cards (the Justice Department indicated in 2005 that Section 215 had never been used to secure library, bookstore, gun sale or medical records).

Section 213 adds a subsection to 18 U.S.C. § 3103a in order to authorize a delayed notice of execution of a search warrant (under specific conditions). The search warrant grants federal agencies the ability to conduct secret searches when armed with the appropriate probable cause judicial warrant. Section 213 of the USA PATRIOT Act simply codifies a law enforcement tool that has been in use for decades by federal judges. The statute eliminates the requirement that law enforcement provide a person subject to a search warrant with contemporaneous notice of the search. Known as "sneak-and-peek," these searches allow law enforcement officers the authority to search and seize any tangible object or record with delayed notification to the owner or possessor when the court finds necessity for action.

Sneak-and-peek authority has stirred debates over the provision's value to the defense of the nation and its attendant harm to civil liberties. Representative C.L. "Butch" Otter (R-Idaho) offered his view at a floor debate: "Sneak-and-peek searches give the government the power to repeatedly search a private residence without informing the residents that he or she is the target of an investigation. Not only does this provision allow the seizure of personal property and business records without notification, but it also opens the door to nationwide search warrants and allows the CIA and the NSA to operate domestically."

Despite the rhetoric of those who oppose the provision, sneak-and-peek searches cannot be carried out without a probable cause search warrant issued by a neutral and detached magistrate. In addition, in order to perform this type of search, the court must find "reasonable cause to believe that providing immediate notification of the execution of the warrant may have an adverse effect" on the investigation. Furthermore, the law does not allow for searches to be conducted without any notification; instead, it simply allows for a delay in notification when there is reasonable belief that prior notification could damage the investigation. Obviously, the sneak-and-peek provision is an extremely valuable tool because it allows the authorities to gather evidence without "tipping their hand." Often, many terrorists, or groups of terrorists in "sleeper cells," maintain only temporary domiciles and are known to move locations very quickly. This provision aids officials in gathering valuable information from a suspect's house or apartment without alerting the suspect of the investigation. In this context, the property that could possibly be seized (or copied) could include laptop computers and other computer records.

Section 206 allows the FISA court to authorize the use of roving wiretap surveillance, permitting the interception of any communications made to or by a suspect without identifying a specific telephone line or computer system to be monitored. In other words, the wiretap authorization is attached to the particular terrorist suspect as opposed to a particular communication technology. Because terrorists are likely to quickly change communication devices to avoid detection, Section 206 provides a vital tool to law enforcement in monitoring their activities. This provision had been used many times against international terrorists and spies. Similarly, Section 207 of the USA PATRIOT Act extends the initial FISA court order time duration from 90 days to 120 days, and such court orders can now be extended for up to one year as opposed to the former requirement of renewable 90 day periods.

Section 212 expands the original law which required that third parties, such as common carriers, be specified in a court order to provide any assistance necessary to conduct surveillance. The new law extends that obligation to any unnamed and unspecified third party. Those parties would include, for instance, any libraries that provide internet access to the public, university computer labs and internet cafes. This allows federal agencies the ability to monitor these facilities if they have probable cause to believe that a terrorist or intelligence target is using the facility to transmit communications. Furthermore, the FBI may issue so-called national security letters demanding a limited amount of information from financial or communication entities.

More recently, Congress passed the Foreign Intelligence Surveillance Act of 1978 Amendments Act of 2008 (FISA Amendments 2008 Act) in order to provide a clearer picture of how the intelligence community can collect actionable intelligence on terrorists in the U.S. and overseas. FISA Amendments 2008 Act was not the first revision of the Foreign Intelligence Surveillance Act (FISA), nor will it be the last. Although some critics chastised Congress for passing the bill, there were certainly a variety of pragmatic reasons for favoring the legislation which followed closely on the heels of the Protect America Act of 2007: Modifications to the Foreign Intelligence Surveillance Act.

The new FISA Amendments 2008 Act provides a positive framework for ensuring that the proper rule of law in this intelligence gathering process keeps pace with the changes in technology, while rightly appreciating the emerging threats to national well-being from both al-Qa'eda-styled terrorism and other foreign machinations. If one couples the phenomenal technical advances in telecommunication technology with an acknowledgement of the growing threats to national security posed by both mega-terrorism and hostile nations, it is fundamentally obvious that the nation's intelligence community must be properly equipped with the necessary tools to protect the nation. Among other things, the Act authorizes the President, through the Attorney General, to conduct electronic surveillance without a court order for the period of one year provided it is only for foreign intelligence information; targeting foreign powers as defined by 50 U.S.C. § 1801(a)(1),(2),(3) or their agents; and there is no substantial likelihood that the surveillance will acquire the contents of any communication to which a U.S. person is a party. The FISA Amendments 2008 Act does require a FISA court order to wiretap Americans who are overseas and provides immunity to telecommunication companies who participated in government wiretap programs in the past.

4.8 Use of the Military in Domestic Law Enforcement

There have been a number of new developments associated with the War on Terror that impact on the use of the United States military. While National Security Presidential Directive 5 designates the Department of Homeland Security as the lead federal agency for consequence management and support to law enforcement, with the FBI as the lead federal agency to handle a terrorist attack in the United States, the President as Commander in Chief retains the authority to directly employ the armed forces in any situation involving homeland defense. To be sure, the use of the military would be a tool of last resort prompted by exigent circumstances.

Recognizing the need to increase military preparedness to fight the War on Terror, Congress has increased defense spending by large percentages over the past five years. Since 2001, the DOD budget has increased from 306 billion to well over half a trillion in 2011. More importantly, in light of the War on Terror, the Pentagon issued its Congressionally mandated *Quadrennial Defense Review* (QDR) on October 1, 2001, which is the official strategic policy of how the United States armed forces should be utilized. The 2001 QDR eliminated the long-standing vision of structuring the United States military to fight two simultaneous wars and envisioned a new military based on a "capabilities-based model" flexible enough to fight asymmetrically and to deal with, among other things, international terrorism. In short, the 2001 QDR placed homeland security as the primary mission of the DOD. Subsequent QDRs have followed suit and concentrated on the many issues associated with the War on Terror. The 2010 QDR acknowledges that U.S. forces must be sized in order to "[p]revail in ongoing conflicts in Afghanistan, Iraq, and in the war against Al Qaeda and its allies." In addition, the creation of a new four-star general combatant command responsible for coordinating military support for defending the territory of the United States has been created. The command is called United States Northern Command (NORTHCOM) and is based in Colorado Springs, Colorado. The commander of NORTHCOM also commands North American Aerospace Defense Command (NORAD). NORTHCOM has no forces other than the approximately 500 personnel at the headquarters. When needed, Northern Command will draw its forces from other commands, depending on the mission.

Even with these changes, the United States has yet to cross the mental bridge from waging conventional warfare on foreign soil to developing action-oriented tactics and strategies to combat international terrorism in the homeland. The 2006 QDR, for the first time, took into account the nation's war against terrorism and the acknowledgement that the War on Terror could be a "long war." This long war is a combination of prolonged irregular combat against al-Qa'eda-styled terror activity that includes Afghanistan, Iraq, and even such places as Somalia, Yemen, or the Philippines. The 2010 QDR recognizes that the forces have to do a better job in addressing non-traditional asymmetric challenges.

One area often revisited in the context of new missions for the American military is the question of whether a long-standing law prohibiting the use of the active military to support domestic law enforcement within the borders of the United States should be revoked or modified. This law is the 1878 Posse Comitatus Act (PCA), 10 U.S.C. § 375; 18 U.S.C. § 1385, which prohibits the use of the military to execute the civil laws of the United States. In full text, the PCA states:

> Whoever, except in cases and under circumstances expressly authorized by the Constitution or Act of Congress, willfully uses any part of the Army or the Air Force as a posse comitatus or otherwise to execute the laws shall be fined under this title or imprisoned not more than two years, or both.

Posse comitatus is Latin for "the force of the country," and refers to the English common law doctrine which empowered the local sheriff to summon able-bodied men to help enforce the law in an emergency situation. With the end of Reconstruction, federal troops employed as a standing army of occupation in the South were finally withdrawn in 1877. In 1878, Congress passed the PCA which stopped the practice of local or federal civilian law enforcement being able to conscript military troops into their posses. Thus, the root cause of the Act came about due to the use of federal troops in the Southern States to assist civilian law enforcement of the Reconstruction Act of 1867 pushed through by radical Republicans following the American Civil War. It originally only applied to the United States Army, but was extended in 1947 to the Air Force. Nevertheless, the DOD views the Act as applying to all services. However, the PCA does not apply to a member of the Reserve component when not on active federal duty, nor to a member of the State National Guard when not in federal service. Finally, the Act does not apply to the Coast Guard.

Apart from the Insurrection Act, which allows the President to deploy troops to "put down law-lessness, insurrection, and rebellion" (used in the 1992 Los Angeles Race Riots), several laws grant specific exceptions to the application of the PCA. United States Code, Title 18, Section 831, provides that if nuclear material is involved in an emergency, the Secretary of Defense may provide assistance to the Department of Justice, notwithstanding the PCA. The Act does not prevent the President from using the military in cases of civil disorders or emergencies. Section 831 defines emergencies as those "that pose a serious threat to the interests of the United States; and in which enforcement of the law would be seriously impaired if the assistance were not provided; and civilian law enforcement personnel are not capable of enforcing the law." In fact, the military has been used hundreds of times in such domestic operations. The Act also does not apply to the use of United States armed forces personnel who either arrest or assist in the arrest of international criminals outside the territory of the United States. In addition, a variety of United States courts have held that military support to domestic law enforcement, short of actual search, seizure, arrest, or similar confrontation with civilians, does not violate the PCA. Specific examples of permitted support to domestic law enforcement include traffic direction; the provision of information, equipment, and facilities; and even training. Violations of the PCA include a fine of $10,000 and/or two years imprisonment.

With the continuing escalation in the War on Terror, the issue of the PCA is sure to be raised again. Arguments that the Act is a Congressional statute and can be repealed in toto does not rest well with the long national tradition of excluding the military from domestic law enforcement. Americans clearly have an aversion to the use of soldiers as a policing force. In a letter sent to Defense Secretary Rumsfeld in October of 2001, then Senator John Warner of Virginia asked if the PCA should "now be changed to enable our active-duty military to more fully join other domestic assets in this war against terrorism?" For now, the answer appears to be no. But the question remains on the table.

One alternative to the use of active duty military force to conduct law enforcement or to respond to a major terrorist attack would be the use of National Guard and Army Reserve to create a rapid deployment force for each state with the attendant funding to develop and train the necessary personnel. Following the 1991 war with Iraq, this idea was quickly put into full force in Israel, where a Home Defense Command was set up. Composed of 97 percent reservists, Israel has established sixty-seven stations throughout the nation in order to better deal with the aftermath of a weapons of mass destruction event. This same idea has not taken hold of policymakers in the United States.

The primary hindrance to a weapon of mass destruction rapid response force in each State rests in the massive amount of funding and training. One way to help reduce costs for developing such a force comes from the State Defense Forces model. United States Code, Title 32, Section 109, provides: "In addition to its National Guard, if any, a state or territory may, as provided by its laws, organize and maintain defense forces." State legislatures in twenty-four states and Puerto Rico have created State defense forces to perform a wide variety of functions from light infantry duties (the Virginia Defense Force) to military police functions (Ohio Military Reserve).

Of particular interest in the mechanics of creating rapid-response forces (RRF) to deal with weapons of mass destruction events is the example set by the Texas State Guard. During 1998, for example, units of the Texas State Guard rapid reaction force "participated in 122 events, which involved 1,865 members who contributed 24,663 man-hours and saved the state's cities $490,860." Activities included crowd control, traffic control, and search-and-rescue operations—just the type of activities sorely needed in the aftermath of a weapon of mass destruction terrorist attack. During the emergency created by Hurricane Katrina in 2005, the Texas State Guard again did active service in a variety of areas.

4.9 Privacy and Immigration

As of 2011, estimates place the number of illegal aliens living in the continental United States at between 11 and 12 million people. On the other side of the equation, there are about 3,000 Homeland Security personnel to police them. With the fact that many of the 9/11 murderers had false identity cards and were here illegally, many blamed the Immigration and Naturalization Service (INS) for the attacks. In 2002 Congress abolished the INS and replaced it with three separate agencies under the DHS: the Bureau of Citizenship and Immigration Services (BCIS), the Bureau of Immigration and Customs Enforcement (BICE), and the Bureau of Customs and Border Protection (BCBP).

Although an in-depth analysis of the new changes authorized by the USA PATRIOT Act is beyond the scope of this book, the provision giving the Attorney General broad powers to take into custody and detain illegal aliens suspected of terrorism will most likely prove to be the most controversial and bears analysis here. The power to indefinitely detain illegal aliens raises at the very least a constitutional due process issue under the Fifth Amendment, a matter which will most certainly require resolution by the federal judiciary.

Specifically, Section 412(a) of the USA PATRIOT Act adds Section 236A to the Immigration and Nationality Act, allowing the Attorney General to take into custody any alien certified to be inadmissible or deportable on one of six grounds: (1) espionage, (2) sabotage, (3) export restrictions, (4) attempt to overthrow the United States Government, (5) terrorist activities, and (6) any other "activity that endangers the national security of the United States." Section 412(a)(5) then requires the government to either begin criminal or deportation proceedings within seven days of the detention. Ostensibly, however, Section 412(a)(6) empowers the government to indefinitely detain certain certified illegal alien terrorists who are not likely to be deported in the foreseeable future due to the continuing nature of the investigation. The question of concern regards the matter of how long a certified individual terrorist may be detained and under what conditions.

The United States Supreme Court has yet to rule on the constitutionality of Section 412(a)(6). Nevertheless, because of a 2001 decision entitled *Zadvydas v. Davis*, it seems likely that the Court will probably find that Section 412(a)(6) is constitutional. In *Zadvydas*, the Court was concerned with the constitutionality of whether the government could detain a removable illegal alien beyond the removable period (i.e., indefinitely, or "only for a period reasonably necessary to secure the alien's removal from the country"). The Court construed the applicable section of the Immigration and Nationality Act narrowly, firmly disapproving the indefinite detention of aliens who were not likely to be deported. Still, the Court in *Zadvydas* did recognize in the opinion that suspected terrorists could be held for indefinite periods in preventive detention. The Supreme Court understood that illegal aliens detained for "terrorism or other special circumstances where special arguments might be made for forms of preventive detention," should not be affected by the general rule disapproving the indefinite detention of resident aliens not likely to be deported. *Zadvydas* seemingly exempted suspected alien terrorists as a "small segment of particularly dangerous individuals" that the government could subject to indefinite detention.

The USA PATRIOT Act's provision on indefinite detention for certified detainees is likely to pass constitutional muster because it actually exceeds the *Zadvydas* standard regarding suspected terrorists held on an indefinite basis. First, Section 412(b) specifically provides that judicial review of detentions of suspected alien terrorists is available via habeas corpus. Second, the new law proscribes fixed time limits for review of the attorney general's certification. Section 412(a)(6) provides that an alien whose "removal is unlikely in the reasonably foreseeable future, may be detained for additional periods of up to six months if release threatens national security or the safety of an individual or the community." Furthermore, Section 412(a)(7) requires the attorney general to review said certification every six months and allows the suspected illegal alien terrorist to request a reconsideration of the certification every six months. If these provisions are satisfied, the said terrorist suspect may be held indefinitely.

Concerns for security measures have caused the United States to revisit the issue of immigration laws regarding who is allowed into the country and under what conditions they are allowed to remain. Each year tens of millions of visas are granted to foreign nationals to enter the United States. The reason for entry into the United States generally includes matters related to education, travel, or to conduct business. Of paramount concern in weighing this figure is the fact that about 40 percent of the nation's undocumented immigrants have overstayed their visas and millions of others simply cross the Mexican border illegally. Still, the government has done little to correct the problem.

One proposal to halt or slow illegal immigration is the creation of a national identity card (NIC), which is standard fare for all nations in Western Europe. Proponents of this highly debated concept argue that such a card would not only stop the flow of illegal aliens into the U.S., but also prevent terrorists from entering and then operating from within America's borders. Opponents not only worry that an NIC would violate the fundamental right of privacy guaranteed by the U.S. Constitution, but cite historical abuses as well ranging from "pass laws" used to enforce slavery in the North and South prior to the War Between the States, to the abuses of the Nazis towards Jews and others.

In 2010, the Democrat-controlled Senate proposed a new social security card to replace the paper blue and white social security card which is probably the simplest document to forge in the history of documents. The social security card was introduced in 1936. Despite President Roosevelt's promise that it would be a confidential document never to be used for identification purposes, the social security account number is *the* identifier for all, e.g., the IRS began to use it in 1962; Medicare in 1965; and DOD in 1967. Recognizing that since 1990, each newborn in America is now issued a social security number, which is recorded on the birth certificate, the 2010 Senate proposal was to create a new foolproof type of social security card for all U.S. citizens and legal immigrants. The new card would be a high-tech, fraud-proof document with biometric identifiers. While the new social security card would not contain medical information or other personal information, the proposed law mandated that all employers would be responsible for swiping the card through a special machine to confirm the person's identity and immigration status. Those who were caught under the new law would be penalized with fines and community service and forced to the back of the line of prospective legal immigrants if they passed a background check. Senator Dick Durbin, who worked on the outline of the proposed bill and had long advocated a national identity card for all driver's licenses, cited the inevitability of a NIC saying: "For a long time it was resisted by many groups but now we live in a world where we take off our shoes at the airport and pull out our identification... people understand that in this vulnerable world we have to be able to present identification."

Perhaps in an ever shrinking world rooted in information and technology, the issue of whether Americans should be required to possess a national identity card that cannot be forged or faked is moot. In reality, the government already "knows" all about the people that are paying taxes and otherwise are here legally. As such, the only people that would potentially suffer harm are those that are illegally present. The question then is really about when and where the government can act on the information. In the 1983 Supreme Court case of *Kolender v. Lawson* the Court struck down a California statute that required individuals "who loiter or wander the streets to identify themselves and to account for their presence when requested by a peace officer" as unconstitutional because it violated the Due Process clause of the Fourteenth Amendment as vague for "failing to clarify what is contemplated by the requirement that a suspect provide 'credible and reliable' identification." The California law was struck down not because people were required to have identification (in the Democrat bill it would be near "full-proof" identification), but because it constituted an illegal request for said identification by the government which also violated the Fourth Amendment. In short, the government may only ask for identification from individuals in limited circumstances. Obviously, if the individual is requesting benefits or services from the government they must present valid identification specified by the government in order to receive said things. The government can demand and specify the type of identification that will be accepted. On the other hand, government agents, to include police, may only ask for valid identification pursuant to a limited set of circumstances. They may ask for valid identification if there is a "reasonable suspicion" that the person committed, is committing, or is about to commit a crime. This judge-made rule was established by the Supreme Court in *Terry v. Ohio* (1968). In all other cases, the police may demand valid identification based on a valid arrest as the Fourth Amendment only protects from unreasonable searches and seizures.

In the final analysis, whatever new changes Congress may make to existing immigration law, it is painfully obvious that a far better job has to be done. This critique extends from screening and background checks of individuals seeking visas to enter the borders of the United States to tracking the millions of illegal aliens who have overstayed their visas or simply have come here without a visa. Despite these troubling facts, concerns must be voiced in the public square that an inordinate tightening of immigration laws may promote "racial profiling" (racial profiling is the practice of targeting individuals solely on the basis of their race or ethnicity in the belief that a particular group is more likely to engage in certain unlawful behavior) or encourage an untoward atmosphere of bigotry and fear in the general population. Still, it is a fact that the vast majority of Islamic terror operatives do fit a certain profile. As Justice Kennedy wrote for the majority in *Ashcroft v. Iqbal* (2009): "It should come as no surprise that a legitimate policy directing law enforcement to arrest and detain individuals because of their suspected link to the attacks [9/11] would produce a disparate, incidental impact on Arab Muslims, even though the purpose of the policy was to target neither Arabs not Muslims." Nevertheless, changes in the law should not negatively affect the vast majority of law-abiding aliens; no American wishes to see a return to the poisoned atmosphere that occurred when, for instance, President Franklin Roosevelt ordered the internment of American citizens of Japanese descent during World War II.

4.10 Privacy and New Information-Gathering Technologies

The revolutionary advancements in the field of technology have made the world a smaller place. Even without the threat of terror, the impact on privacy issues has been phenomenal. Nevertheless, if the ability to engage in preventive measures to defeat terrorism are to be realized, the government will most certainly seek to employ the latest information-gathering technologies which will include, at the very least, the increased use of video surveillance in public places, image-recognition modeling to scan faces, computer data mining, and eavesdropping on electronic message traffic. Within days after September 11, 2001, the Attorney General proposed a laundry list of new wiretap and electronic eavesdropping powers to enable law enforcement officials to "act more quickly in fast-moving cases [of terrorism]." Many of these requests, such as a revision of wiretapping laws pertaining to cell phones and so on, have already been enacted into law; many more issues are sure to be debated as the balance between privacy and security is stretched to the limit. While there exists no specific constitutional right to privacy in public places, some privacy advocates early on feared that the next wave of government requests might short-circuit constitutional safeguards under the guise of counterterrorism.

Two recent federal district court cases have paved the way for such things as random police searches in train stations. One ACLU backed lawsuit against the Massachusetts Bay Transportation Authority saw the court uphold random searches where police teams would take swabs of bag handles and zippers and insert them into an explosive trace detector. To avoid allegations of racial profiling, a predetermined number of subjects were searched at random and the subject was given the right to refuse and depart the public transportation system.

AMERICAN -ARAB ANTI-DISCRIMINATION COMMITTEE, et al.
v.
MASSACHUSETTS BAY TRANSPORTATION AUTHORITY
No. 04-11653-GAO (D. Mass. July 28, 2004)
(Order denying preliminary injunction)

The plaintiffs brought this action to obtain a declaration that a policy adopted by the Massachusetts Bay Transportation Authority ("MBTA") permitting security searches of handbags, briefcases and other items carried by passengers on the MBTA's trains or buses violates the guarantee of the Fourth Amendment to the United States Constitution against unreasonable searches and seizures. The plaintiffs have sought a preliminary injunction against enforcement of the policy. At the hearing held on their motion, the plaintiffs, without waiving their broader objections, narrowed the focus of the requested preliminary relief to one instance of the implementation of the policy.

In connection with the security planning for the Democratic National Convention being held at the Fleet Center in Boston from July 26 through July 29, the United States Secret Service issued directives restricting access to streets and highways that pass near the Fleet Center and requiring all persons who enter within a territorial zone surrounding the Fleet Center to submit to security searches. Some of the MBTA's public mass transit vehicles pass through or very nearly by the designated zone. Specifically, some MBTA buses carry passengers to and from suburban locations via Interstate Route 93, which passes close by the Fleet Center, and the MBTA's Orange Line subway passes either underneath or very nearly underneath the Fleet Center. The MBTA has undertaken to conduct an individual visual search of the hand-carried items of all passengers on buses passing by the Fleet Center on Route 93 and all passengers on Orange Line trains before those trains depart either the Community College station for inbound trains, or the Haymarket station for outbound trains, and pass under the Fleet Center security zone. There is no selectivity in the searches; every passenger's carried-on items are examined.

The MBTA argues that the searches are justified because they are "administrative" security searches similar to the security inspections of personal belongings conducted at airports and the entryways to certain kinds of property, such as courthouses and military installations. Such administrative searches have been upheld in the face of objections that they violated the Fourth Amendment. See *United States v. Doe*, 61 F.3d 107, 109-110 (1st Cir. 1995) (noting that "[r]outine security searches at airport checkpoints pass constitutional muster because the compelling public interest in curbing air piracy generally outweighs their limited intrusiveness"); *Torbet v. United Airlines, Inc.*, 298 F.3d 1087 (9th Cir. 1998) (upholding airport security search); *Morgan v. United States*, 323 F.3d 776 (9th Cir. 2003) (upholding search on military reservation); *McMorris v. Alioto*,567 F.2d 897 (9th Cir. 1978) (upholding search at entrance to courthouse). *See also Chandler v. Miller*, 520 U.S. 305, 323 (1997) (suggesting that "where the risk to public safety is substantial and real, blanket suspicion less searches calibrated to the risk may rank as reasonable' (for example, searches now routine at airports and at entrances to courts and other official buildings.").

There is a catalog of hijackings and other terrorist incidents involving air transportation that now spans decades, and much attention has been given as a result to airport security, as some of the cited cases indicate. But other transportation systems, including urban mass transit systems, have become targets of terrorists as well. The MBTA calls attention to two subway bombings that occurred earlier this year, one in Madrid on March 11, 2004, in which over 200 persons were killed, and one in Moscow on February 6, 2004, in which approximately forty persons were killed. There were many more persons seriously injured in the bombings.

The Department of Homeland Security has warned that credible intelligence indicates that terrorists continue to plan for a large-scale attack within the United States aimed at disrupting the Nation's "democratic process." It is at least plausible, if not likely, that the attack in Madrid was timed to maximize its disruptive effect on the Spanish elections, pointing up the attractiveness to terrorists of timing a terrorist event to have an impact on the democratic process. It is not unreasonable, then, to think that national party nominating conventions could become terrorist targets, and when the conventions are held in cities with significant mass transportation systems that serve the convention locations, it is not without foundation to worry that a terrorist event might be aimed simultaneously at the convention and the transit system.

However, while the existence of a terrorist threat against the MBTA or the Fleet Center or both is real and not imagined, it is much more difficult, if not impossible, to try to assess either the likelihood or the imminence of such an attack. While the Court is advised that there is no specific intelligence information suggesting that either the MBTA or the Fleet Center is an identified target, there is also no reason to believe that specific information is necessarily, or even frequently, available before a terrorist attack, so its absence cannot be taken to indicate that the facilities are *not* likely targets. With respect to airport security measures, the absence of specific threat information about a particular flight or even a particular airport does not vitiate either the authority or the wisdom of conducting security screenings generally for *all* flights. When the threat is to *any* flight, *every* flight may be protected by the security searches. "The essential purpose of the scheme is not to detect weapons or explosives or to apprehend those who carry them, but to deter persons carrying such materials from seeking to board at all." *United States v. Davis*, 482 F.2d 893, 908 (9th Cir. 1973).

There is also no reason to have separate constitutional analyses for urban mass transportation systems and for airline transportation. There may be differences in the security methods that are used or in their manner of implementation, but the fundamental issues should not be substantially affected by the mode of transportation involved.

It seems clear, then, that the first essential question to be asked concerning the validity of an administrative search regime—whether there is a substantial governmental need or public interest that is served by the regime—is to be answered in favor of the MBTA's policy. The next question—just as critical—is whether the privacy intrusion is reasonable in its scope and effect, given the nature and dimension of the public interest to be served.

The intrusion is not insignificant. Passengers are required to open all bags and similar carried on items to visual inspection, exposing to view what they would otherwise have kept unseen, including personal items carried in a purse, papers in a briefcase, and the like. Similar intrusions are routine in airport searches, however, and perhaps in other non-governmental venues as well, such as the entry gates to sporting events or concerts.

The MBTA points to the steps it has taken to mitigate the intrusion. First, it has in a variety of ways published notice to its riders of the prospect that they may be subject to search. The notice broadly advised riders that their carried-on items could be subject to search while they were riding on MBTA facilities. It would perhaps have been desirable for the MBTA specifically to advise Orange Line and Route 93 bus riders that it was not just a possibility, but a certainty, that their belongings would be searched if (or when) their journey would take them through the Fleet Center security zone. This deficiency by itself, however, does not require finding the plan to be "unreasonable" under the Fourth Amendment, because notice, or notice of a particular kind, while an important factor to be considered, is not a necessary element such that its absence automatically vitiates the reasonableness of the search plan.

Notice is a significant factor in the analysis for at least two reasons. First, it tends to reduce the subjective anxiety that MBTA riders might otherwise experience upon being asked to submit to the inspection of their bags if they had no reason to anticipate the inspection. See *United States v. Martinez-Fuerte*, 428 U.S. 543, 558 (1976). It also provides an opportunity for persons who do not want to permit inspection to avoid traveling on the MBTA during the time when security searches are being conducted. *See Davis*, 482 F.2d at 913. For the searches directly at issue now, those affecting riders on the Orange Line between the Haymarket and Community College stations and on Route 93 buses, the plan is to limit the searches to the duration of the Convention, and notice provides riders who object to the intrusion the opportunity to temporarily adjust their plans to avoid it.

The second mitigating factor is related. The particular search plan presently at issue is limited both in scope and duration. Only those riders whose journeys will actually take them through the Secret Service-designated security zone are subjected to the search. Riders on other segments of the Orange Line, for example, are not asked to submit to search under this application of the policy. And as noted, the duration of the plan is limited to the four days of the Convention.

Finally, the plan cedes no discretion to the officers conducting the inspections. All riders on the buses and on the trains about to transit the security zone are subject to the inspection, so the officers do not exercise any choice or judgment about whose bags to inspect. The written plan prescribes the inspection method and defines those items that are deemed "prohibited." The plan provides for supervision of the officers who actually do the inspection, and it requires record keeping so the conduct of the inspections can be reviewed afterward.

In sum, the intrusion experienced by the affected riders is very similar to the intrusions imposed under other, increasingly common, administrative security search regimes. The security concerns that motivated the adoption of the scheme are genuine, the scope and duration of the part of the plan that is the focus of the current request for relief are strictly limited, and the published advice that riders on MBTA facilities may be required to submit personal bags and items for inspection prepared riders to expect such searches. In light of these conclusions, the plaintiffs have not established a likelihood of success on their claim that the inspections as described above violate the Fourth Amendment's guarantee against "unreasonable searches."

The motion for a preliminary injunction, as narrowed by the plaintiffs at the hearing, is therefore DENIED.

July 28, 2004   George A. O'Toole, Jr.
                                                        UNITED STATES DISTRICT JUDGE

A survey of some of the new proposals for combating terrorism clearly adds to the discussion of where the line should be drawn between privacy and security. Indeed, it is largely uncertain where a terrorist attack will most likely originate. Attacks could come from outside an airplane in the form of surface to air missiles, or through the thousands of privately owned planes that can be easily rented. In addition, the 1995 attack on the Tokyo subway by the Aum Shinrikyo religious cult highlights the security challenge posed by terrorists using chemical or biological agents. Still, a favorite target of the radical Islamic terrorist remains commercial aviation as seen in the failed Christmas Day 2009 attack on Delta flight 253 over Detroit.

While metal detection technology has long been used to screen things and people who enter certain government facilities and airports, a new technology called backscatter is now being used to screen airline travelers in a number of American airports. The TSA is also using Backscatter "portals"—21-foot-hihg arch-like machines—for screening vehicles and containers. Backscatter technology uses beams of low-power energy that do not penetrate the subject (as does x-ray technology) to produce a detailed picture image. It is superior to metal detectors in that it can detect with great precision things such as non-metallic weapons, drugs, or bombs. On the other hand, it also reveals the traveler's breasts, buttocks, and genitalia with a detail that can count the number of hairs on a person's back. Does such an intrusion constitute a violation of the Fourth Amendment? Recalling that the Fourth Amendment does not create an absolute right to privacy, but a qualified one to protect individuals from "unreasonable searches," the courts will ultimately decide where the line is to be drawn. Although the Supreme Court has never directly ruled that airport administrative searches are proper, lower courts have. In *United States v. Aukai* (2007), the U.S. Court of Appeals for the Ninth Circuit held that an airport screening process did not violate the Fourth Amendment if conducted in a reasonable fashion.

UNITED STATES V. AUKAI
United States Court of Appeals for the Ninth Circuit
497 F.3d 955 (March 21, 2007)

BEA, Circuit Judge

More than 700 million passengers board commercial aircraft in the United States each year. FN1. The Transportation Security Administration ("TSA") is given the task of ensuring their safety, the safety of airline and airport personnel and, as the events of September 11, 2001, demonstrate, the safety of the general public from risks arising from commercial airplane flights. To do so, the TSA conducts airport screening searches of all passengers entering the secured area of the airport. We have previously held such airport screening searches are constitutionally reasonable administrative searches. Today we clarify that the reasonableness of such searches does not depend, in whole or in part, upon the consent of the passenger being searched.

On February 1, 2003, Daniel Kuualoha Aukai arrived at the Honolulu International Airport intending to take a Hawaiian Airlines flight from Honolulu, Hawaii, to Kona, Hawaii. He proceeded to check in at the ticket counter but did not produce a government-issued picture identification. Accordingly, the ticket agent wrote the phrase "No ID" on Aukai's boarding pass. Aukai then proceeded to the security checkpoint, at which signs were posted advising prospective passengers that they and their carry-on baggage were subject to search. He entered the security checkpoint at approximately 9:00 a.m., placed his shoes and a few other items into a plastic bin, and voluntarily walked through the metal detector or magnetometer. The parties agree that the magnetometer did not signal the presence of metal as Aukai walked through it. Nor did his belongings trigger an alarm or otherwise raise suspicion as they passed through the x-ray machine. After walking through the magnetometer, Aukai presented his boarding pass to TSA Officer Corrine Motonaga.

Pursuant to TSA procedures, a passenger who presents a boarding pass on which "No ID" has been written is subject to secondary screening even if he has passed through the initial screening without triggering an alarm or otherwise raising suspicion. As it was performed here, secondary screening consists of a TSA officer passing a handheld magnetometer, known as a "wand," near and around the passenger's body. If the wand detects metal, it sounds an alarm. The TSA officer then discerns the cause of the alarm, using techniques such as feeling the outside of the passenger's clothes in the area that caused the alarm and, if that area is near a pocket, directing the passenger to empty his pocket.

Because Aukai's boarding pass had the "No ID" notation, Motonaga directed Aukai to a nearby, roped-off area for secondary screening. Aukai initially complied but complained that he was in a hurry to catch his flight which, according to the boarding pass, was scheduled to leave at 9:05 a.m., just a few minutes later. Although Aukai went to the roped-off area as directed, he did not stay there. When Motonaga noticed that Aukai had left the area and was gathering his belongings from the plastic bin, she instructed Aukai that he was not allowed to retrieve his property and that he had to stay in the roped-off area.

Aukai then appealed to TSA Officer Andrew Misajon, who was to perform the secondary screening, explaining again that he was in a hurry to catch his flight. Misajon nonetheless had Aukai sit in a chair and proceeded to use the wand to detect metal objects. At some point, Misajon had Aukai stand, and when Misajon passed the wand across the front of Aukai's body, the wand alarm was triggered at Aukai's front right pants pocket. Misajon asked Aukai if he had anything in his pocket, and Aukai responded that he did not. Misajon passed the wand over the pocket a second time; again the wand alarm was triggered. Misajon again inquired whether Aukai had anything in his pocket; again Aukai said he did not. Misajon then felt the outside of Aukai's pocket and concluded that something was inside the pocket. Misajon could also see the outline of an unknown object in Aukai's pocket. At some point during this screening process, Aukai informed Misajon that he no longer wished to board a plane and wanted to leave the airport.

At this point, TSA Supervisor Joseph Vizcarra approached Misajon and asked whether he needed assistance. Misajon related the events and Vizcarra asked Misajon to pass the wand over Aukai's pocket again. When the wand alarm again was triggered, Vizcarra directed Aukai to empty his pocket. Aukai again protested that he had nothing in his pocket. Using the back of his hand, Vizcarra touched the outside of Aukai's pocket and felt something in the pocket. He again directed Aukai to empty his pocket. This time Aukai reached into his pocket and removed either his keys or change, but a bulge was still visible in his pocket. Vizcarra directed Aukai to remove all contents from his pocket. After claiming at first that there was nothing more, Aukai finally removed an object wrapped in some form of tissue paper and placed it on a tray in front of him.

Suspecting that the object might be a weapon, Vizcarra summoned a nearby law enforcement officer. Vizcarra then unwrapped the object and discovered a glass pipe used to smoke methamphetamine. The law enforcement officer escorted Aukai to a small office near the security checkpoint. Aukai was placed under arrest and was searched incident to his arrest. During the search, the police discovered in Aukai's front pants pockets several transparent bags containing a white crystal substance. Aukai eventually was taken into federal custody, where he was advised of and waived his *Miranda* rights, and then gave a statement in which he inculpated himself in the possession of methamphetamine.

Aukai was indicted for knowingly and intentionally possessing, with the intent to distribute, 50 grams or more of methamphetamine in violation of *21 U.S.C. § 841(a) and 841(b)(1)(A)(viii)*. Aukai filed a motion to suppress the evidence found incident to his arrest at the airport and the statement he later made, which the district court denied. Aukai then pleaded guilty pursuant to a written plea agreement that preserved his right to appeal the denial of his suppression motion. The district court sentenced Aukai to a term of imprisonment of 70 months and a term of supervised release of 5 years. Aukai timely appealed.

We review de novo the district court's legal basis for denying a motion to suppress, but review the district court's findings of fact for clear error. *United States v. Marquez, 410 F.3d 612, 615 (9th Cir. 2005)* (as amended).

The *Fourth Amendment* requires the government to respect "[t]he right of the people to be secure in their persons…and effects, against unreasonable searches and seizures." *U.S. Const. amend. IV.* "A search or seizure is ordinarily unreasonable in the absence of individualized suspicion of wrongdoing. While such suspicion is not an 'irreducible' component of reasonableness, [the Supreme Court has] recognized only limited circumstances in which the usual rule does not apply." *City of Indianapolis v. Edmond, 531 U.S. 32, 37, 121 S. Ct. 447, 148 L. Ed. 2d 333 (2000)* (citations omitted). However, "where the risk to public safety is substantial and real, blanket suspicionless searches calibrated to the risk may rank as 'reasonable'--for example, searches now routine at airports and at entrances to courts and other official buildings." *Chandler v. Miller, 520 U.S. 305, 323, 117 S. Ct. 1295, 137 L. Ed. 2d 513 (1997)* (holding Georgia's requirement that candidates for state office pass a drug test did not fit within this exception) (citing *Nat'l Treasury Employees Union v. Von Raab, 489 U.S. 656, 674-76, 109 S. Ct. 1384, 103 L. Ed. 2d 685 & n.3 (1989)* (upholding warrantless drug testing of employees applying for promotion to positions involving drug interdiction)). Thus, "where a *Fourth Amendment* intrusion serves special governmental needs, beyond the normal need for law enforcement, it is necessary to balance the individual's privacy expectations against the Government's interests to determine whether it is impractical to require a warrant or some level of individualized suspicion in the particular context." *Von Raab, 489 U.S. at 665-66.*

Under this rationale the Supreme Court has repeatedly upheld the constitutionality of so-called "administrative searches." FN2. In *New York v. Burger, 482 U.S. 691, 107 S. Ct. 2636, 96 L. Ed. 2d 601 (1987)*, the Supreme Court upheld the warrantless search of a junkyard's records, permits, and vehicles. The Supreme Court reasoned: "Because the owner or operator of commercial premises in a 'closely regulated' industry has a reduced expectation of privacy, the warrant and probable-cause requirements, which fulfill the traditional *Fourth Amendment* standard of reasonableness for a government search have lessened application...." *Id. at 702* (internal citation omitted). Thus, New York's interest in regulating the junkyard industry, in light of the rise of motor-theft and comprehensive motor vehicle insurance premiums, served as a "special need" allowing inspection without a warrant. *Id. at 708-09*; *see also id. at 702*. The regulatory statute also provided a "constitutionally adequate substitute for a warrant" because the statute informed junkyard operators that inspections would be made on a regular basis and limited the discretion of inspecting officers. *Id. at 711.*

In *Michigan Department of State Police v. Sitz, 496 U.S. 444, 110 S. Ct. 2481, 110 L. Ed. 2d 412 (1990)*, Sitz challenged the constitutionality of suspicionless sobriety checkpoints conducted on Michigan's highways, contending that the program violated the *Fourth Amendment's* protection against unreasonable seizures. *Id. at 447-48*. The Supreme Court upheld the sobriety checkpoints because "the balance of the State's interest in preventing drunken driving, the extent to which [the sobriety checkpoints] can reasonably be said to advance that interest, and the degree of intrusion upon individual motorists who are briefly stopped, weighs in favor of" finding the sobriety checkpoints constitutionally reasonable. *Id. at 455.*

Significantly, the Supreme Court has held that the constitutionality of administrative searches is not dependent upon consent. In *United States v. Biswell, 406 U.S. 311, 92 S. Ct. 1593, 32 L. Ed. 2d 87 (1972)*, the Supreme Court upheld the warrantless search of a pawn shop owner's gun storeroom. The search was authorized by a federal gun control statute. The Court held that, "[i]n the context of a regulatory inspection system of business premises that is carefully limited in time, place, and scope, the legality of the search depends not on consent but on the authority of a valid statute." FN3. *Id. at 315*. Thus, "[w]hen a [gun] dealer chooses to engage in this pervasively regulated business and to accept a federal license, he does so with the knowledge that his business records, firearms, and ammunition will be subject to effective inspection." *Id. at 316.*

The constitutionality of an airport screening search, however, does not depend on consent, *see Biswell, 406 U.S. at 315*, and requiring that a potential passenger be allowed to revoke consent to an ongoing airport security search makes little sense in a post-9/11 world. FN6. Such a rule would afford terrorists (FN7) multiple opportunities to attempt to penetrate airport security by "electing not to fly" on the cusp of detection until a vulnerable portal is found. This rule would also allow terrorists a low-cost method of detecting systematic vulnerabilities in airport security, knowledge that could be extremely valuable in planning future attacks. Likewise, given that consent is not required, it makes little sense to predicate the reasonableness of an administrative airport screening search on an irrevocable implied consent theory. Rather, where an airport screening search is otherwise reasonable and conducted pursuant to statutory authority, *49 U.S.C. § 44901*, all that is required is the passenger's election to attempt entry into the secured area of an airport. FN8. *See Biswell, 406 U.S. at 315*; *49 C.F.R. § 1540.107*. Under current TSA regulations and procedures, that election occurs when a prospective passenger walks through the magnetometer or places items on the conveyor belt of the x-ray machine. FN9. The record establishes that Aukai elected to attempt entry into the posted secured area of Honolulu International Airport when he walked through the magnetometer, thereby subjecting himself to the airport screening process.

Although the constitutionality of airport screening searches is not dependent on consent, the scope of such searches is not limitless. A particular airport security screening search is constitutionally reasonable provided that it "is no more extensive nor intensive than necessary, in the light of current technology, to detect the presence of weapons or explosives [ ] [and] that it is confined in good faith to that purpose." *Davis, 482 F.2d at 913.* We conclude that the airport screening search of Aukai satisfied these requirements.

The search procedures used in this case were neither more extensive nor more intensive than necessary under the circumstances to rule out the presence of weapons or explosives. After passing through a magnetometer, Aukai was directed to secondary screening because his boarding pass was marked "No ID." Aukai then underwent a standard "wanding procedure." When the wand alarm sounded as the wand passed over Aukai's front right pants pocket, TSA Officer Misajon did not reach into Aukai's pocket or feel the outside of Aukai's pocket. Rather, Misajon asked Aukai if he had something in his pocket. When Aukai denied that there was anything in his pocket, Misajon repeated the wanding procedure. Only after the wand alarm again sounded and Aukai again denied having anything in his pocket did Misajon employ a more intrusive search procedure by feeling the outside of Aukai's pocket and determining that there was something in there.

At that point, TSA Supervisor Vizcarra became involved. Vizcarra asked Misajon to pass the wand over Aukai's pocket again. When the wand alarm again sounded, Vizcarra directed Aukai to empty his pocket. Aukai again protested that he had nothing in his pocket. Using the back of his hand, Vizcarra touched the outside of Aukai's pocket and felt something inside. Vizcarra again directed Aukai to empty his pocket. This time Aukai reached into his pocket and removed either his keys or change, but a bulge was still visible in his pocket. Vizcarra directed Aukai to remove all contents from his pocket. After first claiming there was nothing more, Aukai removed an object wrapped in some form of tissue paper and placed it on a tray in front of him. Suspecting that the item might be a weapon, Vizcarra unwrapped the item, discovering drug paraphernalia.

Like the Third Circuit, we find these search procedures to be minimally intrusive. *See Hartwell, 436 F.3d at 180* (holding similar search procedures to be "minimally intrusive," explaining that the procedures are "well-tailored to protect personal privacy, escalating in invasiveness only after a lower level of screening disclosed a reason to conduct a more probing search").

The duration of the detention associated with this airport screening search was also reasonable. Witnesses testified that Aukai entered the checkpoint area at approximately 9:00 a.m. and that the entire search at issue--starting from when Aukai walked through the checkpoint until the TSA's efforts to rule out the presence of a weapon resulted in the discovery of drug paraphernalia--took no more than 18 minutes. Although longer than detentions approved in other cases, *see, e.g., Sitz, 496 U.S. at 448* (average delay of 25 seconds); *United States v. Martinez-Fuerte, 428 U.S. 543, 546-47, 96 S. Ct. 3074, 49 L. Ed. 2d 1116 (1976)* (average detention of 3-5 minutes), the length of Aukai's detention was reasonable, especially in light of Aukai's conduct, because it was not prolonged beyond the time reasonably required to rule out the presence of weapons or explosives. FN10. *See Illinois v. Caballes, 543 U.S. 405, 407, 125 S. Ct. 834, 160 L. Ed. 2d 842 (2005)* (stating that a seizure can become unlawful if it is "prolonged beyond the time reasonably required to complete [its] mission").
AFFIRMED.

FN1. *See* Bureau of Transportation Statistics, February 2007 Airline Traffic Data, http://www.
bts.gov/press_releases/2007/bts022_07/html/bts022_07.html (last visited May 18, 2007).

FN2. The Supreme Court has not specifically *held* that airport screening searches are constitutionally reasonable administrative searches. On three occasions, however, the Supreme Court has *suggested* that airport screening searches are constitutionally reasonable administrative searches. *See Miller, 520 U.S. at 323*; *Edmond, 531 U.S. 47-8* ("Our holding also does not affect the validity of border searches or searches at places like airports and government buildings, where the need for such measures to ensure public safety can be particularly acute.");*Von Raab, 489 U.S. at 675 n.3* [10] (approving of lower court decisions upholding airport screening searches where there was no reason for suspicion).

FN3. The gun shop search in *Biswell* was authorized by *18 U.S.C. § 923(g) (1968). See Biswell, 406 U.S. at 311-12*. Airport screening searches are mandated by a federal law.*See 49 U.S.C. § 44901*; *49 C.F.R. § 1540.107*.

We have held that airport screening searches, like the one at issue here, are constitutionally reasonable administrative searches because they are "conducted as part of a general regulatory scheme in furtherance of an administrative purpose, namely, to prevent the carrying of weapons or explosives aboard aircraft, and thereby to prevent hijackings." *United States v. Davis, 482 F.2d 893, 908 (9th Cir. 1973)*; *see also United States v. Hartwell, 436 F.3d 174, 178 (3d Cir.), cert. denied, 127 S. Ct. 111, 166 L. Ed. 2d 255 (2006)*;*Marquez, 410 F.3d at 616*. Our case law, however, has erroneously suggested that the reasonableness of airport screening searches is dependent upon consent, either ongoing consent or irrevocable implied consent.

FN4. FN5. Omitted

FN6. The concurrence fears that references to 9/11 and terrorists are irrelevant and will invite future litigants to challenge our holding if and when the threat of organized terrorist activity at our airports recedes. But the present threat of organized terrorists using the 9/11 tactic of hijacking commercial aircraft, intending to use the aircraft as a weapon, is relevant to the reasonableness of the search procedures employed. This new terrorist tactic was the impetus behind the Aviation Transportation Security Act, Pub. L. No. 107-71, § 110, 115 Stat. 597, 614-15 (2001), which authorizes the airport screening at issue in this case. *See* H.R. Rep. No. 107-296, at 53-54 (2001) (Conf. Rep.), *as reprinted in* 2002 U.S.C.C.A.N. 589, 590 ("The conferees further note the terrorist hijacking and crashes of passenger aircraft on September 11, 2001, which converted civil aircraft into guided bombs for strikes against the United States, required a fundamental change in the way it approaches the task of ensuring the safety and security of the civil air transportation system."). Here, the search procedures employed included the completion of secondary screening on a passenger who had stated he no longer wished to fly. The concurrence may well be correct that as an original proposition, the present threat of terrorism is not necessary for this procedure to be reasonable under the Fourth Amendment. That had not been our circuit's law prior to 9/11; an intending passenger could refuse to be searched at the airport if he stated he had changed his mind and no longer wished to fly. *See Homburg, 546 F.2d at 1352*. The adoption of a contrary rule based on a factual situation not present--elimination of the historical fact of 9/11 and the lack of an organized terrorist threat--would be speculative. Since we must decide "cases and controversies" only, we should decide only whether the secondary search of Aukai was reasonable under the Fourth Amendment under the circumstances presented and state why. That is what we have strived to do. What search procedures will be "reasonable" when terrorists are no longer threatening us, or when technology is developed that eliminates the present threat, should be decided when, if ever, that happy day dawns. We should also be wary to eliminate historical facts such as 9/11. Orwell warned us: "Who controls the present controls the past...." George Orwell, 1984, Book Three, Chapter II (1949).

FN7. "Terrorists" are those persons who engage in or attempt to engage in acts of "terrorism", as that term is defined in the Homeland Security Act of 2002, Pub. L. No. 107-296, § 101, 116 Stat 2135, 2141 (2002):

The term "terrorism" means any activity that--
(A) involves an act that--
(i) is dangerous to human life or potentially destructive of critical infrastructure or key resources; and
(ii) is a violation of the criminal laws of the United States or of any State or other subdivision of the United States; and
(B) appears to be intended--
(i) to intimidate or coerce a civilian population;
(ii) to influence the policy of a government by intimidation or coercion; or
(iii) to affect the conduct of a government by mass destruction, assassination, or kidnapping.

FN8. "Secured area" is defined as the "portion of an airport, specified in the [TSA] airport security program,...where aircraft operators and foreign air carriers...enplane and deplane passengers...." *49 C.F.R. § 1520.5*. The secured area includes the "sterile area," which "means [the] portion of an airport defined in the [TSA] airport security program that provides passengers access to boarding aircraft and to which the access generally is controlled by TSA...through the screening of persons and property." *Id*. Because of security concerns, the Government has not made public the details of "airport security programs." *See 49 U.S.C. § 114(s); 49 C.F.R. § 1520.5*. Hence, we do not speculate on how far such "sterile" and "secured" areas extend from the airplane boarding gate to the street door. Suffice it to say that such "secured area" extends at least as far as the point at which a prospective passenger places hand luggage on a conveyor belt for inspection, *Torbet, 298 F.3d at 1089*, or passes through a magnetometer, *Marquez, 410 F.3d at 617*. We accept the Government's position at oral argument, on this point.

FN9. The Government asserted during oral argument that regulations and procedures tying this election to an earlier point in time, *i.e.*, entering the airport screening line or the presentation of a boarding pass and I.D. to a TSA officer, would pass constitutional muster. Changes in technology or gains in knowledge as to terrorist operations may prompt the TSA or its successors to claim the need for recognition of danger at an earlier point in the boarding process. However, such a claim, and whatever legal issues it might raise, are not now before us.

> To the extent our cases have predicated the reasonableness of an airport screening search upon either ongoing consent or irrevocable implied consent, they are overruled.

FN10. We note that the detention in this case was prolonged, not by delay on the part of the TSA officers conducting the screening, but by Aukai's repeated lies as to the contents of his pocket. Accordingly, we hold that the airport screening search of Aukai was a constitutionally reasonable administrative search.

A new idea currently in the mill involves the use of electronic profiling. Since the beginning of the War on Terror, the Pentagon has stepped up its testing of various image-recognition technology hardware, developing sophisticated technology that is superior to new automatic teller machines which can scan a customer's face for positive identification. This technology has already been tested in England where thousands of outdoor cameras are used to keep watch on "pedestrians and passerby, employing a facial-recognition system that can automatically pick out known criminals and alert local authorities to their presence." These cameras can compare hundreds of thousands of faces on file against a particular subject face within seconds.

Despite the complaints regarding invasion of privacy, "pod" cameras are rapidly becoming a part of the modern landscape. In fact, the 6,000 cameras set in London's subway system were pivotal in solving the July 7 and July 21, 2005, bombings by al-Qa'eda operatives. Cities across the United States are following suit. In Chicago, for example, over 2,000 camera pods are now in place in high-crime areas and on transit and public buildings. In 2005, the Department of Homeland Security gave over $800 million to 50 cities for surveillance cameras. By 2010, New York City had installed thousands of cameras that record images of everyone who passes through a passenger turnstile or entrance gate for public transportation. The car bomb driven by Faisal Shahzad in the 2010 Times Square terror plot was caught on video.

Baggage screening has also received renewed attention, particularly in wake of the failed August 2006 London based plot to blow up jet airliners bound for the United States. Acting primarily through the rule-making power delegated to administrative agencies such as the DHS, the United States is steadily increasing the security of various public transportation facilities, with a particular emphasis on airports. Congress continues to pass a number of new pieces of legislation including the 2002 Aviation Transportation and Security Act, which requires increased airport screening through the use of advanced detection devices, physical searches, and positive passenger bag match. This new law has proven a burden to both passengers and to the industry in general. Further, starting in 2008, DHS began screening all incoming air cargo with radiation detector machines. The Radiation Portal Monitors cost $450,000 each.

More sophisticated biometric and cryptographic technologies, such as fingerprints on identification cards or iris scans at airports, may soon become common fare. Privacy issues of concern relate to how this data is stored, who should have access, and for what purposes is it to be used?

Although upgrading airport security has received the bulk of the government's attention, with the industry receiving over 30 billion dollars since 9/11, the railways and ports are also prime terror targets. In New York City, doormen at apartment complexes, dock-workers, and other workers are being trained by the city to look for things out of the ordinary. In all, over 28,000 workers have been trained by the police department at a cost of over one million dollars. Other federal programs to train, for example, interstate truck drivers to report possible terrorist situations are also active.

It appears that increased security at public facilities and other public places is rapidly becoming the "new normal." It is perhaps the most obvious signpost that Americans are living in a new time. Paradoxically, it is not only our elected representatives who will decide how much security Americans will receive. Those decisions will be made in part, and implemented in the main, by administrative agencies—the so-called headless "fourth branch" of government.

For example, in late 2005, the DHS Research Projects Agency issued a solicitation to the private sector to provide 26 research and development prototypes in the areas of explosives detection, chemical and biological countermeasures protection, law enforcement, threat assessment and vulnerability testing, critical infrastructure protection, borders and transportation security, emergency preparedness and response, and cyber security in the following areas:

1. Maritime Safety and Security Team (MSST) Explosive Trace Detection—a prototype system demonstrating improved capabilities for explosive trace detection in the maritime environment.

2. Non-invasive Portable Object Examination System—a multi-sensor, person-portable system to assist trained users in expedient, non-invasive examination of unattended bags, mail packages, and other objects.

3. Advanced Capability X-ray System for Bomb Squad—an advanced capability X-ray system that provides improved penetration and resolution to conduct radiographic examination and diagnostics of suspected packages and confirm the presence of Improvised Explosive Devices.

4. Portable Entry Point Screening Portal—a robust, portable, fully automated, walk-through portal that can detect explosive material on clothing or skin using a non-intrusive, non-contact technique that meets the TSA T&E detection criteria and methods.

5. Escape Hood—a small concealable escape mask that will allow personnel to safely leave potentially contaminated areas.

6. Rapid Suspected Bio-agent Screening—a tool and method for rapidly screening suspicious "white powders" to eliminate the probability that the substance is a biological threat agent.

7. Aircraft "Spot" Decontamination—a kit and method for use to provide "spot" decontamination of common aircraft cabin materials.

8. Biosurveillance Detection Algorithms—an algorithmic procedure/model to provide earliest detection of bioterrorist attacks on humans, plants, animals, food, water, or the environment based on correlations between a broad range of low confidence biosurveillance data streams.

9. Rapid Field Identification of High Priority Plant Pathogens (RFIP)—person-portable system that will provide minimally trained users assistance in field identification of plant pathogens.

10. One-Person Portable Chemical Detector—a lightweight, chemical detection device for use in ports of entry (both land and seaport environments) to simultaneously detect and identify high priority chemical threat agents and Toxic Industrial Chemicals (TICs).

11. NIOSH CBRN 60 Tactical Escape Mask—a lightweight, one-time use, NIOSH-approved tactical escape mask with 60-minute endurance in CBRN environments.

12. Transportation Route Risk Analysis and Resource Allocation Tool—a prototype to facilitate transportation route risk analysis. The primary output of the tool will be a list of transportation routes ranked according to relative risk.

13. Significant Encounters Visual Environment (SIEVE)—a real-time port and border encounter monitoring system. This system must incorporate GIS layered data-mapping technologies with established reporting and watch procedures.

14. Modeling the Complex Urban Environment (MCUE)—a near real-time system that maps group and tactic-specific threats to specific vulnerabilities and to emergency preparedness and response within a complex urban environment.

15. Improved Heartbeat Detector System Prototype—a heartbeat detector system for finding concealed passengers or detecting motion in conveyances and cargo containers, using vibration sensors and analysis software with a user interface.

16. Extreme Wide Field-of-View IR/NV Capability—a marine and land-based system that provides vessel and vehicle operators a wide-peripheral awareness, stereoscopic, low moment arm, night-vision system.

17. Tactical Information Sharing System (TISS) Image Analysis Capability—software that performs facial image comparisons for the purpose of identifying possible criminals and terrorists from low resolution images. The system will generate full frontal facial images from partial images and perform digital image comparisons.

18. Advanced 3-D Locator System—a system to accurately locate and track incident responders inside threatened buildings, collapsed buildings, subterranean facilities, or underground.

19. Geospatial Modeling of Homeland Security Capabilities—a capability model in a geospatial system to allow planners to visualize preparedness information and perform quantitative analysis (such as coverage area, deployment time, and mutual aid dependencies).

20. Resource Awareness Data Portal—a shared, virtual data repository of emergency management/emergency response resource data constructed and maintained in a "just in time" manner.

21. Advanced Urban Search and Rescue (US&R) Breaching Approach—an advanced breaching (cutting, coring, burning) and breaking system for faster and safer extrication of victims from disaster sites.

22. BOTNET—a cyber security tool for identifying bots (software agents that interact with network services intended for people as if it were a real person; the term is derived from "robot") and botnets (a collection of such software robots, or bots, which run autonomously, from unwitting host computers, usually for nefarious purposes).

23. Control System Cyber Assessment Tool—a web-based, self-assessment tool for process control systems to assist owners and operators in performing self-assessments of the cyber security of their control system architecture.

24. Exercise Scenario Modeling Tool—a collaborative web-based tool to assist exercise planners in developing cyber security exercise scenarios for use in cyber training incident response teams.

25. Blue Force Tracking Tool and Evaluation of Multi-Agency Maritime Blue Force Tracking (BFT) System—This effort develops a prototype Blue Force Tracking (BFT) Command Center tool to enable the watchstander to simultaneously manage up to 100 Blue Force vessels. Automatic Identification System BFT hardware specified by the Coast Guard will be fabricated and installed in Coast Guard and port partner vessels in the Port of New York. A six month evaluation will be conducted to assess the performance and Command and Control benefits of this new capability.

26. USCG Sector Command Center (SCC) Simulator Testbed—a USCG Sector Command Center Testbed to systematically evaluate the integration of new technologies and improved command and control concepts into SCC operations. The testbed will be simulator based in that vessel movement and sensor output will be synthetic, although based upon realistic performance and behavior.

4.11 Assassination

Osama bin Laden is quoted as saying that "[t]he confrontation that Islam calls for with these godless and apostate regimes does not know Socratic debates, Platonic ideals, nor Aristotelian diplomacy. But it knows the dialogue of bullets, the ideals of assassination, bombing and destruction, and the diplomacy of the cannon and the machine gun." In contrast, the United States is deeply concerned with fighting the War on Terror under the rule of law—domestically and internationally. From a domestic perspective, the continuing dilemma for democratic policymakers is how to protect the nation without curtailing long-recognized civil liberties. From an international perspective, American policymakers are likewise concerned with following all those international laws associated with both the lawfulness of the use of force and the appropriate application of that force. Without question, the most pressing issue in the international realm centers on the Obama Administration's promotion of a legal rationale for the preemptive use of military force against al-Qa'eda-styled terrorists or rogue States who pose a direct or gathering threat to the United States.

Juxtaposed to the issue of crafting a legal basis for the use of preemptive military force is the recurring issue of whether certain individuals—such as high level al-Qa'eda or leaders of totalitarian States which support or sponsor terrorism—can be legally targeted for "assassination." In other words, if preemptive military force is an acceptable addition to the rule of law, can the United States simply kill selected high-level leaders without having to employ large-scale military forces against the offending rogue nation or terrorist organization?

Currently, there are two principle documents associated with these two legal concerns. Respectively, they are the groundbreaking 2002 National Security Strategy of the United States of America released by the Bush White House on September 17, 2002, and the Presidential Executive Order 12333 banning assassination.

The purpose of this section is to provide a policy and legal analysis of the United States' position regarding assassination as viewed in the context of the lawful use of preemptive military force. In doing so, this section examines the deficiencies of the current Executive Order 12333 and suggests that it should be replaced by a new executive order which clearly defines the circumstances under which individuals may be lawfully targeted for death by military forces—either in peacetime or war. Alternatively, if a new and more precise executive order is not issued to replace Executive Order 12333, there are two interlocking principles that argue against overturning Executive Order 12333. The first of these reasons regards properly understanding the most common definition of assassination and the second relates to the proper use of armed force under the rule of law. Taken together, those who advocate that the ban on assassination should be lifted without modification in order to allow the United States to engage in assassination are essentially advocating that the United States should be able to engage in unlawful killing, or murder.

In the days following the September 11, 2001, attacks on the United States the question of retaliation and self-preservation weighed heavily on the minds of policymakers. Instinctively, many in Washington called for an immediate response to the perpetrators behind the attacks, even if it meant engaging in assassination which some clearly viewed to be in violation of longstanding Executive Order 12333, prohibiting assassination by agents of the United States government. Then, prior to the March 2003 war in Iraq, many expressed the idea of toppling the dictator Saddam Hussein by simply killing him. Currently, the Obama Administration utilizes unmanned drone aircraft to kill suspected enemies in such places as Afghanistan, Pakistan, Sudan, Yemen, Somali, and other locations. Some have called these Obama killings illegal and acts of assassination. Accordingly, a proper understanding of Executive Order 12333 and the legal basis for responding to aggression is required.

The genesis of Executive Order 12333 can be traced back to 1977, when President Gerald Ford issued the first executive order prohibiting political assassination. President Ford was prompted to action by a 1975 Congressional Report (commonly known as the Church Commission) headed by Senator Frank Church which held hearings on the question of whether or not the United States had engaged in assassination or assassination plots against certain foreign leaders. The most damning portion of the report found that between 1960 and 1965, "the United States was implicated in several assassination plots to kill Fidel Castro," the ruler of Communist Cuba.

The Church Commission found that the CIA's Operation Mongoose sought to eliminate Castro with a number of unlikely weapons, such as poison tipped pens and cigars, and an exploding seashell that was to be placed near Castro's favorite scuba spots. Issuing a document consisting of hundreds of pages, the Church Commission was unable to make a finding that "assassination plots were authorized by the Presidents or other people above the governmental agency or agencies involved," but the commission did find that the "system of executive command and control was so ambiguous that it [was] difficult to be certain at what levels assassination activity was known and authorized." The Church Commission strongly concluded that assassination was both legally and morally repugnant to a democratic people and should never be associated with the United States of America: "[A]ssassination is incompatible with American principles, international order, and morality. It should be rejected as a tool of foreign policy."

Curiously, despite the exhaustive research done by the Church Commission on assassination and the call for "intervention by Congress to proscribe it as a matter of law," Congress never enacted legislation to legally ban the use of assassination as an instrument of foreign policy, leaving the matter to the Executive Branch via an executive order. Although presidential executive orders are policy and not law, this distinction is functionally irrelevant, particularly in regard to the politically charged issue of assassination.

President Ford's executive order on assassination read: "Prohibition of Assassination. No employee of the United States Government shall engage in, or conspire to engage in, political assassination." Shortly thereafter, President Jimmy Carter followed suit with his own slightly modified version which deleted the term "political," and in 1981, President Ronald Reagan issued Executive Order 12333 on assassination. It reads in full text: "No person employed by or acting on behalf of the United States government shall engage in, or conspire to engage in, assassination." Subsequent presidents have not changed the Reagan order banning assassination by agents of the United States. Executive Order 12333 remains in effect in the Obama Administration.

A common and reoccurring theme of frustration runs across the arguments of those who seek the repeal of Executive Order 12333. This frustration actually reflects a lack of understanding of what assassination actually means or entails, not what Executive Order 12333 actually prohibits. In short, the central problem is that people use the same word—assassination—and assume that everyone is talking about the same meaning. Of course, this situation is aggravated both by the brevity of the executive order, which provides no definition whatsoever for the term assassination, and the fact that it makes no attempt to distinguish between instances of lawful killing verses instances of assassination, or unlawful killing.

Former conservative United States Senator Jesse Helms from North Carolina amplified this confusion when he remarked on September 11, 2001, that he was in favor of taking whatever action was necessary, to include assassination, to punish those responsible for the attacks on the United States: "I hope I will live to see the day when it will once again be the policy of the United States of America to go after the kind of sneaky enemies who created this morning's mayhem." Then, just over a week after the terrorist attacks, liberal minded National Public Radio senior news correspondent, Daniel Schorr, forcefully urged policymakers to do away with the ban on assassination. Schorr wrote: "A 25 year old executive order reflecting the reaction to mindless cold war plotting against President Castro and other third world leaders, seems completely anachronistic after the Sept. 11th. It is time to rescind an assassination ban that has no more reason for existing." In fact, in the days immediately after the attacks on America, Congressman Bob Barr of Georgia proposed a bill in the House of Representatives which would have nullified Executive Order 12333.

Fortunately, cooler heads prevailed and Congress passed no legislation regarding Executive Order 12333. Shortly thereafter, then White House spokesman, Ari Fleischer correctly related to reporters that the assassination ban "does not limit America's ability to act in self-defense." The elimination of terrorists could require, Fleischer remarked, "acts which involve the lives of others."

Although Fleischer rightly understood in September 2001 that the ban on assassination did not prohibit the United States from taking actions in self-defense against specific threats, he later seemed to have lapsed into misunderstanding. At an October 1, 2002, press conference, Fleischer voiced support for non-American actors assassinating Saddam Hussein. When asked about the cost of a possible war with Iraq, spokesman Fleischer remarked, "I can only say that the cost of a one-way ticket is substantially less than that [the estimated cost of nine billion dollars a month]. The *cost of one bullet*, if the *Iraqi people* take it on themselves, is substantially less than that [emphasis added]." While the assassination of Saddam Hussein by his own people would not violate Executive Order 12333, reporters immediately asked Fleischer if the Bush Administration was encouraging assassination. Fleischer shrewdly stopped short of using the term assassination in reference to Saddam Hussein, perhaps remembering that such a call to the Iraqi people would violate the customary law on assassination.

Without question, the traditional concept of assassination absolutely prohibits one nation from encouraging others, in this case the Iraqi people, to murder the leader of an unfriendly government. Nevertheless, as the United States geared up for possible war with Iraq, national news media sources continued to speculate about the assassination of the Iraqi dictator. Numerous newspapers cited "senior intelligence reports" that Saddam Hussein would probably be assassinated by "members of his inner circle in the final days or hours before U.S. forces launch a major ground attack."

Those who call the loudest for abandoning Executive Order 12333 mistakenly feel that it might impede the expeditious prosecution of the War on Terror—either against al-Qa'eda leaders or the senior leaders of those handful of totalitarian regimes that back terrorism. To date, however, neither Congress nor the President have taken steps that would blunt the ban on assassination. The reason for this inactivity rests in a mixed bag of historical, legal, and policy considerations. Still, there are several strong arguments for abandoning the current executive order on assassination, not because it impedes the War on Terror but because it is more confusing than helpful in defining the application of the lawful use of military force against legitimate targets—whether in peacetime or war—to include the senior leadership of hostile governments or terrorist groups.

Before a thing can be properly discussed it must be properly defined. Nowhere is this more applicable than in addressing the issue of assassination *vis-à-vis* Executive Order 12333. Assassination is defined in leading dictionaries as follows:

- *Webster's Dictionary*: "The act of killing or murdering by surprise or secret assault."
- *American Heritage College Dictionary*: "1. To murder (a prominent person) by surprise attack, as for political reasons. 2. To destroy or injure treacherously."
- *Black's Law Dictionary*: "The act of deliberately killing someone, especially a public figure, usually for hire or political reasons."
- *Random House Dictionary*: "1. To kill suddenly or secretively. Murder premeditatedly and treacherously. 2. To destroy or denigrate treacherously and viciously."

A comparison of most definitions reveals that the common meaning associated with the term assassination is that it is "murder by surprise" usually carried out for "political purposes." In a law review article on the topic, Tyler Harder believes that the best way to capture the meaning of assassination is to view it as a combination of three essential elements: "(1) a murder, (2) of a specifically targeted figure, (3) for a political purpose." Thus, an assassination must contain all three elements or the killing will not meet the requirements of an assassination. Harder's approach is a good starting point because it focuses on the elements of murder—always an illegal concept—and politics—a concept generally reserved for activities not in the sphere of warfare.

Since assassination is universally regarded as murder, it is important to distinguish the concept of murdering another human being, which is always illegal *per se*, from the concept of killing another human being, which may or may not be illegal. Unfortunately, the distinction between murder and killing is often blurred in modern society contributing to a lack of clarity on the subject of assassination. Many postmodernists erroneously believe, for example, that it is somehow immoral for the State to take the life of another human being under any circumstances. For them, the concept of *nullen crimen sine poena* (no crime without punishment) does not extend to taking the life of another human. Hence, in their minds, all killing is both immoral and illegal.

Interestingly, definitional problems regarding the lawfulness of killing another human being can be traced back to the Biblical prohibition on this matter found in the Decalogue at Exodus 20:13 and Deuteronomy 5:17, which many widely regarded English translations, such as the King James version of the Bible, incorrectly render as: "Thou shalt not kill." In fact, the correct translation of the Hebrew into the English is: "Thou shalt not *murder* [emphasis added]." The Hebrew word for kill is not used in the prohibitions of Exodus 20:13 and Deuteronomy 5:17. The Hebrew word that is used is *lo tirtzach* and, according to Biblical scholar R.B. Thieme, Jr., "refers only to the criminal act of homicide, not [for instance] taking the life of enemy soldiers in legitimate warfare." In fact, the Mosaic law is filled with detailed laws that specifically mandate that the State should lawfully kill certain humans convicted under the rule of law for such crimes as murder, kidnapping, etc. The Old Testament principle is properly seen as centering on the duty of the State to protect its citizens from domestic criminal behavior.

In turn, the Mosaic law also sets out a detailed law of war codex which provides for the protection of citizens on exterior lines by specifically authorizing the killing of enemy combatants. From the Judeo tradition, killing enemy combatants in battle is not murder.

Assassination, then, is clearly identified and properly classified as a type of killing that is unlawful, i.e., a form of murder, and murder is always defined as the unlawful killing of a human being with malice aforethought. Although Executive Order 12333 does not define assassination, this silence certainly provides no legitimacy to advocating a "new" definition of assassination which would somehow characterize the concept as anything other than what it is—murder. Furthermore, since murder is an intrinsically illegal act, the definitional problem automatically defeats any reasoned advancement of the proposition that murder, e.g., assassination, can somehow be made lawful.

In other words, if murder is a violation of both domestic United States law and international law, Executive Order 12333 really does not make illegal something that was not already illegal. Therefore, doing away with Executive Order 12333 would not allow the United States to engage in assassination, either in peace or war. Indeed, revoking Executive Order 12333 would only send a negative signal, suggesting to the world that the United States did away with the ban so that it could commit an illegal act of murder.

The word "assassination" is derived from the Arabic word *hashishiyyin*, which refers to the practice of an eleventh century Muslim "brotherhood" that was specifically devoted to killing their religious and political enemies in any manner available. To be sure, the concept of assassination is far more ancient and can apply with equal validity to various infamous incidents in history to include the murder by surprise for political purposes of Gaius Julius Caesar by Brutus and his fellow plotters in 44 B.C., as well as to Hebrew Zealots who conducted random acts of assassination against the occupying Romans and those who supported the Romans in Judea prior to the fall of Jerusalem by the legions of Rome under Titus in 70 A.D. Because American history has witnessed the assassination of several presidents by assassins, to include President Abraham Lincoln, most Americans view assassination as something that is carried out against political figures.

There are even historical instances where the concept of assassination was incorporated as an integral part of certain religious beliefs. For example, when the British entered India in the nineteenth century, they encountered a Hindu cult devoted to the goddess Kali that required its members to commit murder by surprise upon random victims as a form of worship. In contrast to other assassinations, these murders by surprise were not for political purposes, but for religious purposes.

Early Western scholars discussed the matter of assassination both in the context of war and peace. They all viewed assassination as an act directed against the leader of a country. Interestingly, some of the earliest commentators, such as theologian and philosopher Thomas Aquinas, felt that killing an evil sovereign for the common good might be legally justified. However, Aquinas' view held little sway with subsequent scholars, particularly following the 1648 Peace of Westphalia and the rise of the nation-state.

In fact, extremely sensitive to the concept of reciprocity as the key element in international intercourse between nation-states, most seventeenth century scholars rejected the idea of assassinating a leader in peacetime under any circumstances and equally frowned on the use of assassination as a legitimate use of armed force during war. Regardless of the method of attack employed during warfare, the attack should never involve treachery, a term commonly associated with assassination but seldom defined. Influenced by Europe's Code of Chivalry, many international jurists in the area felt that assassination should not be employed in order that the "honor of arms be [sic] preserved and public order and safety of sovereigns and generals not be unduly threatened."

Hugo Grotius, the so-called father of international law and author of the first real codification of rules relating to the conduct of warfare, spent a great deal of time exploring the matter of assassination in the context of war. Grotius used treachery or treacherous murder as an analytical starting point in his commentaries. Understanding the issue of reciprocity, he discussed assassination as something that violates an express or tacit obligation between countries. For Grotius, a violation of natural law or the law of nations certainly occurred if a leader was killed by those that had an obligation to him; such an act of assassination would be treacherous. Conversely, if an enemy leader is ambushed or tricked into a trap by opposing soldiers and killed, then natural law was not violated. Grotius wrote, "It is in fact permissible to kill an enemy in any place whatsoever. According to the law of nations, not only those who do such deeds, but also others who instigate others who do them, are considered free from blame." In any event, Grotius strongly disapproved of putting a monetary price on the head of an enemy leader, reasoning that this would encourage the leader's subjects to kill him treacherously, i.e., by assassination.

Alberico Gentili, another prominent scholar of his day, voiced a similar line of argument regarding assassination. A bit more pragmatic in his approach, Gentili cautioned that killing an enemy leader treacherously—by assassination—might actually incite more anger in the enemy population, causing the enemy population to actually fight harder in order to avenge the murder. In addition, Gentili felt that the very act of assassination itself lacked the valor that one might gain in victory on the field of battle. As did Grotius, Gentili distinguished killing an enemy leader by treacherous means from killing an enemy leader in combat. Death on the battlefield was a lawful "battle circumstance."

Writing in the eighteenth century, scholar Emmerich de Vattel of Switzerland also defined assassination as "murder committed by a means of treachery." In his book entitled *Le Droit des Gens, ou Principes de la Loi Naturelle, appliqués a la Conduite dt aux Affaires des Naions et des Souverains*, De Vattel believed that assassination could apply in both peacetime and war, and applied with equal effect whether the deed was done by the people of the leader or subjects of an opposing country. De Vattel wrote:

> Hence I mean by assassination a murder committed by means of treachery, whether the deed be done by persons who are subjects of him who is assassinated, or his sovereign, and who are therefore traitors, or whether it be done by any other agent who makes his way in as a suppliant or refugee, or as a turncoat, or even as an alien; and I assert that the deed is a shameful and revolting one, both on the part of him who executes and of him who commands it.

Furthermore, De Vattel felt that punishing those individuals who assassinated the sovereign was the responsibility of the world community. De Vattel encouraged all civilized nations "[i]n the interest of the common safety of mankind to join forces and unite to punish" those who engaged in assassination.

Thus, the weight of authority from early Western scholars might be encapsulated as follows: First, most defined assassination as an illegal act most commonly associated with targeting and killing enemy leaders in peacetime or war. Second, all early commentators recognized the lawfulness of targeting and killing the enemy leader in war, although some authorities considered killing the enemy leader in a treacherous manner off the battlefield as an act of assassination.

The early American position on the matter held assassination as an illegal tool in both peacetime and wartime. The first significant mention of assassination occurred during the American Civil War with the adoption by Union forces of a codification of the law of war known as the Lieber Code. On April 24, 1863, the Lieber Code was promulgated as Army General Orders Number 100 by the Secretary of War, E.D. Townsend. In a merger of peacetime and wartime scenarios, Section IX, paragraph 148 states:

The law of war does not allow proclaiming either an individual belonging to the hostile army, or a citizen, or a subject of the hostile government an outlaw, who may be slain without trial by any captor, any more than the modern law of peace allows such international outlawry; on the contrary, it abhors such an outrage. The sternest retaliation should follow the murder committed in consequence of such proclamation, made by whatever authority. Civilized nations look with horror upon offers of rewards for the *assassination of enemies* as relapses into barbarism [emphasis added].

Since the somewhat confusing definition of the Lieber Code, subsequent American legal views on assassination have improved only slightly. Surprisingly, the next significant mention of the concept of assassination is not found until 1956, in FM 27-10, The Law of Land Warfare. Paragraph 31 of FM 27-10, entitled Assassination and Outlawry, quotes Article 23, paragraph b of the Annex to the Hague Convention Number IV, dated 18 October 1907: "It is especially forbidden to kill or wound treacherously individuals belonging to the hostile nation or army." FM 27-10 then goes on to describe this sentence in the context of American military law:

This article is construed as prohibiting assassination, proscription, or outlawry of an enemy, or putting a price upon an enemy's head, as well as offering a reward for an enemy "dead or alive." It does not, however, preclude attacks on individual soldiers or officers of the enemy whether in the zone of hostilities, occupied territory, or elsewhere.

To date, one of the very best efforts to handle the legal aspects of assassination *vis-à-vis* Executive Order 12333 is contained in a 1989 legal memorandum written by H. Hays Parks, the Chief of the International Law Branch, International Affairs Division, Office of the Judge Advocate General. In his memorandum entitled, "Executive Order 12333 and Assassination," Parks does an excellent job explaining the term assassination "in the context of military operations across the conflict spectrum." In essence, Parks correctly concludes that the targeting and killing of hostile or enemy leaders in an act of self-defense is not an act of assassination, even if by surprise.

It is well settled in modern international law that no nation may engage in aggression against any other nation. The definition of aggression is spelled out in the 1957 General Assembly's United Nations Definition of Aggression and certainly includes the act of assassination. According to Article 2(4) of the Charter of the United Nations (U.N. Charter), all member states: "[s]hall refrain in their international relations from the threat or use of force against the territorial integrity or the political independence of any state, or in any manner inconsistent with the Purposes of the United Nations." With this premise so stated, it is equally well recognized that the legitimate use of force is rooted in the inherent right of every nation to act in self-defense if it is the object of aggression.

It is also important to realize that aggressive acts are often carried out by one nation against another without the intent to provoke full scale hostilities or war. Likewise, the nation that is attacked with aggressive force will respond in self-defense with proportional military action with no intention of going to war.

Article 51 of the U.N. Charter codifies the right of a nation attacked with aggressive violence to engage in self-defense. The doctrine of self-defense, of course, is a customary right of ancient origin not created by the United Nations Charter. In pertinent part, Article 51 reads: "Nothing in the present Charter shall impair the inherent right of individual or collective self-defense if an armed attack occurs against a Member of the United Nations." Thus, the State that engages in acts of aggression, or the unlawful use of force, may never claim that it is acting under the self-defense provisions of Article 51 of the U.N. Charter. Furthermore, apart from the fundamental requirement of proportionality in the employment of violence in self-defense, the use of self-defense can occur in times of peace as well as war. In other words, even if a state of armed conflict does not exist, the customary principle of self-defense is a separate basis for the use of force. As long as the use of force in self-defense adheres to the customary standards of necessity and proportionally it is lawful.

On numerous occasions, the United States has lawfully exercised the inherent right of self-defense against individuals or States in both peacetime and wartime environments. President Bill Clinton, for example, sent cruise missiles against several al-Qa'eda terrorist training camps in Afghanistan following the 1998 al-Qa'eda attack on the United States embassies in Africa. This military action occurred during peacetime and was permitted under the rule of law regarding self-defense. Even if the leader Osama bin Laden was targeted in the attacks, President Clinton's actions would not be classified as attempted assassination.

Similarly, in the 1991 Gulf War (and the 2003 campaign), Saddam Hussein himself was a legitimate military target and his death by coalition forces would not have been an assassination. As the commander in chief of the Iraqi military, Saddam Hussein could have been legally targeted and killed. In war, enemy combatants are legitimate targets for attack so long as the hostile forces are not killed with treachery, e.g., while legitimately visiting a protected place such as a hospital. The fact that Hussein was not specifically targeted was clearly a political decision, although President George H. Bush is said to have remarked: "We're not in the position of targeting Saddam Hussein, but no one will weep for him when he is gone." Despite the lawfulness of killing the enemy leader in wartime, there often exists an unwillingness to specifically target that individual.

Parks correctly recognizes that a State may use military force in peacetime if it is acting in self-defense. Such acts are not assassination:

> Historically, the United States has resorted to the use of military force in peacetime where another nation has failed to discharge its international responsibilities in protecting U.S. citizens from acts of violence originating in or launched from its sovereign territory, or has been culpable in aiding and abetting international criminal activities.

After listing several historical examples of the United States' use of military force in self-defense, including the 1986 bombing of "terrorist related targets in Libya," Parks concludes: "Hence there is historical precedent for the use of military force to capture or kill individuals whose peacetime actions constitute a direct threat to U.S. citizens or U.S. national security."

Indeed, immediately following the terrorist attacks of September 11, 2001, the Congress of the United States clearly recognized the inherent right of self-defense. Again, while Congress never "declared war" under the provisions of Article I of the Constitution, they quickly passed a joint resolution which left no doubt as to their desire to authorize the President of the United States to use military force in self-defense. Among other things, the Congressional Resolution recognized the inherent right of self-defense,

> under the Constitution to take action to deter and prevent acts of international terrorism against the United States...[and] authorized [the President] to use all necessary and appropriate force

against those nations, organizations, or persons he determines planned, authorized, committed, or aided the terrorist attacks that occurred on September 11, 2001, or harbored such organizations or persons, in order to prevent any future acts of international terrorism against the United States by such nations, organizations or persons.

Congress clearly understood that targeting individual terrorists associated with the attacks on the United States was not assassination, but the appropriate response in self-defense to unlawful aggression. President Obama has most certainly fully embraced this concept.

From a legal perspective, the most challenging issue associated with the continuing War on Terror is the fact that both the nature of the enemy and the nature of the threat has changed dramatically, and so the response under the rule of law has to change. In his State of the Union message of January 29, 2002, President George W. Bush signaled his resolve that the United States of America would "not permit the world's most dangerous regimes to threaten us with the world's most destructive weapons."

In the context of killing individuals, can the United States go beyond the rhetoric and target for death a known terrorist or individual leader of a nation that sponsors or supports terrorism? If the use of a weapon of mass destruction by a fanatical terrorist is on the near horizon, do the traditional international rules related to the use of force, i.e., only used in self-defense, actually work in the real world of the al-Qa'eda virtual State? In other words, must the United States idly wait for a catastrophic terrorist attack before it can respond, or does a threatened nation have the right to engage in preemptive self-defense against those individuals that are planning the attack?

As previously covered, the most striking instance in modern history occurred in the 1967 Six Day War when Israel, anticipating a full-scale armed attack from Egypt, Syria, Jordan, and others, attacked Arab airfields first. The doctrine of preemptive self-defense holds that when a State is faced with an imminent armed attack it may resort to proportional acts of preemptive self-defense. Other scholars view the concept of anticipatory self-defense as inconclusive. For example, one textbook on national security law writes: "Past practice is inconclusive, but it suggests that a state facing an imminent and potentially devastating armed attack may escape condemnation for a preemptive response."

Parks lists three forms of self-defense that the United States recognizes as appropriate for unilateral action under the inherent right of self-defense: "(a) Against an actual use of force, or hostile act. (b) Preemptive self defense against an imminent use of force. (c) Self defense against a continuing threat." Parks agrees that the preemptive use of military force against terrorists would be permissible and would not be assassination. Parks specifically asserts:

This right of self defense would be appropriate to the attack of terrorist leaders where their actions pose a continuing threat to U.S. citizens or the national security of the United States. As with an attack on a guerrilla infrastructure, the level to which attacks could be carried out against individuals within a terrorist infrastructure would be a policy rather than a legal decision.

Nevertheless, the fact that a nation is acting under the rubric of self-defense does not allow that nation to employ military force in any manner it so desires. The State acting in self-defense is still required to adhere to a set of binding international rules associated with how that force is employed. In time of war, these rules are known as the law of war or the law of armed conflict. However, in the modern era, where the line between war and peacetime is inexorably blurred, many of the most basic rules regarding military necessity, unnecessary suffering and proportionality apply equally to the peacetime use of military force.

The law of armed conflict describes lawful targets which can be destroyed in the proper context of military operations. The general principle is that the nation acting in self-defense—whether in a peacetime or wartime environment—may kill the enemy, whether lawful combatants or unprivileged belligerents, and may include in either category civilians who take part in the hostilities. An enemy combatant, whether part of an organized military or a civilian who undertakes military activities, is a legitimate target at all times and may be lawfully killed, even if by surprise. This includes the leader of the hostile forces.

Thus, unannounced attacks involving the element of surprise do not preclude the use of violence. All "combatants are subject to attack if they are participating in hostilities through fire, maneuver and assault; providing logistic, communications, administrative, or other support." In addition, there is "no distinction made between an attack accomplished by aircraft, missile, naval gunfire, artillery, mortar, infantry assault, ambush, land mine or booby-trap, a single shot by a sniper, a commando attack, or other, similar means." It is not an act of assassination to kill individuals in this context.

In turn, the law of armed conflict absolutely prohibits the killing of noncombatants, except as a matter of collateral damage where civilians may be killed ancillary to the lawful attack of a military objective. Civilians that maintain close proximity to a military objective assume the risk of being killed by enemy fire. Since they are neither specifically targeted individuals nor are they killed by the use of treachery, the killing of such civilians is not assassination. On the other hand, specifically targeting innocent civilians as a military objective is always illegal and criminal.

Since President Obama took office, CIA drone attacks (unmanned aircraft) on suspected enemy combatants in Afghanistan, Pakistan, Yemen, and other locations have killed well over 500 people. The vast majority of the 500 are low-level fighters linked to the Taliban or al-Qa'eda. The collateral deaths of civilians in these "death from above" attacks is unknown. Of particular note is President Obama's authorization to kill American-born Anwar al-Awlaki, a notorious al-Qa'eda cleric. As the United States continues to conduct preemptive self-defense strikes against its enemies in the War on Terror, it is efficacious to consider how the Israelis have employed the concept to target and kill known senior terrorist leaders in the continuing Palestinian conflict. In fact, the United States has generally supported the Israeli military's use of preemptive force in regards to the killing of certain Palestinian terrorists. Former United States Deputy Secretary of Defense, Paul Wolfowitz, often cited the Israeli use of preemption with approval, drawing an early parallel to what Americans must do to win the War on Terror. Wolfowitz noted, "Our approach has been to aim at prevention and not merely punishment. We are at war. Self-defense requires prevention and sometimes preemption."

In this light, the killing of known Islamic militant terrorists is not assassination, but an act of preemptive self-defense. Israel, of course, does not call these acts assassination, although the term is often used by various individuals to describe the killings of those responsible for the waves of suicide bombings against innocent Israeli citizens. Instead, the Israelis refer to the acts of killing as "targeted thwarting, liquidation, or elimination." A June 2001 poll taken at Tel Aviv University found that 77 percent of Israeli Jews approved of the policy. Dr. Ely Karmon of the Israel-based Institute for Counter Terrorism believes that the Israeli use of preemptive self-defense is in fact the best means of responding to the terrorists as the practice is largely carried out with concern for collateral civilian casualties. "They [the Israeli military] are not bombing indiscriminately or using heavy weapons as necessary to hit Hezbolla outposts in Lebanon. Here we have much greater control, greater intelligence, and the ability to act."

One of the most high-level public killings was of the Secretary General of the Popular Front for the Liberation of Palestine, Mustapha Zibri, on August 27, 2001. An Israeli helicopter fired two rockets and obliterated his office in Ramallah. Zibri's office was three doors down from Yassir Arafat's. The mechanics for how the killings are carried out generally start with Israeli intelligence that process reports and information from a variety of sources to include Palestinian collaborators. Using this information the government compiles a list of people that they have concluded are definitely involved in terrorist activity. The next step is to give the Palestinian Authority the list of suspects for arrest, which proves futile due to the fact that the Palestinian Authority refuses to act on the information. Thus, when an opportunity to kill the terrorist presents itself, the approval to kill is given and Israeli helicopters or snipers kill the terrorist by surprise attack at a location calculated to reduce collateral damages to civilians.

In summary, assassination is an unlawful killing in violation of the rule of law. Whether conducted in peacetime or wartime, assassination is absolutely forbidden under international law even in the absence of an executive order supposedly banning the practice. Anyone who carries out an act of assassination would be guilty of either murder or a war crime, depending on the circumstances. Furthermore, anyone who ordered the assassination would be guilty of either murder or a war crime under the concept of command responsibility.

At the end of the day, the use of force in legitimate acts of self-defense does not qualify as assassination. Those who think that the United States is somehow restricted by Executive Order 12333 from targeting terrorists or rogue nations that threaten to conduct terrorist acts are mistaken. If it is the case that Executive Order 12333 causes more confusion than not in understanding the applicable rule of law, should it be repealed? One commentator has argued that the "failure of the executive order to outline exactly what it prohibits has set planners and operators adrift." But a stronger case can be made by pointing out that it is the public, politicians, and commentators that are most confused by the executive order, not the military planners and operators. The military generally understands that the proper application of force in self-defense does not violate Executive Order 12333. Politicians and commentators seem most susceptible to succumbing to the temptation to associate an overbroad interpretation to the ban on assassination.

As a practical matter, it is fundamentally obvious that no American president will ever repeal Executive Order 12333 unless he immediately replaces it with a better product. The resulting negative repercussions in the sphere of public relations alone would render such a move remarkably insensate. The better product, of course, would require a document consisting of some pages that clearly defines assassination and then distinguishes those circumstances where the lawful use of force could be applied. As America continues its War on Terror, it is vitally important to operate under clearly framed principles under the rule of law and not shrouded ambiguities and innuendos. Our enemies as well as our friends and allies need to understand that the Untied States of America operates under the rule of law. As Professor John Norton Moore of Virginia so aptly put it:

> Law, however, is vitally important. Even in the short run, law serves as a standard of appraisal for national actions and as a means of communicating intentions to both friend and foe, and perceptions about lawfulness can profoundly influence both national and international support for particular actions.

4.12 The Constitution and the War on Terror

To some, the War on Terror portends a society in which the rights of the individual will more and more have to give way in favor of ever increasing security measures designed to vindicate the expanding desire of protecting the safety of the public from global terrorism. It may be a correct assessment that the continuing War on Terror makes our civil rights *vulnerable* to erosion, but the so-called "slippery slope" argument which resists all changes in the law must be viewed against the clear and present threat of al-Qa'eda-styled terrorist organizations and their possible use of weapons of mass destruction. The all too real specter of mass casualties, billions of dollars in physical damage, and civil disorder absolutely demands that the federal government fulfill its primary mission of ensuring the safety and viability of its citizens. As Supreme Court Justice Robert Jackson remarked in *Terminiello v. Chicago*, "[t]he constitutional Bill of Rights…[is not] a suicide pact." Jackson went on to say: "The choice is not between order and liberty. It is between liberty with order and anarchy without either."

On the other hand, there are many who object to law enforcement tools such as the USA PATRIOT Act as an unconstitutional violation of civil liberties. According to Gregory Nojeim, the former Associate Director of the ACLU's Washington Office: "These new and unchecked powers could be used against American citizens who are not under criminal investigation, immigrants who are here within our borders legally and also those whose First Amendment activities are deemed to be threats to national security by the Attorney General." Despite efforts by various ideologues to demonize the USA PATRIOT Act, the provisions are actually a judicious effort to stop future terror attacks, and in 2006 and 2009 a majority of the members of Congress voted to extend the vast majority of the provisions. Commenting on the number of local governments that had passed resolutions or laws against the USA PATRIOT Act, a Justice Department spokesman noted that many of the ordinances were based on "erroneous" information and that the USA PATRIOT Act "has been one of the most important tools Congress has given the government to fight terrorism and prevent terrorist attacks." In order to thwart future attacks, law enforcement must have the legal ability to gather information on suspected terrorists in order to stop them before they attack.

Another issue of debate that occurred in 2006 was the Bush Administration's "data mining" program that targeted the international calls between terrorist suspects abroad and individuals in the United States. This warrantless program was conducted without a FISA court order by the National Security Agency (NSA) and with the help of the nation's largest telecommunications firms. While the program did not include listening to telephone calls, legal and security experts debated the government's argument that President Bush was acting under his wartime authority as the Commander in Chief under Article II of the Constitution and the Congressional Authorization for Use of Military Force after 9/11. Indeed, echoing Chief Justice John Marshall announcement in *Marbury v. Madison* that "a legislative act contrary to the Constitution is not law," the FISA Court of Review in 2002 affirmed that FISA did not prohibit the President from exercising his independent constitutional power.

While the FISA rules regarding collection of foreign intelligence in the United States is clearly spelled out in statute, the question of whether or not the Executive Branch's Article II power trumps FISA restrictions has never been decided by the United States Supreme Court. In other words, despite the fact that a string of Presidents have operated under the parameters of FISA when conducting foreign intelligence, it is still an open question from the perspective of the Supreme Court as to whether the President's Article II power exempts him from the Fourth Amendment warrant requirements when foreign intelligence is conducted, even if that foreign intelligence collection takes place in the United

States proper. If the rulings of federal circuit courts are measured in this question, it certainly appears that the President possesses independent Constitutional authority to conduct warrantless electronic surveillance in the sphere of foreign intelligence collection. In fact, every federal court of appeals to consider the matter has concluded that the President has independent constitutional authority to conduct warrantless electronic surveillance of foreign powers and their agents.

The last time that the Supreme Court spoke at any length on the issue of the President's authority to conduct warrantless electronic surveillance in foreign intelligence instances was in 1972. In *United States v. United States District Court* (*Keith*) the Court was asked to rule on a number of legal challenges brought on behalf of three defendants who had been convicted of conspiracy to bomb a CIA office in Michigan. The plot had been discovered by use of an electronic wiretap authorized by then Attorney General John Mitchell, without a judicial warrant. While the Court ruled that warrantless domestic electronic surveillance related to ordinary domestic law enforcement was unconstitutional, it clearly drew a strong distinction between such common criminal investigations and the matter of legitimate foreign intelligence electronic surveillance. Discussing a compelling interest by the government in national security matters, the Court indicated that there could be circumstances where a specific electronic surveillance could be conducted without a judicial warrant if it was "reasonable both in relation to the legitimate need of Government for intelligence information and the protected rights of our citizens." The strong distinction between conducting electronic surveillance on domestic targets with no ties to a "foreign power" and the President's surveillance power towards actions of "foreign powers, within or without this country," was set out at both the beginning of the per curium opinion and at the end. At the beginning, the Court stated: "Further, the instant case requires no judgment on the scope of the President's surveillance power with respect to the activities of foreign powers, within or without this country." Near the end of the opinion, the Court wrote:

> We emphasize, before concluding this opinion, the scope of our decision. As stated at the outset, this case involves only the domestic aspects of national security. We have not addressed and express no opinion as to, the issues which may be involved with respect to activities of foreign powers and their agents.

If the *Keith* decision passed on the opportunity to fully address the President's independent constitutional authority to conduct warrantless electronic surveillance when the target was a foreign power or an agent of a foreign power, subsequent federal circuit courts have been rather consistent in their view. Every U.S. Court of Appeals to address the matter—both prior to and after *Keith*—has held that the Executive Branch, by virtue of the President's inherent authority under Article II, has the power to conduct warrantless electronic surveillance for national security reasons related to foreign powers and their agents.

In summary, the government has always taken steps to curtail civil liberties in times of crisis. In the past, some of the measures have been clearly unconstitutional, e.g., President Lincoln's suspension of the writ of habeas corpus for jailed "Northern" American citizens, or President Roosevelt's internment of thousands of U.S. citizens of Japanese descent. Compared with these abuses, the government's efforts in the War on Terror are hardly extreme. In fact, the American people have overwhelmingly approved of the overall performance of the government in finding a working balance between defending their freedoms and protecting their freedoms. Nevertheless, as the federal government makes policy and moves the nation in the War on Terror, it is prudent to well recall the caution of George Washington: "[T]he price of freedom is eternal vigilance." Accordingly, all measures employed to combat terrorism must be within the bounds of democratic principles and the rule of law. More importantly, so-called extraordinary laws should be proportionate to the terrorist threat and frequently reviewed, revised, and rescinded if no longer needed. For instance, the London bombings of July 2005 caused the British to develop new security laws that seriously challenge the foundation of freedom of speech by making it illegal to glorify or indirectly incite terrorism. Obviously, the line between free speech and security is greatly stressed in the War on Terror because this is not a war in the classic sense. This war will not end with a formal surrender. Thus, changes in law that appear necessary in the name of security for the moment may become an unwanted fabric of our society for future generations. If one is to avoid the slippery slope, then marked and clear legal notches must be set out beyond which we as Americans will not pass.

4.13 Questions for Discussion

1. *Legitimate targets.* A major debate exists surrounding the relationship terrorist agents must have to a terrorist organization in order to be considered legitimate military targets in the War on Terror. Considering the different classifications for terrorism discussed in Chapter 1, who is a legitimate target in the War on Terror: individuals or countries? Should individual terrorists be targeted militarily or judicially? Why might the favored response for a nation to a terrorist attack be to use military force as opposed to other methods? If the events of September 11, 2001, had not occurred, would your answer be the same?

2. *Financing terrorism.* The United States Code provides: "Whoever knowingly provides material support or resources to a foreign terrorist organization, or attempts or conspires to do so, shall be fined under this title or imprisoned not more than 15 years, or both, and, if the death of any person results, shall be imprisoned for any term of years or for life." 18 U.S.C.A. § 2339B(a)(1). In *United States v. Hammoud*, 381 F.3d at 316. (4th Cir. 2004) defendant, Mohammed Hammoud challenged his conviction in district court after he was found to have given aid to the foreign terrorist organization, Hizballah. Can this law aimed at criminalizing financial contributions to terrorist organizations do more to deter terrorism than laws which punish terrorist acts?

3. *Why did the United States refuse to sign Protocol I to the Geneva Conventions?* The United States is not a signatory to Protocol Additional to the Geneva Conventions of August 12, 1946, and Relating to the Protection of Victims of International Armed Conflicts, June 8, 1977, 1125 U.N.T.S. 3. Protocol I seeks to extend coverage to non-international conflicts in which "peoples are fighting against colonial domination and alien occupation and against racist regimes in the exercise of their right to self-determination." See generally Abraham Sofaer, *The U.S. Decision Not to Ratify Protocol I to the Geneva Conventions on the Protection of War Victims*, 82 AM. J. INT'L. L. 784 (1988).

4. *Lawful detention?* In September 1868, the U.S. District Court for the Southern District of Florida denied a writ of habeas corpus for Dr. Samuel Mudd, a civilian citizen of Maryland, who had been convicted by a military tribunal for his part in the Lincoln assassination of April 14, 1865. *Ex Parte Mudd*, 17 F. Cas. 954 (S.D. Fla. 1868) (No. 9,899). On June 30, 1865, the military

tribunal convicted Dr. Mudd and sentenced him to life in prison. Dr. Mudd was transferred to a prison in Florida where he filed a writ of habeas corpus relying on *Ex Parte Milligan*. In denying the petition, Judge Thomas J. Boynton distinguished the murder of Lincoln as a military crime, even though the war had arguably ended prior to the assassination of Lincoln. The appeal of this decision reached the United States Supreme Court in February 1869, but was dismissed by Chief Justice Chase as moot due to the fact that President Andrew Johnson had pardoned Dr. Mudd and two other civilians. Was Mudd's detention lawful?

5. *Defining enemy combatants.* DOD Directive 2310.01E, entitled *The Department of Defense Detainee Program,* dated September 5, 2006, describes an enemy combatant as "a person engaged in hostilities against the United States or its coalition partners during *armed conflict* [emphasis added]." Is the DOD term "armed conflict" consistent with the 2009 Military Commissions Act definition of unprivileged enemy belligerents?

6. *Military commission or federal court*? Ahmed Ghailani, was labeled by President Bush as an enemy combatant and detained at Guantanamo Bay. He was involved in the 1998 East African embassy bombings. In 2009 President Obama ordered Ghailani released and had him transferred for criminal trial in a federal court in New York. Should Ghailani have been transferred out of military custody and not tried by military commission? Is it appropriate or legal for the Obama Administration to process some al-Qa'eda members through federal district courts while others are processed through military commissions per the 2009 Military Commissions Act? Should U.S. citizenship really make a difference?

7. *Free speech vs. material support.* In October 2006, Adam Yahiuye Gadahn, an American citizen from California was indicted by a federal grand jury and charged with treason and providing material support to al-Qa'eda per 18 USC § 2339B. Gadahn has appeared in numerous al-Qa'eda videos where he praises the terror group and calls on others to participate in murder and violence against the United States. The form of support is identified as "personnel" and "services." Presumably the theory is that Gadahn provided himself as personnel to al-Qa'eda. Can 2339B lawfully function as the equivalent of a membership prohibition? Due to the expansive reach of the Material Support Act, Professor Norman Abrams urges legal observers to "ask whether and to what extent the residual and preventative uses of these sections are beginning to trespass upon fundamental values of liberty." (Norman Abrams, *The Material Support Terrorism Offenses: Perspectives Derived from the (Early) Model Penal Code*, 1 J. NAT'L SEC. L. POL. 5, 6-7 (2005). Do you agree?

8. *Privacy concerns.* Bomb-sniffing dogs that are trained to smell bomb components that screening devices might miss are being employed at some airports. Is this approach more or less objectionable than the use of TSA airport screeners trained to spot "suspicious behavior" among passengers? What privacy issues are raised?

9. *Advancing the proper rule of law.* In February 2006, the U.N. Commission on Human Rights issued a joint report on the situation of the detainees at Guantanamo Bay. Based on interviews of "former Guantanamo Bay detainee's currently residing or detained in France, Spain and

the United Kingdom," lawyers for detainees and "information available in the public domain" (the Rapporteurs refused to visit the detention facility at Guantanamo Bay for a first hand inspection) they concluded that the United States was engaging in "torture" in violation of international law. The Rapporteurs also found that the detention itself was illegal and that the "United States Government should either expeditiously bring all Guantanamo Bay detainees to trial [via domestic criminal or an international tribunal] or release them without further delay." What premise did the Rapporteurs reject in making the second finding? Why is the first finding flawed?

Selected Bibliography

Aquinas, St. Thomas. ON POLITICS AND ETHICS, (Paul E. Sigmund trans. 1988).

Bank, Aaron. OSS TO GREEN BERETS, 1986.

Chesney, Robert M., *Federal Prosecution of Terrorism-Related Offenses: Conviction and Sentencing Data in Light of the "Soft-Sentence" and "Data-Reliability Critiques*, 11 LEWIS & CLARK L. REV. 862 (Winter 2007).

De Vattel, E. THE LAW OF NATIONS OR THE PRINCIPLES OF INTERNATIONAL LAW APPLIED TO THE CONDUCT AND TO THE AFFAIRS OF NATIONS AND OF SOVEREIGNS, (Charles G. Fenwick trans. 1916).

Dep't of Army, Field Manual 27-10. *The Law of Land Warfare* (July 1956).

Dunoff, Jeffrey L., Steven R. Ratner, and David Wippman. INTERNATIONAL LAW NORMS, Actors Process, 2002.

Elliott, H.W. THE TRIAL AND PUNISHMENT OF WAR CRIMINALS IN THE "NEW WORLD ORDER." (unpublished doctoral of juridical science thesis 1996) (available at the Rare Book Room, U. of Virginia School of Law).

Ford, Franklin L. POLITICAL MURDER: FROM TYRANNICIDE TO TERRORISM, 1985.

Franck, Thomas M., and Michael J. Glennon. FOREIGN RELATIONS AND NATIONAL SECURITY LAW, 1993.

Geneva Convention of August 12, 1949, Relative to the Treatment of Prisoners of War, 6 U.S.T. 3316, T.I.A.S. No. 3364, 75 U.N.T.S. 135.

Gentili, Alberico. DE IURE BELLI LIBRI TRES, John C. Rolfe trans., 1933.

Grotius, Hugo. THE LAW OF WAR AND PEACE (1625), *reprinted in* THE LAW OF WAR: A DOCUMENTARY HISTORY. L. Freidman. (ed.) 1972.

Hartigan, Richard Shelly. LIEBER'S CODE AND THE LAW OF WAR, 1983.

Heddings, Raymond E. U.S. ROLES IN PROVIDING HUMANITARIAN ASSISTANCE FOLLOW-ING NBC ACCIDENTS/INCIDENTS: THE LEGAL CONSIDERATIONS, 1999.

Kerwin, Cornelius M. RULEMAKING: HOW GOVERNMENT AGENCIES WRITE LAW AND MAKE POLICY, 1999.

McHugh, William. *Forcible Self-help in International Law,* 25 NAVAL WAR C. REV. 61 (1972).

Moore, John Norton. LAW AND THE GRENADA MISSION, 1984.

Parks, W. Hays. *Memorandum of Law: Executive Order 12333 and Assassination.* THE ARMY LAW-YER, Dec.1989, at 4.

Pumphrey, Carolyn W. (ed.) TRANSNATIONAL THREATS: BLENDING LAW ENFORCEMENT AND MILITARY STRATEGIES, available at http://carlisle-www.army.mil/usassi/welcome.htm. 2000.

Rosen, Richard D., *America's Professional Military Ethic and the Treatment of Captured Enemy Com-batants in the Global War on Terror*, 5 GEORGETOWN J. OF LAW & PUB. Pol. 113 (Winter 2007).

Scales, Robert H., Jr. FUTURE WARFARE, 1999.

Schindler, Dietrich, and Jiai Toman. THE LAWS OF ARMED CONFLICT 3, 1988.

Schmitt, Michael N. *State Sponsored Assassination in International and Domestic Law.* 17 YALE J. INT'L L. 679 (1992).

Sloan, Steven. BEATING INTERNATIONAL TERRORISM, 1986.

Thieme, R.B., Jr., FREEDOM THROUGH MILITARY VICTORY, 1977.

Chapter 5

Necessity and Rationale for the Law of War—Lessons from My Lai

Nothing is new under the sun.

—Ecclesiastes 1: 9-10

It is often remarked that what we learn from history is that we learn nothing from history. This truism has been attributed to the German philosopher Georg Hegel, but the principle is certainly one of ancient origins, reflecting the fact that the human race has generally exhibited a total inability to learn even the most elementary historical lessons. Of course, the tragedy is that this need not be so; mankind can learn from history. Indeed, if history teaches mankind anything about avoiding the mistakes and disasters of the past, it is that it must first understand the historical lessons—lessons often realized only after the expenditure of incredible amounts of human blood and treasure—and then inculcate those lessons in each succeeding generation.

In the War on Terror, the most critical lesson is that the application of lawful violence is a necessary ingredient in defeating those who employ, or seek to employ, violence in an unlawful manner. The concept of lawful violence, of course, refers to the requirement that the international law of war must be fully followed. Those who violate the law of war commit war crimes.

To a large degree, from Valley Forge (1778) to Afghanistan (2001) and Iraq (2003), the United States military can take full credit for a commendable record in its adherence to the law of war. This is because of its commitment to institutionalizing certain truisms which might be encapsulated in the old saw that "[a] right thing must be done in a right way or it is wrong."

189

Thus, defeating the enemy—a right thing—must be done under the law of war—in a right way—or the entire activity is wrong. This assessment is not only true in the day-to-day functioning of a democratic society, it is fundamentally necessary for the continuation of that democracy. On the other hand, there is no such thing as a "clean" war. In its War on Terror, America has made a significant number of tactical errors in the use of its military, ranging from friendly fire incidents that have killed American soldiers and the soldiers of its coalition partners, to the unintended deaths of non-combatants by coalition military fire power. While these tragedies have been leveraged by some in order to criticize the legitimacy of the American led effort to employ force against its enemies on the battlefield, all such attempts to denigrate the United States pale in the wake of the prisoner abuse scandal at Abu Ghraib. The 2003 release of photographs of American soldiers abusing Iraqi detainees at the Abu Ghraib prison in Iraq created a firestorm of concern that threatened to derail several of the most fundamental policy and legal pillars on which America conducted the War on Terror. While it is now well established that the abuses were not systemic, they provided a propaganda bonanza to the terrorists. The War on Terror is not won or lost on the battlefield; it is won or lost in the sphere of public opinion.

Accordingly, it is necessary to explore the law of war and the rationale and necessity for abiding by those rules. Because these lessons are timeless, the very best lesson plan for the United States flows not from Abu Ghraib, but from a notorious war crime committed by American forces in the Vietnam War—the My Lai massacre.

The War on Terror has involved the use of traditional combat techniques last seen in the 2003 war against Saddam Hussein, where two armed groups of soldiers engaged in open combat. It also involves the more troubling type of combat which Americans continue to face in Iraq and Afghanistan, and encountered in larger measure in the Indo-China conflict, where the Viet Cong and their Communist allies regularly violated the law of war by refusing to wear distinctive uniforms, hiding amongst the civilian population, torturing and murdering American prisoners of war, and murdering noncombatants by the thousands. Tragically, the Vietnam War also saw several instances of abuse of the law of war by American soldiers, the most notorious being the massacre at My Lai. While American forces in Afghanistan and Iraq have generally exhibited broad compliance with the law of armed conflict and an understanding that ethical conduct and military prowess go hand in hand, it is absolutely imperative that the significance of the lessons learned at My Lai are revisited and impressed on every American soldier as the nation once again faces an illegal enemy combatant who engages in the same tactics as the Viet Cong and views our adherence to the rule of law as a weakness.

For many Americans, the knowledge of enemy violations of the law of war elicits a negative reaction to the United States being required to follow the law of war. In other words, if the terrorists and allies of the terrorists do not abide by the rules, e.g., militants in Iraq have decapitated several American soldiers and engaged in the wholesale slaughter of innocent civilians, why should America? For this reason it is imperative that individuals who are unfamiliar with the law of war understand both the basic rationale and the necessity for the law of war. This applies to the American people in general and, more importantly, to the fighting men who actually engage the enemy in the War on Terror.

Again, while it may seem out of place to discuss the law of war in the War on Terror against the lessons learned at My Lai, there is no better model to serve as the perfect vehicle for learning or re-learning the necessity and rationale for the rules of armed conflict. Furthermore, it is equally necessary that American forces impress upon their allies the need to comply with the law of war. In fact, reports filtered out of Afghanistan in 2002 that some of our Afghan allies had engaged in violations of the law of war. One incident is said to have occurred in the case of the deaths of 200 Taliban prisoners of war that died while being transported in shipping containers from the battlefield to internment camps. Similarly, abuses by the new Iraq and Afghan security forces are becoming regular fare. Not only is America relentlessly scrutinized and judged on how it complies with the law of war, but the conduct of our allies is also factored into the assessment. Criminal behavior casts a cloud over both the forces and the new governments of Afghanistan and Iraq.

As a nation that is governed by the rule of law, it is vital that America validate—for itself and for the civilized world—the legitimacy of its War on Terror by the manner in which it conducts that war. Clearly, the United States cannot claim that its forces are the "good guys" unless the rules of armed conflict are meticulously observed. Enforcement of the rules of war is a demonstration to the world and the American people that America is waging a *jus in bello*. No doubt, the attention of the world has shifted from the murderous machinations of the al-Qa'eda and their like, to an extreme focus on how well the United States and its allies adhere to all aspects of the rule of law in battling these people. For better or worse, this phenomenon is a reality. No one shows interest regarding the fact that the "bad guys" behave in gross violation of the law of war as their very *modus vivendi*. After all, that is precisely why they are the "bad guys." On the other hand, the world has an intense interest in how the "good guys" perform. If a State claims that their cause is just, they must act accordingly.

5.1 The Law of War

Warfare is not a novel phenomenon: it is as old as human history itself. Even a cursory review of the practice reveals that all cultures and societies have participated in warfare, either in defense or in aggression. Prior to the adoption of the U.N. Charter, which mandates that the analysis for determining the legitimate use of force turn under the self-defense provisions of Article 51, the concept of waging a just war was known as *jus ad bellum*. *Jus ad bellum* encompassed several elements to include: (1) the nation had a just cause; (2) the nation was acting under the legitimate governing authority; (3) the nation had just intentions; (4) the nation issued a public declaration of the causes for the use of force and the intentions associated with the use of that force; (5) the nation considered the proportionality in the results; (6) the nation demonstrated that the use of force was only used as a last resort; and (7) there existed a reasonable hope of success.

As stated, international law no longer recognizes *jus ad bellum* as a viable legal tool in determining when military force is lawful. Nevertheless, as a practical matter, *jus ad bellum* still has great moral weight in the context of demonstrating the validity of the use of force and ensuring the continuation of public support by a pluralistic society.

In tandem with the concept of *jus ad bellum*, the term *jus in bello* refers to just conduct in war or, simply put, abiding by the law of war. This means that a nation that goes to war engages enemy targets under the concepts of military necessity, proportionality, and unnecessary suffering. In contrast to *jus ad bellum*, *jus in bello* is still a recognized concept in international law. As a matter of fact, as long as mankind has practiced war there have been rules to lessen and regulate the attendant sufferings associated with warfare.

To the uninitiated in the study of war, it seems somewhat incongruent that one of Man's most violent activities should be governed by rules of conduct. Some writers, such as Leo Tolstoy, have even argued that the very establishment of rules which seek to regulate warfare are per se immoral because such rules wrongfully cloak war with a form of legitimacy and are therefore counterproductive to the goal of eliminating the scourge of war. Tolstoy advanced the notion that the waging of war should not be regulated at all: "when it becomes too horrible, rational men will outlaw war altogether."

Fortunately, most serious thinkers reject this utopian attitude, acknowledging the necessity of rules of conduct to mitigate the various categories of sufferings that are the natural consequence of war. The law of war was never intended to be an idealistic proscription against war.

The current corpus of the law of war consists of all of those laws, by treaty and customary principles, which are applicable to warfare. Most nations have bound themselves by international agreements to follow the law of war. Those nations that have not signed these international agreements are nevertheless bound by them if the rules have reached the status of customary international law. Customary international law comes from observing past uniformities among nations of a norm or standard that has reached widespread acceptance in the international community. Evidence of customary international law may be found in judicial decisions, the writing of noted jurists, diplomatic correspondence, and other evidence concerning the practices of States.

The cornerstone of the law of war is the Geneva Conventions of 1949. In the modern era, every nation on the planet is absolutely obligated to abide by the Geneva Conventions of 1949, whether they have signed the Conventions or not. The 1949 Geneva Conventions cover four categories:

- Geneva Convention of August 12, 1949, for the Amelioration of the Condition of the Wounded and Sick in Armed Forces in the Field;
- Geneva Convention of August 12, 1949, for the Amelioration of the Condition of the Wounded, Sick, and Shipwrecked Members of Armed Forces at Sea;
- Geneva Convention of August 12, 1949, Relative to the Treatment of Prisoners of War; and
- Geneva Convention of August 12, 1949, Relative to the Protections of Civilian Persons in Time of War.

In general, the rules of warfare are focused both on the proper targeting of military objectives and the treatment of enemy detainees, prisoners of war, and other noncombatants. Examples of the law of war include such common sense rules as the requirement to treat prisoners and detainees humanely; they may not be abused under any circumstances. Also, the prohibition on targeting for military attack civilians or protected places, such as hospitals and religious sites, and the duty to treat all noncombatants with dignity and respect are integral components of the law of war.

In the War on Terror, Congress has not declared war under the authority granted in Article I of the Constitution. This fact makes absolutely no difference in regard to America's obligation to follow the law of war. In fact, the law of war immediately applies whenever there is an international armed conflict involving two or more States, regardless of how the parties to that conflict care to label the conflict.

Mirroring the Geneva Conventions, the United States military has codified the law of war in FM 27-10. FM 27-10 affirms that the basic goal of the law of war is to limit the impact of the inevitable evils of war by:

- protecting both combatants and noncombatants from unnecessary suffering;
- safeguarding certain fundamental human rights of persons who fall into the hands of the enemy, particularly prisoners of war, the wounded and sick, and civilians; and
- facilitating the restoration of peace.

Violations of the law of war are called war crimes. In FM 27-10: "The term war crime is the technical expression for a violation of the law of war by any person or persons, military or civilian. Every violation of the law of war is a war crime." The definition in FM 27-10 would include both customary and treaty law within the parameters of the law of war. War crimes are categorized as either grave breaches or simple breaches. The term grave breaches is technically only related to those violations set out as such in the Geneva Conventions. Grave breaches would include the following acts committed against persons or property specifically protected by the Geneva Conventions: willful killing; torture or inhuman treatment, including biological experiments; or willfully causing great suffering or serious injury to body or health.

Under the Geneva Conventions, each nation is under a strict obligation to search for all persons alleged to have committed war crimes. They must investigate the allegations of war crimes and if a grave breach of the law of war is discovered, the nation must either prosecute or extradite those so accused. As previously related, it is the policy of the United States that all American military personnel so accused are prosecuted by military courts martial under the substantive provisions of the UCMJ.

5.2 Voices from the Past—My Lai

Every army has its own mythology, its symbols of heroism as well as its symbols of shame. The Army of the United States is no exception. In the sphere of heroism, the American military has an incredible reservoir of noble and fantastic figures to draw from—men whose military proficiency and ethical conduct in combat have maintained an impeccable American reputation for both battlefield excellence and strict adherence to the laws regulating warfare. More than any other army in modern history, the American army is able to proudly claim as its own some of the greatest soldiers in the history of warfare. Robert E. Lee and Douglas MacArthur certainly are two of the very best this country has ever produced and therefore the subject of much study in American military schools.

Unfortunately, the United States military also has its figures of shame; soldiers who have engaged in blatant violations of the most fundamental and civilized rules regulating behavior in combat. While American misconduct is certainly an aberration and not the norm, this fact does not lessen the severity of the shame. Without question, each and every grave breach of the law of war represents a horrible scar on the credibility of the American armed forces, as well as on the civilized democracy which they protect.

The greatest emblem of American military shame in the twentieth century occurred during the Vietnam War, a war many Americans have yet to properly understand. While there were several cases of unlawful killings of unarmed civilians committed by American troops during the Indo-China War, by far the most violent, and hence the most infamous, has come to be called the My Lai massacre.

Of course, any discussion of American violations of the law of war during Vietnam in general, and at My Lai in particular, must be viewed against the background of the enemy's activities. In this context, American violations absolutely pale in comparison to the thousands upon thousands of command directed slaughters that were committed by the Communist regime of then North Vietnam and their Viet Cong allies. With respect to the American presence in Vietnam, My Lai can certainly be characterized as an aberration. Professor Rudy Rummel noted:

> The American record in Vietnam with regard to observance of the law of war is not a succession of war crimes and does not support charges of a systematic and willful violation of existing agreements for standards of human decency in time of war, as many critics of the American in-

volvement have alleged. Such charges were based on a distorted picture of the actual battlefield situation, on ignorance of existing rules of engagement, and on a tendency to construe every mistake of judgment as a wanton breach of the law of war.

As was the case for the Taliban and al-Qa'eda in Afghanistan and the terrorists in Iraq, blatant violations of numerous provisions of the law of war, to include murder, torture, and intimidation, were the policy for the Communists. In the estimate of Rummel, North Vietnam sponsored the slaughter of over one and a quarter million of its own people from 1945 to 1987. Included in this figure, since the fall of South Vietnam in 1975, are over 250,000 boat people and 250,000 other civilians who were either ruthlessly murdered outright or who perished in Communist death camps set up to "re-educate" non-Communists. Sadly, these massive crimes have never been punished, much less acknowledged by numerous human rights groups. According to Rummel: "In sum, re-education was a label for revenge, punishment, and social prophylaxes. But unlike the Khmer Rouge who were too public about their mass killing, the Vietnamese regime at first cleverly hid it from the outside world."

Nonetheless, the enemy's barbaric conduct offers little solace to the American conscience in the wake of My Lai. Misconduct by the enemy, be it the Communists of North Vietnam, the al-Qa'eda-styled terrorists, or the minions of Saddam Hussein, in no way justifies American violations of the law of war. For the Viet Cong and North Vietnamese, the strategy for a Communist victory was intentionally predicated on terror and propaganda; for the United States, the massacre at My Lai was a horrible contradiction.

5.3 Facts of My Lai

The hard facts relating to the My Lai massacre are now fairly certain, thanks to a thorough criminal investigation aimed at the perpetrators of the crime and a collateral administrative investigation ordered by the Secretary of the Army and headed by Lieutenant General W. R. Peers. Despite an initial cover-up by some of those associated with the crime, the enormity of the atrocity made it unlikely that it could long be kept secret, although for well over a year the general public knew nothing of the incident.

On March 16, 1968, an American combat task force of the 23rd Infantry Division (the Americal Division) launched an airmobile assault into the village complex of Son My in the province of Quang Ngai, South Vietnam. As was the case for all such operations, the attack was executed only after the commander of the task force, Lieutenant Colonel Frank Barker (the task force was called Task Force Barker), had assembled the key junior commanders for a final review of the details of the combat operation. This briefing, which took place on March 15, 1968, involved discussions on the positioning of helicopters, artillery preparation, and the specific assignments of the three companies that comprised the task force. While the other two companies provided blocking and support functions, Charlie Company, commanded by Captain Ernest Medina, would take the primary responsibility for battling any enemy resistance encountered in the village.

At the briefing, the commanders were reminded that intelligence reports had indicated that the village complex was a staging area for the 48th Viet Cong local force battalion and that the Americans could expect an enemy force of up to two hundred and fifty soldiers. In short, the United States soldiers anticipated that they would be outnumbered by the enemy. Still, having yet to engage any enemy forces in direct combat, the Barker Task Force saw the operation as an opportunity to finally fight the ever-elusive Viet Cong in the open.

The intelligence regarding a large enemy force proved to be incorrect. When the American combat forces landed they soon found that the village was occupied almost totally by noncombatants. Although the civilians offered no resistance whatsoever, some of the members of Charlie Company went on a command directed killing spree. Under the direct supervision of several company grade officers, First Lieutenant William L. Calley, Jr., being the most notorious, American troops murdered well over 200 unarmed South Vietnamese civilians.

The largest killing of civilians occurred in the hamlet of My Lai, known to the Americans by the nickname of "Pinkville," a part of the Son My complex. Thus, the entire massacre came to be known as the My Lai massacre. The murdered consisted primarily of women, children and old men; some shot in groups, others as they fled. At My Lai proper most of the civilians had been methodically herded into large groups and then gunned down, primarily under the direct supervision of Lieutenant William Calley.

In addition to the unlawful killing of civilians, the soldiers engaged in the destruction of most of the homes and in the killing of the domestic animals in the village. Several cases of rape were also reported to have taken place during the massacre. When it was over, the statistics told the story: one American soldier in Charlie Company had been wounded by friendly fire and hundreds of South Vietnamese women, children, and old men were dead.

The only positive aspect of the incident was the fact that some of the American soldiers had either refused to participate or had openly attempted to halt the killings. Chief Warrant Officer Two (CW2) Hugh C. Thompson, Jr., was one of those who took specific actions to halt the killings. Tasked with piloting one of the helicopters during the operation, CW2 Thompson testified that he noticed large numbers of "wounded and dead civilians everywhere." Assuming that the Americans on the ground would assist those who were wounded—as was the standard procedure—CW2 Thompson began to mark the location of the wounded Vietnamese civilians with smoke canisters as he flew overhead. To his horror, he witnessed the exact opposite. Drawn to the smoke, American soldiers were shooting the wounded that CW2 Thompson had so accurately marked. Still only partially realizing the full impact of what was happening on the ground, CW2 Thompson immediately landed his helicopter in My Lai, near a large drainage ditch filled with dead and dying civilians. As he began to assist those Vietnamese who were still alive to leave the area, Lieutenant Calley and a handful of troops approached.

When CW2 Thompson asked for assistance in caring for the civilians, Lieutenant Calley made it clear that he intended to kill the remaining noncombatants. CW2 Thompson recalled that Lieutenant Calley said: "The only way you'll get them [the civilians] out is with a hand grenade." However, instead of backing down from the designs of his superior officer, CW2 Thompson quickly ordered his M60 machine gunner, Private First Class Lawrence Colburn, to open fire on the American soldiers if they came any closer to the remaining civilians. CW2 Thompson then placed all the civilians he could on his helicopter and ferried them to safety.

5.4 My Lai Comes to Light

The initial attempts to cover up the crime could not quell the nightmares of those who had witnessed the murders. Rumors of the massacre persisted, coming to a boiling point when an ex-serviceman named Ron Ridenhour sent a secondhand account of the massacre to President Richard Nixon, "twenty three members of Congress, the Secretaries of State and Defense, the Secretary of the Army, and the chairman of the Joint Chiefs of Staff." Ridenhour had written a four-page letter that chronicled detailed information from several of the soldiers who had either taken part in the bloody killings or had witnessed it firsthand.

Ron Ridenhour's letter received prompt attention both in the media and in the legislative and executive branches of government. Needless to say, the initial military reaction was one of disbelief; no one believed that a massacre of that magnitude could have been committed by American soldiers or that the massacre "could have remained hidden for so long."

As the horrible truth of the crime became known, the army quickly launched the comprehensive Peers Commission investigation, popularly known as the Peers Report. At the same time the general public tasted the horror of the My Lai massacre through a series of gruesome photographs of the dead which had been taken by a former army photographer named Ronald Haeberle. The color photographs appeared in the December 1969 issue of *Life* magazine.

5.5 Impact of My Lai

In the subsequent judicial actions associated with the murders at My Lai, charges were brought against four officers and nine enlisted men. Twelve other officers were charged with military type offenses associated with the cover-up. Of these, only Lieutenant William Calley was convicted. The other officers and enlisted men either had the charges against them dismissed or were found not guilty at their courts martial.

Tried before a military panel composed of six officers, Lieutenant Calley was found guilty of the premeditated murder of twenty-two noncombatants and of assault with intent to murder a two-year-old child. Although Calley was sentenced to a dismissal and confinement at hard labor for life, the convening authority reduced this to a dismissal and twenty years at hard labor, and the Secretary of the Army further reduced the sentence to a dismissal and ten years at hard labor.

Aside from the issue of individual culpability for those involved in the massacre, My Lai had a devastating impact on the outcome of the Vietnam War. Given the total lack of any semblance of a grand strategy on the part of the United States to win the war, it can be argued that this atrocity did as much to harm the survival of an independent South Vietnam as any other single event in the Indo-China War. The public revelation of this massacre not only solidified the anti-war movement in the United States, but it cast a pall of confusion and shame over the nation at large that significantly contributed to the eventual abandonment of South Vietnam to the Communist forces in the North. Beginning in 1969, a vocal and radical minority of war protestors incorporated opposition to the American ground soldier to their general opposition to the War. For these people, the enemy was now the American soldier, not the Communists. There is no question that the revelation of what happened at My Lai dealt a blow to the *esprit de corps* and professionalism of the United States Army that can still be felt today.

5.6 Why Did My Lai Happen?

Taken out of the context of the social and political climates that were brewing in the United States in the late 1960s and early 1970s and viewed from a purely objective perspective, the immediate focus in the aftermath of the crime was summed up in a single word: "Why?" Why did it happen? How could so many American boys have become involved in such a heinous war crime? And, more importantly, how could the officers in command of the operation have ordered such atrocities or participated in the attempt to cover them up? To realize that some civilians were killed as a collateral matter through military action against legitimate military targets was one thing, to have ground forces intentionally shoot innocent noncombatants in cold blood was incomprehensible.

The Peers Report did not cite any one factor as the cause for the massacre at My Lai. While the panel observed that "what may have influenced one man to commit atrocities had had no effect on another," General Peers was determined that the final report should reflect some explanation as to why the massacre had occurred. Recognizing the inherent difficulty in finger pointing, the panel nonetheless identified several factors that seemed to be conducive to an environment which might have led to the violations of the law of war. In fact, the Peers factors are a witches' brew that would similarly apply to any war, particularly a conflict like Iraq and Afghanistan in which the enemy has no regard for the rule of law.

The lack of proper training in the law of war was a common theme in the interviews of the witnesses and subjects involved in My Lai. Perhaps the most graphic illustration of this factor was reflected at the trial of Lieutenant Calley when he testified that the classes on the Geneva Conventions conducted during Officer Candidate School were inadequate. In any event, the Peers Report entered specific findings that the soldiers that made up Task Force Barker had not received sufficient training in the "Law of War (Hague and Geneva Conventions), the safeguarding of noncombatants, or the Rules of Engagement." Although the requirements set out in United States Army Republic of Vietnam (USARV) Regulation 350-1, dated November 10, 1967, made it clear that, at a minimum, all soldiers were required to have annual refresher training on the Geneva Conventions, in many cases there was no command emphasis on this requirement. Hence, to that degree, the individual soldier did not know what was required of him.

Pocket-sized guidance cards, which were a mandatory issue item to all soldiers to assist in learning and abiding by the law of war, were usually never read and seldom lasted past the first monsoon rains. In addition, Military Assistance Command Vietnam (MACV) Directive 20-4, which required the immediate reporting of all violations of the law of war, was seldom stressed by the command structure.

Regardless of the deficiencies in providing training in the law of war, the Peers Report did not find this to be a significant reason for the grave breaches of multiple murders which occurred at My Lai. Such deficiencies in training might excuse minor or technical breaches of the law of war, but not the grave *malum in se* breaches. The members of the Commission correctly noted that "there were some things a soldier did not have to be told were wrong—such as rounding up women and children and then mowing them down, shooting babies out of mother's arms, and raping." It was patently obvious to the Commission that some of the members of the company were simply cold-blooded criminals dressed in military uniforms, both enlisted and officers. Clearly these individuals found themselves in an environment where there was little, if any, deterrence to the overt expression of their criminal propensities.

A tendency by some of the members of Charlie Company to view the Vietnamese people as almost subhuman was thought to be another factor which may have contributed to the massacre. Of course, the use of derogatory terms to describe the Vietnamese as nothing but "gooks," "dinks," or "slopes" was not uncommon during the Vietnam War. In fact, soldiers in all wars have developed derogatory phrases to describe their enemies; it is easier to dispatch an enemy who can be characterized as different. In the My Lai case, however, the Peers Report concluded that some of the members of Charlie Company had carried this tendency to dehumanize the enemy to an unreasonable extreme, viewing the "Vietnamese [people] with contempt, considering them subhuman, on the level of dogs."

To discover the reason for this degree of hatred, the Peers Report had a detailed background analysis done on each individual in Company C. The results showed nothing unusual. The company was an average unit with 70 percent of the troops having high school diplomas and nineteen having some college credits. The reason for the hatred was a result of a combination of several factors, the greatest of these merely a reflection of the locked-in arrogance inherent in the criminal mind, and the least, but more common, related to the frustration of having to fight an enemy who refused to abide by the law of war.

One of the most telling factors listed in the Peers Report dealt with examining the nature of the enemy that infested South Vietnam, with the implicit criticism that the United States military was never allowed to take the war to the real enemy—North Vietnam. In the South, the United States military was asked to carry out primarily defensive operations against a well-trained and well-equipped guerilla force that could not be distinguished from the local population and that refused to abide by the established principles of the law of war. The Peers Report stated:

> They would set up their bunkers in villages and attack from the midst of helpless civilians. Thus, surrounding themselves with and using innocent civilians to protect themselves is in itself a war crime and makes them criminally responsible for the resulting civilian dead....[T]hey would also directly attack villages and hamlets, kill the inhabitants, including children, in order to panic the civilians in the area and cause social chaos that the communist then could exploit.

Like the al-Qa'eda and the sectarian murderers in Iraq, the Viet Cong and regular North Vietnamese Army soldiers knew their environment; they knew every path, trail, and hut in their areas of operation. In addition, whether by brute force, which included public torture and execution, or by psychological intimidation, the Viet Cong could count on the local support of the civilian population for shelter, food, and intelligence. As such, it was not uncommon for women and children to actively participate in military operations against American forces. With women and children participating in combat activities, by laying booby traps, serving as scouts or actually bearing arms, the American soldier had to disregard the traditional indicators such as sex and age as criteria for categorizing the noncombatant and concentrate instead on the extremely difficult issue of hostile intent. The Peers Report recognized this dilemma:

> The communist forces in South Vietnam had long recognized our general reluctance to do battle with them among the civilian populace and had used that knowledge to our tactical and strategic disadvantage throughout the history of the war in Vietnam. Exploitation of that reluctance by...[the enemy] forces caused a distortion of the classic distinction between combatants and noncombatants.

The difficulty of determining friend from foe was also woefully apparent in regards to the military-aged male Vietnamese. Having developed an incredible system of underground tunnels and caves, members of the Viet Cong and North Vietnamese Army were able to appear and disappear at will. Also, when under pressure, it took only seconds to remove all military insignia or equipment and to blend in with the local population.

Without question, the use of guerilla tactics, characterized by a heavy reliance on booby traps and hit-and-run missions, had a tremendous adverse psychological impact on the American commanders and their troops. In numerous interviews, the Peers Report noted that the general attitude of the soldier was one of extreme tension at engaging this unseen enemy, an enemy who hid behind women and children and would not come out in the open to do battle.

Consequently, every civilian was viewed as a potential threat, every inch of ground as hiding a potential booby trap or mine. Descriptive terms such as "keyed up" were frequently used to describe the apprehension and frustration associated with going out on patrol or, in many cases, just being in friendly villages. It was not uncommon for a friendly village to be visited by the Communists on any given night, setting landmines that would kill Americans the next day. Consequently, some of those who testified before the Peers Commission naturally assumed that the "effects of mines and booby traps were the main reason for the atrocities committed by the task force." This view is incorrect. While such factors undoubtedly contributed to the extraordinary level of tension in the Barker task force, it would be far too simplistic to rely on the illegal warfighting tactics of the enemy as the primary reason for the atrocity. If this factor was the main cause for My Lai, one would have expected many massacres similar to My Lai to have taken place throughout Vietnam.

Taking strong note of the overall organizational problems throughout the Army structure in Vietnam, the Peers Report actually believed that certain specific organizational problems in Task Force Barker "played the most prominent part in the My Lai incident." In focusing on Task Force Barker, it was apparent that the lack of staff personnel was a serious impediment to effective command and control. The task force "could hardly function properly, particularly in such matters as development of intelligence, planning and supervision of operations, and even routine administration."

One of the dominant characteristics of the Vietnam War was the lack of effective organization in the United States Army's force structure. From brigades to platoons, shortages of personnel and frequent rotations resulted in ad hoc arrangements regarding the composition of military units. Adding to the organizational deficiencies was the influx of poorly trained or ill-disciplined troops who were on "short" tours of a year. The short tour ensured problems in command and control; by the time the soldier had gained the necessary experience to be an effective member of the unit, he was eligible for transfer back to the "States." In the realm of directing combat operations, the lack of effective command and control can be disastrous. Indeed, the majority of abuses of detainees in the War on Terror have occurred at the hands of ill-trained and ill-disciplined National Guard and Reserve units.

Along with the general organizational problems in the task force, there was the lack of clear plans and orders concerning the operation into Son My. Because the entire operation was based on intelligence that anticipated a large enemy force in the area, the American soldiers initially expected that they were going to be outnumbered by at least two to one. In addition, the task force leaders regularly employed the term "search and destroy" without providing an adequate definition to the troops. The phrase search and destroy was never meant to provide license to kill whatever was encountered on an operation, despite the connotation of the term. In this regard, the Peers Report found that no instructions were ever given as to how to handle the civilians that might be encountered during the Son My operation.

In the final analysis, the organizational problems outlined above contributed to an overall atmosphere that made the events at My Lai possible. But the real pin in the grenade was the most fundamental aspect of the command and control problem—lack of leadership at the ground level of the operation.

5.7 Leadership

The constant mental and emotional strain associated with combat conditions is certainly exacerbated by having to face enemies like the al-Qa'eda and Iraqi insurgents who engage in violations of the law of war, but the factor that weighed the heaviest in explaining the massacre at My Lai was none of the four discussed above. Rather, it was the lack of responsible leadership at the very level where it was most critical—at the junior officer level. Although the Peers Report faulted all levels of command—"[i]t appears…that at all levels, from division down to platoon, leadership or the lack of it was perhaps the principal causative factor in the tragic events before, during, and after the My Lai operation"—the direct underlying deficiency most certainly rested at the company and platoon level. One of the participants of the massacre, Private Paul Meadlo recalled the orders of his officer:

You know what to do with them, [Lieutenant] Calley said, and walked off. Ten minutes later he returned and asked, "Haven't you got rid of them yet? I want them dead. Waste them.". . .We stood about ten to fifteen feet away from them [a group of 80 men, women and children herded together] and then he [Lieutenant Calley] started shooting them. I used more than a whole clip—used four or five clips.

By virtue of the chain of command structure of the military, the primary responsibility for ensuring adherence to the law of war rests on the officer corps, with particular professionalism demanded of those junior officers at the platoon and company level, where soldiers are most apt to encounter the vast majority of issues associated with the law of war. Simply put, soldiers are expected to obey the law of war and their officers are expected to see that they do.

In their 300-page report on the Abu Ghraib abuse cases, the Department of the Army Inspector General mirrored the Peers Commission finding that "in some cases, abuse was accompanied by leadership failure at the tactical level." Another 2003 report, entitled the Taguba Report, issued by Major General Antonio Taguba, found that leadership failure was a critical problem within the chain of command at the Abu Ghraib prison. Interestingly, although several of the soldiers who were charged with abuse contended that they were ordered to commit the abuses, both reports concluded that the abuses at Abu Ghraib were not the result of soldiers following orders from superiors.

Of course, the difficult issue is not how to deal with those soldiers or officers who in their individual capacities violate the law of war—they are punished by military courts martial. Rather, the real difficulty is presented by the officer who orders his soldiers to commit war crimes, or who knowingly fails to control those under his command who violate the law of war. Clearly, the difficultly at My Lai was a result of command-directed breaches of the law of war in the context of lawful versus unlawful orders. Beginning with the premise that all soldiers are expected to obey lawful orders and are subject to courts martial if they do not, how should one expect the soldier to react to an unlawful order, assuming, of course, that the soldier can even recognize the order as unlawful?

In considering the question of whether a superior order constitutes a valid defense, military courts must take into consideration the fact that obedience to lawful military orders is the duty of every member of the armed forces; that the latter cannot be expected, in conditions of war discipline, to weigh scrupulously the legal merits of the orders received; that certain rules of warfare may be controversial; or that an act otherwise amounting to a war crime may be done in obedience to orders conceived as a measure of reprisal. At the same time, it must be borne in mind that members of the armed forces are bound to obey only lawful orders.

Furthermore, soldiers may not normally rely on the defense of superior orders should they obey an unlawful order; they are responsible for their own acts or omissions. When the defense of superior orders is raised, however, a two-tier test is applied. The first tier is a subjective one concentrating on whether or not the accused knew that the order was illegal. If the accused did not know that the order was illegal then the inquiry shifts to what the accused could reasonably have been expected to know regarding the legality of the order. "The fact that the law of war has been violated pursuant to an order of a superior authority. . .does not constitute a defense. . .unless [the accused] did not know and could not reasonably have been expected to know that the act ordered was unlawful." Although the objective tier of the two-part test draws upon the reasonable man standard, it is really a reasonable man under the stresses present in that particular combat environment.

Moreover, the job of distinguishing the legitimacy of the orders of a superior must be viewed against the backdrop of the entire concept of enforced discipline, extending from boot camp until discharge. The requirement for enforced discipline is absolutely essential to ensure that in the unnatural conditions of the combat environment soldiers will be able to function properly. No army could ever survive without a system promoting genuine and enforced discipline, which is firmly rooted in the requirement to obey the directions of superiors. It follows then, that if soldiers are expected to obey all lawful orders, they cannot be expected to scrupulously weigh the legal merits of orders received under the stresses of combat.

Accordingly, this means that the officer corps of any army must be filled with only the finest available men and women. Nowhere is this requirement more essential than in the selection and placement of the men who serve as officers in combat units. Only men of the highest moral caliber and military skill should be assigned the responsibility of combat command. In commenting on leadership skills for officers, General George S. Patton, Jr., correctly stated, "If you do not enforce and maintain discipline, you [officers] are potential murderers."

Under the concept of command responsibility or indirect responsibility, commanders can be charged with violations of the law of war committed by their subordinates if they ordered the crimes committed or knew that a crime was about to be committed, had the power to prevent it, and failed to exercise that power. In the United States, this standard has come to be called the Medina standard, so named for Captain Ernest Medina.

A second standard for indirect responsibility for commanders that has been the object of much debate and is recognized only in the United States is the Yamashita standard. The Yamashita standard is named for the World War II Japanese general, Tomoyuki Yamashita, who was tried before a military commission for war crimes committed by soldiers under his command. The primary charge against Yamashita revolved around the 20,000 Japanese sailors who went on a murder and rape rampage in Manila near the end of the war. Although the prosecution was unable to prove that Yamashita ordered the crimes or even knew about them, he was convicted under a "should-have-known" standard. This should-have-known theory held that if, through normal events, the military commander should have known of the war crimes and did nothing to stop them, he is guilty of the actions of his soldiers. This should have known standard applies only when the war crimes are associated with a widespread pattern of abuse over a prolonged period of time. In such a scenario, the commander is presumed to have knowledge of the crime or to have abandoned his command.

Herein is the underlying tragedy at My Lai and the essential lesson for battling terrorists, be it in Iraq or Afghanistan: several of the junior officers on the scene were totally inadequate, not only in moral character and integrity, but also in basic military skills. As exhibited by their gross behavior, these officers were completely unworthy of the responsibility of command.

When one details the background of William Calley, the centerpiece of the command-directed killings, it is not surprising to discover that he was not the type of individual who should have been charged with leadership responsibilities of any nature. Having flunked out of a junior college in Miami, Florida, Calley moved west before enlisting in the army in 1966. Once in the army, Calley was somehow selected to attend Officers Candidate School, where he graduated despite poor academic marks. Assigned to the field as a platoon leader in a combat unit, the soldiers under his command quickly discovered that Lieutenant Calley did not even understand basic military combat skills. As one rifleman in the platoon put it, "I wonder how he ever got through Officer Candidate School. He [Calley] couldn't read no darn [sic] map and a compass would confuse his ass."

In summation, the factor that most directly resulted in the crimes at My Lai clearly rests on the shoulders of a few junior officers on the ground, Lieutenant William Calley being one of the worst. All the evidence suggests that it was Lieutenant Calley who initiated much of the murdering, acting both in his individual capacity and, far more shamefully, in his capacity as an officer in charge of subordinates. Abusing the authority of his position, Lieutenant Calley directly ordered the soldiers under his command to commit murder; some of the men obeyed while a few did not. While no one can pardon the behavior of those who carried out the illegal orders, the real tragedy of My Lai was the absence of competent and virtuous leadership.

Instead of setting the standard for moral conduct, Calley performed in the exact opposite fashion. He represented the antithesis of what a commander should be. As Sun Tzu laid out almost 500 years before Christ, "[t]he commander stands for the virtues of wisdom, sincerity, benevolence, courage, and strictness."

5.8 Lack of a Grand Strategy on the Part of the United States

A final factor that must be explored in any war and one that few commentators on Vietnam have properly gauged is the full impact that the lack of a grand strategy by the United States had on the outcome of the Indo-China conflict. In this regard, My Lai was possible due to the total and complete absence of a strategy to deal with the Communist-sponsored aggression against South Vietnam. President George W. Bush established clear objectives in the War on Terror and achieved those objectives in measured steps as American forces have held rogue nations like Iraq, Afghanistan, and Libya to account. Regardless of one's political views, his unequivocal vision for the total defeat of the Taliban government of Afghanistan and the regime of Iraq's Saddam Hussein could not have been clearer. The American military understood that vision and carried it out in a magnificent manner. Although Iraq was not stabilized until Bush's surge in troop strength in 2006-2008, when American forces depart it will be clear to the world that we were victorious and were not "driven out." Obviously, missteps occurred under the Bush Administration, particularly in regard to the faulty intelligence on weapons of mass destruction supplied to both the Clinton and Bush Administrations, as well as the European allies and the United Nations.

On the other hand, Obama's 2009-2010 surge in Afghanistan was done without any clear definition of long term objectives apart from taking and holding ground in Afghanistan from the Taliban. There has never been a definition of victory from President Obama. In fact, when Obama announced the surge he also announced his intention to begin a unilateral withdrawal by summer 2011! The historical parallels between Obama's war in Afghanistan and the war in Vietnam are disturbingly apparent. Indeed, without a clear victory over al-Qa'eda and the Taliban, the narrative will be the same as it was in Vietnam—America was defeated and driven out. This narrative will echo the defeat of the Soviet Union in Afghanistan and result in the swelling of al-Qa'eda ranks by the tens of thousands.

If the concept of a grand strategy is defined as the use of a nation's full national power to achieve a particular objective, it is clear that at no time did the United States have a grand strategy in Vietnam for dealing with the Communist aggression. On the other hand, it is just as obvious that the Communists had from the very beginning a complete and dedicated grand strategy for conquering all of Indo-China through the use of revolutionary warfare. Similarly, the al-Qa'eda attack on September 11, 2001, was certainly motivated by a grand strategy to incite the whole of the Arab world in a crusade against the West and against "moderate" Arab rulers.

The basic mechanics of a sound grand strategy takes advantage of one's strengths and the enemy's vulnerabilities, while neutralizing the enemy's strengths and one's own vulnerabilities. In practically every category of factors associated with the art of waging war, the Communists in Vietnam were able to fulfill this formula; the United States was not. Thus, while the Communists mobilized all of the people under their control in a unity of effort—from the military to the political—the United States consistently sought to disassociate the American people from the war. Fortunately, in the War on Terror, al-Qa'eda has failed to realize their grand strategy and if a pivot of normalcy can be established in Afghanistan or Iraq, al-Qa'eda will not find new safe-havens for planning and training.

In the sphere of combat operations in Vietnam, the Communists were particularly effective in drawing on their strengths. Conversely, the Americans typically refused to rely on their strengths. Aware that they were no match for the far superior power of American combat forces, the Communists primarily employed small hit and run tactics against selected targets; like the Saddam loyalists, they quickly discovered that engaging the United States military in conventional warfare was pure folly. Coupled with guerilla tactics deliberately focused on becoming the unseen enemy, the Communists illegally took advantage of the American respect for the law of war. By hiding themselves in civilian populations, the Communists intentionally sought to blur the distinction between the combatant and the noncombatant. In the words of commentator and author Thomas Begines, they were "hoping either for immunity from attack or to provoke…indiscriminate attack."

Establishing well-stocked sanctuaries in neighboring Cambodia and Laos, they were immune from defeat as long as the United States refused to seriously attack these bases. In the War on Terror, the United States faces a similar situation with al-Qa'eda and Taliban forces taking sanctuary in various countries in the Middle East, including Pakistan, Syria, and Iran. In the war in Vietnam, the United States never effectually used the overwhelming strength of its military to subdue and defeat North Vietnam. Instead, American measures were confined to patrolling efforts in reaction to Communist attacks in the territory of South Vietnam. In the War on Terror, the Bush Administration acknowledged that America had to target the enemy wherever they went. Whether through cooperation with friendly nations or on its own initiative, the United States should remain correctly focused on going after the enemy—in the words of President Bush, to "smoke them out," and in the words of President Obama, to "get Osama bin Laden."

Finally, in tandem with their guerilla tactics, the Communists relied heavily on all forms of propaganda, placing special emphasis on the ambiguity of words to erode the will of the United States to continue the war. For example, they falsely portrayed the conflict as a protracted war waged by agrarian reformers with no end in sight, while simultaneously promising a negotiated settlement at any moment. Al-Qa'eda, on the other hand, has not entirely failed in its use of violence and propaganda. Before his death by U.S. forces in June 2006, Abu Musab al-Zarqawi managed to organize so many attacks on Shias and their holy places of worship that a bitter sectarian war broke out with such violence that many in America pronounced a defeat for the United States.

In summation, the ultimate success of the Communist strategy in Vietnam rested primarily in the fact that the United States never developed a coherent overall strategy of its own. Necessarily, this mandated that the Communist's grand strategy would eventually prevail. What is surprising is that it was not until 1968 that the impact of not having a viable grand strategy became apparent to the American soldier. When it did, however, the painful beginning of the demoralization of the United States military quickly followed. As the attendant anti-war protests at home increased, many soldiers questioned the efficacy of their sacrifices in Vietnam. More importantly, the soldiers realized that the emphasis of the American leadership was not on achieving peace through a military victory, but on peace through negotiations—negotiations which constantly promised an end to the war at any time. As a consequence, no one wanted to be the last casualty in a war that was not supported at home and which the United States government refused to let the military win.

5.9 Lessons of My Lai

The massacre at My Lai cannot be undone. However, in developing a methodology for preventing future atrocities which could occur in the War on Terror, the images of the horror of My Lai perfectly illustrate the necessity for abiding by the law of war. Certainly, the Peers Report was a valuable tool in attempting to explain some of the factors that seemed to create an environment in which violations of the law of war were more likely to occur. Taken together, these factors can be reduced to three fundamental lessons.

One of the most troubling issues for American soldiers is the realization that in many of the wars the United States has fought, the enemy has openly and repeatedly violated numerous provisions of the law of war. In the Vietnam War, the Communist forces regularly engaged in command-directed atrocities on a massive scale. Just in relation to the treatment of prisoners, for example, every single American prisoner of war was subjected to torture and maltreatment in flagrant violation of the Geneva Conventions.

For many American soldiers, knowledge of enemy violations presents an immediate negative response to the law of war. The realization that the enemy may often refuse to abide by the law of war prompts an immediate gut response: Why should I care about the rules if the enemy doesn't? Faced with such questions, it is not enough to simply inform the soldier that he will be punished for violations, it is imperative that the soldier understand the rationale for abiding by the law of war. Thus, it is critical that the soldier's question be answered so that he possesses a basic understanding of the entire concept of the development of rules regulating combat.

5.10 Lesson One—Rationale for the Law of War

Many people have some vague notion that rules regulating warfare came out of the aftermath of World War II or, at the most, World War I. Nothing could be further from the truth. As long as there have been wars there have been rules established to reduce the suffering to both the environment and to other humans. While some of these ancient rules would not be consistent with the modern humanitarian concepts reflected in the current law of war, it is interesting to note that many of the provisions in the modern law of war are derived directly from some of the earliest formulations of rules regulating warfare.

For example, in the book of Deuteronomy, the ancient Hebrews were given specific instructions on the protections that were to be afforded to the persons and property of an enemy city under siege. Generally, if the city surrendered, the inhabitants were not to be harmed. If the city refused to surrender, but was subsequently captured, no women or children were to be molested. In all cases, torture was absolutely prohibited. Similarly, protection for the environment was also codified; fruit trees located outside of a besieged city were protected from unnecessary damage; the fruit could be eaten but it was unlawful to cut down the trees.

To observe that the modern law of war rests firmly upon an ancient foundation of humanitarian concerns that are intrinsically acceptable is only one reason why the rules have enjoyed universal acceptance through time—the fact that such rules are morally valuable axioms only captures part of the truth as to their development and utility. Clearly, the historical development of rules regulating warfare also follows a general pattern of what might be termed pragmatic necessity. While many of the rules limiting suffering were undoubtedly based on humanitarian concerns, it can be argued that the basic rationales for having a law of war are rooted in several collateral principles of self-interest.

First, under the concept of reciprocity, nations would develop and adhere to laws of warfare because they were confident that the enemy would also do the same under a quid-pro-quo theory. This mutual assurance theory has long been recognized as not only a primary motivator for establishing rules regulating warfare, but as the centerpiece in almost every other function of international intercourse.

The second element in the historical development of the law of war centers on a similar vein of self interest, reflected so aptly by Alexander the Great's admonitions to his incredible army on the eve of practically every battle: "Why should we destroy those things which shall soon be ours?" Under this reasoning, particularly in the context of securing limited amounts of spoil, the destruction of anything beyond military targets to subdue the enemy's military forces would be neither beneficial nor reasonable. Under modern principles, similar violations of the law of war would not contribute to the goal of the collection of legitimate reparations, a measure often employed against the aggressor nation.

A third line of reasoning draws on the related fact that abuses seldom shorten the length of the conflict and are never beneficial in facilitating the restoration of peace. The targeting of nonmilitary property usually produces unwanted effects for those who engage in such activities. Despite the best efforts of historical revisionists to brush over the war crimes of Union General William T. Sherman, the event in American history that best illustrates this point comes from the illegal activities of General Sherman during the American Civil War. General Sherman's widespread looting and burning of Southern—black and white—civilian homes and personal property, coupled with the deliberate slaughter of all domesticated animals on his march through Georgia and the Carolinas in the last two years of the War did not significantly contribute to the collapse of the Confederacy. On the contrary, his brutal actions simply strengthened the resolve of Southerners to resist while sowing the seeds of hatred against "Yankees" for generations to come.

Clearly, the intelligent warfighter makes every effort to comply with and even exceed the requirements of the law of war, particularly in regard to the treatment of prisoners of war and noncombatants. Not only does humane treatment demonstrate the best evidence that your side is the one that is waging a *jus in bello*, but it often serves as the best avenue to counter enemy propaganda concerning law of war violations. As the pragmatic Prussian soldier and author, Karl von Clausewitz observed, "If we find that civilized nations do not…devastate towns and countries, this is because their intelligence exercises greater influence on their mode of carrying on war, and has taught them a more effectual means of applying force.…"

A fourth factor approaches the matter from a purely military perspective. Plainly put, the use of limited military resources for the destruction of civilian targets is a waste of assets and hence, detrimental to the goal of defeating the enemy's military. In short, such conduct is simply counterproductive because "it rarely gains the violator a distinct military advantage."

The final rationale, albeit of greater impact in an era characterized by the widespread dissemination of information, rests in the very nature of the modern civilized nation-state. States that adhere to the principles of democratic institutions and fundamental human rights will not tolerate activities that are conducted in defiance of the rule of law. As brought out so strongly by the My Lai incident, civilized societies will not provide the necessary homefront support for an army that is perceived as acting in violation of the law of war. Although in the radical totalitarian regime this factor is generally ignored, in the United States, as in all democratic societies, this element of homefront support is absolutely essential to any deployment and sustainment of military forces. The basic minimum standards of morality transcend national boundaries.

The necessity of homefront support is not always easy for the military to sustain. In part the difficulty rests in the associated phenomenon of "imputed responsibility." With reference to any military in a democratic society, the term imputed responsibility recognizes the fact that the acts of a few soldiers who engage in egregious abuses of the law of war are immediately imputed to the entire military establishment. For instance, because Lieutenant Calley and a handful of others murdered babies at My Lai, large segments of the public might tend to view all American soldiers in Vietnam as baby killers. To a large degree, the mass media feeds this phenomenon, as reflected by almost every Hollywood movie concerning the Vietnam War. In American cinema, the soldier is routinely depicted as engaging in abuses of the law of war or ingesting large quantities of illegal drugs. The fact that the vast majority of American soldiers did neither is not shown. Accordingly, the best way for the military to combat the concept of imputed responsibility is to make every effort to see that abuses do not occur and, if they do, promptly investigate and punish those proven to be guilty. Complete transparency must be the guide. Under no circumstances can a cover-up be justified—the light must be shed promptly and fully on all allegations of war crimes. The U.S. military learned this lesson from My Lai as demonstrated by the handling of the prisoner abuse cases in Iraq. Again, the military self-reported the individual acts of criminal behavior to the media and also launched its own investigation (the Taguba Report) prior to the photographs appearing in the media.

In the modern era, then, the law of war is based on a combination of rationales reflecting a mixture of pragmatism and moral concerns. The competent warfighter should understand that the factors include:

- humanitarian concerns based on moral precepts;
- the concept of reciprocity in behavior;
- the desire for reparations;
- the desire to limit the scope and duration of the conflict and to facilitate the restoration of peace;
- the effective use of military resources; and
- the necessity for securing homefront support.

5.11 Lesson Two—Soldiers Must Be Trained in the Law of War

The second lesson from My Lai needs little introduction—to be effective the law of war must be constantly taught to soldiers. To a large degree the United States military has long held an outstanding reputation for adherence to the law of war because of its commitment to training. Unfortunately, there have been periods where training has not been properly emphasized, providing fertile ground for violations of the law of war. Colonel H. Wayne Elliott, former Chief of the International Law Division at the Army's Judge Advocate General's School wrote that, the massacre at My Lai served as the "catalyst for a complete review of Army training in the law of war."

The United States Army has proponency for the law of war for all branches of the military. This means that the Army is responsible for developing and publishing the written doctrine. The current methodology for teaching the law of war attempts to tailor the training to the particular unit.

Since Special Operations Forces are a primary tool used on the ground in the War on Terror, it is efficacious to review the current level of training that these forces receive in the law of war. In short, Special Operations Forces not only receive constant classroom instruction on the law of war but also have difficult law of war questions dealing with special operations built into their training missions which are constantly practiced. The much-reported event in the 1991 Gulf War in which an Army Special Forces team had to choose between killing an Iraqi girl or being discovered by enemy forces was actually a well-rehearsed scenario resulting in a correct application of a very difficult law of war issue. The girl was spared.

A red thread that runs throughout the issue of training in the law of war is the role of the military lawyer or judge advocate. Since Vietnam, the Army has dramatically expanded its use of military attorneys to ensure that its forces comply with all aspects of the law of war. All combat forces have an operational law attorney assigned at the Division level. Likewise, all Army Special Forces Groups have a specialized military attorney assigned. The function of this judge advocate is not only to ensure compliance with and adherence to the law of war, but to examine the full range of international and domestic laws that affect specifically legal issues associated with the planning for and deployment of United States forces overseas in both peacetime and combat environments. This is a major change from the role of the judge advocate in Vietnam—a role primarily delegated to the administration of criminal law, well behind the front lines of combat.

Currently, the function of the judge advocate in the field can be divided into two elements—he has both preventive and active roles. In the preventive role, the judge advocate advises commanders on potential issues dealing with rules of engagement, targeting enemy military objectives, and all other relevant aspects of the law of war. In addition, the judge advocate is deeply involved in providing instruction and training to soldiers within his particular command.

In the active role, the judge advocate is involved in the investigation of allegations of war crimes. The requirement to investigate is either carried out directly by the legal officer or is closely monitored by the judge advocate. Finally, judge advocates will be called upon to either prosecute or defend those charged with violations.

5.12 Lesson Three—Preventing Violations of the Law of War in the War on Terror

As noted, the importance of professional conduct on the battlefield extends to the strategic, political, and social realms. In turn, the primary responsibility for inculcating professional conduct falls directly on the officer corps. Nowhere is the need for training in the law of war more critical than in the proper development of the military's officer corps. Thus, no officer should be given the responsibility of leadership without two essential factors: (1) technical proficiency in the profession of arms; and (2) the highest ethical and moral courage. Under the ancient Roman adage that no man can control others until he can first control himself, officers must be thoroughly prepared in both of these areas. Combat command should only be offered to officers who have been thoroughly scrutinized and put through extensive field training exercises designed to test their reaction under combat pressures.

There can be no question that the primary cause of My Lai was the lack of disciplined control, i.e., the lack of any real leadership. Such leadership is absolutely essential in preventing war crimes. The associated tensions set out by the Peers Report were not the real problem at My Lai—tensions of combat will always be present in one form or another. The real problem was in the effective control of those tensions. Control of warfighting pressures rest not only with the individual soldier but directly with his commanding officer. Sadly, many of the officers in Charlie Company not only allowed the illegal manifestations of battlefield stress to be exhibited by their troops, but through their orders and example they initiated and actively participated in the atrocities. There can be little doubt that proper officer leadership could have prevented the murders at My Lai. Consequently, the primary responsibility for these crimes is on their heads. The function of leadership is to hold up the professional torch at all times, at all costs.

Great armies are neither created, nor sustained, by accident. To a large degree, great armies are maintained by officers who understand, and then are able to apply, the lessons of military history. In this respect, no officer can truly be called a professional without a firm commitment to the moral and ethical rules regulating combat. Quite naturally, this objective requires constant training, as well as a comprehensive understanding of one's moral roots. Consequently, the military of the United States must constantly reaffirm its commitment to the positive values of military proficiency and ethical integrity.

Currently, U.S. Army training doctrine places a great deal of emphasis on the concept of duty and uses General Robert E. Lee as its illustration to all soldiers. For instruction, inspiration and inculcation, American officers can find no better role model than General Lee. While some may forget, ignore, or purposefully deny the role that Lee has had in shaping our modern military, to those who are objective, his impact on American tactics and humanitarian concerns can never be obscured.

Lee's tactics and civility have become ingrained into the character of the United States military establishment. Although these qualities certainly existed before the emergence of Lee the general, his genius and humanity have epitomized and translated them into the very fabric of subsequent American military doctrines. For this reason, any analysis of the United States military, either in terms of tactics or comportment with the law of war, that ignores the tremendous contributions of General Lee can never be more than a fraction of the truth.

For example, although some Southerners criticized Lee for not authorizing lawful reprisals to deter Union violations of the law of war, General Lee firmly believed that reprisals were not the answer. Responding to a letter from the Confederate Secretary of War regarding possible Confederate responses to widespread Union atrocities, Lee reiterated his position in the summer of 1864:

> As I have said before, if the guilty parties could be taken, either the officer who commands, or the soldier who executes such atrocities, I should not hesitate to advise the infliction of the extreme punishment they deserve, but I cannot think it right or politic, to make the innocent…suffer for the guilty.

With Americans fighting Americans, Lee knew that the long-term effects of engaging in reprisals would not be profitable for the nation or the South. He was undoubtedly correct; Lee's strict adherence to the rules regulating warfare, coupled with his firm policy prohibiting reprisals, contributed greatly to the healing process after the War. This same thinking colors the activities of American forces who face the cowardly and unlawful tactics of the terrorists.

One of the driving forces that created the legend of Lee, the ultimate gentleman, was his unmatched sense of humanity. In a 1902 article, the Southern Historical Society Papers called Lee "the soldier-gentleman of tradition, generous, forgiving, silent in the face of failure…a hero of mythology." No matter how great the temptation for legitimate reprisals, a concept well-recognized in international law, R. E. Lee would not stoop to the level of his enemies. This is one of the reasons he has been called the "Christian General," as reflected in his address to the troops as they marched into Pennsylvania during the Gettysburg campaign of 1863: "It must be remembered that we make war only on armed men, and that we cannot take vengeance for the wrongs our people have suffered without lowering ourselves in the eyes of…Him to whom vengeance belongeth." Instructing his officers to arrest and punish all soldiers who committed any offense on the person or private property of Northern civilians, he reminded them that "the duties exacted of us by civilization and Christianity are not less obligatory in the country of the enemy than in our own."

Perhaps the most telling tribute to Lee came from his former enemies. When General Lee died in 1870, newspapers throughout the North universally praised his military genius and morality. The *New York Herald* said, "In him the military genius of America was developed to a greater extent than ever before. In him all that was pure and lofty in mind and purpose found lodgment. He came nearer the ideal of a soldier and Christian general than any man we can think of."

Unfortunately, despite America's rich tradition in fairness in combat operations, even the best lessons of history quickly fade unless they are inculcated. Future My Lai's cannot be prevented unless the answers to the "why" of My Lai are repeated over and over until they are ingrained into every warfighter in uniform. Just as Americans must never forget their rallying cries of honor and nobility—"Remember the Alamo"—they must be forced to deal with their nightmares—"My Lai." On the other hand, it is precisely because of its horror and repulsiveness that My Lai is uniquely suited to serve as the primary vehicle to address the entire issue of adherence to the law of war as well as the necessity for effective leadership in the extremely trying War on Terror.

The final caveat in the War on Terror is that the American military cannot afford to take these lessons lightly. Given the fact that knowledge acquired beyond basic trial and error methodologies requires varying degrees of academic effort, it is not surprising that over time, both individually and collectively, many lessons of history will be forgotten and thus, repeated. This fact is particularly devastating when viewed in the context of Man's efforts to reduce the continuing pattern of human warfare and terrorism. Accordingly, not only must the lessons of My Lai be remembered—they must be inculcated.

5.13 Questions for Discussion

1. *Responding to war crime allegations.* Considering the lessons of My Lai, what is the best course of action for the military command to take when it receives allegations of war crimes committed by American forces?

2. *Role of propaganda in the War on Terror.* How does the al-Qa'eda terror network employ the media as a tool of warfare? Is it effective?

3. *Grand strategy.* What impact does a grand strategy have in the War on Terror? Does the Obama Administration have a clearly focused grand strategy in Afghanistan?

4. *Why follow the law of war if the enemy does not*? The Roman practice of offering Roman citizenship to tribes who agreed to serve in the Roman army as auxiliary troops greatly benefited the expansion of the empire. For example, the *Honariani Atecotti Seniores* were formed from captured pirates from the Scottish Atecotti tribe circa 300 A.D. and served in the *Auxilium Palatinum*. On the other hand, the later Roman practice of slaughtering civilians only stiffened resistance amongst the barbarians who eventually conquered Rome. Caleb Carr, THE LESSONS OF TERROR: A HISTORY OF WARFARE AGAINST CIVILIANS, WHY IT HAS ALWAYS FAILED AND WHY IT WILL FAIL AGAIN (2002).

5. *Did the Calley trial follow the rules of war that were set in the aftermath of World War II at the Tokyo and Nuremberg War Crimes Tribunals?* The Tribunals had set the precedent that no soldier could rely on the excuse that he was following orders from a superior in order to excuse his war crimes. Then Secretary of the Army Howard H. Callaway stated to the *New York Times* that Lt. William Calley believed he was following orders, and thus his sentence was reduced. This contradicted the standards set in Tokyo and Nuremberg, where some Japanese and German soldiers were executed for their purported war crimes despite the fact that they raised the defense of superior orders. *See* Burke Marshall and Joseph Goldstein, *Learning From My Lai: A Proposal on War Crimes*, NY TIMES, Apr. 2, 1976 at 26. In light of these facts did the United States set a precedent that it did not have to abide by international law? Could a subordinate in a terrorist organization rely on the same defense Lt. Calley used if he were charged with a war crime?

Selected Bibliography

30 SOUTHERN HISTORICAL SOCIETY PAPERS 94, 1902.

Addicott, Jeffrey F. *Operation Desert Storm: R. E. Lee or W. T. Sherman?* 136 MILITARY LAW REVIEW 115 (1992).

Elliott, H. Wayne. *Theory and Practice: Some Suggestions for the Law of War Trainer*, THE ARMY LAWYER, July 1983, at 1.

Generous, Kevin M. Vietnam, THE SECRET WAR, 1985.

Goldstein, Joseph, et al. THE MY LAI MASSACRE AND ITS COVER-UP: BEYOND THE REACH OF LAW? 1976.

Graham, David E. *Operational Law (OPLAW)—A Concept Comes of Age*, THE ARMY LAWYER, July 1987, at 9.

Hall, David K., et al. FORCE WITHOUT WAR, 1979.

Henkin, Louis, et al. MIGHT V. RIGHT, 1991.

Jones, J. William. LIFE AND LETTERS OF GENERAL ROBERT EDWARD LEE, 1906.

Moore, John Norton. LAW AND THE INDO-CHINA WAR, 1972.

Nagel, Paul C. THE LEES OF VIRGINIA, 1990. Lee's view on Christian salvation was devoid of any form of human merit or morality although by the measure of any society, his own moral standards were impeccable. Grace oriented to biblical Christianity, he wrote, "I can only say that I am a poor sinner, trusting in Christ alone for salvation."

O'Brien, William V. THE CONDUCT OF JUST AND LIMITED WAR, 1981.

Peers, Lt. Gen. W.R. THE MY LAI INQUIRY, 1979.

Samenow, Stanton E., Jr. INSIDE THE CRIMINAL MIND, 1984.

Schindler, Dietrich, ed., and Jiri Toman. THE LAWS OF ARMED CONFLICTS, 1988.

Taylor, Lawrence. A TRIAL OF GENERALS, 1981.

Tinkle, Lon. 13 DAYS TO GLORY: THE SIEGE OF THE ALAMO, 1958.

von Clausewitz, Karl. ON WAR. J. Graham trans, 1918.

Walsh, Gary L. *Role of the Judge Advocate in Special Operations*, THE ARMY LAWYER, Aug. 1989, at 6-8.

Weigley, Russel F. HISTORY OF THE UNITED STATES ARMY, 1984.

Williamson, Porter B. PATTON'S PRINCIPLES: A HANDBOOK FOR MANAGERS WHO MEAN IT, 1979.

Chapter 6

Interrogation Techniques

If interrogators step over the line from coercion to outright torture, they should be held personally responsible. But no interrogator is ever going to be prosecuted for keeping Khalid Sheikh Mohammed awake, cold, alone and uncomfortable. Nor should he be.

—Mark Bowden

In discussing the issue of American interrogation practices, most are reminded of the Abu Ghraib prison abuse incident or the spurious "water boarding is torture" allegation. In the former case, was the prison abuse a reflection of a systemic policy—either *de jure* or *de facto*—on the part of the United States to illegally extract information from detainees, or was the abuse simply isolated acts of criminal behavior on the part of a handful of soldiers amplified by a grossly incompetent tactical chain of command at the prison facility? In the later case, did the Department of Justice approve CIA interrogation techniques, to include water boarding, which constituted torture?

Along with Abu Ghraib and water boarding, the central concern associated with interrogation methodologies centers on the time period from 2002-2005, the years before the enactment of a series of laws and the Supreme Court *Hamdan* ruling causing serious limitations on the use of various forms and levels of physical and physiological force to extract information from certain detainees. In turn, juxtaposed to all this is the matter of rendition, where it is alleged that the United States purposefully sent detainees to other nations knowing that they were going to be subjected to interrogations that employed torture or other illegal techniques.

Without question, numerous elements of the government have direct roles to play in gathering timely intelligence about terrorist networks in the War on Terror. The primary responsibilities are shared by the CIA, the FBI, and the DOD. The CIA has primary responsibility for terrorist matters outside the United States and the FBI has primary responsibility for terrorist matters in the United States. The

DOD relies chiefly on the Defense Intelligence Agency (DIA), a DOD support agency with over 7,000 military and civilian employees stationed throughout the world.

As covered in Chapter 4 of this book, starting in 2005 three important developments have shaped U.S. policy and law in terms of interrogation techniques. In the context of enemy combatants under the control of the U.S. government, the Detainee Treatment Act of 2005 adopted international human rights terminology in setting out interrogation limits. In short, American interrogators could not engage in "cruel, inhuman and degrading treatment or punishment of persons under detention, custody, or control of the United States Government." Pursuant to the so-called McCain Amendment, "cruel, unusual, and inhuman treatment or punishment" covers all those acts prohibited by the Fifth, Eighth, and Fourteenth Amendments to the Constitution, as previously stated in the U.S. reservations to the Torture Convention. The second development was the *Hamdan* case and the resulting 2006 Military Commissions Act which applied the provisions of Common Article 3 of the Geneva Conventions to all detainees. Finally, Executive Order 13441 issued by President Obama in January 2009, now requires all U.S. agencies (to include the CIA) to comply with the new Bush-era Army Field Manual on interrogations (FM 2-22.3) which specifically outlaws: (1) forcing the detainee to be naked, perform sexual acts, or pose in a sexual manner; (2) placing hoods or sacks over the head of the detainee, or using duct tape over the eyes; (3) applying beatings, electric shock, burns, or other forms of physical pain; (4) water boarding; (5) using military working dogs; (6) inducing hypothermia or heat injury; (7) conducting mock executions; and (8) depriving the detainee of necessary food, water, or medical care. Still, President Obama's order does allow federal agencies to employ non-coercive techniques and established a High-Value Detainee Interrogation Group (HIG), composed of experienced interrogators and support personnel from law enforcement, the DOD, and the intelligence community.

Allegations of torture roll off the tongue with ease. In the context of American interrogation practices and treatment of detainees, charges of torture are regularly raised by a variety of individuals and interest groups often associated with fixed political agendas. Recognizing that not every alleged incident of mistreatment necessarily satisfies the legal definition of torture, it is imperative that one views such allegations with a clear understanding of the applicable legal standards set out in law and judicial precedent. In this manner, claims of illegal interrogation practices can be properly measured as falling above or below a particular legal threshold. Only then can one hope to set aside the shrilly voiced rhetoric by such groups as the American Civil Liberties Union (ACLU) or Amnesty International, who once called the Guantanamo detention facility the "gulag of our time," and objectively establish whether or not the United States stands in violation of the rule of law.

In tandem with investigating American interrogation practices, the matter of how authorities should deal with the so-called "ticking time bomb" terrorist merits serious scrutiny in America's war against the unrestrained savagery of fanatical al-Qa'eda suicide bombers bent on using weapons of mass destruction. The concern is so great that a number of prominent voices both in and outside of the government have advocated that a judicial exception should be carved out to allow torture as an interrogation tool in special instances. Perhaps one of the most prominent and unexpected voices to advocate such a position is Professor Alan Dershowitz of Harvard Law School.

While some may claim that Dershowitz is reluctantly reflecting a new and ugly pragmatism associated with fighting terrorism, America cannot allow itself to slip into a Star Chamber mentality where torture is mandated by the State as a necessary evil. Understanding the need to find the appropriate balance between civil liberties and security concerns, the purpose of this chapter is twofold. First, the interrogation practices used by the United States to get information from various categories of detainees will be measured in light of both the domestic and international laws on torture and other forms of mistreatment. Bluntly put, did the United States employ illegal interrogation methods in the War on Terror, particularly between the years 2002-2005, as some have charged? Second, in the special case of the ticking time bomb terrorist, should the United States openly disregard the rule of law and officially sanction the use of torture?

The American position on the question of illegal interrogation practices is that the United States does not engage in torture or other ill-treatment, either in questioning or housing detainees. During the Bush Administration, U.S. National Security Council spokesman, Sean McCormack, exemplified the official stand: "The United States is treating enemy combatants in U.S. government control, wherever held, humanely and in a manner consistent with the principles of the Third Geneva Convention of 1949." Of course, this is not to say that the United States did not then and does not now fully question detainees at a variety of levels. Government officials responsible for gathering information from detainees certainly employ the full range of permissible interrogation tactics measured against the existing law at the time. In other words, some "legal" interrogation practices from 2002-2005 would be clearly "illegal" today.

6.1 Defining Torture

Torture as an instrument of the State to either punish or extract information from certain individuals has a long and dark history which need not be fully recounted here. Suffice it to say that in the West, the practice can be traced to the Romans who codified the use of torture as part of the Roman criminal law (Roman citizens were generally exempt).

In England, the earliest authoritative records regarding State use of torture appears in the Privy Council registers in the year 1540, which extends, with some gaps in the reports, for a hundred years. (Anyone familiar with the reign of Henry VIII knows that the State practice of torture surely predated these official warrants.) The number of official warrants issued by the Crown during this period was less than 100, an amazingly low figure relative to the number of felony investigations which occurred in any given year. This low statistic demonstrates that the predominant use of torture was interrogational in nature and not for punishment. The 1597 case of Jesuit priest John Gerard typifies the goal of torture. The Crown's warrant directed Gerard's torture in the Tower of London by means of "the manacles" and other "such torture" in order to make Gerard "utter directly and truly his uttermost knowledge" concerning certain traitors to the Crown.

In the modern era, by fixed law and customary practice, the prohibition on torture is now universal in nature; a majority of States have ratified the various international agreements associated with banning torture. Nevertheless, even though no State allows torture in its domestic law, the practice continues to flourish. It is estimated that one in four States regularly engages in the torture of various prisoners and detainees. Added to this paradox is the dilemma that some of the acts that should clearly constitute torture do not enjoy a uniformity of definition within the international community. As one legal commentator rightly pointed out, "The prohibition of torture…is not, itself, controversial. The prohibition in application, however, yields endless contention as each perpetrator [State actor] seeks to define its own behavior so as not to violate the ban."

Before exploring the common international legal definition of torture, it is useful to survey the general understanding of the term. Torture comes from the Latin verb "torquere" (to twist) and is defined in leading Anglo-Saxon dictionaries as follows: "Infliction of severe physical pain as a means of punishment or coercion;" "[t]he act of inflicting excruciating pain, as punishment or revenge, as a means of getting a confession or information, or for sheer cruelty;" "[t]he infliction of intense pain to the body or mind to punish, to extract a confession or information, or to obtain sadistic pleasure."

Certainly the red thread in these definitions is a combination of two essential elements: (1) the infliction of severe physical pain to the body or mind used to; (2) punish or obtain information. International law adopts this formula but sharpens it by stipulating that a State actor must carry out the act of torture and that the act must be intentional. Thus, one may describe certain criminals as torturing their victims during the commission of a particularly gruesome murder, but such criminal acts carried out by non-State actors are not violations of the international law on torture. In addition, international law expands the prohibition of torture to include other less abusive acts commonly designated in the world community as "other acts of cruel, inhuman, or degrading treatment or punishment," which is shortened simply to "ill-treatment."

6.2 The Torture Convention

Like the concept of human rights, international law really had little to say about the practice of State torture until the close of World War II. With the establishment of the United Nations in 1945, the prohibition of torture and ill-treatment are now core rights found in all of the most important international documents and treaties.

Article 5 of the 1948 Universal Declaration of Human Rights serves as the foundation for all subsequent efforts outlawing torture. Article 5 of the Declaration consists of only one brief sentence: "No one shall be subjected to torture or to cruel, inhuman, or degrading treatment or punishment." Later, the widely influential and legally binding International Covenant on Civil and Political Rights tracked the Universal Declaration of Human Rights. In pertinent part, Article 7 of the Covenant utilizes the exact same language found in the Universal Declaration on Human Rights: "No person shall be subjected to torture or to cruel, inhuman or degrading treatment or punishment." In binding itself to the International Covenant on Civil and Political Rights, the United States Senate sought to clarify the meaning of Article 7 and attached a reservation which defined "cruel, inhuman or degrading treatment or punishment" as meaning "the cruel and unusual treatment or punishment prohibited by the Fifth, Eighth, and Fourteenth Amendments to the Constitution of the United States."

In 1975, the United Nations adopted the Declaration on the Protection of all Persons from Being Subjected to Torture or Other Cruel, Inhuman or Degrading Treatment or Punishment. Although this document was a declaration only, it served as the basis for the 1984 United Nations Convention Against Torture, and Other Cruel, Inhuman or Degrading Treatment or Punishment (Torture Convention), the primary international agreement governing torture and ill-treatment. As suggested by the title, the point which had served as a source of controversy was more fully addressed in the Torture Convention—the distinction between "torture" and "other acts of cruel, inhuman, or degrading treatment or punishment." While both acts were previously prohibited in other documents, for the first time, the Torture Convention spelled out the obligations and consequences attendant to each type of act. Still, the Torture Convention did not exhibit the same care in defining what it meant by "other cruel, inhuman or degrading treatment or punishment" as it did with regard to torture. Without question, the Torture Convention devoted far more attention to crafting the meaning of the term torture, which it defined as:

[A]ny act by which severe pain or suffering, whether physical or mental, is intentionally inflicted on a person for such purposes as obtaining from him or a third person information or a confession, punishing him for an act he or a third person has committed or is suspected of having committed, or intimidating or coercing him or a third person, or for any reason based on discrimination of any kind, when such pain or suffering is inflicted by or at the instigation of…a public official or other person acting in an official capacity. It does not include pain or suffering arising only from, inherent in or incidental to lawful sanctions.

According to the Torture Convention, for torture to exist in the context of an interrogation the following criteria must be present: (1) the behavior must be based on an intentional act; (2) it must be performed by a State agent; (3) the behavior must cause severe pain or suffering to body or mind; and (4) it must be accomplished with the intent to gain information or a confession. In adopting the Torture Convention, the United States Senate provided the following reservations which require specific intent and better define the concept of mental suffering:

[T]he United States understands that, in order to constitute torture, an act must be *specifically intended* to inflict severe physical or mental pain or suffering and that mental pain or suffering refers to *prolonged mental harm* caused by or resulting from: (1) the intentional infliction or threatened infliction of severe physical pain or suffering; (2) the administration or application, or threatened administration or application, of mind altering substances or other procedures calculated to disrupt profoundly the senses or the personality; (3) the threat of imminent death; or (4) the threat that another person will imminently be subjected to death, severe physical pain or suffering, or the administration or application of mind altering substances or other procedures calculated to disrupt profoundly the senses or personality [emphasis added].

Article 2 of the Torture Convention absolutely excludes the notion of exceptional circumstances to serve as an excuse to the prohibition of torture. "No exceptional circumstances whatsoever, whether a state of war or a threat of war, internal political instability or any other public emergency, may be invoked as a justification for torture."

As noted, the phrase "other acts of cruel, inhuman, or degrading treatment or punishment," e.g., ill-treatment, is not defined in the Torture Convention. It is just stated. The Torture Convention certainly obliges each State party to the document to "undertake to prevent…other acts of cruel, inhuman, or degrading treatment or punishment," but Article 16 of the Torture Convention is the only part of the entire treaty that addresses ill-treatment.

Since the Torture Convention desires to "make more effective the struggle against torture and other cruel, inhuman or degrading treatment or punishment throughout the world," the distinction rests in the fact that torture and ill-treatment are viewed as two limbs of the same formula with torture, quite understandably, being predominant. Thus, while all acts of torture must necessarily encompass ill-treatment, acts of ill-treatment do not constitute torture. Clearly, a greater stigma is associated with the insidious evil of torture so that all intuitively realize that international law forbids torture, even if few are cognizant of the fact that ill-treatment is also prohibited. In turn, interrogation practices that do not rise to the level of ill-treatment may be repugnant by degree, but may be perfectly legal under international law. This being the case, it is efficacious to carefully note the differences between torture and ill-treatment as they have significant ramifications regarding State Party obligations.

Article 3 of the Torture Convention prohibits any State Party to "expel, return ("*refouler*") or extradite any person to another State where there are substantial grounds to believe that the person will be subjected to torture." The more common euphemism for this illegal practice is "extraordinary rendition," although it should be properly categorized as "illegal rendition." In making the determination of whether an illegal rendition has occurred, the State Party is required at Article 3(2) "to take into account all relevant considerations" with particular regard to whether or not there exists "a consistent pattern of gross, flagrant or mass violations of human rights." Even though the combined factors of "substantial grounds," coupled with "a consistent pattern of gross, flagrant or mass violations of human rights," provide considerable flexibility for a State Party to justify a particular rendition, at least the prohibition is established and a standard is established, albeit a subjective one. Surprisingly, Article 16 has no similar requirement regarding rendition to a country that engages in ill-treatment. This means that a State Party to the treaty is absolutely free to hand over an individual to a State that it knows engages in ill-treatment.

Article 4 requires each State Party to ensure that torture is a criminal offense under its domestic criminal law and Article 12 dictates that each State Party investigate any allegations of torture under its jurisdiction when reasonable grounds exist to believe that such acts have occurred. Article 7 further requires the State Party to either extradite the alleged torturer or "submit the case to competent [domestic] authorities for the purpose of prosecution." Also, Article 15 excludes all statements elicited through torture from evidence in a court of law, while Article 14 requires the State Party to make compensation to the victims of torture.

In contrast, Article 16 has no similar requirements mandating that ill-treatment be criminalized in domestic penal codes, requiring the prosecution of individuals charged with ill-treatment, or limitations on rendition. In addition, Article 16 has no requirement that victims of ill-treatment be compensated or that statements obtained as the fruit of ill-treatment must be excluded from evidence at a criminal trial. According to commentator Matthew Lippman, "[t]he failure to strengthen article [sic] 16 appears to have been based on a belief that the concept of cruel, inhuman or degrading treatment or punishment was too vague a legal standard upon which to base legal culpability and judgments."

Once one understands the basic statutory language prohibiting torture, the question of whether certain acts constitute torture or ill treatment can only be addressed by looking at leading judicial decisions and extrapolating the facts in those cases to the particulars at hand. Thus, while many individuals may cavalierly brand the CIA's practice of water boarding as "torture," the question can only find resolution in a competent judicial ruling. In this context, the inherent vagueness of ill-treatment and the reluctance of the Torture Convention to fully define the concept or to provide even a minimum level of sanction to the practice are further amplified by the leading international case dealing with unlawful interrogation practices. The often cited European Court of Human Rights ruling, *Ireland v. United Kingdom* provides the most useful barometer of the international legal view concerning what acts would and would not amount to torture.

The *Ireland* court found certain interrogation practices of English authorities to investigate suspected terrorism in Northern Ireland to be "inhuman and degrading," i.e., ill-treatment, under the European Convention on Human Rights, but not severe enough to rise to the level of torture. According to the Court, the finding of ill-treatment rather than torture "derives principally from a difference in the intensity of the suffering inflicted." In *Ireland*, the Court considered the use of five investigative measures known as "the five techniques" which were practiced by British authorities for periods of "four or five" days pending or during interrogation sessions. By a lopsided vote of 13-4, the Court ruled that the following interrogation techniques did not constitute torture:

- Wall-standing: Forcing the detainees to stand for some period of hours in a stress position described as "spread-eagled against the wall, with their fingers put high above their head against the wall, the legs spread apart and the feet back, causing them to stand on their toes with the weight of the body mainly on the fingers." Wall-standing was practiced for up to 30 hours with occasional periods for rest.

- Hooding: Placing a dark hood over the head of the detainee and keeping it on for prolonged periods of time except during interrogation.
- Subjection to noise: Holding the detainees in a room where there was a continuous loud and hissing noise.
- Deprivation of Sleep: Depriving detainees of sleep for prolonged periods of time.
- Deprivation of Food and Drink: Reducing the food and drink to suspects pending interrogations.

Although *Ireland* was decided prior to the 1984 Torture Convention, the language of the European Convention on Human Rights is identical to the Torture Convention's definition of torture and ill-treatment. Indeed, in *Selmouni v. France* (1999), the European Court of Human Rights cited *Ireland* with approval.

In order to determine whether a particular form of ill-treatment should be qualified as torture, the Court must have regard to the distinction, embodied In Article 3, between this notion and that of inhuman or degrading treatment. As the European Court has previously found, it appears that it was the intention that the Convention should, by means of this distinction, attach a special stigma to deliberate inhuman treatment causing very serious and cruel suffering (see the *Ireland v. the United Kingdom* judgment cited above …).

IRELAND v. UNITED KINGDOM
European Court of Human Rights
2 EHRR 25 (1978)

PANEL: Judge Balladore Pallieri (President), Judges, Wiarda, Zekia, Cremona, O'Donoghue, Pedersen, Thsr Vilhjalmsson, Ryssdal, Ganshof Van Der Meersch, Sir Gerald Fitzmaurice, Bindschedler-Robert, Evrigenis, Teitgen, Lagergren, Liesch, Gvlc Kl, Matscher, Mr M-A Eissen, Registrar, and Mr H Petzold, Deputy Registrar.

AS TO THE FACTS
I. The Emergency Situation and its Background
The tragic and lasting crisis in Northern Ireland lies at the root of the present case. In order to combat what the respondent Government describe as "the longest and most violent terrorist campaign witnessed in either part of the island of Ireland," the authorities in Northern Ireland exercised from August 1971 until December 1975 a series of extrajudicial powers of arrest, detention and internment. The proceedings in this case concern the scope and the operation in practice of those measures as well as the alleged ill-treatment of persons thereby deprived of their liberty.
…
15. Northern Ireland is not a homogeneous society. It consists of two communities divided by deep and long-standing antagonisms. One community is variously termed Protestant, Unionist

or Loyalist, the other is generally labeled as Catholic, Republican or Nationalist. About two-thirds of the population of one and a half million belong to the Protestant community, the remaining third to the Catholic community. The majority group is descended from Protestant settlers who emigrated in large numbers from Britain to Northern Ireland during the seventeenth century. The now traditional antagonism between the two groups is based both on religion and on social, economic and political differences. In particular, the Protestant community has consistently opposed the idea of a united Ireland independent of the United Kingdom, whereas the Catholic community has traditionally supported it.

16. The Irish Republican Army (IRA) is a clandestine organisation with quasi-military dispositions. Formed during the troubles prior to the partition of the island and illegal in the United Kingdom as well as in the Republic of Ireland, the IRA neither accepts the existence of Northern Ireland as part of the United Kingdom nor recognizes the democratic order of the Republic. It has periodically mounted campaigns of terrorism in both parts of the island of Ireland and in Great Britain. After 1962, the IRA was not overtly active for some years.

During the time covered by the complaints of the applicant Government, that is from 1971 to 1975, virtually all those members of the IRA living and operating in Northern Ireland were recruited from among the Catholic community.

...

47. At the beginning of 1972, despite a small drop, the level of violence remained higher than at any time before 9 August 1971. On 30 January 1972, 13 people were killed by army gunfire in the course of disorders taking place in the predominantly Catholic town of Londonderry. This incident led to a new upsurge in support for the IRA amongst the Catholic community.

In the first three months of 1972, 87 people were killed, including 27 members of the security forces. Two assassinations carried out in March, one of a Protestant and the other of a Catholic, were the only deaths attributed to Loyalist activity. 421 explosions, the vast majority attributed to the IRA, were caused during the same period.

48. From August 1971 until 30 March 1972 there had been in Northern Ireland 1,130 bomb explosions and well over 2,000 shooting incidents. 158 civilians, 58 soldiers and 17 policemen had been killed, and 2,505 civilians, 306 soldiers and 107 RUC members injured.

Throughout these months the numbers held under detention or internment orders proceeded to rise until a total of over 900 persons, all suspected of involvement with the IRA, were held at the end of March 1972. At the same time, the ordinary processes of the criminal law continued to be used, against Protestants as well as Catholics, whenever there was thought to be sufficient evidence to ground a criminal conviction. Thus, between 9 August 1971 and 31 March 1972, over 1,600 people were charged with "terrorist-type" offences.

49. In March 1972, in view of the deteriorating circumstances, the Government in London decided that they should assume direct responsibility for the administration of law and order in Northern Ireland if there was to be any hope of political progress. This decision was unacceptable to the Government of the province and accordingly it was announced on 24 March 1972 that direct rule from Westminster not only on law and order but on all matters was to be introduced.

Under the Northern Ireland (Temporary Provisions) Act 1972 (hereinafter referred to as the "Temporary Provisions Act"), which was passed by the United Kingdom Parliament and came into force on 30 March 1972, temporary provision was made for the exercise of the executive and legislative powers of the Northern Ireland Parliament and Government by the United Kingdom authorities. The Belfast Parliament was prorogued and the Queen empowered to legislate in its stead by Order in Council. The executive powers of the Belfast Government were transferred to the Secretary of State for Northern Ireland. This was a new office created for the purpose; its holder was a member of the United Kingdom Government and answerable to the United Kingdom Parliament. The legislation was enacted for a period of one year but was subsequently extended.

…

68. On 8 August 1973, the Northern Ireland (Emergency Provisions) Act 1973 (hereafter abbreviated to the "Emergency Provisions Act") came into force. This Act, which was based mainly on the recommendations of the Diplock Commission (see paras. 58 and 59 above), repealed the 1922 Special Powers Act, Regulations 10 and 11(1) and the 1972 Terrorists Order, while retaining in substance the procedure laid down in the latter Order. Briefly, the extrajudicial powers introduced under the Emergency Provisions Act were:

(i) arrest and detention for 72 hours;
(ii) interim custody for 28 days; and
(iii) detention (see paras. 88 and 89 below for a fuller explanation). These emergency powers remained in force for a period of one year unless renewed. The Act also dealt with the trial and punishment by the ordinary courts of certain scheduled offences, for the most part offences concerned with violence. One provision, s.6, is referred to below at para. 136.

69. Between 1 February 1973 and 31 October 1974, interim custody orders were served on 99 Protestants and 626 Catholics; at all times many more Catholics than Protestants were actually held. Shortly before Christmas 1973, 65 detainees, 63 of whom were Catholics, were released.

70. During the same period, 2,478 persons were charged with "terrorist-type offences", the total being made up as follows: 1,042 Protestants, 1,420 Catholics and 16 soldiers. These figures included 60 Protestants and 66 Catholics charged with murder. In addition, searches were being conducted and arms recovered in relation to both sides.

…

III. Allegations of Ill-Treatment
A. Introduction
92. As recounted above at paras. 39 and 41, on 9 August 1971 and thereafter numerous persons in Northern Ireland were arrested and taken into custody by the security forces acting in pursuance of the emergency powers. The persons arrested were interrogated, usually by members of the RUC, in order to determine whether they should be interned and/or to compile information about the IRA. In all, about 3,276 persons were processed by the police at various holding centres from August 1971 until June 1972. The holding centres were replaced in July 1972 by police offices in Belfast and at Ballykelly Military Barracks.

93. Allegations of ill-treatment have been made by the applicant Government in relation both to the initial arrests and to the subsequent interrogations. The applicant Government submitted written evidence to the Commission in respect of 228 cases concerning incidents between 9 August 1971 and 1974....

95. The Commission grouped the cases into five categories, according to the place where the ill-treatment was said to have been inflicted, namely:

    (1) the unidentified interrogation centre or centres;
    (2) Palace Barracks, Holywood;
    (3) Girdwood Park Barracks;
    (4) Ballykinler Regional Holding Centre; and
    (5) various other miscellaneous places.

B. The unidentified interrogation centre or centres

96. Twelve persons arrested on 9 August 1971 and two persons arrested in October 1971 were singled out and taken to one or more unidentified centres. There, between 11 to 17 August and 11 to 18 October respectively, they were submitted to a form of "interrogation in depth" which involved the combined application of five particular techniques.

These methods, sometimes termed "disorientation" or "sensory deprivation" techniques, were not used in any cases other than the fourteen so indicated above. It emerges from the Commission's establishment of the facts that the techniques consisted of:

    (a) wall-standing: forcing the detainees to remain for periods of some hours in a "stress position," described by those who underwent it as being "spread-eagled against the wall, with their fingers put high above the head against the wall, the legs spread apart and the feet back, causing them to stand on their toes with the weight of the body mainly on the fingers;"
    (b) hooding: putting a black or navy coloured bag over the detainees' heads and, at least initially, keeping it there all the time except during interrogation;
    (c) subjection to noise: pending their interrogations, holding the detainees in a room where there was a continuous loud and hissing noise;
    (d) deprivation of sleep: pending their interrogations, depriving the detainees of sleep;
    (e) deprivation of food and drink: subjecting the detainees to a reduced diet during their stay at the centre and pending interrogations.

The Commission's findings as to the manner and effects of the application of these techniques on two particular case-witnesses are referred to below at para. 104.

97. From the start, it has been conceded by the respondent Government that the use of the five techniques was authorised at "high level." Although never committed to writing or authorised in any official document, the techniques had been orally taught to members of the RUC by the English Intelligence Centre at a seminar held in April 1971.

98. The two operations of interrogation in depth by means of the five techniques led to the obtaining of a considerable quantity of intelligence information, including the identification of 700 members of both IRA factions and the discovery of individual responsibility for about 85 previously unexplained criminal incidents.

…

103. The Irish Government referred to the Commission 8 cases of persons submitted to the five techniques during interrogation at the unidentified centre or centres between 11 and 17 August 1971. A further case, that of T 22, considered in the Commission's report in the context of Palace Barracks, concerned the use of the five techniques in October 1971. The Commission examined as illustrative the cases of T 6 and T 13, which were among the 11 cases investigated by the Compton Committee.

104. T 6 and T 13 were arrested on 9 August 1971 during Operation Demetrius. Two days later they were transferred from Magilligan Regional Holding Centre to an unidentified interrogation centre where they were medically examined on arrival. Thereafter, with intermittent periods of respite, they were subjected to the five techniques during four or possibly five days; neither the Compton or Parker Committees nor the Commission were able to establish the exact length of the periods of respite.

The Commission was satisfied that T 6 and T 13 were kept at the wall for different periods totaling between twenty to thirty hours, but it did not consider it proved that the enforced stress position had lasted all the time they were at the wall. It stated in addition that the required posture caused physical pain and exhaustion. The Commission noted that, later on during his stay at the interrogation centre, T 13 was allowed to take his hood off when he was alone in the room, provided that he turned his face to the wall. It was not found possible by the Commission to establish for what periods T 6 and T 13 had been without sleep, or to what extent they were deprived of nourishment and whether or not they were offered food but refused to take it.

The Commission found no physical injury to have resulted from the application of the five techniques as such, but loss of weight by the two case-witnesses and acute psychiatric symptoms developed by them during interrogation were recorded in the medical and other evidence. The Commission, on the material before it, was unable to establish the exact degree of any psychiatric after-effects produced on T 6 and T 13, but on the general level it was satisfied that some psychiatric after-effects in certain of the fourteen persons subjected to the techniques could not be excluded.

…

107. T 13 and T 6 instituted civil proceedings in 1971 to recover damages for wrongful imprisonment and assault; their claims were settled in 1973 and 1975 respectively for £15,000 and £14,000. The twelve other individuals against whom the five techniques were used have all received in settlement of their civil claims compensation ranging from £10,000 to £25,000.

…

PROCEEDINGS BEFORE THE COMMISSION

144. In their original application, lodged with the Commission on 16 December 1971, and later supplemented, the Irish Government made various allegations of violations by the United Kingdom of Articles 1, 2, 3, 5, 6 and 14 of the Convention.

145. On 1 October 1972, the Commission declared the application inadmissible as regards Article 2 but accepted the allegations that:

—the treatment of persons in custody, in particular the methods of interrogation of such persons, constituted an administrative practice in breach of Article 3;

…

147. In its report, the Commission expressed the opinion:

(i) unanimously, that the powers of detention and internment without trial as exercised during the relevant periods were not in conformity with Article 5(1) to (4), but were "strictly required by the exigencies of the situation" in Northern Ireland, within the meaning of Article 15(1);

…

(iv) unanimously, that the combined use of the five techniques in the cases before it constituted a practice of inhuman treatment and of torture in breach of Article 3;

(v) unanimously, that violations of Article 3 occurred by inhuman, and in two cases degrading, treatment of

—T 6, in an unidentified interrogation centre in August 1971,

—T 2, T 8, T 12, T 15, T 9, T 14 and T 10 at Palace Barracks, Holywood, in September, October and November 1971,

—T 16, T 7 and T 11, at various places in August, October and December 1971;

(vi) unanimously, that there had been at Palace Barracks, Holywood, in the autumn of 1971, a practice in connection with the interrogation of prisoners by members of the RUC which was inhuman treatment in breach of Article 3 of the Convention;

…

The report contains various separate opinions.

DECISION-1:

AS TO THE LAW

148. Paragraph (d) of the application of 10 March 1976 states that the object of bringing the case before the Court (r.31(1)(d)) of the Rules of Court) is:

"to ensure the observance in Northern Ireland of the engagements undertaken by the respondent Government as a High Contracting Party to the Convention and in particular of the engagements specifically set out by the applicant Government in the pleadings filed and the submissions made on their behalf and described in the evidence adduced before the Commission in the hearings before them."

"To this end," the Court is invited:

"to consider the report of the Commission and to confirm the opinion of the Commission that breaches of the Convention have occurred and also to consider the claims of the applicant Government with regard to other alleged breaches and to make a finding of breach of the Convention where the Court is satisfied that a breach has occurred."

In their written and oral pleadings before the Court, the Irish Government allege breaches of Articles 1, 3, 5 (taken together with Article 15), 6 (taken together with Article 15) and 14 (taken together with Articles 5 and 6).

They also maintain—though they do not ask the Court to make a specific finding—that the British Government failed on several occasions in their duty to furnish the necessary facilities for the effective conduct of the investigation. The Commission does not go as far as that; however, at various places in its report, the Commission points out, in substance, that the respondent Government did not always afford it the assistance desirable. The Court regrets this attitude on the part of that Government; it must stress the fundamental importance of the principle, enshrined in Article 28, sub-paragraph (a) in fine, that the Contracting States have a duty to cooperate with the Convention institutions.

149. The Court notes first of all that it is not called upon to take cognizance of every single aspect of the tragic situation prevailing in Northern Ireland. For example, it is not required to rule on the terrorist activities in the six counties of individuals or of groups, activities that are in clear disregard of human rights. The Court has only to give a decision on the claims made before it by the Irish Republic against the United Kingdom. However, in so doing, the Court cannot lose sight of the events that form the background to this case.

I. On Article 3

150. Article 3 provides that "no one shall be subjected to torture or to inhuman or degrading treatment or punishment."

A. Preliminary questions

151. In their memorial of 26 October 1976 and at the hearings in February 1977, the United Kingdom Government raised two preliminary questions on the alleged violations of Article 3. The first concerns the violations which they no longer contest, the second certain of the violations whose existence they dispute.

1. Preliminary question on the non-contested violations of Article 3

152. The United Kingdom Government contest neither the breaches of Article 3 as found by the Commission (see para. 147 above), nor—a point moreover that is beyond doubt—the Court's jurisdiction to examine such breaches. However, relying inter alia on the case-law of the International Court of Justice (Northern Cameroons case, judgment of 2 December 1963, and Nuclear Tests cases, judgments of 20 December 1974), they argue that the European Court has power to decline to exercise its jurisdiction where the objective of an application has been accomplished or where adjudication on the merits would be devoid of purpose. Such, they claim, is the situation here. They maintain that the findings in question not only are not contested but also have been widely publicised and that they do not give rise to problems of interpretation or application of the Convention sufficiently important to require a decision by the Court. Furthermore, for them the subject-matter of those findings now belongs to past history in view of the abandonment of the five techniques (1972), the solemn and unqualified undertaking not to reintroduce these techniques (8 February 1977) and the other measures taken by the United Kingdom to remedy, impose punishment for, and prevent the recurrence of, the various violations found by the Commission.

This argument is disputed by the applicant Government. Neither is it accepted in a general way by the delegates of the Commission; they stated, however, that they would express no conclusion as to whether or not the above-mentioned undertaking had deprived the claim concerning the five techniques of its object.

153. The Court takes formal note of the undertaking given before it, at the hearing on 8 February 1977, by the United Kingdom Attorney-General on behalf of the respondent Government. The terms of this undertaking were as follows:

> "The Government of the United Kingdom have considered the question of the use of the 'five techniques' with very great care and with particular regard to Article 3 of the Convention. They now give this unqualified undertaking, that the 'five techniques' will not in any circumstances be reintroduced as an aid to interrogation."

The Court also notes that the United Kingdom has taken various measures designed to prevent the recurrence of the events complained of and to afford reparation for their consequences. For example, it has issued to the police and the army instructions and directives on the arrest, interrogation and treatment of persons in custody, reinforced the procedures for investigating complaints, appointed commissions of enquiry and paid or offered compensation in many cases (see paras. 99-100, 107, 110-111, 116-118, 121-122, 124, 128-130, 132, 135-139 and 142-143 above).

154. Nevertheless, the Court considers that the responsibilities assigned to it within the framework of the system under the Convention extend to pronouncing on the non-contested allegations of violation of Article 3. The Court's judgments in fact serve not only to decide those cases brought before the Court but, more generally, to elucidate, safeguard and develop the rules instituted by the Convention, thereby contributing to the observance by the States of the engagements undertaken by them as Contracting Parties (art 19).

The conclusion thus arrived at by the Court is, moreover, confirmed by para. 3 of r.47 of the Rules of Court. If the Court may proceed with the consideration of a case and give a ruling thereon even in the event of a "notice of discontinuance, friendly settlement, arrangement" or "other fact of a kind to provide a solution of the matter", it is entitled a fortiori to adopt such a course of action when the conditions for the application of this Rule are not present.
…

C. Questions concerning the merits

162. As was emphasized by the Commission, ill-treatment must attain a minimum level of severity if it is to fall within the scope of Article 3. The assessment of this minimum is, in the nature of things, relative; it depends on all the circumstances of the case, such as the duration of the treatment, its physical or mental effects and, in some cases, the sex, age and state of health of the victim, etc.

163. The Convention prohibits in absolute terms torture and inhuman or degrading treatment or punishment, irrespective of the victim's conduct. Unlike most of the substantive clauses of the Convention and of Protocols Nos. 1 and 4, Article 3 makes no provision for exceptions and, un-

der Article 15(2), there can be no derogation there from even in the event of a public emergency threatening the life of the nation.

164. In the instant case, the only relevant concepts are "torture" and "inhuman or degrading treatment", to the exclusion of "inhuman or degrading punishment".

...

165. The facts concerning the five techniques are summarized at paras. 96-104 and 106-107 above. In the Commission's estimation, those facts constituted a practice not only of inhuman and degrading treatment but also of torture. The applicant Government ask for confirmation of this opinion which is not contested before the Court by the respondent Government.

166. The police used the five techniques on fourteen persons in 1971, that is on twelve, including T 6 and T 13, in August before the Compton Committee was set up, and on two in October whilst that Committee was carrying out its enquiry. Although never authorised in writing in any official document, the five techniques were taught orally by the English Intelligence Centre to members of the RUC at a seminar held in April 1971. There was accordingly a practice.

167. The five techniques were applied in combination, with premeditation and for hours at a stretch; they caused, if not actual bodily injury, at least intense physical and mental suffering to the persons subjected thereto and also led to acute psychiatric disturbances during inter-rogation. They accordingly fell into the category of inhuman treatment within the meaning of Article 3. The techniques were also degrading since they were such as to arouse in their victims feelings of fear, anguish and inferiority capable of humiliating and debasing them and possibly breaking their physical or moral resistance.

On these two points, the Court is of the same view as the Commission.

In order to determine whether the five techniques should also be qualified as torture, the Court must have regard to the distinction, embodied in Article 3, between this notion and that of inhuman or degrading treatment.

In the Court's view, this distinction derives principally from a difference in the intensity of the suffering inflicted.

The Court considers in fact that, whilst there exists on the one hand violence which is to be condemned both on moral grounds and also, in most cases, under the domestic law of the Contracting States, but which does not fall within Article 3 of the Convention, it appears on the other hand that it was the intention that the Convention, with its distinction between "torture" and "inhuman or degrading treatment," should by the first of these terms attach a special stigma to deliberate inhuman treatment causing very serious and cruel suffering.

Moreover, this seems to be the thinking lying behind Article 1 in fine of Resolution 3452 (XXX) adopted by the General Assembly of the United Nations on 9 December 1975, which declares: "Torture constitutes an aggravated and deliberate form of cruel, inhuman or degrading treatment or punishment."

Although the five techniques, as applied in combination, undoubtedly amounted to inhuman and degrading treatment, although their object was the extraction of confessions, the naming of others and/or information and although they were used systematically, they did not occasion suffering of the particular intensity and cruelty implied by the word torture as so understood.

168. The Court concludes that recourse to the five techniques amounted to a practice of inhuman and degrading treatment, which practice was in breach of Article 3.

(b) Ill-treatment alleged to have accompanied the use of the five techniques
169. The applicant Government claim that the fourteen persons subjected to the five techniques, or some of those persons including T 6 and T 13, also had to undergo other kinds of treatment contrary to Article 3.

The Commission has found such treatment only in the case of T 6, although it regarded it as probable that the use of the five techniques was sometimes accompanied by physical violence (see para. 105 above).

170. As far as T 6 is concerned, the Court shares the Commission's opinion that the security forces subjected T 6 to assaults severe enough to constitute inhuman treatment. This opinion, which is not contested by the respondent Government, is borne out by the evidence before the Court.

171. In the thirteen remaining cases examined in this context, including the contested case of T 13, the Court has no evidence to support a finding of breaches of Article 3 over and above that resulting from the application of the five techniques.

172. Accordingly, no other practice contrary to Article 3 is established for the unidentified interrogation centre or centres; the findings relating to the individual case of T 6 cannot, of themselves, amount to proof of a practice.
…
246. The Court accordingly considers that it is not necessary to apply Article 50 in the present case.

FOR THESE REASONS, THE COURT
I. On Article 3
1. holds unanimously that, although certain violations of Article 3 were not contested, a ruling should nevertheless be given thereon;
2. holds unanimously that it has jurisdiction to take cognisance of the cases of alleged violation of Article 3 to the extent that the applicant Government put them forward as establishing the existence of a practice;
3. holds by sixteen votes to one that the use of the five techniques in August and October 1971 constituted a practice of inhuman and degrading treatment, which practice was in breach of Article 3;
4. holds by thirteen votes to four that the said use of the five techniques did not constitute a practice of torture within the meaning of Article 3;
5. holds by sixteen votes to one that no other practice of ill-treatment is established for the unidentified interrogation centres;

6. holds unanimously that there existed at Palace Barracks in the autumn of 1971 a practice of inhuman treatment, which practice was in breach of Article 3;

7. holds by fourteen votes to three that the last-mentioned practice was not one of torture within the meaning of Article 3;

…

Another source of guidance to distinguish a reasonable interrogation from an interrogation that crosses the line into ill-treatment or torture is found in the 1999 Israeli High Court decision entitled, *Public Committee Against Torture v. State of Israel (Public Committee)*. In the context of outlawing certain interrogation practices by Israeli officials, the High Court considered how otherwise reasonable interrogation practices could become illegal if taken to an extreme point of intensity. Playing music to disorient a subject prior to questioning is not illegal per se, but if the music is played in a manner that causes undue suffering, it is arguably a form of ill-treatment or torture. Depriving subjects of sleep during a lengthy interrogation process may be legitimate, but depending on the extent of sleep deprivation, could also constitute ill-treatment or torture. The use of handcuffing for the protection of the interrogators is a common and acceptable practice, so long as the handcuffs are not unduly tightened so as to cause excess pain. Similarly, the use of blindfolds is acceptable if done for legitimate security reasons, while the use of sacks over the head without proper ventilation is unacceptable.

The backdrop for *Public Committee* is as follows. The General Security Service of Israel (GSS) is responsible for conducting investigations of suspected terrorists who commit crimes against the State of Israel. As part of this responsibility, the GSS engages in the detention and interrogation of suspected terrorists. Up until the late 1980s, the official position of the government of Israel was that GSS interrogators did not use "coercive" methods during terrorist interrogations. In 1987, the government appointed the Landau Commission to investigate the methods of interrogation used by the GSS. In November 1987, the Landau Commission issued its report, recognizing the terrorist threat to the nation and the attendant necessity for the GSS to engage in what it termed euphemistically as "a moderate measure of physical pressure" during interrogations of suspected terrorists. In a separate secret part of the report, the Landau Commission set out limits in the types of physical pressure that the GSS might employ. In the publicly released section of the report, the commission advised that GSS agents should combine "non-violent psychological pressure of a vigorous and extensive interrogation…with…a moderate amount of physical pressure." In short, the Landau Commission provided the green light for the GSS to use "moderate…physical pressure" when conducting interrogations.

Adopting the recommendations of the Landau Commission, the Israeli government issued directives authorizing the GSS to use various physical means in certain cases. In taking the unprecedented step of trying to regulate the use of physical pressure during the interrogation of suspected terrorists, the government contended that such methods did not constitute torture. The Supreme Court of Israel found that the primary techniques used by the GSS (which had until then remained secret) involved the following:

- Shaking: The practice of shaking was deemed to be the most brutal and harshest of all the interrogation methods. The method is defined as "the forceful shaking of the suspect's upper torso, back and forth, repeatedly, in a manner which causes the neck and head to dangle and vacillate rapidly."
- Shabach Position: The practice of binding the subject in a child's chair "tilted forward towards the ground, in a manner that causes him real pain and suffering." Other reports amplify the

method and add that the subject's head is "covered in a hood while powerfully deafening music is emitted within inches of the suspect's head."

- Frog Crouch: The practice of making the subject crouch on the tips of their toes for five-minute intervals.
- Excessive Tightening of Handcuffs: The practice of inflicting injury to a suspect by excessive tightening of handcuffs or through the use of small handcuffs.
- Sleep Deprivation: The practice of intentionally keeping the subject awake for prolonged periods of time.

In ruling that there existed an absolute prohibition on the use of torture or ill-treatment as a means of interrogation, the Supreme Court held some of the practices of the GSS violated Israel's Basic Law—Human Dignity and Liberty. Specifically, the Court found that shaking, the use of the shabach, the use of the frog crouch, and, in certain instances, the deprivation of sleep, were all illegal and prohibited investigation methods. The fact that the Court did not characterize any of these techniques as having the severity of pain or suffering indicative of torture indicates that the Court viewed them as ill-treatment only, as in *Ireland*.

PUBLIC COMMITTEE AGAINST TORTURE IN ISRAEL v. ISRAEL
Supreme Court of Israel Sitting as High Court of Justice
H.C.J. 5100/94 (1999)

OPINION by President A. Barak:

The General Security Service (hereinafter, the "GSS") investigates individuals suspected of committing crimes against Israel's security. Is the GSS authorized to conduct these interrogations? The interrogations are conducted on the basis of directives regulating interrogation methods. These directives equally authorize investigators to apply physical means against those undergoing interrogation (for instance, shaking the suspect and the "Shabach" position). The basis for permitting such methods is that they are deemed immediately necessary for saving human lives. Is the sanctioning of these interrogation practices legal? These are the principal issues presented by the applicants before us.

Background

1. The State of Israel has been engaged in an unceasing struggle for both its very existence and security, from the day of its founding. Terrorist organizations have established as their goal Israel's annihilation. Terrorist acts and the general disruption of order are their means of choice. In employing such methods, these groups do not distinguish between civilian and military targets. They carry out terrorist attacks in which scores are murdered in public areas, public transportation, city squares and centers, theaters and coffee shops. They do not distinguish between men, women and children. They act out of cruelty and without mercy (For an in depth description of this phenomenon see the Report of the Commission of Inquiry Regarding the GSS' Interrogation Practices with Respect to Hostile Terrorist Activities headed by (ret.) Justice M. Landau, 1987—hereinafter, "Commission of Inquiry Report") published in the Landau Book 269, 276 (Volume 1, 1995).

The facts presented before this Court reveal that one hundred and twenty one people died in terrorist attacks between 1.1.96 to 14.5.98. Seven hundred and seven people were injured.

A large number of those killed and injured were victims of harrowing suicide bombings in the heart of Israel's cities. Many attacks—including suicide bombings, attempts to detonate car bombs, kidnappings of citizens and soldiers, attempts to highjack buses, murders, the placing of explosives, etc.—were prevented due to the measures taken by the authorities responsible for fighting the above described hostile terrorist activities on a daily basis. The main body responsible for fighting terrorism is the GSS.

In order to fulfill this function, the GSS also investigates those suspected of hostile terrorist activities. The purpose of these interrogations is, among others, to gather information regarding terrorists and their organizing methods for the purpose of thwarting and preventing them from carrying out these terrorist attacks. In the context of these interrogations, GSS investigators also make use of physical means. The legality of these practices is being examined before this Court in these applications.

...

Shaking

9. A number of applicants (H.C. 5100/94; H.C. 4054/95; H.C. 6536/95) claimed that the shaking method was used against them. Among the investigation methods outlined in the GSS' interrogation regulations, shaking is considered the harshest. The method is defined as the forceful shaking of the suspect's upper torso, back and forth, repeatedly, in a manner which causes the neck and head to dangle and vacillate rapidly. According to an expert opinion submitted in one of the applications (H.C. (motion) 5584/95 and H.C. 5100/95), the shaking method is likely to cause serious brain damage, harm the spinal cord, cause the suspect to lose consciousness, vomit and urinate uncontrollably and suffer serious headaches.

The State entered several countering expert opinions into evidence. It admits the use of this method by the GSS. To its contention, there is no danger to the life of the suspect inherent to shaking; the risk to life as a result of shaking is rare; there is no evidence that shaking causes fatal damage; and medical literature has not to date listed a case in which a person died directly as a result of having been only shaken. In any event, they argue, doctors are present in all interrogation compounds, and instances where the danger of medical damage presents itself are investigated and researched.

...

Waiting in the "Shabach" Position

10. This interrogation method arose in numerous applications (H.C. 6536/95, H.C. 5188/96, H.C. 7628/97). As per applicants' submission, a suspect investigated under the "Shabach" position has his hands tied behind his back. He is seated on a small and low chair, whose seat is tilted forward, towards the ground. One hand is tied behind the suspect, and placed inside the gap between the chair's seat and back support. His second hand is tied behind the chair, against its back support. The suspect's head is covered by an opaque sack, falling down to his shoulders. Powerfully loud music is played in the room. According to the affidavits submitted, suspects are detained in this position for a prolonged period of time, awaiting interrogation at consecutive intervals.

The aforementioned affidavits claim that prolonged sitting in this position causes serious muscle pain in the arms, the neck and headaches. The State did not deny the use of this method before this Court. They submit that both crucial security considerations and the investigators' safety require tying up the suspect's hands as he is being interrogated. The head covering is intended to prevent contact between the suspect in question and other suspects. The powerfully loud music is played for the same reason.

The "Frog Crouch"

11. This interrogation method appeared in one of the applications (H.C. 5188/96). According to the application and the attached corresponding affidavit, the suspect being interrogated was found in a "frog crouch" position. This refers to consecutive, periodical crouches on the tips of one's toes, each lasting for five minute intervals. The State did not deny the use of this method, thereby prompting Court to issue an order nisi in the application where this method was alleged. Prior to hearing the application, however, this interrogation practice ceased.

Excessive Tightening of Handcuffs

12. In a number of applications before this Court (H.C. 5188/96; H.C. 7563/97), various applicants have complained of excessive tightening of hand or leg cuffs. To their contention, this practice results in serious injuries to the suspect's hands, arms and feet, due to the length of the interrogations. The applicants invoke the use of particularly small cuffs, ill fitted in relation to the suspect's arm or leg size. The State, for its part, denies any use of unusually small cuffs, arguing that those used were both of standard issue and properly applied. They are, nonetheless, prepared to admit that prolonged hand or foot cuffing is likely to cause injuries to the suspect's hands and feet. To the State's contention, however, injuries of this nature are inherent to any lengthy interrogation.

Sleep Deprivation

13. In a number of applications (H.C. 6536/96; H.C. 7563/97; H.C. 7628/97) applicants have complained of being deprived of sleep as a result of being tied in the "Shabach" position, being subjected to the playing of powerfully loud music, or intense non-stop interrogations without sufficient rest breaks. They claim that the purpose of depriving them of sleep is to cause them to break from exhaustion. While the State agrees that suspects are at times deprived of regular sleep hours, it argues that this does not constitute an interrogation method aimed at causing exhaustion, but rather results from the prolonged amount of time necessary for conducting the interrogation.

…

The Means Employed for Interrogation Purposes

21. As we have seen, the GSS investigators are endowed with the authority to conduct interrogations. What is the scope of these powers and do they encompass the use of physical means in the course of the interrogation in order to advance it? Can use be made of the physical means presently employed by GSS investigators (such as shaking, the "Shabach" position, and sleep deprivation) by virtue of the investigating powers given the GSS investigators? Let us note that the State did not argue before us that all the means employed by GSS investigators are permissible by virtue of the "law of interrogation" per se….

22. An interrogation, by its very nature, places the suspect in a difficult position. "The criminal's interrogation," wrote Justice Vitkon over twenty years ago, "is not a negotiation process between two open and fair vendors, conducting their business on the basis of maximum mutual trust" (Cr. A 216/74 *Cohen v. The State of Israel*) 29(1) P.D. 340 at 352). An interrogation is a "competition of minds," in which the investigator attempts to penetrate the suspect's thoughts and elicit from him the information the investigator seeks to obtain. Quite accurately, it was noted that:

> Any interrogation, be it the fairest and most reasonable of all, inevitably places the suspect in embarrassing situations, burdens him, intrudes his conscience, penetrates the deepest crevices of his soul, while creating serious emotional pressure. (Y. Kedmi, On Evidence, Part A, 1991 at 25).

…

23. It is not necessary for us to engage in an in-depth inquiry into the "law of interrogation" for the purposes of the applications before us. These vary from one matter to the next. For instance, the law of interrogation, as it appears in the context of an investigator's potential criminal liability, as opposed to the purpose of admitting evidence obtained by questionable means. Here, by contrast, we deal with the "law of interrogation" as a power activated by an administrative authority (See Bein supra.). The "law of interrogation" by its very nature, is intrinsically linked to the circumstances of each case. This having been said, a number of general principles are nonetheless worth noting:

> First, a reasonable investigation is necessarily one free of torture, free of cruel, inhuman treatment of the subject and free of any degrading handling whatsoever. There is a prohibition on the use of "brutal or inhuman means" in the course of an investigation (F.H. 3081/91 *Kozli v. The State of Israel*, 35(4) P.D. 441 at 446). Human dignity also includes the dignity of the suspect being interrogated. (Compare H.C. 355/59 *Catlan v. Prison Security Services*, 34(3) P.D. 293 at 298 and C.A.4463/94 *Golan v. Prison Security Services*, 50(4) P.D. 136). This conclusion is in perfect accord with (various) International Law treaties—to which Israel is a signatory—which prohibit the use of torture, "cruel, inhuman treatment" and "degrading treatment" (See M. Evans and R. Morgan, Preventing Torture (1998) at 61; N.S. Rodley, The Treatment of Prisoners under International Law (1987) at 63). These prohibitions are "absolute." There are no exceptions to them and there is no room for balancing. Indeed, violence directed at a suspect's body or spirit does not constitute a reasonable investigation practice. The use of violence during investigations can potentially lead to the investigator being held criminally liable. (See, for example, article 277 of the Penal Law: Pressure on a Public Servant; supra at 130, 134; Cr. A. 64/86 *Ashash v. The State of Israel* (unpublished)).

> Second, a reasonable investigation is likely to cause discomfort. It may result in insufficient sleep. The conditions under which it is conducted risk being unpleasant. Indeed, it is possible to conduct an effective investigation without resorting to violence. Within the confines of the law, it is permitted to resort to various machinations and specific

sophisticated activities which serve investigators today (both for Police and GSS). Similar investigations—accepted in the most progressive of societies—can be effective in achieve their goals. In the end result, the legality of an investigation is deduced from the propriety of its purpose and from its methods. Thus, for instance, sleep deprivation for a prolonged period, or sleep deprivation at night when this is not necessary to the investigation time wise may be deemed a use of an investigation method which surpasses the least restrictive means.

From the General to the Particular

24. We shall now turn from the general to the particular. Plainly put, shaking is a prohibited investigation method. It harms the suspect's body. It violates his dignity. It is a violent method which does not form part of a legal investigation. It surpasses that which is necessary. Even the State did not argue that shaking is an "ordinary" investigation method which every investigator (in the GSS or police) is permitted to employ. The submission before us was that the justification for shaking is found in the "necessity" defence. That argument shall be dealt with below. In any event, there is no doubt that shaking is not to be resorted to in cases outside the bounds of "necessity" or as part of an "ordinary" investigation.

25. It was argued before the Court that one of the investigation methods employed consists of the suspect crouching on the tips of his toes for five minute intervals. The State did not deny this practice. This is a prohibited investigation method. It does not serve any purpose inherent to an investigation. It is degrading and infringes upon an individual's human dignity.

26. The "Shabach" method is composed of a number of cumulative components: the cuffing of the suspect, seating him on a low chair, covering his head with an opaque sack (head covering) and playing powerfully loud music in the area. Are any of the above acts encompassed by the general power to investigate? Our point of departure is that there are actions which are inherent to the investigation power. Therefore, we accept that the suspect's cuffing, for the purpose of preserving the investigators' safety, is an action included in the general power to investigate. Provided the suspect is cuffed for this purpose, it is within the investigator's authority to cuff him. The State's position is that the suspects are indeed cuffed with the intention of ensuring the investigators' safety or to prevent fleeing from legal custody. Even the applicants agree that it is permissible to cuff a suspect in similar circumstances and that cuffing constitutes an integral part of an interrogation. Notwithstanding, the cuffing associated with the "Shabach" position is unlike routine cuffing. The suspect is cuffed with his hands tied behind his back. One hand is placed inside the gap between the chair's seat and back support, while the other is tied behind him, against the chair's back support. This is a distorted and unnatural position. The investigators' safety does not require it. Therefore, there is no relevant justification for handcuffing the suspect's hands with particularly small handcuffs, if this is in fact the practice. The use of these methods is prohibited. As was noted, "Cuffing causing pain is prohibited." Moreover, there are other ways of preventing the suspect from fleeing from legal custody which do not involve causing the suspect pain and suffering.

27. This is the law with respect to the method involving seating the suspect in question in the "Shabach" position. We accept that seating a man is inherent to the investigation. This is not the

case when the chair upon which he is seated is a very low one, tilted forward facing the ground, and when he is sitting in this position for long hours. This sort of seating is not encompassed by the general power to interrogate. Even if we suppose that the seating of the suspect on a chair lower than that of his investigator can potentially serve a legitimate investigation objective (for instance, to establish the "rules of the game" in the contest of wills between the parties, or to emphasize the investigator's superiority over the suspect), there is no inherent investigative need for seating the suspect on a chair so low and tilted forward towards the ground, in a manner that causes him real pain and suffering. Clearly, the general power to conduct interrogations does not authorize seating a suspect on a forward tilting chair, in a manner that applies pressure and causes pain to his back, all the more so when his hands are tied behind the chair, in the manner described. All these methods do not fall within the sphere of a "fair" interrogation. They are not reasonable. They impinge upon the suspect's dignity, his bodily integrity and his basic rights in an excessive manner (or beyond what is necessary). They are not to be deemed as included within the general power to conduct interrogations.

28. We accept that there are interrogation related considerations concerned with preventing contact between the suspect under interrogation and other suspects and his investigators, which require means capable of preventing the said contact. The need to prevent contact may, for instance, flow from the need to safeguard the investigators' security, or that of the suspects and witnesses. It can also be part of the "mind game" which pins the information possessed by the suspect, against that found in the hands of his investigators. For this purpose, the power to interrogate—in principle and according to the circumstances of each particular case—includes preventing eye contact with a given person or place. In the case at bar, this was the explanation provided by the State for covering the suspect's head with an opaque sack, while he is seated in the "Shabach" position. From what was stated in the declarations before us, the suspect's head is covered with an opaque sack throughout his "wait" in the "Shabach" position. It was argued that the sack (head covering) is entirely opaque, causing the suspect to suffocate. The edges of the sack are long, reaching the suspect's shoulders. All these methods are not inherent to an interrogation. They do not confirm the State's position, arguing that they are meant to prevent eye contact between the suspect being interrogated and other suspects. Indeed, even if such contact should be prevented, what is the purpose of causing the suspect to suffocate? Employing this method is not connected to the purpose of preventing the said contact and is consequently forbidden. Moreover, the statements clearly reveal that the suspect's head remains covered for several hours, throughout his wait. For these purposes, less harmful means must be employed, such as letting the suspect wait in a detention cell. Doing so will eliminate any need to cover the suspect's eyes. In the alternative, the suspect's eyes may be covered in a manner that does not cause him physical suffering. For it appears that at present, the suspect's head covering—which covers his entire head, rather than eyes alone,—for a prolonged period of time, with no essential link to the goal of preventing contact between the suspects under investigation, is not part of a fair interrogation. It harms the suspect and his (human) image. It degrades him. It causes him to lose sight of time and place. It suffocates him. All these things are not included in the general authority to investigate. In the cases before us, the State declared that it will make an effort to find a "ventilated" sack. This is not sufficient. The covering of the head in the circumstances described, as distinguished from the covering of the eyes, is outside the scope of authority and is prohibited.

29. Cutting off the suspect from his surroundings can also include preventing him from listening to what is going on around him. We are prepared to assume that the authority to investigate an individual equally encompasses precluding him from hearing other suspects under investigation or voices and sounds that, if heard by the suspect, risk impeding the interrogation's success. Whether the means employed fall within the scope of a fair and reasonable interrogation warrant examination at this time. In the case at bar, the detainee is found in the "Shabach" position while listening to the consecutive playing of powerfully loud music. Do these methods fall within the scope or the general authority to conduct interrogations? Here too, the answer is in the negative. Being exposed to powerfully loud music for a long period of time causes the suspect suffering. Furthermore, the suspect is tied (in place) in an uncomfortable position with his head covered (all the while). The use of the "Shabach" method is prohibited. It does not fall within the scope of the authority to conduct a fair and effective interrogation. Powerfully loud music is a prohibited means for use in the context described before us.

30. To the above, we must add that the "Shabach" position includes all the outlined methods employed simultaneously. Their combination, in and of itself gives rise to particular pain and suffering. This is a harmful method, particularly when it is employed for a prolonged period of time. For these reasons, this method does not form part of the powers of interrogation. It is an unacceptable method. "The duty to safeguard the detainee's dignity includes his right not to be degraded and not to be submitted to sub-human conditions in the course of his detention, of the sort likely to harm his health and potentially his dignity."

A similar—though not identical—combination of interrogation methods were discussed in the case of *Ireland v. United Kingdom* (1978) 2 EHRR 25. In that case, the Court probed five interrogation methods used by England for the purpose of investigating detainees suspected of terrorist activities in Northern Ireland. The methods were as follows: protracted standing against the wall on the tip of one's toes; covering of the suspect's head throughout the detention (except during the actual interrogation); exposing the suspect to powerfully loud noise for a prolonged period and deprivation of sleep, food and drink. The Court held that these methods did not constitute "torture." However, since they treated the suspect in an "inhuman and degrading" manner, they were nonetheless prohibited.

31. The interrogation of a person is likely to be lengthy, due to the suspect's failure to cooperate or due to the information's complexity or in light of the imperative need to obtain information urgently and immediately. Indeed, a person undergoing interrogation cannot sleep as does one who is not being interrogated. The suspect, subject to the investigators' questions for a prolonged period of time, is at times exhausted. This is often the inevitable result of an interrogation, or one of its side effects. This is part of the "discomfort" inherent to an interrogation. This being the case, depriving the suspect of sleep is, in our opinion, included in the general authority of the investigator…

The above described situation is different from those in which sleep deprivation shifts from being a "side effect" inherent to the interrogation, to an end in itself. If the suspect is intentionally deprived of sleep for a prolonged period of time, for the purpose of tiring him out or "breaking" him—it shall not fall within the scope of a fair and reasonable investigation. Such means harm the rights and dignity of the suspect in a manner surpassing that which is required.

…

35. Indeed, we are prepared to accept that in the appropriate circumstances, GSS investigators may avail themselves of the "necessity" defence, if criminally indicted. This however, is not the issue before this Court. We are not dealing with the potential criminal liability of a GSS investigator who employed physical interrogation methods in circumstances of "necessity." Moreover, we are not addressing the issue of admissibility or probative value of evidence obtained as a result of a GSS investigator's application of physical means against a suspect. We are dealing with a different question. The question before us is whether it is possible to infer the authority to, in advance, establish permanent directives setting out the physical interrogation means that may be used under conditions of "necessity." Moreover, we are asking whether the "necessity" defence constitutes a basis for the GSS investigator's authority to investigate, in the performance of his duty. According to the State, it is possible to imply from the "necessity" defence, available (post factum) to an investigator indicted of a criminal offence, an advance legal authorization endowing the investigator with the capacity to use physical interrogation methods. Is this position correct?

36. In the Court's opinion, a general authority to establish directives respecting the use of physical means during the course of a GSS interrogation cannot be implied from the "necessity" defence. The "necessity" defence does not constitute a source of authority, allowing GSS investigators to make use physical means during the course of interrogations. The reasoning underlying our position is anchored in the nature of the "necessity" defence. This defence deals with deciding those cases involving an individual reacting to a given set of facts. It is an ad hoc endeavour, in reaction to a event. It is the result of an improvisation given the unpredictable character of the events. Thus, the very nature of the defence does not allow it to serve as the source of a general administrative power….

A Final Word

39. This decision opens with a description of the difficult reality in which Israel finds herself security wise. We shall conclude this judgment by re-addressing that harsh reality. We are aware that this decision does not ease dealing with that reality. This is the destiny of democracy, as not all means are acceptable to it, and not all practices employed by its enemies are open before it. Although a democracy must often fight with one hand tied behind its back, it nonetheless has the upper hand. Preserving the Rule of Law and recognition of an individual's liberty constitutes an important component in its understanding of security. At the end of the day, they strengthen its spirit and its strength and allow it to overcome its difficulties….

40. Deciding these applications weighed heavy on this Court. True, from the legal perspective, the road before us is smooth. We are, however, part of Israeli society. Its problems are known to us and we live its history. We are not isolated in an ivory tower. We live the life of this country. We are aware of the harsh reality of terrorism in which we are, at times, immersed. Our apprehension is that this decision will hamper the ability to properly deal with terrorists and

terrorism, disturbs us. We are, however, judges. Our brethreen require us to act according to the law. This is equally the standard that we set for ourselves. When we sit to judge, we are being judged. Therefore, we must act according to our purest conscience when we decide the law.

In terms of American legal jurisprudence related to rendition, the Ninth Circuit case of *Bellout v. Ashcroft* provides a typical view of the standard legal burden and how it is evaluated. Not only is the burden on the defendant, the concept of what constitutes an illegal rendition which would violate the Torture Convention is also set at a high level.

BELLOUT v. ASHCROFT
United States Court of Appeals for the Ninth Circuit
363 F.3d 975 (April 12, 2004)

SILVERMAN, Circuit Judge:

Mouloud Bellout, a native and citizen of Algeria, petitions for review of the BIA's summary affirmance of the IJ's denial of Bellout's application for asylum, withholding of removal, and protection under the Convention Against Torture (CAT). The IJ found Bellout statutorily ineligible for relief from deportation because he engaged in terrorist activity when he joined "Armed Islamic Group (GIA)," a State Department-recognized terrorist organization, in 1995 and lived in GIA camps in Algeria for three years. Bellout has been removed to Algeria.

We hold as follows: First, because the IJ found that there are reasonable grounds to believe that Bellout engaged in or is likely to engage in terrorist activity under *8 U.S.C. § 1158(b)(2)(a)(v)*, we lack jurisdiction to review the IJ's determination that Bellout is ineligible for asylum by virtue of *8 U.S.C. § 1158(b)(2)(D)*. Second, substantial evidence supports the IJ's conclusion that Bellout is ineligible for withholding of removal. Finally, substantial evidence supports the IJ's denial of deferral of removal under CAT.

I. FACTS

Bellout attempted to enter the United States at Los Angeles International Airport on January 6, 1999, using a fraudulent Belgian passport. After the INS initiated removal proceedings, Bellout applied for asylum, withholding of deportation, and relief under CAT, alleging that he would be tortured by terrorists or police if he returned to Algeria. At his hearing, Bellout testified that he joined GIA in 1995, lived in GIA mountain camps, made friends with other members, read GIA's pamphlets and literature, discussed ideology with other members of the group, and carried weapons and ammunition. When GIA divided into a second group in 1996, Bellout went with the second group—"Algamma El-Salafia Lel-Daawa Wal Ketal." He remained with this group until 1998, when he left Algeria.

The IJ found that Bellout was statutorily barred from asylum, withholding of removal and relief under CAT as an alien "who the Attorney General knows, or has reasonable grounds to believe, is engaged in or is likely to engage after entry in any terrorist activity."

8 U.S.C. § 1189(a) authorizes the Secretary of State to designate foreign terrorist organizations by providing notice and findings to congressional leaders and publishing the designation in the Federal Register. Unless Congress disapproves the designation, it becomes effective upon publication in the Federal Register. *Id. § 1189(a)(2)(B)*. Although the designation is effective for two years, the Secretary may redesignate a foreign terrorist organization after the two years expire. *Id. § 1189(a)(4).*

The Secretary has designated and redesignated the "Armed Islamic Group (GIA)" as a terrorist organization under *8 U.S.C. § 1189. Designation of Foreign Terrorist Organizations, 62 Fed. Reg. 52650 (Oct. 8, 1997); 64 Fed. Reg. 55112 (Oct. 8, 1999); 66 Fed. Reg. 51088 (Oct. 5, 2001); 68 Fed. Reg. 56860 (Oct. 2, 2003).* According to the State Department Office of Counterterrorism's 1999 Report of Foreign Terrorist Organizations, GIA is an extremely violent terrorist group that frequently and brutally attacks and kills civilians, journalists, and foreign residents. The Report says that GIA uses assassinations and bombings and favors kidnapping victims and slitting their throats. According to the Report, GIA's activities are not limited only to Algeria; GIA hijacked an Air France flight in December 1994 and is suspected of a series of bombings in France in 1995.

Because Bellout had been a member of a State Department-designated terrorist organization, the IJ found that Bellout engaged in terrorist activity and, in the alternative, posed a danger to security in the United States. He was therefore ineligible for asylum. He likewise was ineligible for withholding of deportation. The IJ also concluded that Bellout was not entitled to deferral of removal under CAT because he had failed to establish that he would more likely than not be tortured if he returned to Algeria. The BIA affirmed the IJ's decision, adopting that decision as the final agency determination pursuant to 8 C.F.R. § 3.1(a)(7) (2002).

Bellout argues that the IJ erred in finding that he was ineligible for asylum and withholding of removal because he engaged in terrorist activity, and in denying him relief under CAT.

II. ASYLUM

An alien is ineligible for asylum if he is inadmissible or removable for engaging in terrorist activity or if "the Attorney General determines" that "there are reasonable grounds for regarding an alien as a danger to the security of the United States." *8 U.S.C. § 1158(b)(2)(A) (iv)–(v).* "Terrorist activities" include membership in "a foreign terrorist organization, as designated by the Secretary [of State] under [8 U.S.C.] section 1189." *Id. § 1182(a)(3)(B)(i)(v).*

The asylum statute deprives this court of jurisdiction to review the Attorney General's determination under *8 U.S.C. § 1158(b)(2)(A)(v)* that an alien is ineligible for asylum because the alien is inadmissible or removable because of terrorist activity. See *8 U.S.C. § 1158(b)(2)(D).* The statute provides:

> (D) No judicial review
> There shall be no judicial review of a determination of the Attorney General under subparagraph (A) (v) [ineligibility for asylum because the alien is inadmissible for terrorist activity].

Thus, this court lacks jurisdiction to review the IJ's determination that Bellout is ineligible for asylum pursuant to *§ 1158(b)(2)(A)(v)* because Bellout is inadmissible or removable because of terrorist activity. This portion of the petition for review is dismissed.

III. WITHHOLDING OF REMOVAL

We affirm the IJ's denial of relief if there is reasonable, substantial, and probative evidence to support the decision based on the record as a whole, and we may not reverse the IJ's findings unless the evidence compels a contrary conclusion. *INS v. Elias-Zacarias, 502 U.S. 478, 481, 117 L. Ed. 2d 38, 112 S. Ct. 812 (1992).*

An alien is ineligible for withholding of removal if "the Attorney General decides that… there are reasonable grounds to believe that the alien is a danger to the security of the United States."…Reasonable grounds exist to believe that an alien is a danger to security if the alien "has engaged, is engaged, or at any time after admission engages in any terrorist activity (as defined in *section 1182(a)(3)(B)(iv)*…)." Terrorist activities include membership in "a foreign terrorist organization, as designated by the Secretary [of State] under [*8 U.S.C. §*] *1189*."

Consistent with the statutory provision for withholding of removal, federal regulation provides for mandatory denial of withholding of removal under CAT if the Attorney General has "reasonable grounds to believe that the alien is a danger to the security of the United States." *8 U.S.C. § 1231(b)(3)(B)(iv); 8 C.F.R. § 1208.16(d)(2) (2003).* Thus, if the alien is barred from withholding of removal under *§ 1231(b)(3)(B)(iv)*, he is also barred from withholding of removal under CAT.

Substantial evidence supports the IJ's conclusion that Bellout engaged in or was likely to engage in terrorist activity because Bellout testified that he was a member of GIA for three years. Because Bellout engaged in terrorist activity, there are reasonable grounds to believe that he is a danger to the security of the United States, and he is ineligible for statutory withholding of removal and withholding of removal under CAT. *See 8 U.S.C. § 1231(b)(3)(B); 8 C.F.R. § 1208.16(d)(2).*

Interpreting a prior version of the asylum statute, we recently held that an alien who engaged in terrorist activity against a foreign country is not necessarily a danger to the security of the United States. *Cheema v. INS, 350 F.3d 1035, 1040–41 (9th Cir. 2003). Cheema* does not control this case because the court's reasoning in *Cheema* was premised on prior versions of the asylum and withholding statutes. The prior asylum statute barred aliens who engaged in terrorist activity from eligibility for asylum and withholding of removal *unless* the Attorney General found that there were not reasonable grounds for regarding the alien as a danger to the security of the United States. We held that the Attorney General could not collapse the two-prong statutory test and focus only on terrorist activity.

However, the statute has changed so there is no longer a two-prong test. The Illegal Immigration Reform and Immigrant Responsibility Act of 1996 (IIRIRA) amended the asylum statute to provide that an alien is ineligible for asylum if the Attorney General decides that there are reasonable grounds for regarding the alien as a danger to the security of the United States *or* that the alien is inadmissible or removable for terrorist activity. Either ground will support the IJ's denial of asylum. Pub. L. 104-208, § 604, 110 Stat. 3009-691 (1996) (codified at *8 U.S.C. § 1158(b)(2)(A) (I(v))-(v)).* In addition, the Antiterrorism and Effective Death Penalty Act of 1996 (AEDPA) amended the withholding of removal statute to specifically provide that an alien who engages in terrorist activity "shall be considered to be an alien for whom there are reasonable grounds for regarding as a danger to the security of the United States." Pub. L. 104-132, § 413(a), 110 Stat. 1214 (1996) (codified at *8 U.S.C. § 1231(b)(3)(B)(iv)).*

IV. RELIEF UNDER CAT

Bellout argues that the IJ should have granted him deferral of removal under the Convention Against Torture because, he claims, the police will torture him if he returns to Algeria. Article

3 of the United Nations Convention Against Torture or Punishment prohibits removal to a state where there are substantial grounds to believe the alien would be tortured. *Al-Saher v. INS, 268 F.3d 1143, 1146 (9th Cir. 2001)*. Although barred from "withholding of removal" under CAT, Bellout remains eligible for "deferral of removal" under CAT. *8 C.F.R. § 1208.17(a) (2003)*. We review the denial of relief under CAT for substantial evidence. *Zheng v. Ashcroft, 332 F.3d 1186, 1194 (9th Cir. 2003)*.

To be eligible for deferral of removal under CAT, Bellout must establish that he "is more likely than not to be tortured" if he returns to Algeria. *8 C.F.R. § 1208.17(a) (2003); see also Zheng, 332 F.3d at 1194*. Bellout testified to one incident of abuse by the police in 1994 before he joined GIA. There is no evidence in the record that the Algerian government is aware that Bellout joined GIA or is interested in him. The IJ found that there was no evidence that members of militant groups who leave Algeria will be persecuted or tortured upon return and that Bellout did not meet his burden of establishing it is more likely than not that he will face torture if returned to Algeria. The evidence does not compel a contrary conclusion. *Zheng, 332 F.3d at 1194*.

PETITION FOR REVIEW DISMISSED IN PART AND DENIED IN PART.

Real world enforcement mechanisms to ensure compliance with the Torture Convention's prohibition of torture and ill-treatment are wholly inadequate. This is because the individual State Party is expected to self-police and, if this fails, the only remaining hope for meaningful pressure is international condemnation from the court of world opinion. While the Torture Convention did create an investigatory body called the Committee Against Torture, its responsibilities revolve around a complex maze of reports and recommendations which, as one might anticipate, have generally accomplished very little. In fact, the biggest stick that the Committee Against Torture wields is the threat that it may provide an unfavorable summary of a particular country in its yearly report. As always, the chief enforcement tool in a democracy is the rule of law coupled with the judgment of its citizens; civilized peoples are repulsed by the concept of torture. Levels of compliance in totalitarian regimes are dismal, and the minimal progress that is achieved occurs only through the economic and political pressure applied by democracies.

6.3 United States Domestic Law

The American experience has not been guiltless in terms of the sanctioned use of torture and ill-treatment to elicit confessions in criminal investigations, particularly in the early part of the last century. By 1931, the appalling practice of torture by local law enforcement had become so common throughout the nation that a special government fact-finding commission was set up to investigate the matter. The Wickersham Commission issued a report on abusive police interrogation practices that not only educated the public, but also energized the United States Supreme Court to hand down a string of cases in which police interrogation abuses that "shocked the conscience" of the Court were equated with torture.

Currently, torture is defined in 18 U.S.C. § 2340 as:

[A]n act committed by a person acting under the color of the law specifically intended to inflict severe physical or mental pain or suffering (other than pain or suffering incidental to lawful sanctions) upon another person within his custody or physical control.

While domestic acts of torture are punished as common law crimes, 18 U.S.C. § 2340A makes it a federal offense for an American national to either commit or attempt to commit torture outside the United States. In 1992, Congress passed the Torture Victim Protection Act of 1991, which opened United States courts to civil law damage suits by any individual "who, under actual or apparent authority, or color of law, of any foreign nation," violates international law regarding torture.

In the context of what techniques would be lawful for interrogators to use in the United States, a 2003 United States Supreme Court decision entitled *Chavez v. Martinez* provides some current guidance. The central issue in *Chavez* involved the issue of coercive questioning by a police officer.

The facts of the case are as follows. While "investigating suspected narcotics activity" near a vacant lot, police in Oxnard, California, stopped Oliverio Martinez as he was riding his bike down a darkened path. The police conducted a *Terry* patdown frisk of Martinez and discovered a knife in his waistband. An altercation ensued and police officers claim that Martinez took one of the officer's "gun from its holster and pointed it at them." Officer Pea then drew her service pistol and shot Martinez five times, leaving him blinded and paralyzed. Martinez was placed under arrest and taken by ambulance to the hospital. Sergeant Ben Chavez, the patrol supervisor, "accompanied Martinez to the hospital and then questioned Martinez while he was receiving treatment from medical personnel." The interrogation in the emergency room of the hospital "lasted a total of about 10 minutes, over a 45-minute period, with Chavez leaving the emergency room for periods of time to permit medical personnel to attend to Martinez."

During the interrogation, Chavez never read Martinez his *Miranda* warnings. There can be no question that Martinez was disoriented and in extreme pain throughout the process of interrogation. At first Martinez was uncooperative. "At one point, Martinez said 'I am not telling you anything until they treat me,' yet Chavez continued the interview." Later, Martinez admitted taking the gun and pointing it at police. This act resulted in Martinez being shot by Pea.

Although Martinez was never charged with any crime and his statements were never used against him in a criminal proceeding, he subsequently filed a claim for damages in the United States District Court for the Central District of California under 42 U.S.C. § 1983, alleging that Sergeant Chavez had violated his Fifth Amendment right against self-incrimination as well as his Fourteenth Amendment substantive due process right. The Court of Appeals for the Ninth Circuit affirmed the District Court's denial of Chavez's defense of qualified immunity and entered summary judgment in favor of Martinez for both claims. With Justice Thomas delivering the opinion for the majority, the Supreme Court granted certiorari and reversed and remanded the case.

In seeking guidance for questioning suspected terrorists within the United States, the case is significant for two reasons. First, by overturning the Ninth Circuit's ruling that "the mere use of compulsive questioning, without more, violates the Constitution," the Court clearly established that the Fifth Amendment is not violated when law enforcement agents who do not intend to use statements in subsequent criminal proceedings interrogate with coercion an unwilling suspect without providing *Miranda* warnings. The Court related that "mere coercion does not violate the text of the Self-Incrimination Clause absent the use of compelled statements in a criminal case against the witness." Thus, the Court held that "the absence of a 'criminal case' in which Martinez was compelled to be a 'witness' against himself defeats his core Fifth Amendment claim" and voids any § 1983 action. Still, the Court was quick to note that they were not condoning the use of torture or ill-treatment by law enforcement:

[O]ur views of the proper scope of the Fifth Amendment's Self-Incrimination Clause do not mean that police torture or other abuse that results in a confession is constitutionally permissible so long as the statements are not used in trial; it simply means that the Fourteenth Amendment's Due Process Clause, rather than the Fifth Amendment's Self Incrimination Clause, would govern the inquiry in those cases and provide relief in appropriate circumstances.

Second, the ruling left in place the subjective "shock the conscience" standard, taken from the 1952 case of *Rochin v. California*, for determining when the police cross the threshold for conduct that violates the Fourteenth Amendment. In *Rochin*, police officers witnessed the defendant swallow two capsules which they suspected were illegal substances. Rochin was handcuffed and taken to a hospital where a doctor forced an emetic solution through a tube into Rochin's stomach and against Rochin's will. Rochin vomited two morphine capsules and was subsequently convicted. Overturning the conviction, the Supreme Court held that obtaining evidence by methods that are "so brutal and so offensive to human dignity" stands in violation of the Fourteenth Amendment's due process clause:

> [W]e are compelled to conclude that the proceedings by which this conviction was obtained do more than offend some fastidious squeamishness or private sentimentalism about combating crime too energetically. This is conduct that *shocks the conscience*....They are methods too close to the rack and screw to permit of constitutional differentiation [emphasis added].

As to whether the facts of *Chavez* would constitute a violation of the Fourteenth Amendment, the Court remanded that issue back to the lower court although at least five of the justices apparently were not "shocked" that Sergeant Chavez engaged in a repetitive interrogation even though Martinez was suffering "excruciating pain." Despite the fact that Sergeant Chavez may have indeed benefited from the situation if Martinez subjectively thought that he had to answer questions as a condition of getting medical treatment, this was not the case and medical personnel were treating Martinez throughout the interrogation period. Justice Thomas wrote that "we cannot agree with Martinez's characterization of Chavez's behavior as egregious or conscience shocking." The fact that Chavez did not interfere with medical treatment and did not cause the pain experienced by Martinez (the bullet wounds to Martinez occurred prior to and totally apart from the questioning process) were certainly important factors which influenced some, but not all, of the justices.

Expressing an opposite view, Justice Stevens dissented and saw the interrogation conducted by Sergeant Chavez as tantamount to torture and a clear violation of the Fourteenth Amendment:

> As a matter of fact, the interrogation of respondent was the functional equivalent of an attempt to obtain an involuntary confession from a prisoner by torturous methods. As a matter of law, that type of brutal police conduct constitutes an immediate deprivation of the prisoner's constitutionally protected interest in liberty.

Unfortunately, the Court did not provide any new approaches to assist in defining what would constitute interrogation behavior that would "shock the conscience." The Court was content to cite previous examples from past cases, traced from the 1936 case of *Brown v. Mississippi*.

In *Brown*, the Court ruled that convictions based on confessions extracted by law enforcement through methods tantamount to torture violated the Fourteenth Amendment. The facts of the case involved the hanging and whipping of a murder suspect by local police until a confession was obtained. Other defendants were also tortured—they "were made to strip and...were laid over chairs and their backs were cut to pieces with a leather strap with buckles on it…and in this manner the defendants confessed to the crime." All of the defendants were convicted of murder and sentenced to death. In reversing the convictions, the Supreme Court stated the following:

> [The] state is free to regulate the procedure of its courts in accordance with its own conceptions of policy, unless in so doing it offends some principle of justice so rooted in the traditions and conscience of our people as to be ranked as fundamental. But freedom of the state in establishing its policy is the freedom of constitutional government and is limited by the requirement of due process of law. Because a state may dispense with a jury trial, it does not follow that it may substitute trial by ordeal. The rack and torture chamber may not be substituted for the witness stand.

Not all fact patterns are as easy to associate with torture as *Brown*, which is clearly torture. Indeed, those familiar with the "shock the conscience" test understand that the Court has often interpreted the test with a great degree of flexibility, particularly when judging the actions of law enforcement officers faced with exigent circumstances related to governmental needs such as public safety issues. For example, in the 1998 case of *County of Sacramento v. Lewis* the Court denied a § 1983 claim based on an alleged substantive due process violation. In *Lewis*, a passenger on a motorcycle was killed as the result of a high-speed police chase ending when the fleeing motorcycle tipped over and a police car in close pursuit struck and killed the respondent's sixteen-year-old son.

In discussing the threshold for shocking the conscience, the *Lewis* decision "made it clear that the due process guarantee does not entail a body of constitutional law imposing liability whenever someone cloaked with state authority causes harm." Indeed, "[i]n a due process challenge to executive action, the threshold question is whether the behavior of the governmental officer is so egregious, so outrageous, that it may fairly be said to shock the contemporary conscience."

Interestingly, an equally important aspect of *Lewis* centered on the Court's view that not only does the conduct have to be egregious, but that "conduct intended to injure in some way unjustifiable by any government interest is the sort of an official action most likely to rise to the conscience-shocking level." This means that the Court will provide greater deference if the government can demonstrate a justification for its conduct based on the totality of the circumstances. The stronger the justification, the more flexibility allowed.

This deference factor certainly played out in a 1966 Ninth Circuit case entitled *Blefare v. United States*. In a fact pattern similar to *Rochin*, the appellants were suspected of swallowing narcotics which were lodged in their rectums or stomachs. Appellants were searched by U.S. officials at a border crossing from Mexico into the United States where they consented to a rectal probe by a doctor. When the rectal probe found no drugs, a "saline solution was…given the appellants to drink to produce vomiting." Blefare, one of the suspects, "was seen by the doctor to have regurgitated an object and reswallowed it." Then, without Blefare's consent the doctor forcefully passed a soft tube into the "nose, down the throat and into the stomach," through which fluid flowed in order to induce vomiting. This resulted in the discovery of packets of heroin and the subsequent conviction of Blefare.

The Ninth Circuit refused to hold that the involuntary intrusion into Blefare's stomach shocked the conscience. The Court attempted to distinguish the case from *Rochin* by noting that Blefare had at first consented to the rectal probe and the drinking of saline, and that, in any event, the actions to induce vomiting were not brutal. Arguably, the ruling hinged on the fact that the State had an important governmental interest in keeping heroin from entering the United States. In the Court's view, it would have been shocking had they overturned the conviction based on the due process clause. The Court felt that it would "shock the conscience" if Blefare's conviction were set aside:

> It would shock the conscience of law abiding citizens if the officers, with the knowledge these officers had, were frustrated in the recovery and use of this evidence. It is shocking to know that these appellants swallowed narcotics to smuggle it into and through the United States for sale for profit....If we were mechanically to invoke Rochin to reverse this conviction, we would transform a meaningful expression of concern for the rights of the individual into a meaningless mechanism for the obstruction of justice.

To be sure, there are a number of cases that proponents of coercive questioning techniques can cite to buttress the view that in exigent circumstances the police may be obliged to use force to get life saving information. For instance, in *Leon v. Wainwright* the Eleventh Circuit brushed aside the fact that police officers had used "force and threats" on kidnap suspect Jean Leon in order to get the suspect to reveal the location of his kidnap victim. When apprehended by a group of police officers in a Florida parking lot, Leon refused to reveal the location of his kidnap victim (the victim, Louis Gachelin, had been taken by gunpoint to an apartment where he was undressed and bound to a chair). In order to get the suspect to talk, police officers physically abused Leon by twisting his arm and choking him until he revealed where the victim was being held. Later, Leon was taken to the police station where he made a second confession which the Court ruled as admissible at his trial. In speaking to the use of brutal force to get the information needed to protect the victim, the Court deemed that the action of the officers was reasonable given the immediate concern to find the victim and save his life.

> We do not by our decision sanction the use of force and coercion by police officers. Yet this case does not represent the typical case of unjustified force. We do not have an act of brutal law enforcement agents trying to obtain a confession in total disregard of the law. This was instead a group of concerned officers acting in a reasonable manner to obtain information they needed in order to protect another individual from bodily harm or death.

Returning to *Chavez*, the government brief attempted to draw together the concept of governmental interest by arguing that the Court in *Chavez* should take the opportunity to create a "terrorist exception" which would accord protection to police officers from § 1983 suits when questioning suspected terrorists. This matter was not directly addressed by the justices. Nevertheless, if one adds *Chavez* to *Lewis* and its progeny, certain constitutional parameters for interrogating a terrorist suspect can now be staked out. Simply put, even if a terrorist suspect asks for a lawyer and demands that all questioning cease, law enforcement may justifiably refuse these requests and engage in interrogation that may consist of coercive techniques so long as the techniques utilized fall below the threshold of shocking the conscience (which equates to actions not in violation of the Torture Convention). In addition, under the concept of governmental interest, the more the suspected terrorist matches the scenario of the ticking time bomb terrorist, the more deference given to police interrogators under the umbrella of public safety.

Critics of *Chavez* such as Brooklyn law professor and President of the ACLU, Susan Herman, fear that allowing the use of coercive interrogation techniques short of the ambiguous "shock the conscience" standard leaves open the door for abuse to those not suspected of terrorism. Others are dismayed that the *Chavez* Court refused to even acknowledge the existence of the Torture Convention and its place in the matter of coercive interrogations.

6.4 Allegations of United States Sanctioned Torture

Keeping in mind that the goal of any antiterrorism effort is to stop or eliminate the terrorists before they commit murderous attacks, there are four general law enforcement means that mesh together in this effort: (1) using informants and undercover agents to infiltrate the terror cell (known as HUMINT sources); (2) using surveillance, searches, and wiretaps to learn of locations, organizational structure and plans for future attacks; (3) arresting and detaining individuals before they commit a terrorist attack; and (4) interrogation of individuals. Only the last category, interrogating those detained as suspected foot soldiers of terrorism, is discussed herein.

Since the advent of the War on Terror, the United States has detained thousands of individuals which can be grouped into one of four categories: (1) those suspected of having links to the al-Qa'eda, or a similar radical Islamic fundamentalist, terror movement; (2) those designated by the President as enemy combatants; (3) those detained as prisoners of war in the Iraq military campaign; and (4) those who were apprehended in Iraq and Afghanistan and designated as "security detainees." Most of those detained in the first category were apprehended by federal law enforcement personnel on the heels of the attacks of September 11, 2001, and, after questioning, the majority were deported as illegal aliens. Those in the third group have since been released.

Detainees in the second group are members of the al-Qa'eda network or Taliban captured on the battlefields of Afghanistan, although the United States has also included other suspected members of al-Qa'eda apprehended in places other than the military combat zone of Afghanistan. Along with Yaser Esam Hamdi, at least two enemy combatants, Ali Saleh Kahlah Al-Marri and Jose Padilla, were arrested in the United States. With the 2006 release of the 14 detainees held by the CIA in "undisclosed" locations, almost all of the individuals in the second category are currently being housed in Guantanamo Bay, Cuba, or Bagram Air Force Base in Afghanistan. Some of the detainees have been held in detention as enemy combatants since 2002 without being charged with a crime. With the drawdown of American combat forces from Iraq, all those in the fourth group have been turned over to the Iraqi government and the Afghan government in Afghanistan for the security detainees. Some detainees in the second and fourth group of individuals—enemy combatants and security detainees—were subjected to extended interrogation by programs administered by the DOD and the CIA.

Once a terrorist enemy combatant suspect is detained, what do American interrogators do? In the first few years following 9/11 (2002-2005) the answer to that question was difficult to ascertain. It was not until the passage of the Detainee Treatment Act of 2005 that uniform standards for interrogation of individuals in the custody of the DOD were set out. The Detainee Treatment Act expressly prohibited cruel, inhuman, or degrading treatment of detainees in the custody of any U.S. agency. Then, in 2006, the Supreme Court in *Hamdan* ruled that the detainees must be given all the provisions set out at Common Article 3 of the Geneva Conventions. Common Article 3 of the Geneva Conventions requires the following, with special reference to (1) (c) below:

ARTICLE 3 COMMON TO THE GENEVA CONVENTIONS OF 1949

In the case of armed conflict not of an international character occurring in the territory of one of the High Contracting Parties, each Party to the conflict shall be bound to apply, as a minimum, the following provisions:

(1) Persons taking no active part in the hostilities, including members of armed forces who have laid down their arms and those placed *hors de combat* by sickness, wounds, detention, or any other cause, shall in all circumstances be treated humanely, without any adverse distinction founded on race, colour, religion or faith, sex, birth or wealth, or any other similar criteria.

To this end, the following acts are and shall remain prohibited at any time and in any place whatsoever with respect to the above-mentioned persons:
(a) violence to life and person, in particular murder of all kinds, mutilation, cruel treatment and torture;
(b) taking of hostages;
(c) outrages upon personal dignity, in particular humiliating and degrading treatment;
(d) the passing of sentences and the carrying out of executions without previous judgment pronounced by a regularly constituted court, affording all the judicial guarantees which are recognized as indispensable by civilized peoples.
(2) The wounded and sick shall be collected and cared for.
An impartial humanitarian body, such as the International Committee of the Red Cross, may offer its services to the Parties to the conflict.
The Parties to the conflict should further endeavour to bring into force, by means of special agreements, all or part of the other provisions of the present Convention.
The application of the preceding provisions shall not affect the legal status of the Parties to the conflict.

The quickly enacted 2006 Military Commissions Act also provided similar protections:

(c) Additional Prohibition on Cruel, Inhuman, or Degrading Treatment or Punishment—
(1) IN GENERAL—No individual in the custody or under the physical control of the United States Government, regardless of nationality or physical location, shall be subject to cruel, inhuman, or degrading treatment or punishment.
(2) CRUEL, INHUMAN, OR DEGRADING TREATMENT OR PUNISHMENT DEFINED—In this subsection, the term 'cruel, inhuman, or degrading treatment or punishment' means cruel, unusual, and inhumane treatment or punishment prohibited by the Fifth, Eighth, and Fourteenth Amendments to the Constitution of the United States, as defined in the United States Reservations, Declarations and Understandings to the United Nations Convention Against Torture and Other Forms of Cruel, Inhuman or Degrading Treatment or Punishment done at New York, December 10, 1984.
(3) COMPLIANCE—The President shall take action to ensure compliance with this subsection, including through the establishment of administrative rules and procedures.

Returning to the time period of 2002-2005, the reluctance to release the exact interrogation techniques early on centered on the fear that the release of such information would allow enemy forces to develop counter-intelligence techniques to frustrate American efforts to get meaningful intelligence. Consequently, U.S. officials remained silent about the techniques, telling the public that its agents were employing the full range of robust interrogation tactics to include offering various incentives such as money or engaging in trickery.

Perhaps the most well-known official source available to the public early on regarding the need for secrecy in the use of interrogations in the War on Terror was the Jacoby Declaration. The Jacoby Declaration consisted of a nine page sworn statement issued to the District Court for the Southern District of New York in the case of *Padilla v. Bush* by Vice Admiral Lowell E. Jacoby (USN), the Director of the DIA.

In a section of the declaration entitled "Interrogation Techniques," Jacoby stated that the "approach to interrogation is largely dependent upon creating an atmosphere of dependency and trust between the subject and the interrogator." Creating this atmosphere can take a prolonged period of time. Then, in a section entitled "Use of Interrogations in the War on Terrorism," Jacoby devoted several paragraphs describing asymmetric warfare and the unique threats posed by terrorists who "have also clearly demonstrated their willingness—and in fact have expressed their intent—to use any type of potential weapon, including weapons of mass destruction" against the United States. Still, Jacoby refused to provide any information as to the methods used by American interrogators. Jacoby stated only that the "United States is now engaged in a *robust* program of interrogating individuals who have been identified as enemy combatants in the War on Terrorism [emphasis added]." Then, in a last amplification he stated: "As detainees collectively increase their knowledge about United States detention facilities and *methods of interrogation*, the potential risk to national security increases *should those methods be released* [emphasis added]."

Suggestions by various ideologues and other "unnamed" government sources that American interrogators might be forced to engage in physical pressure, e.g., torture or ill-treatment, to get information from suspected terrorists surfaced almost immediately after the terror attacks of September 11, 2001. In October 21, 2001, a *Washington Post* article served as the information source of choice to those who accuse the United States of engaging in torture. The article quoted the perennial "unnamed" FBI agent as stating:

> We are known for humanitarian treatment, so basically we are stuck….Usually there is some incentive, some angle to play, what you can do for them. But it could get to that spot where we could go to pressure…where we don't have a choice, and we are probably getting there.

Then, in March of 2002, the *Washington Post* once again relied on "unnamed sources" to alert its readers that the United States government had turned over dozens of suspected terrorists "to countries, including Egypt and Jordan, whose intelligence services have close ties to the CIA and where they can be subjected to interrogation tactics—including torture and threats to their families—that are illegal in the United States." As previously noted, rendition is a common practice which is only improper under international law if, for instance, the United States knowingly delivers a suspect to a nation that it has substantial grounds to believe engages in "a consistent pattern of gross, flagrant or mass violations of human rights." While an "unnamed source" in a media article may view a particular country as a nation that satisfies this test, it is ultimately a question for the government of the United States and the international community to answer.

Without more evidence than that provided by unnamed sources, it is impossible to accurately gauge what interrogation methods are being used in a particular State. In addition, from a legal perspective, there is no international prohibition against rendering a suspected terrorist to a nation that engages in interrogation practices that would constitute ill-treatment. For example, assuming for the sake of argument that Jordan does use some amount of physical or physiological pressure in its interrogation practices, one would need to determine whether or not the type of pressure rises to the level of torture, or is ill-treatment only.

In April 2002, a *Wall Street Journal* article examined some of the interrogation methods currently taught to students at the Army's interrogation school in Fort Huachuca, Arizona. The reporter began the piece by making the following observation:

> *Interrogators*—the Pentagon renamed them "human intelligence collectors" last year—are authorized not just to lie, but to prey on a prisoner's ethnic stereotypes, sexual urges and religious prejudices, his fear for his family's safety, or his resentment of his fellows. They'll [Army interrogators] do just about anything short of torture, which officials say is not taught here, to make their prisoners spill information that could save American lives.

The *Wall Street Journal* piece went on to list some of the techniques that are taught at the school to get prisoners to talk. These techniques include the "incentive" approach, the "fear-up" approach, the "fear-down" approach, the "pride and ego down" approach, and the "pride and ego up" approach. The article concluded by noting that stress positions—placing prisoners in uncomfortable positions until they talk—are not taught at the school and that a military lawyer is "on hand during interrogations for quick decisions on the degree of physical or mental pressure allowed."

It was not until December 26, 2002, that the public was alerted to the concept of "stress and duress" tactics allegedly used by American interrogators. According to the initial story in the *Washington Post*, various unnamed government sources suggested that the United States was using a laundry list of questionable techniques to get uncooperative detainees housed outside the United States to talk. The article stated: "At times they [uncooperative detainees] are held in awkward, painful positions and deprived of sleep with a 24-hour bombardment of lights—subject to what are known as 'stress and duress'." Other examples of stress and duress listed were so-called "false flag" operations in which the detainee is deceived into believing he has been turned over to a "country with a reputation for brutality," or having female interrogators question the detainee, "a psychologically jarring experience for men reared in a conservative Muslim culture where women are never in control."

The article also alleged that when detainees were first apprehended, "MPs [military police] and U.S. Army Special Forces troops…[would] beat them [detainees] up and confine them in tiny rooms." To buttress this view, the article then quoted another unnamed American official as saying: "[O]ur guys may kick them around a little bit in the adrenaline of the immediate aftermath [of the arrest]."

Ultimately, if such stress and duress tactics failed to glean meaningful results, the article reported that the detainees were rendered to third countries where they could be subjected to mistreatment or "mind-altering drugs such as sodium pentothal." However, the *Washington Post* article piece placed a caveat on its claims about rendition practices by noting that the CIA's "Directorate of Operations instructions, drafted in cooperation with the general counsel, tells case officers in the field that they may not engage in, provide advice about or encourage the use of torture by cooperating intelligence services from other countries." As expected, with the publication of the stress and duress story, similar secondhand reports also found their way into the media, most of them parroting the mantra that America tortures detainees as an official policy.

Throughout the War on Terror, the Red Cross has regularly criticized the United States for alleged violations of international law by conducting interrogations of non-uniformed combatants and terrorists taken into custody. The legal basis that the Red Cross asserts is Additional Protocol I to the

Geneva Conventions of August 12, 1949, which would accord prisoner of war status to these people. The problem with this charge is that the United States has never ratified Protocol I. On the contrary, the United States specifically rejected Protocol I for the very reason that it bestowed a legal status on non-uniformed combatants. Thus, the idea that Protocol I is binding on the United States as a principal of "customary international law" is correct only in part. The United States is not bound by Protocol I in this regard and is perfectly within its legal rights to interrogate non-uniformed combatants; these individuals are not entitled to the protections given to prisoners of war. The Red Cross is unquestionably a valuable early warning system for any democracy that wants to respect the rule of law, but its credibility is weakened each time it uses the guise of Protocol I to criticize the United States.

6.5 DOD Interrogation Practices 2002-2005

With the breaking of the Abu Ghraib prison abuse story in mid 2004 the question of American interrogation techniques could no longer remain in the dark; the public could no longer be left to wonder whether the techniques used by the military were lawful or actually involved torture. The propaganda value of Abu Ghraib demanded transparency to combat the negative press. In June 2004 the government released a 10-centimeter pile of previously classified internal memos and documents from senior policymakers in the Bush Administration detailing the approved interrogation tactics for conducting interrogations of uncooperative detainees at Guantanamo Bay by the military. Much later, with the advent of the Obama Administration, the public was also given access to portions of the DOJ memorandums concerning the interrogation practices of the CIA.

The volume of information now available to the public makes it possible to set out a fairly detailed chronology of the what, when, where, and how of interrogation practices. The discussion is best divided between the DOD's military interrogation actions at Guantanamo Bay and the CIA's interrogation actions at undisclosed locations overseas (not Guantanamo Bay).

First, in terms of the military's interrogation practices, under the law of war the purpose of detaining enemy combatants is to ensure that they do not return to join enemy forces and, in this unique situation, to allow American officials the opportunity to gather any necessary intelligence about the terrorists' organizational infrastructure, financial network, communication system, weapon supply lines, and plans for future terror attacks. As is the practice in all wars, the purpose of detention is not to punish the enemy combatant, but to protect the host nation from future acts of violence by the enemy. In this light, over 450,000 German and Italian enemy combatants were held in the United States during World War II. They were not charged with crimes, afforded lawyers, or allowed access to U.S. courts to file habeas corpus petitions.

The precise status of enemy combatant is pivotal in determining what interrogation techniques can be used to gather information from the subject detainee. Article 17 of the Third Geneva Convention provides that prisoners of war are only required to give their "surname, first names and rank, date of birth, and army regimental, personal or serial number, or failing this, equivalent information." The prisoner of war is not required to give any further information upon questioning. To leave no doubt on this point, Article 17 goes on to provide the following:

No physical or mental torture, nor any other form of coercion, may be inflicted on prisoners of war to secure from them information of any kind whatever. Prisoners of war who refuse to answer may not be *threatened, insulted, or exposed to any unpleasant or disadvantageous treatment of any kind* [emphasis added].

Certainly, if the full provisions of the Third Geneva Convention covered the detainees, American authorities would not be entitled to interrogate them or obtain additional information. Conversely, enemy combatants who are not prisoners of war do not fall under the full protections of the Third Geneva Convention and may therefore be questioned by American interrogators on additional topics of interest.

By far the group that has received the most attention consists of the more than 800 men once held at Guantanamo Bay, Cuba, at a specially built facility named Camp Delta. President Obama has still not closed the Guantanamo Bay within one year, as promised in January 2009. As of 2011, the more than 150 detainees at Guantanamo Bay continue to receive regular visits by ICRC, diplomats from their respective nations, military attorneys, and various other fact finding groups.

Again, the majority of the illegal enemy combatants were captured on the battlefields of Afghanistan. Although all of the detainees were said to be participants in the War on Terror, initially the Bush Administration did not recognize these detainees as eligible for prisoner of war status under the Third Geneva Convention, nor did the Bush Administration apply Common Article 3 of the Geneva Conventions. The reason that the Bush Administration did not apply the Third Geneva Convention was because both the Taliban fighters and the al-Qa'eda fighters failed to qualify as lawful enemy combatants under the applicable provisions of international law. Specifically, prisoner of war status is only conferred on persons who are "[m]embers of armed forces of a Party to the conflict" or "members of other militias and members of other volunteer corps, including those of organized resistance movements, belonging to a Party…provided that such…fulfill[s]" four specific conditions:

- That of being commanded by a person responsible for his subordinates;
- That of having a fixed distinctive sign recognizable at a distance;
- That of carrying arms openly; and
- That of conducting their operations in accordance with the laws and customs of war.

Despite the fact that the Third Geneva Convention was not applied to these enemy combatants, the Bush Administration pledged that all detainees were treated in accordance with the humanitarian concerns set out in the Geneva Conventions. Nevertheless, they were all subject to being interrogated.

A review of the 2004 memorandums show that the most severe technique that was approved by Secretary of Defense Rumsfeld for Guantanamo Bay detainees was the use of "mild, non-injurious physical contact—poking, grabbing, lightly shoving" against selected high-value detainees, like one Guantanamo detainee named al-Qahtani.

The documents reveal that on October 11, 2002, Major General Michael Dunleavy, the Joint Task Force Commander for Guantanamo Bay, submitted a request for approval to use non-standard interrogation techniques on three detainees held at Guantanamo Bay. The requested interrogation techniques were divided into three categories:

Category I:
1. Yelling at the detainee;
2. Deceiving the detainee by:
 a. Using multiple interrogators; or
 b. Posing as interrogators from a country with a reputation for harsh treatment of detainees;

Category II:
1. Placing the detainee in stress positions;
2. Using falsified documents or reports to deceive the detainee;
3. Placing the detainee in isolation;
4. Interrogating detainees in non-standard interrogation environments or booths;
5. Depriving detainee of light and auditory stimuli;
6. Hooding detainee during interrogation;
7. Interrogating detainee for twenty-hour sessions;
8. Removing all "comfort items" (including religious items);
9. Switching detainee from hot food to cold rations;
10. Removing all clothing;
11. Forced grooming (shaving facial hair);
12. Exploiting individual phobias (such as fear of dogs) to induce stress;

Category III:
1. Convincing the detainee that death or severe pain is imminent for him or his family;
2. Exposing the detainee to cold weather or water (with medical monitoring);
3. Water boarding;
4. Using light physical contact, such as grabbing, pushing, or poking with a finger.

On December 2, 2002, Rumsfeld authorized all Category I and II techniques, but only a single Category III approval was given for interrogators to use "mild, noninjurious physical contact" (grabbing or pushing). According to the released documents, some FBI agents who were cooperating with the military interrogators as well as other military personnel themselves objected to the approved techniques and voiced those concerns up their respective chains of command. Six weeks later, on January 15, 2003, Rumsfeld rescinded the approval of the use of all Category II techniques and the one Category III technique. In doing so, Rumsfeld ordered: "In all interrogations, you should continue the humane treatment of detainees, regardless of the type of interrogation technique employed." In April 2003, Rumsfeld issued a new set of directives that applied only to the detainees in Guantanamo Bay, Cuba. This memorandum set out dozens of interrogation techniques that essentially tracked the guidelines of then Army FM 34-52, Intelligence Interrogation.

No. 596-04
IMMEDIATE RELEASE June 22, 2004
DOD Provides Details on Interrogation Process

The Department of Defense today released documents related to the development of interrogation procedures at Guantanamo. These documents are made available to demonstrate that the actions of the U. S. Defense Department are bound by law and guided by American values.

The Department is providing this level of detail realizing that we are still a nation at war and we must be careful in what we disclose to our enemies. Throughout this conflict the interrogation procedures have been reviewed and modified when deemed necessary and appropriate. These documents demonstrate the concern to balance law with the need to obtain intelligence on the war on terrorism. The interrogations procedures discussed are an important tool to attempt to prevent further attacks by the terrorists intending to do Americans harm.

Development and approval of interrogation techniques is done in a deliberate manner with strict legal and policy reviews to ensure the protection of the detainees, our institutions, and our troops responsible for carrying out these operations. The President's February 2002 determination set the guidelines for detainee operations in the war on terrorism. The processes and procedures that followed reflected America's values and called for all detainees in the war on terrorism in our custody to be treated humanely, and to the extent appropriate and consistent with military necessity, in a manner consistent with the principles of the Geneva Convention.

The release of these declassified documents will demonstrate the transparency in which we are conducting inquiries into allegations of detainee abuse. What follows is a brief timeline that lead to the development of these documents and the interrogation procedures that are in effect today at Guantanamo.

On Jan. 11, 2002, the first detainees arrived at JTF-Guantanamo. The doctrine contained in Field Manual 34-52 guided interrogations from January to December 2002.

FM 34-52 sets forth the basic principles for interrogations for the U.S. Armed Forces in a conventional military conflict.

The initial approaches governing interrogations at Guantanamo were in accordance with the standing doctrine outlined in FM 34-52. These procedures include 17 techniques such as direct questioning and providing incentives.

During the summer and fall of 2002, the United States was in a high-threat environment, and intelligence continued to indicate planning by al-Qaeda for attacks in the U.S. and elsewhere. Among the detainees at Guantanamo were individuals with close connections to al-Qaeda leadership and planning figures.

These individuals include financiers, bodyguards, recruiters and operators. There were detainees assessed to possess significant information of al-Qaeda plans. They were also demonstrating training in al-Qaeda resistance methods to the approaches set out in FM 34-52.

On Oct. 11, 2002, the commander of Joint Task Force Guantanamo requested the use of additional interrogation techniques for Muhammad, Mani Ahmed and S'hal Lan al Qahtani, individuals believed to have close al-Qaeda connections. The Commander requested approval for 20 other interrogation techniques.

On Oct. 25, 2002, the commander of the U.S. Southern Command forwarded the request to the Chairman of the Joint Chiefs of Staff for approval. The request included 20 techniques.

On November 27, 2002, General Counsel, after discussing the request with Deputy Secretary of Defense, Under Secretary of Defense (Policy) and the Chairman of the Joint Chiefs of Staff, recommended that the Secretary of Defense approve 17 of the 20 techniques requested by Southern Command.

On Dec. 2, 2002, the Secretary of Defense approved the 17 techniques recommended by the General Counsel. The techniques approved were arranged on a three-tiered system that required approval from different levels of the chain of command before they could be used. A number of the techniques that were approved were never used. These guidelines were in effect from Dec. 2, 2002 until Jan. 15, 2003.

On Jan.15, 2003, the Secretary of Defense rescinded the Dec. 2 guidance when he learned of concern about the implementation of the techniques. The Secretary of Defense directed the Department of Defense General Counsel to establish a working group to assess the legal, policy, and operational issues relating to the interrogation of detainees held by the U. S. Armed Forces in the war on terrorism.

The working group consisted of representatives of the military departments, service general counsels, the Judge Advocates General of the armed services, defense policy, the joint staff, and the Defense Intelligence Agency. The Department of Justice advised the working group in its deliberations. The working group reported 35 techniques as appropriate for consideration for use and rejected several as either inappropriate or lacking sufficient information to permit review. The final product of the working group included a list of techniques and procedures. (Note: This working group was the subject of a Department of Defense background briefing on May 20, 2004. The briefing transcript can be located at http://www.defenselink.mil/transcripts/2004/tr20040520-0788.html.)

After this deliberate and determinative legal and policy review, the Secretary of Defense approved the use of 24 techniques for use at Guantanamo on April 16, 2003. Seventeen of the techniques approved for use at Guantanamo come from FM 34-52. Four of the techniques require notification to the Secretary before use.

It is the policy and practice of the Department of Defense to treat detainees in the War on Terrorism humanely and, to the extent appropriate and consistent with military necessity, in a manner consistent with the principles of the Geneva Convention.

No procedures approved for use ordered, authorized, permitted, or tolerated torture. Individuals who have abused the trust and confidence placed in them will be held accountable. There are a number of inquiries that are ongoing to look at specific allegations of abuse, and those investigations will run their course.
...

In relation to "security detainees" in Iraq, the then head of U.S. forces, Lieutenant General Ricardo Sanchez, issued a one-page directive in October 2003, titled "Interrogation Rules of Engagement" which would be applicable to non-POWs. This directive allowed for practices, vetted by Army lawyers as lawful under the Fourth Geneva Convention and Common Article 3, that included silence, repetition of questioning, emotional love/hate techniques, and the use of fear (where the interrogator behaves in a heavy overpowering manner by yelling or throwing things).

In September 2006, the DOD issued its new military detainee and terror suspect treatment guidelines. The DOD Directive 2310.01E is entitled: The Department of Defense Detainee Program. In addition, Army Field Manual (FM) 2-22.3, Human Intelligence Collector Operations (September 2006), supersedes FM 34-52, Intelligence Interrogation. FM 2-22.3 absolutely prohibits the use of torture or physical stress techniques in conducting interrogation.

6.6 CIA Interrogation Policies 2002-2005

In announcing the new interrogation rules, President Bush also informed the public that 14 "high value" terror suspects had been transferred from undisclosed CIA locations overseas to Guantanamo Bay. This speech was the first official acknowledgement of the existence of the previously secret CIA detainee program. President Bush said that the CIA program had been authorized by a secret presidential directive issued on September 17, 2001. Relating that the program was subject to internal legal review, the Bush Administration promoted the legal view that the CIA detainees were wartime detainees held under the law of war; international human rights law, which applies in peacetime, was not applicable. Believing that the CIA program had "saved lives," President Bush confirmed that with the transfer of the 14 there were "now no terrorists in the CIA program." Further, the Bush Administration denied that any of the CIA detainees were subjected to interrogation techniques that violated international or domestic law. The water boarding interrogation technique used on a handful of detainees in the CIA program was viewed as constituting a level of force that did not rise to the level of torture under the Torture Convention.

The clandestine "black-site" detention facilities were established by the CIA in order to interrogate suspected high value al-Qa'eda leaders. The interrogations were initially conducted jointly by the CIA and FBI. With the capture of senior al-Qa'eda leader Abu Zubaydah during a raid in Pakistan in late March 2002, the CIA determined that it needed permission to use more aggressive interrogation techniques. The CIA psychologists proposed 12 so-called "enhanced interrogation techniques" (EITs) which they modeled entirely from practices used in the U.S. military's Survival, Evasion, Resistance, and Escape (SERE) training program (except for the use of non-poisonous insects).

The SERE program is used to train pilots and special operations forces to withstand harsh and abusive treatment by the enemy should they be captured. Begun after the Korean War, tens of thousands of military personnel have gone through the program which subjects the participants to such things as stress positions, sleep deprivation, exposure to extreme cold or heat, and water boarding.

Understanding that the CIA would use the EITs on only senior members of al-Qa'eda who had knowledge of imminent terrorist threats against the United States, on August 1, 2002, the Office of the Legal Counsel (OLC), Department of Justice, issued two legal memorandums under the signature Jay S. Bybee, Assistant Attorney General, OLC. The classified version issued to the CIA, was entitled: Memorandum for John Rizzo, Acting General Council of the Central Intelligence Agency, Interrogation of al-Qa'eda Operative (classified Bybee memo). After reviewing the applicable international and domestic law to include statutes and case law, the classified Bybee memo concluded that "because the acts inflicting torture are extreme, there is sufficient range of acts that though they might constitute cruel, inhuman, or degrading treatment or punishment [ill-treatment] fail to rise to the level of torture." In addition, the classified Bybee memo concluded that the infliction of severe physical or mental pain or suffering must be the "defendant's precise objective." Thus, noting that the SERE techniques produced no prolonged mental harm that would violate the Torture Convention, the classified Bybee memo authorized the CIA to use 10 of the 12 proposed EITs. Each technique was carefully described in the legal memorandum, along with restrictions and safeguards which required, for instance, the presence of psychologists and medical personnel along with the interrogator. The approved techniques were:

(1) Attention grasp: The interrogator grasps the subject with both hands, with one hand on each side of the collar opening, in a controlled and quick motion, and draws the subject toward the interrogator.

(2) Walling: The subject is pulled forward and then quickly and firmly pushed into a flexible wall so that his shoulder blades hit the wall. His head and neck are supported with a rolled towel to prevent whiplash.

(3) Facial hold: The Interrogator holds the subject's head immobile by placing an open palm on either side of the subject's face, keeping fingertips well away from the eyes.

(4) Facial or insult slap: With fingers slightly spread apart, the interrogator's hand makes contact with the area between the tip of the subject's chin and the bottom of the corresponding earlobe.

(5) Cramped confinement: The subject is placed in a confined space, typically a small or large box, which is usually dark. Confinement In the smaller space lasts no more than two hours and in the larger space, up to 18 hours.

(6) Insects: A harmless insect is placed in the confinement box with the detainee.

(7) Wall standing: The subject may stand about four to five feet from a wall with his feet spread approximately to his shoulder width. His arms are stretched out in front of him and his fingers rest on a wall to support all of his body weight. The subject is not allowed to reposition his hands or feet.

(8) Stress positions: These positions may include having the detainee sit on the floor with his legs extended straight out in front of him with his arms raised above his head or kneeling on the floor while leaning back at a 45 degree angle.

(9) Sleep deprivation: The subject is prevented from sleeping, not to exceed 11 hours at a time.

(10) Waterboard: The subject is restrained on a bench with his feet elevated above his head. His head is immobilized and an interrogator places a cloth over his mouth and nose while pouring water onto a cloth. Airflow is restricted for 20 to 40 seconds; the technique produces the sensation of drowning and suffocation.

Later, other OLC legal memorandums were issued in 2005 and 2007. The 2005 so-called Bradbury legal memorandum superseded the classified Bybee memo, but confirmed the basic conclusions of the classified Bybee memo regarding the use of EITs. The Bradbury memo held that 13 EITs would not constitute torture: (1) dietary manipulation; (2) nudity; (3) attention grasp; (4) walling; (5) facial hold; (6) facial slap or insult slap; (7) abdominal slap; (8) cramped confinement; (9) wall standing; (10) stress positions; (11) water dousing; (12) sleep deprivation (more than 48 hours); and (13) water boarding.

Despite the many gross distortions which continue to circulate about the CIA program in general, and water boarding in particular (which was deemed to be the worst of the EITs), the water boarding approved EIT was only used on three of the high value detainees in CIA hands: Abu Zubaydah, Abd Al-Rahim Al-Nashiri (captured in November 2002), and Khalid Sheik Muhammed (captured in March 2003). Abu Zubaydah was waterboarded 83 times, the majority of which lasted less than ten seconds and Khalid Sheik Muhammed was waterboarded 180+ times. Apparently, however, there is evidence that some of the interrogators may have engaged in illegal conduct in their individual capacities. Allegations of verbal threats to Abu Zubaydah and pointing an unloaded pistol next to Al-Nashiri's head have surfaced and are being investigated by the Obama Administration. In any event, in the fall of 2005, as Congress was crafting the Detainee Treatment Act of 2005, the CIA removed water boarding from the list of EITs. No one has been waterboarded (with the exception of US military personnel) since 2005. Although the 2006 Military Commissions Act attempted to circumvent the ruling in *Hamdan* as applying to the CIA (by redefining certain abuses that could be considered to constitute a war crime under the War Crimes Act, 18 U.S.C. § 2441) President Obama's Executive Order 13491 issued in January 2009, directs the CIA and all federal agencies to proceed with interrogations "strictly in accord with the principles, processes, conditions, and limitations [FM 2-22.3] prescribed." Today there is no difference between what the military and other federal agencies can do in terms of conducting an interrogation.

In July 2009, the DOJ Office of Professional Responsibility (OPR) issued a report entitled: Investigation into the Office of Legal Counsel's Memoranda Concerning Issues Relating to the Central Intelligence Agency's Use of "Enhanced Interrogation Techniques" of Suspected Terrorists. The OPR report concluded that former OLC lawyers "John Yoo and Jay Bybee had engaged in professional misconduct by failing to provide 'thorough, candid, and objective' analysis in memoranda regarding the interrogation of detained terrorist suspects." The OPR indicated that it would refer its findings of misconduct to the State legal bar for disciplinary action. In January 2010, however, the DOJ Office of the Deputy Attorney General issued its own memorandum objecting to the findings of the OPR report and refused to "authorize OPR to refer its findings to the state [sic] bar disciplinary authorities in the jurisdictions where Yoo and Bybee are licensed." In short, the DOJ determined that Yoo and Bybee had not engaged in professional misconduct in advising the CIA on the legality of EITs based on existing law at the time.

In summary, given the following facts, it is clear that the CIA did not engage in unlawful interrogation practices during the time frame 2002-2005. First, existing international case law such as *Ireland* and *Public Committee* clearly set an extremely high bar for what would constitute torture. Even the worst of the CIA EITs, water boarding, is clearly not torture when measured against *Ireland*. Second, the techniques used by the CIA (with the exception of the harmless insect) are all used on American military personnel in SERE training courses. If the techniques were torture as claimed by some then the Torture Convention would demand that the SERE interrogators and those who approved the program be prosecuted. There is no exception in the Torture Convention for military "training."

6.7 The Ticking Time Bomb Scenario

Those associated with the art of interrogation know that the initial goal is to get the suspect to start talking and that the best way to get reliable and useful information is to treat the subject humanely; in other words, to not engage in torture or ill-treatment. In fact, when faced with torture, individuals will most likely say anything to stop the pain, making their statements sometimes questionable. According to a former Colonel in Army intelligence, "Anything you can do to disconnect someone is going to help…[b]ut it's a myth that torture is effective. The best way to win someone over is to treat them kindly." On the other hand, to say that torture never produces accurate information is simply naive. In fact, if the subject has information, he will at some point "break." Recognizing this reality, the DOD only requires American soldiers in the military's Code of Conduct to resist torture to the best of their ability. The fact is that torture does work on someone who has information.

Many legal scholars who understand the threat of al-Qa'eda-styled terrorism often paraphrase with approval former Supreme Court Justice Jackson's observation that "the Constitution is not a suicide pact." One issue that gains a tremendous amount of attention in this debate is how to deal with a suspected terrorist in a ticking time bomb scenario. Even noted civil rights advocates like Harvard law professor Laurence Tribe understand that the landscape has changed. After 9/11 he wrote: "The old adage that it is better to free 100 guilty men than to imprison one innocent describes a calculus that our Constitution—which is no suicide pact—does not impose on government when the 100 who are freed belong to terrorist cells that slaughter innocent civilians, and may well have access to chemical, biological, or nuclear weapons."

Different commentators have varying turns on the theme of the ticking time bomb, but it commonly goes something like this. Suppose a terrorist suspect is taken into custody in a major city and is found to be in possession of nuclear bomb-making materials and detailed maps of the downtown area. The terrorist blurts out to police that he is a member of al-Qa'eda and that a nuclear car bomb is on a timer set to detonate in ten hours (the time he had estimated he could safely get away from the blast). The suspect then demands a lawyer and refuses to answer any more questions. Of course, law enforcement may legitimately ignore his demands and conduct a reasonable interrogation as long as they do not engage in torture, ill-treatment or employ techniques that would shock the conscience. But what if reasonable interrogation techniques yield no information—the suspect refuses to talk? This Hobson's choice poses one of the strongest arguments for the use of non-lethal torture.

Given the premise of the ticking time bomb scenario, it is difficult to portray oneself as a centrist—either one uses whatever means necessary to get the information to stop the blast or one simply allows the slaughter of innocent civilians. Should a reasonable law enforcement officer with a spouse and children residing in the blast zone simply resign himself to the fact that they are all going to perish since it is unlawful under both international and domestic law to use torture? Or is it more likely that the law officer faced with this scenario would in fact engage in torture and then raise the defense of necessity at a subsequent criminal trial?

Alternatively, one might attempt to overcome the moral dilemma if the government created a justification defense which sanctioned the use of torture in special circumstances. In this manner one could eschew hypocrisy—the government would sanction the use of torture and the law officer would not face prosecution for his acts.

As noted in the *Public Committee* decision, the Supreme Court of Israel was clearly apprehensive about the sweeping scope of its decision, particularly in the context of a ticking time bomb terrorist. In rendering its decision, the Court strongly signaled that the Knesset (legislative branch of Israel) might find it efficacious at some point to "sanction physical means in interrogations…provided, of course, that a law infringing upon a suspect's liberty…is enacted for a proper purpose, and to an extent no greater than is required." To date, the Israeli legislature has not enacted any such legislation.

In addition, despite its absolute stance rejecting the legality of moderate physical pressure and the associated administrative directives promulgated to regulate the use of moderate physical pressure *vis-à-vis* the interrogation of terrorist suspects, the Supreme Court of Israel went on to recognize the defense of necessity if individual GSS investigators were charged with employing such prohibited interrogation techniques in the case of a ticking time bomb scenario. Citing Israeli penal law regarding necessity—engaging in illegal conduct in order to promote a greater good—the Court recognized that GSS interrogators would have the right to raise the defense of necessity in a subsequent prosecution. The Court stated that "[o]ur decision does not negate the possibility that the 'necessity' defense be available to GSS investigators [in ticking time bomb scenarios]…if criminal charges are brought against them, as per the Court's discretion." The Court said that "if a GSS investigator—who applied physical interrogation methods for the purpose of saving human life—is criminally indicted, the 'necessity' [defense] is likely open to him in the appropriate circumstances."

Indeed, the Court seemed to anticipate that any reasonable GSS investigator, charged with protecting innocent lives, would apply "physical interrogation methods for the purpose of saving human life" when confronted with a ticking time bomb terrorist. In other words, GSS investigators would use whatever means necessary to avert the explosion of the bomb. The Court noted, however, that the threat of the explosion must be a "concrete level of imminent danger:"

> [The] "necessity" exception is likely to arise in instances of "ticking time bombs," and that the immediate need…refers to the imminent nature of the act rather than that of the danger. Hence, the imminence criteria is satisfied even if the bomb is set to explode in a few days, or perhaps even after a few weeks, provided the danger is certain to materialize and there is no alternative means of preventing its materialization. In other words, there exists a concrete level of imminent danger of the explosion's occurrence.

The defense of necessity is a doctrine well-known to the common law. It is defined as "[a] justification defense for a person who acts in an emergency that he or she did not create and who commits a harm that is less severe than the harm that would have occurred but for the person's actions." Professor Wayne Lafave's criminal law text amplifies this definition by explaining that "the harm done is justified by the fact that the action taken either accomplished a greater good or prevented a greater harm."

The general understanding of the necessity defense at common law was that it was in response to circumstances emanating from the forces of nature and not from people. "With the defense of necessity, the traditional view has been that the pressure must come from the physical forces of nature (storms, privations) rather than from human beings." When the pressure is from human beings, the defense, if applicable, is duress, not necessity.

In the modern era, the distinction between the pressure coming from nature or human beings has merged. According to Lafave, defense of necessity extends to both instances.

> [T]he reason is of public policy: the law ought to promote the achievement of high values at the expense of lesser values, and sometimes the greater good for society will be accomplished by violating the literal language of the criminal law….The matter is often expressed in terms of choice of evils: when the pressure of circumstances presents one with a choice of evil, the law prefers that he avoid the greater evil by bringing about the lesser evil.

Still, the defense of necessity is not available to a defendant in situations where the legislature has previously made a determination of values. This concept is clearly stated in the Model Penal Code: "Neither the Code nor other law defining the offense provides exceptions or defenses dealing with the specific situation involved; and a legislative purpose to exclude the justification claimed does not otherwise plainly appear." For instance, a person may not take a human life in order to save himself.

It is no secret to those familiar with the debate on civil liberties in the War on Terror that Harvard Law School's Alan Dershowitz has publicly advocated a far more aggressive approach to dealing with such things as the ticking time bomb terrorist. Dershowitz opposes the use of a necessity defense because relying on a necessity defense allows for torture to be carried on "below the radar screen," which invites greater abuse by law enforcement agents. Without bantering words, Dershowitz acknowledges the utility of nonlethal torture to get life saving information from a ticking time bomb terrorist. To be sure, Dershowitz's views spawned a firestorm of debate, not because he has advocated something new, but because it was Alan Dershowitz, the well-known civil libertarian, who made the case for State approved torture.

According to Dershowitz, such instruments of non-lethal torture could include the use of "a sterilized needle inserted under the fingernails to produce unbearable pain without any threat to health or life." The authority to engage in non-lethal torture would come from a torture warrant issued by a judge. In this manner, Dershowitz argues that the process of torture is judicially sanctioned and the chances of abuse by individual investigators is thereby reduced. "I believe…that a formal requirement of a judicial warrant as a prerequisite to nonlethal torture would decrease the amount of physical violence directed against suspects."

Those who oppose the use of torture under any circumstance whatsoever, to include the ticking time bomb scenario, invariably attempt to change or avoid the premise. Those who flatly reject Dershowitz's proposal for judicial torture warrants for a ticking time bomb terrorist are prone to engage in avoidance. For example, a recent law review article noted that "[b]y expanding the narrow framework of Dershowitz's inquiry, it is possible to focus our debate on alternative means of maintaining national security that do not violate [the] human dignity [of the terrorist]." Of course, the only way to lessen the likelihood of a ticking time bomb scenario is to neutralize the bomb before the fuse is lit, i.e., increasing police powers to break up the terrorist organizations and to prevent the unthinkable from coming to fruition.

No one can disagree that the rule of law and democracy are cherished values that must be protected. However, Dershowitz counters that in time of war it is sometimes necessary to, as Abraham Lincoln advocated, suspend our liberties to protect our liberties. In fact, Lincoln denied habeas corpus and unilaterally jailed thousands of American citizens (in the North) who expressed dissent.

Interestingly, Dershowitz's argument would require lawyers to chart a legal course around the Fourth, Fifth, and Fourteenth Amendment protections of the United States Constitution, while simultaneously ignoring the binding obligations of the Torture Convention which clearly states in Article 2: "No exceptional circumstances whatsoever, whether a state of war or a threat of war, internal political instability or any other public emergency, may be invoked as a justification for torture."

Dershowitz also fails to consider the matter of war crimes in his argument. To add judicial torture warrants to the corpus of America's rule of law would not only make a mockery of the rule of law, it would subject the United States to allegations of international war crimes. As noted, all of the existing international laws relating to armed conflict—to include the Geneva Conventions, the Hague Conventions, and customary principles—are codified by the military in FM 27-10, Law of Land Warfare. Violations of the law of war are labeled as war crimes. FM 27-10, paragraph 499 defines the term war crime as a "technical expression for a violation of the law of war by a person or persons, military or civilian." War crimes are divided into simple breaches and grave breaches. Grave breaches are set out in the Geneva Conventions to include such acts as torture or inhuman treatment, including biological experiments, or willfully causing great suffering or serious injury to body or health. FM 27-10, paragraph 502 defines the following acts as "grave breaches" of the Geneva Convention of 1949 if committed against persons or property protected by the Conventions: willful killing, torture or inhuman treatment, including biological experiments, willfully causing great suffering or serious injury to body or health, and extensive destruction and appropriation of property, not justified by military necessity and carried out unlawfully and wantonly.

Each nation is under a strict legal obligation to search for all persons alleged to have committed war crimes and to investigate all allegations of war crimes. If a grave breach of the law of war is discovered, that nation has the obligation to either prosecute or extradite the accused offender. FM 27-10, paragraph 498 indicates that:

> [a]ny person, whether a member of the armed forces or a civilian, who commits an act which constitutes a crime under international law is responsible therefore and liable to punishment. Such offenses in connection with war comprise: a. Crimes against peace, b. Crimes against humanity, and c. War crimes.

The United States policy is that American soldiers accused of violations of the law of war will be prosecuted under the provisions of the Uniform Code of Military Justice (UCMJ) for the substantive offense. For example, killing unarmed civilians is a war crime and also a substantive crime of murder. A deliberate attack on noncombatant civilians clearly violates the codified and customary laws of war. Indeed, the law of war was designed to protect innocent civilians.

If one accepts the premise that the United States is at war with the al-Qa'eda network, then it certainly follows that the law of war is violated should an American investigator, civilian or military, engage in torture. Acts of torture constitute a grave breach of the law of war and the United States has an obligation to investigate and, if allegations of torture are valid, to either prosecute or extradite the offender to a nation that desires to prosecute. There are no exceptions for a ticking time bomb terrorist. The al-Qa'eda are clearly illegal enemy combatants, but that does not provide the United States with a license to torture them.

It is easy to choose between a right and a wrong, but the ticking time bomb scenario forces one to choose between the lesser of two wrongs. Disregarding the legal issues associated with torturing a ticking time bomb terrorist, is it possible to morally justify the use of torture to extract information? Those who believe so point to the so-called utilitarian principle best developed by philosopher Jeremy Bentham. Under the concept of utilitarianism, the pain inflicted on the ticking time bomb terrorist by means of otherwise prohibited interrogation techniques is weighed against the potential pain and death that would be inflicted on the community. Accordingly, the utilitarian argument is cited with approval by those who believe that the community's welfare is of greater value than the welfare of the terrorist who seeks to destroy the community.

There are a great number of words in the English language to describe a person who not only does the *right thing* in a given situation, but performs that action in the *right way*. Such a person may be described as exhibiting virtue, integrity, honor, courage, etc. (Chapter 9.4). The formula of doing a right thing in a right way is an essential ingredient for the establishment and development of a just and democratic society based on the rule of law. Conversely, deviations from the formula are destructive to the individual and to society. For instance, I regularly inform my students that getting an "A" on a Civil Procedure exam in law school is a right thing, but cheating to accomplish this goal can only be characterized as a wrong way to achieve the "A." Thus, doing a right thing (getting an "A") must be done in a right way (by studying and not cheating) or the result is wrong.

In dealing with the ticking time bomb terrorist scenario, the right thing is simple enough to appreciate—law enforcement must get the information that could save the lives of thousands or, if the bomb is a weapon of mass destruction, tens of thousands. The more difficult part of the formula is the second half—getting the needed information in the right way.

Prior to *Public Committee*, the government of Israel had taken the unusual step of trying to regulate the use of torture if not by means of a judicial torture warrant, then by administrative rules. In short, the government directives had provided a justification defense to an interrogator who engaged in torture. This practice was struck down as unlawful. A similar move to regulate torture in the United States would certainly meet the same end—a democracy cannot sanction torture. Once it does, it has abandoned the moral high ground; it is no longer a democracy. Whether justification flows from the legislative, executive, or judicial branch, it is anathema to a freedom loving people.

If an interrogator engages in torture, he must be charged for his crimes. Drawn from the Israeli approach in *Public Committee*, a defense of necessity would require him to satisfy a four pronged test: (1) the investigator had reasonable grounds to believe that the suspect had direct knowledge which could be used to prevent the weapon from detonating; (2) that the weapon posed an imminent danger to human life; (3) that there existed no alternative means of preventing the weapon from exploding; and (4) that the investigator was acting to save human life.

The War on Terror provides Americans an opportunity to reexamine much of what this nation represents to the world. In this light, the sanctioned use of torture must surely strike the vast majority as inconsistent with civilized values. Accordingly, while there could very well exist an emergency ticking time bomb scenario in which torture of a particular terrorist is necessary, the interrogator must face criminal liability. To approach the issue in any other manner would send the wrong signal to friends and foe alike. Those who believe that the United States can defend freedom by subverting our own values are as misguided as those who demand that the government fight the War on Terror without altering civil liberties by jot or tittle. Torture is illegal and must remain on the books as such.

6.8 Abu Ghraib and the Search for the Smoking Gun

This chapter would not be complete without a section on the so-called Abu Ghraib scandal and the associated implications for the War on Terror. While the end to major combat operations was declared by President Bush on May 1, 2003, a new and deadly chapter in the Iraq War quickly took hold—coalition forces and Iraqi civilians were now targeted for murder by various groups of sectarian guerrilla fighters, common criminals and al-Qa'eda linked terrorists. Even the capture of the dictator Saddam Hussein on December 15, 2003, did not stem the growing volume of terrorist attacks.

The rising intensity of the insurgency in mid 2003 also mandated that the large number of detainees that were being apprehended had to be categorized and housed. As already detailed, the United States grouped the detainees into one of three categories: (1) Iraqi soldiers who qualified as prisoners of war (POWs) under the Geneva Conventions; (2) those suspected of having links to a variety of terrorist groups (to include Saddam loyalists and radical Islamic fundamentalists), called "security detainees;" and (3) common criminals.

Those in the first category were quickly processed and released back into Iraqi society within a few months. While most of the prisoners were treated in accordance with the protections of the Geneva Conventions, the U.S. military reported some incidents of physical abuse by American guards. The most common type of abuse seemed to occur at or near the point of capture and included physical assaults and petty larceny. In general terms, however, the vast majority of POWs were treated in accordance with international law protections. Most importantly, as POWs, this particular class of detainees was not required to give any further information upon additional questioning by American forces.

Those in the second category were held for indefinite periods of time pending interrogation and eventual transfer to the nascent Iraqi judicial system. The reason that these security detainees were not given the protections of the Third Geneva Convention was because they failed to qualify as lawful enemy combatants. Again, prisoner of war status is conferred only on those persons who are "[m]embers of armed forces of a Party to the conflict" or "members of other militias and members of other volunteer corps, including those of organized resistance movements, belonging to a Party…provided that such…fulfill[s]" four specific conditions: (a) being commanded by a person responsible for his subordinates; (b) having a fixed distinctive sign recognizable at a distance; (c) carrying arms openly; and (d) conducting their operations in accordance with the laws and customs of war.

Unless a detainee in the post major combat phase of the Iraq War met these requirements, he was not entitled to the status of prisoner of war but was rather a security detainee. At most, such an individual would be protected only by the Fourth Geneva Convention covering civilians held during the occupation and the humanitarian protections provided by Common Article 3 of the Geneva Conventions. Common Article 3 protects all unlawful combatants taken captive from "(a) violence to life and person, in particular murder of all kinds, mutilation, cruel treatment and torture; (b) taking hostages; [and] (c) outrages upon personal dignity, in particular humiliating and degrading treatment.…" Essentially, the detainee must be treated humanely, but can be questioned to gain information.

Although determinations were often hard to make between a security detainee and a common criminal, the Bush Administration repeatedly made it clear that all detainees were to be treated in accordance with the humanitarian concerns set out in the Geneva Conventions. Accordingly, all detention facilities received regular visits by the ICRC (Red Cross). In fact, the Red Cross served a valuable function in Iraq by alerting the United States to a number of abuse allegations.

The establishment of detention facilities to house the detainees was aggravated by the sheer number of detainees. This required the coalition to utilize prison structures that had been used in the Saddam era to include the infamous prison at Abu Ghraib, located about 20 miles west of Baghdad. Abu Ghraib was the largest U.S. run detention facility and, at a high point in the tempo of operations, housed up to 7,000 detainees in October 2003. It was a vast complex of six separate compounds on a 280 acre site circled by over 2 miles of fences and 24 guard towers. The Red Cross reported that they made regularly scheduled visits to a total of 14 U.S. run facilities to include the infamous Tier 1 (cellblock 1a), "a darkened, two-story isolation wing used for interrogations" and the site of the prisoner abuse at Abu Ghraib. During the visit to Tier 1 at Abu Ghraib, they reported that they did not notice anything "as bad as the abuses portrayed in the…photos." About 35 people were held in Tier 1 during the Red Cross visit.

The public was first shown the infamous photographs taken inside of the U.S. military run prison at Abu Ghraib in a CBS show called *60 Minutes II* which aired on April 28, 2004. The widely circulated photos showed a handful of U.S. military police soldiers engaged in a variety of abusive and sexually sadistic acts against mostly blindfolded Iraqi detainees. Among other things, the photos showed naked prisoners stacked in pyramids, connected by wires, on dog leashes, and threatened by dogs. In addition, a handful of U.S. military police charged in the abuse scandal had forced naked prisoners to simulate sex acts.

The chronology of how the Abu Ghraib abuse story was revealed began on January 13, 2004, when Army Specialist Joseph Darby, a military policeman at Abu Ghraib, gave a computer disc containing the abuse photos to a military investigator. On January 14, 2004, the Army immediately initiated a criminal investigation and the United States Central Command (the four-star combatant command located in Florida) informed the media in a press release on January 16, 2004, that it was investigating detainee abuse at an unspecified U.S. prison in Iraq. On February 23, 2004, the military informed the U.S. press that 17 Army personnel had been suspended of duty pending further criminal investigations about the detainee abuse. Then, on March 20, 2004, the military reported to the media that it had charged six soldiers with detainee abuse to include criminal charges of assault, cruelty, indecent acts, and mistreatment. Interestingly, however, the press did not fully respond to the growing story as the mere fact that soldiers were being punished for misconduct did not constitute news that was out of the ordinary—the military regularly punishes soldiers who violate the law. In fact, the media only became energized on April 28, 2004, when *60 Minutes II* aired the photos.

Pursuant to evidence of criminal misconduct contained in a U.S. Army Criminal Investigation Division (CID) Report, seven enlisted reserve soldiers, all from the 372nd Military Police Company, 320th Military Police Battalion, 800th Military Police Brigade, were charged with an assortment of violations of provisions of the UCMJ. The central figure in the scandal was a reservist Private First Class (PFC) named Lynndie England who is known for poses in which "she pointed at the genitals of a naked detainee while a cigarette dangled from her lips" and "holding a [dog] leash around a naked prisoner's neck." The other soldiers were Specialist Charles Graner, Staff Sergeant Ivan Frederick, Sergeant Javal Davis, Specialist Jeremy Sivits, Specialist Sabrina Harman, and Specialist Megan Armbuhl. All of those charged were reservists and all worked the night shift at Tier 1 in Abu Ghraib, where the abuses took place in the last months of 2003.

The particulars relating to the Abu Ghraib abuse story are now well settled thanks to the CID's criminal investigation and a number of collateral administrative investigations. In chronological order they are: (1) the April 2004 Taguba Report, prepared by Major General Antonio Taguba; (2) the July 2004 Army Inspector General Report, prepared under Lieutenant General Paul Mikolashek; (3) the August 2004 Fay Report, prepared by Major General George Fay; and (4) the August 2004 Schlesinger Report, headed by the former Secretary of Defense in the Nixon administration, James Schlesinger. In addition, there are other related examinations to include: (1) Vice Admiral Albert Church, Navy Inspector General, looking into interrogation and detention rules in Iraq, Afghanistan and elsewhere; (2) Secretary of Defense Donald Rumsfeld, looking into all prisoner operations and interrogation procedures; (3) CID investigation, looking into prisoner deaths in Iraq and Afghanistan; and (4) Lieutenant General James Helmly, Chief of the Army Reserve, looking into Army Reserve training procedures with special attention to military police and military intelligence.

The overriding question regarding the prisoner abuse echoes the thoughts of Senator Lindsey Graham (R-S.C.), a member of the Armed Services Committee: "How could we let this prison melt down and become the worst excuse for a military organization I've seen in my life?" None of the reports found that there was an official policy—either written or oral—to torture or abuse prisoners. According to the Schlesinger Report, the most far reaching investigation to date and the one which the *Wall Street Journal* deemed the "definitive assessment of what went wrong," "no approved procedures called for or allowed the kinds of abuse that in fact occurred." In fact, the Schlesinger Report found "no evidence of a policy of abuse promulgated by senior officials or military authorities." In addition, none of the Reports cite any direct abuse of prisoners by officers or by superiors ordering subordinates to commit the abuses. In short, the Schlesinger Report concurs with all the Reports to date in finding that the individuals that conducted the sadistic abuse are personally responsible for their acts.

Nevertheless, taking a broader examination of what happened at Abu Ghraib, the Schlesinger Report did find fault with the senior levels of command; there were "fundamental failures throughout all levels of command, from the soldiers on the ground to [the United States] Central Command and to the Pentagon" that set the stage for the abuses to occur.

The Schlesinger Report agreed with the calls for disciplinary action in the Fay Report for a number of officers in the immediate tactical chain of command who knew, or should have known, about the abuses at Abu Ghraib. "The commanders of both brigades—800 Military Police Brigade Commander Janis Karpinski and Military Intelligence Brigade Commander Thomas Pappas—either knew, or should have known, abuses were taking place and taken measures to prevent them." Certainly, however, this would include not only Brigadier General Karpinski and Colonel Pappas, but those subordinate commanders and on down the chain of command to the battalion, company, and platoon level. The chaotic environment at the prison existed in large part due to the dereliction of tactical commanders on the ground at Abu Ghraib.

The Schlesinger Report and all other investigations found that the culpability of commanders rested at the tactical level. The Schlesinger Report found "no evidence that organizations above 800th MP Brigade—or the 205 MI Brigade—level" were directly involved in the incidents at Abu Ghraib.

While all the Reports talked about a number of factors that contributed to an atmosphere that allowed the abuses at Abu Ghraib to occur, the Schlesinger Report did the best job of providing a clear summation. These factors included:

- A lack of planning for detainee operations—from the Pentagon to the commanders on the ground in Iraq—and an inability to react to the marked spike in the insurgency that occurred in the summer of 2003;
- A confusing chain of command at Abu Ghraib where a military intelligence officer, Colonel Pappas, was placed in command of military police units;
- Lack of equipment and troops at Abu Ghraib; and
- A failure of the immediate chain of command to supervise and train soldiers under their command.

Finally, the Schlesinger Report did an excellent job of placing the problem of detainee abuse in a wider "real world" perspective. Noting that the U.S. military has handled about 50,000 detainees from all theaters of conflict since the start of combat operations in Afghanistan in 2001, the Schlesinger Report then compared that figure with the number of reported allegations of abuse, including some deaths. With around 300 cases of abuse reported, the Schlesinger Report noted that about one-third of the allegations occurred at the "point of capture or [at a] tactical collection point." As of August 2004, about half of the 300 cases had been investigated with 66 substantiated cases.

At the end of the day, it is simply false that the American military engaged in command directed torture or ill-treatment at Abu Ghraib, particularly when it was the military itself that self-reported to the media the fact that individual soldiers were being investigated and punished in accordance with the rule of law for wartime abuses at the prison. Clearly, the best indicator that the senior leadership is not culpable (with the exception of the direct tactical chain of command for dereliction of duty) is found in its continuing commitment to criminally investigate and prosecute those soldiers accused of committing detainee abuses. Numerous soldiers have already been prosecuted and sentenced for their crimes, and criminal trials will continue for others.

When one considers that the number of detainees in the War on Terror—including Afghanistan, Iraq, and other operations—is well over 50,000, it is unrealistic to expect that abuses will not occur.

Violations of rules occur in every human endeavor, to include war. In an interview with the *Wall Street Journal*, Mr. James Schlesinger correctly noted that the "behavior of our troops is so much better than it was in World War II." The so-called "bad apple" syndrome is in fact the primary causative issue at Abu Ghraib—a handful of closely knit reserve personnel engaged in acts of sadism as they worked the night shift from October to December of 2003.

It is equally true that the Abu Ghraib story has been devastating to the United States war effort. While each and every case of abuse is repulsive to American standards of decency and justice, the terrorists have certainly become "media-savvy" in their quest to parlay these individual cases into marketable propaganda. For example, many nations that are opposed to the United States are quick to exploit the individual cases of abuse at Abu Ghraib by painting the entire conduct of all American soldiers as immoral and illegal. Of course, Americans do not need to be told that the abuses are beyond the pale of conduct expected of its military. A CNN Gallup poll taken in May 2004 showed that three in four Americans agreed that the abuses at Abu Ghraib could not be justified.

The investigative reports have done a great service to the American people and the world by dispelling the shrill cries of those who blame a secret Pentagon "culture of permissiveness" for the abuses at Abu Ghraib. While the Schlesinger Report found institutional and even personal responsibility in the tactical chain of command for allowing conditions for abuse to occur at Abu Ghraib, the Report specifically found that "[n]o approved procedures called for or allowed the kinds of abuse that in fact occurred. There is no evidence of a policy of abuse promulgated by senior officials or military authorities." The investigative reports exonerate the military from any charges of a systemic use of abuse to gain intelligence.

The abuses at Abu Ghraib should not have happened. The damage to American credibility and the War on Terror is incalculable. In the long run, the fact that the military prosecuted the Abu Ghraib offenders speaks volumes to the world about the true character of the United States and its military. To its great credit, the senior military leadership certainly learned the lessons of My Lai. Understanding that the best approach to dealing with criminal events is to act with alacrity and transparency, the tragedy at Abu Ghraib by a few has been thoroughly investigated and justice has been handed out to the perpetrators and, as the process moves forward, it is hopeful that the sword of justice will turn to those in the tactical chain of command. Two quotes sum up the entire affair: Senator Ben Nighthorse Campbell: "I don't know how the hell these people got into our Army;" and Secretary of Defense Donald Rumsfeld: "I failed to identify the catastrophic damage that the allegations of abuse could do to our operations in the theater, to the safety of our troops in the field, to the cause to which we are committed."

6.9 Conclusion

The story of "Half-Dead Bob" reported by *U.S. News and World Report* typifies the al-Qa'eda mindset while illustrating the American policy of humane treatment of detainees in accordance with the principles of the Geneva Conventions. An Arab captured on the battlefield of Afghanistan was nicknamed "Half-Dead Bob" by the Americans when he arrived at Guantanamo Bay. His nickname derived from the fact that he came to the detention center weighing 66 pounds, suffering from tuberculosis, shrapnel wounds, and having only one lung. The article states:

> Army Maj. Gen. [Major General] Michael Dunlavey vividly remembers his first encounter with "Bob." Dunlavey ran interrogations at the base until November of last year. By the time they met, Bob was making a rapid recovery. He had put on 50 pounds and, sitting across a table from

Dunlavey, he thanked him for the food and medical treatment. "General, you are probably a good Christian," Dunlavey recalls him saying. "And you are probably a good man. But, if I ever get free, I will kill you."

In the early years following 9/11, weighing the credibility of charges that the United States engaged in torture or ill-treatment as a standard practice was difficult at best. On the one hand, suggestions of torture generally came from media reports based on unnamed sources and anecdotal evidence. On the other hand, the government's penchant for secrecy regarding interrogation tactics made it next to impossible to make an independent assessment. Today, it is now clear that the United States did not engage in a systemic command directed interrogation regime that violated international or domestic law. In tandem with the June 2004 document release, President Bush declared, "Look, let me make very clear the position of my government and our country. We do not condone torture. I have never ordered torture. The values of this country are such that torture is not a part of our soul and being."

Again, apart from the moral argument and speaking strictly from a legal perspective, the United States cannot engage in torture. This is in violation of the Torture Convention and is penalized under domestic law. This is the baseline legal consideration. Following 9/11 both the military and CIA employed tactics that entered an ambiguous legal zone from 2002-2005. As foreboding as some of the outlined techniques may have appeared, there were many techniques that involved acts which were clearly permissible under any analysis. For example, one would be hard pressed to argue that the reported use of female interrogators, trickery, or a day long interrogation session would have ever constituted a prima facie case of even ill-treatment as some have suggested. Further, one could not automatically conclude that the use of awkward positioning of a particular detainee violated legal norms.

Accordingly, from 2002-2005 top legal advisors concluded that the United States could legitimately engage in interrogation practices that did not rise to the level of torture. By late 2005, however, the law quickly changed and continued to the point of absurdity where interrogators today may essentially not question a detainee without the express permission of the detainee. In fact, at Guantanamo Bay, it is forbidden for an American soldier who is not a Muslim to hand any religious object to a detainee as this would be "degrading" and in violation of Common Article 3! In short, our interrogation programs are now driven by "political correctness."

A factor that lends a tremendous amount of credibility to the government's contention that it abides by the international law prohibiting torture is the military's continuing commitment to criminally investigate and prosecute those soldiers accused of torture or ill-treatment. From the beginning of the War on Terror, the United States has responded well to verifiable instances of criminal activity that could be even remotely interpreted as torture or ill-treatment with relentless criminal investigation, prosecution, and punishment. For instance, a number of convictions have been handed down in a variety of cases as a result of the Army's criminal investigations. Indeed, if the government is sincere about prohibiting torture and ill-treatment, one would certainly expect that those who engaged in such illegal acts would be investigated and punished to the full extent of the law. The sincerity of the United States to reject the practice of illegal interrogations is further boosted by the fact that the initial stories concerning abuse are generally made by military officials. Again, the initial story about the prisoner abuse at Abu Ghraib was by the military, not the media. The media simply paid no attention to the March 2004 self reported information that several soldiers were going to be punished under UCMJ until a media source was given the photographs in April of 2004. The military's prompt and thorough investigation of the Abu Ghraib scandal and the transparency of the trials of the soldiers who were involved in these atrocities should reassure observers that the military command structure will not allow torture or ill-treatment tactics to become institutionalized.

Of course, to the naive the most direct source of information on torture would obviously come from those detainees who claim to have been tortured by the Americans. Consequently, as small groups of detainees are released from custody, Western reporters have attempted to glean first hand testimony as to the issue of torture. As one would expect from the mouths of ruthless terrorists devoted to a Nazi-like ideology of hate (if one can murder innocent civilians, one can certainly lie), many of these newly released members of the Taliban and al-Qa'eda alleged that they were horribly tortured by their American captors.

Unexpectedly, others in the same group are sometimes quite open in proclaiming that all the detainees were treated well and not tortured. For instance, in a group of 27 detainees released from Guantanamo Bay in July 2003, 16 Afghans were interviewed by *Associated Press* correspondents as they were transferred to a Red Cross bus in Afghanistan. Those who alleged they were tortured complained in general terms of "cold rooms," "crowded rooms" and "beatings." Only one in the group, Abdul Rahman, specifically alleged that he had been "badly punished 107 times," and had been chained and beaten with "a metal rod on his legs and back." Interestingly, when pressed by reporters to show any scars or evidence left by the torture, Rahman "refused to show scars that may have resulted from any abuse."

In contrast, another detainee in the group, Nate Gul, told reporters that none of the detainees were beaten during interrogation: "They didn't beat us during the interrogation. They wrote down anything we said. They interrogated me about 30 to 40 times." In fact, as terrorist expert Mark Bowden revealed in the following comments from two former Pakistani detainees at Guantanamo, Americans do not engage in abuse as a fixed policy:

> Shah Muhammad and Sahibzada Osman Ali told me that except for some roughing up immediately after they were captured they were not badly treated at Camp X-Ray. They both felt bored, lonely, frustrated, angry, and helpless (enough for Shah Muhammad to attempt suicide), but neither believed that he would be harmed by his American captors, and both regarded the extreme precautions (shackles, handcuffs, hoods) that so outraged the rest of the world as comical.

At the end of the day, the reasonable observer must conclude that allegations that the United States condones and uses torture and ill-treatment as interrogation tools are vastly overstated and often simply taken for granted even by those who should know better. For instance, in his book, *The Case for Israel*, Dershowitz charged that the United States engages in "modified forms of torture that include physical and psychological components."

The purpose of detainee interrogation is to glean as much intelligence as possible from individuals who have information associated with the al-Qa'eda terrorist network and all associated terror networks. The goal is to apprehend as many of the terrorists as possible and to prevent future acts of terror on our people with particular concern for the likelihood that our enemies will surely use weapons of mass destruction against us. To date, interrogations have yielded much valuable information. According to the Jacoby Declaration the United States thwarted over 100 terrorist attacks worldwide based on information provided in part from detainee interrogations conducted in 2002. Hopefully, the Obama Administration will release similar reports showing how many lives were saved because of the CIA interrogation program.

One matter is fundamentally certain: if al-Qa'eda is to be kept at bay, the United States must rely on detainee interrogation as an integral antiterrorist tool. The need for the interrogator to get information to protect the lives of innocents is a legitimate and perfectly lawful exercise. By its very nature, even the most reasonable interrogation places the detainee in emotional duress and causes stress to his being—both physical and mental. Still, a reasonable interrogation must necessarily be free of torture or ill-treatment.

Those who regularly claim that the United States oversteps the line regarding interrogation techniques tend to invoke the worn slippery slope argument, but that does not mean the potential for abuse does not exist. The old saw attributed to Lord Acton that "power tends to corrupt" has great validity.

6.10 Questions for Discussion

1. *Is it wise to advocate the use of an advance judicial approval for nonlethal torture?* Alan Dershowitz, WHY TERRORISM WORKS: UNDERSTANDING THE THREAT, RESPONDING TO THE CHALLENGE 141, 148 (2002). Dershowitz writes: "When I respond by describing the sterilized needle being shoved under the fingernails, the reaction is visceral and often visible—a shudder coupled with a facial gesture of disgust."

2. *Do we need rules?* In a FOX NEWS channel interview on *DaySide with Linda Vestor* (Oct. 31, 2003), Professor Addicott supported the pending criminal charges against an Army Lieutenant Colonel charged with assault in the interrogation of an Iraqi detainee. The Colonel allegedly threatened the Iraqi detainee with a pistol to get information about a future ambush of American soldiers. The live audience was largely opposed to the military's criminal investigation of the officer and displayed displeasure with the author's legal support for the referral of courts martial charges. *See also* Rowan Scarborough, *Colonel in Iraq Refuses to Resign*, WASH. TIMES, Oct. 31, 2003, at A3. Why?

3. *Does politics trump reason?* Professor Addicott provided oral and written testimony before the Senate Committee on the Judiciary, Subcommittee on Administrative Oversight and the Courts hearing entitled: "*What Went Wrong Torture and the Office of the Legal Counsel in the Bush Administration*," Washington, DC. The Democrat Senators used the 1983 case of *U.S. v. Lee* (744 F.2d 1124 (5th Cir. 1984) to conclude that the CIA's use of the waterboard was torture. While the *Lee* case used the term "water torture" as one of the things that four Texas police officers did to obtain confessions from prisoners, the court never described the technique. In turn, the Democrat Senators used the fact that several Japanese soldiers were convicted by American war crimes trials after World War II for engaging in "water torture" of American POWs. They failed, of course, to mention that the Japanese technique caused either death or unconsciousness when used and was nothing like the CIA technique. Professor Addicott was the only witness called to testify that defended the CIA's program. The text can be viewed in entirety at: http://jurist.law. pitt.edu/paperchase/2009/05/bush-era-interrogation-techniques.php.

4. *Releasing enemy combatants.* What dangers face a nation if it releases enemy combatants prior to the end of a conflict? American news media have confirmed U.S. official findings that some detainees released from Guantanamo Bay have returned to Afghanistan and Pakistan in order

to rejoin their comrades in fighting the United States and its allies. *See* John Mintz, *Released Detainees Rejoining the Fight*, WASH. POST, Oct. 22, 2004 at A01. How can released enemy combatants be prevented from returning to the fight? How might prolonged confinement help or hinder United States efforts in the War on Terror?

Selected Bibliography

42 U.S.C. § 1983.

> Every person who, under color of any statute, ordinance, regulation, custom, or usage, of an State or Territory or the District of Columbia, subjects or causes to be subjected, any citizen of the United States or other person within the jurisdiction thereof to the deprivation of any rights, privileges, or immunities secured by the Constitution and laws, shall be liable to the party injured in an action at law, suit in equity, or other proper proceeding for redress, except that in any action brought against a judicial officer for an act or omission taken in such officer's judicial capacity, injunctive relief shall not be granted unless a declaratory decree was violated or declaratory relief was unavailable.

Balz, Dan. *Durbin Defends Guantanamo Comments*, WASH. POST, June 17, 2005, at A11 (discussing the reactions of the White House and other politicians to Illinois Senator Richard J. Durbin's speech on the Senate floor, comparing interrogation procedures and conditions for detainees at Guantanamo Bay to those of Nazi concentration camps and Soviet gulags).

Bowden, Mark. *The Dark Art of Interrogation*, ATLANTIC MONTHLY, Oct. 2003, at 76.

Cohn, Marjorie. *Dropping the Ball on Torture: The U.S. Supreme Court Ruling in Chavez v. Martinez*, June 10, 2003, available at http://jurist.law.pitt.edu/forum/forumnew113.php.

Commission of Inquiry Into the Methods of Investigation of the General Security Service Regarding Hostile Terrorist Activity, reprinted in 23 ISR. L. R. 146 (1989).

Cooperman, Alan. *CIA Interrogation Under Fire; Human Rights Group Say Techniques Could Be Torture*, WASH. POST, Dec. 28, 2002, at A9 (detailing Human Rights Watch's accusations that the United States violated international law by torturing detainees and turning detainees over to states that engaged in torture).

Dershowitz, Alan. THE CASE FOR ISRAEL, 2004.

Dershowitz, Alan. WHY TERRORISM WORKS: UNDERSTANDING THE THREAT, RESPONDING TO THE CHALLENGE, 2002.

Gellman, Barton, and Dana Priest. *U.S. Decries Abuse But Defends Interrogations; 'Stress and Duress' Tactics Used On Terrorism Suspects Held in Secret Overseas Facilities*, WASH. POST, Dec. 26, 2002, at A1.

Langbein, John H. TORTURE AND THE LAW OF PROOF, 1987.

Levinson, Sanford. *"Precommitment" and "Postcommitment:" The Ban On Torture In The Wake Of September 11*, 81 TEX. L. REV., 2013 (2003).

Parry, John T. *What Is Torture, Are We Doing It, And What If We Are?* 64 U. PITT L. REV. 237 (2003).

Schofield, Phillip. FIRST PRINCIPLES PREPARATORY TO CONSTITUTIONAL CODE: COLLECTED WORKS OF JEREMY BENTHAM, 1989.

Schulz, William F. *The Torturer's Apprentice*, THE NATION, May 13, 2002, at 25 (reviewing Alan M. Dershowitz's 2002 publication "Shouting Fire: Civil Liberties in a Turbulent Age").

Sofaer, Abraham. *The U.S. Decision Not to Ratify Protocol I to the Geneva Conventions on the Protection of War Victims*, 82 AM. J. INT'L. L. 784 (1988).

Taylor, Stuart, Jr. *Rights, Liberties, and Security*, BROOKINGS REVIEW. Volume 21, Issue 1, Jan. 1, 2003.

Willson, David Jarris. A HISTORY OF ENGLAND, SECOND EDITION. 1972.

Chapter 7

Contractors on the Battlefield

The American military cannot function without the support of civilian contractors and other government civilians.

—Col. Michael Stripling

Providing adequate protection, antiterrorism (AT) training and, if necessary, personnel recovery for civilian contractors deployed to support United States military operations presents significant legal and policy challenges that both the military and civilian contractor companies have yet to fully appreciate, let alone properly institutionalize. Although many Americans still visualize the United States military as a monolithic force of uniformed personnel only, the reality is far different. Due to federally imposed personnel limitations for the armed forces, the need for specialized skills in the modern high-tech military, and cost savings, hundreds of activities once performed by the military are now privatized and outsourced to thousands of civilian contractors. These civilian contractors routinely provide a wide array of important and essential activities in support of the full range of military operations to include infrastructure improvements, rebuilding, and security services. In other words, civilian contractors now work shoulder-to-shoulder with military personnel during both armed conflict and what is now termed "contingency operations," once called Military Operations Other Than War (MOOTW). While armed conflict refers to traditional combat operations associated with internationally recognized warfare, contingency operations include activities such as combating terrorism, counter-narcotic operations, peacekeeping operations, and other high-risk missions around the globe.

One of the consequences of the War on Terror is that American and coalition contractors—particularly in Iraq and Afghanistan—are subjected to kidnappings, torture, and murder by terrorists, criminal elements, and other insurgency forces. Without question, civilian contractors will continue to be integral participants in the ongoing War on Terror. Therefore, it is imperative that issues of force protection, AT training, and personnel recovery be fully delineated and the related legal contours more clearly defined. This is particularly important in light of the ever-evolving nature of terrorism and the attendant responses.

Both the DOD and the companies that provide civilian contractors have core moral and legal responsibilities to provide contract personnel with adequate security, AT training and, in certain circumstances, rescue from capture. In tandem with identifying the legal and policy considerations associated with these issues, this chapter will also address the matter of civil liability to the contracting company should it fail to provide adequate protection and/or appropriate AT training to their civilian employees serving overseas in hostile environments.

7.1 History and Status of Contractors

The military's use of civilian defense contractors certainly did not begin with the military campaigns and counter-terror operations in Afghanistan and Iraq. Since the inception of the American republic over 200 years ago, civilian contractors have provided a wide array of essential goods and services to military personnel operating both in garrison and in the field. The role of and need for contractor support began to expand greatly during the war in Vietnam and has dramatically increased in the War on Terror. With the accelerated use of civilian contractors who accompany the military, the issue of status looms as a central matter of concern. Are they combatants, non-combatants, or a hybrid?

Civilians accompanying military forces, also known in the DOD lexicon as contractors deploying with the force (CDF), fall into three broad categories, each governed by somewhat different legal and regulatory guidance. These three categories are: DOD civilian employees, civilian contractor personnel, and other non-affiliated civilians. As the primary topic of interest for these three categories, civilian contractor personnel includes "any individual, firm, corporation, partnership, association, or other legal nonfederal entity that enters into a contract directly with the [DOD] to furnish services, supplies, or both, including construction." In addition, many of the civilian contractors who accompany the military on contingency operations are designated as "mission-essential" (M-E) personnel (similar to the designation of DOD civilian employees as "emergency-essential" personnel). In essence, an M-E contractor is someone who works in a position in an overseas contingency operation that is required to ensure the success of the operation.

Given the scope and pace of the modern military, military planners no longer consider civilian contractors as a luxury or a "nice to have" addition to the force structure. Indeed, contractors accompanying the military on operations are a necessity without which the modern military could not conduct combat or engage in contingency operations. Because contractors now provide a wide range of technical, logistical, maintenance, and security support services to DOD missions, America's unparalleled military superiority now requires contractor support to maintain military readiness and operational capabilities. As noted, governmental limits on the number of DOD personnel authorized in a particular area, the increasing sophistication of military technologies, and the ever present need to conserve DOD resources for other potential activities make contractor personnel support vital. Working for American contractor companies under DOD contracts, thousands of engineers, technicians, construction workers, food service providers, weapon specialists, etc., make up a "privatized Army." This privatized Army is currently deployed closer than ever before to imminently dangerous areas, including the actual battlefield. To be sure, this fact has resulted in untoward consequences. Tragically, as of 2011, over 1,000 civilian contractors working in Iraq and Afghanistan (many of them Americans) have been killed, with an unknown number wounded.

Furthermore, relative to the size of the uniformed armed forces during the Cold War, today's active duty military is a significantly smaller force. This increases the importance of contractor support to maintain the overall flexibility of the active and reserve forces. While no one really knows exactly how many civilian contractors are currently supporting DOD contingency operations overseas, low ranging estimates reveal that in Iraq and Afghanistan there is approximately one civilian contractor for every two active duty military personnel. This amounts to over 75,000 civilian contractors, a number sure to increase over the next few years as the pace of infrastructure support in Iraq and Afghanistan increases. The high end number is one to one, which includes Private Military Firms (PMFs) like Blackwater (now renamed X-E Services), conducting security missions.

All civilian contractors operate under a specific contract, either directly with the DOD or subcontracted to another contractor who is under contract with the DOD. The duties of all contractors are "established solely by the terms of their contract." Usually, the military contract will fall into one of three general categories. First, Theater Support Contracts are contracts associated with providing support to the regional combatant command, for instance, in Colombia the combatant command is United States Southern Command. These contracts are typically for day-to-day recurring services at the deployed site, to include minor construction projects, repair parts, equipment rental, etc. The second type of contract is called External Support Contracts and are awarded by commands outside the pertinent combatant command, such as the Defense Logistics Agency. Again, under these civilian contracts, civilian contractors are expected to provide services at the deployed locations. Finally, Systems Contracts, the third category of contracts, provide the required logistics support to maintain and operate weapons systems and various mechanical systems used in the field. Regardless of the type of contract, the realities of military exigencies necessitate that civilian contract personnel "shall be prepared to respond rapidly, efficiently, and effectively to meet mission requirements for all contingencies and emergencies."

Some contracts may require contractor personnel to be United States citizens, reflecting security considerations associated with intelligence concerns or other sensitive issues. In fact, vetting contractors who might have access to particular DOD military sites is a necessary force protection measure. For example, the threat posed by in-country contractors with regular access to coalition military facilities was vividly demonstrated in December 2004, at Forward Operating Base (FOB) Marez in Mosul, Iraq. In this tragic incident, a suicide bomber penetrated base security measures and killed twenty-two people, including several civilian contractors. While the suicide bomber was not a civilian contractor (he was most probably a terrorist who disguised himself in an Iraqi military uniform), the event illustrated the fact that a non-American civilian who falsely gained employment under the pretense of an in-country contractor could accomplish the same act of terrorism.

The United States clearly adopts the international law prohibiting contractors from engaging in hostilities, but the reality is that contractors can be deployed throughout the battlefield, including forward-deployed positions (relative to enemy forces) to support operations during armed conflict or in other hostile environments associated with contingency operations. As evidenced by contractor casualties at the FOB Mosul attack, civilian contractors are regularly exposed to the risks of physical harm similar to that of military personnel. An enemy that blends in with the civilian population is far more able to employ violence. To prepare for the physical dangers inherent in such asymmetrical conflicts, contractors must be properly informed, trained and equipped not only to understand their own rights and obligations, but also to understand those of the United States military and the contractor company.

Unlike military personnel, civilian contractors accompanying the armed forces in the field do not fit neatly into well-defined arenas of military law and procedure. While the military has always carefully outlined its own command structure for its uniformed personnel, the picture is far less certain for civilians accompanying the forces. In fact, prior to the John Warner National Defense Authorization Act for

Fiscal Year 2007, which now authorizes trial by military courts-martial for crimes committed by civilian contractors who accompany military forces in both declared wars by Congress and on contingency operations, the Court of Military Appeals in *U.S. v. Averette* (1970) had made it clear that except in a Congressional declaration of war (which last occurred in 1941 during World War II), civilian contractors were not subject to the provisions of the Uniform Code of Military Justice (UCMJ), that is, military law.

There are three statutory avenues by which civilian contractors could be subject to criminal liability, the Special Maritime and Territorial Jurisdiction of the United States (SMTJ), the Military Extra-territorial Jurisdiction Act (MEJA), and the UCMJ. The USA PATRIOT Act amended the SMTJ and allowed for jurisdiction for offenses committed by or against a U.S. citizen or national, or on a facility used for U.S. foreign missions, or operations to include a location outside the jurisdiction of any nation (like Somalia). To date only one person has been prosecuted under the SMTJ. David Passaro, a contract employee of the CIA, was convicted in a federal court in North Carolina for the death of Abdul Wali in Afghanistan.

MEJA authority rests with the Attorney General via the respective federal districts and provides jurisdiction for crimes committed by civilian employees and contractors of the DOD operating with or near the U.S. military outside of U.S. territory, for felonies (offenses punishable by more than one year imprisonment). In 2010, two former Blackwater contractors were charged under MEJA in a federal court in Virginia for killing two Afghan nationals.

As noted UCMJ authority is the most recent development and is based on a revision of Article 2(a)(10) which provides for jurisdiction over any civilian contractor accompanying the military on "contingency operations." To date only one case has been tried. In 2008, Alaa Mohammad Ali, a contract interpreter plead guilty in a military courts-martial to stabbing another civilian employee.

Apart from criminal matters, military commanders have extremely limited authority to take any type of direct disciplinary action against contractors to make them perform their duties, contractors are generally not required to do anything outside of the terms of their specific contract. Simply stated, commanders must look to the contracting officer for enforcement of the terms of the contract. DOD Instruction 3020.41 in paragraph 6.1.1, entitled, International Law and Contractor Legal Status, states:

> Under applicable law, contractors may support military operations as civilians accompanying the force, so long as such personnel have been designated as such by the force they accompany and are provided with an appropriate identification card under the provisions of the 1949 Geneva Convention Relative to the Treatment of Prisoners of War....If captured during armed conflict, contingency contractor personnel accompanying the force are entitled to prisoner of war status.

The reason for this dilemma revolves around the exact nature of the civilian contractor as measured against the concept of armed conflict. To begin with, traditional international law has focused sharply on the distinction between international and internal armed conflict with most of the concern on the former. Even under the international law of war, the precise status of contractors is still the subject of some debate. The current corpus of the law of war, which consists of all laws created by treaty and customary principles applicable to international warfare, is largely encompassed by the 1949 Geneva Conventions. The Geneva Conventions serve as the primary source of law in the event of an international armed conflict. While the Geneva Conventions require all militaries to distinguish between combatants (armed forces) and non-combatants (civilians), civilian contractors are neither combatants nor non-combatants in the traditional sense of the terms. Contractors are simply civilians who are authorized to accompany regular military forces on assorted military operations to include times of international armed conflict (the United States' policy is to handle all hostile adversaries consistent with the spirit and terms of the Geneva Conventions irrespective of the nature of the conflict).

When taking a broader meaning of the term non-combatant, that is, the general civilian population, the concept actually embraces "certain categories of persons who, although members accompanying the armed forces, enjoy special protected status, such as medical officers, corpsmen, chaplain[s], technical (i.e., contractor) representatives, and civilian war correspondents." In fact, the Geneva Convention III provides that prisoner of war (POW) protected status is given to "[p]ersons who accompany the armed forces without actually being members thereof, such as civilian members of military aircraft crews, war correspondents, supply contractors, [and] members of labor units or of services responsible for the welfare of the armed forces...." Thus, contractors are viewed as separate from the general civilian population and must be treated as POWs if captured by enemy forces during an international armed conflict.

Ultimately, the legal fate of any contractor turns on how one interprets "direct participation." As long as the civilian contractor takes no direct part in hostilities, he must be given POW status. Even PMFs are not "mercenaries" or outside of the law because they act only in self-defense. Still, this non-combatant status does not insulate contractors from the exigencies of the battlefield, including the possibility of capture, injury, or death. This fact should always be stressed to civilian contractors before they are assigned to work in hostile environments outside of the United States.

Furthermore, with the defeat of the radical Taliban regime and the dictatorship of Saddam Hussein, a state of international armed conflict no longer exists between the United States (and its allies) and Afghanistan or Iraq. In this environment of contingency operations, the protections of the Geneva Conventions are not applicable. In fact, the ongoing terrorist activities in Afghanistan would probably not even qualify as an internal armed conflict. Although one could argue that the basic protections associated with basic humanitarian law and human rights law would protect the captured contractor from abuse or torture, the sad reality of the War on Terror is that civilian contractors are often specifically targeted by terrorists who recognize no law whatsoever and hold no distinction between civilians and the military. Humanitarian law has no value to terrorists. Thus, self-defense, AT training, and a personnel recovery policy are best viewed from the perspective of the adversary. In other words, will the hostile forces abide by the applicable legal norms and standards of civilized behavior?

During contingency operations, either the normative law of the host nation or any applicable Status of Forces Agreements (SOFAs) will determine the rights and privileges bestowed on civilian contractors while they are present in the host nation (special diplomatic arrangements may also exist for particular deployments). Unless a state of international armed conflict exists or some other set of special circumstances, e.g., the United States serving in an occupation role as it did in Iraq and Afghanistan, the use of civilian contractors will be strictly limited by these parameters. Again, as stated in the June 2005 Defense Federal Acquisition Regulation Supplement (DFARS): "Contractor personnel are not combatants and shall not undertake any role that would jeopardize their status."

7.2 Force Protection

Force protection is not simply providing armed military escorts to civilian contractors. Instead, it is a process of events that begins long before the civilian contractor is deployed. In recognition of this fact, force protection is defined as "actions taken to prevent or mitigate hostile actions against DOD personnel, resources, facilities, and critical information." Thus, the process of force protection clearly encompasses AT training, to include such things as ensuring that civilian contractors have "an understanding of [the] threat and the development of a system of indications and warnings that will facilitate a proactive, predictive response to enemy and terrorist action."

Force protection is the shared obligation of the military and the contractor company, tempered by the restriction that while accompanying the forces during an armed international conflict, civilian contractors cannot conduct force protection measures that would be tantamount to engaging in hostilities. Further, if armed contractors are used to provide security during a contingency operation, such activities must be spelled out in the contract and "[r]equests for permission to arm contingency contractor personnel to provide security services shall be reviewed on a case-by-case basis by the appropriate Staff Judge Advocate to the geographic Combatant Commander to ensure there is a legal basis for approval. The request will be approved or denied by the geographic Combatant Commander...."

Although the responsibility for force protection "starts with the combatant commander, extends downward, and includes the contractor," the exact extent of force protection afforded to the contractors as a general class is not entirely clear. The recently adopted June 2005 DFARS on contractors deployed on contingency operations offers only general guidance for the Combatant Commander. Of course, as a practical matter, the military's failure to adequately protect the civilian contractor may compromise the contractor's ability to perform the tasks (or terms) of the contract, thereby hampering the ability of the deployed military force to conduct operations. With the continuing cycle of violence in Iraq, some contracting companies have decided that the atmosphere is simply too dangerous and have pulled out. For instance, in December 2004, American contracting company Contrack International abandoned a $325 million contract in which they supervised a consortium that rebuilt transportation infrastructure in Iraq. In making their announcement to withdraw, a Contrack spokesman confided that "work [in Iraq] was too dangerous and costly."

As stated, if the contract allows, the military may position civilian contractors anywhere in the theater of operations. While they can never be used in "direct support" of hostile operations, the dangers of the battlefield and the limitations of the military to provide adequate force protection may subject contractors to bodily harm, necessitating the contractors' possession of firearms for self defense.

DOD policy discourages contractor personnel from possessing firearms for self-defense (although United States law does not preclude the possession of firearms for DOD employees under certain conditions). If weapons are authorized, they must be a military specification sidearm (the 9mm automatic pistol), utilizing military specification ammunition. A new draft DOD Instruction provides that the combatant commander may "authorize issuance of standard military sidearms or appropriate weapons to selected contractor personnel for individual self-defense," but only on those "rare occasions when military force protection is deemed unavailable." The June 2005 DFARS states that the "Combatant Commander will determine whether to authorize in-theater contractor personnel to carry weapons and what weapons will be allowed."

While a hostile environment and the limits of force protection may favor the possession of weapons by civilian contract personnel, other factors weigh heavily against it. First, arming contractors may distort their battlefield status as civilians accompanying the force. Second, contractors—especially those with prior military experience—may use the weapon in an unauthorized manner, further blurring the line between combatant and non-combatant. Furthermore, possession of a sidearm may cause the enemy to mistake a contractor for a soldier, thereby having the unintended effect of increasing the risk of physical harm to the contractor. To prevent accidents and misuse, contractors must be properly trained in use of firearms for self-defense only and must comply with all applicable local laws.

Even if the contractor gains approval from the Combatant Commander to carry a sidearm in theater, the terms of the contract or parent company policy may forbid it. In reality, contractors who wish to possess a firearm for self-defense must not only gain the approval of the Combatant Commander but must also be authorized (or not expressly forbidden) by the terms of the contract under which they are employed. In the majority of cases, civilian contractors may be provided with protective clothing such as bulletproof vests and helmets, but few are ever allowed to carry firearms. Additionally, in some circumstances, host nation laws may also prohibit contractors from possessing firearms. The exception, of course, would be those PMFs who are specifically hired to provide armed security protection. Depending on the agreement with the host nation, in times of non-international armed conflict, these individuals are armed with firearms other than pistols.

Army doctrine clearly provides that civilian contractors accompanying the force must be protected: "[T]he Army's policy has become that when contractors are deployed in support of Army operations/ weapons systems, they [contractors] will be provided force protection commensurate with that provided to DAC personnel." Still, force protection measures necessary to safeguard contract personnel will vary depending on the circumstances, taking into account known and perceived risks. This is a directly proportional relationship; a more direct threat requires greater force protection to safeguard contract personnel. For instance, during military operations in Somalia in 1993, the risks to contract personnel supporting DOD operations in theater were acute—armed gangs hostile to the American presence and the humanitarian mission presented a serious threat to the safety of civilian contract personnel. As a result, some contract personnel required an armed military escort at all times. Conversely, other military operations present lower levels of threat. In the late 1990s, civilian contract personnel traveled "nearly one million miles a month on the open roads of Bosnia, Croatia, and Hungary…for the most part without the benefit of any force protection."

In the War on Terror, ample evidence demonstrates that contractors, particularly those who have not received training on the rudimentary aspects of battlefield risks or how to manage them, are more likely the targets of kidnapping or other acts of violence. Within the general class of contractors, it is apparent that those without prior military experience or those who operate without the benefit of weapons for self-defense are at the greatest risk. Nevertheless, even if the contractor is former military, "the currency of their conditioning, both mental and physical, must be taken into account."

Army policy regarding contractor force protection must be juxtaposed more generally against Joint DOD doctrine, which relates to all the military services. Interestingly, Joint Publication (JP) 4-0, issued by the Chairman of the Joint Chiefs of Staff in 2000, provides that "[f]orce protection responsibility for DOD contractor employees is a contractor responsibility, unless valid contract terms place that responsibility with another party…." Consistent with JP 4-0, DOD force protection makes it clear that contractors are private American citizens and, accordingly, "[t]he Commanders do not have the same legal responsibility to provide security for [DOD] contractors as that provided for military forces or direct hire employees." Thus, while commanders may feel a moral or practical obligation to provide active and comprehensive force protection, in the sphere of legality, "[c]ontractors working within a U.S. military facility or in close proximity of U.S. Forces shall receive incidentally the benefits of measures undertaken to protect U.S. Forces."

The Draft DOD Instruction entitled Contractor Personnel Authorized to Accompany U.S. Armed Forces provides that contractors "shall receive incidentally the benefits of measures undertaken to protect U.S. forces...." However, the draft also mandates a higher level of responsibility in certain instances: "[C]ommanders shall provide force protection, commensurate with the level of force protection provided to military forces, when contractor personnel are integral to the military forces and providing essential contractor services (e.g., contractor logistics convoys)."

While the Combatant Commander will make the final decision "to provide force protection to participating contractors," the degree of force protection civilian contractors receive can also be a contractual matter that is determined by the contract itself. Consequently, astute negotiations on the part of civilian contractors seeking to provide services to DOD operations in hostile environments could obligate military personnel to provide increased levels of force protection. Yet, even if a particular contract absolves the military of formal force protection responsibilities, military policy maintains that commanders assume some duty to protect civilians accompanying the force, particularly those who are deemed to be M-E personnel. The June 2005 DFARS simply acknowledges that the military should at least provide training to those contractors who are issued special equipment: "The deployment center, or the Combatant Commander, shall issue OCIE [organizational clothing and individual equipment] and shall provide training, if necessary, to ensure the safety and security of contractor personnel."

Obviously, commanders should ensure that contractor security provisions are incorporated into the operational plans (OPLANs) and operational orders (OPORDs) when determining the size of theater security forces. Given the importance of certain categories of contract personnel to certain missions, it is likely that the commander will willingly assume the responsibility of providing appropriate force protection commensurate with the risks and resources available.

Paradoxically, although the military requires force protection for civilian contract personnel accompanying the forces, it is an impossible task to perform. In turn, a lack of precise (and often contradictory) guidance can certainly hamper the ability of contractor companies to fulfill their obligations *vis-à-vis* providing viable AT training to their employees. In short, to protect their employees from harm (and themselves from time consuming and costly lawsuits), contracting companies must assume high levels of force protection because AT training may not be provided by the military.

Equally disadvantaged by the absence of a uniform standard, military commanders must "work with requirements that vary according to the services and the individual contracts" between the military and the contractor. Indeed, the confusing nature of the contractor force protection doctrine has led "the Combatant Commanders [to request] DOD-wide guidance on the use of contractors to support deployed forces to establish a baseline [force protection policy] that applies to all the services." Until uniform DOD guidance is fully developed regarding force protection, the only alternative is to ensure that proper and adequate AT training is provided by the parent contracting company to help close the gap.

7.3 AT Training

Major General (Ret.) Alfred A. Valenzuela remarked at a June 2005 conference on "Contractors on the Battlefield," sponsored by the Center for Terrorism Law in San Antonio, Texas, and TATE, Inc., that "[a]lthough AT training is clearly a central theme of force protection in general, it is an area that requires special attention, particularly since the parent contracting company has a much larger role to play in AT training." The current reality of the War on Terror has merged traditional force protection concerns with antiterrorism policies and security initiatives. It is now DOD policy that "[DOD] Components and the [DOD] Elements and Personnel shall be protected from terrorist acts through a high priority, comprehensive AT program." Again, military commanders have the primary "responsibility and authority to enforce appropriate security measures to ensure the protection of [DOD] Elements and Personnel subject to their control and shall ensure AT awareness and readiness of all [DOD] Elements and Personnel…assigned or attached." Unfortunately, this Directive does not define what constitutes "appropriate security measures." Instead, the matter is left to the discretion of the commander on the ground, who is in the best position to understand the most salient threats and the proper methodologies to counter them.

DOD policy provides that training—both in certain basic legal issues and in techniques to manage personal security in hostile environments—should always be a prerequisite to deployment. Preventing the need for the military to engage in personnel recovery of captured civilians, military doctrine is clear on the need to provide appropriate AT training:

> Before entering a theater of operations or an area of responsibility…identified [DOD] civilian employees, [DOD] contractors (under the terms of the contract), and other designated personnel shall receive or already have completed the training necessary to survive isolation in a hostile environment, including captivity, and to return home safely and with honor.

Consistent with military doctrine, it seems entirely logical that all civilian contractors should be processed and trained through a DOD training site. Unfortunately, while a Draft DOD Instruction illustrates this basic need, it is not currently the case. In reality, AT training is approached in an extremely fragmented and ad hoc manner. Although the military may provide AT training at Individual Deployment Sites (IDS) or Continental United States (CONUS) Replacement Centers (CRC), it does not always happen. In fact, the use of IDS or CRC facilities by contract personnel is determined based upon the terms of the contract between the contractor and DOD. Then again, if contract personnel do require IDS or CRC pre-deployment processing, they may not get meaningful AT training since the IDS/CRC is tasked with actions to "screen contractor personnel records, conduct theater specific briefings and training, issue theater specific clothing and individual equipment, verify that medical requirements… for deployment have been met, and arrange for transportation to the theater of operations." Moreover, CRC focus is on military unit training versus training of individual survival skill sets.

The fact "that [DOD] contracts have varying and sometimes inconsistent language addressing deployment requirements" creates a sloppy training model for contractors engaged in contingency operations. Sending contractors into harm's way, absent a basic understanding of the threat or of the basic principles associated with terrorism law, places the contractors and the military forces they support at great risk. Thus, while military doctrine provides that "[c]ontractors arriving in theater must receive appropriate processing," specified AT training is not a mandatory component of contractor pre-deployment. Certainly, the rise of terrorism and the challenges of providing support to the armed forces in urban settings necessitate additional AT training for contractors in these high-risk environments. Yet, commanders are only required to offer "AT training to contractors under the terms specified in the contract," leaving many contract personnel ill-prepared and under-equipped to operate in locations plagued by the threat of car bombs, suicide bombers, or other ambushes.

The 2003 DOD guidance on isolated personnel training for civilian contractors does outline certain AT training requirements for contractors accompanying the force, but the level of training is not uniform—it varies based on the level of threat determined by the Combatant Commander. The guidance designates three levels of training regarding specific principles of resistance: Level A, if the perceived threat by hostile forces is low; Level B, for a medium threat level; and Level C, for a high threat level.

The mechanics of the training is often accomplished through the use of videos and is designed to help the contractor survive capture and exploitation by hostile forces. The training is not representative of comprehensive SERE (Survival, Evasion, Resistance, Escape) training given to certain categories of military personnel.

Another glaring deficiency associated with AT training is the lack of a Civilian Code of Conduct for civilian contractors who may be captured by hostile forces, to include terrorists. Civilian contractors sorely need "guidelines to increase their chance of survival in captivity, and to avoid potential criminal sanctions upon repatriation." For example, all Americans owe an unconditional allegiance to the United States and that allegiance is not cut-off simply because of capture by hostile forces.

DOD guidance regarding the provision of basic AT training has not kept up with the volume of contractors pouring into Iraq, Afghanistan, and other places around the globe. In effect, civilian contractor companies operating under the United States Army's Logistics Civil Augmentation Program (LOGCAP) are left to provide their own AT training. Unfortunately, in far too many cases, the AT training is sorely inadequate or is simply not done. The case of Thomas Hamill of Macon, Mississippi, is typical of how this process plays out in the real world. In late 2003, Hamill was hired by Kellogg Brown and Root (KBR) to serve as a driver of large tanker trucks in Iraq. Hamill's case is noteworthy because he is one of the few civilian contractors to have ever survived a terrorist kidnapping—he escaped from his terrorist captors 24 days after a brutal ambush of his truck convoy. His escape in 2004 is all the more amazing because he received only limited training from KBR in basic force protection related solely to his driving duties. He had no training whatsoever from the military in how to survive, evade, resist, or escape from the terrorists. Military SERE experts who interviewed him after the ordeal were impressed by Hamill's level-headed dealings with his terrorist captors, stating, "We don't know how you did it. You aren't a soldier, and you haven't been trained [in AT techniques]."

Hamill was only slightly better prepared from the KBR training than if he had received no AT training at all. When first hired in 2003, Hamill was flown to KBR headquarters in Houston, Texas, for "a seven-day orientation class." A month after the course, Hamill was flown to Kuwait where he was given a second round of training courses. "They had us attend a defensive-driving course where we discussed things such as convoy formations, how to spot explosive devices, booby traps, and how to recognize and avoid suspicious automobiles." Then, before each convoy was started on the road for its destination, Hamill, now a convoy commander, would receive a safety briefing from KBR as to road conditions and possible danger from terrorist attacks. Beyond this, Hamill never received any other type of AT training.

In light of the Hamill experience, it is imperative that either the military or the parent contracting company provides a higher level of meaningful and realistic AT training that prepares DOD contract personnel for high-risk deployments. For the contractor, adequate AT training provides "the first opportunity to get the contractor's head in the current joint operational and tactical situation" present within the theater. Obviously, the preferred point of contact for this obligation should be the military. "As it becomes the primer for theater specific force protection and personnel recovery readiness of contractors en route from [the continental United States] to high-threat overseas venues," the CRC has the potential to provide near real-time information that will improve contractor safety and survivability. Training also facilitates contractor compliance with an understanding of security-related DOD regulations, such as those regarding temporary duty travel abroad, made applicable to contract personnel through the DOD AT Program Directive.

If the military does not provide the proper AT training, parent contracting companies need to hire specialists to provide in-house training to ensure that their employees are as ready as possible to handle the exigencies associated with contingency operations and possible capture by hostiles. Not only is there a moral duty to see that this is accomplished, but the parent company who fails in this regard may be subjecting itself to possible civil liability. Just as contracting companies must ensure that employees have proper equipment, clothing, and supplies to perform the contract, they are also responsible to provide AT awareness training to their employees similar to that provided to military personnel.

In short, contractors who receive AT and security-related training prior to deployment are better positioned to avoid and manage the risks encountered on MOOTW or in armed conflict. This, in turn, takes pressure off the Combatant Commander in terms of force protection concerns and the conservation of military resources.

7.4 Contractor Company Liability Issues

With the increasing number of terrorist-related deaths and wounding of civilian contractors accompanying the military in the War on Terror, the question of civil liability for contracting companies has become an important concern. Considering the rapid rate in which individual employee contractors are prepared, processed, and trained to go into dangerous environments, such as Iraq, Afghanistan, and Colombia, it is inevitable that civil litigation against parent contract companies will arise. A 2004 civil lawsuit, filed in Wake County Superior Court, Raleigh, North Carolina, against the contracting company Blackwater Security Consulting and other named defendants, illustrates the concern.

Nordan v. Blackwater Security Consulting was filed by the survivors of four deceased independent civilian contractors and was the first in the nation to be lodged against a private contracting company for death during action in Iraq. The four contractors were hired as security consulting contractors and were viciously murdered on March 31, 2004, while escorting a civilian convoy through Fallujah, Iraq, a known hostile environment at the time. Among a list of allegations of wrongdoing, the families contended that Blackwater sent the contractors into this hostile environment without proper equipment or armed escorts as promised in the contract. The families also thought the amount of AT training given to the deceased contractors was insufficient. The formal allegations lodged by the survivors consisted of fraud in the inducement of the contract and wrongful death because the contractors had been promised protection and proper information (associated with AT training) when they signed the contracts.

After a long series of pleadings and various motions (to include two attempts by Blackwater to remove to federal court), in 2007, North Carolina Eastern District Court Judge James Fox sent the case into secret arbitration based on an independent service agreement. Although the *Nordan* case was disposed of in 2007, the arguments raised in the pleadings and motions are illustrative of the tactics employed by both sides. For example, Blackwater argued that the Defense Base Act, a federal law capping death benefits for contractors working outside of the United States, entirely preempted State law relevant to this matter. Second, Blackwater asserted that the political question doctrine rendered the case non-justiciable.

Before detailing the issue of the political question doctrine, it is important to consider some of the possible reasons that many civilian contractors might be motivated to sign on to work for companies operating overseas, particularly in dangerous environments. Apart from fulfilling a sense of patriotism to the nation at war, in all probability, a significant incentive rests in the increased pay that the civilian contractor can receive. Not only do most companies pay danger premiums for work in hostile environments, but much of the pay earned overseas may be excluded from U.S. Federal taxable income. For example, the United States Army allows contracting officers to negotiate increased amounts of pay when the employee operates in areas considered to be equivalent to a war type environment. For many civilians, the increase in pay is a sufficient element to subject themselves to a hostile, even deadly work environment.

On the other hand, many contracting companies seek to insulate themselves from any liability whatsoever by crafting language in the contract that leaves the contractor (or the heirs) with virtually no ability to sue the company. Again, the *Nordan* case is quite telling concerning the methodology of how the contractor company attempts to absolve itself of liability. A typical Blackwater contract related to employment duties in Iraq or Afghanistan contains a clause regarding contract performance during hostilities:

Contractor agrees and acknowledges that the Services performed in the Duty Station…have been identified as being essential to BSC's [Blackwater] complete performance under the terms of the contract between BSC and the Customer [the United States] and notwithstanding the existence of hostilities or a state of war, whether declared or undeclared, Contractor agrees to perform his or her assigned duties until released from such duties by the Contractor's supervisor or the supervisor's designated representative.

Next, the sample Blackwater contract has a clause headlined as "Contractor Acknowledgement, Release and Waiver." Spelling out an assumption of the risk, the clause graphically reads:

Contractor agrees and acknowledges that due to the hazardous nature of the Duty Station and the Services to be provided hereunder, Contractor hereby expressly and voluntarily agrees to assume any and all risks of personal injury including, without limitation, death and disability which may result from contractor providing Services pursuant to this Agreement. Contractor understands and acknowledges that the Duty Station [place where the contractor works] is volatile, hostile and extremely dangerous and in some instances, military forces may be conducting continuing military operations in the region.

The assumption of the risk clause then continues with a lengthy list of the dangers and risks that the Contractor acknowledges and "voluntarily, expressly and irrevocably assum[es]."

Contractor understands and acknowledges that by voluntarily agreeing to participate in the Engagement [accompanying the military on a contingency operation or actual armed conflict], he is voluntarily, expressly, and irrevocably assuming any and all known and unknown, anticipated and unanticipated risks which could result in physical or emotional injury, paralysis, death, or damage to himself, to his property, or to third parties, whether or not such injury or death is caused by other independent contractors to BSC, known and unknown domestic and foreign citizens or terrorist or U.S. governmental employees.

In addition to the above exculpatory clauses, Blackwater further attempts to release liability for any acts of negligence on its part by including the following language in a clause entitled "Release":

Contractor, on behalf of Contractor and Contractor's spouse, heirs, administrators, estate, personal representatives, successors and assigns (collectively referred to as "Contractor's Group"), hereby releases and forever discharges BSC…(collectively referred to as "Releasees") from any and all claims, judgments, awards, actions and causes of action which may be asserted now or in the future by Contractor's Group for any liability whatsoever for accident, injury (including without limitation, death or disability), losses, loss of consortium, expenses, loss of income and other damages based upon or in any way arising from Contractor's performance of Services pursuant to this Agreement and the transportation of Contractor, including, without limitation, loss of life...*whether as a result of negligence, gross negligence, omissions or failure to guard or warn against dangerous conditions*, use, structure or activity, or any other cause, arising from Contractor's participation in the Engagement...even if such injury was caused in whole or in part by the negligence of Releasees [emphasis added].

To further reinforce the position that the company cannot be sued in civil court, the contract specifically spells out the following in a separate paragraph entitled, "Covenant Not to Sue":

Contractor further agrees and covenants not to file, prosecute, bring, maintain or in any way proceed on any claim, suit, civil action, complaint, arbitration or administrative action or proceeding of any kind in any municipal, state, federal agency, court, or tribunal against Releasees with respect [sic] any of the foregoing facts, occurrences, events, transactions, damages, injuries, claims, causes of action and other matters released in Section 11.2 [the "Release" clause set out above].

Then, in a separate clause entitled, "Liquidated Damages," the Blackwater contract expressly sets out:

The parties hereto expressly agree that in the event of Contractor's death or injury based upon or in any way arising from Contractor's performance of Services pursuant to this Agreement and the transportation of Contractor, even if such injury was caused in whole or in part by the negligence of Releasees, Contractor's Group has no recourse whatsoever against BSC. Contractor understands and agrees that if he is hurt or killed during Contractor's performance of Services pursuant to this Agreement or the transportation of Contractor, Contractor has no recourse whatsoever against Releasees.

Finally, at the end of the lengthy contract, the contractor employee agrees to a final waiver:

By signing this document, Contractor acknowledges that if Contractor is hurt or his property is damaged while providing Services hereunder, the intent is that Contractor and Contractor's Group is bound by this Release and Indemnification and therefore will be found by a court of law to have waived his right to maintain a lawsuit against BSC on the basis of any claim from which Contractor has released them herein.

Obviously, an employment contract such as the detailed Blackwater example serves as a formidable shield to any legal responsibility on the part of the parent company. Because many contracts are interpreted within the "four-corners" of the contract, these iron-clad provisions are generally viewed as binding, leaving contract personnel with little recourse against the company if that contractor is harmed or killed. Likewise, there appears to be little incentive for the company to take responsibility for its contractors as the contract language precludes the contractor from suing, even for the company's negligent behavior.

In response to the plaintiffs in a *Nordan*-styled lawsuit, the contracting company could raise the following defenses: the contract specifically spelled out the dangers; the workers signed a release giving up most of their rights to sue if something untoward happened to them, even if the deaths were the result of the company's negligence or gross negligence; and the contractors signed on willingly, were being paid a large sum of money, and were fully aware of all of the risks since all of them were military veterans. Furthermore, the company would argue that the Defense Base Act is the contractor's remedy, particularly if the dependents of the contractors have already started to receive payments for the deaths. However, if the court finds that the decedents were independent contractors and not employees, the applicability of the statute would be brought into question. The test to determine whether the decedents were independent contractors will center on a number of factors to include: (1) the extent of control exercised over the work by the employer; (2) the presence of independent skills, knowledge and training of the decedents; (3) the method of payment and taxes; (4) the length of time of employment; and (5) the provision of equipment. Indeed, if the court finds that the relationship between the plaintiffs and the company were not that of employee/employer, then the Act will not bar recovery.

Aside from relying on the contract provisions themselves, contracting companies can also rely on a "Government Contract Defense" to further absolve themselves of responsibility. First raised in the context of a contractor's liability for a manufacturing defect, this defense is set out by the United States Supreme Court in *Boyle v. United Technologies*. *Boyle* arose in the context of a tort claim asserting that a defense contractor had negligently designed a helicopter escape hatch resulting in the death of the pilot when the helicopter crashed. The Court applied a three-prong test to determine whether the contractor was immune from suit. The Court concluded that the Government Contract Defense was applicable where: (1) the contractor has taken actions at the direction of agency officials exercising their discretionary authority; (2) the directions involved reasonably precise specifications created by the Government with which the contractor complied; and (3) the contractor did not fail to warn the Government of known dangers associated with the Government's design. Therefore, the contractor was immunized from tort liability for damages arising from the alleged helicopter design defects.

Currently, the immunity arising under *Boyle* is a potentially valuable tool for those contract companies that provide a weapons system in a battlefield environment. Providing such equipment in a combat or contingency operation raises the stakes for all parties involved. This is true because the failure of a weapons system can have direct adverse consequences in terms of property damage and combat casualties. Such adverse consequences could then give rise to potentially enormous financial liability for the contractor.

While this scenario no doubt makes reliance on the *Boyle* defense a potentially important shield for contractors, it is important to note that the *Boyle* case involved a contract for production of a weapons system. Currently, many overseas contractor efforts in support of contingency operations usually involve contracts for services. At least two federal district courts have undertaken detailed analyses of this issue, and both have held that the rationale for the defense outlined in *Boyle* and its progeny dictates that the defense is also available to civilian contractors performing service contracts, not just manufacturing.

Another possible line of defense for a contracting company is the so-called "Government Agency Defense." This defense basically holds that if a contractor engages in a valid legal activity in furtherance of the performance of a government contract, the contractor is immune from suit for that activity to the extent that the government would be immune if sued directly. The treatment of this defense by federal courts in recent decades has been woefully inconsistent and, therefore, it unfortunately provides little real guidance.

Despite the rigid language of Blackwater-styled contracts and the above mentioned defenses, plaintiffs (like those in *Nordan*) may still be able to recover significant monetary damages even if they entered into an iron-clad contract. First, the claims will be filed in individual State courts and therefore the applicable State law may provide some relief, for example, under a wrongful death statute that allows for financial compensation or an expansive strict liability theory. Apart from the fact that the parent company may be held liable for intentional or reckless conduct, strict liability may prove to be a viable option.

The Second Restatement of Torts establishes strict liability for defendants who engage in ultra-hazardous or abnormally dangerous activities. Clearly, sending contractors into hostile combat zones would be considered an abnormally dangerous activity. Section 519 of the Restatement generally declares that "[o]ne who carries on an abnormally dangerous activity is subject to liability for harm to the person, land or chattels of another resulting from the activity, although he has exercised the utmost care to prevent the harm." Naturally, this section also limits the liability "to the kind of harm, the possibility of which makes the activity abnormally dangerous."

The subjective factors for determining whether or not an activity is abnormally dangerous are set out in Section 520 of the Restatement. These factors include: (1) the "existence of a high degree of risk of some harm to the person, land or chattels of others;" (2) the "likelihood that the harm that results from it will be great;" (3) the "inability to eliminate the risk by the exercise of reasonable care;" (4) the "extent to which the activity is not a matter of common usage;" (5) the "inappropriateness of the activity to the place where it is carried on;" and (6) the "extent to which its value to the community is outweighed by its dangerous attributes."

In assessing each of the factors listed in Section 520, it should be noted that none of them are dispositive, and it is not necessary to prove each of them in order to find that an activity qualifies as abnormally dangerous. Moreover, none of the factors have to be given equal weight. In short, the framers of the Restatement grant courts wide latitude in using these factors to determine the dangerousness of the activity. Section 522 takes things a step further, imposing strict liability on a defendant engaged in an abnormally dangerous activity "for the resulting harm although it is caused by the unexpectable (1) innocent, negligent, or reckless conduct of a third person, or (2) action of an animal, or (3) operation of a force of nature."

Applying all of these factors to the plaintiffs' claims in a *Nordan*-styled case, it appears on the surface that a solid case for strict liability can certainly be made against the defendant. It is difficult, if not impossible, to argue that the defendant's business does not qualify as an abnormally dangerous activity. The representations made to the plaintiffs when they signed on with the contracting company to serve as security contractors certainly sent a message that their job would include specific hazards that required special equipment and training (to include AT training). It also appears that most of the six factors listed in Section 520 can be applied. The first four factors are particularly applicable, as it is obvious that the situation security contractors face in hostile environments constitute "a high degree of risk of some harm…[to] others," with the likelihood that the resulting harm "will be great" and could not be eliminated with "the exercise of reasonable care." Moreover, it would be difficult for the defendant to demonstrate that the activity they hired the contractors to engage in was "a matter of common usage."

Nevertheless, the last two factors are more problematic for the plaintiff. It is less likely that a court would find the defendants' activities in hostile environments to be inappropriate for that locale. For example, in the *Nordan* case, Fallujah was a well-known hostile zone where terrorists regularly operated. Additionally, the court could subjectively find that the valuable service that the defendants supplied to the Iraqi civilian population and American troops in the Fallujah community outweighed the dangerous attributes of the activity itself.

At the end of the day, of course, the Restatement grants the court the power to exercise a great amount of discretion in assessing the criteria. Accordingly, the formula the court would use to assign weight and persuasiveness to each of the factors makes prognostication nearly impossible. Still, Section 519 of the Restatement reveals that a defendant can exercise the utmost care and still be liable for the harm that another suffers as a result of the defendant's abnormally dangerous activity. As such, in *Nordan* the precautions taken and the equipment supplied by Blackwater would not shield them from strict liability for the harms that befell the plaintiffs in Fallujah on March 31, 2004. A *fortiori*, if the plaintiff can show that Blackwater was actually deficient in providing the proper equipment or AT training, the strict liability case becomes stronger.

On the other hand, it must be admitted that other factors make the imposition of strict liability on the defendant, based on their engagement in an abnormally dangerous activity, much more difficult. Most significantly, Section 523 of the Restatement makes a "plaintiff's assumption of the risk of harm from an abnormally dangerous activity" an absolute bar from recovery. The defendant is likely to argue the plaintiff was aware of all of the dangers associated with the job and still signed an employment contract in which they were specifically informed of the risks and assumed the risks. If the court finds this argument to be credible, it could prove fatal to the plaintiffs' claims of strict liability based on the exercise of an abnormally dangerous activity. Nevertheless, many courts view assumption of the risk language to be calculated risks that do not automatically bind contractor employees, particularly when viewed in the light of any promises made by the parent contracting company.

Faced with the assumption of the risk obstacle, which is included as boilerplate contract language for all of the contracting companies, the plaintiffs could still use some of the strict liability elements to buttress their negligence claims. As counterintuitive as it might appear, in arguing for imposition of strict liability, plaintiffs could cite the amount of increased training they were required to undertake as evidence of the abnormal and hazardous nature of the activity. As more often is the case, in arguing a strict liability or negligence theory of recovery, the plaintiffs would argue that they received no extensive AT training and therefore were more likely to suffer the harms that they did, in fact, suffer. Thus, since they were not properly provided AT training, they could not form the required level of understanding to appreciate the dangers they were waiving. In other words, the injuries the plaintiffs suffered were directly attributable to the lack of information and AT training offered by the parent contracting company. Indeed, inadequate and nonexistent training has been cited frequently by contractors in Iraq as an ongoing and potentially dangerous problem.

In addition, plaintiffs can claim, as in *Nordan*, that they relied on the defendant's promises of proper AT training and force protection in making their decision to sign the subject contract. As in *Nordan*, the four plaintiffs could allege that the parent company neglected its duty to provide AT training and force protection, or engaged in intentional fraud (perhaps in the interest of greater profits) to induce the deceased to enter the contract. Stated specifically, fraud in the inducement applies when the defendant knowingly makes a false representation of a material fact, intending that action to be acted upon. Additionally, the plaintiff must have incurred damages in its reasonable reliance and action upon the false representation. In the event that fraud in the inducement of a contract is found, the court orders rescission of the entire contract. In short, the so-called iron clad contract is gone.

Finally, the matter of the political question doctrine has created a division of opinion in the federal courts. Given the fact that military operations give rise to their fair share of untoward activities to include wrongful deaths and accidents—by negligence and/or intentional acts—it is not surprising that parent contracting companies have faced a number of civil lawsuits during the War on Terror emanating from civilian employees, other contractors, military personnel, and host nation foreigners. An often raised defense employed by the contacting company early on in the litigation process is the political question doctrine which, if adopted by the court, serves as complete jurisdictional bar to the lawsuit. As set out in the Supreme Court case of *Japan Whaling Association v. American Cetacean Society*, "the political question doctrine excludes from judicial review those controversies which revolve around policy choices and value determinations constitutionally committed for resolution in the halls of Congress or the confines of the Executive Branch." In other words, even if the plaintiff's lawsuit meets every other procedural and substantive matter, the political question doctrine renders the case non-justiciable. Although the court may have subject matter jurisdiction, the type of issues at hand are deemed to be inappropriate for judicial resolution and left for resolution to the other two branches of the federal government. Accordingly, since the case can be disposed of as non-justiciable, defense counsel representing the subject contracting company invariably include the political question doctrine either as a pre-answer motion or as an integral part of the responsive pleading.

The political question doctrine is firmly set in separation of powers concerns and originates under the case and controversy requirement of Article III of the Constitution. In essence, courts should refuse to intrude on those matters that are properly the dominion of the more accountable branches of the federal government. The question of how to identify a non-justiciable political question is set out by the Supreme Court in *Baker v. Carr*. The so-called *Baker* inquiry lists six separate factors, any one of which renders the case non-justiciable. The six *Baker* factors are:

> (1) a textually demonstrable constitutional commitment of the issue to a coordinate political department; or (2) a lack of judicially discoverable and manageable standards for resolving it; or (3) the impossibility of deciding without an initial policy determination of a kind clearly for nonjudicial discretion; or (4) the impossibility of a court's undertaking independent resolution without expressing lack of the respect due coordinate branches of government; or (5) an unusual need for unquestioning adherence to a political decision already made; or (6) the potentiality of embarrassment form multifarious pronouncements by various departments one question.

While the test in *Baker* is broadly defined and listed in descending order of importance, with the first and second factors providing the most weight, it is well established that not all matters regarding foreign policy would automatically trigger exclusion from judicial review. Each case mandates "a discriminating analysis of the particular question posed, in terms of the history of its management by the political branches, of its susceptibility to judicial handling in the light of its nature and posture in the specific case, and of the possible consequences of judicial action." Because each case must be evaluated in light of the factors in *Baker*, it is not surprising that lower courts will place great emphasis on previous judicial rulings dealing with whether the actions of a particular contracting company involved issues barred from review under the political question doctrine. The problem, of course, is that the various contingency operations associated with the War on Terror have so far only provided a handful of cases against contracting companies where federal courts have been able to make comparisons and extrapolate common areas of agreement.

Ibrahim v. Titan Corp., decided in 2005, provided one of the early attempts to address the political question doctrine. In *Ibrahim*, seven Iraqi nationals brought suit in federal court seeking compensation against two private contracting companies (Titan and CACI) operating under government contract in Iraq as interpreters and interrogators for the U.S. military at the infamous Abu Ghraib prison. The plaintiffs alleged various acts of assault and battery, false imprisonment, intentional infliction of emotional distress, wrongful death, and torture at the hands of the contractors and also sought recovery under the Alien Tort Statute and the Racketeer Influenced and Corrupt Organizations Act (RICO). Although the defendants moved to dismiss the lawsuit as non-justiciable because they implicated political questions, the court flatly ruled that the plaintiffs' claims were not barred by the political question doctrine. While the ruling was clear, the accompanying legal analysis for the decision was extremely weak. With only a passing acknowledgment of the six-part *Baker* criteria, the court held that the "political question doctrine may lack clarity…but it is not without standards." Instead of flushing out the specifics of the *Baker* factors, the court simply parroted a phrase from the 2004 Supreme Court case of *Hamdi v. Rumsfeld*, and declared that not every dispute that "can arguably be connected to 'combat'" is excluded from judicial review by a separation of powers argument. The court wrote that "[a]n action for damages from the acts of private contractors and not seeking injunctive relief does not involve the courts in" overseeing foreign policy or the use of military force. Indeed, the court's shallow justification for rejecting the political question doctrine seems to have been based on the fact that the suit was against a private contracting company, not the United States government, for "actions of a type that both violate clear Untied States policy…and have led to recent high profile court martial proceedings against United States soldiers."

The 2006 case of *Smith v. Halliburton Co.*, involved a suit against a civilian contractor who operated a dining facility at Forward Operating Base (FOB) Marez, in Mosul, Iraq. In December 2004 a suicide bomber entered the dining facility and murdered twenty-two people. In contrast to *Ibrahim*, the *Smith* court actually spent some time and effort in applying the *Baker* factors and determined that the contractor was "operating pursuant to the military's orders, instructions and regulations." As a result of this finding, the court ruled that the case was non-justiciable. Indeed, the heart of the *Baker* analysis speaks to the issue of the court substituting its own judgment for the military, which the court would surely have to do in the context of FOB security measures.

In *Lessin v. Kellogg Brown & Root*, the defendant moved for dismissal based on the political question doctrine. The facts of the case revealed that plaintiff Lessin, a U.S. Army active duty military police (MP) solider, suffered traumatic brain injury in Iraq while providing a military escort for a truck convoy owned and operated by private contracting company Kellogg Brown & Root. Attempting to assist the civilian driver of a Kellogg Brown & Root truck that had stopped on the side of the road, Lessin was struck in the head by the truck's ramp. The 2006 lawsuit, filed in the United States District Court for the Southern District of Texas, alleged that the contracting company was negligent in "inspecting, maintaining, and repairing the truck that injured Lessin, and in supervising the driver who was operating the truck." The defendant asserted that the case should be dismissed based on one or more of the first four factors of the *Baker* test. Respectively, the defendant argued that: (*Baker* factor one) adjudicating the plaintiff's claims would require a detailed inquiry by the court into military regulations and orders associated with military escort procedures for civilian convoys; (*Baker* factor two) there are no judicially discoverable standards to determine whether or not the military exercised reasonable judgment in regard to allowing the subject truck to be a part of the convoy, halting and assisting the subject truck in a combat zone, and overseeing proper maintenance standards for the convoy truck; and (*Baker* factors three and four) the court would be required to undertake a policy decision *vis-à-vis* the military and civilian contractors in a combat zone which would "express a lack of respect due to coordinate branches of government that oversee such war efforts."

The *Lessin* court disagreed, noting that the case at hand was a mere traffic accident raising standard tort issues related to negligence by the civilian driver coupled with allegations that the company failed to properly train and supervise the employee. The court wrote that the incident "was, essentially, a traffic accident, involving a commercial truck alleged to have been negligently maintained, as well as a civilian truck driver who was allegedly negligent in operating the truck and insufficiently trained…[c]laims of negligence arising from this type of incident are commonly adjudicated by courts, using well-developed standards." Still, the court did agree that Discovery might reveal additional facts to support dismissal based on the political question doctrine. The court ruled that at this stage of the lawsuit "it is by no means clear that the policies or decisions of the military or of the executive branch itself will be implicated in this case."

A month after the 2006 ruling in *Lessin*, a similar set of facts was presented to a federal district court in Georgia. This time, however, the court ruled that the case was barred under the political question doctrine. In *Whitaker v. Kellogg Brown & Root, Inc.*, the court found that a U.S. Army soldier killed in a vehicle accident while escorting a truck supply convoy operated by Kellogg Brown & Root posed a non-justiciable political question. The soldier, Whitaker, was serving duty as part of a military escort for a civilian convoy delivering supplies under a government contract in Iraq. During the convoy, Whitaker died as the result of being struck by a civilian contractor driving a civilian truck over the Tigris River in Iraq—Whitaker fell into the Tigris River and drowned. Whitaker's parents, as plaintiffs, alleged negligence against the contracting company Kellogg Brown & Root under the doctrine of respondeat superior for the negligence of its drivers.

Using the *Baker* factors as its guide, the court refused to characterize the incident as a traffic accident involving standard negligence claims, but instead viewed the matter as a wreck that occurred in a combat zone during wartime involving "strategic and tactical military decisions made in a combat zone." Paying great attention to a variety of U.S. Army regulations which authorize the use of civilian contractors "to perform selected services in wartime to augment Army forces," the court went into great detail about how these orders and regulations impacted across the full range of the *Baker* factors. Further, the court ruled that there were no judicially discoverable and manageable standards to apply to the incident because the standard for review is not what a reasonable driver would have done, but what a reasonable driver in a wartime environment would have done. Finally, the court specifically recognized that because the military was accomplishing "its mission by partnering with government contractors who are subject to the military's orders, regulations, and convoy plan," due deference had to be given to the political branches of Congress and the Executive. "The Army will fight as a total force—active and reserve components and *civilians* [emphasis added]."

In *Fisher v. Halliburton, Inc.*, another 2006 ruling, employees of a civilian contractor in Iraq filed suit alleging that the parent contracting company had committed a wide variety of actionable wrongs to include wrongful death, intentional infliction of physical and emotional distress, fraud, etc. The case arose from an attack on a convoy by anti-American forces in Iraq on the morning of April 9, 2004, resulting in the deaths and injury of several civilian contractors. Defendant's motion for dismissal based on the political question doctrine was granted. In short, the court determined that decisions regarding when and where the convoy would be sent that day were "so interwoven with Army decisions," that it touched at least three of the *Baker* factors. "The case at bar meets not one, but three of the formulations described in *Baker v. Carr*." In fact, the court actually listed four of the *Baker* factors. Specifically, the court found that *Baker* factor one applied even if the Army had no direct control over the civilian members of the convoy. "Even assuming the court found this statement to be true [that the civilian contractor company deployed, directed, and controlled the convoy's civilian members], the private character of the actions do not preclude the application of the political question doctrine." The *Fisher* court reasoned that it could not "try a case set on a battlefield during wartime without an impermissible intrusion into powers expressly granted to the Executive by the Constitution." In addition, the court found that the second *Baker* factor applied since a lack of judicially discoverable and manageable standards existed by which it could measure the responsibility of the military in the context of the attack. Finding that the Army played an integral part in the decision to deploy and protect the convoy, the court noted that it would have to "substitute its judgment for that of the Army," a function prohibited by *Baker*. Finally, the court listed the third and fourth Baker factors together—"nonjudicial policy determination and lack of respect [due to coordinate branches of government]" as the final reasons for granting dismissal of the civil action. The court recognized that it was not equipped to formulate an examination of the many questions associated with the incident—ranging from the wisdom of sending the convoy on a particular route to the use of civilian contractors to drive the trucks.

Stemming from a plane crash in Afghanistan, in *McMahon v. Presidential Airways, Inc.* the 11th Circuit U.S. Court of Appeals upheld the lower court's denial of a motion to dismiss based on the political question doctrine. The facts of the case show that civilian contractor company Presidential Airways (Presidential) was under military contract to provide transportation and operational support to the DOD in Afghanistan. On one such flight in Afghanistan, the plane crashed, killing all aboard. Survivors of United States soldiers brought suit against Presidential Airways in a federal district court in Florida, claiming negligence regarding the staffing, equipping, and operation of the subject flight. In the opinion, the court dismissed the first *Baker* factor, finding that while the military was involved in choosing the start and end points of various Presidential flights, the military role in directing the activities were "relatively discrete." The court reasoned that because the contract provided that Presidential was responsible for supervision, management, and administration of its operations, the trial court would not be challenging the duties given by the military, but the duties performed by Presidential. The court found that the second *Baker* factor did not present matters that were inherently unmanageable since the standards to assess the issue were "the same as in any tort suit involving a plane crash." Since the court felt that the facts demonstrated minimal military involvement and the type of claim was squarely in the realm of a negligence claim, the remaining *Baker* factors were disposed of in quick step.

In the 2006 case of *Potts v. Dyncorp Intern. LLC*, an Alabama federal district court also addressed the issue of the political question doctrine. Potts, a civilian contractor in Iraq, sued another contractor company over personal injuries he suffered as a result of a car accident in Iraq. Potts was a passenger in one of the vehicles in a convoy traveling on the main supply route from Trebil, Jordan to Baghdad, Iraq. The driver of the vehicle was a Dyncorp employee who crashed the vehicle at a high rate of speed while trying to avoid a "black object in the road."

Analogizing to *Lessin* the *Potts* court found that the case did not satisfy any of the *Baker* factors. The court found that the first and third *Baker* factors were not satisfied because the incident at hand related to assessing Dyncorp's internal policies related to its contract with the Coalition Provisional Authority (CPA) which did not "involve decisions regarding foreign policy at such a level where judicial review would encroach upon the constitutional authority of one or both of the political accountable branches." In contrast to the *Whitaker* approach, which focused heavily on a variety of military directives and orders associated with civilian contractors and the fact that convoy operations are controlled by the military, the court in *Potts* focused on the terms of the specific contract between Dyncorp and the CPA and ignored any connection with the military that would activate the first *Baker* factor. In discounting the second *Baker* factor, the court ruled that because the vehicle accident was a claim of negligence commonly adjudicated under well established legal parameters, it was able to "assess whether the private contractor was negligent or wanton, even when performing services in a war zone."

In 2008, a federal district court in Georgia held in *Carmichael v. Kellogg Brown & Root, Inc.*, that a civil action brought against Kellogg Brown & Root was non-justiciable under the political question doctrine. After first denying a motion to dismiss based on the political question doctrine, the court allowed Kellogg Brown & Root to renew the motion to dismiss at the close of Discovery. Taking cognizance of the 11th Circuit's ruling in *McMahon*, which spoke favorably about the *Whitaker* finding of a non-justiciable political question, *Carmichael* ruled in favor of the motion to dismiss. Clearly, the facts in *Carmichael* were very similar to the facts of *Whitaker*. In *Carmichael,* a United States Army soldier was injured in a convoy accident. The solider was an armed escort passenger in a tractor-trailer driven by a civilian contractor in a convoy in Iraq when the vehicle's driver lost control, drove off the road, and the vehicle overturned. In finding that the first *Baker* factor applied, the court concluded that "the army did in fact control every aspect of the organization, planning and execution of the convoy in question." Accordingly, the court determined that it would have to pass judgment on military decisions "of the type typically insulated from judicial review." This same analysis flowed into the second *Baker* factor. In finding that the second *Baker* factor was applicable, the court placed great emphasis on the fact that it would have to question the military's decisions regarding "the planning and conduct of the convoy" which would be unmanageable. The court refused to consider the remaining *Baker* factors in the opinion, since only one factor would bar the case under the political question doctrine.

A final case worth noting is the 2008 ruling in *Lane v. Halliburton* from the U.S. Court of Appeals, Fifth Circuit. The case involved a civil action by a group of Halliburton civilian employees against Halliburton for injuries sustained while working in Iraq as truck drivers. The district court had dismissed the case as non-justiciable under the political question doctrine, but the Fifth Circuit reversed and remanded noting that the case needed "further factual development before it can be known whether that doctrine is actually an impediment [to jurisdiction]." The Fifth Circuit spent a great deal of effort going over all of the *Baker* factors and setting out all of the arguments—pro and con—regarding the political question doctrine warning that the matter would certainly require additional analysis at the district court level, but that it "may be possible to resolve the claims without needing to make a constitutionally impermissible review of wartime decision-making." It remains to be seen what the focused legal framework outlined by the Fifth Circuit will produce as the case is reconsidered at the district level.

Political questions are deemed to be non-justiciable, but the determination can only be made after a "discriminating inquiry into the precise facts and posture of the particular case." While it is undeniable that civilian contractors provide essential combat related services on the battlefield—as evidenced in reality and in a variety of official military instructions and regulations deeming them part of the military "total force"—this does not mean that civilian contractors will be provided the same protections accorded to the military under the political question doctrine. A central element in distinguishing the conflicting opinions emanating from recent cases that have dealt with the political question doctrine in the context of civilian contractors on the battlefield turns on an examination of the particular contractor's relationship to the military and the actual military operation in question.

It is clear that the political question doctrine will not preclude judicial review simply because there exists some nexus between the contractor and the military. In the words of the 11th Circuit ruling in *McMahon*, in order for the political question doctrine to serve as a bar to jurisdiction, the nexus between the contractor and the military must strike at "core military decisions, including [military] communication, training, and drill procedures." Closely associated with the nature and closeness of the military/contractor relationship is the question of whether a particular court will have to second-guess the particulars of a military operation, or whether the court can determine that it need only evaluate the civilian contractor's performance under the subject contract.

Finally, it is not surprising that the developing trend for dealing with motions for dismissal based on the political question doctrine is for the subject court to delay political question determinations until the close of Discovery when the fullest amount of information is available to measure against the *Baker* factors. Given the consequences of a finding of non-justiciability, each side deserves the fullest opportunity to present all the facts at hand.

At the end of the day, the repercussions of any lawsuit to the contracting company can extend far beyond compensatory or even punitive damages. The injury to reputation can impact negatively on developing new business contacts and cause difficulty in recruiting new hires.

7.5 Personnel Recovery

According to the DOD, "[p]reserving the lives and well-being of...contractors placed in danger of being isolated, beleaguered, detained, captured or having to evade while participating in U.S.-sponsored activities or missions is one of the highest priorities of the Department of Defense."

As stated, contractors who have "fallen into the power of the enemy" during an international armed conflict are considered POWs and are to be afforded all the protections of the Geneva Conventions. As such, during captivity the contractor is now a POW and must receive adequate food, water, shelter, and clothing. Following the cessation of active hostilities between the two warring parties, the contractor must be released. Toward this end, DOD policy requires that:

> Before entering a theater of operation or an area of responsibility, identified [DOD] civilian employees, [DOD] contractors (under the terms of the contract), and other designated personnel shall know their personal legal status under the Geneva Conventions. Knowledge of their personal legal status shall assist those who become captured or isolated to apply properly the rights and privileges afforded to them under international law.

Ironically, DOD issued this broad-reaching Instruction on August 20, 2003, more than three months after the cessation of the international armed conflict in Iraq and almost three years after the cessation of the international armed conflict in Afghanistan. Still, since most of the contractor casualties in the War on Terror have not occurred during the rather brief periods of international armed conflict against totalitarian regimes, international law of war protections are not applicable.

The vast majority of contractor deaths, kidnappings, and woundings have occurred during contingency operations, particularly in the context of the ongoing terror attacks by al-Qa'eda, insurgents and other criminals. In contingency operations, civilians accompanying the force represent easy targets for enemy forces set on hostage-taking. There is no question that the terrorists recognize the propaganda value of exploiting the media and sensationalizing the kidnappings. Because contractors are typically unarmed, have little knowledge of or training in evasion techniques (i.e., no AT training), and may receive only incidental protection from combatant personnel, the risk of capture is often high. Once captured, many are viciously tortured and murdered.

Although the terrorist attacks are not considered to be under the umbrella of any international set of rules, the distinction has little meaning to terror groups like al-Qa'eda or the FARC in Colombia who have no regard for any civilized rules regulating armed conflict. Terrorists, insurgents, and criminal gangs who prey upon contractors do not subscribe to the law of war or civilized behavior, thereby making the protections afforded by any rule of law hollow with little practical or perceived value. Considering the prospect of torture and other violence likely to befall the captured civilian contractor, the issue of personnel recovery is a pressing matter.

While a primary purpose of AT training is to provide contractors with the skills necessary to avoid capture, it is also concerned with providing skills to allow them to cope with possible capture and return to U.S. control. Thus, AT training should always be viewed as a venue for SERE training. The very purpose of AT training is to avoid potential threats.

> It is DOD policy that preserving the lives and well-being of U.S. military, [DOD] civilian and contract service employees placed in danger of being isolated, beleaguered, detained, captured or having to evade while participating in a U.S.-sponsored activity or mission is one of the highest priorities of the Department of Defense. The Department of Defense has a moral obligation to protect its personnel, prevent exploitation of its personnel by adversaries, and reduce the potential for captured personnel being used as leverage against the United States.

Nevertheless, it is no secret that personnel recovery matters are fragmented and a National Security Presidential Directive is sorely needed. Although the military has attempted to recover captured contractors in Iraq, whether or not such a rescue attempt is made may be limited not only by operational constraints (e.g., a lack of intelligence as to the location of the contractor), but also due to a lack of clear, high-level guidance. Each military service plan for individual operations, the training/preparation for such operations and even the terminology is defined differently. Indeed, the term "personnel recovery" is defined differently within the military establishment. One source defines personnel recovery as follows:

> [A]ggregation of military, civil, and political efforts to recover captured detained, evading, isolated or missing personnel from uncertain or hostile environments and denied areas. Personnel recovery may occur through military action, action by non-governmental organizations, other U.S. Government-approved action, and diplomatic initiatives, or through any combination of these options.

In effect, the term personnel recovery is an umbrella term that envisions a combination of military, civil, and political efforts united to obtain the immediate release of those detained against their will or isolated from a hostile environment either via coordinated negotiation or forcible recovery.

Given the current high-risk environments of not only Iraq and Afghanistan, but also of places like Colombia and other hostile zones around the globe, one might conclude that all personnel recovery operations are conducted by either the Air Force or Special Operations Forces (SOF). This is not the case. While SOF provides flexibility as well as the unique knowledge and equipment required for high-risk, personnel recovery missions, there is no "dedicated" personnel recovery force. Based on each case, the Combatant Commander will rely on a combination of assets to form a rescue mission. The much-publicized April 2003 rescue of Jessica Lynch does not represent the model for recovery operations, although in that personnel recovery operation SOF soldiers successfully rescued Private Jessica Lynch from an Iraqi hospital during a nighttime raid without suffering a single American casualty.

The use of the military to conduct personnel recovery missions is defined, in part, by the DOD policy on Non-Conventional Assisted Recovery, which covers not only United States military personnel, but also "DOD civilian employees, contractors and other designated personnel isolated during military operations or as a direct result of developing or ongoing crisis prior to U.S. military intervention." The significance of this DOD Instruction cannot be overstated for two reasons. First, the DOD Instruction specifically includes, by its terms, "contractors" as a covered entity without limitations or qualification (that is, under the terms of the contract). Second, the DOD Instruction's applicability is broad—arguably, by using the term "military operations," the policy accounts for personnel recovery operations in both war and contingency operations. As such, Non-Conventional Assisted Recovery (NAR) encompasses:

All forms of personnel recovery conducted by an entity, group of entities, or organizations that are trained and directed to contact, authenticate, support, move and exfiltrate U.S. military and other designated personnel from enemy-held or hostile areas to friendly control through established infrastructure procedures. NAR includes unconventional assisted recovery.

Though frequently the result of hostilities, personnel recovery options are not limited to hostilities *per se*:

The scope of persons for whom the United States will undertake Personnel Recovery is not limited to situations involving hostile action or circumstances suggestive of hostile action. Personnel Recovery measures may be initiated for personnel (U.S., allied, or coalition) who become unaccounted for as a result of training exercises, operations other than war wherein hostile action is not involved and operational environments not involving hostile action.

Individuals who become missing as a result of non-hostile action do not automatically gain the benefits of personnel recovery operations initiated on their behalf. DOD policy provides that "the specific persons for whom Personnel Recovery may be initiated will vary based upon the circumstances unique to each situation."

While the implementing regulations are the province of DOD, Congress has provided the statutory framework within which DOD conceptualizes and formulates personnel recovery policy specifically and missing persons policy more generally. The Secretary of Defense established the Defense Prisoner of War/Missing Personnel Office pursuant to 10 U.S.C. § 1501:

The Secretary of Defense shall establish within the Office of the Secretary of Defense an office to have the responsibility for Department of Defense Policy relating to missing persons....Subject to the authority, direction, and control of the Secretary of Defense, the responsibilities of the office shall include...policy, control, and oversight...of the entire process for investigation and recovery related to missing persons (including matters related to search, rescue, escape, and evasion)....

The Defense Prisoner of War/Missing Personnel Office (DPMO) is charged with coordinating the full range of policy issues associated with personnel recovery throughout DOD and the interagency community. Perhaps more significant for the civilian contractor, Congress defines the term "missing person" to mean:

> [A] member of the armed forces on active duty who is in a missing status; or a civilian employee of the Department of Defense or an employee of a contractor of the Department of Defense who serves in direct support of, or accompanies, the armed forces in the field under orders and who is in a missing status.

Contractors are also considered "covered persons" for the purposes of DOD action to investigate the circumstances of their absence and, possibly, to evaluate and implement personnel recovery options. As a result, 10 U.S.C § 1502 states:

> After receiving information that the whereabouts and status of a [covered] person…is uncertain and that the absence of the person may be involuntary, the commander of the unit, facility, or area to or in which the person is assigned shall make a preliminary assessment of the circumstances. If, as a result of that assessment, the commander concludes that the person is missing, the commander shall recommend that the person be placed in missing status and…transmit a report containing that recommendation to the Secretary concerned.…

The application of the statute to personnel recovery provides some overarching bright-lines and the opportunity for Congressional supervision, but does not limit or preclude the need for more clarification of personnel recovery *vis-à-vis* the specific and increasingly important role of the contractor.

7.6 Conclusion

There can be no doubt that the use of civilian contractors by the modern United States military is an absolute necessity for successful mission accomplishment. This is certainly true in the context of the War on Terror, but it is also true in other contingency operations from South America to the Far East. Unfortunately, "the regulatory scheme governing civilians accompanying the force is in a rapid state of flux" and DOD lacks a "comprehensive policy to ensure that contractors are adequately protected…or that the risks to them are adequately managed in high-threat, overseas locations." In fact, most of the regulatory guidance dealing with civilians accompanying the military was written prior to the War on Terror.

Congress has recognized a number of the shortcomings in the areas of civilian contractors and personnel recovery, and has taken steps to address some of these gaps. Mitigating the risk of injury or capture of civilian contractors is a shared responsibility of the United States and the parent contracting company. Not only does DOD need to fully develop an institutional approach to contractor force protection, it is imperative that parent contracting companies develop a better system of providing the necessary AT training for their employees who are sent to high-risk overseas locations. Until the government develops a systemic approach (e.g., providing the full range of force protection training at military pre-deployment sites), the prudent parent contracting company will ensure that their employees have the necessary information to prepare them for the exigencies of their overseas assignments. At a minimum, this means that the parent company should include an appropriate level of AT training so that contractors are better able to avoid or survive capture or injury when operating in high-risk environments.

7.7 Questions for Discussion

1. *Civilian or combatant?* Thomas Hamill & Paul T. Brown, ESCAPE IN IRAQ: THE THOMAS HAMILL STORY 150 (2004). When captured by terrorists in Iraq, Hamill noted that he was considered a solider by the terrorists:

    "What do you do?" asked the well-dressed man [Iraqi terrorist].
    "I am a civilian contractor," I replied.
    "You are a soldier," pronounced the well-dressed man. "You haul supplies and fuel to the soldiers for the trucks, tanks, and planes that bomb Fallujah."
    "You are a soldier!" said the man in the red wrap [Iraqi terrorist].
    "No I am not a soldier," I said. "I am here to support the military. I am a truck driver."
    "You were driving military trucks, no?" said the well-dressed man.
    "Yes, I was, but I am a civilian," I said.
    "You are a soldier," he said.

2. *Protection from lawsuits.* What impact will a civil lawsuit on contractor companies have on the continued viability of the "total force?"

3. *Code of Conduct.* Should independent civilian contractors have a Code of Conduct similar to the DOD Code of Conduct?

4. *Prosecuting civilians in a military court.* The John Warner National Defense Authorization Act for Fiscal Year 2007, authorizes trial by military courts-martial for crimes committed by civilian contractors who accompany military forces both in declared wars by Congress and on contingency operations. Is this provision constitutional? Is it wise?

Selected Bibliography

Campbell, Gordon L. *Contractors on the Battlefield: The Ethics of Paying Civilians to Enter Harm's Way and Requiring Soldiers to Depend on Them*, JOINT SERVICES CONFERENCE ON PROFESSIONAL ETHICS, January 27–28, 2000.

Defense Federal Acquisition Regulation Supplement (DFARS). CONTRACTOR PERSONNEL SUPPORTING A FORCE DEPLOYED OUTSIDE THE UNITED STATES, 70 Fed. Reg. 23790, May 5, 2005 (eff. June 6, 2005).

Dep't of the Army Field Manual 100-21. CONTRACTORS ON THE BATTLEFIELD, Jan. 2003, at ¶ 6-1.

Dep't Of Defense Dir. 2310.2. PERSONNEL RECOVERY, ¶ 3.1. Dec. 22, 2000. (defining personnel recovery as the "aggregation of military, civil, and political efforts to recover captured, detained, evading, isolated or missing personnel from uncertain or hostile environments and denied areas").

General Accounting Office. *Military Operations: Contractors Provide Vital Services to Deployed Forces but Are Not Adequately Addressed in DOD Plans*, GAO-03-695, at 2-9 (June 2003).

Govern, Kevin H. & Bales, Eric, C, *Taking Shots at Private Military Firms: International Law Misses Its Mark (Again)*, 32 FORDHAM INT'L L.J. 55 (2008-2009).

Hamill, Thomas, and Paul T. Brown. ESCAPE IN IRAQ: THE THOMAS HAMILL STORY, 2004.

Interagency National Personnel Recovery Architecture: Final Report, INST. FOR DEFENSE ANALYSES, P-3890, July 2004, at F-1.

Legal Lessons Learned From Afghanistan And Iraq, Vol. 1, CENTER FOR LAW AND MILITARY OPERATIONS, THE JUDGE ADVOCATE GENERAL'S LEGAL CENTER & SCHOOL 172, August 1, 2004.

Liegl-Paul, Charlotte M. *Civilian Prisoners of War: A Proposed Citizen Code of Conduct*, 182 MILITARY L. REV. 106 (2004).

Taylor, Guy. *Legal Limbo Shadows Civilians in War Zone*, WASH. TIMES, July 6, 2004, at A1.

Tiron, Roxana. *Pentagon Still Undecided on Policies to Protect Contractors*, NAT'L DEF., Nov. 2004, at 39.

Turner, Lisa L., and Lynn G. Norton. *Civilians at the Tip of the Spear*, 51 A. F. L. REV. 1 (2001).

U.S. Dep't of the Army Pamphlet 715-16. CONTRACTOR DEPLOYMENT GUIDE ¶ 3-1(c). Feb. 27, 1998.

U.S. Dep't Of Defense Dir. 2000.12. DOD ANTITERRORISM (AT) PROGRAM, ¶ 4.6. Aug. 18, 2003.

U.S. Dep't Of Defense instruction 1300.23. ISOLATED PERSONNEL TRAINING FOR DOD CIVILIAN AND CONTRACTORS ¶ E1.1.1. Aug. 20, 2003. (defining DOD civilian employees as "U.S. citizens or foreign nationals employed by the [DOD] and paid from appropriated or non-appropriated funds under permanent or temporary arrangement").

U.S. Dep't Of Defense instruction 1300.23. ISOLATED PERSONNEL TRAINING FOR DOD CIVILIAN AND CONTRACTORS ¶ 4.1. Aug. 20, 2003.

U.S. Dep't Of Defense instruction 2310.5. ACCOUNTING FOR MISSING PERSONS ¶ E3.1.6. Jan. 31, 2000.

U.S. Dep't Of Defense instruction 2310.6. NON-CONVENTIONAL ASSISTED RECOVERY IN THE DEPARTMENT OF DEFENSE ¶ 1. Oct. 13, 2000.

U.S. Dep't of the Army Regulation 715-9. CONTRACTOR PERSONNEL IN GERMANY—TECHNICAL EXPERT, TROOP CARE, AND ANALYTICAL SUPPORT PERSONNEL ¶ 1-4, Apr. 2, 2003.

Chapter 8

Cyberterrorism

We have learned from the tragedy of September 11 that our enemies will increasingly strike where they believe we are vulnerable...our cyberspace infrastructure is ripe for attack today.

— Senator Joseph Lieberman

While many trace the beginning of the War on Terror to September 11, 2001, it is now clear to all that the United States has been a primary target for terrorist attacks by radical Islamic terrorist groups for many years. Unfortunately, in hindsight, it is equally apparent that the United States was not adequately prepared to defend the homeland from the innovative al-Qa'eda terror attacks of September 11, 2001. The 9/11 Commission described the lack of preparedness of American intelligence and law enforcement agencies as a "failure of imagination." The government simply did not take seriously the possibility of terrorists using commercial airlines as precision weapons to attack buildings. The failure to appreciate the sophistication of the al-Qa'eda terrorist network opened the door for devastating attacks. Consequently, the United States was caught completely by surprise, resulting in the loss of 3,000 lives and billions of dollars in property loss.

Since the attacks of September 11, 2001, the government has crafted a variety of robust antiterrorism responses designed to disrupt terrorist networks and lessen the probability of future al-Qa'eda-styled terrorist attacks. Trying to anticipate emerging threats, these responses include the passage of the National Strategy to Secure Cyberspace, the National Strategy for the Physical Protection of Critical Infrastructure and Key Assets and the passage of the USA PATRIOT Act. Without question, shifting the tactical focus from punishing those individuals, organizations, or nations who commit terrorist crimes or engage in aggression to new broad methodologies designed to thwart such criminal acts in the first place has caused "a sea of change" in how the government approaches terrorism prevention.

Nevertheless, a new and deadly terrorist threat called cyberterrorism is now emerging that may, as many commentators predict, catch the United States totally off guard. The same failure of recognition and lack of awareness prior to the terrorist air attacks of September 11, 2001, might be mimicking itself in the cyber world, and the attacks could prove to be more crippling and deadly than anything imaginable. Fortunately, some in the government have recognized that if portions of our physical world could be destroyed as it was in the attacks of 9/11, a *fortiori*, our cyber world, which regulates all aspects of modern society, is an extremely vulnerable sector of our society, ripe for terrorist attack.

Until the April-May 2007 coordinated cyber attacks which shut down the entire nation of Estonia, the full destructive potential of cyberterrorism was something that the world had not adequately appreciated. When one considers that terrorist organizations such as al-Qa'eda and HAMAS have been using computers, e-mail, and encryption to support and finance their organizations for years, it is only logical to conclude that they are fully aware that cyberterrorism offers a low cost method of inflicting major damage that is very difficult to trace. Indeed, it is simply naive to believe that terrorists will not adapt their thinking to attack cyber space.

Ultimately, the real issue is one of cybersecurity. Does a sufficient cybersecurity framework exist that can adequately protect cyberspace and the information it contains, processes, and transmits? While the government has embarked on a variety of initiatives with private and public entities to protect against the threat of cyberterrorism, a growing number of legal and policy issues remain unanswered. The purpose of this chapter is to provide a basic framework for understanding the threat of cyberterrorism and to explore the current state of preparedness from government and private industry perspectives.

8.1 Defining Cyber Terms

The modern world we have created is totally dependent on the workings of the Internet, computer databases and software of the cyber world. Without question, the cyber realm is fully incorporated into our everyday lives and touches almost everything we do or think. Apart from serving as a fantastic communication medium, the cyber world regulates all aspects of our infrastructure to include water, electricity, banking, transportation, technology, agriculture, medical, nuclear facilities, waste management, government services, etc. This fact has not only spawned the era of cyber crime, costing billions of dollars a year, but it has also given rise to the specter of cyberterrorism.

Dozens of new and unfamiliar terms associated with cyberspace have now entered the lexicon. Accordingly, before one can fully discuss the dangers associated with cyberterrorism, certain foundational terms require definition.

Cyberspace. The term cyberspace has many connotations and is used in a variety of contexts. Synonyms include the terms virtual space and cyber world (sometimes spelled cyberworld). In common understanding cyberspace refers to the entire function of computer-centric information technology—hardware and software—as it is created, stored and transmitted in the non-physical and physical terrain. A 2005 Congressional Research Service Report (CRS) (Creating a National Framework for Cybersecurity: An Analysis of Issues and Options) refers to cyberspace as "the combination of the virtual structure, the physical components that support it, the information it contains, and the flow of that information within it." The 2008 Department of Defense Dictionary of Military and Associated Terms defines cyberspace as: "A global domain within the information environment consisting of the interdependent network of information technology infrastructures, including the Internet, telecommunications networks, computer systems, and embedded processors and controllers." As a global phenomenon, cyberspace is largely controlled by private companies.

Cyberterrorism. Similar to the problem of obtaining universal agreement on defining the term "terrorism," there is no generally accepted definition for cyberterrorism (sometimes spelled cyber terrorism). All intentional attacks on a computer or computer network involve actions that are meant to disrupt, destroy, or deny information. These attacks may be motivated by monetary gain, vandalism, terrorism, or as acts of war. Thus, most cyber attacks may be categorized as cyber crimes, but not all cyber attacks are deemed to be an act of cyberterrorism or war. Clearly, the key difference between cyber crime and cyberterrorism is the concept of *terror*. If a universal definition of the term terrorism does not exist, one can at least list four key characteristics of terrorism that better reflect the nature of the activity:

1. The illegal use of violence directed at civilians to produce fear in a target group.
2. The continuing threat of additional future acts of violence.
3. A predominately political or ideological character of the unlawful act.
4. The desire to mobilize or immobilize a given target group.

Combining these four key characteristics, then Secretary General of the United Nations, Kofi Annan, offered a succinct 2005 definition for terrorism:

[A]ny action constitutes terrorism if it is intended to cause death or serious bodily harm to civilians or non-combatants, with the purpose of intimidating a population or compelling a Government or an international organization to do or abstain from doing any act.

Adopting the general definitional theme of terrorism set out above, cyberterrorism is the improper use of various computing technology to engage in terrorist activity. Since the terror motivated cyber attack would most likely be against the critical infrastructure of a nation to intimidate or coerce another (usually a nation) in furtherance of specific political objectives, one commentator has defined cyberterrorism as "the premeditated, politically motivated attack against information, computer systems, computer programs, and data which results in violence against non combatant targets by sub-national groups or clandestine agents." On the other hand, some commentators like Rollins and Wilson contend that the use of the term cyberterrorism to describe an attack on the critical infrastructure is inappropriate "because a widespread cyber attack may simply produce annoyances, not terror, as would a bomb, or other chemical, biological, radiological, or nuclear explosive (CBRN) weapon."

Nevertheless, given the nation's complete dependency on cyberspace, if a cyber attack caused widespread damage to computer networks associated with the critical infrastructure, the level of fear from the resulting economic disaster and/or civilian fatalities would rapidly qualify as terrorism. Certainly the digital fears that emerged from the month-long denial of service (DDoS) cyber attack on the small Baltic country of Estonia (orchestrated from Russian sources apparently in response to the removal of a bronze statue of a World War II era Soviet soldier from a park) would qualify as cyberterrorism and perhaps, as some argued, as an act of war. The Estonian cyber attacks resulted in a digital infrastructure disaster as websites for government officials, government agencies, daily newspapers, and Estonia's biggest banks were overwhelmed and shut down due to the cyber onslaught of "unknown" digital information attacks.

Perhaps a more useful way to encapsulate the term cyberterrorism can be found in a 2005 CRS Report where the authors present cyberterrorism in two related categories:

- Effects-based: Cyberterrorism exists when computer attacks result in effects that are disruptive enough to generate fear comparable to a traditional act of terrorism, even if done by criminals [as opposed to terrorists].
- Intent-based: Cyberterrorism exists when unlawful or politically motivated computer attacks are done to intimidate or coerce a government or people to further a political objective, or to cause grave harm or severe economic damage.

Critical Infrastructure. The predominate concern that most drives the discussion of cyberterrorism is that a cyber attack will target one or more of the nation's critical infrastructures. The term critical infrastructure is defined with more or less uniformity in a variety of documents and laws. The 2003 National Strategy for the Physical Protection of Critical Infrastructure and Key Assets provides a detailed list of assets of national importance and critical infrastructure to include: information technology; telecommunications; chemicals; transportation; emergency services; postal and shipping services; agriculture and food; public health and healthcare; drinking water/water treatment; energy; banking and finance; national monuments and icons; defense industrial base; key industry/technology sites; and large gathering sites. The Department of Homeland Security (DHS) lists five general types of critical infrastructure:

(1) production industries: energy, chemical, defense industrial base;
(2) service industries: banking and finance, transportation, postal and shipping;
(3) sustenance and health: agriculture, food, water, public health;
(4) federal and state: government, emergency services;
(5) Information Technology (IT) and cyber: information and telecommunications.

Section 1016(b)(2) of the Critical Infrastructures Protection Act (CIPA) of 2001 specifically identifies as critical infrastructures "telecommunications, energy, financial services, water, and transportation sectors," all of which have not only physical components, but cyber components as well. In addition, section 1016(e) of CIPA expands the concept of critical infrastructure to mean all "systems and assets, whether physical or virtual, so vital to the United States that the incapacity or destruction of such systems and assets would have a debilitating impact on security, national economic security, national public health or safety, or any combination of those matters." Both the Uniting and Strengthening America by Providing Appropriate Tools Required to Intercept and Obstruct Terrorism Act of 2001 (USA PATRIOT Act) (renewed in 2006) and the Homeland Security Act of 2002 adopt the same definition set out below:

SEC. 1016. CRITICAL INFRASTRUCTURES PROTECTION

(a) SHORT TITLE.--This section may be cited as the "Critical Infrastructures Protection Act of 2001."

(b) FINDINGS.--Congress makes the following findings:

(1) The information revolution has transformed the conduct of business and the operations of government as well as the infrastructure relied upon for the defense and national security of the United States.

(2) Private business, government, and the national security apparatus increasingly depend on an interdependent network of critical physical and information infrastructures,

including telecommunications, energy, financial services, water, and transportation sectors.

(3) A continuous national effort is required to ensure the reliable provision of cyber and physical infrastructure services critical to maintaining the national defense, continuity of government, economic prosperity, and quality of life in the United States.

(4) This national effort requires extensive modeling and analytic capabilities for purposes of evaluating appropriate mechanisms to ensure the stability of these complex and interdependent systems, and to underpin policy recommendations, so as to achieve the continuous viability and adequate protection of the critical infrastructure of the Nation.

(c) POLICY OF THE UNITED STATES.--It is the policy of the United States—

(1) that any physical or virtual disruption of the operation of the critical infrastructures of the United States be rare, brief, geographically limited in effect, manageable, and minimally detrimental to the economy, human and government services, and national security of the United States;

(2) that actions necessary to achieve the policy stated in paragraph (1) be carried out in a public-private partnership involving corporate and non-governmental organizations; and

(3) to have in place a comprehensive and effective program to ensure the continuity of essential Federal Government functions under all circumstances.

(d) ESTABLISHMENT OF NATIONAL COMPETENCE FOR CRITICAL INFRASTRUCTURE PROTECTION.

(1) SUPPORT OF CRITICAL INFRASTRUCTURE PROTECTION AND CONTINUITY BY NATIONAL INFRASTRUCTURE SIMULATION AND ANALYSIS CENTER.--There shall be established the National Infrastructure Simulation and Analysis Center (NISAC) to serve as a source of national competence to address critical infrastructure protection and continuity through support for activities related to counterterrorism, threat assessment, and risk mitigation.

(2) PARTICULAR SUPPORT.--The support provided under paragraph (1) shall include the following:

(A) Modeling, simulation, and analysis of the systems comprising critical infrastructures, including cyber infrastructure, telecommunications infrastructure, and physical infrastructure, in order to enhance understanding of the large-scale complexity of such systems and to facilitate modification of such systems to mitigate the threats to such systems and to critical infrastructures generally.

(B) Acquisition from State and local governments and the private sector of data necessary to create and maintain models of such systems and of critical infrastructures generally.

(C) Utilization of modeling, simulation, and analysis under subparagraph (A) to provide education and training to policymakers on matters relating to--

(i) the analysis conducted under that subparagraph;

(ii) the implications of unintended or unintentional disturbances to critical infra-structures; and

(iii) responses to incidents or crises involving critical infrastructures, including the continuity of government and private sector activities through and after such incidents or crises.

(D) Utilization of modeling, simulation, and analysis under subparagraph (A) to provide recommendations to policymakers, and to departments and agencies of the Federal Government and private sector persons and entities upon request, regarding means of enhancing the stability of, and preserving, critical infrastructures.

(3) RECIPIENT OF CERTAIN SUPPORT.--Modeling, simulation, and analysis provided under this subsection shall be provided, in particular, to relevant Federal, State, and local entities responsible for critical infrastructure protection and policy.

(e) CRITICAL INFRASTRUCTURE DEFINED.--In this section, the term "critical infrastructure" means systems and assets, whether physical or virtual, so vital to the United States that the incapacity or destruction of such systems and assets would have a debilitating impact on security, national economic security, national public health or safety, or any combination of those matters.

SCADA. Cyberterrorism is not simply an attack on the Internet. As previously stated, the primary concern is that a cyberterrorist attack will target the electronic control systems that regulate the operational functions of a critical infrastructure so that the flow of essential services are disrupted. Such a scenario is possible because the thousands of interconnected computers, servers, routers, and switches associated with the myriad physical and virtual tasks inherent in operating and maintaining the nation's most important critical infrastructures, such as defense systems, chemical and hazardous materials, water supply systems, transportation, energy, finance systems, and emergency services are no longer predominately handled by people, but are rather electronically monitored and controlled by centralized computer networks called Industrial Control Systems (ICS), Supervisory Control and Data Acquisition (SCADA) systems, or any equivalent system in function such as distributed control systems or programmable logic control systems.

SCADA systems, or their equivalent, digitize and automate almost every imaginable task associated with a given critical infrastructure—from opening and closing valves in nuclear facilities, to operating circuit breakers on electrical power grids, to managing air traffic in the sky. Since SCADA systems provide the "brain power" to manage critical infrastructures a successful cyberterrorist attack on even a single SCADA could cause massive economic and physical damage across broad sections of the country.

Approximately 85 percent of the nation's critical infrastructures are owned and operated by private business where the predominate emphasis for SCADA is on maintaining system reliability and efficiency, not cybersecurity. In most cases, the SCADAs are connected to their associated private corporate networks which are in turn primarily connected directly or indirectly to the Internet. This cyberspace vulnerability presents an open door for a terrorist with the necessary skills to hack into a SCADA and, for example, disable the valves at the nuclear facility, shut down an entire electrical power grid, or redirect air traffic to harmful flight patterns.

Techniques Employed in Cyber Attacks. Not all disruptions of an information system's confidentiality, integrity, or availability (CIA) constitute a cyber attack. In fact, most disruptions of information systems are caused by unintentional human error and are called cyber incidents. A cyber attack refers only to the intentional disruption of an information system's CIA. The National Institute of Standards and Technology Federal Information Processing Standards Publication 200, Minimum Security Requirements for Federal Information and Information Systems, March 2006, defines a cyber incident as:

> An occurrence that actually or potentially jeopardizes the confidentiality, integrity, or availability (CIA) of an information system or the information the system processes, stores, or transmits or that constitutes a violation or imminent threat of violation of security policies, security procedures, or acceptable use policies. Incidents may be intentional or unintentional.

Taken from a Government Accountability Office Report, GAO-07-705, dated June 2007, the chart below lists the most common techniques employed in conducting a cyber attack, along with a brief description. The individuals making such attacks range from juveniles (so-called "script-kiddies"), to disgruntled ex-employees, to thieves, to competitors, to terrorists, to agents of foreign governments. Terrorists wishing to launch a cyberterror attack would employ one or more of the tools listed below:

Type	Description
Spamming	Sending unsolicited commercial e-mail advertising for products, services, and websites. Spam can also be used as a delivery mechanism for malware and other cyber threats.
Phishing	A high-tech scam that frequently uses spam or pop-up messages to deceive people into disclosing their credit card numbers, bank account information, Social Security numbers, passwords, or other sensitive information. Internet scammers use e-mail bait to "phish" for passwords and financial data from the sea of Internet users.
Spoofing	Creating a fraudulent website to mimic an actual, well-known website run by another party. E-mail spoofing occurs when the sender address and other parts of an e-mail header are altered to appear as though the e-mail originated from a different source. Spoofing hides the origin of an e-mail message.
Pharming	A method used by phishers to deceive users into believing that they are communicating with a legitimate website. Pharming uses a variety of technical methods to redirect a user to a fraudulent or spoofed website when the user types in a legitimate Web address. For example, one pharming technique is to redirect users—without their knowledge—to a different website from the one they intended to access. Also, software vulnerabilities may be exploited or malware employed to redirect the user to a fraudulent website when the user types in a legitimate address.
Denial-of-service attack	An attack in which one user takes up so much of a shared resource that none of the resource is left for other users. Denial-of-service attacks compromise the availability of the resource.

Distributed denial-of-service	A variant of the denial-of-service attack that uses a coordinated attack from a distributed system of computers rather than from a single source. It often makes use of worms to spread to multiple computers that can then attack the target.
Viruses	A program that "infects" computer files, usually executable programs, by inserting a copy of itself into the file. These copies are usually executed when the infected file is loaded into memory, allowing the virus to infect other files. A virus requires human involvement (usually unwitting) to propagate.
Trojan horse	A computer program that conceals harmful code. It usually masquerades as a useful program that a user would wish to execute.
Worm	An independent computer program that reproduces by copying itself from one system to another across a network. Unlike computer viruses, worms do not require human involvement to propagate.
Malware	Malicious software designed to carry out annoying or harmful actions. Malware often masquerades as useful programs or is embedded into useful programs so that users are induced into activating them. Malware can include viruses, worms, and spyware.
Spyware	Malware installed without the user's knowledge to surreptitiously track and/or transmit data to an unauthorized third party.
Botnet	A network of remotely controlled systems used to coordinate attacks and distribute malware, spam, and phishing scams. Bots (short for "robots") are programs that are covertly installed on a targeted system allowing an unauthorized user to remotely control the compromised computer for a variety of malicious purposes.

A review of the listed techniques point to four general types of attack. First, the most common type of cyber attack is service disruption or the distributed denial of service (DDoS) attack, which aims to flood the target computer with data packets or connection requests, thereby making it unavailable to the user or, in the case of a website, unavailable to the website's visitors. DDoS attacks are often conducted utilizing "zombies"—computer systems controlled by a "master" through the utilization of "bots" or "botnets." Service disruption could directly affect any aspect of the critical infrastructure causing regional or even global damage. A second, but related, type of cyber attack is designed to capture and then control certain elements of cyberspace in order to use them as actual weapons. The third category of cyber attack is aimed at theft of assets from, for example, financial institutions. This activity includes not only theft, but also extortion and fraud. Finally, a cyber attack can also manifest itself in a conventional explosive attack on a physical structure, such as a building that houses a SCADA.

Cybersecurity. There is no commonly accepted definition for the term cybersecurity (sometimes spelled cyber security). Obviously, responding to the task of protecting cyberspace requires, at a minimum, the adoption of a unified government definition. Different uses of the term cybersecurity can be found in a wide variety of federal laws, executive orders, presidential directives, and other agency directives. Taken together, cybersecurity is concerned with protecting the basic security of computerized systems from unauthorized access. The central focus of cybersecurity is protection of an information system's CIA. According to the 2005 CRS Report, Creating a National Framework for Cybersecurity: An Analysis of Issues and Options, cybersecurity refers to:

> a set of activities and other measures intended to protect—from attack, disruption, or other threats—computers, computer networks, related hardware and devices software [sic], and the information they contain and communicate, including software data, as well as other elements of cyberspace. The activities can include security audits, patch management, authentication procedures, access management, and so forth. They can involve, for example, examining and evaluating the strengths and vulnerabilities of the hardware and software used in the country's political and economic electronic infrastructure. They also involve detection and reaction to security events, mitigation of impacts, and recovery of affected components. Other measures can include such things as hardware and software firewalls, physical security such as hardened facilitates, and personnel training and responsibilities.

8.2 Cyberterrorism Threats

Those unfamiliar with the term cyberterrorism simply view the concept to mean an attack on the Internet. This is far too simplistic a view. A cyber attack could be used to destroy not only the electronic, but also the physical infrastructures that hold the nation together. Such a scenario is possible because some of the nation's most important infrastructures, such as defense systems, chemical and hazardous materials, water supply systems, transportation, energy, finance systems, and emergency services are electronically controlled by centralized computer networks ICSs or SCADAs. A successful cyber terror attack on even a single ICS of SCADA could cause massive economic and physical damage throughout large portions of the United States. For example, in 2002, the FBI uncovered information emanating out of the Middle East that certain hackers were studying the electrical generation, transmission, water storage, distribution and gas facilities of SCADA digital systems used to control the utilities of the San Francisco Bay area in California. Theoretically, hackers could disrupt the SCADA or even take command of the system in order to disable the flood gates or control hundreds of thousands of volts of electric energy. In fact, this type of activity has already occurred.

Along with the growth in cyberspace is a growth in cyber attacks. The almost seamless interconnectivity of the Internet presents a readily available and inexpensive opportunity for computer network cyber attack. Each day uncountable numbers of people gain access, or attempt to gain access, without authorization to computers in order to read, modify, or destroy information. Although the vast majority of harmful cyber attacks on U.S. interests to date—both government and private—have involved criminal activity, common sense and reason dictate that cybersecurity must better prepare for the real possibility of an Estonian-styled cyberterror attack. New forms of digital attacks are constantly emerging so that future cyber attacks will result from vulnerabilities in software that hackers find and exploit. During the week of July 17, 2006, alone, the United States Computer Emergency Response Team (US-CERT) listed more than 30 new vulnerabilities in cyberspace that fell in what they deemed a "high risk" category. Some of the security breaches that actually caused widespread damage received much publicity and still linger in the collective memory of society, e.g., computer worms such as the Love Bug, Slammer, and Blaster. The Log Bug virus, which caused billions of dollars in losses, was caused by a single university student in the Philippines.

In 2000, a hacker was arrested in Australia for breaking into the SCADA of an Australian sewage and water treatment plant and directing the pumping of one million liters of sewage into the environment. The culprit, Vitek Boden, was apprehended during a routine traffic stop in Queensland, Australia. Boden was found in possession of a stolen computer and radio transmitter which he used to turn his vehicle into a mobile "command center." Boden had breached the SCADA system of an Australian water and sewage treatment plant off Australia's Sunshine Coast. Over the course of two months, Boden directed the system, on forty-six separate occasions, to pump massive amounts of raw sewage into the local environment. This was the first reported instance of a hacker successfully breaking into a critical infrastructure, causing massive damage and being apprehended. It is a harbinger of things to come.

To be sure, the activity of all kinds of cyber crime is on the increase. A study released in June 2004 found that cyber attacks on financial institutions have more than doubled from the previous year. Studies regularly demonstrate that the majority of Internet professionals believe a major attack on Wall Street or other banking institutions is imminent. It is well known that al-Qa'eda is especially attracted to financial institutions where they can steal funds, disrupt day-to-day business, or even create a major assault on the system to cause panic. A coordinated cyber attack could mean far more than the inconvenience of shutting down an ATM machine. It could encompass the transfer of millions of dollars from banking accounts.

Apart from a cyber attack, law enforcement must also consider a scenario in which terrorists conduct an actual conventional explosives attack on a ICS or its equivalent, perhaps in conjunction with a cyber attack. A terrorist suicide attack aimed at a building that contains a major Internet service provider would be devastating.

Other possibilities for attack are equally possible. In a 2004 article in *Computerworld* magazine, security expert Peiter Zatka expressed concerns about a different type of cyber threat. Zatka warned that the real destruction might not occur from cyber attacks, but from insider threats. An insider threat exists when a hacker infiltrates an internal network and then, instead of causing an immediate denial of service or other type of harm, remains invisible inside the network in order to spy. The infiltrators use a technique called "sniffing" in order to acquire account information needed to access the network. This allows the interceptors the ability to obtain all the information that passes along the network line, including usernames and passwords.

Remaining undetected, the insider often alters encryption and communication applications in order to copy input and output data from the control terminals to various hidden sections on the system. Universities and network service providers are tempting targets for the harvesting of accounts and credentials. In testimony before the United States Senate in 2004, the Deputy Director of the FBI's cyberterrorism division stated: "The FBI predicts that terrorist groups will either develop or hire hackers, particularly for the purpose of complementing large scale attacks with cyberattacks." There is no doubt that al-Qa'eda-styled terrorists are studying means to attack the West's infrastructure by means of cyber space. If they are successful, the world could suffer an "electronic Pearl Harbor."

Representing the tip of the cyber jihad iceberg, one recent case from England illustrates what is occurring across the world in growing intensity. In 2007, a 21-year-old biochemistry student named Tariq al-Daour, a 24-year-old law student named Waseem Mughal and 23-year-old Younes Tsouli were convicted in the United Kingdom of using the Internet to incite murder. These Islamic terrorists employed a wide range of computer viruses and stolen credit card accounts to set up a sophisticated network of communication links and websites that hosted videos of al-Qa'eda suicide bombings, beheadings, and detailed tutorials on computer hacking and bomb-making. Tsouli was the administrator of the online jihadist website, "Muntada al-Ansar al-Islami," the once main Internet propaganda outlet for Abu Musab al-Zarqawi, al-Qa'eda's notorious chief lieutenant in Iraq (Zaraqwi was killed by American forces in

2006). According to British investigators, the trio used scores of stolen credit card accounts to register almost 200 website domains at 95 different Web service providers in the U.S. and Europe. A single computer found in the London apartment of al-Daour had 37,000 stolen credit card numbers with detailed personal information cross-referenced for each holder.

In summary, the threat domain can come from outside by means of communications channels or from inside by those with knowledge and ability to access. Actors include terrorists and State sponsors of terrorism.

8.3 Prosecuting Cyber Attacks

To even the cursory viewer, the advances in technology have caused a shift in law enforcement techniques that are stretching the protections of the Constitution's Fourth Amendment (unreasonable searches and seizures). For example, one area that is not covered in the USA PATRIOT Act involves the question of whether law enforcement should be able to unscramble an encrypted communication back into a readable form. It is common knowledge that sophisticated terrorists are now using cloaking devices provided by encryption companies to keep police from reading their communications. Thus, even if law enforcement can intercept the scrambled communications sent by terror suspects, they have no way of translating the information back into readable form. Consequently, legislation is probably necessary to more fully force encryption companies to provide a "back door" to allow law enforcement agencies access.

The primary law enforcement mechanism to deal with attacks on computers is the 1984 Counterfeit Access Device & Computer Fraud and Abuse Act (18 U.S.C. § 1030). It was amended in 1994, 1996, and in 2001 by the USA PATRIOT Act. The Counterfeit Access Device & Computer Fraud and Abuse Act makes it a federal crime to gain unauthorized access to, damage, or use illegally, certain "protected" computers and computer systems. The term protected applies to those computer systems used by the nation's financial institutions, a federal government entity, or for interstate and foreign commerce. In addition to addressing acts of trafficking in passwords, espionage and fraud, the Counterfeit Access Device & Computer Fraud and Abuse Act also covers damage to such protected computers by the use of a virus, worm, or other device. The seven areas of interest in 18 U.S.C. § 1030(a) include:

- computer trespassing, e.g., hacking, associated with a government computer, § 1030(a)(3);
- computer trespassing resulting in exposure to certain governmental, credit, financial, or commercial information, § 1030(a)(2);
- damaging either a government computer, a bank computer, or a computer that is used in interstate or foreign commerce, § 1030(a)(5);
- committing fraud where an integral part involves unauthorized access to a government computer, a bank computer, or a computer used in interstate or foreign commerce, § 1030(a)(4);
- threatening to damage a government computer, a bank computer, or a computer used in interstate or foreign commerce, § 1030(a)(7);
- trafficking in passwords used for a government computer, a bank computer, or a computer used in interstate or foreign commerce, § 1030(a)(6); and
- accessing a computer to commit espionage, § 1030(a)(1).

Section 1030(b) makes it a crime to attempt to commit any of the offenses in § 1030(a). Section 1030(c) sets out the penalties, which range from imprisonment for not more than a year for simple violations to a maximum of life imprisonment should death result from intentional computer damage. Section 1030(g) creates a separate civil cause of action for victims.

Under § 218, the USA PATRIOT Act increased the scope and penalties associated with hackers where violators only need to intend to cause damage generally, and a second offense is punishable by up to a 20 year prison sentence. The USA PATRIOT Act also enlarged the definition for criminal acts associated with terrorism, 18 U.S.C. § 2332b(g)(5)(B), to include intentionally damaging a protected computer if the offense involves either impairing medical care, causing physical injury, threatening public health or safety, or damaging a governmental justice, national defense, or national security computer system.

Other federal statutes address illegal wire fraud, 18 U.S.C. § 1343; aggravated identity theft, 18 U.S.C. § 1028A; fraud in connection with identification documents, authentication features and information, 18 U.S.C. § 1028; intentional interference with computer-related systems used in interstate commerce, 18 U.S.C. § 1030(a)(5); deceptive practices affecting commerce, 15 U.S.C. § 45(a)(1); and installing "sniffer" software to record keystroke and computer traffic, 18 U.S.C. § 2510-2421.

The case of *U.S. v. Mitra*, 405 F.3d 492 (2005), United States District Court for the Western District of Wisconsin, serves as a good illustration of the application of the Counterfeit Access Device & Computer Fraud and Abuse Act in terms of defining offenses that fall under its umbrella. In *Mitra* the defendant was convicted of two counts of intentional interference with computer-related systems used in interstate commerce, in violation of 18 U.S.C. § 1030(a)(5). The judge in the case noted that even though the statute violated does not directly address the acts committed by the defendant, that Congress had written a general statute not intended to list each and every particular forbidden act. The judge rightly explained that "[e]lectronics and communication change rapidly, while each legislator's imagination is limited." The conviction was upheld on appeal.

UNITED STATES v. MITRA
United States Court of Appeals for the Seventh Circuit
405 F.3d 492 (April 18, 2005)

EASTERBROOK, Circuit Judge. Wisconsin's capital city uses a computer-based radio system for police, fire, ambulance, and other emergency communications. The Smartnet II, made by Motorola, spreads traffic across 20 frequencies. One is designated for control. A radio unit (mobile or base) uses the control channel to initiate a conversation. Computer hardware and software assigns the conversation to an open channel, and it can link multiple roaming units into "talk groups" so that officers in the field can hold joint conversations. This is known as a "trunking system" and makes efficient use of radio spectrum, so that 20 channels can support hundreds of users. If the control channel is interfered with, however, remote units will show the message "no system" and communication will be impossible.

Between January and August 2003 mobile units in Madison encountered occasional puzzling "no signal" conditions. On Halloween of that year the "no system" condition spread city-wide; a powerful signal had blanketed all of the City's communications towers and prevented the computer from receiving, on the control channel, data essential to parcel traffic among the other 19 channels. Madison was hosting between 50,000 and 100,000 visitors that day. When disturbances erupted, public safety departments were unable to coordinate their activities because the radio system was down. Although the City repeatedly switched the control channel for the Smartnet system, a step that temporarily restored service, the interfering signal changed channels too and again blocked the system's use. On November 11, 2003, the attacker changed tactics. Instead of blocking the system's use, he sent signals directing the Smartnet base station to keep channels open, and at the end of each communication the attacker appended a sound, such as a woman's sexual moan.

By then the City had used radio direction finders to pin down the source of the intruding signals. Police arrested Rajib Mitra, a student in the University of Wisconsin's graduate business school. They found the radio hardware and computer gear that he had used to monitor communications over the Smartnet system, analyze how it operated, and send the signals that took control of the system. Mitra, who in 2000 had received a B.S. in computer science from the University, possessed two other credentials for this kind of work: criminal convictions (in 1996 and 1998) for hacking into computers in order to perform malicious mischief. A jury convicted Mitra of two counts of intentional interference with computer-related systems used in interstate commerce. See *18 U.S.C. § 1030(a)(5)*. He has been sentenced to 96 months' imprisonment. On appeal he says that his conduct does not violate *§ 1030*—and that, if it does, the statute exceeds Congress's commerce power.

Section 1030(a)(5) provides that whoever
(A)
   (i) knowingly causes the transmission of a program, information, code, or command, and as a result of such conduct, intentionally causes damage without authorization, to a protected computer;
   (ii) intentionally accesses a protected computer without authorization, and as a result of such conduct, recklessly causes damage; or
   (iii) intentionally accesses a protected computer without authorization, and as a result of such conduct, causes damage; and
(B) by conduct described in clause (i), (ii), or (iii) of subparagraph (A), caused (or, in the case of an attempted offense, would, if completed, have caused)—
   (i) loss to 1 or more persons during any 1-year period (and, for purposes of an investigation, prosecution, or other proceeding brought by the United States only, loss resulting from a related course of conduct affecting 1 or more other protected computers) aggregating at least $5,000 in value;
   (ii) the modification or impairment, or potential modification or impairment, of the medical examination, diagnosis, treatment, or care of 1 or more individuals;
   (iii) physical injury to any person;
   (iv) a threat to public health or safety; or
   (v) damage affecting a computer system used by or for a government entity in furtherance of the administration of justice, national defense, or national security...
shall be punished as provided in subsection (c) of this section.

Subsection (e)(1) defines "computer" as "an electronic, magnetic, optical, electrochemical, or other high speed data processing device performing logical, arithmetic, or storage functions, and includes any data storage facility or communications facility directly related to or operating in conjunction with such device, but such term does not include an automated typewriter or typesetter, a portable hand held calculator, or other similar device." Subsection (e)(2)(B) defines a "protected computer" to include any computer "used in interstate or foreign commerce or communication." Finally, subsection (e)(8) defines "damage" to mean "any impairment to the integrity or availability of data, a program, a system, or information."

The prosecutor's theory is that Smartnet II is a "computer" because it contains a chip that performs high-speed processing in response to signals received on the control channel, and as a whole is a "communications facility directly related to or operating in conjunction" with that computer chip. It is a "protected computer" because it is used in "interstate...communication"; the frequencies it uses have been allocated by the Federal Communications Commission for police, fire, and other public-health services. Mitra's transmissions on Halloween included "information" that was received by the Smartnet. Data that Mitra sent interfered with the way the computer allocated communications to the other 19 channels and stopped the flow of information among public-safety officers. This led to "damage" by causing a "no system" condition citywide, impairing the "availability of...a system, or information" and creating "a threat to public health or safety" by knocking out police, fire, and emergency communications. *See § 1030(a)(5)(A)(i), (B)(iv)*. The extraneous sounds tacked onto conversations on November 11 also are "information" sent to the "protected computer," and produce "damage" because they impair the "integrity" of the official communications. This time subsection *§ 1030(a)(5)(B)(v)* is what makes the meddling a crime, because Mitra hacked into a governmental safety-related communications system.

Mitra concedes that he is guilty if the statute is parsed as we have done. But he submits that Congress could not have intended the statute to work this way. Mitra did not invade a bank's system to steal financial information, or erase data on an ex-employer's system, see *United States v. Lloyd, 269 F.3d 228 (3d Cir.2001)*, or plaster a corporation's website with obscenities that drove away customers, or unleash a worm that slowed and crashed computers across the world, see *United States v. Morris, 928 F.2d 504 (2d Cir.1991)*, or break into military computers to scramble a flight of interceptors to meet a nonexistent threat, or plant covert programs in computers so that they would send spam without the owners' knowledge. All he did was gum up a radio system. Surely that cannot be a federal crime, Mitra insists, even if the radio system contains a computer. Every cell phone and cell tower is a "computer" under this statute's definition; so is every iPod, every wireless base station in the corner coffee shop, and many another gadget. Reading *§ 1030* to cover all of these, and police radio too, would give the statute wide coverage, which by Mitra's lights means that Congress cannot have contemplated such breadth.

Well of course Congress did not contemplate or intend this particular application of the statute. Congress is a "they" and not an "it"; a committee lacks a brain (or, rather, has so many brains with so many different objectives that it is almost facetious to impute a joint goal or purpose to the collectivity). See Kenneth A. Shepsle, *Congress is a "They," Not an "It": Legislative Intent as Oxymoron, 12 Int'l Rev. L. & Econ. 239 (1992)*. Legislation is an objective text approved in constitutionally prescribed ways; its scope is not limited by the cerebrations of those who voted for or signed it into law.

Electronics and communications change rapidly, while each legislator's imagination is limited. Trunking communications systems came to market after 1984, when the first version of *§ 1030* was enacted, and none of the many amendments to this statute directly addresses them. But although legislators may not know about trunking communications systems, they *do* know that complexity is endemic in the modern world and that each passing year sees new developments. That's why they write general statutes rather than enacting a list of particular forbidden acts. And it is the statutes they enacted—not the thoughts they did or didn't have—that courts must apply. What Congress would have done about trunking systems, had they been present to the mind of any Senator or Representative, is neither here nor there. See *West Virginia University Hospitals, Inc. v. Casey, 499 U.S. 83, 100-01, 111 S.Ct. 1138, 113 L.Ed.2d 68 (1991).*

Section 1030 is general. Exclusions show just *how* general. Subsection (e)(1) carves out automatic typewriters, typesetters, and handheld calculators; this shows that other devices with embedded processors and software are covered. As more devices come to have built-in intelligence, the effective scope of the statute grows. This might prompt Congress to amend the statute but does not authorize the judiciary to give the existing version less coverage than its language portends. See *National Broiler Marketing Ass'n v. United States, 436 U.S. 816, 98 S.Ct. 2122, 56 L.Ed.2d 728 (1978).* What protects people who accidentally erase songs on an iPod, trip over (and thus disable) a wireless base station, or rear-end a car and set off a computerized airbag, is not judicial creativity but the requirements of the statute itself: the damage must be intentional, it must be substantial (at least $5,000 or bodily injury or danger to public safety), and the computer must operate in interstate or foreign commerce.

Let us turn, then, to the commerce requirement. The system operated on spectrum licensed by the FCC. It met the statutory definition because the interference affected "communication." Mitra observes that his interference did not affect any radio system on the other side of a state line, yet this is true of many cell-phone calls, all of which are part of interstate commerce because the electromagnetic spectrum is securely within the federal regulatory domain. See, e.g., *Radovich v. National Football League, 352 U.S. 445, 453, 77 S.Ct. 390, 1 L.Ed.2d 456 (1957); Federal Radio Commission v. Nelson Brothers Bond & Mortgage Co., 289 U.S. 266, 279, 53 S.Ct. 627, 77 L.Ed. 1166 (1933).* Congress may regulate all channels of interstate commerce; the spectrum is one of them. See *United States v. Lopez, 514 U.S. 549, 558, 115 S.Ct. 1624, 131 L.Ed.2d 626 (1995); United States v. Morrison, 529 U.S. 598, 608-09, 120 S.Ct. 1740, 146 L.Ed.2d 658 (2000).* Mitra's apparatus was more powerful than the Huygens probe that recently returned pictures and other data from Saturn's moon Titan. Anyway, the statute does not ask whether the person who caused the damage acted in interstate commerce; it protects computers (and computerized communication systems) used in such commerce, no matter how the harm is inflicted. Once the *computer* is used in interstate commerce, Congress has the power to protect it from a local hammer blow, or from a local data packet that sends it haywire. (Indeed, Mitra concedes that he could have been prosecuted, consistent with the Constitution, for broadcasting an unauthorized signal. See *47 U.S.C. § 301, § 401(c).*) Section 1030 is within the national power as applied to computer-based channel-switching communications systems.

Mitra offers a fallback argument that application of *§ 1030* to his activities is so unexpected that it offends the due process clause. But what cases such as *Bouie v. Columbia, 378 U.S. 347, 84 S.Ct. 1697, 12 L.Ed.2d 894 (1964),* hold is that a court may not apply a clear criminal statute in a way that a reader could not anticipate, or put a vague criminal statute to a new and unexpected use. Mitra's problem is not that *§ 1030* has been turned in a direction that would have surprised reasonable people; it is that a broad statute has been applied *exactly as written,* while he wishes that it had not been. There is no constitutional obstacle to enforcing broad but clear statutes. See *Rogers v. Tennessee, 532 U.S. 451, 458-62, 121 S.Ct. 1693, 149 L.Ed.2d 697*

(2001) (discussing *Bouie's* rationale and limits). The statute itself gives all the notice that the Constitution requires.

During deliberations the jury inquired about the meaning of the word "intentionally." The judge referred them to the instructions, which included a definition. Mitra says that the judge should have drafted a new definition, because the first must have been confusing (though he concedes that it was correct). This sort of problem is one for the district judge to resolve on the spot; there would be little point in Monday morning quarterbacking.

Sentencing requires but little discussion. The district judge added offense levels under *U.S.S.G. § 2B1.1(b)(13)(A)(iii) and (B)* after concluding that Mitra had disrupted a "critical infrastructure." (Our citations are to the 2003 Manual, which the district judge used; the current version is substantively identical but numbered a little differently.) Application Note 12 defines that term; Mitra concedes that an emergency radio system fits the definition. Emergency services are one of the note's examples. Once again his argument takes the form that the authors of this language just couldn't have meant what they said. It is not as if the note were a linguistic garble, or that it is impossible to fathom why any sane person would think that the penalty for crippling an emergency-communication system on which lives may depend should be higher than the penalty for hacking into a website to leave a rude message. The district judge was right to apply the guideline and note as written.

Mitra was sentenced before *United States v. Booker*, ____ *U.S.* ____ , *125 S.Ct. 738, 160 L.Ed.2d 621 (2005)*, and did not argue in the district court that the sixth amendment limits the judge's role in sentencing. Review now is limited to a search for plain error. The approach developed in *United States v. Paladino, 401 F.3d 471 (7th Cir.2005)*, applies to this sentence, which falls within a properly calculated guideline range. Accordingly, although the judgment of conviction is affirmed, we remand to the district court under the terms of *Paladino* so that the district judge may inform us whether the additional discretion provided by *Booker* 's remedial holding would affect Mitra's sentence.

Without question, the most well known piece of legislation associated with the terror attacks of September 11, 2001, is the USA PATRIOT Act. Designed as a tool to assist law enforcement to disrupt terrorist cells and their base of operations, the USA PATRIOT Act was passed by an overwhelming majority of the Congress and signed into law by President Bush on October 26, 2001, and renewed with amendments on March 26, 2006.

The USA PATRIOT Act contains a mixed variety of criminal provisions aimed at both the investigation of suspected terrorists and the disruption of the sources of funding and support for terrorist organizations. However, because almost all of the provisions in the USA PATRIOT Act amend or add language to existing federal statutes, it is often difficult to encapsulate the full impact of many of the provisions at first glance. In terms of cyberterrorism, a number of legislative changes were instituted that expanded the ability of both law enforcement and intelligence agencies regarding surveillance and investigative powers. In short, the USA PATRIOT Act allows federal authorities far greater freedom in monitoring the Internet and provides for a streamlined system of sharing gathered information with other federal and State agencies.

The USA PATRIOT Act authorizes electronic communications interception for the collection of evidence related to terrorism, computer fraud, and abuse at § 201 and § 202. The Act also clarifies the definition of "protected computers" and increases fines and prison terms for damage at § 814. Other important tools are found in the ability of law enforcement agents to employ "pen registers," "trap and trace" devices, "sneak and peek" searches, and "roving wiretaps" (which permits surveillance on the person and not, for example, on the phone or phone number). Section 214 of the USA PATRIOT Act is entitled: "Pen Register and Trap and Trace Authority under FISA." This section expands the scope of the Foreign Intelligence Surveillance Act of 1978 (FISA) and provides greater powers to the FISA courts to grant court orders for surveillance. Section 217 sets out detailed definitions regarding interception of computer trespasser communications. Among other things it clearly defines "wire communications," "electronic communications," "user," and "computer trespasser." A computer trespasser "means any person who accesses a protected computer without authorization and thus has no reasonable expectation of privacy in any communication transmitted to, through, or from the protected computer."

In addition, both the USA PATRIOT Act at § 214 and the Cyber Security and Enhancement Act (CSEA) have eased the warrant and subpoena requirements under the old Electronic Communications Privacy Act of 1986 (ECPA). Under the CSEA (which amends certain sections of Title 18 of the United States Code), the government official need not obtain a warrant if he has a "good faith" belief regarding the prevention of death or serious bodily harm. In addition, the CSEA amends 18 U.S.C. § 3125(a)(1) to allow a government official to use a pen register or a trap and trace device without a warrant or a court order if there is a "threat to national security and an ongoing attack on a protected computer system."

In traditional terms, a pen register is simply a process that collects the outgoing phone numbers from a specific telephone line, while a trap and trace device captures the incoming numbers placed to a specific phone or computer line. Prior to the enactment of the USA PATRIOT Act, pen registers and trap devices could only be used to intercept the numbers dialed or transmitted on the telephone line that was specifically attached to the device. In addition, the old statutory language limited the use of such devices to telephone lines. Understanding the fantastic growth in electronic devices used to communicate information, the USA PATRIOT Act redefined pen register to mean "a device or process which records or decodes dialing, routing, addressing, or signaling information transmitted by an instrument or facility from which a wire or electronic communication is transmitted."

In short, the use of pen registers under the USA PATRIOT Act now allows for the tapping of all sorts of private activity on the Internet and allows law enforcement to collect some private information communicated even from personal e-mails. A pen register and trap and trace device that is used in association with the Internet allows federal agencies to capture all the e-mail headers going to and from an e-mail account, list all servers that a suspect accesses, track anyone that accesses a certain web page and track all web pages that a particular suspect may access. Thus, armed with the new definitions, pen registers and trap and trace now allow federal agencies to include not only telephone lines, but also the Internet, electronic mail, Web surfing and any other form of electronic communication. Although the law prohibits the collection of "content," this can be an ambiguous term—valuable data can still be collected that is more personal than a home telephone number.

Another example of the USA PATRIOT Act providing an avenue to link the private industry and the government is § 105, which allows the United States Secret Service to develop a national network of Electronic Crimes Task Forces (ECTF). The goal of this section of the Act is to take a formula designed by the United States Secret Service and spread that concept throughout the continental United States. The model is based on the New York Electronic Crimes Task Force, a task force created to combat various forms of electronic crimes, including potential terrorist attacks against critical infrastructure and financial institutions. Since its inception in 1995, the New York Electronic Crimes Task Force has initiated investigations resulting in more than 800 people being charged with computer crimes that resulted in losses exceeding $500 million. In 2002, the New York Task Force was comprised of over 50 law enforcement agencies, 100 private companies, and nine regional universities.

Since the passage of the USA PATRIOT Act, the United States Secret Service has begun operating these task forces all over the United States, including locations in San Francisco, Las Vegas, Los Angeles, Dallas, Houston, Miami, Chicago, Cleveland, Boston, New York, Washington, DC, Charlotte, and Columbia. These ECTF's are designed to adapt to the type of industry that is prevalent in that geographical area. Since combating cyberterrorism as a partnership is imperative, the addition of private corporations is a pivotal component to the success of the ECTF and is a partnership that not only enhances the role of law enforcement, but provides mutually beneficial rewards for private corporations. The private sector is able to directly bring issues to the ECTF that affect their particular industry and do so in a secure law enforcement environment. Private corporations are also able to view how criminals violate current computer technology, and therefore, they are better able to protect their own corporate assets. One of the many perks for the government is that it is able to connect with companies that have a particular expertise and resources that many law enforcement agencies are lacking. One such example is AT&T Laboratories. AT&T is able to break encryption codes with greater speed than most law enforcement entities and this can be invaluable in an investigation, particularly when gathering evidence in an expeditious manner.

A 2007 report issued by the Government Accountability Office (GAO) noted that government and private sectors face a number of serious obstacles in securing cyberspace particularly in the context of law enforcement and operational security. The four main categories of concern in the GAO report touched on cyber crime, but would also be equally pertinent in regards to any type of cyber attack to include cyberterrorism:

(1) accurately reporting cyber crime to law enforcement;
(2) ensuring adequate law enforcement analytical and technical capabilities: obtaining and retaining investigators, prosecutors, and cyber forensics examiners and keeping up to date with current technology and criminal techniques;
(3) working in a borderless environment with laws of multiple jurisdictions; and
(4) protecting information and information systems and raising awareness about criminal behavior.

Individual States have also enacted laws associated with cyberterrorism concerns. These laws address a wide range of issues from improving security measures for wireless networks to criminalizing the installation of software on another's computer which is then used in deceptive methods. In addition to criminal laws, civil actions based on commercial code unfair competition prohibitions can also serve to punish hackers.

The fear of cyberterrorism as a destructive force has caused at least 48 States to pass non-release provisions to their State open government laws—State freedom of information laws (patterned after the federal Freedom of Information Act) and State Sunshine laws (providing for public access to government meetings). An examination of the legislative thrust of most of these non-release provisions is to deny potential terrorists access to certain information that could aid them in conducting a disabling physical or cyber attack on the critical infrastructure. For instance, the Ohio Revised Code makes specific exceptions to the Ohio Open Government law regarding non-release of information related to *acts of terrorism*, *critical infrastructures*, and *security records*. Under § 149.433(B): "A record kept by a public office that is a security record or an infrastructure record is not a public record under § 149.433 of the Revised Code and is not subject to mandatory release or disclosure under that section." Under § 149.433(A)(3), the term "security records" is broadly construed to include:

(a) Any record that contains information directly used for protecting or maintaining the security of a public office against attack, interference, or sabotage, and

(b) Any record assembled, prepared, or maintained by a public office or public body to prevent, mitigate, or respond to acts of terrorism, to include any of the following:

(i) Those portions of records containing specific and unique vulnerability assessments or specific and unique response plans either of which is intended to prevent or mitigate acts of terrorism, and communication codes or deployment plans of law enforcement or emergency response personnel;

(ii) Specific intelligence information and specific investigative records shared by federal and international law enforcement agencies with state and local law enforcement and public safety agencies; and

(iii) National security records classified under federal executive order and not subject to public disclosure under federal law that are shared by federal agencies, and other records related to national security briefings to assist state and local government with domestic preparedness for acts of terrorism.

The term "infrastructure record" under the Ohio Revised Code § 149.433(A)(2) means:

Any record that discloses the configuration of a public office's critical systems including, but not limited to, communication, computer, electrical, mechanical, ventilation, water, and plumbing systems, security codes, or the infrastructure or structural configuration of the building in which a public office is located. However, the term infrastructure record does not mean a simple floor plan that discloses only the spatial relationship of components of a public office or the building in which a public office is located.

The term "act of terrorism" under the Ohio Revised Code § 149.433(A)(1) has the same statutory meaning as is found in Ohio Revised Code § 2909.21:

'Act of terrorism' means an act that is committed within or outside the territorial jurisdiction of this state or the United States, that constitutes a specified offense if committed in this state or constitutes an offense in any jurisdiction within or outside the territorial jurisdiction of the United States containing all of the essential elements of a specified offense, and that is intended to do one or more of the following:

(1) Intimidate or coerce a civilian population;

(2) Influence the policy of any government by intimidation or coercion; or

(3) Affect the conduct of any government by the act that constitutes the offence.

Limitations have also been imposed on the federal FOIA. These restrictions have drawn wide and vocal criticism from a variety of sources and leads to the question: "How much information should be suppressed in the interests of national security?"

8.4 Government and Private Sector Partnership

Starting with the Clinton Administration and continuing to the Obama Administration, the government's approach to cybersecurity for owners/operators of private computer systems has been one of cooperative engagement and not mandatory regulation. The general feeling was that since the civilian sector invented and developed cyberspace, security should be left to market forces. In short, despite the rapidly expanding reliance on the Internet by American businesses, consumers, and government agencies, the government provides extremely little affirmative regulatory laws in terms of cybersecurity functions for non-government computer systems. Instead, the concept of engagement stresses the promotion of voluntary public-private alliances to combat cyber attacks of all kinds with particular regard to protecting the nation's critical infrastructure. With but minor exceptions, aimed at government computer systems, the theme of engagement predominates all of the federal laws, executive orders and presidential directives associated with cyberspace. These include the following: Internet Integrity and Critical Infrastructure Protection Act (2000); Cyber Security Research and Development Act; National Strategy to Secure Cyberspace (2003); National Strategy for the Physical Protection of Critical Infrastructures and Key Assets (2003); Presidential Decision Directive (PDD) 63; Executive Order 13821, Critical Infrastructure Protection in the Information Age; and Homeland Security Presidential Directive No. 7 (HSPD-7). The two strategies are designed to help America secure the cyber world by establishing three main objectives: (1) prevent cyber attacks against America's critical infrastructure; (2) reduce national vulnerability to cyber attacks; and (3) reduce damage and recovery time from cyber attacks when they do occur.

The National Strategy to Secure Cyberspace specifically recognizes that cyberspace constitutes "the control system of our country." In addition, the document recognizes that a comprehensive national strategy must protect against such cyber attacks which "can have serious consequences such as disrupting critical operations, causing loss of revenue and intellectual property, or loss of life." The main goal of the National Strategy to Secure Cyberspace calls for the entire society—the federal government, state and local government, private industry and the American public—to engage in coordinated and focused efforts to secure cyberspace. To expedite this goal, the primary focus of the National Strategy to Secure Cyberspace is the establishment of a national cyber space security response system consisting of federal, state and local governments as well as the private sector. Thus, not only does the National Strategy to Secure Cyberspace reinforce the private sector's involvement in critical infrastructure protection, it also expands on the Clinton era 1998 PDD 63. PDD 63 recognizes that addressing cyber risks to the nation's critical infrastructures requires close coordination and cooperation across federal agencies and among the private sector. Since the policy of engagement depends on public and private sector coordination, research and preparation to repel a cyber attack, PDD 63 specifically tasks federal agencies with developing critical infrastructure protection plans (CIP) and establishing relationships with private industry sectors. It calls for those private commercial enterprises working in any of the identified 14 vertical industries such as banking, commerce, telecommunications, power, water, utilities, and transportation, to have assessments conducted of their network infrastructure.

In 2001, President Bush expanded this effort with Executive Order 13821, Critical Infrastructure Protection in the Information Age, which continues many of the initiatives begun by PDD 63 to include the creation of the President's Critical Infrastructure Protection Board to better coordinate all federal cyber security efforts. In addition, the 2003 HSPD-7 designates certain federal agencies to work with private sector counterparts; designates the DHS as the lead agency for information and telecommunications critical infrastructure; and assigns the Secretary of Homeland Security with the task of coordinating all matters dealing with protecting the nation's critical infrastructure. In fact, numerous public entities have individual and collaborative responsibilities to ensure that the cyber world is protected. For example, DHS established the National Cyber Security Division as part of its Information Analysis and Infrastructure Protection Directorate to better fulfill its oversight responsibilities. One of DHS's main objectives is to structure a response system that fully joins the government and the private sector together in order to promote the creation of a viable crisis management response in the event of a major cyber attack. In addition, DHS seeks to identify and remediate existing vulnerabilities by developing new security systems and technologies. Along with DHS, the Department of Justice (DOJ), the Federal Trade Commission (FTC), and the Department of Defense (DOD) are all focused on responding to intentional, unlawful cyber attacks that threaten the confidentiality, integrity, and availability of information networks.

DHS also encourages the development of voluntary partnerships with the private sector through information sharing and analysis centers (ISACs). Currently DHS lists 14 ISACs across the nation. The Cyber Security Research and Development Act authorizes a multi-year grant effort to promote computer security measures from private sources as well as universities and the establishment of multi-disciplinary Centers for Computer and Network Security Research. US-CERT is another joint endeavor between DHS and the public and private sectors. It is charged generally with protecting the nation's infrastructure and is responsible for coordinating defense and response against cyber attacks nationwide.

The development of effective tools to protect cyberspace is of paramount importance. Realizing that the superhighway of the cyber world is composed of hundreds of thousands of interconnected computers, servers, switches, and fiber optics that allow our critical infrastructures to function, the threat of cyberterrorism requires urgent cybersecurity measures. As demonstrated by the cyber attack on Estonia in 2007, the threat is no longer a topic of academic debate. Considering that approximately 85 percent of America's critical infrastructure is privately owned and operates via control systems that are largely connected to the Internet, it is imperative that the government—law enforcement and military—not only partner with private industry in a unified manner to establish both reactive and proactive strategies, but also conduct realistic training exercises. Unfortunately, the pace of progress in this regard is slow.

In February 2006, DHS hosted the first ever government-led real world cyber exercise called Cyber Storm (Cyber Storm 2 was held in 2008). Costing over 3 million dollars, this invitation-only exercise provided over 100 public and private agencies from over 60 locations in five countries with a platform to address a variety of technical and cooperative issues associated with a realistic "staged" mega cyber attack against large-scale critical infrastructure elements to include energy, transportation and information technology. Considering that reviews of the exercise showed that many of the participants did not even know of the existence of the National Cyber Response Coordination Group, which serves as the primary federal organization to respond to major cyber attacks, it is evident that a key component of the engagement strategy demands increased training exercise. In addition, considering that 90 percent of the threat from cyberterrorism exists in the private sector, it is equally evident that relying on voluntary engagement practices may not be adequate—regulatory mandates are needed.

There can be absolutely no question that the threat of cyberterrorism is a grave concern that has the potential for significant damage to vast areas of the public domain. Indeed, because of cyberterrorism's great potential for harm to the basic pillars of society many commentators argue that cyberspace has passed into the realm of a societal "commons" that obliges the government to exert greater protection. If cyberspace is considered a commons, *a fortiori*, cybersecurity demands that the government provide solid protection and regulation for the common good of the general public. From this perspective many question the wisdom of a federal policy to secure cyberspace that fails to incorporate strict cybersecurity standards or regulations on the private sector as part of the strategy.

Because it is impossible to immediately determine the source of a cyber attack—it may be an amateur "script kiddie," a terrorist, or even a nation-state—the so-called "response baton" will originate with the private sector and then may be passed to law enforcement and next, perhaps, to the military. Clearly, the main thrust of a commons oriented cybersecurity strategy would involve two key elements: (1) a program that required the sharing of timely and accurate information all along the continuum from private to government and (2) the adoption of industry-specific cybersecurity standards and certification for all information systems.

The concept of "standards" is defined by the National Standards Policy Advisory Committee as: "a prescribed set of rules, conditions, or requirements concerning definitions of terms; classification of components; specification of materials, performance, or operations; delineation of procedures; or measurement of quantity and quality in describing materials, products, systems, services, or practices." As suggested by the government's current engagement strategy, the federal government only promulgates cybersecurity standards for federal computer systems, except national security systems. The federal standards are developed by the National Institute of Standards and Technology (NIST) and set out as Federal Information Processing Standards (FIPS). FIPS are promulgated under the simple rule-making procedures (notice and comment) of the Administrative Procedure Act.

In accordance with National Security Directive 42, standards regarding national security systems are developed and controlled by the Committee on National Security Systems. The Federal Information Security Act of 2002, defines a national security system as:

> Any computer system (including any telecommunications system, used or operated by an agency or by a contractor of an agency, or other organization on behalf of an agency...
> (i) the function of which—
> > (I)   involves intelligence activities;
> > (II)   involves cryptologic activities related to national security;
> > (III)   involves command and control of military forces;
> > (IV)   involves equipment that is an integral part of a weapon or weapons system;
> > (V)   ...is critical to the direct fulfillment of military or intelligence missions; or
> (ii) is protected at all times by procedures established for information that have been specially authorized under criteria established by an Executive Order or an Act of Congress to be kept classified in the interest of national defense or foreign policy.

In 2008, President Bush signed National Security Presidential Directive 54 and Homeland Security Presidential Directive 23. The classified directives expand the intelligence communities' role in cybersecurity for federal agencies' computer systems and expand DHS's ability to work with the DOD on cybersecurity threats.

To be sure, numerous public and private studies offer various proposals for sound security and best practices needed to reduce vulnerabilities from cyber attack. The studies usually prescribe a standardized integration of cybersecurity technology associated with all critical infrastructure systems in order to ensure an acceptable national level of cybersecurity. While various approaches have been advanced, the 2005 CRS report RL32777, observed that none of them are "likely to be widely adopted in the absence of sufficient economic incentives for cybersecurity."

Those who believe that the federal government should not require the development and enforcement of mandatory cybersecurity standards in the private sector, often argue that apart from issues of intrusiveness and technical feasibility, that such requirements would simply be too costly. Although the argument related to cost would be dwarfed into insignificance when measured against the monetary damage incurred in the event of a mega cyberterrorist attack, technical matters ranging from how to develop said standards in the rapidly changing world of cyberspace to how the government would measure compliance pose significant challenges.

Those who critique the engagement strategy argue that absent the impetus that would be provided by a massive cyberterrorist attack on the nation's critical infrastructure, efforts to actually create a meaningful cooperative proactive and reactive strategy between the government and private industry are piecemeal. Even the more immediate negative consequences to businesses caused by the impact of cyber crime (which drains billions of dollars from consumers and private industry each year) have not resulted in the necessary strides to produce stronger and more secure computer networks.

In May 2009, the Obama Administration released its Cyberspace Policy Review with a key recommendation centered on the engagement strategy of improving partnerships between the private sector and the government. According to the Cyberspace Policy Review:

> Some members of the private sector continue to express concern that certain federal laws might impede full collaborative partnerships and operational information sharing between the private sector and government. For example, some in industry are concerned that the information sharing and collective planning that occurs among members of the same sector under existing partnership models might be viewed as 'collusive' of contrary to laws forbidding restraints on trade.

The basic reason for the lack of cooperation is that private companies are largely unwilling to share information about security breaches with other companies or the government. First, they are concerned that competitors might gain access to exclusive company data that is shared with the government through a public Freedom of Information Act (FOIA) request or by means of other sources (the Critical Infrastructures Protection Act exempts such revelations to the government from FOIA). Second, because the private sector operates in a competitive market-based economy, public revelations about security breaches at the company could have serious negative responses from stockholders or consumers.

Unfortunately, it is a hard fact that very few private companies have exhibited interest in joining the cybersecurity effort to the degree that the various government strategies so strongly desire. In short, the private sector does not trust the government. The frustration is that without a cooperative effort to identify breaches and the possible weak points of security systems, the vulnerabilities to cyber attack are magnified and countermeasures remain far behind. For certain, when the West suffers its first "Pearl Harbor cyber attack," the government will adopt a more draconian stance in order to force private industry to share information and to develop better cybersecurity systems. For the time being, apart from suffering economic loss, there are no driving incentives for private industry to work together to combat cyberterrorism.

8.5 Cyber as a Weapon of War

In July 2009, a multi-day DDoS cyber attack on American and South Korean websites occurred at the same time that North Korea was conducting ballistic missile tests over the Sea of Japan. This incident made headlines worldwide and caused many to consider the use of cyber as a weapon of war.

A number of nation-states, to include the United States, are rapidly developing the operational doctrine and functional tools necessary to conduct what is termed cyber warfare. There is no doubt that cyber warfare with its non-kinetic use of force will be the next area for weapon development by militaries around the world. In fact, according to a variety of open source documents, the People's Republic of China openly boasts that it intends to develop the capability to win a cyber war by the mid-21st century. In fact, scores of nation-states are actively involved in developing cyber war capabilities. In keeping with the Obama theme of internationalism, the Obama Cyberspace Policy Review states that "the United States needs to develop a strategy … to shape the international environment and bring like-minded nations together on a host of issues, including acceptable norms regarding territorial jurisdiction, sovereign responsibility and the use of force."

Cyber warfare involves the action of conducting a cyber information attack on the computer network of an adversary in order to limit their ability to obtain or use information. Of course, this matter is not restricted to the activity of nation-states—hackers and terrorists are not constrained by any rule of law and might engage in coordinated cyber attacks that could equally disrupt a nation's computer network system. Nevertheless, since the rule of law would certainly encompass the use of cyber information activity conducted by a nation-state, it is necessary to examine the law and policy issues related to cyber warfare.

The use of "information warfare" or cyber warfare is a new concept; the use of cyber tactics are emerging as a key component of 21st century warfighting. For instance, the U.S. military conducted successful cyber attacks in both the 1991 Gulf War and the 2003 Iraq War (to a lesser degree) to disrupt Iraqi command and control networks and the operation of other essential physical facilities. Currently, the Joint Functional Component Command for Network Warfare (JFCCNW) functions under the United States Strategic Command (STRATCOM), to coordinate cyber information actions for the DOD. In 2008, the U.S. Air Force established a Cyber Command to prepare its forces for fighting wars in cyberspace by protecting those information systems which operate U.S. critical infrastructures and to be able, if tasked, to attack an adversary's computer networks. The U.S. Navy has the Naval Network Warfare Command in Norfolk, Virginia. In short, DOD is developing both offensive and defensive capabilities to conduct war in cyberspace.

Like a number of legal issues that have emerged in the post-9/11 world, the question of addressing cyber attacks from an international law of war perspective remains unsettled. The central legal issue poses the following question: Does the use of a cyber attack constitute a sufficient "use of force" in the context of the law of war to be deemed an "armed attack" or an "act of war?"

The use of the term act of war traditionally refers to the use of aggressive force against a sovereign State by another State in violation of the United Nations (U.N.) Charter and/or customary international law. In almost every instance in the modern era, such illegal acts occur without a formal declaration of war and the aggressive act itself triggers the ensuing armed conflict, i.e., war. The application of the traditional law of war principles (also known as the law of armed conflict) was developed by the international community in response to readily recognized deliberate armed attacks by soldiers, aircraft, or vessels on the military, citizens, or territory of another nation-state. At the time of the development of the law of war, cyberspace did not exist. Thus, the question of whether or not a computer network attack is an act of war requires extrapolation from the existing norms related to the law of war.

Any analysis of the matter must begin with the U.N. Charter. The goal of the U.N. Charter is to restrict the unfettered power of member States to pursue activities and policies that threatened international peace and security. Understanding that the U.N. Charter does not outlaw the use of force—it only outlaws the use of *aggressive* force—there are four primary provisions of the U.N. Charter under which the use of force is analyzed.

First, Articles 2(3) and (4) set out the general obligations of all member States to settle disputes in a peaceful manner and to refrain from "the threat or use of force." U.N. Charter Article 2(3) requires that, "[a]ll Members shall settle their international disputes by peaceful means in such a manner that international peace and security, and justice are not endangered." U.N. Charter Article 2(4) states, "[a]ll Members shall refrain in their international relations from the threat or use of force against the territorial integrity or political independence of any State, or in any other manner inconsistent with the purposes of the United Nations." In 1970, the General Assembly elaborated on Article 2(4), with U.N. General Assembly Resolution 2625, Declaration on Principles of International Law Concerning Friendly Relations and Cooperation among States in Accordance with the Charter of the United Nations. Although General Assembly resolutions are considered as non-binding recommendations they often prove useful, particularly to the extent that they contain authoritative restatements of customary international law. General Assembly Resolution 2625 states:

> Every State has the duty to refrain from organizing, instigating, assisting, or participating in acts of civil strife or terrorist acts in another State or acquiescing in organized activities within its territory directed towards the commission of such acts, when the acts referred to in the present paragraph involve a threat or use of force.

Second, if a State engages in the use of aggressive force, Article 24 of the U.N. Charter gives the Security Council the "primary responsibility for the maintenance of international peace and security." Article 27 requires that all permanent members of the U.N. Security Council (China, France, Russia, the United States, and Britain) must agree on enforcement provisions, e.g., authorizing member States to engage in the defensive use of armed force.

The third element in the analytical framework is Article 51 of the U.N. Charter, which expresses the "inherent right of self-defense" in the case of an armed attack. The inherent right of self-defense refers to the ancient customary right of a country to unilaterally engage in acts of self-defense in response to an armed attack regardless of what any other nation or organization, to include the United Nations, may or may not do.

Article 51 of the U.N. Charter states:

> Nothing in the present Charter shall impair the inherent right of individual or collective self-defense if an armed attack occurs against a Member of the United Nations, until the Security Council has taken measures to maintain international peace and security. Measures taken by Members in the exercise of the right of self-defense shall be immediately reported to the Security Council and shall not in any way affect the authority and responsibility of the Security Council under the present Charter to take at any time such action as it deems necessary in order to maintain or restore international peace and security.

While a cyber attack has the potential to do great harm to the critical infrastructure of a given nation-state, would such an action rise to the level of what Article 51 deems as an "armed attack"? Clearly, a cyber attack of sufficient scope on either the military network or the critical infrastructure could constitute a violation of Article 2(3) and 2(4), but would that be considered enough to constitute an armed attack triggering the customary right of self-defense now codified under Article 51 of the U.N. Charter?

Common sense would dictate that a cyber attack of sufficient magnitude should be considered an armed attack, but when the U.N. Charter was drafted in 1945, the founders clearly did not foresee the potential for devastation that could come from cyberspace. For instance, Article 41 of the U.N. Charter views the "complete or partial interruption of…telegraphic, radio, and other means of communication" as measures not rising to the level of the use of armed force. In turn, the definition of aggression as adopted by the 1974 General Assembly Resolution 3314, excludes the concept of cyber attacks as an act of aggression that would constitute an armed attack (see Chapter 2.3).

Finally, because there is no absolute requirement that a "threat to the peace, breach of the peace, or act of aggression," take the form of a traditional styled armed attack, Article 39 of the U.N. Charter ultimately provides the Security Council with the final authority to determine whether a particular cyber attack would constitute a breach of the peace, and to what degree. Obviously, for the Security Council to take action, the cyber attack would have to be extensive in nature. In other words, the consequences of a cyber attack would be a central ingredient in their decision making process. Article 39 of the U.N. Charter states:

> The Security Council shall determine the existence of any threat to the peace, breach of the peace, or act of aggression and shall make recommendations, or decide what measures shall be taken in accordance with Articles 41 and 42, to maintain or restore international peace and security.

A related issue in the analysis is the issue of State-sponsorship. The law of war recognizes acts of self-defense in the context of the acts of a hostile nation-state, not of individual actors or groups of individuals that act in their private capacity. The expectation is that the aggrieved State will notify the nation-state where the private actors are located and then request assistance and cooperation. If the host nation is unwilling or unable to provide assistance and cooperation, then the aggrieved State may be justified to use force as was the case with the United States *vis-à-vis* the Taliban's support for the terrorist al-Qa'eda network in Afghanistan. On the other hand, if the cyber attack cannot be traced to a nation-state, the matter of retaliation is greatly limited.

Clearly, the international laws associated with the use of force are woefully inadequate in terms of addressing the threat of cyber warfare. Without a clear set of rules addressing cyber warfare, individual nation-states will no doubt operate within the framework of existing legal norms by extrapolation, much like the North Atlantic Treaty Organization (NATO) did when it invoked the NATO collective self-defense clause under Article 5 of its Charter, declaring that the terror attacks of 9/11 constituted an "armed attack" under international law despite the fact that al-Qa'eda is not a nation-state.

The international community needs to agree on the application of cyber warfare to the international rules of armed conflict. To date, however, periodic calls for the development of international rules dealing with information warfare have gone unanswered. In 1998 and 1999, for example, Russia was unsuccessful in its bid to get the United Nations to explore the need for an information warfare weapons arms control protocol. The Russian resolution asked member States to provide input on the "advisability of elaborating international legal regimes to ban the development, production and use of particularly dangerous information weapons."

The only real significant international agreement on cyber matters to date is the 2001 Council of Europe Convention on Cybercrime, which has been ratified by at least 26 nations, including the United States (July 1, 2004). There is hope that this convention, which focuses on cyber crime and not cyber warfare, may at least present a starting point for future efforts in the realm of cyber warfare.

Currently, DOD views the use of cyber technology in military operations as a part of what is termed Information Operations (IO). IO consists of five subcategories: Psychological Operations (PSYOP); Military Deception (MILDEC); Operations Security (OPSEC); Computer Network Operations (CNO); and Electronic Warfare (EW). While the domestic guidelines that detail how and when the United States would conduct a computer network attack is classified information in National Security Presidential Directive 16 (February 2003), there are a number of unclassified DOD policy directives that speak to IO operations which would certainly have impact on cyber warfare. For instance, in regard to PSYOP, only non-domestic audiences can be targeted. This restriction would certainly apply to electronic warfare.

From a military perspective, the use of cyber technology in warfare is something that is clearly viewed as a new and powerful weapon. Cyber warfare offers a cheap method of employing targeted force against an adversary—it requires no deployment of soldiers, vehicles, or vessels. As is the case for all weapons, however, the American military command structure responds to lawful commands from the government and uses force in accordance with the Standing Rules of Engagement (SROE). Depending on the objective of the military operation, the SROE are further amplified by multiple levels of Rules of Engagement (ROE) which are developed by commanders and their lawyers. Designed for offensive and defensive uses of force, these rules ensure compliance with the law of war as well as domestic law. Even though no review has yet been produced, the DOD has recommended a legal review to determine what level of data manipulation constitutes an attack. In addition, because cyber weapons can transit global networks and produce far-reaching and unforeseen results, considerations need to be addressed regarding the impact on neutrals.

At the end of the day, if directed by lawful authority, DOD can and will attack an adversary's computer system—private or government. No new authority is needed. The issue that is seldom discussed centers on the mechanics—the U.S. military relies significantly on the computer systems of the private sector and would presumably have to use those private assets in any large scale cyber attack.

8.6 Civil Liability in the Private Sector

A variety of cyberspace-related legal issues are developing in the private sector. At the forefront of most Internet users' minds is the question of privacy. As they venture online, users and consumers look for reassurance that the personal information they submit will remain protected by their own computer, their Internet service provider (ISP) and the website they are visiting. Conversely, the chief concern of technology developers, manufacturers and owner/operators is the question of legal responsibility regarding the type and level of cybersecurity protection.

As noted in the discussion on the government's overall cybersecurity strategy in the private sector, the understated theme of engagement continues to characterize the approach for user privacy and cyber system integrity. The matter of cybersecurity in general and security standards in particular are left in the hands of civilian technology developers, manufacturers and owner/operators.

Federal legislation mandating protective measures in terms of computer security is restricted to federal agencies only, e.g., the Federal Information Security Management Act of 2002. Apart from a few specific laws associated with protecting financial and health-related information from disclosure, government efforts to set security standards or make private entities responsible for protecting their computer systems has not yet come of age. A brief survey of federal involvement in this area reveals only two major pieces of legislation—one in health and one in financial reporting—and even those two indirectly address cybersecurity concerns. The Health Insurance Portability and Accountability Act of 1996 requires certain private entities to establish security programs that protect the health-related information in their possession, and the Sarbanes-Oxley Act of 2002 requires corporate executives of publicly held companies to annually certify the integrity of their financial reporting under penalty of fines or imprisonment. While the Sarbanes-Oxley Act was passed in the wake of the accounting scandals at Enron and WorldCom, it spurred a massive increase in cybersecurity spending by private companies now concerned about the operating effectiveness of computerized internal controls and fraud prevention.

Liability issues associated with breaches of computer security rubricate cyber discussions from both ISPs and private companies. Liability for failure to protect customers from cyber attacks and liability for (unknowingly) hosting a DDoS attacker are two significant concerns that will soon find their way into court as civil actions in tort or product liability claims. Currently, however, there are no federal laws holding a technology developer, manufacturer, or owner/operator liable if they sell or offer a product that has inadequate cybersecurity protections or design flaws. As a practical matter, licensing agreements or terms of service agreements include disclaimer protections.

In tandem with these cyber "defensive" concerns, i.e., responsibility for damage done to third parties as a result of inadequately providing security protection as a technology developer, manufacturer, or owner/operator, is the emerging issue of the increased use of "offensive" or self-defense responses to a cyber attack, e.g., actions employed by private network security personnel in response to a cyber attack on their system. Known as hackback—an offensive response against a cyber attacker—this offensive process may also damage the computer networks of innocent third parties used by the attacker. While hackback illustrates a desire by some in the civilian sector to take cybersecurity matters into their own hands, it also raises a number of legal issues.

Identification of the source(s) of a cyber attack, including the Internet Protocol (IP) address of the attacker, is vital to the identification of the attacker, the deployment of effective countermeasures and the development of new cybersecurity defense tools. However, due to a number of techniques that can be used to hide the identity of an attacker, manually tracing the multiple sources of a DDoS attack generally proves overly burdensome and requires more time to conduct than the actual attack itself. As a practical matter, then, the best way to identify the source of an attack is through an automated process. One such program is known as "IP Traceback." Southwest Research Institute (SWRI), San Antonio, Texas is currently working on a project to develop an Autonomous System Traceback (AST) solution to combat cyber attacks, including DDoS attacks. As such, AST provides a useful platform in the discussion of a variety of legal issues that are not only integral in the context of developing and deploying the AST solution, but in dealing with liability and privacy issues associated with both defensive and offensive cybersecurity actions.

Experts correctly refer to the IP traceback concept as a problem because tracing an attack to its source is complicated by the fact that attackers typically forge, or "spoof," the IP address from which the attack packet is sent. Spoofed packets will contain an invalid or false IP address in the packet header making the packet appear as though it originated from the "spoofed" IP address. To complicate matters further, the traditional method of tracing the source of an attack is largely a manual process that must be conducted during the course of an attack (this is further aggravated because the attack can be carried out from a multitude of sources). The complexity of such attacks thereby renders traditional tracing of IP addresses impractical for commercial networks in terms of cost effectiveness.

Four main types of IP traceback exist: packet marking; packet or hash-based logging; link testing; and Internet Control Message Protocol (ICMP) traceback. In general, each of these approaches has suffered technical, policy and legal restrictions. The need for additional hardware, software upgrades, modifications to network configurations and filtering the enormous amount of data processed on computer networks have presented technical obstacles. Further, one of the key limitations to successful deployment of IP traceback systems is the necessity for cooperation among ISPs. According to one report on the matter:

> Tracking an anonymous attack is not a trivial task. An individual or organization would find this task difficult, if not impossible, without involving their upstream ISPs. Today, tracing an anonymous attack even within a single ISP remains a manual task. ISPs and enterprise networks do not have incentives to monitor for attack packets....The lack of incentives comes from the fact that monitoring for such packets has no immediate benefit to the ISP itself or its subscribers. Furthermore, participating in traceback may mean disclosure of internal topology, investment in additional equipment, upgrades to existing equipment, and additional operational costs for the ISP. Consequently, IP traceback solutions should not assume complete cooperation of ISPs.

Looking at the final goal of the traceback process—identifying and blocking the source of the attack—the AST method of IP traceback focuses not on identifying a specific computer as the attack source but rather locating the Autonomous System (AS) from which the attack originated. AST monitors record hashes of the packet signature—in this case, specific fields in the packet header—for each packet that crosses their borders. The route of an attack packet may then be traced back by identifying each AS it crossed, without the need to examine internal network paths. Additionally, and most importantly for privacy concerns, the contents of the traffic are never viewed or stored. Only a hash of the packet's header information is stored by the AST. In other words, no internal network topology is disclosed to the AST, only whether an AS saw the packet and where it received the packet from. Since AST does not utilize any of the active traceback techniques such as "active defense" or hackback, an AST model remains within the passive realm. Because there is no expectation of privacy from routing information, the Electronic Communications Privacy Act (ECPA), which generally prohibits the interception, use, or disclosure of e-mail contents while they are being transmitted, does not protect packet headers which are used to route information from point A to point Z.

Accordingly, AST developers express two specific concerns in the area of liability: (1) what liability might a company or ISP have for failing to use AST technology (if it were one day viewed as an industry standard practice, for instance) in its network cybersecurity program; and (2) what liability might attach if a company or ISP became host to a DDoS attacker?

Answering the first question, without the benefit of significant judicial case law on the subject, mandates reference to traditional notions of common law tort liability. For an ISP, or other commercial firm, to be liable under tort law requires that the provider breach a legal duty to exercise a level of care imposed by either statute or common law.

Sources for common law tort liability require consideration as to the developing legal standard for information security, which in this case would be discovered by reviewing trends in the area of cybersecurity. At a minimum, there exists at least a general obligation to provide some level of cybersecurity. Specifically, legal obligations for technology developers, manufacturers and owner/operators regarding information security derive from multiple sources—enacted federal and state laws; regulations and government enforcement actions; and common law fiduciary duties and obligations to provide reasonable care. The legal obligation to implement cybersecurity measures can be classified as either industry-specific, data-specific, or focused on public companies.

As previously noted, a handful of federal laws have been enacted in order to protect personal data and financial reporting of individuals, customers, or prospects held by certain private companies. The Sarbanes-Oxley Act and the Gramm-Leach-Bliley Act require the integrity of financial reporting, and the Health Insurance Portability and Accountability Act mandates cybersecurity protections for personal information. The Children's Online Privacy Protection Act of 1998 requires protection of personal information regarding children. The Securities Exchange Commission (SEC) also imposes regulations regarding cybersecurity standards for internal financial controls over information systems.

The Federal Trade Commission (FTC) possesses a series of enforcement actions and consent decrees which extend security obligations to certain private industries. Originally, the FTC facilitated cases based on the alleged failure by companies to provide adequate information security contrary to representations they made to customers (deceptive trade practices claims). In June 2005, the FTC significantly broadened the scope of its enforcement by asserting that a failure to provide appropriate information security was, itself, an unfair trade practice—even in the absence of any false representations by the defendant as to the state of its security.

A variety of federal and State E-transaction laws (E-SIGN and UETA) now require all companies to provide security for storage of electronic records relating to online transactions. In addition, sector-specific regulations are experiencing proliferation. This includes the Internal Revenue Service's (IRS) requirement for companies to implement information security to protect electronic tax records and SEC regulations on cybersecurity concerns as a condition to engage in certain E-transactions. The Food and Drug Administration (FDA) also has agency regulations that require security for certain types of records.

Many legal commentators suggest that corporate directors have a duty of care rooted in a fiduciary obligation that includes responsibility for the security of the company's information systems. They also argue that there may be a common law duty to provide cybersecurity, the breach of which constitutes a tort.

State laws also impose certain cybersecurity obligations to ensure the security of personal information. These laws are known as security breach laws. In 2003, California enacted the California Database Protection Act, Cal. Civil Code § 1798.82 (2006), becoming the first state in the nation to enact legislation requiring any government or private entity that possessed confidential personal information (e.g., social security numbers) to notify the owners of said information in the event of a disclosure to an unauthorized person resulting from a security breach. Additionally, § 1798.81.5 (2006) of the Act added an unprecedented statutory duty on businesses that own or authorize the use of personal information to "implement and maintain reasonable security procedures and practices appropriate to the nature of the information, to protect the personal information from unauthorized access, destruction, use, modification, or disclosure." Thus, businesses obtaining the personal or confidential information of California customers now have a statutory duty to not only provide notification to individuals regarding security breaches but also provide reasonable care for securing such data. California's approach has served as a model for statutes in dozens of other states. As of 2007 at least thirty-five states require businesses to notify their customers or clients if there is a security breach involving sensitive personal information. These laws generally apply to any business maintaining the information of a resident of the state which enacts the statute.

For instance, in 2005, the Texas legislature passed Senate Bill 122, which amended the Texas Code of Criminal Procedure and Texas Business and Commerce Code. The relevant portion of the Texas Business and Commerce Code, § 48.102(a) (2006) reads: "A business shall implement and maintain reasonable procedures, including taking any appropriate corrective action, to protect and safeguard from unlawful use or disclosure any sensitive personal information collected or maintained by the business in the regular course of business." Like the approach in California, the Texas legislature statutorily defined that businesses within the state owe a duty to their customers to implement reasonable procedures to safeguard personal data. Section 521.053 of the Texas Business & Commerce Code provides:

> Any person who *maintains computerized data* that includes *sensitive personal information* not owned by the person *shall notify the owner* or license holder of the information of *any breach of system security immediately after discovering the breach*, if the sensitive personal information was, or is *reasonably believed* to have been, acquired by an unauthorized person.

The law defines sensitive personal data as:

> "Sensitive personal information" means, subject to Subsection (b), an individual's first name or first initial and last name in combination with any one or more of the following items, if the names and the items *are not encrypted*:
> (A) social security number;
> (B) driver's license number or government-issued identification number; or account number or credit or debit card number in combination with any required security code, access code, or password that would permit access to an individual's financial account.

What, then, is considered reasonable care in the context of cybersecurity protection? Some analysts argue that the very fact that a security breach occurs indicates a breach of a common law duty owed by the ISP or a commercial firm to provide reasonable security for its customers' personal information. The more reasoned approach is to look at industry standards. In fact, in various cyberspace arenas a number of standards, best-practices and guidelines have been developed. While adherence to an existing industry standard is not dispositive to the determination of reasonable care owed, it is relevant. Indeed, a given court could determine that a party was negligent and did not take reasonable security precautions even if the industry standard was met. Accordingly, although implementation of IP traceback technology is not yet an industry custom, the availability of the AST technology may help determine a new standard of reasonable care owed to protect customer data from intruders. Of course, other factors would also be relevant, such as the cost of using the technology, the availability of alternative technologies and any evidence of problems with the technology (e.g., security breaches in networks using IP traceback methods).

Another approach would be for the federal or State government to allow plaintiffs to sue manufacturers under various product liability laws. This has not occurred at the federal level.

The second question regarding liability issues for hosting a DDoS attacker poses a more difficult challenge. No court has thus far held an ISP liable for the actions of its users. Most cases involving ISP liability have involved questions of copyright and trademark infringement or responsibility for offensive content posted on the Internet. In fact, many of the court decisions find that ISPs are statutorily immune from liability for the actions of their customers under, for example, the Communications Decency Act. The Communications Decency Act states that "no provider or user of an interactive computer service shall be treated as the publisher or speaker of any information provided by another information content provider."

Do ISPs enjoy the same protection in the case of security breaches by intruders that harm ISP customers? While it may seem a stretch to extend the Communications Decency Act to this area, at least one court has already done so. In *Green v. America Online, Inc.*, 318 F.3d at 471 (3rd Cir. 2003) the court extended the language of the Communications Decency Act to a "punter" program. The court first "not[ed] that the dictionary includes 'signal' as a definition of 'information'," and it then asserted that the punter program was in fact a signal; therefore, it was information.

The current approach of some courts to provide immunity is consistent with the way ISPs view their role. Universally, ISPs take the position that they are only providing a "pipe" through which customers connect and information flows. Additionally, most ISPs have a "Terms of Use" agreement with their customers in which the customer agrees not to engage in certain prohibited or criminal activities. In *Green v. America Online, Inc.*, the court held that an ISP was not liable for the actions of two of its subscribers, including posting offensive messages about the plaintiff in a chat room. The *Green* opinion was in line with a 1997 ruling from the 4th Circuit in *Zeran v. America Online, Inc.*, 129 F.3d 328 (4th Cir. 1997). The court in *Zeran* ruled that the defendant was not liable for damages caused by the defamatory messages posted by an unidentified third party. In *Noah v. AOL Time Warner*, 261 F. Supp.2d 532 (E.D. Va. 2003), the district court held that a "chat room" was not a place of public accommodation under the Civil Rights Act and that the ISP was not liable for defamatory messages posted in the chat room.

Aside from the limited amount of firm case law, new distinctions in terminology will certainly impact on future regulatory issues. In *Nat'l Cable & Telecomm. Assoc. v. Brand X Internet Serv.*, 125 S.Ct. 2688, 2711-12 (2005), the Supreme Court held that broadband cable companies provided "information services" rather than "telecommunication services." This means that cable companies, functioning as ISPs, are not common carriers, yet telecommunication companies, which function as ISPs, are common carriers and subject to regulation under the Telecommunications Act of 1996. While the Telecommunications Act focuses almost exclusively on rates of service and interchange between carriers, any future legislation that affects one industry, should be carefully worded to include both telecommunication and information providers.

In a DDoS attack, the actual attacker is the immediate wrongdoer, but courts may extend liability to other tortfeasors who have contributed to the attacks. The most common civil action following a DDoS cyberattack will most likely be under a negligence theory of some sort. In this vein, an emerging negligence theory is the so-called "Encourage Free Radicals" (EFR) doctrine. The EFR doctrine preserves the liability of an original tortfeasor if the second tortfeasor is a "free radical" and the case exhibits factors that influence the courts to hold the original tortfeasor liable for encouraging free radicals. Mark Grady, the originator of the doctrine, describes free radicals as "those individuals who are shielded from liability by anonymity, insufficient assets, lack of mental capacity, or a lack of good judgment." Cyber criminals clearly fit the description of free radicals because they are judgment-proof, elusive and protected by anonymity. Cyberterrorists, in particular DDoS attackers, exemplify free radicals because their judgment is blinded by ideological or religious motivations. Additionally, a DDoS attacker spoofs or hides the true origin of the attack, making identification of the attacker difficult.

The second factor necessary for applying the EFR doctrine is that the original tortfeasor's encouragement of the free radical constituted negligent behavior. Liability in a negligence action requires that the victim of a DDoS prove: (1) that the defendant had a duty to the plaintiff to take reasonable care to avoid the attack or reduce its risk; (2) that defendant breached this duty; (3) that the breach was the actual and legal cause of the attack; and (4) that the breach resulted in actual harm. While courts have not explicitly identified a duty of care for Internet cybersecurity a willingness to recognize such a duty is developing. For instance, some courts have recognized that in certain circumstances a failure to apply a security patch constitutes a breach of duty. The AST system is a logical and cost-effective precaution to protect against DDoS because if implemented by ISPs, it operates as a central element of the ISP's information security protocol by mitigating or preventing the attack and resulting damage.

The court will consider other factors in holding the original tortfeasor liable for damage caused to third parties by encouraging free radicals. These factors include such things as whether the defendant (ISP) by lax cybersecurity measures, created an opportunity for the free radical; whether the free radical's behavior was foreseeable; whether the foreseeable harm was serious; the deliberateness of the defendant's behavior; and whether a special relationship existed between the defendant, the third party victim, or both (a defendant who encourages a free radical through a nonfeasance as opposed to a misfeasance will not be liable unless there was a special relationship). The court also factors in the seriousness of the harm as measured by the economic impact of the cyber attack.

While the law is currently in the early stages of development, ISPs and others need to anticipate developments and implement risk management strategies for cyber attacks. Clearly, advancements in DDoS fighting technologies will shape the future of ISP tort liability.

Another statute warranting attention in the context of the AST and other new cybersecurity tools is the federal Support Anti-Terrorism by Fostering Effective Technologies Act (SAFETY Act). The SAFETY Act provides a legal liability shield to designated anti-terrorism technologies thereby encouraging the adoption of innovative technologies that will help protect cyberspace. Under the terms of the SAFETY Act, "sellers" of a technology that would "be effective in facilitating the defense against acts of terrorism, including technologies that prevent defeat or respond to such acts" can petition the Secretary of Homeland Security to designate the technology as a Qualified Anti-Terrorism Technology (QATT). Specifically, the sellers of "any product, equipment, service, device, or technology designed, developed, modified, or procured for the specific purpose of preventing, detecting, identifying, or deterring acts of terrorism" can apply for government certification from DHS. Once the Secretary has certified that the proposed "goods" conform to the seller's specifications, a rebuttable presumption is established that can "only be overcome by evidence showing that the seller acted fraudulently or with willful misconduct in submitting information to the Secretary during the course of the Secretary's consideration of such technology." A cybersecurity technology certified as a QATT, means that any liability actions regarding the use of the QATT must be brought in federal court. The SAFETY Act also restricts the legal claim to actual damages, removing punitive or exemplary damages from the claim.

Furthermore, the SAFETY Act approach departs from the government contractor's defense set out in *Boyle v. United Technologies Corp*, where the private party contractor obtained immunity only if it conformed to the "government's specifications." Not only does the SAFETY Act provide the designer of a QATT certified technology the ability to raise a government contractor defense (which absolves the manufacturer of liability outright), but it actually departs from the criteria that such a defense can only be raised in products liability where the product was developed and manufactured according to government contract and specifications required by such contract. Again, the SAFETY Act standard is simply that the goods conform to the seller's specifications. This presumption may only be rebutted by a showing of evidence that the seller acted fraudulently or with willful misconduct in submitting information to the Secretary during the QATT application process. Moreover, it should be noted that this presumption follows the QATT no matter where the customer is located. Therefore, the defense would be viable in situations where the technology was sold to non-federal government customers, in addition to instances where the federal government is the customer.

Finally, sellers of QATTs are required to obtain liability insurance for themselves, "contractors, subcontractors, suppliers, vendors, customers of the seller" and vendors of those customers. Thus, if the AST, or any new cybersecurity technology, could be certified as a QATT, potential customers would certainly be more inclined to adopt the technology.

At a minimum, technology developers, manufacturers and owner/operators should ensure that they craft judicious licensing agreements or terms of service agreements that make clear to potential customers the following: (1) they (ISPs in particular) are not liable for the actions of third parties which result in damages; (2) they will use network monitoring technologies for performance and security purposes; and (3) they reserve the right to terminate connections that threaten their customers. Acceptance of such an agreement could signify approval of the technology's use.

From a defensive perspective, the issue of liability to customers in the context of safeguarding private information and securing networks against cyber attack is of great concern. Unfortunately, from a legal perspective, because of the rapid pace at which technological developments occur, the law in this area is substantially behind.

8.7 Conclusion

America's technological advances in cyber technology are unmatched. As often is the case, however, a country's greatest strength can also prove to be a critical weakness. America's dependency on the cyber world opens new vulnerabilities to a different type of terrorist attack. A cyber attack can target an actual computer networking system that can cripple a critical infrastructure. It can also manifest itself in a conventional explosive attack on physical structures. Former FBI Director Louis Freech claimed that "the FBI believes cyber-terrorism, the use of cyber-tools to shut down, degrade, or deny critical national infrastructures, such as energy, transportation, communications, or government services, for the purpose of coercing or intimidating a government or civilian population, is clearly an emerging threat."

The use of ICSs and SCADAs to digitize and automate almost every aspect of the workings of electric utilities; chemical, gas, and oil refineries; public transportation; or hospital services makes them a tempting target for cyber terrorists who desire to cripple some component(s) of the nation's critical infrastructure. Since American ICS and SCADA systems are designed for efficiency not security—SCADAs are predominately linked to the Internet—the opportunity for a significant cyber attack is greatly enhanced. Making ICS and SCADA systems safe and secure is further frustrated by the absence of a strong federal strategy that mandates information sharing and cybersecurity standards. In addition, the widespread technical ignorance of security managers and the false sense of security due to the absence of a major cyberterrorist incident on America's infrastructure contribute to the vulnerability equation. The threats can come from hostile foreign nations, terror groups, hackers, criminal organizations, and embittered inside employees. The impact can include massive human casualties, wide-scale economic damage, wide-scale disruption to public order, and significant disruption of national readiness for war.

The cyber threat must be met with the same recognition and gravity as a physical terrorist attack. In order to secure the nation against cyberterrorism, security officials must not be lured into believing that terrorist organizations, such as al-Qa'eda, lack the necessary equipment and knowledge needed to implement such an attack. Top al-Qa'eda officials have already expressed their intent to attack the American economy and infrastructures by using the Internet. Al-Qa'eda suicide bombers routinely depend on the Internet for training and tactical support for terror operations; the migration from the physical world to the cyber world has already begun. It is only a matter of time before a computer savvy jihadist will deal a devastating blow to the United States.

The United States must heed these warnings. A valuable tool in this effort is the USA PATRIOT Act coupled with the general framework set out by the National Strategy to Secure Cyberspace. In order to thwart future attacks, law enforcement must have the legal ability to gather information on suspected terrorists. Still, cyber security has not benefited from the increase in dollars seen elsewhere in homeland security. Partnering the private industry with the government is in its infancy but it is imperative that long-term research and development be encouraged. Eventually, the government may be forced to implement programs to ensure that private industry shares information and develops security systems. Unfortunately, the complacent habit of dealing only with realized threats has not imparted a sense of urgency that will ultimately be necessary to protect the cyber world. The government must work so that in the upcoming years the cyber world is as safe a place as the physical world.

8.8 Questions for Discussion

1. *Applying the "terrorism" label to a cyber attack.* In *R v. Boden*, The Supreme Court of Queensland in Australia upheld 20 of the 26 convictions that Vitek Boden was sentenced to for his cyber attacks on the SCADA system of an Australian water and sewage treatment plant in the year 2000. 2002 WL 969399 (QCA), [2002] QCA 16. In his appeal, Boden contended that he was not a terrorist, but a disgruntled ex-employee, and the severe sentencing he received hurt his future marketability in the workplace. Boden was not found to have had any known connections to a terrorist organization. Does the fact Boden was a disgruntled ex-employee mean he should have been granted leniency? Was Boden a terrorist?

2. *Developing new tools to fight cyber attacks.* Locating the source of a DDoS attack is important for purposes of criminal prosecution, deploying effective countermeasures and development of new defense tools. Southwest Research Institute (SwRI) and CIAS are partnered on a project to develop an automated IP traceback solution to combat DDoS attacks. Although the IP Traceback concept faces additional challenges such as the need for cooperation among Internet Service Providers (ISPs) and the future potential for government regulation, there are legal concerns as well. What specific legal issues should the project's managers be concerned with? Why?

3. *Open Government laws.* What impact could each State's Open Government laws have on restricting or prohibiting private industry from taking measures to protect themselves from a cyberterrorism attack?

Selected Bibliography

Cyberspace Policy Review (May 2009)

Grady, Mark F. *Proximate Cause Decoded*, 50 UCLA L. REV. 293 (2002).

Johnson, Vincent R. *Cybersecurity, Identity Theft, and the Limits of Tort Liability*, 57 SOUTH CARO-
   LINA L. REV. 255 (2005).

Krim, Jonathan. *U.S. Goals Solicited on Software Security; Task Force Suggests Limited Regulation.*
   WASH. POST, 7. Apr. 2, 2003, at E2.

Malcolm, John. *Virtual Threat, Real Terror: Cyberterrorism in the 21st Century.* Testimony of the
   Deputy Assistant Attorney General John G. Malcolm on Cyberterrorism, Senate Judiciary Committee, Subcommittee on Terrorism, Technology and Homeland Security, February 24, 2004.

McLemore, David. *On the Cyberterror Front Lines San Antonio Carving a Niche by Helping Protect
   Vital Systems,* DALLAS MORNING NEWS, Sept. 21, 2003, at A31.

Pollitt, Mark. *Cyberterrorism: Fact or Fancy?* PROCEEDINGS OF THE 20TH NATIONAL INFOR-
   MATION SYSTEMS SECURITY CONFERENCE. October 1997, at 285–289.

Rollins, John, and Clay Wilson. *Terrorist Capabilities for Cyberattack: Overview and Policy Issues.*
   CRS Report RL33123. Oct. 20, 2005.

Stohs, Brett. *Protecting the Homeland Exemption: Why the Critical Infrastructure Information Act of
   2002 will Degrade the Freedom of Information Act*, BERKELEY TECHNOLOGY L. J. (Summer
   2003).

Verton, Dan. BLACK ICE: THE INVISIBLE THREAT OF TERRORISM, 2003.

Zatko, Peiter. *Inside the Insider Threat*, COMPUTER WORLD, June 10, 2004.

Chapter 9

Terrorism Avoidance

Before we bring all the U.S. troops and all the coalition troops out of here [Afghanistan]…we must set conditions that prevent a reintroducing of the sorts of people that caused us to be standing where you and I are standing right now.

—General Tommy Franks

Apart from the fact that the United States emerged from the Cold War as the sole remaining super-power, a promising by-product of the disintegration of the Communist dictatorship was the addition of dozens of nascent democracies into the community of nations. At the time, little thought was given to the long-term effect of this phenomenon. Nevertheless, some recognized very quickly that the world was more secure, not only because an evil system of government had been swept into the dust bin of history, but because it witnessed a series of new governments that earnestly wanted to embark on the road to democracy. Strongly advocating the need for the "world community" to foster the develop-ment of these new and struggling democracies, the Director of the Center for International Studies at New York University School of Law noted the utopian ideal: "The world will certainly miss the boat if it does not use the end of the cold war to create a global system for the new millennium, one which preserves peace, fosters economic growth, and prevents the deterioration of the human physical and environmental condition." Other scholars were happy to settle on advancing a very simple truth in both war and terrorism avoidance. As previously noted, this truth was best summed up in the words of Anthony Lake: "[D]emocracies tend not to wage war on each other and they tend not to support terror-ism—in fact, they don't. They are more trustworthy in diplomacy and they do a better job of respecting the environment and human rights of their people." Can the War on Terror result in a similar shift? Are the winds of freedom poised to fan across the Arab world? This hopeful theme was the heart and soul of the Bush Administration's war aims. President Bush best summed up this ideal in his second Inaugural Address in 2005: "The best hope for peace in our world is the expansion of freedom in all the world."

Although it is true that the Islamic and Arab community of nations are plagued with non-democratic governments, it is erroneous to label that corner of the globe as a monolithic conglomerate of countries that embrace the radical Nazi-like totalitarianism of Iran, Syria, and the virtual-State of the al-Qa'eda movement. In addition, it is equally erroneous to assume that the vast majority of people who live under the tyranny of these dictatorships do so with any welcomed degree of loyalty or enthusiasm. In the words of former Secretary of State Condoleezza Rice: "We reject the condescending view that freedom will not grow in the soil of the Middle East—or that Muslims somehow do not share in the desire to be free." Basic denials of human rights are not a matter of "cultural heritage." Given the choice between freedom and dictatorial rule, rational humans—those who have not been brainwashed in "Hitler youth camps"—will always choose freedom. This basic truth was demonstrated with the fall of the Taliban regime. Even without a viable frame of reference for what democracy really entails, the common people of Afghanistan enthusiastically welcomed the promise of liberation and freedom. Over 1.8 million Afghans have returned since the fall of the Taliban, the largest movement in thirty years. The window of opportunity, then, centers on the hope that as dictatorships fall in the War on Terror, they will be replaced with something better. This certainly is the ultimate goal in Afghanistan and Iraq.

The international community, especially the well-established democracies led by the United States, has a critical role to perform in the promotion of democratic values and human rights. The task of promoting genuine democratic standards of behavior in whatever new governments take hold will not be a simple undertaking. In far too many instances, forces of intolerance—ethnic, nationalistic, racial, and religious—permeate both the new governments and the societies from which they are formed. For instance, the new government in Iraq may desire the concepts associated with democracy, but a general pattern of ethnic and sectarian fragmentation has introduced an escalating and often uncontrollable level of disorder and violence. Thus, if America and the international community do not find a realistic way to promote and foster at least the most fundamental categories of democratic values and human rights, the flames of terrorism and aggressive war will burn bright once again. Totalitarianism always stands hungrily at the door of freedom.

9.1 The Causes of Aggression and Terrorism
The most troubling aspect of all in addressing terrorism and war avoidance begins with the question of what causes people, or more precisely governments, to commit gross violations of human rights and unlawful violence. Clearly, this is a critical issue as it is directly related to the attendant matter of how to best halt terrorism and aggression. Thus, the question becomes whether there is a way to rid the planet of these scourges apart from the use of armed force.

In reviewing the human experience of the last six thousand years, one could list a host of factors related to a country's use of aggression against both its own people and its neighbors to include such things as religious conflict, ethnic strife, territorial disputes, population pressures, and competition for limited resources. While all of these external factors may be catalysts for aggression, any discussion that fails to examine the basic nature of man can never capture more than a part of the real truth. Biblical theologians such as the late R. B. Thieme, Jr., often stressed that the root of the matter centers on the makeup of Man, a morally flawed being: "In our beings are all the seeds of great conflicts." Holocaust victim Anne Frank also amplified this point in her diary:

I don't believe that the big men, the politicians and the capitalists alone, are guilty of war. Oh no, the little man is just as guilty, otherwise the peoples of the world would have risen in revolt long ago. There's in people simply an urge to destroy, an urge to kill, to murder and rage, and until all mankind, without exception, undergoes a great change, wars will be waged, everything that has been built up, cultivated, and grown will be destroyed and disfigured, after which mankind will have to begin all over again.

Moreover, nations are made up of people. The troubles of the world are not beamed onto earth from some hostile alien force. Since violations of the rule of law in terms of aggression and terrorism are generally associated with corresponding human lusts for power and approbation, one must put the responsibility for violations not only on the external factors created by Man, but on the darker angles of mankind itself. Although numerous excuses are always voiced by the perpetrator, violations are ultimately a reflection of the problems that rest inside each individual, who, according to the basic tenets of every major religion, is morally flawed. Thus, the question of what causes a person to commit a *malum in se* crime can be asked collectively of a government that engages in a consistent pattern of aggression and human rights violations.

On the individual level, observations about the sinister side of some societies strongly reinforce the Judeo-Christian doctrine of the total depravity of Man. However, the view that there will always be aggressive warfare and terrorism in the world, like crime in society, is only partially correct. Crime on the national level and aggressive violence on the international level can be controlled. The concept of the total depravity of Man voiced by Anne Frank applies primarily to theological questions, e.g., the mechanics of salvation. The concept does not mean that mankind is in a state of total helplessness and wickedness *vis-à-vis* other people. On the contrary, operating under the principles of freedom and self-determination, freedom-oriented peoples have come together to form national entities so that they might produce the by-products of privacy, justice, and economic prosperity.

Under such a model, nation-states have prospered and flourished, but only to the extent that they have recognized the collateral need to protect those rights on interior and exterior lines. On interior lines, States must recognize the legitimate functions of a police and judicial system to punish criminal behavior; on exterior lines, nation-states must recognize the need for a strong military establishment to protect the nation from the aggressive behavior of dictatorships and international terrorism.

Objectively, much of what we know about the nature of governments created by Man comes from the record of our histories, records written in streams of blood. For example, to observe that various governments have engaged in horrendous acts of aggression against their own people and others simply describes their behavior, but only partially explains it. In fact, no one has ever satisfactorily explained why certain societies—ancient Assyria, Soviet Russia, Nazi Germany, North Vietnam, Communist China, or Saddam's Iraq—turned into aggressive war machines that committed murderous human rights violations against their own people and engaged in war with neighboring countries.

What has been established are the characteristics of those nations that have a high propensity for engaging in aggressive war, terrorism, and human rights abuses. National Security law expert and Director of the Center for National Security Law, Professor John Norton Moore, argues that totalitarian regimes like the Taliban and Saddam's Iraq are considerably more likely to resort to aggressive violence than democracies. Professor Moore terms this phenomenon the "radical regime" syndrome:

A radical totalitarian regime…seems to blend together a mixture of a failing centrally planned economy, severe limitations on economic freedom, a one-party political system, an absence of an independent judiciary, a police state with minimal human rights and political freedoms at home, a denial of the right to emigrate, heavy involvement of the military in political leadership, a large percentage of the GNP devoted to the military sector, a high percentage of the population in the military, leaders strongly motivated by an ideology of true beliefs including willingness to use force, aggressively anti-Western and antidemocratic in behavior, and selective support for wars of national liberation, terrorism, and disinformation against Western or democratic interests.

Tyrants seek the destruction of freedom loving people. Some, like the Taliban and current Iranian regime, cloak themselves in radicalized versions of Islam; others, like Saddam's Iraq and the current regime in Syria, have no driving religious affiliation. All of these regimes are linked, however, by a common bond of hate, power lust, and aggression to gain, maintain, and extend power. Human rights, the rule of law, capitalism, and civilian control of the military are alien concepts to totalitarian governments because the freedom inherent in these concepts cannot coexist with tyranny.

9.2 Religion and the War on Terror

Some have tried to depict the War on Terror as a war against all of Islam. This is simply not true. The War on Terror is a term that is generally used to describe the ongoing armed conflict against a select group of fanatics that embrace a highly radicalized Islam—a view of Islam that encourages and directs aggressive violence against the United States of America as well as all who do not share their militant jihadism. In 1996, Osama bin Laden, the founder of al-Qa'eda, issued his first declaration that he was at war with the United States. After listing a rambling series of so-called grievances against the "Zionist-Crusaders," he stated:

The walls of oppression and humiliation cannot be demolished except in a rain of bullets. The freeman does not surrender leadership to infidels and sinners. My Muslim Brothers of the World: Your brothers in Palestine and in the land of the two Holy Places are calling upon your help and asking you to take part in fighting against the enemy—your enemy and their enemy—the Americans and the Israelis.

As even the novice student of history knows, the relationship between religion and war has existed for a very long time. A brief review of human history reveals that various individuals, groups, and nations have wrongfully used religious dogma as a pretext to engage in aggression against others. For instance, reflecting the idea that God was on their side, the Nazis in World War II issued a metallic military belt buckle to their infantry that was stamped with the phrase: Gott Mit Uns ("God With Us"). Accordingly, it is no surprise that the Islamic radicalism that fuels the War on Terror employs what it calls the "true" Moslem religion in order to cloak a lust for domination through despicable expressions of unlawful violence, primarily targeting innocent civilians (Muslims, Christians, and Jews). In short, al-Qa'eda-styled militants claim that their religious beliefs justify the use of illegal and aggressive violence.

On the other hand, when it comes to confronting the forces of al-Qa'eda-styled aggression, it is not surprising that democracies like the United States of America will also employ religious ideology, i.e.,

Christianity, and other religious symbolism to support the necessary use of force in self-defense. However, despite the fact that all American presidents, to include George W. Bush, have invoked religious themes in time of war, the use of religion in this context is generally subordinate to the more predominant and commonsense themes of self-defense and national patriotism.

When Karl Marx (1818-1883) wrote that religion is the "opium of the people," he was referring to the fact that religion has long been used by those in power to control the social, political, and cultural behavior of the masses, with little or no concern for the content or validity of the underlying theological principles. Indeed, to any serious student of history, there is no question that the psychological forces associated with religion have played a powerful role in controlling and channeling human behavior across a broad spectrum, even to the point where monstrous horrors have been committed in the name of God. People of all religions are guilty. This does not mean that the religion itself is at fault; only the people that have used (or misused) the religion are at fault.

In general terms, all of the major religions discourage the use of aggressive violence, to include terrorism; the moral codes of all religions are the same. Clearly, the basic themes of the various religious beliefs are not the problem. Even without religion, groups intent on aggression and terror would find some excuse to justify their unlawful use of violence.

In the current War on Terror, various individuals and groups have engaged in aggressive violence against innocent civilians in the name of Islam. The response by the United States has taken the form of the use of violence in self-defense, but has generally not been cloaked in any specific religious ideology. Paradoxically, the voices in the West that have most loudly employed religious beliefs in this context have been those that seek to tie Christianity with pacifism. In their search for the panacea of universal brotherhood, these voices intentionally blur the difference between lawful and unlawful uses of force. While voices of restraint, proportionality, and negotiation must always be considered in the equation of responding to aggression, the use of lawful force under the rule of law must remain as a primary option. Just as it is wrong that al-Qa'eda-styled terrorists and the dictators that harbor them murder in the name of religion, it is wrong to ignore or excuse these voices of appeasement who cry out in the name of religion (see Chapter 10.2 and 10.4).

Like many words, the term "religion" is subject to a variety of meanings. According to the American Heritage College Dictionary, the most ordinary definition would mean "[b]elief in and reverence for a supernatural power or powers regarded as creator and governor of the universe," but it also means, "[a] set of beliefs, values, and practices based on the teachings of a spiritual leader." Interestingly, however, a generalized comparative study of the world's major religions reveals that one can actually subdivide the term into two categories—"works-religion" and "grace-religion."

Each day, around the world, there are those who begin and end their day by turning to the "sacred" writings of their religious traditions for comfort and guidance, understanding, and enlightenment. In the brief sojourn of mankind, seven major world religions have arisen and set out their beliefs in writing. These works are Hinduism's *Bhagavad Gita*, Judaism's *Tanakh*, Confucianism's *Analects*, Taoism's *Tao Te Ching*, Buddhism's *Dhammapada*, Christianity's *New Testament,* and Islam's *Koran.*

Religious books are not texts for the study of life sciences, but rather books that claim to be about God and His plan and purpose for mankind. In this regard, Hindus, Jews, Confucians, Taoists, Buddhists, Christians, and Muslims each claim that their book best reveals God(s) and offers the better—or, in some cases, the only—answer to the meaning of life. Such being the case, critics ask how it is possible to know which religion, if any, is correct. This, of course, sums up the real intellectual challenge associated with religion and raises the most profound question one can ask: What is the truth?

Surprisingly, a predominating factor one encounters in studying this matter revolves around an astonishing amount of apathy; most people simply have no desire to challenge themselves to even frame the question: which religion is true? Content to incorporate as their own whatever religious belief system they were born into—no matter how illogical or ill-conceived—independent thinking and reasoning have little, if anything, to do with how the mass of humanity comes to personalize a religious belief. For instance, you are a Hindu for no other reason except that your parents were Hindus.

Still, people have free will, and in each generation there are those who find this follow-the-leader approach to religion wholly unsatisfactory. These are the *truth seekers*: men and women who base their personal religious beliefs not on the happenstance of their cultural birthright or other environmental factors (such as conversion due to marriage), but on a foundation which evaluates the full range of religious options and then makes an informed decision. Many would argue that for someone deeply concerned with truth, there is absolutely no subject more important to which the human mind can address itself. Unlike the infamous Pontius Pilate who disingenuously asked, "What is [the] truth?" and then refused to intellectually consider the answer, the truth-seeker is not discouraged by the fact that various world religions compete for consideration. Of necessity, truth should encourage honest scrutiny.

So what can be said about the origin of religion? As long as humans have looked out into the night sky, it seems apparent that some have set aside the obvious social and cultural forces associated with religion and given a great deal of careful thought about what constitutes the true nature of God. Accordingly, if one accepts the premise that God exists, it is entirely reasonable to assume two points. First, God makes sense. And second, He purposefully reveals Himself in a sensible fashion, in the language and culture of the particular time frame in which any human resides, to those individuals who desire to know Him. As R.B. Thieme notes, God does not "hide the ball" to the truth seeker.

Unfortunately, from a historical perspective, much of this God-directed activity towards people is difficult to chronicle, as the vast majority of the human experience in this regard has been based on oral traditions, leaving few traces of record. We can only say with certainty that archeological evidence associated with some of the earliest human sites unequivocally demonstrates that humans have always held some kind of belief in an afterlife. Therefore, meaningful information about God's revelations can only be found in the historic period of Man's sojourn, when people developed writing. This era did not begin until a mere 5,000 years ago in the Euphrates River valley. Since that time, seven major religions have emerged, each leaving written records to stand for consideration.

Anyone who has taken the time to engage in the study of comparative religion realizes that it is impossible to catalogue all the many variations and sub-groupings that reside in each of the major religions. Nevertheless, certain broad generalities can be drawn. Thus, apart from all the things that can be said about Hinduism, Buddhism, Confucianism, Taoism, Islam, Judaism, or Christianity, when one boils each of them down to their bottom lines—to their basic beliefs—there emerge four central themes that are shared as base commonalities:

(1) All religions agree that the nature of each human either is, or becomes, tainted with sin. Man is a morally flawed creature relative to God(s).
(2) All religions share a common moral code that reflects similar, if not identical, values for human behavior. For all practical purposes, the basic moral laws for how all members of any religion should behave are identical to the moral and ethical laws found in all other major religions and, for that matter, in any significant human social structure. It is a fundamental commonality that all religions prohibit the evils of murder, larceny, lying, brawling, and

hatred, while encouraging love, self-control, self-discipline, charity, and helping the less fortunate.

(3) All religions share a system of rituals designed to assist the adherent in some fashion associated with the belief system.

(4) All religions proclaim that the primary goal of the religion is for the human soul to obtain eternal union with God(s) or some other supreme sublime force in the afterlife.

The real issue that sharply and forever divides the major religions rests in the mechanics of how one fulfills the goal of obtaining this relationship with God under the fourth commonality above. In this regard, there are two, and only two, diametrically opposed answers to how this is achieved—(1) by a system of *human merit*, or (2) through a system of unmerited *grace*. Those religions that teach that the mechanics by which Man achieves eternal union are via human effort or works (human morality coupled with the performance of various rituals) are properly termed as *works-religion*. All religions except Christianity fall into the camp of works-religion. In contrast, Biblical Christianity rejects the concept that Man can achieve relationship with perfect God based on any system of morality, ritual, or human effort. Christianity holds that relationship with God is automatically and irrevocably achieved when one accepts the salvation work of Jesus Christ on the cross by a simple act of non-meritorious faith. Biblical Christianity is properly termed as *grace-religion*.

Islam is a works-religion. Islam was introduced into the Middle East in A.D. 622 by an Arab named Muhammad (570-632). Muhammad was born into the Koreish tribe in Mecca, in what is now Saudi Arabia. Although he was orphaned young and grew up poor and disadvantaged, Muhammad married a wealthy older widow and entered a life of ease at the age of 25. Freed from the need to work, Muhammad spent long hours in a mountain cave outside the city. Here he claimed to have received a series of revelations from Allah, the leading god worshipped in the polytheistic city of Mecca. Muhammad soon declared that Allah was the only god in existence and that all the other gods were false. An illiterate, Muhammad attracted a small band of followers to document everything he said. At the age of forty Muhammad began to preach in public, only to be greeted with skepticism and hostility by the ruling merchants of Mecca. Eventually, he was forced to flee about 300 miles to the rival city of Yathrib, later called Medina, where he raised an army of 10,000 warriors. After a series of battles between Medina and Mecca lasting several years, Muhammad took the city of Mecca by force and the surviving inhabitants converted to Islam. From Mecca, the new religion spread rapidly, primarily on the wings of military expansionism.

When Muhammad died in 632, he left behind a battle-hardened army, united as never before and ready to move into Europe. Muhammad's primary military chief, Abu Bakr (573-634), swiftly took control of the ever-expanding Islamic army and violently crushed all opposition to his claim as successor. Abu Bakr was the first caliph of Mecca and launched the Islamic forces on a blitzkrieg across Arabia, conquering region after region in the name of the new religion. By 710, the Arab Muslims had even entered Spain, only to be turned back from France by the Frankish ruler Charles Martel (688-741) and his knights at the Battle of Tours in 732.

Abu Bakr was also responsible for collecting all of the sayings of Muhammad and incorporating them into a book called the *Koran*. The *Koran*, more than any other item, is central to the Muslim religion. In order for the soul of the deceased to go to heaven or paradise, one must strictly follow the dictates of the *Koran*.

The religion is divided into Five Pillars of Islam and Six Pillars of Faith. The pillars focus on various rituals and beliefs that every Muslim must accept and perform. In general terms, to be a Muslim requires the following:

(1) One must confess the core Islamic beliefs in the proper manner, that Allah is god and that Muhammad the Prophet is his messenger: "*La ilaha illa Allah; Muhammad rasul Allah.*" Although Islam recognizes that there have been prophets before him (e.g., Moses and Jesus), Muhammad is the culmination and no legitimate prophets will succeed him. (Certain parts of the Old Testament and even limited aspects of the New Testament are accepted as valid.)

(2) One must pray in a particular manner that requires the faithful to prostrate himself in the direction of Mecca five times a day. A caller delivers the call to prayer from a tall tower, a symbol to all that the nation is strictly tied to a communion with god and to a social brotherhood.

(3) One must give money to the poor and to the religious organization in compliance with a set mathematical formula. The *Koran* is explicit on this matter; annually, two and one-half percent of the Muslim's property must be given to the poor.

(4) One must fast once a each year, during the month of Ramadan.

(5) One must go on a sacred pilgrimage; the greatest—required for all during their lifetime, if at all possible—is the trip to Mecca. The annual pilgrimage to Mecca is called the *Hajj*.

(6) One must take part in "holy" war, if required. The holy war concept can apply in the real sense of taking up arms against an enemy, but it also speaks of an inner spiritual cleansing of wicked thoughts and deeds. As such, the *Koran* lays down a meticulous code of moral and ethical behavior. Drinking intoxicants, gambling, larceny, lying, eating pork, and unlawful sexual relations (a man can be married to several wives) are just a few of the sins detailed in the *Koran*.

In conclusion, Muhammad founded a religion that prescribes an extremely strict moral, social, political, and legal code, coupled with a series of demanding rituals. Muhammad stressed that he was not divine; he was only a human whom God had chosen to be the messenger. His message was that one must strictly follow all of the Islamic moral laws and codes of behavior to pass muster at a final judgment where the follower will be evaluated as to whether or not he is deemed worthy enough to enter into heaven.

Of all the major religions, Christianity has the largest number of followers and is the most widespread. Christians claim a direct extension from Judaism, and the Christian Bible incorporates with its New Testament all of the books of the *Tanakh* (the Old Testament). The testimony of Christ's person and work is recorded in the New Testament, a series of documents written by either eyewitnesses or those directly associated with eyewitnesses, from A.D. 40 (the earliest estimate for the book of Matthew) to A.D. 100 (the latest estimate for the book of John). Although there are three major divisions—Roman Catholicism, Eastern Orthodoxy, and Protestantism—Christianity is a system of belief that begins and ends with the person of Jesus of Nazareth. Biblical Christianity holds that Jesus is the promised Messiah written about in the Old Testament—the Christ, the God/man—who, while suspended on a Roman cross, willingly bore God's judgment for all human sins. This unlimited atonement for each human's sin—past, present, and future—provides instantaneous and irrevocable salvation to any member of the human race who believes in Him, regardless of personal merit or worthiness in the past or future. Since entrance into a relationship with God in time and eternity requires only a single speck of non-meritorious faith alone in Christ alone, this central doctrine for salvation is called the "gospel" or good news.

Unlike other religions, whose founders could be entirely removed without destroying the noetic (intellectual) aspects of the religion, without the person and work of Jesus Christ, Christianity would cease to be. This is because the path set forth by Christianity to an eternal relationship with God (salvation) is not based on a system or formula of human works (morality, rituals, and so on) or philosophy, as all other types of works-religion dictate. Rather, it is based on the work of Jesus Christ while on the cross. R.B. Thieme encapsulates this point in his book, *The Plan of God*: "Biblical Christianity asserts that only the work of God through Jesus Christ provides the means of salvation and eternal relationship with God (John 8:12). Christianity proclaims God's way of salvation for the human race."

In the early years of Christianity, when the Roman persecution was heaviest, believers would use the symbol of the fish as a recognition sign. As an encapsulated illustration to what biblical Christians believe—then and now—the Greek letters that spell "fish" correspond to the words "Jesus Christ God's Son [the] Savior."

In Christianity, one's eternal relationship with God is based absolutely and solely on a single act of personal belief in the redeeming work of the God/man Jesus Christ on the death-cross where He suffered "spiritual death" and became the substitute sacrifice for mankind's sin. Since Jesus Christ was the perfect God/man, He was qualified to bear the sins of the world and provide salvation to all who believe. This grace policy excludes all human merit as a means of salvation and thus stands in sharp contrast to all of the other major religions. Ephesians 2:8-9: "For by grace are you saved through faith; and that not of yourselves, it is the gift of God: Not of works lest any man should boast."

Although the grace system of belief revealed in Christianity is totally antithetical to the works formula for salvation found in the other world religions, the concept of human morality and works as a vehicle to gain the approbation of God is a constant plague to Christian doctrine. To be sure, Christians are commanded to follow the moral laws set out in the Bible, but this obligation is not a requirement for salvation. Salvation is appropriated freely based on a one-shot decision in a moment of time to believe in Christ. For example, when a Roman official asked what he had to do to be saved, the book of Acts records that Paul and Silas said: "Believe on the Lord Jesus Christ, and thou shalt be saved, and thy house [should also do the same]."

In his multi-volume work on systematic theology, Dr. Lewis Sperry Chafer, late president and professor of systematic theology at Dallas Theological Seminary, wrote:

> The idea that man will stand on a basis of personal worthiness has been the chief heresy, opposing the central doctrine of grace, from the time of Christ's death to the present hour. It so permeates the church that few who preach are able to exclude it from their attempts at gospel preaching. It is safe to say that wherever the element of human merit is allowed to intrude into the presentation of the plan of salvation, the message is satanic to that extent.

Thus, grace-religion is all that God is free to do for Man on the basis of the work of Jesus Christ on the cross. For Biblical Christians, grace is God's policy and plan. Works-religion is a progressive process; grace is non-meritorious and instantaneous.

In sum, regardless of the fact that Christianity and Islam are diametrically opposed as to the means of salvation, it is vitally important that the West understand that the War on Terror is not a religious conflict that pits Islam against Christianity. It is rather a war against religious fanatics who wrongfully invoke the Islamic religion as a justification for aggression. History has seen these fanatics many times before as they have pillaged and murdered in the name of the other major religions, to include Christianity. This generation of free people must squarely face the evil that confronts it. The War on Terror must be fought with the moral courage to employ legitimate and lawful force in the name of justice, not religion.

9.3 The New Paradigm for War and Terrorism Avoidance

Recognizing a nexus between the nation that mistreats its own citizens and the nation that fosters aggression against its neighbors, "[b]oth the preamble and Article 1 of the United Nations Charter make crystal clear that the drafters were under the impression that the unleashing of aggressive war occurred at the hands of those States in which the denial of the value...of the individual human being...was most evident." Furthermore, with the outstanding research of eminent scholars such as Professor Rudy Rummel, it is now possible to demonstrate numerically the validity of the proposition that totalitarian regimes are the chief abusers of human rights:

> War is not the most deadly form of violence. Indeed, I have found that while about 37,000,000 people have been killed in battle by all foreign and domestic wars in our century, government democide [genocide and mass murder] have killed over 148,074,000 more. Plus, I am still counting. Over 85 percent of these people were killed by totalitarian governments.

So, the new paradigm for war and terrorism avoidance is a very simplistic and common sense model: If democracies make better neighbors, *a fortiori*, it is certainly in the best interests of the United States to do all it can to foster democratic values and human rights in the other nations and to thereby enlarge respect for the rule of law in international relations. In the words of Professor B. Russett, "[D]emocracies have almost never fought each other....By this reasoning, the more democracies there are in the world, the fewer potential adversaries we and other democracies will have and the wider the zone of peace."

All can understand the simplicity of Russett's argument. In fact, Professor Moore firmly believes this simple fact represents a "new and more accurate paradigm about war, peace, and democide." It replaces the old thinking of peace through appeasement and rubricates the only hope for reducing the threat of weapons of mass murder, terrorism, and human rights abuse. Appeasement leads to more aggression. This view is further amplified by a RAND study:

> The failure of regimes to provide for peaceful political change and the phenomenon of economies unable to keep pace with population growth and demands for more evenly distributed benefits can provide fertile ground for extremism and political violence affecting U.S. interests. For this reason, the United States has a stake in promoting political and economic reform as a means of reducing the potential for terrorism, some of which, as in Latin America, the Middle East, and the Gulf, may be directed at us.

Unfortunately, the paradigm seems to be extremely difficult to propagate. In part, this is because democratic ideals are not spread through the use of force—of fire and sword—so that windows of opportunity for change generally only appear in the aftermath of the collapse of a totalitarian regime.

This occurred in the Axis powers of Germany, Italy, and Japan following World War II and then again with the end of the Cold War in the former territories of the Soviet Union. In addition, the paradigm is difficult to advance because people in democracies are often lulled into complacency and apathy about the horrendous conditions of fellow humans on the planet. They forget the truth that democracies are far better systems of government than any other. To borrow a phrase from the British novelist Rebecca West: "The trouble with man is twofold; he cannot learn those truths that are too complicated and he forgets those truths that are too simple." The realization that democracies do not engage in terrorism or aggressive war is clearly a "simple truth" that must be reinforced at every turn.

In the War on Terror, the United States needs to accelerate efforts to encourage the full development of any fledgling democracy under the truism that democracies do not wage war or allow terrorism to flourish. If the RAND study is correct, this strategy will go far in reducing the root causes of terrorism.

The primary criterion for winning the War on Terror, then, must concentrate on a realistic examination and application of this simple, yet powerful, formula, a formula related directly to the enhancement of United States' interests as it addresses the long-term goal of curtailing the aggressive use of force. In fact, the truism about the behavior of democracies is predicated upon United States' interests; in no way does it pit American domestic interests against issues of international concern. In the context of either peace or deterrence, they are one and the same.

If one accepts the paradigm as valid, three issues immediately arise. First, what precisely are the values associated with democracy? Second, are these values merely a Western ethnocentric assertion of power over other non-democratic nations or are they self-evident truths? Third, what is the best way to promote these values?

9.4 Defining Democratic Values and Democracy

In 1788, Massachusetts adopted a State Bill of Rights which proclaimed: "A frequent recurrence to fundamental principles is absolutely necessary to preserve the blessings of liberty and to maintain a free government." These fundamental principles generally refer to all of those basic rights associated with democratic forms of government and are best encapsulated in the Constitution's Bill of Rights approved by Congress in 1789 and ratified in 1791.

Before America stood up as a republic, early Western scholars such as John Locke, David Hume, Adam Smith, Baron de Montesquieu, and Jean-Jacques Rousseau wrote extensively on the subject of "civic humanism" or "natural rights" and the proper function of government in relation to the citizen. These scholars agreed with the premise that individuals came together to form national entities so that the individual could, within the framework of a government, better protect and advance his inherent rights to life, liberty, and property.

Contrary to the practice of the majority of the countries of their day, men like Rousseau claimed that Man "is born free" but "is everywhere in chains." These men pointed out that the government was formed to be the guardian of basic human freedoms, not the usurper. For instance, in his *Second Treatise of Government*, John Locke wrote: "The legislative or supreme authority cannot assume to itself a power to rule by extemporary, arbitrary decrees, but is bound to dispense justice, and to decide the rights of the subject by promulgated, standing laws, and known authorized judges."

The writings of these early scholars had a tremendous impact on the American rebels of 1776. Faced with the task of articulating a moral justification for their armed secession against the colonial rule of Great Britain, Thomas Jefferson and others were obliged to carefully translate Locke's natural rights into legal and enforceable rights. Apart from properly dealing with the continued evil of human servitude, which most assumed would die a natural death within a few decades, the American drafters were largely successful. In their Declaration of Independence to the British Crown, they declared that the individual, simply by virtue of his God-given being, possessed the "right to life, liberty, and the pursuit of happiness." The Declaration of Independence's powerful opening showed that the framers were not inventing out of whole cloth the ideas and ideals they embraced. The men who penned the Constitution and the Declaration of Independence were drawing on the wisdom of Biblical principles to bring together a proper balance between freedom and authority. Recognizing that freedom without authority is anarchy, and authority without freedom is tyranny, the Declaration of Independence proclaimed:

> We hold these truths to be self-evident, that all men are created equal, that they are endowed by their Creator with certain inalienable rights that among these are Life, Liberty, and the pursuit of Happiness. That to secure these rights, Governments are instituted among Men, deriving their just powers from the consent of the governed.

In two sentences, the framers laid out a fantastic manifesto that recognized the right of men exercising their God-given rights through a democratic government formed to protect the fundamental freedoms of its citizens. For the Americans, these rights were rooted in Divine providence which made them inalienable and morally justified ab initio. As Benjamin Franklin remarked at the Constitutional Convention in 1787, "I have lived, Sir, a long time, and the longer I live, the more convincing proofs I see of this truth: that God governs the affairs of men."

With their freedom purchased through six long years of bloodshed on the battlefield, the colonial Americans produced one of the most phenomenal documents in the history of mankind—the Constitution of the United States of America. The Constitution established a republican government operating under concepts which forever united the terms freedom and democracy. In the minds of many, the terms are synonymous. Understandably, when one speaks of the desirability of promoting "democratic values," this does not necessarily imply the adoption of a direct democracy as the ideal form of government.

In point of fact, the United States of America was created as a representative democracy, i.e., a republic; it is not a true direct democracy in the fashion of the ancient Greek city-states. The founding fathers were extremely careful in their choice of government. They rejected the concept of a pure democracy where all citizens have an equal and direct voice in government and chose instead a representative democracy. The framers restricted the franchise of participants and established three separate independent branches of government, with checks and balances, to ensure that the authority of the central government was truly limited. *Webster's Third New International Dictionary* defines a representative democracy as "a form of government in which the supreme power is vested in the people and exercised by them indirectly through a system of representation and delegated authority in which the people choose their officials and representatives at periodically held free elections...."

Tragically, inherent in every democracy rest the seeds which will ultimately destroy it, for the real power rests not in the structure of government but in the character of the people that make up the nation. Robert E. Lee, the great Confederate general and iconic symbol of all that is good about the South, once observed that when virtue is absent from a people, the nation will collapse. In other words, the freedoms and blessings associated with capitalism and free enterprise cannot function without virtue.

When the employer possesses virtue there is no need for workers to form unions because the boss will take better care of the wants and needs of the employees than any union ever could. In contrast, an employer without virtue will operate the company with selfish interests without regard to honesty and integrity. In turn, a worker with genuine virtue will work earnestly. Without virtue, a worker will produce little except slothfulness and deceit.

Virtue cannot be legislated, it must be taught in the home and reflected in the values of the society. In short, virtue can be defined as "doing a right thing in a right way." America, which once prided itself on the "Protestant work ethic," increasingly rejects so-called "family values," and instead looks to a central government to provide for its needs from the cradle to the grave. In tracing the life expectancy of great democracies, it is interesting to note the words of historian Alexander Fraser Tytler (1748–1813), who wrote about the decline and fall of the Athenian Republic. Tytler concluded:

A democracy cannot exist as a permanent form of government. It can only exist until the voters discover that they can vote themselves money from the public treasury. From that moment on, the majority always votes for the candidates promising the most benefits from the public treasury with a result that a democracy always collapses over loose fiscal policy always followed by dictatorship.

Considering that the United States of America is just over 200 years old, Mr. Tytler went on to develop a fascinating general trend in the rise and fall of the great nations. He wrote:

The average age of the world's greatest civilizations has been 200 years. These nations have progressed through the following sequence:

From bondage to spiritual faith;
From spiritual faith to courage;
From courage to liberty;
From liberty to abundance;
From abundance to selfishness;
From selfishness to complacency;
From complacency to apathy;
From apathy to dependency;
From dependency back to bondage.

If democratic principles do not always mesh with democracy as the best form of government, they certainly do equate to what Daniel Webster envisioned as "a state of society characterized by tolerance toward minorities, freedom of expression, and respect for the essential dignity and worth of the human individual with equal opportunity for each to develop freely to his fullest capacity in a cooperative community." It is certainly possible that a government that is honest, accountable, predictable, and efficient can conform to democratic principles and protect human rights. However, the modern era has demonstrated repeatedly that a representative democracy is best suited to produce democratic principles and is, therefore, the government of choice in reference to the paradigm for war and terrorism avoidance.

Still, governmental authority in a State may be vested in one person, a small group, a large group, or the entire body. Measured in the light of human rights and democratic principles, none of these systems are necessarily per se worse than any other; it is just that representative democracies have institutional safeguards (such as checks and balances on power) that can guarantee fundamental freedoms over a longer term.

For instance, the framers instituted three basic types of activities for the federal government. First, a system of checks and balances was established to ensure that the government fulfilled its obligation to protect the life, freedom, privacy, and property of law-abiding citizens. Second, laws were instituted to better regulate commercial and social disputes between individuals. And third, the government was asked to set up certain physical infrastructures to provide essential services that were beyond individual capabilities, such as providing for basic primary education, law enforcement, and a military establishment.

The factor that divides good government from bad government is in the degree to which the government allows the functioning of democratic principles under the framework of the law. Dictatorships have a pseudo "rule of law," but it is not based on principles of freedom. Accordingly, any so-called elections held in a totalitarian system can never be more than a cruel perversion of the concept. Clearly, a ruling system that provides its citizens with freedom of expression, peaceful assembly, a free market economy, and some degree of participation in government rests on democratic principles and a true rule of law. Thus, a monarchy, an aristocracy, or a representative democracy that rules for the common good of the citizen under democratic principles can each be positive manifestations of legitimate government. Other forms of government such as a tyranny or an oligarchy wield authority based solely on the self-interest of the ruling elite and refuse to embrace freedom.

In addressing the issue of writing democratic constitutions for the emerging democracies of Eastern Europe following the collapse of the Soviet Empire, Professor A. E. Dick Howard of the University of Virginia School of Law commented on this friction concerning what government is all about:

> The Bill of Rights of the United States Constitution declares what government may not do; it is what Justice Hugo Black once called a list of "thou shalt nots." The document reflects the view that the function of a bill of rights is to limit government's powers. Central and East European drafters have enlarged this meaning of "rights." A legacy of the twentieth-century notion of positive government, an age of entitlements, is bills of rights that declare affirmative rights. Such bills include, of course, the traditional negative rights, but they also spell out claims upon government, such as the right to an education, the right to a job, or the benefits of care in one's old age.

Forced equality through social engineering is the policy and propaganda of the totalitarian system. As Professor Howard discovered, many of the emerging democracies out of the former Soviet Union have still not shaken this old thinking. The true function of good government emphasizes freedom and self-determination which will always lead to varying degrees of social inequality. Faced with Lord Acton's often quoted truism that "power tends to corrupt, and absolute power corrupts absolutely," the government that adheres to principles of freedom and limited powers is much preferred. The siren song of "affirmative rights" for the people always leads to poverty and misery for the national entity.

But what if people want to choose a political system that denies fundamental freedoms? Coming out of the Nazi era, the post World War II German government was quick to address this question by enacting in their Basic Law a provision which holds that no citizen may use his freedom to destroy freedom. In other words, no political party that endorses non-democratic principles will be allowed to stand for office. At Article 21:

(1) Political parties shall participate In the formation of the political will of the people. They may be freely established. Their internal organization must conform to democratic principles. They must publicly account for their assets and for the source and use of their funds.

(2) Parties that, by reason of their aims or the behavior of their adherents, seek to undermine or abolish the free democratic basic order or to endanger the existence of the Federal Republic of Germany shall be unconstitutional. The Federal Constitutional Court shall rule on the question of unconstitutionality.

Indeed, once a totalitarian party takes office, it will abolish all systems of freedom because it is the antithesis of freedom. A recent historical example of this strange paradox—where an extremist party manages to win at the ballot box—is found in the Algerian experience. When the first round of balloting in December 1991 went to the radical Taliban-styled Islamic Salvation Front (better known by its French acronym FIS), the Algerian military intervened to stop the extremists from taking power. Understanding that the FIS would not endorse principles of freedom if they took power, the Algerian Army banned the FIS and supported the secular State apparatus. Showing their true colors, the FIS then accelerated a murder and terror campaign (their tactic of choice was to slit the throat of anyone who did not agree with the Islamic movement) against the civilian population, resulting in the murder of nearly 200,000 people. Fortunately, the FIS's armed wing, the so-called Islamic Salvation Army, disbanded in January of 2000 and Algerians elected President Abdelaziz Bouteflika shortly thereafter. Although much remains to be done, President Boutelflika's Charter for Peace and National Reconciliation put the nation on the road to democratic reforms.

In the modern era, the terms democratic principles and fundamental freedoms have been joined by the concept of human rights. The report of the June 1993 World Conference on Human Rights, held in Vienna and attended by 171 States, defined the relationship between democracy, fundamental freedoms, and human rights as follows:

Democracy, development, and respect for human rights and fundamental freedoms are interdependent and mutually reinforcing. Democracy is based on the freely expressed will of the people to determine their own political, economic, social and cultural systems and their full participation in all aspects of their lives....The international community should support the strengthening and promoting of democracy, development and respect for human rights and fundamental freedoms in the entire world.

Finally, since some wrongly criticize the concept of democracy as a Western value, it may be more appropriate to speak to the world politic in terms of the normative concept of human rights. Human rights evoke a more inclusive standard, which can apply to all the peoples and nations of the world. As a practical matter, of course, there is no difference between democratic values and basic human rights.

9.5 Origins of Human Rights

When the framers of the Constitution wrote about the Law of Nations, they were addressing those principles of international law that governed State-to-State contacts. At most, the individual was viewed only as an object in the process. As recently as sixty years ago, the leading treatise on international law reflected the absence of a legal recognition of the issue of international human rights. International law scholar Lassa Oppenheim wrote: "[A]part from obligations undertaken by treaty, a State is entitled to treat both its own nationals and stateless persons at discretion and that the manner in which it treats them is not a matter with which International Law, as a rule, concerns itself."

While general humanitarian concerns for individuals have always been around in the marketplace of world ideas, it has only been since the close of the Second World War that legal norms in the context of human rights have emerged. Before this period, humanitarian concerns such as eradicating the evil of slavery were handled to a large degree by each individual State. Nevertheless, as each of the Western powers eradicated the institution, the abolition of slavery gradually became a principle of customary international law. Thus, fueled by the formation of the United Nations in 1945, an entire system of human rights legal principles, some by treaty and some by custom, slowly emerged.

In the last half of the twentieth century, no concept has done more to advance positive change in the social and political spheres of human experience than human rights. In the quest for bettering the quality of human life, human rights have had a major impact in shaping world opinion and events. In this context, human rights have increasingly served as the basis for reaching consensus on defining the fundamental pillars upon which all "just" governments should be anchored. As the preamble to the Universal Declaration of Human Rights asserts, human rights serve "as a common standard of achievement for all peoples and all nations."

In the modern era, human rights have emerged as a significant moral and legal force in modern domestic and international relations. In its most comprehensive meaning, human rights encompass all those principles and concerns associated with ensuring respect for the inherent dignity of the individual human being. In this sense alone can individuals ever be called equal, since each human being, regardless of his abilities or handicaps, possesses the same right of respect for his person and property. The problem, of course, is in the extent to which individual governments are willing to define, recognize, and then enforce the inherent human rights each citizen possesses.

Because mankind is organized into national entities or States, human rights have their primary meaning as they relate to the relationship of the individual and the national entity. In contrast to the situation of only a few generations ago, when the sovereignty of the State was the fundamental principle upon which international law was based, the rapid development of international human rights norms and standards now requires the sovereignty of the State to be weighed and measured against what might be called the sovereignty of the individual.

Despite the phenomenal inroads that human rights have made in the world arena, the goal of universal acceptance and adherence has not been achieved; the path continues to be strewn with adversity. Although the term human rights rolls off the tongue with great ease, one of the most frustrating issues associated with the study of human rights is the fact that there is no standard definition of the term human rights. The legal definition of rights usually refers to claims recognized and enforced by law, but human rights can encompass a far broader category of issues, many not deemed to be legally binding in the context of either domestic or international law. Thus, without a clear definition, the range of matters human rights should encompass continues to be debated.

Juxtaposed to the strict definitional problem, another obstacle in reaching a universal consensus on defining human rights rests in the polarization of the term. Without question, the term human rights has numerous connotations, making it extremely popular over the entire political and social spectrum to describe, with equal vigor, almost any and every aspect of the human condition. Furthermore, because the term is freely used by groups with diametrically opposed agendas and ideologies—often without honest assessment or examination—human rights are often treated as a disposable tool to achieve a political end. The result is that the unwary or casual observer is left with a term that is saddled with wide-ranging ambiguities as to its meaning and goal.

For example, during the Cold War both the Soviet Union and the United States routinely accused one another of human rights abuses. The United States would accuse the Soviets of violating human rights, pointing to the systematic denial of all categories of human freedom related to person and property as a function of the totalitarian regime. In turn, the Soviets would vehemently charge the United States and other capitalist countries with "headline grabbing" human rights abuses (in order to divert attention from their own abuses and to further ongoing machinations to advance Communist ideology throughout the globe).

Of course, in the debate of which system of government commits the worst violations of human rights, one point is generally clear: totalitarian governments are hypocritical in their professed support for human rights; democracies are not. Although individual acts of human rights abuse can occur under any form of government, there is a vast difference between totalitarian regimes and democratic governments. Totalitarian regimes are guilty of institutional denials of human rights, routinely carried out as the *modus vivendi* of government.

In contrast, human rights violations in democracies are generally caused by individuals operating under their own authority and outside of normal institutional safeguards and procedures. Accordingly, democracies are far more likely to care about human rights and to investigate and punish those public officials guilty of human rights violations.

Another mark of the phenomenal degree of support for human rights in democracies is that human rights are accepted as vitally important considerations across the entire political spectrum. For instance, in democracies, all major political platforms, be they conservative or liberal, recognize and endorse the need for the promotion of the most fundamental categories of human rights, both in America and throughout the globe. Liberals and conservatives may disagree on the degree or method of promotion, but both advocate the pursuit of human rights as the primary vehicle for the advancement of peace and stability.

As a consequence of the support given to human rights by the democracies, the world community, by treaty and custom formed essentially since the close of World War II, has arrived at a general consensus on certain basic human rights which all mankind should enjoy. Because this basic category of international human rights is universally recognized, it is commonly referred to as "international human rights." In the realm of international law, international human rights can be generally defined as that body of universally recognized inalienable rights that every individual is entitled to and that every government must guarantee.

At least in the sphere of this consensus, international law no longer recognizes the unrestricted right of the State to deal with its citizens or aliens in any manner it so desires. International human rights law transcends international borders. The often-heard quip of England's King George when asked for help during France's reign of terror no longer applies: "If a country chooses to go mad within its own borders, it may do so."

Without question, the lynchpin of international human rights law advocates one of the most fundamental functions of the national entity—to protect the human rights of the individual. In this sense, respect for international human rights is the *sine qua non* of civilized society and failure of the State to afford such protection can lead to a wide range of sanctions—political, economic, and even judicial.

Apart from the desire to halt external aggression, the U.N. Charter was also designed to address fundamental issues related to international human rights. If the desire for curtailing aggressive war was the justification for restricting some aspects of the external exercise of a State's sovereignty, the drafters intended human rights to be the justification for examining a State's internal ability to generally treat its citizens in any manner it wished.

Although the references to human rights in the U.N. Charter are set out in extremely general terms, they nonetheless clearly set the tone for all future treaties and covenants related to human rights. For example, the preamble to the U.N. Charter states that the peoples of the United Nations have determined to "reaffirm faith in fundamental human rights, in the dignity and worth of the human person [and] in the equal rights of men and women...." This is followed by language in Article 1 (3) which, under the purpose of the U.N., calls for member nations to promote and encourage "respect for human rights and for fundamental freedoms for all without distinction as to race, sex, language, or religion...."

With the creation of the United Nations, work quickly began on a series of international agreements and instruments designed to accomplish the two major themes in the Charter—restricting war and promoting human rights. Many of the efforts resulted in widespread and immediate acceptance of various international agreements throughout the nations of the world, including the 1949 Geneva Conventions. While the Geneva Conventions do not deal with restricting warfare, *jus ad bellum*, they are deeply concerned with *jus in bello*.

It was at this time that human rights moved from a "vision in the minds of some men, of an ideal aspiration towards universal values of law," to the reality of a world that began to acknowledge the existence and validity of international human rights. Next to the U.N. Charter, the primary document that frames the basic principles, as well as the future aspirations, for an international legal corpus for human rights is the U.N. Universal Declaration of Human Rights. The Universal Declaration was passed unanimously (eight abstentions) by the General Assembly in 1948, just three years after the creation of the United Nations.

Unlike the U.N. Charter, the U.N. Universal Declaration of Human Rights is not yet regarded as legally binding among the nations of the world. The Universal Declaration is a declaration of the international body relating to moral and political issues of governments. Although it is not legally binding, the Universal Declaration has gained considerable authority as a legal guide to all member States and serves as a foundation for future expansion of international human rights law.

Another problem with the Universal Declaration is that it lacks machinery for enforcing any of the human rights that it lists. The Universal Declaration has, however, inspired two major covenants which contain more detailed assertions of fixed categories of human rights. Approved by the General Assembly in 1966, these are the International Covenant on Civil and Political Rights and the International Covenant on Economic, Social, and Cultural Rights. Both of these covenants continue to receive growing acceptance from many nations of the world community.

Other treaties that relate to human rights speak to a whole series of specific concerns such as the International Convention on the Elimination of All Forms of Racial Discrimination, the Convention on the Elimination of All Forms of Discrimination Against Women, the Convention on the Prevention and Punishment of the Crime of Genocide, and the Torture Convention.

Obviously, the evolution of the international corpus for human rights law is still ongoing. As with all aspects of international law, international human rights law develops as States become bound by treaty or by custom. Even absent consent via treaty, nations can still be obligated. Again, when a norm or standard has reached widespread acceptance in the international community, it is said to have passed into the realm of customary international law. For example, in respect to the U.N. Charter, even those few nations who are not members of the United Nations are bound by the provisions of the Charter under the concept of customary international law.

9.6 The Corpus of Human Rights Law

What then is the current corpus of human rights and how much of it falls into the category of recognized international human rights law? Many scholars view human rights as chronologically evolving in "generations." For the purposes of this study, it is particularly helpful to divide human rights into three generations.

The first generation of human rights deals basically with the individual's right to be secure in the most sacred asset of all—his person. All nations are bound by treaty and custom to observe these basic protections which are clearly included as the most fundamental of international human rights. Specifically, a State violates international human rights law if, as a matter of State policy, it practices, encourages, or condones seven types of actions that have gained universal recognition. Codified in the Restatement (Third) of the Foreign Relations Law of the United States (1987), Section 702, Customary International Law of Human Rights, those actions consist of:

1. genocide;
2. slavery or slave trade;
3. the murder or causing the disappearance of individuals;
4. torture or other cruel, inhuman, or degrading treatment or punishment;
5. prolonged arbitrary detention;
6. systematic racial discrimination; and
7. a consistent pattern of gross violations of internationally recognized human rights.

Any nation that violates these first generation human rights is deemed to have committed a "gross violation of international human rights." No exceptions.

The second generation of human rights is related to political and civil claims. In short, the individual has the right to be free from the State in all civil and political endeavors. Second category rights are set forth in the International Covenant on Civil and Political Rights and include the broader civil and political freedoms of religion, movement, peaceful assembly, association, expression, privacy, family rights, fair and public trial, and participation in government—all sacred principles related directly to democratic principles of individual freedom. Unfortunately, while many countries have adopted these rights, nations who do not enter into international agreements to follow these rights are not obligated to do so. In other words, second generation rights are not yet customary international law.

Second generation human rights are fundamental to the complete development of the individual, for without the basic guarantees of freedom which these rights speak to, the full potential of the individual can never be realized. However, for those who mistakenly equate human rights with social equality, second generation rights are a paradox, as individuals are free to enjoy the consequences of their own decisions without government interference, good or bad. Furthermore, second generation human rights directly parallel the fundamental freedoms in democracies, concepts that are never offered under totalitarianism. A government committed to second generation human rights is tantamount to a democracy.

In contrast to the second generation of human rights, there is no great or growing international movement toward agreeing on the status of the third generation of human rights. Third generation rights are different from first and second generation rights because they move from restricting governmental behavior toward the individual, to mandating that the government perform numerous social and welfare actions for the individual. Third generation human rights include such issues as working conditions, social security, education, health care, resource development, food, the environment, humanitarian assistance, and peace.

While good government can certainly be measured by how closely it protects and provides for first and second generation human rights, it is not true that the promotion of the third category of human rights is beneficial to society as a whole, especially over the long term. Apart from very basic obligations for any government to provide for the general welfare, which all democracies pledge to do, good governments should shun panaceas. The obligation of the State is not to provide third generation human rights such as food, shelter, or employment to its citizens, but to protect the individual's freedom in the lawful pursuit of these things. Under this reasoning, the primary function of the State is to protect, not to engage in socialism and the redistribution of wealth.

9.7 United Nations Efforts to Promote Human Rights

Thomas Paine once wrote: "Had we a place to stand upon, we might raise the world." If a program's success is ultimately measured by how effectively its goals are achieved, it is clear that the world community, embodied especially in the United Nations, has so far failed to develop any viable program to assist in institutionalizing the observance of first and second generation human rights in many of its member States. In short, the United Nations has not materialized as Paine's place upon which to stand. Indeed, the only true place upon which to stand are God-given individual freedoms.

To be sure, the United Nations has been extremely effective in codifying a body of binding international law so that basic human rights are clearly defined. Nevertheless, restricted by the sovereignty of its members, this tremendous contribution to the advancement of human rights has not been followed by a viable mechanism to ensure compliance with human rights standards within the community of nations. The United Nations thus far has proven to be more suited to building consensus among States about the nature of human rights than to enforcing observance of these rights by individual countries. If the new paradigm for war and terrorism avoidance is to flourish, gaining individual State commitment to at least first generation human rights must be the foundational basis of a workable and realistic plan of action.

One of the major challenges of the War on Terror centers on what steps the United Nations can take to encourage member countries, particularly the Islamic and Arab nations, to follow first and second generation human rights standards. In the long term, totalitarianism will fail only when these human rights flourish. The question, of course, is whether the United Nations has both the will and ability to offer the type of long-term assistance that is needed. The answer seems to be no.

Although a key purpose of the United Nations is to promote and encourage respect for human rights, the human rights provisions that actually guide the United Nations are set out in extremely general terms. Nowhere in the Charter is the term human rights defined; this work is left to later conventions and declarations. Article 1, paragraph 3, of the U.N. Charter lists as the purposes of the organization: "To achieve international cooperation in solving international problems of an economic, social, cultural, or humanitarian character, and in promoting and encouraging respect for human rights and fundamental freedoms for all without distinction as to race, sex, language, or religion." Article 55 of the U.N. Charter provides:

> With a view to the creation of conditions of stability and well-being which are necessary for peaceful and friendly relations among nations based on respect for the principle of equal rights

and self-determination of peoples, the United Nations shall promote…universal respect for, and observance of, human rights and fundamental freedoms for all without distinction as to race, sex, language, or religion.

In turn, Article 56 states that "[a]ll members pledge themselves to take joint and separate action in cooperation with the Organization for the achievement of purposes set forth in Article 55." The burden for enforcement and compliance is clearly placed on the individual States.

Under the U.N. Charter, the U.N. General Assembly does have a defined role with respect to the promotion of human rights. Article 13 of the U.N. Charter provides that the General Assembly "shall initiate studies and make recommendations for the purpose of…assisting in the realization of human rights and fundamental freedoms for all without distinction as to race, sex, language, or religion." Within the framework of this mandate, the General Assembly's role has been to adopt numerous declarations or conventions concentrating on human rights matters.

Since the adoption of the Charter, the General Assembly has expended considerable effort to codify principles of human rights that nations should follow to guarantee the prosperity and well being of their citizens. These principles now form an important part of international law. Although codification has been a major contribution, so no nation can seriously contend that first generation human rights are not binding universal international law, mechanisms to curb the actual violations of these codified principles have been difficult to establish. In fact, the United Nations currently relies chiefly on what some have termed the "mobilization of shame"—the embarrassment of being under investigation, or even condemned, by the United Nations—as the primary means of motivating governments to comply with internationally recognized standards of human rights in the treatment of their citizens. Obviously, public condemnation means very little to totalitarian regimes, as was so clearly demonstrated by a decade of indifference by Saddam Hussein to almost twenty Security Council resolutions. Paradoxically, it is democracies such as the United States, who have far superior records in respecting human rights, that are often singled out for criticism by the General Assembly. Driven by political agendas, the world body of the United Nations often looks at the speck of sand and ignores the boulder in the eye of dictatorships.

During the Cold War, the United Nations seemed to restrict its active concerns to resolving disputes between sovereign States, thereby not dealing with human rights abuses committed within the borders of sovereign States. Even in the process of resolving international disputes, U.N. forces had to be invited to play such a role by both parties to a conflict. While the term is not used in the U.N. Charter, the phrase "peacekeeping" was coined to describe this process.

With the end of the Cold War, the United Nations has attempted to enlarge its active concern to "peace-building," a concept inexorably linked to human rights concerns. Peace-building involves "actions to identify and support structures which will tend to strengthen and solidify peace in order to avoid a relapse into conflict." In this context, the United Nations has been involved in numerous peace-building operations designed to help alleviate the suffering of a particular State through promoting human rights, democratization, and economic development.

As with the United Nation's attempt to shift from peacekeeping to peace-building, the War on Terror demands strong new approaches to promote the observance of human rights in such emerging nations as the new Iraq. Robust approaches will not come under the United Nations' umbrella, but only by efforts of a coalition of democracies.

Always reluctant to employ or authorize the more forceful categories of sanctions such as the use of military force or embargoes, the United Nations traditionally draws on a series of weak sanctions based on embarrassing the government that has engaged in human rights violations. To better track human rights violators, the United Nations relies on several commissions and committees that derive their authority from key international human rights instruments or from the U.N. Charter itself.

Because many of the instruments that established these organizations are not binding or, if binding, drafted in terms that are ambiguous with respect to the responsibilities of individual member States, it is sometimes difficult to evaluate the specific obligations of individual U.N. member States. Also, each United Nations committee or commission generally has the task of reporting, commenting and studying only a specific category of human rights. As a result, these instrumentalities have proven adept in developing human rights principles in specific areas of concern, but have been of little use in working toward the enforcement of these principles in practice.

The proponent for most actions taken by the General Assembly is the Economic and Social Council (ECOSOC). Under the terms of the U.N. Charter, the ECOSOC may:

1. make recommendations for the purpose of promoting respect for, and observance of, human rights and fundamental freedoms for all;
2. prepare draft conventions for submission to the General Assembly, with respect to matters falling within its competence; and
3. call…international conferences on matters falling within its competence.

The ECOSOC may also ask member States to fully report on their own compliance with human rights obligations. The ECOSOC meets several times annually and matters related to human rights issues are typically handled by the ECOSOC's Second (Social) Committee. Under the U.N. Charter, the ECOSOC has the right to establish commissions for, *inter alia*, the promotion of human rights. Pursuant to this authority, the ECOSOC has formed a major commission: the Commission on Human Rights (also known as the Human Rights Commission). The ECOSOC established the Commission on Human Rights on February 16, 1946. The Human Rights Commission's role in the process of advancing human rights includes the following:

Draft an international bill of rights; draft international declarations or conventions on civil liberties, the status of women, freedom of information and similar matters; protect minorities; prevent discrimination on grounds of race, sex, language, or religion; handle any other matter concerning human rights and…assist the [ECOSOC] in coordination of activities concerning human rights in the United Nations System.

The crowning achievements of the Human Rights Commission include the drafting of the Universal Declaration of Human Rights; the International Covenant on Economic, Social and Cultural Rights; and the International Covenant on Civil and Political Rights. Taken together, these instruments comprise what has commonly become known as the International Bill of Human Rights.

In addition to functioning as a vehicle to codify and promote human rights, the Human Rights Commission also monitors and identifies human rights violations. However, since its enforcement powers are limited, the Human Rights Commission relies primarily on persuasion and dialogue to curb human rights violations.

The Human Rights Commission generally operates through the appointment of a special rapporteur or special envoy who acts as a fact-finder, investigating general human rights issues or a particular country's human rights record. The Human Rights Commission also recommends measures for State compliance and will act in an advisory capacity to governments that request such assistance. At other times, the special rapporteur will assist a particular government on specific human rights issues. The Human Rights Commission has also established several working groups which tackle such projects as drafting new international instruments.

Another organization under the United Nations umbrella is the Human Rights Committee. The Human Rights Committee serves as the chief administrator of the International Covenant on Civil and Political Rights. Established in 1977, the Human Rights Committee is responsible for studying, commenting, and transmitting reports from United Nations member States to the Secretary General on the progress of implementing the obligations assumed by the member States under the International Covenant on Civil and Political Rights. Those obligations include:

1. ensuring to all individuals the rights enunciated in the covenant;
2. enacting legislation to give effect to those rights; and
3. guaranteeing to individuals remedies that can be exercised if those rights are violated.

The Human Rights Committee generally receives periodic reports from member nations in response to a series of questions and issues that the Committee wishes that nation to address. In compliance with Article 40 of the Covenant on Political and Civil Rights, the committee then passes a report on to the General Assembly. For example, in response to a Human Rights Committee request, a nation will usually send a delegation of public officials to Geneva with extensive written remarks on concerns raised by the Committee. The Committee will consider the written remarks and the oral input by the host nation delegation before issuing their report.

The Optional Protocol to the International Covenant on Civil and Political Rights contains provisions for a final implementation mechanism. In this regard, the Committee may consider individual complaints alleging human rights violations by State parties. Although the Committee may reach a decision on the merits and forward that decision to the State and individual concerned, it may not issue judgments. It is a paper tiger.

9.8 Non-Governmental Organizations Devoted to Human Rights

Non-governmental organizations (NGOs) serve an important function as watch dogs for human rights issues. The most widely recognized human rights NGO is Amnesty International. It is a worldwide movement premised on the "conviction that governments must not deny individuals their basic human rights." Although from a political perspective the organization is often unbalanced in its views, Amnesty International was awarded the 1977 Nobel Peace Prize for its continuing efforts to promote the Universal Declaration of Human Rights.

The three primary goals of Amnesty International are to work for:

1. the release of prisoners of conscience-men, women and children imprisoned for their beliefs, color, sex, ethnic origin, language or religion, provided they have neither used nor advocated violence;
2. fair and prompt trials for all political prisoners; and
3. an end to torture and executions in all cases.

With the exception of Amnesty International's opposition to the long recognized right of a State to exercise the death penalty, all of its stated goals are clearly consistent with the common body of first generation international human rights. The major problem with the organization is that it exhibits an untoward bias against some of the world's leading democracies to include the United States and Israel.

One powerful NGO that has attempted to actually implement human rights promotion programs in individual States is the International Committee of the Red Cross (ICRC). Beginning in 1976, the ICRC has sponsored scores of human rights symposia for numerous developing countries. From the establishment of the International Institute of Humanitarian Law in San Remo, Italy, to specific training programs for various militaries worldwide, the ICRC has taken the NGO lead in trying to promote institutional change. While other NGOs have sponsored human rights conferences, absolutely no organization has made as much progress as the ICRC in getting governments to at least address the issue of institutional change in the conduct of armed forces *vis-à-vis* human rights and the law of war. Unfortunately, because the ICRC constantly strives for neutrality, it can have difficulty establishing the necessary rapport with the host nation military to carry out significant training programs.

9.9 Regional Organizations to Promote Human Rights

In accordance with the provisions of the U.N. Charter regarding regional organizations, there are several major regional organizations that have been formed to better represent the desires of sovereign nations in the same geographic location. Like the United Nations approach in dealing with and enforcing compliance with human rights, all of the regional approaches rely simply on categorizing human rights abuses and little else.

For example, the Charter of the Organization of American States (OAS), which is the largest regional organization in the Americas (consisting of 32 members States), includes the same generalist human rights language that is found in the U.N. Charter. Article 3(j) holds that OAS member States will "proclaim the fundamental rights of the individual without distinction as to race, nationality, creed, or sex." Article 16 states that in exercising the right to freely develop its cultural, political, and economic life, the member States agree to "respect the rights of the individual and the principal of universal morality."

Similar to the United Nations' approach to further define human rights by means of the Universal Declaration on Human Rights, the OAS passed the American Declaration of the Rights and Duties of Man (American Declaration) to provide a clear indication of what was meant by human rights. Indeed, when the OAS created the Inter-American Commission on Human Rights, it specified that the human rights listed in the American Declaration were the ones to be used by the Commission in evaluating evidence and issuing reports. The American Declaration includes in its list of human rights: the right to life, liberty, and security of person (Article 1); the protection from abusive attacks on honor, reputation, and family (Article 5); the inviolability of the home and correspondence (Articles 9 and 10); and due process of laws (Articles 18, 25, and 26).

As noted, the OAS has not created an enforcement mechanism. The OAS has passed the American Convention on Human Rights in 1978 which requires all members to respect "the rights and freedoms recognized herein and to ensure to all persons subject to their jurisdiction the free and full exercise of those rights and freedoms." To promote compliance, Articles 34 through 73 of the American Convention on Human Rights established the Inter-American Commission on Human Rights and the Inter-American Court on Human Rights. The Inter-American Commission on Human Rights is authorized to receive individual or State complaints alleging violations of human rights. After ensuring that all domestic remedies have been exhausted, the Commission can conduct investigations, make reports, and release information.

The Inter-American Court on Human Rights, located in San Jose, Costa Rica, is authorized to hear human rights cases, but only from parties who voluntarily submit to the jurisdiction of the court. If the parties do submit to the court's jurisdiction, they pledge obedience to the judicial findings which may include reparations.

9.10 Traditional Efforts of the United States in Promoting Human Rights

If the United Nations, NGOs, and regional organizations have been less than effective in developing a serious methodology to promote the institutionalization of first and second generation human rights in new democracies, the United States government has only been slightly more effective. Recognizing that promoting human rights is in its best interest, as well as a responsibility to the world community, the United States relies on two means to achieve this end—foreign assistance funding and political pressure.

Political pressure is difficult to gauge in its success and varies according to each situation. In terms of politics, for example, the United States has signaled that it will not subordinate perceived security interests in Asia to the desire to promote human rights; the consequences for regional stability could be jeopardized if China is the recipient of an intensified human rights crusade. Under the Clinton, Bush, and Obama administrations, even linking China's trade benefits to its human rights record has been viewed as counterproductive—China might become resentful and retaliate in ways that would be destabilizing for the region, such as not cooperating in the Security Council or making irresponsible arms sales.

The traditional mechanism for encouraging countries to develop acceptable human rights records rests with the policy of denying foreign assistance aid or security assistance to countries who are human rights abusers. Security assistance is generally defined as the complete body of statutory programs and authorities under which the United States provides defense articles, military training, and other defense-related services to foreign governments and international organizations for the purpose of enhancing American national policies and objectives. Without question, the security assistance program is a principal element of American foreign policy.

The main objective of security assistance is to enhance American strategic objectives, not only from a regional perspective, but also in key countries within the region. Thus, the basic elements of security assistance involve assisting allies and friendly nations in meeting security threats, securing route access over flight and base rights essential to rapid deployment of United States forces, promoting force commonalities, and improving or maintaining access to critical raw materials.

It is well known that there are also domestic benefits associated with the security assistance program. Not only does the production of defense items provide domestic employment, it generates capital investment and improves the nation's industrial defense mobilization base.

Although the Department of State is responsible for the operation of the security assistance program, it is the National Security Council (NSC) that establishes the overall strategic planning and goals of the program. From the military aspect of security assistance, the Defense Security Assistance Agency (DSAA) is the primary Department of Defense office.

Each United States military Unified Command (collectively they have responsibility for all major regions in the world where American forces are stationed) is required to develop a security assistance program for their region which will assist in achieving assigned strategic goals and missions. After developing a security assistance program, the Commander of each Unified (and Specified) Command (CINC) forwards his security assistance proposal to the Joint Chiefs of Staff (JCS) in Washington where they are evaluated and passed to the NSC for final incorporation into the overall United States strategic plan.

The subordinate component commands of Unified Commands are responsible for the actual implementation of security assistance programs within individual countries in the region. Furthermore, in the countries that are major recipients of security assistance, a Security Assistance Organization (SAO) operates on the ground as part of the Country Team to the American Ambassador in the country. The SAO includes all DOD elements located in the foreign country with assigned responsibilities for carrying out the various security assistance programs for that country. Because of their position, SAOs are afforded a great deal of deference by both the host nation and other Americans working in the host country.

Chief among the legislative authorities for security assistance is the Foreign Assistance Act (FAA) of 1961 (as amended). This act authorizes five basic types of programs as follows:

1. The Foreign Military Financing Program (FMFP). Under this program, defense articles are transferred to friendly nations either through grants, loans, or sales. Defense articles include such things as weapons, munitions, aircraft, vessels, and military equipment.
2. International military education and training (IMET). This program allows the United States military to provide training to foreign military students, primarily in the United States. A primary goal of IMET is to expose the foreign military students to the benefits of a free and democratic society based on the rule of law. Key in this process is the demonstration to the foreign soldiers of how a military is properly subordinated to civilian control. Not only are channels of communication opened between United States and foreign nationals, but it is hoped that the personal contacts made as a result of the training will encourage the promotion of democratic values and human rights in the future.
3. Antiterrorism assistance. A relatively new program, the antiterrorism program attempts to assist those democratic nations that are plagued by terrorist organizations.
4. Economic support fund. This program provides direct grant monies to the recipient nation in an effort to assist in economic recovery or development.
5. Peacekeeping operations. This provision authorizes assistance in the form of personnel and equipment to friendly countries and international organizations for peacekeeping operations.

The second major piece of security assistance legislation is the Arms Export Control Act (AECA). The AECA directly ties in with the applicable provisions of the FAA and provides for the sale of defense articles and services to other countries. The definition of what constitutes a defense article remains the same as under the FAA. A defense service includes any service, test, inspection, repair, training, publication, or other assistance, or defense information used for the purpose of making military sales.

A key element in the AECA defense service definition is "training." As defined in the act:

Training includes formal or informal instruction of foreign students in the United States or overseas by officers or employees of the United States, contract technicians, or contractors (including instruction at civilian institutions), or by correspondence courses, technical, educational, or information publications and media of all kinds, training aid, orientation, training exercise, and military advice to foreign military units and forces.

Depending on the type of training mission, American training teams fall into one of three general types: (1) mobile training teams; (2) technical assistance teams; or (3) technical assistance field teams. A letter of offer and acceptance of the training is executed in all cases. Besides the standard issues related to providing the service, this letter also spells out the status DOD team members will have while performing training duties in the foreign country. The status is usually the same privileges and immunities accorded to the administrative and technical staff at the American embassy in that country.

As stated, the Department of State is the executive branch agency charged with the operation of security assistance. Congress, however, through its power over the authorization and appropriation of funds, has actually become the key policy player in the process. In fact, much to the chagrin of the executive branch, Congress views security assistance as a prime opportunity to influence and even establish foreign policy.

Congress exercises its authority in two ways: through the budget process and through the legislative process. Under the budget process, Congress does not simply allocate a fixed sum of money to the Department of State to allow them to operate the security assistance program through DSAA. Exercising their "power of the purse," Congress engages in micro-management by earmarking specific dollar amounts to specific countries.

From the earmarking of about half of the security assistance budget in the 1980s, Congress now earmarks about 90 percent of all security assistance monies. In addition, not content with earmarking monies to individual recipient States, Congress increasingly directs through functional accounts exactly how the earmarked money for a particular country will be spent. This Congressional practice has taken almost all of the flexibility away from the State Department and hence, the security assistance administrators.

In an effort to further increase its management role, Congress now establishes "mission accounts." For example, under the IMET funding Congress sets up specific mission accounts in which money can be spent for particular countries. In one year's budget, these accounts were listed as: Middle East Peace, Promotion of Democracy and Human Rights, Counter-narcotics, Regional Stability and Defense Cooperation, and Promote Professional Military Relationships. For the year in question, all IMET money had to be spent in one of these mission accounts or returned to the general treasury.

The second manner in which Congress has inserted itself in the process rests in myriad legislative prohibitions on providing security assistance. Apart from numerous country-specific restrictions, a sampling of the general prohibitions reveals just how complex the administration of security assistance program has become:

1. The prohibition against American personnel performing defense services of a combatant nature. Set out at 21(c)(1) of the AECA, 22, "Personnel performing defense services sold under this act may not perform any duties of a combatant nature, including any duties related to training and advising that may engage United States personnel in combat activities outside the United States in connection with the performance of those defense services." Thus, if American military personnel find themselves in any situation where hostilities occur, or are imminent, they must cease training and withdraw from the area. This has oc-

curred on many occasions in the past, particularly in situations where Army Special Forces are training host nation soldiers in unstable countries.

2. The prohibition against American forces training police forces, found at Section 660 of the FAA, provides that foreign assistance funds cannot be used to "provide training, advice, or financial support to police, prisons, or other law enforcement forces of a foreign government or for any program of internal intelligence or surveillance on behalf of a foreign government." This section has been amended to allow such training to longtime democracies with no standing armed forces and which do not violate human rights. Costa Rica, for example, has no military.

3. The Kennedy Amendment, at 502B of the FAA, requires that all federal assistance be cut off to any country that "engages in a consistent pattern of gross violations of internationally recognized human rights."

4. The Hickenlooper Amendment, at 620(e)(1) of the FAA, deals with halting aid to any nation that engages in the expropriation of American property.

5. The Symington-Glenn Amendments, at 669 and 670 of the FAA, deal with issues associated with the transfer of and receipt of nuclear materials. The intent is to keep nuclear arms from spreading to other countries.

6. The Brooke Amendment, at 620(q) of the FAA, mandates the complete termination of foreign assistance (to include United States military assistance) to any country more than twelve months in arrears on payment of debts accrued.

As disruptive as these restrictions appear on the ability of the executive branch to conduct foreign affairs, Congress has given the President special authorities in both the FAA and AECA that allow him to override almost all Congressional restrictions. Because the entire process of planning, budgeting, and delivering security assistance requires substantial lead-time, the President is given this special authority to deal with exigent circumstances. This authority is exercised only as an exception to the rule, generally requires written notification, and is limited by dollar ceilings.

Through a series of federal statutes and directives, the United States government is required to consider human rights in conducting foreign relations with other countries. Countries that engage in a consistent pattern of gross violations of human rights are generally restricted from American foreign aid—military and economic. Obviously, this advantage is significant only in those areas that receive foreign aid from the United States.

In regard to the major legislative authority through which foreign assistance is rendered, the Kennedy Amendment and Harkin Amendment leave no doubt that the promotion of human rights is a key objective of American foreign policy. Indeed, Section 502B(a)(3) of the Kennedy Amendment directs the President to administer security assistance in a manner which promotes human rights and avoids "identification of the United States...with governments which deny to their people internationally recognized human rights and fundamental freedoms...."

Section 502B(a)(1) establishes as "a principal goal of the foreign policy of the United States...to promote the increased observance of internationally recognized human rights by all countries." Section 502B(a)(2) prohibits security assistance to countries which "engage in a consistent pattern of gross violations of internationally recognized human rights."

As with most pieces of legislation, there is a limited exception clause in the Kennedy Amendment. Section 502B(e) allows the President to waive the restrictions imposed if he finds that "extraordinary circumstances exist warranting provision of such assistance," or if the President finds "that the human rights record in that country has significantly improved."

Similarly, Section 116(e) authorizes and encourages the President to identify and conduct "programs and activities which will encourage or promote increased adherence to civil rights, as set forth in the Universal Declaration of Human Rights...." The Harkin Amendment also has an exception clause which prohibits economic assistance to "the government of any country which engages in a consistent pattern of gross violations of internationally recognized human rights...unless such assistance will directly benefit the needy people of such country."

Gross violations of internationally recognized human rights are defined under both Sections 502B(d)(1) and 116(a) as the types of violations falling under the first generation of international human rights. The language describes gross violations as:

> [A] consistent pattern of gross violations of internationally recognized human rights, including torture or cruel, inhuman, or degrading treatment or punishment, prolonged detention without charges, causing the disappearance of persons by the abduction and clandestine detention of those persons, or other flagrant denial of the right to life, liberty, and the security of person.

Finally, both Sections 5O2B and 116 require the State Department to submit to Congress an annual status report on human rights for all countries receiving economic or security assistance. The process of collecting information for the report is conducted by the Assistant Secretary of State for Human Rights and Humanitarian Affairs. Information is gathered chiefly from the applicable American embassy and various respected human rights NGOs.

There exist numerous other legislative provisions that deal with the issue of providing assistance to nations that exhibit an unwillingness to abide by first generation human rights. For example, Section 701 of the International Financial Institutions Act requires the United States to do everything in its power to influence international financial institutions to prevent the grant of economic aid to countries whose governments engage in "a consistent pattern of gross violations of internationally recognized human rights." Because the United States exercises tremendous influence in organizations like the World Bank and International Finance Corporation over loans and grants to specific countries, it is able to act as an overseer for human rights issues.

Congress also enacts country-specific legislation which attempts to link American assistance to a particular country and that country's compliance with specific human rights standards. This conditional funding may be triggered by an unacceptable country report issued by the State Department. These violations mirror those found in Common Article 3 of the Geneva Conventions:

1. violence to life and person, in particular, murder of all kinds, mutilation, cruel treatment, and torture;
2. taking hostages;
3. outrages upon personal dignity, in particular, humiliating and degrading treatment;
4. the passing of sentences and carrying out of executions without previous judgment pronounced by a regularly constituted court affording all the judicial guarantees which are recognized as indispensable by civilized peoples.

Another force multiplier speaks to the long-term goal of developing and institutionalizing a democratic ethos in the new militaries of the liberated lands. One of the greatest force multipliers imaginable would be to develop a methodology to encourage the growth of democracies throughout the community of nations. Since, for all practical purposes, democracies do not engage in aggressive warfare or terrorism, it is only logical for the United States to find ways to encourage the solidification of the new democracies that have emerged in the post-Cold War era and might emerge in the wake of the War on Terror.

The use of the United States military to promote democracy and human rights values to newly liberated countries will take on a much added significance in the War on Terror. In particular, the new governments of Afghanistan and Iraq look to American soldiers to assist them in establishing both order in the land and a law-based military whose policies, rules, and practices are rooted in human rights. Many of these efforts are being conducted by American Special Operations Forces.

Although the terms human rights and democratic values do not immediately bring to mind images of Special Forces soldiers in action, the last three decades actually witnessed, for example, the use of "Green Berets" in missions that clearly reflect America's desire to inculcate human rights values within the militaries of our friends and allies. Special Forces soldiers have proved themselves to be a premier vehicle in this regard and are now heavily engaged in Afghanistan and Iraq in this same effort. Given the new paradigm of democracy building, promoting human rights is clearly a priority mission for which Special Forces are uniquely qualified.

9.11 New Non-Traditional Roles—Human Rights as a Force Multiplier

Rubricated by the disintegration of the Soviet Union in 1991, the world has changed drastically and with breathtaking speed. Just two short decades ago, the free world was focused on containing a heavily armed and expansionist Soviet Empire. Suddenly, primarily through internal aspirations for greater human rights (first and second generation), the Soviet Union and its ideology of repression were gone, and the attendant winds of freedom had blown to peoples and nations throughout the world. While these winds did not much impact the Middle East, other formerly repressed peoples of the world have expressed aspirations leading to hurried attempts to establish democratic governments and free market economies, the principal coins of the realm of human rights.

The Cold War period was the classic example of the traditional use of military force to deter aggression-combat soldiers trained and prepared to go to war at any moment. The American armed forces were war-fighters, pure and simple.

As the Soviet Union began to implode, the free world realized that it was not only the military might of the United States that defeated communism—it was the ideals represented by the United States. It was what Americans have always represented to the world—respect for human rights and freedom. It can be argued that the United States military fixed the Soviets in place, but freedom ultimately caused Soviet communism to disintegrate.

Unfortunately, the United States entered the post-Cold War era with only a vague and ill-defined understanding that fostering democracies was vital to American national security interests. Nevertheless, in the War on Terror, the export of human rights values is a powerful weapon against those renegade nations and peoples who still seek to wage war and terrorism. Without question, democratic values and promoting human rights are needed force multipliers in the War on Terror, primarily because the new-styled terrorists cannot be deterred by the threat of force.

The promise of a new era, where the world strives to be free from the constant evils of war, terrorism and human rights abuse, demands that the United States military expand its traditional role of war-fighter and actively enter into new, nontraditional roles. Indeed, beginning in the 1980s, the United States military has, in limited areas, responded by assisting in such things as drug reduction, disaster relief, humanitarian assistance, peace operations, and nation building.

In the War on Terror, the United States military has a much-needed role to play in two key force multipliers—humanitarian assistance and nation building. In fact, the concern for human rights, in general, mirrors the overall United States national security policy of peacetime engagement by maintaining contacts with allies and friendly governments for the purpose of imparting values and ideals associated with democratic principles. These forces must also be brought to bear on terrorist regimes.

One of the force multipliers in the War on Terror is the use of the United States military for humanitarian peacemaking missions or peace operations. The term peace operation is now defined in United States military doctrine. The United States military definition is drafted in broad terms to capture the full range of possible activities associated with maintaining or restoring peace. According to the United States Army's Center for Strategy and Force Evaluation, the term "peace operation" is defined as:

> The umbrella term encompassing observers and monitors, traditional peacekeeping, preventive deployment, internal conflict resolution, security assistance to a civil authority, protection and delivery of humanitarian relief, guaranteeing and denial of movement, imposing sanctions, peace enforcement, high intensity operations, and any other military, paramilitary or non-military action taken in support of a diplomatic peacemaking process.

In assessing the efficacy of a peace operation, from both a legal and a practical perspective, it is preferable to engage the backing and support of the United Nations as well as the financial assistance of fellow States. Not only do deepening fiscal concerns at home militate against the United States becoming the policeman for the world, common sense dictates that if the world is to move forward, all peace loving nations must join together in the effort. For these reasons, it is critical that other nations also share the burden and responsibility of future peace operations.

The other nontraditional role of the United States military is in the realm of nation building. This is what is happening in Afghanistan and in Iraq, although the continuing violence has slowed the efforts in Afghanistan. The United States military defines nation building as "assisting a host nation in its efforts to restructure, reinforce, or rebuild its formal and informal institutions." Starting in the 1960s, the United States military has been involved in providing nation assistance, through the Foreign Assistance Act of 1961 and other Congressional authority, to friends and allies throughout the world.

In the War on Terror, many of these activities will be centered on helping new nations develop the military capability to defend themselves from internal and external aggression. The United States military is currently utilizing special Congressional authority to undertake activities designed to improve the standard of living for the inhabitants of Afghanistan and Iraq. As a result of this specific authority, United States military forces are engaged in numerous humanitarian and civic action (HCA) projects such as road building, medical care, well drilling, and other minor construction projects.

The hope for conducting these humanitarian efforts is that by raising the standard of living for the local population, the causes of internal unrest associated with conflict can be curtailed before they start. This concept has reaped tremendous benefits in fledgling democracies as far apart as Honduras and Thailand.

Of course, the most immediate concern in fostering the new Afghan and Iraqi governments is the formation of a military establishment that respects human rights and adheres to democratic principles.

The new militaries of Afghanistan and Iraq have little frame of reference for a nation, or, for that matter, a military establishment that is ruled by law and guided by human rights concerns. These new militaries will undoubtedly be absolutely essential in protecting the fledgling nations as they find their paths on the road to democracy. Ironically, although totalitarian-based militaries were the chief violators of international human rights in the old non-democratic Hussein and Taliban systems, the new military forces of Afghanistan and Iraq must establish themselves as the most influential institutions during their transition periods to democracy.

Because the chief violators of human rights in the old Taliban and Hussein systems were the military, it is absolutely essential that the new military arm of the Afghan and Iraqi governments be fully exposed to the basic norms and standards of behavior commonly held by militaries in a democratic society. At a minimum, they must be apolitical, respectful of human rights, personally accountable, and responsive to the civilian leadership in a democratic process.

The hallmark of a successful democracy is the military's acceptance of human rights concerns. In a democracy, the military cannot be an abuser of human rights; it must respect human rights and be held accountable to civilian authority under a rule of law for the way it carries out its missions. The military must understand that soldiers are not just people who have technical and fighting skills, but citizens who understand their role as a member of an organization with rights and responsibilities in a constitutional democracy.

Obviously, this goal can only be achieved through a systemic program designed to institutionalize these concepts. In past efforts with other emerging democracies since the fall of the Soviet Union, the United States relied on a variety of military security assistance programs to try to instill human rights values compatible with democratic principles in the host nation military. Since the United States' effort was geared only at exposing the individual foreign soldier to human rights ideals, institutional reform within the host nation military never occurred. Essentially, the promotion of human rights and democracy was an indirect benefit at best, rather than an explicit goal.

By their very nature, the promotion of human rights and democratization of the new Afghan and Iraqi governments involve matters that cannot be assigned to the jurisdiction of any single department of the United States government. However, the promotion of human rights and democratic principles in the military of any new democracy is best left to the United States military.

The primary concern for the Afghan and Iraqi governments rests with how, over the long term, the host nation military can be encouraged to accept a reduced and more professional role appropriate to a democracy. Ideally, this concern exceeds the minimally accepted standards for human rights and extends to the fullest possible range of meaningful human rights. These rights include freedom of religion, freedom of association, freedom of speech, and all of those principles indicative of a truly democratic society.

One of the major obstacles in imparting concepts relating to human rights and democratic principles is the fact that both Afghanistan and Iraq are faced with the social and economic turmoil traditionally associated with lesser developed countries—from economic chaos to actual armed insurgency by bands of terrorists and bandits. Thus, the effectiveness of any program of assistance must be measured against the realities associated with the specific problems facing Afghanistan and Iraq.

A successful strategy for achieving these democratization goals must be based on three clearly focused themes directed to the host nation military (and appropriate civilian government officials):

1. instilling a greater respect for internationally recognized standards for human rights;
2. fostering greater respect for and an understanding of the principle of civilian control of the military; and
3. improving military justice systems and procedures to comport with internationally recognized standards of human rights.

More than any other single endeavor one might imagine, the institutionalization of human rights values has the potential to directly reduce the threat of aggressive warfare. To be sure, true democracy cannot exist without a military establishment dedicated to the principles associated with a healthy respect for human rights. In his book on warfare in the twenty-first century, *Race to the Swift*, Richard Simpkin encapsulates this concept by noting that the militaries of democratic governments "rest on the rule of law, [of which human rights is the core] and must so rest." While such values may be taken for granted in societies resting on stable democratic traditions, this is clearly not the case in Afghanistan, Iraq, or other nondemocratic states wishing to abandon totalitarian rule.

It is a simple fact that those militaries who truly abide by human rights will support and not threaten democratic development. In turn, healthy democracies are less likely to resort to aggressive warfare to settle international disputes.

9.12 The Role of Special Forces

History has shown that one of the most vital components of any democratic society is its military establishment. True democracy cannot exist without a military establishment dedicated to the principles associated with civilian control of the military and respect for fundamental human rights. While such principles are taken for granted in societies resting on stable democratic traditions, this is not the case in the militaries of totalitarian States. The antithesis of a democratic military, the military under the totalitarian system wields tremendous power over the internal affairs of the State; in many cases they are the government.

For better or worse, the United States has entered a period of profound change in the use of military capabilities to meet the new circumstances of the War on Terror. Not only has the use of overt military force as a tool of national security reemerged, but the War on Terror has led to a rethinking of military roles and missions with a search for "force multipliers." The term force multipliers applies in many ways, but in the War on Terror there are two significant force multipliers. First, as demonstrated in the Afghanistan campaign, the American strategy of using local indigenous fighters to help displace a totalitarian regime is a tremendous force multiplier in the short term. Coupled with a small cadre of United States Special Operations Forces, President George W. Bush correctly used these local forces in conjunction with America's strongest military suit—its fantastic air and sea power.

The 2001 military campaign in Afghanistan was easily won and the new government easily established because the war was seen more as American help for the oppressed people to retake their own country than as an American invasion. When the War on Terror reached Iraq in 2003, the elements were similar despite the continuing sectarian and al-Qa'eda sponsored violence. Considering that the city of Baghdad has over five million people, it is clear that the vast majority of Iraqis are not in conflict with the coalition forces or the new Iraqi government; they want a better life that offers freedom.

The goal of creating a law-based Afghan and Iraqi military has, to be sure, many challenges. Apart from the issue of funding such a force, they must be properly trained. Nevertheless, the training aspect is not as difficult as it may sound due to the fact that, in large part, militaries of many emerging democracies have always looked to the American military in general, and the Army Special Forces in particular, as a model to assist them in defining how human rights concerns should properly function in their respective military establishments and how the military itself should fit into a more democratic form of government.

The genesis of modern Special Forces is most closely identified with President Kennedy who first officially authorized the wearing of the distinctive green beret for Army Special Forces. Although the entire force structure virtually disappeared with the end of the Vietnam era, revitalization of Special Forces occurred in the 1980s, culminating with the 1987 Congressional creation of a separate unified command—the United States Special Operations Command. This command has direct responsibility for every type of special operational force in the Navy, Army, Air Force, and Marines. Congress further helped structure the types of forces and named specific mission activities: direct action, strategic reconnaissance, unconventional warfare, foreign internal defense, counterterrorism, civil affairs, psychological operations, humanitarian assistance, theater search and rescue, and other activities. Army Special Forces are one component of Special Operations Forces. They are elite professionals, trained to operate in any type of environment. Because they know the language, culture, and environment, the soldiers foster an atmosphere of unity with the indigenous people.

The public mystique of the Green Beret as the ultimate jungle fighter capable of single-handedly defeating entire enemy battalions clearly belies the real importance of these specialized and highly skilled soldiers. While they certainly have significant wartime missions, Special Forces are most effective when executing their dual peacetime roles of prevention and deterrence. Paradoxically, when executing their peacetime role, it is in part because of, not in spite of, the aura of invincibility that they enjoy public support and successes far in excess of what their limited numbers would imply. Currently, the Army has five active-duty, brigade-size Special Forces groups, each group operationally directed toward a particular segment of the world. In the War on Terror, prevention and deterrence roles are proving just as important as the fighting mission.

The Special Forces' role covers a full range of activities in the Third World, the principal purpose being to prevent escalation of conflict. This is done by training indigenous people to defend themselves and, to a lesser degree, engaging in limited humanitarian missions in the more remote parts of the country. This civic action includes providing medical and veterinary aid, conducting various public services, and other activities aimed at improving living conditions. The primary mission in the prevention role is training. It was during the Vietnam era that Special Forces earned the coveted reputation of being premier trainers of indigenous forces in military skills. Thousands of tribesmen and local Vietnamese were successfully organized into effective self-defense forces. Then, as now, the secret to their achievements was hard training, common sense, and empathy. These professionals were required not only to be experts in their technical skills, but they also had to be proficient in the host language, totally familiar with the culture, and able to literally live in the same, often-times primitive, environments. To accomplish these tasks, these men underwent extensive, intensive, and expensive training.

Carrying on this tradition, Special Forces continue to teach host nation forces fundamental military skills, as well as more advanced tactics in desert, jungle and urban warfare. The training activities are directly aimed at assisting the host nation through long-term, in-depth courses and instruction. Accordingly, the mission to train and help organize indigenous local forces remains the cornerstone of modern Special Forces. The efforts crystallize as the host nation is better prepared to deal with overt manifestations of conflict through strengthened military capabilities.

When used in their preventive capacity, Special Forces are inherently successful in establishing an excellent rapport with the local population. This, quite naturally, helps defeat terrorism at its roots. One Special Forces medic conducting missions in Honduras described the typical attitude of the locals: "[I]t is also a morale boost for them [Hondurans]; if we're out in the field with them, sweat with them, eat their food and drink their beer, then, by God, they appreciate what we're doing and what we're going through."

The other critical role of Special Forces is that of deterrence, a role that is particularly important in a crisis situation. In this role, the Special Forces are used to "wave the flag," to be nothing less than concrete evidence that America is strongly committed to the host nation. A good illustration of this function occurred in 1987. Soldiers from the 1st Special Forces Group were sent to Thailand at the request of that government in order to demonstrate American support. At the time, the Thais were fighting North Vietnamese forces seeking to exert control over Cambodian resistance fighters. In keeping with the deterrent function, the Special Forces were directed to perform numerous well-publicized mass parachute jumps and exercises with their Thai counterparts along the Cambodian border. More recently this role of deterrence assigned to Special Forces has been illustrated by numerous events in Afghanistan. Special Forces operatives assigned to a bodyguard detail for Afghan President Karzai thwarted an assassination attempt on Karzai. These Special Forces soldiers killed the would-be assailant, while sustaining only one casualty to an American soldier.

Show of force functions are relatively well-suited to the Special Forces, due again in part to their universal reputation as America's elite fighters. In 1987 the *Soviet Military Review* described them as being "professional killers...with...a brutal hatred of the Communist countries." Such puffing aside, these soldiers never fail to make an impression; no matter the story line, headlines always start with the same two words: "Green Berets."

Now, in the War on Terror, Special Forces are the preferred weapon of choice when it comes to ground operations with local counterparts and, just as critical, in the task of promoting democratic values. Host nation forces that join the fight against terrorism instinctively turn to United States Army Special Forces for the following reasons.

First, Army Special Forces are uniquely positioned to influence the attitudes and, in some cases, even the structure and function of the host nation military. Why? Because they go where no other element of the United States military can. As noted by Major General (U.S. Army, ret.) Kenneth R. Bowra, the former commanding general of the Army's Special Forces (1996–1998), "Other than Special Forces, there is no element of the United States military forces that is more capable of instilling human rights into the militaries of emerging democracies."

Special Forces soldiers perform hundreds of missions each year in support of the war fighting combatant commands and other government agencies. These operations span the entire spectrum of conflict, to include direct action, foreign internal defense, special reconnaissance, unconventional warfare, security assistance training, humanitarian assistance, counter-narcotics, de-mining, and combating terrorism. Simply put, when it comes to operating with host nation forces, Green Berets are everywhere, doing everything. The deployment figures tell the tale. In fiscal year (FY) 2001, for instance, United States Army Special Forces soldiers were deployed on over 2,500 missions to over 200 countries throughout the world.

Second, since Special Forces soldiers are extensively trained in the language, culture, religion, and politics of the countries in which they operate, they are best able to foster genuine military-to-military relationships. This fact applies to individual host nations, as well as to the geographic region as a whole. Thus, based on cultural nuances only they can appreciate, Special Forces can tailor each particular mission in order to make the maximum impression on their military counterparts regarding the importance of human rights concerns.

Third, more than any other arm of the United States military, Special Forces exemplify to foreign militaries the success story of how a professional military force can maintain a superb operational record while functioning in accordance with human rights concerns. Almost without exception, foreign soldiers are deeply impressed with how human rights and military efficiency can go hand-in-hand. Foreign forces know that, for the Green Berets, concern for human rights has always been the *sine que non* for United States military operations.

Indeed, the promotion of international human rights and democratic behavior has long been a critical theme of the United States Army's Special Forces, regardless of the mission that they happen to be performing. President Kennedy routinely praised this unique quality, and no one who has followed the success story of Army Special Forces soldiers in Operations Provide Comfort (Iraq/Turkey), Restore Hope (Somalia), Just Cause (Panama), Desert Storm (Middle East), Uphold Democracy (Haiti), IFOR (Bosnia), Enduring Freedom (Afghanistan), and Iraqi Freedom (Iraq) can doubt their value in this regard.

In short, Army Special Forces soldiers are universally recognized and respected as efficient, professional, and humanitarian. The former United States Army Special Operations Commander, Lieutenant General (ret.) James T. Scott, stressed this truism during a speech given in the summer of 1996, "I can tell you that Special Forces soldiers will…continue to serve as the conscience and the example for lesser developed nations regarding human rights."

The motto of Special Forces, *De Oppresso Liber* (To Free the Oppressed), reflects a profound concern for the inherent dignity of those who are denied international human rights. Crossing all cultural and societal boundaries, this mentality makes Special Forces soldiers an ideal model as they train host nation forces and assist in alleviating many of the conditions that breed human rights abuses. By word and deed, Special Forces promote the message that the hallmark of a professional military serving the interests of a democratic nation is its commitment to human rights. This message is not lost on the host nation.

The four basic themes taught and stressed to the developing Afghan and Iraqi militaries are:

1. human rights abuses are never tolerated by a democratic populace;
2. such violations do not shorten a conflict, be it internal or external in nature, but usually have the opposite effect;
3. the soldiers guilty of human rights violations must be punished, or similar abuses will certainly follow; and
4. in order to maintain discipline and esprit de corps, the chain of command must constantly train soldiers to respect internationally recognized human rights and the law of war.

Shortly after assuming command of the Army Special Forces Command at Fort Bragg, North Carolina, Major General Bowra took affirmative action to ensure that all Special Forces soldiers thoroughly understood their rights and responsibilities regarding human rights issues and interaction with any host nation military. A first ever Special Forces Human Rights Policy Memorandum was issued by General Bowra, directing that all Special Forces soldiers who deploy overseas must:

1. be trained in the full range of human rights issues, both generally and as they may apply to the host nation to which they are deploying; and
2. report through the chain of command all gross violations of human rights they may encounter while overseas.

The four-page policy memorandum also requires commanders, whenever practicable, to integrate human rights training as a part of the training provided to the host nation military. In addition, senior commanders must review all exercise and deployment "after action reports" to evaluate the impact that human rights training initiatives have had on host nation military forces and then make recommendations for improvements to higher headquarters.

Special Forces soldiers and their commanders have many resources available to them to promote human rights. The most important resource, other than a soldier's solid moral compass, is the group judge advocate (GJA) assigned to each of the Special Forces groups. Each GJA is thoroughly trained in human rights law and has compiled an extensive collection of information dealing with human rights issues related to the group's area of responsibility. Apart from providing the mandatory pre-deployment legal briefings to all soldiers deploying to foreign soil, these specialized military attorneys stay abreast of current doctrine in the form of international agreements, human rights doctrine, and political and social changes in the region concerned. They are currently on the ground in Afghanistan and Iraq, taking a proactive view and performing crucial implementation missions with the local Afghan and Iraqi leaders as new Afghan and Iraqi militaries stand up.

9.13 New Challenges and New Thinking

In terms of promoting peace and advancing human rights, the Middle East remains the most difficult area of the world for the United States to influence. A continuing pattern of violence and bloodshed accurately defines the character of the region, a pattern which was brought home to America with the heinous attacks by al-Qa'eda operatives on the United States, on September 11, 2001, and continues with terror attacks by Islamic radicals against United States forces in Afghanistan and Iraq.

The policy of the United States toward the Middle East is still rooted primarily on maintaining stability in this oil-rich region, with human rights concerns often taking a back seat to financial concerns. Accordingly, the United States spends billions of dollars each year (in equal amounts) in military and economic assistance for the two major powers in the region—Israel and Egypt.

Unfortunately, Islamic radicalism that engages in hostilities against the United States and its allies is seeking to fill the ideological power vacuum in the region left by the decline of communism and could easily engulf other Arab countries in the same manner as it did with Iran, Afghanistan, and the Sudan. Islamic radicalism, which is diametrically opposed to most of the normative values of human rights, is offered as the only alternative to the moderate, yet non-democratic, Muslim and Arab leaders who are unwilling or unable to address the economic and social disparities of their people.

In the context of advancing human rights issues in the region, only Israel can be considered as a stable democratic environment. Egypt, by constitution, is a socialist democratic republic in which the Islamic Sharia is a principal source of legislation. Unfortunately, Egypt has shown little willingness to improve its record. Tragically, the majority of countries considered by the State Department of the United States as sponsors of terrorism are located in the Middle East, e.g., Iran and Syria.

The pivot for democratic advancement is certainly at stake in Iraq and Afghanistan. Only time will tell if the policy of offering a more democratic form of government is a "bridge too far" or a "bridge too soon."

9.14 Questions for Discussion

1. *Causes of aggression.* Dr. Stanton E. Samenow, Jr., INSIDE THE CRIMINAL MIND, 1984:

    > Criminals cause crime—not bad neighborhoods, inadequate parents, television, schools, drugs, or unemployment. Crime resides in the minds of human beings and is not caused by social conditions. Once we as a society recognize this simple fact, we shall take measures radically different from current ones. To be sure, we shall continue to remedy intolerable social conditions for this is worthwhile in and of itself. But we shall not expect criminals to change because of such efforts.

    Is Dr. Samenow's observation correct?

2. *Correct analysis but flawed execution?* Reflecting the fact that democracies do not engage in aggression and do a better job at promoting human rights concerns, democratization was a central core of the Bush Administration's policy for the Middle East. How can democratization be achieved when it appears that centrifugal forces of violence have now been unleashed in many parts of the Middle East? Will the Obama Administration's policy of "mutual respect" achieve positive results, particularly with Iran?

3. *Have Mideast democracy concepts provided a boost to Islamic militants?* 2006 elections in Lebanon provided Hizballah, an Iranian Shiite backed terrorist organization, seats in the parliament and a post in the government's Cabinet. Similarly, HAMAS' rise to power in the "free" elections in the Palestinian territories replaced the secular Fatah party. Discuss.

4. *Is the War on Terror a battle of religions?* The 2006 National Security Strategy of the United States of America states:

    > While the War on Terror is a battle of ideas, it is not a battle of religions. The transnational terrorists confronting us today exploit the proud religion of Islam to serve a violent political vision: the establishment, by terrorism and subversion, of a totalitarian empire that denies all political and religious freedom. These terrorists distort the idea of jihad into a call for murder against those they regard as apostates or unbelievers—including Christians, Jews, Hindus, other religious traditions, and all Muslims who disagree with them. Indeed, most of the terrorist attacks since September 11 have occurred in Muslim countries—most of the victims have been Muslims.

    Is any one religion more likely to engage in terrorism than another? Although Biblical Christianity is distinguished from all other major world religions in that it rejects any system of human good deeds, morality, or ritual as the vehicle to achieve eternal relationship with God, Christians have engaged in terrorism. *See* Jeffrey F. Addicott, *The Misuse of Religion in the War on Terror*, 7 BARRY L. J. 109 (Fall 2006).

5. *What role does the concept of virtue play in the survivability of a democracy?* Tytler's observation about the rise and fall of nations seems to imply that democracies work only when a majority of the people are virtuous. R. E. Lee once observed that "when virtue is absent from the people, the nation will collapse." Define virtue. Explain how virtue is necessary for capitalism to function. Can socialism promote virtue?

Selected Bibliography

Burns, John F. *Traces of Terror: Kandahar and Kabul; Afghan President Escapes Bullets; 25 Killed by Bomb*, NY TIMES, Sept. 6, 2002, at A1.

Defense Institute of Security Assistance Management. THE MANAGEMENT OF SECURITY ASSISTANCE, 12th ed. 1992.

Foreign Assistance Act of 1961, as amended, 22 U.S.C. 2347, which provides the authority for security assistance under the International Military Education and Training (IMET) program.

Halberstadt, H. GREEN BERETS: UNCONVENTIONAL WARRIORS, 1988.

Howard, A.E. Dick. CONSTITUTION MAKING IN EASTERN EUROPE, 1993.

Humphrey, John T. NO DISTANT MILLENNIUM: THE INTERNATIONAL LAW OF HUMAN RIGHTS, 1989.

Hutchins, Robert Maynard, ed. GREAT BOOKS OF THE WESTERN WORLD, 1952.

Klare, Michael T., and Peter Kornbluh, eds. LOW-INTENSITY WARFARE, 1988.

Lesser, Ian O., et al. COUNTERING THE NEW TERRORISM, 1999.

Lillich, Richard B., and Frank C. Newman. INTERNATIONAL HUMAN RIGHTS, 1991.

O'Brien, William V. THE CONDUCT OF JUST AND LIMITED WAR, 1981.

Oppenheim, Lassa. INTERNATIONAL LAW: A TREATISE, 1955.

Privileged Killers, SOVIET MILITARY REVIEW, Jan. 1987, at 4.

Russett, B. GRASPING THE DEMOCRATIC PEACE: PRINCIPLES FOR A POST-COLD WAR WORLD, 1993.

Simpkin, Richard. RACE TO THE SWIFT: THOUGHTS ON TWENTY-FIRST CENTURY WARFARE, 1985.

THE NATIONAL INTELLIGENCE STRATEGY OF THE UNITED STATES OF AMERICA, Aug. 2009.

Thieme, Robert B., Jr. THE INTEGRITY OF GOD. Houston, TX: R.B. Thieme, 1979.

U.S. Army's Center for Strategy and Force Evaluation. Peacekeeping Operations, Sept. 1993.

USASFC (A) Policy Memorandum, dated August 13, 1996. Special Forces Human Rights Policy, issued by MG Kenneth Bowra, CG, USASFC (A).

USASFC (A) Human Rights Handbook (on file with the OSJA, USASFC(A), Fort Bragg, NC).

Chapter 10

Leading the Way—
Pax Americana or the Rule of Law?

Let he who desires peace, prepare for war.

—Flavius Vegetius Renatus (first century A.D.)

The fact that the United States saved Western Europe and the free world in two World Wars by the use of its magnificent military establishment, coupled with its even greater industrial complex, does not imply that the ongoing military campaigns in the War on Terror will set the stage for a pax Americana. Much like President Roosevelt's attempt to color the participation of the United States in World War II with a far greater purpose than national self-interest, President Bush's concern for protecting the United States was also cognizant of promoting world stability. To his great credit, President Bush chose the rule of law as his rallying point and did not fall into the trap of embracing issues and matters that appealed to utopian ideals beyond the scope of the War on Terror. This error was made by his father, President George H. Bush, in his desire to advance an idea known as the *New World Order* in the context of the Gulf War. To date, President Obama has viewed the role of the United States in a far more limited fashion. For instance, after taking over four months to reach a decision, in 2009 Obama ordered a significant increase in American troop involvement in Afghanistan. Other than that, he has shown a great reluctance to fully address the threat of radical Islam or the threat posed by a nuclear Iran and North Korea.

10.1 The United States Global Strategic View

Although the War on Terror has seen a dramatic shift to homeland security as the primary mission of the United States military, the overall strategy since the end of the Cold War has been one of active engagement or deterrence through power projection. At least in theory, active engagement also has a positive aim of promoting democracy, regional stability, and economic prosperity. However, in the context of conducting "operations other than war," the orientation has shifted from containing the menace posed by an expansionist Soviet Union to responding to regional conflicts throughout the world.

Since regional conflicts may vary and are far less monolithic than the old Soviet threat, ad hoc coalitions have replaced formal alliances. This was seen in the 1991 Gulf War as well as in the ongoing War on Terror. To support the active engagement theory, force generation has also changed from forward deployment to forward presence—no longer are large numbers of United States forces permanently stationed in foreign countries to ensure the peace. Despite the continued presence of a large force in Iraq and now Afghanistan, the new strategy in the War on Terror envisions a force projection of small contingents of American forces deployed on the foreign soil of other States, such as Yemen and the Philippines, to assist in blunting the impact of al-Qa'eda forces and other like-minded terrorist groups. In conjunction, President Obama has utilized drone attacks on specific targets in a variety of other nations to include Sudan, Yemen, Somalia, Pakistan, and Afghanistan.

Another purpose of these small scale deployments of American fighters is to deter aggression simply by being present in the region. Ultimately, deterrence remains a key component of strategic policy in the War on Terror, with the United States threatening the full scale use of force to punish aggression should the challenge arise.

Undoubtedly, the projection of its forces in this engagement strategy requires a strong leadership role by the United States. In the post-Cold War era, the cement of anti-communism that held democratic alliances together is no longer valid and many allies and friends no longer have the same degree of need for American protection. Consequently, America is required to walk a thinner line between leadership and dominance, as selected coalitions are temporarily built to deal with the threat of terrorism. Furthermore, to be successful under the collective engagement strategy, American leadership must be exercised in conjunction with the interests of the people of the host nation. Indeed, the strongest coalition partners in defeating a totalitarian terrorist regime are the people enslaved in their own country.

Still, in the face of drastic military reductions in United States military forces since the 1990s, the elite ground forces available for these unique missions are being stretched to the breaking point. Demanding that the military do more with less causes many to express skepticism about maintaining the required effectiveness to fight and win a conflict with the ever elusive al-Qa'eda and the renegade States like Iran who seek access to weapons of mass murder.

One fact stands certain. The United States cannot continue the War on Terror or take a strong leadership role in promoting democracy in liberated lands with an emasculated military. There is no historical basis to validate the proposition that a nation can successfully increase its influence in the world while simultaneously reducing its armed forces. In the context of deterring future aggression and winning the War on Terror, this proposition is extremely disturbing. If history has proven anything, it is that the machinations of aggressor nations bent on expansion are not stopped by negotiation or peace overtures. In dealing with aggressor nations, the avenues of unilateral military reduction, negotiation, or appeasement do not lead to the path of peace—all are false concepts washed in utopian nonsense. The shared revulsion against war and terrorism that all free people possess will have no good effect unless it is coupled with an enforcement mechanism rooted in the application of lawful violence or the threat of lawful violence.

10.2 American Leadership in National Security

Collective security has always required a dominant leader with a sufficient military establishment. Devoid of any military arm of its own, the United Nations could not deal with, for example, Saddam Hussein and his continued violations of international law. In the twentieth century, that has always meant the United States. This is true in every case in which international collective security has functioned. The lesson of the War on Terror is the same as that of the 1991 Gulf War and the Korean War: the United Nations does not have the capacity to guarantee the security of its members absent the direct participation of the United States.

In the real world, the question will be the same as it has always been. Will the people of the United States continue to possess the resolve to assist in the struggle to halt major acts of aggression in the future? As demonstrated in the War on Terror, it is probable that a majority of Americans will continue to possess such resolve, although there are clear signs that the pivot of patriots in the United States that truly understand these truths is shrinking. Apart from matters of self-interest, the United States of America does have a continuing responsibility to the world to enforce the rule of law. Judged by any positive standard, be it in the field of human rights, self-determination, economic opportunity, or privacy related to property and person, the United States still stands out as the pearl of all that is possible for any given nation to achieve. Furthermore, America, like great nations before it, has related all of these positive values to a strong heritage of law. The framers of the nation established certain democratic values, and subsequent generations have generally exhibited the discipline and courage to maintain and expand those values. America is exceptional.

America's most fundamental asset does not reside in her military might or industrial complex. Those pillars merely provide support for the United States' most precious commodity—freedom as related to the rule of law. Although the United States military most certainly deterred the aggressiveness of the Soviet Empire from 1945 to 1991, it was the beacon of American freedom and capitalism that ultimately dispelled the darkness of communism. To the world, then, the United States offers a pattern of prosperity and freedom under the rule of law. This is the message that the United States must continue to send to the world.

The world is still a very dangerous place and, as never before, it is time for forward thinking in the long term as the nation prosecutes the War on Terror. Coming out of the Cold War, millions of people in Central Asia and Eastern Europe still have little frame of reference for a nation or, for that matter, a world that is ruled by law. Indeed, the governments of the Middle East lag far behind in fulfilling the requirements of first and second generation human rights.

Under the leadership of the Bush Administration, the United States successfully validated the logic and necessity for following the rule of law. Undeniably, the legitimate interest of the United States in halting international terrorism in the era of weapons of mass destruction has benefited the entire civilized world. For freedom loving peoples everywhere, the 2001 victory in Afghanistan and the successful conclusion of the Iraq War ensured that the cost of maintaining freedom was paid by another generation of patriotic Americans. To a large degree, this sacrifice not only enforces the rule of law, but undoubtedly serves as a deterrent to other tyrants and terrorists. Unfortunately, memories of both tyrants and democracies are short and the struggle for freedom must be played out in each and every generation.

It is a fundamental principle that all free States have a common interest in maintaining peace. However, peace, like security, is a precious commodity rarely attained without great sacrifice. In addition, peace is far more than the absence of war; it is an elusive intangible which only takes on meaning when related to freedom. Although the goal of abolishing war, like eradicating crime, is certainly commendable, given the basic nature of man, neither goal is totally feasible. As long as there are demagogues like Sennacherib, Hitler, Stalin, Saddam Hussein, and Ahmadinejad, nation-states must have strong military establishments to protect themselves. Under this truism, the symbol of freedom for Americans is not a cracked Liberty Bell in Philadelphia, but the military uniform of its fighting men.

Accepting the premise that human beings are morally flawed creatures (Chapter 9.1 and 9.2), it stands to reason that the best that mankind can ever hope to achieve is to control aggression. Like criminals, aggressive nations and terrorists can only be deterred through the proper functioning of two principles: (1) the threat of lawful force; or (2) the application of lawful force. To the extent that the function of these two principles fail, wars will certainly continue to exist. Paradoxically, those groups who resist this truism, demonstrated by irrational demands for peace through the continued restriction of all categories of force, blissfully lay the groundwork for the next war.

The oft-heard saying, "violence never solves anything," is a favorite catch phrase for so-called "peace activists" and progressives. Of course, as is the case for many such glib expressions, it is a falsehood that does not stand up to reason or historical scrutiny. As illustrated by the Allied defeat of the Axis powers in World War II, only the application of lawful violence ultimately solved the problem of Axis aggression and murder. In short, the use of lawful violence in self-defense is a hard reality of life that must always remain as the number one legitimate option to secure the peace. While nonviolence expressed in the form of public demonstrations, boycotts, "sit-ins," etc., may be efficacious when confronting social injustice in certain organizations and governments that are based to some degree on democratic foundations, such activities seldom make any progress when used to confront committed totalitarian forces. Even Martin Luther King, an American champion of nonviolence, conceded that this tactic would be useless against tyrants.

> I felt that while war could never be a positive or absolute good, it could serve as a negative good in the sense of preventing the spread and growth of an evil force. War, as horrible as it is, might be preferable to surrender to a totalitarian system—Nazi, Fascist, or Communist.

Sadly, in the course of the human experience, it is sometimes the case that nothing except the employment of lawful violence will thwart the use of aggressive violence and the correct moral course is to employ lawful violence. Understanding this truth is fundamental to penetrating the state of mind of those who simply reject violence under any circumstances. Tragically, those most devoted to peace above all values seem ill prepared to recognize that the cost of not using lawful violence may only ensure a continuation of aggressive violence that often spirals out of control.

Peace activists who use religion (primarily their reading of "Christianity") to justify a rejection of force come in many varieties. Some try to mask their refusal to engage in violence with Bible verses taken out of context, while others simply make broad religious generalizations about the matter. For instance, William H. De Lancey, bishop of the Episcopal Diocese of New York, wrote a letter to President Abraham Lincoln in 1863 invoking religion to avoid participating in the American Civil War. He demanded that he and all other bishops and priests be exempted from the federal conscription laws. De Lancey wrote, "[I]t is contrary to their consciences as officers of Christ's kingdom to bear arms as soldiers and shed blood." Continuing with the letter, Bishop De Lancey reminded Lincoln that in the garden of Gethsemane on the occasion of his arrest, Christ told Peter in Matthew 26:52 that, "[t]hey that take the sword shall perish with the sword." Of course, in making his case, the bishop rejected the more sensible and Biblically correct view that this passage refers to the societal consequences of criminal behavior, i.e., criminals will be lawfully executed by the State for their crimes, and not the lawful use of force in combat activities.

If peace at any price, with compromise as the only means to achieve it, is the major concern of a national entity, then the destruction of that nation will be the inevitable consequence. Freedom, not peace, must always be the issue for free nations; when nations are no longer willing to pay the price of freedom, then they, too, will lose their freedom. As Woodrow Wilson so wisely reflected in May of 1917: "It is not an army that we must train for war; it is a nation."

Tragically, every democratic nation has within it the very seeds which will eventually destroy it, for the choice between freedom or peace must be made by each successive generation. With freedom, war is periodically inevitable. By choosing peace without maintaining the power to enforce the peace, however, war will come more often and with a greater probability of resulting in the annihilation of the nation. Just as crime increases when society gets sentimental about the criminal and forgets about the victim, so too will the probability of war increase as the nation emphasizes peace instead of freedom.

When Spain was attacked by a series of coordinated bombings in March 2004, killing 200 commuters, the response to the al-Qa'eda-linked terrorists was to withdraw all Spanish military personnel from Iraq. This step signaled to the terrorists that terror attacks can produce a desired outcome. In quick step, the terrorists used terror threats and acts of terror to intimidate the Philippines, who withdrew their forces early from Iraq in response to a kidnapping and threat of beheading. On the other hand, threats to Italy and Australia to withdraw from Iraq were not successful. In July of 2004, the Australians were warned that "we will shake the earth under your feet as we did in Indonesia [referring to the 2002 Bali bombing which killed over 200 people, mostly Australians on vacation], and lines of car bombs will not cease." Similarly, the Abu Jafs al-Masri Brigades' threat to "shake the earth" everywhere in Italy, unless the Italians withdrew from Iraq, did not cause the Italians to budge. The Italian and Australian leadership remembered the lesson of Munich—appeasement only encourages aggression.

Ultimately, the cost of achieving freedom can only be understood by those who have paid the price. Indeed, there is no permanent guarantee that the United States will continue to function as a national entity beyond a strong military-industrial complex coupled with the people who have the will to fight if necessary.

For this reason, it is dangerous rhetoric to blur the fundamental distinction between the need for the legitimate use of force and unlawful aggression. Despite disclaimers that the concept of "world peace" should not be related to restricting the use of force or promoting unilateral disarmament, the connotation is otherwise. No anti-war movement has ever been premised on maintaining a strong and viable military, and no proponent of the use of lawful violence can ever hope to be immune from the wishful thinking of those who demand the dismantling of the very forces that sustain and protect the freedom of the nation—the military establishment.

On the other hand, the concept of the rule of law does not necessarily carry with it the connotation that man is ever capable of achieving the panacea of world peace. For the rule of law, it is enough if aggressive war can be controlled. As international law expert Professor Bob Turner noted during the Gulf War of 1991: "At the root of United States policy in the Gulf War was the principle of upholding the Rule of Law. Article 2 (4) of the U.N. Charter outlaws armed international aggression, and the massive Iraqi invasion of Kuwait was a direct challenge to that principle."

In short, how does one react to those nations or groups who either contemplate the use of unlawful force or who actually engage in such unlawful force? To date, the U.N. Charter is undeniably the foremost legal tool in dealing with and deterring aggression; it is an integral component of the rule of law. The classic McDougal and Feliciano, *Law and Minimum Public Order*, states:

The most difficult problem which today confronts world public order is that of characterizing and preventing unlawful violence. The history is familiar how over the centuries—through *bellum justum*, the Covenant of the League of Nations, the Pact of Paris, the judgments at Nuremberg and Tokyo, and the U.N. Charter—the public order of the world community has at long last come to a prohibition of certain coercion as a method of international change and to a distinction between permissible and nonpermissible coercion.

Although history has proven time and again that the curtailment of aggression can only come through the threat of force, or the application of force, the authority for those responses must be firmly rooted in law. Despite this truism, the necessity for and legality of Article 51 is, nonetheless, constantly under attack by those groups who intentionally blur the difference between lawful and unlawful uses of force. In their search for the panacea of brotherhood, various peace groups refuse to acknowledge any distinction regarding the use of force. Left unchallenged, this attitude will only encourage aggression, not forestall it.

President Bush performed admirably in the task of articulating to the world the distinction between the unlawful use of force by an aggressor and the lawful use of force under the rule of law by civilized nations. In fact, those who advocate ending war by destroying the forests of bayonets (i.e., unilateral disarmament) hinder the validity of the rule of law to that extent.

Historically, the desire of numerous organizations to curtail or eliminate the use of force as a national option, regardless of the justification for the employment of that force, is always present in any debate on how to best answer aggression. While these voices are helpful if kept in proper perspective, appeasement is nothing new. The Biblical prophet Jeremiah heard the same voices almost 2,500 years ago as peace activists in the Southern Kingdom of Judah proposed how to deal with the aggression of Chaldean militarism. Jeremiah analyzed the peace at any cost advocates as follows: "They allege to solve the problems of my people, [they cry] 'Peace, peace' when there is no peace."

10.3 Peace, Freedom and Appeasement—Lessons from the Gulf War of 1991

The voices in the War on Terror who call for peace at any price say nothing new—the same voices occurred in the Gulf War of 1991, although far more loudly. Calling for peace in the Gulf War at any price, some paid little regard for even the most clearly worded rules and norms associated with the rule of law as it applies to the lawful use of force. This phenomenon extended all the way from the highest levels of the United Nations to, as to be expected, an assortment of politically active anti-war groups.

At the top echelon, this phenomenon was brought out rather dramatically on November 8, 1990, when none other than the Secretary General of the United Nations, Perez de Cuellar, opined that because no nation had taken military action against Iraq since the occupation of Kuwait in August 1990, "the passage of three months time had terminated the right of individual states to use force against Iraq under the 'collective self-defense' provisions of Article 51." Not only did de Cuellar's statement exhibit a gross misunderstanding of the U.N. Charter, it did nothing but encourage the continued aggression of the Iraqi military.

Certainly, de Cuellar knew that Article 51 did not create the right of self-defense, but that such a right was an inherent right which Article 51 simply acknowledged and reinforced. Furthermore, Iraq's aggression did not end on August 2, 1990, but was a continuing offense, since none of the Security Council resolutions demanding that Iraq leave Kuwait had succeeded in "maintaining international peace and security."

The policy implications of the Secretary General's position revealed its total absurdity; a rule that requires nations to respond immediately to an armed attack or else forfeit their rights to take defensive action effectively nullifies the principles embodied in Article 2(3) and 2(4) of the U.N. Charter. By making a mockery of this critical rule of law, de Cuellar sent two disastrous signals, one to Saddam Hussein and one to the community of nations. First, the Secretary General's total misreading of Article 51 only encouraged Iraq's continuing occupation of Kuwait and was completely counterproductive to the international movement to force Iraq out of Kuwait short of armed force. Second, the requirement that nations act immediately in self-defense is the antithesis of what the United Nation encourages, i.e., the peaceful settlement of disputes through diplomacy and every other peaceful channel for resolution of conflict. Finally, the longer the hesitation in the use of legitimate force (give peace a chance), the more probable that the same peace activists would view the coalition forces as the aggressor!

The more common variety of anti-war groups also hoped that the end of the Cold War would be the catalyst for their simplistic notions concerning the abolition of war. Advocating peace, but having no idea of what the concept must necessarily entail—the willingness to fight for peace—numerous anti-war activists demanded appeasement. Paradoxically, the loud demands for peace during the six month Iraqi occupation of Kuwait probably ensured that the threat of force as a deterrence would most surely fail, leaving no alternative but the use of lawful violence.

As Saddam Hussein held firm in Kuwait with no signs of withdrawal, various religious groups also voiced dismay over those who contemplated the exercise of lawful armed force against Iraq under Article 51. For example, both the Vatican daily newspaper, *Losservatore Romano*, and the official publication of the Jesuit order, *La Civilta Cattolica*, spoke out against using force to expel Iraq from Kuwait. On November 17, 1990, *La Civilta Cattolica* wrote, "The [coming] war in the Gulf will be a moral shame and a political disaster."

In his traditional Christmas message, Pope John Paul II gave the following heartfelt warning to those who contemplated the use of force to expel Saddam Hussein: "May leaders be convinced that war is an adventure with no return. By reasoning, patience, and dialogue with respect for the inalienable rights of people and nations, it is possible to identify and travel the paths of understanding and peace." In the final analysis, the Pope's sincere desire for "[n]o more war, war never again" is a beautiful ideal but, unfortunately, can sometimes prove counterproductive in the maintenance of world peace. Often, such signals encourage aggression if no room is left for the use of lawful force to halt aggression *ab initio* or to challenge aggression once it has become entrenched. In fact, one commentator observed that of the thirty-eight times the Pope spoke out against the Gulf War, "[t]here was not an echo of a hint of a suggestion that the United States and its allies (including Italy) were in a battle against a tyrant who had just invaded and [sic] occupied and brutally destroyed a small neighbor...."

Some religious leaders, emotionally obsessed by the fact that large numbers of soldiers were going to be killed in war, irrationally concluded that all war in the modern era was immoral, regardless of the motivation. Fueled by reports that some Iraqi soldiers had been buried alive in their defensive positions by American tanks, a religious publicist, Guy Munger, concluded that "any discussion of whether Desert Storm was a just war seem[s] to border on the insane. Indeed, practical application of the theory may have ended with the crossbow." According to Munger, "modern war is always immoral." Of course, the argument is totally fallacious for two reasons. First, long before the crossbow, battle casualties could easily mount into the hundreds of thousands. For example, during the Second Punic War (219–202 B.C.), the Carthaginian forces under Hannibal killed in combat over 60,000 Roman soldiers in a single day. And second, Munger fails to understand the real world consequences associated with a refusal to defend oneself.

Claiming to be a spokesperson for morality and justice, the wife of Martin Luther King, Jr., Coretta King, also attempted to derail the United States-led military coalition to eject Saddam Hussein from

Kuwait. She referred to the American actions as a "low [point] since the death of Dr. King." Speaking on January 11, 1991, Mrs. King called on a new anti-war movement to be launched on January 15, 1991, the date of the United Nations' deadline for Iraq to withdraw from Kuwait or face the use of force: "And so I am urging everyone who believes in Martin Luther King, Jr.'s dream of peace to use this holiday to launch a new anti-war movement that will not rest until a peaceful resolution of the conflict in the Persian Gulf is secured."

Failing to elaborate on how this peace movement could force a brutal dictator to relinquish his death grip on Kuwait, Mrs. King called the American participation in the Gulf War "wrong and immoral." Like the other peace activists who refuse to consider the application of force under any circumstances, Mrs. King's call for "peace-loving people everywhere to accelerate their efforts to stop it" did nothing except encourage the ruthlessness of the Iraqi occupation.

Similarly, the president of the Southern Christian Leadership Conference, Reverend Joseph Lowery, objected to the United States military action on moral grounds saying, "Let us call upon the nations to spend our resources on medical supplies, not military supplies; to make tractors, not tanks; to beat missiles into morsels of bread to feed the hungry; to build housing, not foxholes." Again, if history has demonstrated anything, it has demonstrated that utopian rhetoric about turning "swords into plowshares" is not helpful in deterring people and nations who exhibit aggressive tendencies.

Obviously, Man is always confronted with aggression; a world without conflict is not something that is in the here and now. The attitude of any free people is being well prepared for war so that the nation may either rattle the saber or, if necessary, employ the saber against forces of aggression. Pacifism finds its origin in many of the statements of the Bible regarding the future millennium reign of Jesus Christ on the earth. Those who wish to enter a new world order in which "swords are turned into plowshares" need to recall the comments of Haynes Johnson of the *Washington Post*: "[this] is not the millennium; the new world order has not arrived." Unfortunately, the sincere but unrealistic belief that war can be curtailed by third-party dispute settlement processes or by massive disarming processes was not buried in the lessons of the Gulf War of 1991.

10.4 Peace, Freedom and Appeasement—Lessons from the War on Terror

While the murderous machinations of al-Qa'eda-styled militant Islam constantly invoke religious beliefs to justify the use of the most horrible forms of illegal violence, some voices in the West appropriate their own system of religious beliefs as a justification to advance platforms of pacifism in dealing with the terrorists. Many religious leaders in the West will align themselves with anti-war activists and then employ religion as the reason to reject all forms of violence whatsoever, self-defense or otherwise. For these voices of appeasement, a misapplication of religious belief is used as a justification *not* to use lawful violence to curtail aggression. Paradoxically, as history has proven time and time again, appeasement—be it in the name of religion or not—cannot long curtail those intent on aggression. Such wishful thinking simply emboldens the aggressor and inevitably leads to an increase in the butcher's bill of human suffering. A sampling of remarks during the War on Terror is all that is necessary to address the theme of those who call for peace at any price, with little or no regard for the long standing norms and rules associated with the lawful use of force.

In her 2006 book, *The Mighty and the Almighty*, even the liberal-minded Madeleine Albright opposed the voices of appeasement that protested the pending military campaign against the Taliban regime in Afghanistan following the attacks of 9/11. Not only did she disagree with the official 2001 call by the World Council of Churches to not strike back against the terrorists, but she also questioned the soundness of prize winning author Alice Walker's naive admonishment that "the only punishment that works is love."

In November of 2002, as the United States and its coalition of the willing were gearing up to expand the War on Terror to Iraq, over 70 religious leaders in the United States and the United Kingdom issued a joint statement that condemned the contemplated use of what they termed "preemptive war" against the regime of Saddam Hussein. Recognizing that the Iraqi government had a duty to "stop its internal repression, to end its threats to peace, to abandon its efforts to develop weapons of mass destruction, and to respect the legitimate role of the United Nations in ensuring that it does so," the religious leaders nevertheless insisted that as "Christians" they were certain that the United States, Britain, and the international community could only employ the tools of "moral principles, political wisdom, and international law" to confront Saddam:

> As Christians, we seek to be guided by the vision of a world in which nations do not attempt to resolve international problems by making war on other nations. It is a long held Christian principle that all governments and citizens are obliged to work for the avoidance of war.

In closing the statement, the group quoted the familiar Biblical passage "nation shall not lift up sword against nation," which, although very popular in anti-war circles, is grossly distorted from its proper scriptural context. The passage clearly deals with eschatological teachings about the future and not the current world we reside in. They wrote: "We reaffirm our religious hope for a world in which 'nation shall not lift up sword against nation.' We pray that our governments will be guided by moral principles, political wisdom, and legal standards, and will step back from their calls for war."

Similarly, in late 2002, the President of the United Methodist Council of Bishops wrote a pastoral letter to the United Methodist congregation, of which President Bush and Vice President Cheney are both members, stating that "war by the United States against a nation like Iraq goes against the very grain of *our understanding of the gospel*, our church's teachings, and our conscience [emphasis added]."

With the defeat of Saddam Hussein and the end of the international armed conflict with Iraq in May 2003, the Bush Administration was faced with an unexpected deadly level of sectarian violence fueled in part by a variety of criminal groups, al-Qa'eda terrorists, and Saddam loyalists. Nevertheless, the theme of religious-based anti-war activists remained the same. When Reverend Al Sharpton met anti-war activist Cindy Sheehan at an interfaith service on Sunday, August 28, 2005, outside of Crawford, Texas, he did so based on his "moral obligation" to oppose the war. In March of 2003, two well-known bishops and one church official were among 65 people arrested during an anti-war protest near the White House. United Methodist Bishop Joseph Sprague; Jim Winkler, the general secretary of the United Methodist Board of Church and Society; and Roman Catholic Bishop Thomas Gumbleton of Detroit were included among those arrested. Winkler said that his religious board had "stated that the war is wrong."

After receiving the 2002 Nobel Peace Prize in Oslo, Norway, former President Jimmy Carter concluded his December 10, 2002 remarks by asserting that God gives mankind the capacity for choice and that war is always an evil, even when necessary, and "never a good."

> War may sometimes be a necessary evil. But no matter how necessary, it is always an evil, never a good. We will not learn to live together in peace by killing each other's children. The bond of

our common humanity is stronger than the divisiveness of our fears and prejudices. God gives us the capacity for choice. We can choose to alleviate suffering. We can choose to work together for peace. We can make these changes—and we must.

While many leading religious leaders have issued statements condemning the use of force in both Iraq and in the Bush-era war in Afghanistan, the majority of Christians prior to the war in Iraq supported the use of force. For example, the 16 million-strong Southern Baptist Convention, the largest denomination in America (made up of Southern conservatives), sent a letter to President Bush "assuring him that the Iraqi threat satisfied the conditions of a 'just war.'" (Current opposition by the American public is not based on moral or religious grounds, but on a sense that the mission of bringing democratic reforms cannot be accomplished.) In addition, George Weigel, a biographer of Pope John Paul II as well as a leading Catholic commentator and Senior Fellow of the Ethics and Public Policy Center, also believed that the 2003 war against Iraq was justified.

In the case of Iraq, the crucial issue in the moral analysis is what we mean by an "aggression under way." When a vicious regime that has not hesitated to use chemical weapons against its own people and against a neighboring country, a regime that has no concept of the rule of law and that flagrantly violates its international obligations, works feverishly to obtain and deploy further weapons of mass destruction, I think a compelling moral case can be made that this is a matter of an "aggression under way." The nature of the regime, which is the crucial factor in the analysis, makes that plain. It surely makes no moral sense to say that the U.S. or the international community can only respond with armed force when an Iraqi missile carrying a weapon of mass destruction has been launched, or is being readied for launch. To be sure, there are serious questions of prudence to be addressed in thinking through the question of military action against the Iraqi regime. At the level of moral principle, however, it seems to me that there are, in fact, instances where it is not only right to "go first," but "going first" may even be morally obligatory. And I think this may well be one of those instances.

Weigel also criticized other "clerical opponents of war...[as giving] themselves over to a functional pacifism, a conviction that there are virtually no circumstances in which the proportionate and discriminate use of armed force can serve the goals of peace, order, justice and freedom." Indeed, some of the more extreme pacifists go so far as to blame the "Christian God" and President Bush as instigating an "American Inquisition" in the War on Terror. Curiously, when a liberal President, like Barack Obama, engages in combat activities to include the unprecedented use of drone attacks and the huge 2009-2010 deployment of U.S. soldiers in Afghanistan, the pacifists and leftists remain muted. There are no "Cindy Sheehans" or "World Council of Churchs" taking to the streets in massive outrage.

Still, for the committed pacifist, there simply should be no relationship between religion and warfare. Their interpretation of religion prohibits all forms of violence whatsoever. Further, they steadfastly oppose people who invoke God to justify violence in self-defense. While one can certainly agree with the utopian idea that war, crime, poverty, and a whole host of evils should not exist in the world, it is a fact that they do. When asked by his disciples what would be the signs that would signal His second coming to the world, Jesus Christ himself declared that wars would continue to be a part of the landscape until His return: "And you will be hearing of wars and rumors of wars; see that you are not frightened, for those things must take place, but that is not yet the end."

To some, pacifism is a fundamental aspect of being a Christian. Liberals think that they are somehow reflecting the attitude and concepts of Jesus Christ by trying to abolish war. This is absurd. To use the Bible to justify an uncompromising belief in pacifism requires one to distort, ignore, or otherwise explain away vast areas of scripture that speak approvingly of specific instances where violence is justified and necessary to protect various values and objects. Jesus Christ himself engaged in violence and would be considered by religious pacifists as quite "anti-Christian" in his dealings with the religious leaders and legalists of the day—calling them, among other things, "of your father the Devil" (Jn. 8:44a).

A fair understanding of the Bible does not support the human viewpoint expressed by the religious anti-war activist. In A.D. 425, Augustine, the Bishop of Hippo, strongly affirmed the idea that the Bible does not prohibit or condemn a Christian from engaging in combat on the battlefield. In a letter to a Roman Christian by the name of Boniface, Augustine told him to fight the invading tribes called the Vandals because "[w]ar is waged in order that peace may be obtained." As stated in Ecclesiastes and echoed throughout the Bible, in the affairs of mankind there is clearly "[a] time for war, and a time for peace." The hope is that when a soldier goes to war, he will be militarily prepared, per Psalms 144:1—"[God] teach my hands to war and my fingers to fight"—and that the national leadership will heed Proverbs 20:18, by choosing to "make war by wise guidance."

10.5 Stay with the Rule of Law

To a large degree, history is defined by the workings of spheres of power which are commonly categorized into eras. Within these eras, the trends of history are replete with great wars whose goal was to end all wars. While the natural tendency of mankind is to promote and to nourish the resulting periods of peace between wars, history gives no encouragement to the notion that war will be no more or that peace will be more than a mere handful of years. The collective memory of the world has traditionally proved to be very short.

With the liberation of Kuwait in 1991, President George H. Bush became the primary proponent of an ambiguous phrase which he called the "New World Order." President George H. Bush attempted to advance this phrase as an international rallying cry for the future of the world. The New World Order was to herald a new era in international affairs, an era of collective security sponsored and reinforced by the United Nations. Expectations for the fulfillment of this goal were understandably high and recalled the old Roman proverb, "For he who desires to become rich also wishes that desire to be soon accomplished." In reality, however, the natural desire to create some form of a New World Order quickly met with failure. Even more disturbing, the promotion of the term New World Order by President Bush served only to minimize or cast doubt on the viability of the rule of law. President George W. Bush has been careful not to repeat this mistake as the War on Terror progresses. Catchy utopian phrases are counterproductive to the critical mission of promoting the rule of law and democratic behavior.

To the serious student of history, the concept of the New World Order is neither new in its origin, nor, as the concept might imply, universal in its interpretation; it has existed in many forms. From the *pax Romana* of ancient Rome to the *novus ordo seclorum* printed on the reverse side of the one-dollar bill, the concept of the New World Order has been used by public figures to represent a variety of agendas associated, of course, with a vision for how the world should be ruled.

In the past century, both the Germans under Adolf Hitler and the British under Winston Churchill used the concept to describe their respective notions about the world's future. Although both were seeking to rally public opinion to support a particular objective, they were diametrically opposed in their meaning and application of the concept. Hitler envisioned *Die neue Ordnung* (the New Order) as a world ruled by the master German race, while Churchill wielded it as a sword of international force against Nazi expansionism.

Addressing the League of Nations in 1936, Churchill warned of Hitler's continued pattern of aggression and announced that the "fateful moment [had] arrived for choice between the New Age and the Old." For Churchill, the new age for the world was squarely based on establishing a defensive alliance to defeat the Nazi's quest of conquering Europe and the world.

Adolf Hitler employed the concept in its most aggressive connotation and irrationally believed that he had a sacred mission to establish a New Order through terror, violence and warfare. The Axis powers set out the parameters of their New Order for the world by signing a joint agreement in Berlin, January 1942. Linking their New Order to economic prosperity, the Germans envisioned the world divided into four *Grossraumwirtschaften* (great economics), each led by an authoritarian leader under the ultimate control of Germany. Once the Axis forces had won World War II, "a conclave was to be held in Vienna to legalize Nazi Germany's hegemony within the New Order." Hitler's New Order would initially be made up of German-dominated Europe, Africa, and the Near East, but ultimately it would encompass the entire world.

In the end, Hitler's "New Order for the World" collapsed in a bloody inferno while "Churchill's New Age for the World" silently slipped into the bookshelves of history after it helped to inspire the formation of the United Nations. Although the concepts were similar, the meanings were not.

The New World Order witnessed its latest reincarnation during the Iraqi invasion of Kuwait in August of 1990. In an unprecedented use of the United Nations, President George H. Bush used the concept of the New World Order as the focal point for gathering world opinion against the Iraqi occupation of Kuwait. In an effort to consolidate support for the possible use of military force against Iraq, President Bush not only followed Churchill's example against Hitler, but simultaneously offered this old term to describe American foreign policy in the post-Cold War era.

Just a month after the invasion, President George H. Bush proclaimed that the New World Order "would be a world where the rule of law supplants the rule of the jungle. A world in which nations recognize the shared responsibility for freedom and justice. A world where the strong respect the rights of the weak." As the months passed and Iraq became more entrenched in Kuwait, the Bush Administration increased the usage of the concept. In a statement delivered on December 5, 1990, before the Senate Foreign Relations Committee, Secretary of State James Baker said, "Historically, we must stand with the people of Kuwait so that the annexation of Kuwait does not become the first reality that mars our vision of the new world order."

Without a doubt, America's vision of the New World Order was to be firmly rooted in the new-founded efficacy of the United Nations to function as the primary legal instrument for maintaining peace in the world, the assumption being that Gorbachev's Russia would no longer use its veto power to hinder the effectiveness of the Security Council. By the close of the Gulf War, the tenets of the New World Order were set: "Peaceful settlements of disputes, solidarity against aggression, reduced and controlled arsenals and just treatment of all peoples."

Unfortunately, from the viewpoint of epistemology, the concept of New World Order was not very successful for the administration of President George H. Bush. First, although the New World Order was undeniably catchy, the concept was not really a simple phrase to understand. In reality, the New World Order stood for a whole regime of policies, ranging all the way from universal human rights issues to the peaceful settlement of international disputes. Apart from a handful of scholars devoted to the study of those topics, the hope that a wider audience would understand the concept, without fully grasping the categories behind it, was the primary failure of its proponents.

Second, because President George H. Bush chose as his rallying cry a phrase that, throughout the past hundred years, had been used to stand for various propositions, he should have necessarily exerted an even greater amount of time and effort to achieve a minimum amount of association to his meaning. In other words, if a concept is to gain acceptance, the rate of forgetting must not exceed the rate of learning. This, too, was never accomplished, reflected in part by a remarkable lack of attention given to the phrase by the public media.

In his September 1991 address to the United Nations, President Bush specifically stressed the concept of the New World Order several times, even deliberately choosing the theme of the New World Order to close out his final remarks to the world body. Seeking to establish a straightforward definition, the President dramatically spelled out the elements of the New World Order.

> [The] new world order [is] an order in which no nation must surrender one iota of its own sovereignty; an order characterized by the rule of law rather than the resort to force; the cooperative settlement of disputes, rather than anarchy and bloodshed; and an unstinting belief in human rights.

Unfortunately, this definition was not really the same given at the close of the Gulf War. Then it was "peaceful settlements of disputes, solidarity against aggression, reduced and controlled arsenals and just treatment of all people." In addition, despite a conscious effort by President Bush to fully sponsor the phrase, the domestic media concentrated on the President's condemnation of Iraqi interference with United Nations inspection teams and the ill-conceived "Zionism is racism" General Assembly resolution. Predictably, the news reports that followed Bush's speech failed to mention the New World Order even once. While one might criticize the news media for exhibiting a total failure to publicize the concept, judged by the standards of keeping it simple and promoting repetition, the blame also rested with the Bush administration.

As to simplicity, President George H. Bush erred by expanding his initial meaning of the New World Order, most associated with the enforcement of the international rule of law against the raw aggression of Iraq, to a definition which equated the New World Order to various categories of international principles, each requiring a sophisticated level of comprehension. By lumping other concepts ranging from nuclear disarmament to human rights with the concept of the New World Order, the vast majority of the public had no idea what the New World Order "really" entailed. At the time, Harvard's Joseph S. Nye, Jr., remarked, "No one really knows what it means."

Most of the world can quickly grasp the idea of halting an aggressor who has broken the law (e.g., Iraq broke the most critical provision of the rule of law, the prohibition of aggression, in its use of force against Kuwait). But, when one adds, for example, the concept of creating norms for international human rights to the concept of the New World Order, the audience is lost. A brief survey of the concept of humanitarian law reveals that it is, at best, an evolving idea that is not very well understood.

As to repetition, when the public was told that President George H. Bush was going to issue a major address to the nation on sweeping nuclear arms initiatives, many "New World Order watchers" anticipated that the concept would be woven throughout the speech. Set for September 27, 1991, the address would follow soon after the United Nations address, which provided President Bush with the perfect opportunity to promote the concept, but this time at the domestic level. Indeed, in President

Bush's September 1990 address to the United Nations, he had already set the precedent and employed the concept of the New World Order to urge a worldwide ban on chemical weapons and to continue the efforts to stop the proliferation of nuclear and biological weapons. At that time, President Bush said, "It is in our hands to leave these dark machines [nuclear, chemical and biological weapons] behind, in the dark ages where they belong…to cap a historic movement toward a new world order, and a long era of peace."

When the 1991 address to the nation was made, President George H. Bush did not invoke the concept of the New World Order even once. President Bush concentrated on an entirely new concept called "the new age." Pointing out that not only had the Cold War ended, but the Soviet Union was undergoing drastic change, President Bush preferred to justify his proposals for disarmament as in keeping with the new age. Once again, the press exhibited no interest in reporting unfamiliar terminology; the new age was unmentioned.

In summation, after a full year-and-a-half of being in the marketplace of ideas, the New World Order was still unfamiliar to the American public. Consequently, the general domestic understanding of what the New World Order really meant remained inexorably clouded. Of course, if the American public could not understand the New World Order, it was certain the rest of the world was at an even greater disadvantage. This was especially true for emerging democracies. For example, having a vague frame of reference for the notion of a State ruled by law, the vast territories of the old Soviet Empire had only just begun to awaken from a seventy-year nightmare of the most vicious brutality. Although the republics had renounced the twisted and flawed premise upon which the Communist party had rested for seven decades, there was tremendous confusion. Indeed, even with the dawn of the twenty-first century, it will be some time before the former Communist States will be able to implement many of the components associated with democratic values. It is difficult enough for them to grasp the concept of being ruled by law and not by force.

Catchy phrases such as the New World Order have nothing positive to offer those who seek to foster, strengthen and advance the rule of law. If the United States is serious about promoting the rule of law as the basis for its War on Terror, then it must stand as the chief champion of the rule of law as the basis for the War on Terror. The challenge must be to abandon all such new age and new world phrases and to concentrate fully on the never ending business of promoting the rule of law in word as well as deed. In the never-ending struggle to move the credibility of the concept forward, the United States must exhibit a faithful sponsorship of the rule of law in every international forum available.

Many of the most fundamental values, particularly those dealing with the illegality of aggressive war, have been translated into well-rooted rules of law at the cost of untold blood and fortune. Hope remains that many more democratic values will be added to that book, and that the attendant sacrifices will not have been in vain. Although there is no need to speak of the United States as the world's policeman, there is a need for the United States to fully sponsor the rule of law, which remains the best hope to those nations that wish to exist in a sphere of freedom. As the United States fights the War on Terror, it must continuously place emphasis on the rule of law and avoid the use of any descriptive phrase that casts doubt on the supreme function of the rule of law.

10.6 America Must Stay the Course

Since the events of September 11, 2001, the world has entered into a period fraught with uncertainty and yet, strangely, there shines a renewed hope to enlarge the peace and advance human rights. Although it is true that the chief characteristic of the War on Terror is the fact that the United States stands alone as the world's only remaining superpower, this is not the central focus of the post-9/11 era. The central hope rests in the great promise of a world more fully based on governments who adhere to human rights and democratic values.

Unlike other historical eras, the War on Terror offers a chance to advance human rights and democracy in areas of the world heretofore untouched. There is an intense global interest in securing the blessings of peace, prosperity, and human rights that the West has so long enjoyed. The positive aspect of the War on Terror is that it will create one of those rare moments in history where a window of opportunity opens for the world to make serious and lasting strides toward the ever elusive goals of controlling aggressive warfare and terrorism, and at the same time improving respect for human rights.

If the international community, led by the United States, does not find ways to realistically promote and foster at least the most fundamental categories of human rights, the horrific terrorism exemplified by the attacks on America is sure to be only a taste of things to come. Radical Islam must be confronted. However, battlefield victories alone will not bring a peace that can extend beyond a handful of years. Long-term periods of peace and stability require an attendant advance in institutionalizing the blessings of democratic values.

America must learn to take the long view of history and ignore the snapshots which invariably portray the American led effort as a failure or a Viet Nam-like quagmire. Unfortunately, the news item of the day seldom takes the long view of things. For example, an article in *Life Magazine* by one of their star correspondents, John Dos Passos, dated January 7, 1946, featured a major story entitled: "Americans are Losing the Victory in Europe." The article then went on to catalogue all of the mistakes that were being made in occupied Germany and how the war had been a waste. Of course, as it turned out, the American effort to promote democracy in Germany was a resounding success story. Certainly, winning the War on Terror will require patience, leadership and optimism, but it can be accomplished. As in all wars, strategic and tactical errors have been made in the War on Terror, particularly in Iraq following the 2003 defeat of the Iraqi military. But the al-Qa'eda-styled terrorists will not allow America to retreat to "a live and let live policy."

Assisting in the incorporation of human rights values into the institutional framework of, for example, the new Iraqi government is not merely an end worthy unto itself, but in the quest for war avoidance and promoting the full range of human rights benefits it creates a society which can peacefully coexist with the whole of the world community. It appears fundamentally obvious that activities pursued by democracies are substantially better than the activities pursued by totalitarian regimes like Cuba, North Korea, Sudan, Iran, and Syria. While it has long been suspected that stable democracies firmly committed to human rights do not make war on each other, nor do they abuse their own people, the empirical evidence now demonstrates this correlation. Debate on this point is over.

Thus, the central question now becomes how best to quickly impress solid human rights values on other national entities. Most certainly, human rights values become solid and irreversible only through the development of institutions designed to promote them. Institutionalization must be the criterion. While the desires for freedom will ultimately destroy a totalitarian system, freedom and human rights are not self-perpetuating; they can only be sustained through the creation of concrete law-based institutions.

In order to foster democratic ideals and human rights in countries like Afghanistan and Iraq, the United States must learn from its failure to liberate the people of Iraq from the evil of Saddam Hussein at the close of the 1991 Gulf War. The United States must accept that it has an obligation to assist any country endeavoring to create a government grounded in basic human rights. Liberated nations in the War on

Terror may eagerly embrace the principles of liberal democracy and self-determination, but will need immediate assistance to implement an institutional framework to accommodate their desires for the full range of human rights. Without meaningful assistance to translate the battle cry of human rights into an institutional framework, it is naive to assume that democratic values and human rights will germinate.

Apart from the normal pressures associated with building democratic institutions, the escalating and often uncontrollable level of disorder and violence in many of the new democracies forcefully supports the idea that the United States must assist in the creation and maintenance of fledgling democratic governments. Aside from country-specific issues, whether one concentrates on sectarian fragmentation or religious bias, the euphoric hope for instant world peace and greater human rights in the wake of the War on Terror is presumptuous—the globe is a dangerous place. Indeed, the danger of global terrorism is far more pronounced than ever before. In the first two years of the Obama Administration, more terror plots by radical Muslims occurred than any other two year period in American history. Today, due to the growth of terrorist activities throughout the world, it is not only uncertain where the next attack will occur, but virtually impossible to take a defensive posture against every potential attack. The modern al-Qa'eda-styled terrorist cannot be deterred by the threat of force—these murderers welcome death.

America, like great nations before her, has related all of these positive human rights values to a strong heritage of law institutionalized into its government. The founders of the nation established certain fundamental democratic institutions, and subsequent generations have generally exhibited the moral values and discipline required to maintain those institutions. American democracy continues to boast that men can rise to eminence in nearly any profession unaided by the advantages related to hereditary preferment. For over 200 years, this boast of freedom and human rights has echoed throughout the world, penetrating even the strongest iron curtain of communism. As a consequence, together with American force of arms, several totalitarian regimes have been swept into the dust of history. More than any other nation, America has demonstrated that human rights and the by-products of human rights—economic success and social well being—are worth promoting and protecting.

Therefore, if democracies shun aggression, terrorism, and hate, it is in the best interest of the United States to expend the necessary time, effort, and money to adequately assist those nations who have exhibited the will to embark on democracy's path. In this context, the United States has rapidly assessed the ramifications of this important responsibility and offered assistance to the fledgling Iraqi government before the window of opportunity closed and the chance for democracy was lost. But not all nations are ripe for democratic reform as seen in the continuing struggle to promote even the most basic concepts of democracy in Afghanistan. The most significant danger in the War on Terror is that the global movement toward democratic reform, which started with the collapse of the Soviet Union, will fail, signaling a return to totalitarianism, a more dangerous world, or even a Third World War.

Arguments that the Western European nations should take the lead in fostering the development of greater human rights and democracy have proven to be contentious. One need look no further than the conflict in the backyard of the European community itself, the former Yugoslavia, to conclude that either individually or collectively, Western Europe is not able to quickly solve even its own problems. Although Germany may be best suited to take on a leadership role in Europe, the historical suspicion of German militarism makes such an event highly unlikely.

For similar reasons, the Far East will not allow Japan, a powerhouse of the region, to assert a more dominant leadership role. It remains for the United States to continue to extend its influence in the region, particularly in the face of the destabilizing effect of an aggressive and nuclear armed North Korea.

It is naive to believe that the United Nations might one day fill some part of the vacuum. Hopes that the United Nations might evolve into a truly effective world collective security organization have not materialized and, given its track record, it seems unlikely that the United Nations can fulfill such a position. Clearly, an organization that allows totalitarian regimes an equal voice is inherently flawed and largely worthless.

In the final analysis, there is as yet no viable substitute for United States dominance in the international arena. For the time being, it is apparent that history has chosen the United States as the nation most suited to assist in promoting human rights in the War on Terror. This is true for three reasons. First, the United States emerged from the Cold War as the foremost power in the world, a power that possesses the necessary capability to influence change. Second, many governments in Western Europe, East Asia, and the Middle East, whether allies of the United States or not, want the United States to continue to lead. Third, despite its own internal faults and shortcomings in the realm of human rights, it is well-recognized that the United States has always been the foremost champion of values related to human rights and democratic ideals.

Interestingly, many of these impressions have not been made by the civilian arm of the United States, but by its military forces stationed throughout the world. The United States military has been—and continues to be—an excellent ambassador for positive change.

Finally, those who argue that the United States should not become involved in assisting the growth of human rights and democratic movements because there is no domestic benefit are incorrect. The United States chose not to become involved after World War I, and the resulting costs in terms of life lost and property destroyed were extremely high. Conversely, as pointed out in an article by Brigadier General James R. Harding and John A. Pitts (*Military Review* July 1999), the United States did choose to become actively engaged after World War II and the resulting benefits were substantial, producing "the longest period of uninterrupted peace in Europe in 400 years, the highest level of economic prosperity and sustained economic growth in the history of the Western World, and the defeat of totalitarianism in Eastern Europe." The United States wisely rolled up its sleeves and rooted out Nazi ideology, Italian fascism, and Japanese militarism. These evils were replaced with liberal democratic values which led to strongly rooted constitutional democracies at peace with their people and with the world community.

The spread of human rights and democracy around the world helps United States security, improves global stability, and increases economic prosperity. Thus, promoting governments who desire human rights and democracy benefits American national security directly—a more democratic world is a safer world. Unfortunately, according to the group Freedom House, the number of electoral democracies stands at 116, down significantly from the burst of freedom associated with the collapse of the Soviet Union. Many wonder if the spread of democracy may be coming to a halt.

The events of September 11, 2001, initially unleashed a tremendous moral clarity in America and the civilized world for the creation of governments that are truly based on protecting human rights and living with their neighbors in peace and prosperity. Unfortunately, as the War on Terror grinds on into its tenth year, many have "hit the snooze button" and fallen into a false sense of security. The fight against the rather substantial forces of al-Qa'eda-styled terrorism will not end with the signing of a peace treaty with the enemy visibly vanquished. This war will follow our children into adulthood.

In order to push the global movement towards expanding human rights, America must develop a strong and practical strategy that can truly assist the struggling and emerging governments to get out of the totalitarian shadows in which they stand by institutionalizing human rights values. If the doctrines of human rights can be inculcated, for example, in Iraq, the benefits will lead to a stabilized nation capable perhaps of contributing as a full partner to a more peaceful, humane, and free world. This goal may or may not be achieved in the short term, but there are no other alternatives.

On the homefront, the balance between civil liberties and security demands has changed. To be sure, the debate on where the balance should rest must be deliberate and inclusive of all voices, but the hard premise that accentuates the call for robust debate must rubricate the discussion—these al-Qa'eda-styled fanatics are in our midst and mean to slaughter us wholesale if they can. Many well know this fact. Yet they are naive in considering the real world ramifications of advocating that no revisions need to be made to existing authorities, laws, and processes. For certain, the world of pre-9/11 will never return, and evil forces of terror remain fixed on the horizon. In the technological age of weapons of mass destruction, we need only be unlucky once for catastrophe to cripple the nation and the civilized world. As General Tommy Franks warned, such an event would "cause our population to question our own Constitution and to begin to militarize our country in order to avoid [another weapon of mass destruction event]."

The quote by former Chief Justice William H. Rehnquist cited at the Introduction to this book speaks to the challenge of achieving or maintaining a proper balance between freedom and order in a time of national crisis. Rehnquist's words bear repeating: "In wartime, reason and history both suggest that this balance shifts to some degree in favor of order—in favor of the government's ability to deal with conditions that threaten the national well-being." While his observation is undoubtedly correct in terms of past wars in our history, the uniqueness of the War on Terror poses a far more difficult dilemma for those concerned with civil liberties. In brief, the War on Terror may never "be over" so that the on-going conflict presents a fundamentally new and potentially devastating threat to civil liberties. If the War on Terror has no end in sight, Rehnquist's premise that order must trump freedom in wartime could mean that freedoms quickly relinquished in this war may never return. Accordingly, calls for greater "order" must be carefully weighed, debated, and incrementally enacted. Another Chief Justice of the United States, Warren E. Burger (1969–1986), noted in his capacity as the Chairman for the Commission on the Bicentennial of the United States Constitution, "Ever since people began living in tribes and villages, they have had to balance order with liberty, individual freedom had to be weighed against the need for security of all."

More importantly, America's strongest weapon in the War on Terror does not rest with our military might or police functions. In the long run, America's strongest weapon is our uncompromising commitment to the freedoms and civil liberties embodied in our Constitution and reflected in the U.N. Charter. If we engage in tactics that violate the democratic principles that make up our rule of law, are we different from the terrorists at our gates? The United States of America can only ride the crests of the waves of history so long as it follows a rule of law rooted in human rights and democratic principles. America will drown in the sea of hypocrisy if it trades civil liberties for a mess of pottage. Terrorism consultant Brian Jenkins agrees that the best defense against the terrorists calls for a "continuing commitment to the basic values that…the nation stands for." The real genius of the United States is that it is a nation of immigrants that has managed to unite its disparate parts through common values of freedom. These values are embodied in the Constitution and in the Declaration of Independence's expression of a people yearning to be free and to develop the talents given them by their Creator.

10.7 Questions for Discussion

1. *What is the proper role of nationalism in war?* See Edward Gibbons, THE HISTORY OF THE DECLINE AND FALL OF THE ROMAN EMPIRE, Vol. I, 85-86 (1914). Literally, the "peace of Rome," *Pax Romana* refers to the peace and prosperity in the known world, i.e., the Mediterranean, brought about by Roman rule from 27 B.C. to 180 A.D. Gibbon, widely recognized as the foremost modern scholar on the Roman empire, places the high point of *pax Romana* at 96 to 180 A.D., the period of the Antonine Caesars:

   If a man were called to fix the period in the history of the world during which the condition of the human race was most happy and prosperous, he would without hesitation, name that which elapsed from the death of Domitian [A.D. 96] to the accession of Commodus [A.D. 180]. The vast extent of the Roman Empire was governed by absolute power, under the guidance of virtue and wisdom. The armies were restrained by the firm but gentle hand of four successive emperors, whose characters and authority commanded in voluntary respect. The forms of the civil administration were carefully preserved by Nerva, Trajan, Hadrian, and the Antonines [Pius], who delighted in the image of liberty, and were pleased with considering themselves as the accountable ministers of the law.

2. Does Obama believe in American exceptionalism? Critics paint Obama as "apologizing" for American behavior in the past and not promoting the values and virtues of America.

3. *Should foreign policy only be concerned with human rights? See* Madeleine Albright, THE MIGHTY AND THE ALMIGHTY (2006). In her chapter entitled, Good Intentions Gone Astray: Vietnam and the Shah, Albright talks about how the Carter policy of not sufficiently supporting the Shah of Iran in the late 1970s led to far greater human rights abuses under the mullahs:

   Many rejoiced when the monarch was brought down, but from any objective standpoint, the practices of Iran's successor governments with regard to human rights have been far worse than the shah's. In the first few years alone, thousands of people were executed for political dissent and "moral crimes." The shah's secret police were replaced by religious "guardians of the faith," who were even more ruthless.

Selected Bibliography

Ajami, Fouad. *Where the Warrior Comes to Rest*, U.S. NEWS AND WORLD REPORT. Oct. 7, 1991, at 10.

Albright, Madeleine. THE MIGHTY AND THE ALMIGHTY, 2006.

Bonds, Russell S. *Pawn Takes Bishop*, CIVIL WAR TIMES, May 2006, at 53.

Campanile, Carl. *Rev. Al Will Join GI Ma in Anti-War Texas Vigil*, N.Y. POST. Aug. 26, 2005, at 10.

Carty, Anthony, and Gennady Danilenko. *Perestroika and International Law*, CURRENT ANGLO-SOVIET APPROACHES TO INTERNATIONAL LAW, 1, 1990.

Coates, Sam. *Sharpton Adds Voice to Antiwar*, WASH. POST. Aug. 29, 2005, at A4.

Colombo, Furio. *Vatican: The Pope's War Record*, NEW REPUBLIC. Apr. 8, 1991, at 12. (The article compiled some of the Pope's statements about the use of force by the United States and its allies. On January 10, 1991: "This war is an adventure with no return." On January 16: "International law cannot be seen as a protection for hegemonic interests." On January 21: "The intoxication of war has prevailed over the courage of peace." On January 26: "This war is a threat to humanity." On February 4: "This war is a virus of death.")

Duke, Lynne. *Coretta Scott King Deplores Decision*, WASH. POST. Jan. 17, 1991, at A30 (quoting Rev. Joseph Lowery).

Elsner, Alan. *Christian Leaders Prominent in Anti-War Movement*, REUTERS, Feb. 8, 2003.

Gellman, Barton. *Reaction to Tactic They Invented Baffles 1st Division Members*, WASH. POST, Sept. 13, 1991, at A21.

Haberman, Clyde. *Pope, In Christmas Message, Warns on a Gulf War*, NEW YORK TIMES, 26. Dec. 1990, at A19 (quoting Pope John Paul II).

Interview by Zenit Daily Dispatch with George Weigel, a biographer of Pope John Paul II as well as a leading Catholic commentator, and Senior Fellow of the Ethics and Public Policy Center, Washington, D.C. Sept. 22, 2002. (discussing the Catholic moral teaching regarding what many claimed to be a pre-emptive strike in Iraq and the Catholic views of just war theory).

Jackson, Fred, and Jody Brown. *Arrest of Anti-War Methodist Leaders Called 'Embarrassment' for Denomination: Bishop, others from 'Radical Fringe' Protest Near White House*, AGAPE PRESS, *available at* http://headlines.agapepress.org/archive/3/282003a.asp. Mar. 28, 2003.

Johnson, Haynes. *Renewed Perils to Peace*, WASH. POST. Sept. 27, 1991, at A2.

King, Martin Luther, Jr. STRIDE TOWARD FREEDOM: THE MONTGOMERY STORY, 1958.

Kramer, Michael. *Kuwait: Back to the Past*, TIME. Aug. 5, 1991, at 32.

Munger, Guy. *Lessons From the Desert Death Plow*, NC CATHOLIC. Sept. 22, 1991, at 4.

President Orders Sweeping Reductions in Strategic and Tactical Nuclear Arms, WASH. POST. Sept. 28, 1991, at A1.

Przetacznik, Frank. *The Catholic Concept of Peace as a Basic Collective Human Right*, 39 REVUE DE DROIT MILITAIRE ET DE DROIT DE LA GUERRE, 523, (1990).

Rich, Norman. HITLER'S WAR AIMS. 1973.

Safire, William. *The New New World Order*, NEW YORK TIMES. Feb. 17, 1991, at 14 (quoting President George H. Bush).

Schaff, Philip, ed. ST. AUGUSTINE, NICENE AND POST-NICENE FATHERS OF THE CHRISTIAN CHURCH, 1983.

Smothers, Ronald. *Thousands Recall Quest for Equality*, NEW YORK TIMES. Jan. 22, 1991, at A18.

Steinfels, Peter. *War in the Gulf: Religious Leaders; Cardinal Says Iraqi's Acts Prove Bush Right*, NEW YORK TIMES. Jan. 26, 1991, at A9 (quoting Pope John Paul II).

Turner, Robert F. *The Gulf War—and Its Fallout*, FREEDOM REV, May–June 1991, at 17, 19.

U.S. and U.K. Statement. *Disarm Iraq Without War: A Statement from Religious Leaders in the United States and United Kingdom*, SOJOURNERS, Nov. 26, 2002.

Walker, Richard. *Martin Luther King's Widow Urges New Anti-War Movement*, REUTER LIBRARY REP, Jan. 11, 1991.

We Stand...Before a New World of Hope and Possibility for Our Children, WASH. POST. Dec. 26, 1991, at A35.

Wilgoren, Debbie. *Peaceful Protest Ends in Peaceful Arrest: Nobel Winners Among 68 Detained Activists*, WASH. POST, Mar. 27, 2003, at B.01.

Chapter 11

Civil Litigation

In the face of this universal criminal liability it is hardly a stretch to ask how the civil justice system might more effectively also contribute to deterrence against such heinous acts [international terrorism].

—John Norton Moore

The area of civil litigation encompasses two major themes in the realm of terrorism. The first relates to cases brought by victims of terrorism against an "affected target" of terrorism under the sphere of tort law. The second relates to lawsuits directed against those individuals, groups, or States (or State agents) who commit or sponsor a terrorist attack. To be sure, the new and developing area of civil liability in either context is an open invitation for the courts to play a significant role in the realm of terrorism law.

11.1 Tort Liability Against Affected Targets

As in all cases of tort law, suits brought by individual victims against an affected target of terrorism, such as an owner of a building or an airline, must satisfy the common law elements of basic tort law: (1) the affected target owed a duty to the plaintiff; (2) the duty was breached; (3) there existed a causal relationship between the breach and the resulting injury; (4) and the plaintiff suffered an actual loss.

The new and developing area of civil liability in the context of civil actions brought by victims of terrorism against an affected target of terrorism, i.e., a particular business entity, under the sphere of tort law is extremely relevant to the issue of developing adequate business security—both in the physical world and cyberspace. Indeed, while no business can protect against every form of terrorist threat, courts will ultimately determine whether or not the affected business had developed appropriate and reasonable security methods and procedures. Accordingly, all business entities must take cognizance of at least four main themes.

- Understand the aims and objectives of the global terror threat posed by al-Qaeda-styled terror groups, sub-State terror groups, and "lone wolf" terrorists.

399

- Understand the specific threats to American business sectors that are deemed part of the nation's "critical infrastructure," i.e. energy, petro-chemical, electric utilities, communication, transportation, health, etc.
- Understand the varied legal issues associated with terrorism and criminal negligence claims against businesses that have suffered a terror attack or serious criminal act in cyberspace or the physical world.
- Develop a comprehensive review of how to develop appropriate security methods and procedures to mitigate potential legal liability to the business.

The most notable case related to these types of terrorism negligence claims is *In re September 11*. While most of the liability issues associated with the terror attacks of 9/11 were settled by a Special Master (using a seven billion dollar "pot" of money) established under the Air Transportation Safety and System Stabilization Act of 2001, *In re September 11* was a major tort liability case in which a handful of the victims who were injured, survivors of victims who were killed, and some who sustained property damage in the al-Qa'eda terror attacks on September 11, 2001, brought civil actions against airlines, airport security companies, owners and operators of buildings destroyed in the crash, and aircraft manufacturers. *In re September 11* rendered some significant insight in its early rulings: (1) under New York law, the duty of airlines and airport security companies to secure aircraft against potential terrorists and weapons smuggled aboard extended to ground victims of crashes; (2) the crash of the planes hijacked by terrorists was within the class of foreseeable hazards resulting from negligently performed security screening by airlines; (3) federal statutes and regulations providing for protection of passengers and property on aircraft in the event of air piracy did not preempt plaintiff's negligence claim under New York law; (4) owners and operators of office buildings owed a duty under New York law to the building's occupants to create and implement adequate fire safety measures; (5) plaintiffs pleaded sufficient facts to alleged legal proximate cause against owners and operators; (6) plaintiff's allegations were sufficient to establish manufacturer's duty under Virginia and Pennsylvania law; and (7) the failure of manufacturers to design an impenetrable cockpit door was a proximate cause of the crashes.

In re SEPTEMBER 11
United States District Court for the Southern District of New York
280 F.Supp.2d 279 (Sep. 9th 2003)

OPINION BY: HELLERSTEIN, J.

The injured, and the representatives of the thousands who died from the terrorist-related aircraft crashes of September 11, 2001, are entitled to seek compensation. By act of Congress, they may seek compensation by filing claims with a Special Master established pursuant to the Air Transportation Safety and System Stabilization Act of 2001, Pub.L. No. 107-42, 115 Stat. 230 (2001) (codified at 49 U.S.C. § 40101) "the Act." Or they may seek compensation in the traditional manner, by alleging and proving their claims in lawsuits, with the aggregate of their damages capped at the limits of defendants' liability insurance. If they choose the former alternative, their claims will be paid through a Victim Compensation Fund from money appropriated by Congress, within a relatively short period after filing. Claimants will not have to prove fault or show a duty to pay on the part of any defendant. The amount of their compensation, however, may be less than their possible recovery from lawsuits, for non-economic damages are limited to $250,000, economic damages are subject to formulas that are likely to be less generous than those often allowable in lawsuits, and punitive damages are unavailable. I have discussed, and upheld, certain portions of the Act and regulations related to the Fund in *Colaio v. Feinberg , 262 F.Supp.2d 273 (S.D.N.Y. 2003)*, appeal filed, June 6, 2003. Approximately seventy of the injured and representatives of those who died, and ten entities which sustained property damage, have chosen to bring lawsuits against defendants whom they claim are legally responsible to compensate them: the airlines, the airport security companies, the airport operators, the airplane manufacturer, and the operators and owners of the World Trade Center. The motions before me challenge the legal sufficiency of these lawsuits, and ask me to dismiss the complaints because no duty to the plaintiffs existed and because the defendants could not reasonably have anticipated that terrorists would hijack several jumbo jet airplanes and crash them, killing passengers, crew, thousands on the ground, and themselves. I discuss in this opinion the legal duties owed by the air carriers, United and American Airlines, and other airlines and airport security companies affiliated with the air carriers to the plaintiffs who were killed and damaged on the ground in and around the Twin Towers and the Pentagon; by the Port Authority of New York and New Jersey "Port Authority" and World Trade Center Properties LLC "WTC Properties" to those killed and injured in and around the Twin Towers; and by the Boeing Company, the manufacturer of the "757" jets that were flown into the Pentagon and the field near Shanksville, Pennsylvania, to those killed and injured in the two crashes. I hold in this opinion that each of these defendants owed duties to the plaintiffs who sued them, and I reject as well defendants' alternative arguments for dismissal.

I. Background
A. Exclusive Jurisdiction and the Governing Law

The Air Transportation Safety and System Stabilization Act of 2001, Pub.L. No. 107-42, 115 Stat. 230 (2001) (codified at 49 U.S.C. § 40101) "the Act", passed in the weeks following the September 11 attacks, provides that those who bring suit "for damages arising out of the hijacking and subsequent crashes" must bring their suits in the United States District Court for the Southern District of New York. The Southern District has "original and exclusive jurisdiction" "over all actions brought for any claim (including any claim for loss of property, personal injury, or death) resulting from or relating to the terrorist-related aircraft crashes of September 11, 2001," with the exception of claims to recover collateral source obligations and claims against terrorists and their aiders, abettors and conspirators, Act § 408(c). The Act provides that the governing law shall be "derived from the law, including choice of law principles, of the State in which the crash occurred unless such law is inconsistent with or preempted by Federal law." Act § 408(b)(2). Thus, all cases, whether arising out of the crashes in New York, Virginia, or Pennsylvania, must be brought in the Southern District of New York, to be decided in accordance with the law of the state where the crash occurred.

B. The Complaints

Plaintiffs' individual pleadings have been consolidated into five master complaints, one for the victims of each crash and one for the property damage plaintiffs. Plaintiffs allege that the airlines, airport security companies, and airport operators negligently failed to fulfill their security responsibilities, and in consequence, the terrorists were able to hijack the airplanes and crash them into the World Trade Center, the Pentagon, and the field in Shanksville, Pennsylvania, killing passengers, crew, and thousands in the World Trade Center and the Pentagon and causing extensive property damage. The complaints allege that the owners and operators of the World Trade Center, World Trade Center Properties LLC and the Port Authority of New York and New Jersey, negligently designed, constructed, maintained, and operated the buildings, failing to provide adequate and effective evacuation routes and plans. Plaintiffs who died in the crashes of American flight 77 and United flight 93 also sue Boeing, the manufacturer of the two "757" airplanes, for strict tort liability, negligent product design, and breach of warranty.

C. Motions to Dismiss

I heard oral argument on May 1 and 2, 2003 on six motions by the several categories of defendants. I previously have decided three of the motions, by most of the airport operators, by three airlines that did not carry any of the victims or alleged hijackers, and by Fiduciary Trust Company International and Franklin Templeton Investments, an employer of one of the victims. The three motions which remain, and which I now decide are: by the airlines and airport security companies (the "Aviation Defendants"); by the Port Authority and World Trade Center Properties LLC (together, the "WTC Defendants"); and by Boeing.

The airport operators that joined in this motion are: the Massachusetts Port Authority, the Metropolitan Washington Airport Authority, the City of Portland, Maine, and the Port Authority of New York and New Jersey. I denied their joint motion without prejudice. (Order of May 5, 2003, *In re September 11 Litigation, 21 MC 97.*) The City of Portland, Maine and the Port Authority of New York and New Jersey brought separate supplementary motions to dismiss. I granted Portland's motion, dismissing it as a defendant from those cases where plaintiffs had failed to file a timely notice of claim. *In re September 11 Litigation, 265 F.Supp.2d 208 (S.D.N.Y.2003).* The Port Authority's supplementary motion will be decided herein, see infra Part II.B.iv.

The three non-carrier airlines are Continental Airlines, Air Canada, and America West Airlines. I denied their motion for summary judgment without prejudice. (Order of May 5, 2003, *In re September 11* (Order of May 13, 2003, *Greene-Wotton v. Fiduciary Trust Co. Int'l, 02 Civ. 7245.*) The plaintiff's husband had worked for Fiduciary Trust/Franklin Templeton in Tower Two and was allegedly asked to remain at the office after Tower One had been struck. I held that the New York workers' compensation statute precluded plaintiff's negligence claims and that she had failed to state a claim for intentional infliction of emotional distress.

The Aviation Defendants who joined in the motion to dismiss include: AirTran Airlines, American Airlines, America West Airlines, AMR Corp., Argenbright Security, Atlantic Coast Airlines, Burn International Services Corp., Burns International Security Services Corp., Colgan Air, Continental Airlines, Delta Air Lines, Globe Aviation Services Corp., Globe Airport Security Services, Inc., Huntleigh USA Corp., Northwest Airlines, Pinkerton's Inc., and United Air Lines.

The Aviation Defendants concede that they owed a duty to the crew and passengers on the planes, but contend that they did not owe any duty to "ground victims." The Port Authority and WTC Properties argue that they did not owe a duty to protect occupants in the towers against injury from hijacked airplanes and, even if they did, the terrorists' actions broke the chain of proximate causation, excusing any negligence by the WTC Defendants. Boeing argues that it did not owe a duty to ground victims or passengers, and that any negligence on its part was not the proximate cause for the harms suffered by the plaintiffs.

II. Discussion

Defendants' motions were made pursuant to Fed.R.Civ.P. 12(b)(6). A Rule 12(b)(6) motion requires the court to determine if plaintiff has stated a legally sufficient claim. A motion to dismiss under Rule 12(b)(6) may be granted only if "it appears beyond doubt that the plaintiff can prove no set of facts in support of his claim which would entitle him to relief." *Conley v. Gibson, 355 U.S. 41, 45-46, 78 S.Ct. 99, 2 L.Ed.2d 80 (1957); Branum v. Clark, 927 F.2d 698, 705 (2d Cir.1991).*
...

A. Aviation Defendants' Motion to Dismiss

The Aviation Defendants argue that they did not owe a duty to the ground victims; that the injuries suffered by the plaintiffs were beyond the scope of any foreseeable duty that may have been owed; and that the federal laws that regulate aviation preempt any state law to the contrary.

i. Choice of Law

Section 408(b)(2) of the Act provides that the substantive law "shall be derived from the law, including choice of law principles, of the State in which the crash occurred unless such law is inconsistent with or preempted by Federal law." Ground victims of the planes that crashed into the World Trade Center and the Pentagon have filed suit against the Aviation Defendants, and thus the choice of law principles of New York and Virginia apply.

New York typically analyzes choice-of-law issues in tort cases according to two categories of rules: conduct-regulating and loss-allocating. The issue of duty—whether duty exists and its scope—is conduct-regulating. New York choice of law dictates that the state in which the tort took place has the strongest interest in applying its conduct-regulating rules. *Schultz v. Boy Scouts of Am., Inc., 65 N.Y.2d 189, 491 N.Y.S.2d 90, 480 N.E.2d 679, 684- 85 (1985).* Thus, the substantive law of New York governs the issue of duty in relation to the crashes at the World Trade Center.

Virginia's choice of law rules apply to the ground damage claims arising from the crash of American flight 77 into the Pentagon. Under Virginia law, the substantive law of the place of the tort controls. *McMillan v. McMillan, 219 Va. 1127, 253 S.E.2d 662, 664 (1979).* The parties agree that the law of Virginia does not differ materially from New York law with respect to the issue of duty and rely on New York law for their arguments.

ii. Existence of Duty to Ground Victims

"The threshold question in any negligence action is: does the defendant owe a legally recognized duty of care to plaintiff?" *Hamilton v. Beretta U.S.A. Corp., 96 N.Y.2d 222, 727 N.Y.S.2d*

7, 750 N.E.2d 1055, 1060 (2001). In New York, the existence of a duty is a "legal, policy-laden declaration reserved for judges." *Palka v. Servicemaster Mgmt. Servs. Corp., 83 N.Y.2d 579, 611 N.Y.S.2d 817, 634 N.E.2d 189, 192 (1994).* The injured party must show that a defendant owed not merely a general duty to society but a specific duty to the particular claimant, for "without a duty running directly to the injured person there can be no liability in damages, however careless the conduct or foreseeable the harm." *Lauer v. City of New York, 95 N.Y.2d 95, 711 N.Y.S.2d 112, 733 N.E.2d 184, 187 (2000).* Courts traditionally "fix the duty point by balancing factors, including the reasonable expectations of parties and society generally, the proliferation of claims, the likelihood of unlimited or insurer-like liability, disproportionate risk and reparation allocation, and public policies affecting the expansion or limitation of new channels of liability." *Palka, 611 N.Y.S.2d 817, 634 N.E.2d at 193.*

New York courts have been cautious in extending liability to defendants for their failure to control the conduct of others, "even where as a practical matter [the] defendant can exercise such control." *D'Amico v. Christie, 71 N.Y.2d 76, 524 N.Y.S.2d 1, 518 N.E.2d 896, 901 (1987).* "This judicial resistance to the expansion of duty grows out of practical concerns both about potentially limitless liability and about the unfairness of imposing liability for the acts of another." *Hamilton, 727 N.Y.S.2d 7, 750 N.E.2d at 1061.* However, courts have imposed a duty when the defendant has control over the third party tortfeasor's actions, or the relationship between the defendant and plaintiff requires the defendant to protect the plaintiff from the conduct of others. As the New York Court of Appeals ruled, "The key in each [situation] is that the defendant's relationship with either the tortfeasor or the plaintiff places the defendant in the best position to protect against the risk of harm." *Id.* One additional consideration, the Court of Appeals added, is that "the specter of limitless liability is not present because the class of potential plaintiffs to whom the duty is owed is circumscribed by the relationship." *Id.*

Plaintiffs allege that the Aviation Defendants negligently failed to carry out their duty to secure passenger aircraft against potential terrorists and weapons smuggled aboard, enabling the terrorists to hijack and crash four airplanes. Plaintiffs argue that the Aviation Defendants employed their security measures specifically to guard against hijackings, and knew or should have known that the hijacking of a jumbo jet would create substantial risks of damage to persons and property, not only to passengers and crew, but also to people and property on the ground. Plaintiffs assert also that terrorism was a substantial international concern, and that suicidal acts by terrorists seeking to cause death, injury and havoc to as many innocent people as possible had become a frequently used strategy.

I must test this dispute over duty even before a record has been established. In New York, duty is a legal question, for the judge to decide. I must assume, for the purpose of the motion, that all well-pleaded facts about the defendants' negligence are true and will in time be proved, and that defendants' negligence proximately caused the injuries and deaths upon which plaintiffs filed their lawsuits.

Airplane crashes in residential areas are not unknown. In January 1952, an American Airlines Convair crashed into a residential area of Elizabeth, New Jersey on its approach to Newark airport, killing passengers and crew, as well as seven residents of houses it struck. Elizabeth Recalls First of 3 Crashes, N.Y. Times, Dec. 17, 1952, at 27. A month later, another plane out of Newark, a National Airlines DC-6, struck an apartment house in New Jersey, killing 29 passengers and four tenants of the apartment house. Id. Military airplanes have had to make emergency landings on highways, and have collided with automobiles. See *Rehm v. United States, 196 F.Supp. 428 (E.D.N.Y.1961)*. On July 9, 1982, a Pan American World Airways jet crashed shortly after takeoff, killing all on board and eight individuals on the ground. The airline and the government acknowledged liability for the crash, which was caused by windy conditions. Pan Am and U.S. Accept Responsibility for Crash, N.Y. Times, May 13, 1983, at 6. In January 1990, a Columbian passenger airplane exhausted its fuel supply while circling La Guardia Airport waiting for clearance to land, and crashed into a residential backyard in Long Island's populated North shore. See *In re Air Crash Disaster at Cove Neck, 885 F.Supp. 434 (E.D.N.Y.1995)*. On November 12, 2001, two months after the aircraft crashes of September 11, 2001, a jumbo-jet passenger airplane lost its stability in take-off from JFK airport and crashed into a populated area of the Rockaways, causing the deaths of over two hundred passengers and crew members and five people on the ground. Dan Barry and Elissa Gootman, 5 Neighbors Gone, N.Y. Times, Nov. 14, 2001, at D11. Such incidents are inevitable in the context of the sheer number of miles flown daily in the United States. None matches the quantity or quality of tragedy arising from the terrorist-related aircraft crashes of September 11.

Airlines typically recognize responsibility to victims on the ground. See, e.g., *Rehm, 196 F.Supp. at 428; Cove Neck, 885 F.Supp. at 439-40*. Assuming negligence and assuming there is damage to houses on the ground that is the type of traditional ground damage negligent maintenance cases in which the courts have imposed duty….[W]e would concede in those circumstances assuming the facts of liability are proven there is a legal duty. (Tr. of May 1, 2003 at 8.) However, counsel did not concede duty in relation to those killed and injured on the ground in the September 11, 2001 aircraft crashes. The "potential for a limitless liability to an indeterminate class of plaintiffs," he argued, made the instant cases distinguishable. Id. The distinction, in his opinion, is "no[t][a] difference in kind," but "the law of extraordinary consequences [which] can sometimes draw a distinction based on degree." *Id.* at 9-10. He explained:

> We are in an area of policy and there are lines to be drawn that may occasionally seem arbitrary. But what really distinguishes our case from [the hypothetical example of an airplane crash into Shea Stadium while taking off from, or landing at, La Guardia airport] is the intentional intervening acts of the third party terrorists.

While defense counsel raised the issue of proximate causation during the oral argument, the issue was not briefed. Counsel suggested, without legal citation, that the extraordinary nature of the attacks, involving intervening acts by the terrorists, should negate the duty air carriers owed to ground victims. Id. As defense counsel commented, "we are in an area of policy," where "the existence and scope of a tortfeasor's duty is…a legal question for the courts," *532 Madison Ave. Gourmet Foods, Inc. v. Finlandia Center, Inc., 96 N.Y.2d 280, 727 N.Y.S.2d 49, 750 N.E.2d 1097, 1101 (2001)* (Kaye, Ch. J.). It is the court's job to "fix the duty point by balancing factors," including the following: the reasonable expectations of parties and society generally, the proliferation of claims, the likelihood of unlimited or insurer-like liability, disproportionate risk and reparation allocation, and public policies affecting the expansion or limitation of new channels of liability. *Id.* (citation omitted). *532 Madison Avenue* involved collapses of a high-rise office building and a 48-story construction elevator tower, both in midtown Manhattan and both causing busy areas of the city to be closed for a two-week period. The lawsuits sought recovery of financial losses resulting from the closures; plaintiffs had not suffered personal injury or property damage. Applying the considerations set out above, the Court of Appeals limited the scope of defendants' duty "to those who have, as a result of these events, suffered personal injury or property damage," but held that those who suffered merely financial losses could not recover. *Id.* at 1103. The Court of Appeals acknowledged that "[p]olicy-driven line-drawing is to an extent arbitrary because, wherever the line is drawn, invariably it cuts off liability to persons who foreseeably might be plaintiffs." Id. If those who suffered financial losses were to be allowed to sue, the Court of Appeals held, "an indeterminate group in the affected areas" would be able to recover. Id. If, however, the field of plaintiffs was to be limited to those who "suffered personal injury or property damage" as a result of defendants' negligence, the limitation would "afford[ ] a principled basis for reasonably apportioning liability," and be "historically" consistent with New York precedents. *Id.*

The cases before me involve claims to recover for personal injuries, death, or property damage. They fall within the line drawn by the New York Court of Appeals in *532 Madison Avenue*. There may be more plaintiffs within the ambit of duty at issue here than those contemplated under the rule set forth in *532 Madison Avenue*, but that is not a principled basis of distinction. I therefore hold that the Aviation Defendants owed a duty of care, not only to their passengers to whom they concede they owed this duty, but also to victims on the ground.

In terms of the *532 Madison Avenue* analysis, plaintiffs are favored by the first of the factors set out above, for plaintiffs and society generally could have reasonably expected that the screening performed at airports by the Aviation Defendants would be for the protection of people on the ground as well as for those in airplanes. Ours is a complicated and specialized society. We depend on others charged with special duties to protect the quality of the water we drink and the air we breathe, to bring power to our neighborhoods, and to enable us to travel with a sense of security over bridges, through tunnels and via subways. We live in the vicinity of busy airports, and we work in tall office towers, depending on others to protect us from the willful desire of terrorists to do us harm. Some of those on whom we depend for protection are the police, fire and intelligence departments of local, state and national governments. Others are private companies, like the Aviation Defendants. They perform their screening duties, not only for those boarding airplanes, but also for society generally. It is both their expectation, and ours, that the duty of screening was performed for the benefit of passengers and those on the ground, including those present in the Twin Towers on the morning of September 11, 2001.

Nothing that I hold or say should be considered as any form of ruling on the reasonableness of the Aviation Defendants' conduct. Nor should it be construed as a finding on whether their conduct was the proximate cause of plaintiffs' damages, or whether that of the terrorists' constituted an intervening act breaking the chain of causation. I simply hold that the Aviation Defendants, and plaintiffs and society generally, could reasonably have expected that the screening methods at Logan, Newark, and Dulles airports were for the protection of people on the ground as well as for those on board the airplanes that the terrorists hijacked.

...

The fourth factor of *532 Madison Avenue* is "disproportionate risk and reparation allocation." This inquiry probes who was best able to protect against the risks at issue and weighs the costs and efficacy of imposing such a duty. The airlines, and the airport security companies, could best screen those boarding, and bringing objects onto, airplanes. The same activities reasonably necessary to safeguard passengers and crew are those that would protect the public as well. Hijacking presents a substantial elevation of risks, not only to those aboard the hijacked airplane, but also to those on the ground. This case is thus distinguishable from other cases where courts did not find a duty to protect against third-party conduct. *In Waters v. New York City Housing Authority*, the court held that the owner of a housing project did not owe a duty to a passerby when she was dragged off the street into the building and assaulted. *69 N.Y.2d 225, 513 N.Y.S.2d 356, 505 N.E.2d 922 (1987)*. Imposing such a duty on landowners would do little to minimize crime, and the social benefits to be gained did not warrant the extension of the landowner's duty. See *id.* at 924. Similarly, in *Hamilton, 727 N.Y.S.2d 7, 750 N.E.2d at 1062*, the court held that gun manufacturers did not owe a duty to victims of gun violence for negligent marketing and distribution of firearms. The connection between the manufacturers, criminal wrongdoers, and victims was too remote, running through many links in a long chain, from manufacturer, distributor or wholesaler, retailer, legal purchasers, unlawful possessors, and finally to the victims of gun violence.

...

Unlike *Hamilton* and *Waters*, the *Aviation* Defendants could best control the boarding of airplanes, and were in the best position to provide reasonable protection against hijackings and the dangers they presented, not only to the crew and passengers, but also to ground victims. Imposing a duty on the Aviation Defendants best allocates the risks to ground victims posed by inadequate screening, given the Aviations Defendants' existing and admitted duty to screen passengers and items carried aboard.

Lastly, recognition of a duty on the part of the Aviation Defendants would not substantially expand or create "new channels of liability," the fifth and last factor of *532 Madison Avenue*. New York courts have found on other occasions that aircraft owners and operators owe a duty to those on the ground who may be harmed or sustain property damage resulting from improper or negligent operation of an aircraft.

...

The Second Circuit has recognized that airlines have a duty not only to passengers on the flights they operate, but also to passengers on connecting flights, and thus may be liable when they allow terrorists to board planes. In *Stanford v. Kuwait Airways Corp., 89 F.3d 117 (2d Cir.1996)*, the airline failed adequately to screen passengers against terrorists. The hijacking occurred, not on the airplane initially boarded, but on the connecting flight. The Second Circuit, relying on general tort principles including New York law, upheld the air carrier's duty of care as to the passengers on the connecting flight. *Id.* at 125. Clearly, the duty of care extends to cover those embraced by the risk of the terrorists' conduct.

Accordingly, I hold on the pleadings that the Aviation Defendants owed a duty of care to the ground victim plaintiffs.

iii. Scope of Duty to Ground Victims: the Issue of Foreseeability

Defendants argue that the ground victims lost their lives and suffered injuries from an event that was not reasonably foreseeable, for terrorists had not previously used a hijacked airplane as a suicidal weapon to destroy buildings and murder thousands. Defendants contend that because the events of September 11 were not within the reasonably foreseeable risks, any duty of care that they would owe to ground victims generally should not extend to the victims of September 11.

The scope of duty to a particular class of plaintiffs depends on the relationship to such plaintiffs, whether plaintiffs were within a zone of foreseeable harm, and whether the harm was within the class of reasonably foreseeable hazards that the duty exists to prevent. *Di Ponzio v. Riordan, 89 N.Y.2d 578, 657 N.Y.S.2d 377, 679 N.E.2d 616, 618 (1997)* (citations omitted). See also *Palsgraf v. Long Island R.R. Co., 248 N.Y. 339, 162 N.E. 99, 100-01 (1928)....*

In order to be considered foreseeable, the precise manner in which the harm was inflicted need not be perfectly predicted. As *Di Ponzio v. Riordan* explained: "Where an individual breaches a legal duty and thereby causes an occurrence that is within the class of foreseeable hazards that the duty exists to prevent, the individual may be held liable, even though the harm may have been brought about in an unexpected way. On the other hand, no liability will result when the occurrence is not one that is normally associated with such hazards....

...

Construing the factual allegations in the light most favorable to the plaintiffs, I conclude that the crash of the airplanes was within the class of foreseeable hazards resulting from negligently performed security screening. While it may be true that terrorists had not before deliberately flown airplanes into buildings, the airlines reasonably could foresee that crashes causing death and destruction on the ground was a hazard that would arise should hijackers take control of a plane. The intrusion by terrorists into the cockpit, coupled with the volatility of a hijacking situation, creates a foreseeable risk that hijacked airplanes might crash, jeopardizing innocent lives on the ground as well as in the airplane. While the crashes into the particular locations of the World Trade Center, Pentagon, and Shanksville field may not have been foreseen, the duty to screen passengers and items brought on board existed to prevent harms not only to passengers and crew, but also to the ground victims resulting from the crashes of hijacked planes, including the four planes hijacked on September 11.

Defendants point to two decisions in cases brought against manufacturers and distributors of ammonium nitrate utilized in the Oklahoma City bombing and the 1993 attack on the World Trade Center. Relying on either New York or New Jersey law and on Oklahoma law, the courts found that the fertilizer products were not themselves dangerous and served socially useful purposes. *In Gaines-Tabb v. ICI Explosives USA, Inc.*, the district court ruled that the manufacturer did not owe a duty to the plaintiffs because the manufacturer did not expose the plaintiffs to a "recognizable high degree of risk of harm through the misconduct of third persons which a reasonable person would take into account." *995 F.Supp. 1304, 1317 (W.D.Okla.1996)* (citation omitted). On appeal, the Tenth Circuit affirmed, but on the ground that the terrorists' actions served as the supervening cause for the plaintiffs' injuries. 160 F.3d 613, 620 (10th Cir.1998). *In Port Authority of New York and New Jersey v. Arcadian Corp.*, the Third Circuit held that the manufacturers and distributors of ammonium nitrate did not owe a duty to the plaintiffs, because the product had been substantially altered after leaving the defendants' control, and because only the altered product created the danger to the plaintiff. 189 F.3d 305, 317 (3d Cir.1999). "[D]efendants' products were not in and of themselves dangerous but were merely the raw materials or components that terrorists used in combination with other ingredients to build a bomb." *Id.* at 313.

The cases are distinguishable. Ammonium nitrate is a socially and economically useful product. To require manufacturers to prevent the appropriation of their products for an unin-

tended purpose when manufacturers have no control over who purchases and alters the fertilizer would be an undue burden. Unlike the manufacturers, however, the Aviation Defendants
controlled who came onto the planes and what was carried aboard. They had the obligation to
take reasonable care in screening precisely because of the risk of terrorist hijackings, and the
dangerous consequences that would inevitably follow. The consequences that in fact followed
were within the scope of the duty that the Aviation Defendants undertook to carry out.

I hold at this stage of the litigation, on the pleadings and before any discovery has taken
place, that the injuries suffered by the ground victims arose from risks that were within the
scope of the duty undertaken by the Aviation Defendants.

...

B. World Trade Center Defendants' Motions to Dismiss
i. Background

The Port Authority of New York and New Jersey and WTC Properties LLC move to dismiss
all claims brought against them as owners and operators of the World Trade Center for loss of
life, personal injury, and damage to nearby property and businesses resulting from the collapse
of the Twin Towers. The claims are alleged in two Master Complaints regarding Flights 11
and 175 in the consolidated litigation, and in numerous individual complaints. Plaintiffs allege
that the WTC Defendants: 1) failed to design and construct the World Trade Center buildings
according to safe engineering practices and to provide for safe escape routes and adequate
sprinkler systems and fireproofing; 2) failed to inspect, discover, and repair unsafe and dangerous conditions, and to maintain fireproofing materials; 3) failed to develop adequate and safe
evacuation and emergency management plans; 4) failed to apply, interpret and/or enforce applicable building and fire safety codes, regulations and practices; and 5) instructed Tower Two
occupants to return to their offices and remain in the building even while the upper floors of
Tower One were being consumed by uncontrolled fires following the airplane crash into Tower
One. See Plaintiffs' Flight 11 Master Liability Complaint ¶ 85; Plaintiffs' Flight 175 Master
Liability Complaint ¶ 82.

A number of other defendants whose interests are aligned with the Port Authority and World
Trade Center Properties LLC—those who were named as defendants because they designed,
constructed, operated, or maintained the World Trade Center buildings—were voluntarily dismissed earlier in the litigation.

The WTC Defendants argue that the complaints against them should be dismissed because
they had no duty to anticipate and guard against deliberate and suicidal aircraft crashes into
the Towers, and because any alleged negligence on their part was not a proximate cause of the
plaintiffs' injuries. The Port Authority argues also that it is entitled to immunity because the
complained-of conduct essentially consisted of governmental functions.

...

ii. Existence and Scope of Duty

The WTC Defendants contend that they owed no duty to "anticipate and guard against crimes
unprecedented in human history." Plaintiffs argue that defendants owed a duty, not to foresee
the crimes, but to have designed, constructed, repaired and maintained the World Trade Center
structures to withstand the effects and spread of fire, to avoid building collapses caused by fire

and, in designing and effectuating fire safety and evacuation procedures, to provide for the escape of more people.

The existence of a duty owed by the WTC Defendants to its lessees and business occupants has been clearly set out in New York law. "A landowner has a duty to exercise reasonable care under the circumstances in maintaining its property in a safe condition,"

...

The duty of landowners and lessors to adopt fire-safety precautions applies to fires caused by criminals. "[L]andowners have a duty to protect tenants, patrons or invitees from foreseeable harm caused by the criminal conduct of others while they are on the premises."...

The criteria for establishing the existence of duty, discussed previously in the context of the Aviation Defendants' duty to ground victims, applies as well to the duty of landowners to lessees and business occupants. See *532 Madison Ave., Gourmet Foods, Inc. v. Finlandia Ctr., 96 N.Y.2d 280, 727 N.Y.S.2d 49, 750 N.E.2d 1097, 1101 (2001); Palka v. Servicemaster Mgmt. Servs. Corp., 83 N.Y.2d 579, 611 N.Y.S.2d 817, 634 N.E.2d 189, 193 (1994)*. First, the parties and society would reasonably expect that the WTC Defendants would have a duty to the occupants of the Twin Towers in designing, constructing, repairing and maintaining the structures, in conforming to appropriate building and fire safety codes, and in creating appropriate evacuation routes and procedures should an emergency occur. Second, although a large number of claims have been filed against the WTC Defendants, there is no danger that the number will proliferate beyond those who died in the collapse of the structures or were injured while trying to escape. Similarly, the WTC Defendants are not subject to unlimited or insurer-like liability, for they can be held liable only after a showing of fault and only to those who suffered death, personal injury, or property damage resulting from their alleged negligence. Furthermore, by specific provision of the Air Transportation Safety and System Stabilization Act, their liability is limited to their insurance coverage. Act § 408(a)(1). Fourth, the defendants' relationship with the plaintiffs, as their landlord or the landlord of their employer, placed the WTC Defendants in the best position to protect against the risk of harm. And fifth, as discussed above, imposing a duty on the WTC Defendants in the situation at hand will not create new channels of liability, for the New York courts have held traditionally that landlords owe duties of safety and care to the occupants of leased premises and their invitees.

A finding of duty also requires a consideration of the nature of plaintiffs' injuries, and the likelihood of their occurrence from a particular condition. "Defining the nature and scope of the duty and to whom the duty is owed requires consideration of the likelihood of injury to another from a dangerous condition or instrumentality on the property; the severity of potential injuries; the burden on the landowner to avoid the risk; and the foreseeability of a potential plaintiff's presence on the property." *Kush, 462 N.Y.S.2d 831, 449 N.E.2d at 727*. The criteria are clearly satisfied, for the severity and likelihood of potential injuries of people unable to escape from a heavily occupied building before fires envelope evacuation routes is high. The more difficult question is whether the injuries arose from a reasonably foreseeable risk.

Plaintiffs argue that the WTC Defendants had a duty to exercise reasonable care in order to mitigate the effects of fires in the Twin Towers. They allege that defendants knew about the fire safety defects in the Twin Towers, as evident by the Allied litigation concerning inadequate fireproofing in the construction of the buildings; that defendants could have reasonably foreseen crashes of airplanes into the Towers, given the near miss in 1981 of an Aerolineas Argentinas Boeing 707 and the studies conducted during the Towers' construction reporting that the Towers would be able to withstand an aircraft crash; that defendants were aware of numerous fires and evacuations that had occurred at the World Trade Center since its creation, including arson fires in 1975 and the 1993 terrorist-caused explosion in the garage under Tower One; and that the World Trade Center continued to be a prime target of terrorists. A finding of duty does not require a defendant to have been aware of a specific hazard. See *Sanchez v. State of New York, 99 N.Y.2d 247, 754 N.Y.S.2d 621, 784 N.E.2d 675, 679-81 (2002)*. It is enough to have foreseen the risk of serious fires within the buildings and the goal of terrorists to attack the building.

This is a very early point in the litigation. There has been no discovery, and defendants' motions to dismiss accept, as they must, all allegations of the complaints. I hold that the WTC Defendants owed a duty to the plaintiffs, and that plaintiffs should not be foreclosed from being able to prove that defendants failed to exercise reasonable care to provide a safe environment for its occupants and invitees with respect to reasonably foreseeable risks.

iii. Proximate and Supervening Causation

The WTC Defendants argue that even if they are held to have owed a duty to the plaintiffs and even if a jury ultimately finds that they acted negligently, their negligence was not the proximate cause of plaintiffs' damages. This is because, they claim, the terrorist-related aircraft crashes into the Twin Towers were so extraordinary and unforeseeable as to constitute intervening and superceding causes, severing any link of causation to the WTC Defendants.

When an intervening act "is of such an extraordinary nature or so attenuates defendants' negligence from the ultimate injury that responsibility for the injury may not be reasonably attributed to the defendant," proximate cause is lacking. *Kush v. City of Buffalo, 59 N.Y.2d 26, 462 N.Y.S.2d 831, 449 N.E.2d 725, 729 (1983)*. Thus, "when such an intervening cause 'interrupts the natural sequence of events, turns aside their course, prevents the natural and probable result of the original act or omission, and produces a different result that could not have been reasonably anticipated,' it will prevent a recovery on account of the act or omission of the original wrongdoer." *Sheehan v. City of New York, 40 N.Y.2d 496, 387 N.Y.S.2d 92, 354 N.E.2d 832, 835-36 (1976)* (citations omitted). The "negligence complained of must have caused the occurrence of the accident from which the injuries flow." *Rivera v. City of New York, 11 N.Y.2d 856, 227 N.Y.S.2d 676, 182 N.E.2d 284, 285 (1962)*.

Generally, an intervening intentional or criminal act severs the liability of the original tort-feasor. *Kush, 462 N.Y.S.2d 831, 449 N.E.2d at 729*. But that "doctrine has no application when the intentional or criminal intervention of a third party or parties is reasonably foreseeable." *Id. In Bonsignore v. City of New York*, a New York City police officer shot and seriously wounded his wife. *683 F.2d 635 (2d Cir.1982)*. The wife sued the City, alleging that it was negligent in failing to identify officers who were unfit to carry guns and who would likely use them without proper restraint and in inappropriate circumstances, and in not recognizing that her husband was such an officer. The City defended on the ground of independent and supervening cause, arguing that the officer's intentional and criminal act severed any link of causation to its own alleged negligence. The Court of Appeals held in favor of the wife, ruling that since the officer's act was precisely that which the City should reasonably have foreseen, the police officer's intentional and criminal act was not an independent and supervening break between the City's negligence and the plaintiff's injury. See *id.* at 637-38.

At this early stage of the case and in the absence of a factual record, I find that plaintiffs have pleaded sufficient facts to allege legal proximate cause....

iv. Governmental Immunity

The Port Authority claims that it is immune from liability to the extent that the plaintiffs complain that the Port Authority was negligent in its performance of governmental functions such as planning for public safety and responding to a public emergency. The Port Authority agrees, however, that it does not enjoy a blanket immunity to suit. See N.Y. Unconsol. Laws § 7106 (2003) ("Although the port authority is engaged in the performance of governmental functions, the said two states [NY and NJ] consent to liability on the part of the port authority in such suits, actions or proceedings for tortious acts committed by it and its agents to the same extent as though it were a private corporation"). The allegations and proofs have to be parsed in order to determine whether, and to what extent, the defense of government immunity applies.

The defense of governmental immunity requires a court to scrutinize specific claims. "It is the specific act or omission out of which the injury is claimed to have arisen and the capacity in which that act or failure to act occurred which governs [governmental] liability, not whether the agency involved is engaged generally in proprietary activity or is in control of the location in which the injury occurred." *Weiner v. Metro. Transp. Auth.*, 55 N.Y.2d 175, 448 N.Y.S.2d 141, 433 N.E.2d 124, 127 (1982). The inquiry is to determine a point "along a continuum of responsibility," one side of which may be considered as proprietary, and the other, governmental. See *Miller v. State*, 62 N.Y.2d 506, 478 N.Y.S.2d 829, 467 N.E.2d 493, 496 (1984). "[The continuum] begins with the simplest matters directly concerning a piece of property for which the entity acting as landlord has a certain duty of care, for example, the repair of steps or the maintenance of doors in an apartment building. The spectrum extends gradually out to more complex measures of safety and security for a greater area and populace, whereupon the actions increasingly, and at a certain point only, involve governmental functions, for example, the maintenance of general police and fire protection." *Id.* When a public entity acts in a proprietary capacity as a landlord, it is held to the same duty as private landlords. See id.

Miller illustrates the issue. The plaintiff, a student at a SUNY college, was assaulted in the college dormitory by an intruder and sued the State for the university's failure to keep doors locked and maintain adequate security. *478 N.Y.S.2d 829, 467 N.E.2d at 495.* The Court of Appeals held that while the state could not be liable for failure to provide police protection, the state in its capacity as landowner had the duty to maintain minimal security measures to protect occupants against foreseeable criminal intrusions. See *id.* at 496.

As a landowner, the State must act as a reasonable [person] in maintaining his property in a reasonably safe condition in view of all the circumstances, including the likelihood of injury to others, the seriousness of the injury, and the burden of avoiding the risk. Under this standard, a landlord has a duty to maintain minimal security measures, related to a specific building itself, in the face of foreseeable criminal intrusion upon tenants. *Id.* at 497 (citations omitted).

Plaintiffs allege negligence by the Port Authority in a number of respects: 1) failure to design and construct the World Trade Center buildings according to safe engineering practices and to provide for safe escape routes and adequate sprinkler systems and fireproofing; 2) failure to inspect, discover, and repair unsafe and dangerous conditions, and to maintain fireproofing materials; 3) failure to develop an adequate and safe evacuation plan and emergency management plan; 4) failure to apply, interpret and/or enforce applicable building and fire safety codes, regulations and practices; and 5) instructing Tower Two occupants to remain in the building rather than evacuate. See Plaintiffs' Flight 11 Master Liability Complaint ¶ 85; Plaintiffs' Flight 175 Master Liability Complaint ¶ 82. Based only on the pleadings and before any discovery has occurred, I have been given no basis to determine where, on the continuum between functions that are essentially proprietary and those that are essentially governmental, these various allegations should fall. It would seem, from the pleadings alone, that it would be difficult for the Port Authority to establish its defense with respect to claims of negligent design, construction, inspection, repair, maintenance, and application and enforcement of building codes, for these functions are not likely to differ from those required of private landowners. The same is true regarding allegations relating to inadequate evacuation and emergency management plans and procedures, but these allegations may touch also upon the functions of the Port Authority police force within the Twin Towers, and come closer to the governmental end of the continuum. This may be even more so for the allegation that occupants of Tower Two were told, before the crash into that Tower, to return to, and remain in, their offices, rather than evacuate. The record does not yet show who gave this instruction, whether a member of the Port Authority's security force or some other employee, and for what reasons the instruction was given.

...

At this point, the Port Authority has not shown that it will prove its defense of governmental immunity as to the negligence allegations made by WTC occupants.

The Port Authority argues also that it should have immunity in its capacity as operator of Newark Airport, for alleged negligence in permitting terrorists and weapons aboard United Air Lines flight 93, and for the hijacking and deaths that resulted. The Port Authority claims that it was performing a governmental function. Again, however, the Port Authority has not shown that it was performing a governmental function with respect to the "specific act or omission out of which the injury is claimed to have arisen and the capacity in which that act or failure to act occurred." *Weiner, 448 N.Y.S.2d 141, 433 N.E.2d at 127.* Further development of the record is required.

For the reasons stated, I deny the WTC Defendants' motion to dismiss the complaints.

C. Boeing's Motions to Dismiss

Some of those who were injured and the successors of those who died in the Pentagon, in American Airlines flight 77 which crashed into the Pentagon, and in United Air Lines flight 93 which crashed into the Shanksville, Pennsylvania field, claim the right to recover against Boeing, the manufacturer of the two "757" jets flown by United and American. Plaintiffs allege that Boeing manufactured inadequate and defective cockpit doors, and thus made it possible for the hijackers to invade the cockpits and take over the aircraft. Boeing moves to dismiss the lawsuits.

I hold that plaintiffs have alleged legally sufficient claims for relief under the laws applicable to the claims, Virginia and Pennsylvania, respectively. I therefore deny the motion except for certain claims, as discussed below....

ii. Motion to Dismiss Claims Arising out of the Crash of American Airlines Flight 77
a. Background

Thus far, three individual complaints have been filed with respect to the flight 77 crash. They charge Boeing with strict tort liability and negligent design based on an unreasonably dangerous design of the cockpit doors. See *Edwards v. American Airlines, Inc.*, No. 02 Civ. 9234 (brought on behalf of a decedent who was a passenger on flight 77); *Powell v. Argenbright Security, Inc.*, *No. 02 Civ. 10160* (brought on behalf of a decedent who died while working at the Pentagon); *Gallop v. Argenbright Security, Inc.*, *No. 03 Civ. 1016* (plaintiffs injured at the Pentagon site).

The Plaintiffs' First Amended Flight 77 Master Liability Complaint contains three counts applicable to Boeing. Count Six alleges strict tort liability for an unreasonably dangerous design of the cockpit doors. Count Seven alleges that Boeing breached its duty of care by failing to design the cockpit doors and accompanying locks in a manner that would prevent hijackers and/or passengers from accessing the cockpit. Count Eight alleges that Boeing violated its express or implied warranty that the aircraft structure and frame, with respect to the cockpit doors, were fit for the purposes for which they were designed, intended and used.

b. Strict liability claims

Virginia does not permit recovery on a strict liability theory in product liability cases. See *Sensenbrenner v. Rust, Orling & Neale, Architects, Inc.*, *236 Va. 419, 374 S.E.2d 55, 57 n. 4 (1988)*. Thus, Count Six in the Flight 77 Master Complaint, and the underlying related claims in the individual complaints—Count Three in *Edwards*, Count Five in *Powell*, and Count Five in *Gallop*—are all dismissed.

c. Negligent design and breach of warranty claims

Boeing moves to dismiss both the claims of negligent design and breach of warranty, arguing that it did not owe a duty to prevent the use of the plane as a weapon, and that the independent and supervening acts of the terrorists, not Boeing's acts, caused the injuries of the plaintiffs. A plaintiff, to state a claim of negligence, must allege the existence of a legal duty, violation of that duty, and proximate causation which results in injury. *Marshall v. Winston, 239 Va. 315, 389 S.E.2d 902, 904 (1990)*. In order to state a claim of breach of warranty, plaintiff may invoke the Virginia law of an implied warranty of merchantability, which guarantees that a product "was reasonably safe for its intended use when it was placed in the stream of commerce." *Turner v. Manning, Maxwell & Moore, Inc., 216 Va. 245, 217 S.E.2d 863, 868-69 (1975)*.

In order to recover under either a negligence or breach of warranty theory against a product manufacturer, "a plaintiff must show (1) that the goods were unreasonably dangerous either for the use to which they would ordinarily be put or for some other reasonably foreseeable purpose, and (2) that the unreasonably dangerous condition existed when the goods left the manufacturer's hands." *Morgen Indus., Inc. v. Vaughan, 252 Va. 60, 471 S.E.2d 489, 492 (1996)*. Thus, a manufacturer owes a duty to supply a product "fit for the ordinary purposes for which it is to be used" and safe notwithstanding a reasonably foreseeable misuse that could cause injury, *Jeld-Wen, Inc. v. Gamble, 256 Va. 144, 501 S.E.2d 393, 396 (1998)*. However, "a manufacturer is not required to supply an accident-proof product." *Besser Co. v. Hansen, 243 Va. 267, 415 S.E.2d 138, 144 (1992)* (citation omitted).

The existence of duty in the products liability context is a question of law. "[T]he purpose of making the finding of a legal duty as a prerequisite to a finding of negligence, or breach of implied warranty, in products liability is to avoid the extension of liability for every conceivably foreseeable accident, without regard to common sense or good policy." *Jeld-Wen, 501 S.E.2d at 396* (citations omitted). Legal duty may extend to a user of the product, as well as to its purchaser. See *Morgen Indus., 471 S.E.2d at 492.*

...

Boeing argues that its design of the cockpit was not unreasonably dangerous in relation to reasonably foreseeable risks, and that the risk of death to passengers and ground victims caused by a terrorist hijacking was not reasonably foreseeable. The record at this point does not support Boeing's argument. There have been many efforts by terrorists to hijack airplanes, and too many have been successful. The practice of terrorists to blow themselves up in order to kill as many people as possible has also been prevalent. Although there have been no incidents before the ones of September 11, 2001 where terrorists combined both an airplane hijacking and a suicidal explosion, I am not able to say that the risk of crashes was not reasonably foreseeable to an airplane manufacturer. Plaintiffs have alleged that it was reasonably foreseeable that a failure to design a secure cockpit could contribute to a breaking and entering into, and a take-over of, a cockpit by hijackers or other unauthorized individuals, substantially increasing the risk of injury and death to people and damage to property. I hold that the allegation is sufficient to establish Boeing's duty.

Boeing also argues that the regulations of the Federal Aviation Administration ("FAA") relating to design of passenger airplanes did not require an impenetrable cockpit door, and thus its designs, which satisfied FAA requirements, could not be defective. However, the only support provided by Boeing for its argument is an after-the-fact FAA policy statement, issued to explain why the FAA, in 2002, was requiring airplane manufacturers to provide such doors even though the FAA previously had not done so.

Flight crew compartment doors on transport category airplanes have been designed principally to ensure privacy, so pilots could focus their entire attention to their normal and emergency flight duties. The doors have not been designed to provide an impenetrable barrier between the cabin and the flight crew compartment. Doors have not been required to meet any significant security threat, such as small arms fire or shrapnel, or the exercise of brute force to enter the flight crew compartment. *67 Fed.Reg. 12,820-12,824 (Mar. 19, 2002).*

Boeing has not proffered the parameters that existed when it manufactured its "757" jumbo-jet airplanes that United and American flew on September 11, 2001. Boeing also has not shown the extent to which FAA regulations determined how passenger airplanes were to be constructed. Although a FAA promulgation of standards for the design and manufacture of passenger aircraft may be entitled to weight in deciding whether Boeing was negligent, see, e.g., *Curtin v. Port Auth. of N.Y. and N.J., 183 F.Supp.2d 664, 671 (S.D.N.Y.2002)* (concluding that the standard of care with respect to aircraft evacuation procedures is a matter of federal, not state, law), statements by the FAA characterizing what its former regulations required does not dictate the totality of the duty owed by aircraft manufacturers. Boeing's argument is not sufficient to support its motion to dismiss the complaints against it.

d. Proximate Causation

Boeing next argues that its design of the cockpit doors on its "757" passenger aircraft, even if held to constitute an "unreasonably dangerous condition," was not the proximate cause of plaintiffs' injuries. Boeing argues that the criminal acts of the terrorists in hijacking the airplanes and using the airplanes as weapons of mass destruction constituted an "efficient intervening cause" which broke the "natural and continuous sequence" of events flowing from Boeing's allegedly inadequate design. See *Sugarland Run Homeowners Ass'n v. Halfmann, 260 Va. 366, 535 S.E.2d 469, 472 (2000)* (a "proximate cause of an event is that 'act or omission which, in natural and continuous sequence, unbroken by an efficient intervening cause, produces the event, and without which that event would not have occurred,' " quoting *Beale v. Jones, 210 Va. 519, 171 S.E.2d 851, 853 (1970))*. Plaintiffs have the burden to prove proximate cause and, generally, the issue is a question of fact to be resolved by a jury. *Sugarland, 535 S.E.2d at 472.* However, when reasonable people cannot differ, the issue becomes a question of law for the court. *Id.*

The record at this point does not support Boeing's argument that the invasion and take-over of the cockpit by the terrorists must, as a matter of law, be held to constitute an "efficient intervening act" that breaks the "natural and continuous sequence" flowing from Boeing's allegedly inadequate design. Plaintiffs allege that Boeing should have designed its cockpit door to prevent hijackers from invading the cockpit, that acts of terrorism, including hijackings of airplanes, were reasonably foreseeable, and that the lives of passengers, crew and ground victims would be imminently in danger from such hijackings. Virginia law does not require Boeing to have foreseen precisely how the injuries suffered on September 11, 2001 would be caused, as long as Boeing could reasonably have foreseen that "some injury" from its negligence "might probably result." See *Blondel v. Hays, 241 Va. 467, 403 S.E.2d 340, 344 (1991)* ("[A] reasonably prudent [person] ought under the circumstances to have foreseen that some injury might probably result from that negligence"). Given the critical nature of the cockpit area, and the inherent danger of crash when a plane is in flight, one cannot say that Boeing could not reasonably have foreseen the risk flowing from an inadequately constructed cockpit door.

...

In re Korean Air Lines Disaster of September 1, 1983, No. 83-3442, 1985 WL 9447, 1985 U.S. Dist. LEXIS 17211 (D.D.C.1985), involved lawsuits by the legal successors of passengers who died when Korean Airlines passenger flight 007 was shot down by Russian fighter planes. The passenger plane had flown off course and over a sensitive military zone in Russia. Russian fighter pilots intercepted the plane and, instead of following international protocol for causing the plane to return to international routes over the high seas or to land at a selected landing field, shot it down. Plaintiffs sued Boeing, the manufacturer of the airplane, alleging that a product defect in its navigation systems caused it to fly off course and over Soviet territory, and that Boeing's improper and unsafe design was therefore the proximate cause of plaintiffs' damages. The court dismissed the complaint, holding that Boeing could not foresee that the Soviet Union would destroy an intruding aircraft in violation of international conventions, and had no ability to guard against such conduct. See *id., 1985 WL 9447, **5-6, 1985 U.S. Dist. LEXIS 17211, at *17-20.* The court held, consequently, that Boeing did not owe a duty to passengers with respect to such risks, and that the actions of the Russian pilots were independent and supervening causes that broke the chain of causation.

...

Accordingly, I deny Boeing's motion to dismiss the complaints against it arising from the crash of flight 77 into the Pentagon.

iii. Motion to Dismiss Claims Arising out of the Crash of United Air Lines Flight 93
a. Background

The successors of the passengers who died in the crash of United Air Lines flight 93 in Shanksville have filed four lawsuits: *Burnett v. Argenbright, 02 Civ. 6168; Lyles v. Argenbright, 02 Civ. 7243; Cashman v. Argenbright, 02 Civ. 7608; and Driscoll v. Argenbright, 02 Civ. 7912.* Their allegations are encapsulated in Plaintiffs' Flight 93 Master Liability Complaint, which mirrors the Plaintiffs' First Amended Flight 77 Master Liability Complaint. The Flight 93 Master Complaint alleges claims against Boeing based on strict tort liability, for an unreasonably dangerous design of the cockpit doors (Count Five); negligence, for failure to design cockpit doors and accompanying locks in a manner that would prevent hijackers and/or passengers from accessing the cockpit (Count Six); and express or implied warranty, for creating a product that was unfit for the purposes for which it was designed, intended and used (Count Seven).

b. Strict tort liability and breach of warranty claims

Under Pennsylvania law, following section 402A of the Restatement (Second) of Torts, a plaintiff pressing a product liability or strict tort liability claim must allege and prove that the product was defective, that the defect existed when it left the defendant, and that the defect proximately caused the harm. See *Weiner v. American Honda Motor Co. Inc., 718 A.2d 305, 307 (Pa.Super.1998).* The elements of breach of warranty and strict product liability are the same. *Cucchi v. Rollins Protective Servs. Co., 377 Pa.Super. 9, 546 A.2d 1131, 1136 (1998),* rev'd on other grounds, *524 Pa. 514, 574 A.2d 565 (1990).*

...

Because the decision of whether the product was unreasonably dangerous and unsafe for its intended use is a question of law, Boeing argues that the judge should not be influenced by conclusory allegations of the complaint. The reason, Boeing argues, is that "the trial court is not bound by any party's legal conclusions as to the intended purpose of a product, even if those conclusions are couched as averments of fact or presented as expert evidence. To hold otherwise would force trial courts (and reviewing courts) to accept unrealistic, generalized or distorted views of the product's purpose simply because they are presented as factual evidence." *Schindler, 774 A.2d at 773.*

But this is not the situation in the case before me. The cockpit door, like any door, is intended as a separation, a "movable barrier of wood or other material, consisting either of one piece, or of several pieces framed together, usually turning on hinges or sliding in a groove, and serving to close or open a passage into a building, room, etc." Oxford English Dictionary (Second Edition 1999). A door may be fitted with, and without, locks, depending on who may be allowed to enter and in what circumstances. The intended users of a door, and in particular a locked door, are those within, in order to assure their privacy, and possibly those without who may have an interest in allowing those within to perform their jobs without unwanted intrusion.

Boeing asks me to hold that since the terrorists who hijacked the airplanes were not the intended users of the cockpit doors, one cannot say that the doors were unreasonably dangerous or unsafe in relation to the use that terrorists would be expected to make of the doors. Clearly, however, the intended users of the cockpit doors were not the terrorists who broke through them, but the pilots who had the right to protection from unwanted intrusion, and the passengers who had the right to believe that the pilots could continue to guide the plane, free from intrusion, to ensure their safe arrival at their intended destination. If, as Boeing argues, a person who breaks through a door is considered to be an unintended user, no manufacturer of a door and lock system could ever be liable. The intended user of a door is the person who wishes it to be closed and stay closed, not the person who can easily force it open. The pilots and passengers are not mere "casual bystanders," but people with a vital stake in the door's performing its intended purpose. See Restatement (Second) Torts § 402A, Comments (l) and (o) (intended users include "those who are passively enjoying the benefit of the product, as in the case of passengers in automobiles or airplanes,…casual bystanders, and others who may come in contact with the product, as in the case of employees of the retailer, or a passer-by injured by an exploding bottle, or a pedestrian hit by an automobile have been denied recovery").

Boeing may be able to show that the cockpit doors were not unreasonably dangerous, and that it was not unreasonable to design them to provide privacy without making them impenetrable. At this point, it would be inappropriate for a judge to make this determination. The record will have to be developed to show if the cockpit doors, incapable of keeping out unwanted intruders, were unreasonably dangerous, taking into consideration: 1) the gravity of the danger posed by the design; 2) the likelihood that the danger would occur; 3) the feasibility of a safer design; 4) the adverse consequences to the product and to the consumer that would result from a safer design; 5) the usefulness and desirability of the product; 6) the likelihood that the product will cause injury and the probable seriousness of the injury; 7) the availability of a substitute product which meets the same needs and is not unsafe; 8) the manufacturer's ability to eliminate the unsafe character of the product without impairing usefulness or making the product too expensive; 9) the user's ability to avoid danger by the exercise of care in the use of the product; 10) the user's anticipated awareness of the dangers inherent in the product and their avoidability; and 11) the ability of the manufacturer to spread loss through price-setting or insurance coverage. See *Schindler, 774 A.2d at 772; Riley, 688 A.2d at 225*.

In order to prevail on their strict liability and breach of warranty claims, the plaintiffs must also show that the defect was the proximate cause for the injuries; this will be discussed in the negligent design analysis below. *Weiner, 718 A.2d at 307*.

c. Negligent design claims

Boeing argues that the plaintiffs' negligent design claims must be dismissed because it did not owe a duty of care to the plaintiffs, and because its alleged negligence was not the proximate cause of plaintiffs' damages. The elements of a claim of negligence are: the existence of a duty to plaintiffs; the breach of that duty; a causal relationship between the breach and the resulting injury; and actual loss by the plaintiff. See *Brisbine v. Outside In School, 2002 PA Super 138, 799 A.2d 89, 93 (2002)* (citation omitted). Because Pennsylvania and Virginia law do not appear to differ significantly, the analysis is similar to that for Flight 77.

Duty is "imposed on all persons not to place others at risk of harm through their actions. The scope of this duty is limited, however, to those risks which are reasonably foreseeable by the actor in the circumstances of the case." *J.E.J. v. Tri-County Big Brothers/Big Sisters, Inc., 692 A.2d 582, 584 (1997)* (citation omitted). "In the context of duty, the concept of foreseeability means the likelihood of the occurrence of a general type of risk rather than the likelihood of the occurrence of the precise chain of events leading to the injury." *Huddleston v. Infertility Ctr. of Am., Inc., 700 A.2d 453, 460 (Pa.Super.1997)* (citation omitted). Plaintiffs have alleged that Boeing reasonably should have foreseen that a negligently designed cockpit door, permitting unauthorized individuals to enter the cockpit, would lead to risk of injury or death. For the same reasons as I have discussed previously, Boeing's motion to dismiss based on the absence of a duty of care to plaintiffs is denied.

To determine whether proximate cause exists, "the court must determine whether the injury would have been foreseen by an ordinary person as the natural and probable outcome of the act complained of." *Reilly v. Tiergarten Inc., 430 Pa.Super. 10, 633 A.2d 208, 210 (1993)*. The existence of a concurring cause responsible for producing injury does not relieve a defendant of liability, if "a jury could reasonably believe that a defendant's actions were a substantial factor in bringing about the harm." *Powell v. Drumheller, 539 Pa. 484, 653 A.2d 619, 622 (1995)*. "Among the factors to consider in determining whether a subsequent force is an intervening or superseding cause are whether the force is operating independently of any situation created by the first actor's negligence and whether it is a normal result of that situation." *Rabutino v. Freedom State Realty Co. Inc., 809 A.2d 933, 942 (Pa.Super.2002)*. Plaintiffs allege that without defendant's negligence, the hijackers would not have been able to intrude into the cockpit and take over the airplane. Again, for the reasons previously discussed, the terrorists' unauthorized entry into the cockpit was not unforeseeable, and did not constitute an "intervening" or "superseding" cause that could, as a matter of law, break the chain of causation.

Accordingly, I deny Boeing's motion to dismiss the complaints against it arising from the crash of flight 93 into Shanksville.

III. Conclusion

For the reasons stated, the motions to dismiss the complaints by the Aviation Defendants and the WTC Defendants are denied. The motion of Boeing to dismiss Counts Four and Six in the Flight 77 Master Complaint, Count Four in the Flight 93 Master Complaint, Count Three in *Edwards v. American Airlines, Inc., No. 02* Civ. 9234, Count Five in *Powell v. Argenbright Security, Inc., No. 02* Civ. 10160, and Count Five in *Gallop v. Argenbright Security, Inc., No. 03* Civ. 1016, is granted; the remainder of the motion is denied.

By this decision, substantially all preliminary matters have been resolved, with the exception of the Port Authority's motion to dismiss Mayore Estates LLC, 02 Civ. 7198(AKH). We are now ready to proceed with the discovery stages of the lawsuits. To this end, I will meet with all counsel for case management purposes on September 26, 2003, at 9:30 A.M., in Courtroom 14D, 500 Pearl Street, New York, N.Y. 10007. Liaison Counsel shall submit a proposed agenda by September 24, 2003.

SO ORDERED.

11.2 Suits Against State-Sponsors of Terrorism

Monetary damages associated with civil actions against terrorists and their sponsors serve as a key ingredient in combating international terrorism and fulfill United Nations Security Council Resolution 1368 (issued in the wake of the terror attacks of September 11, 2001): "The international community [must] redouble their efforts to prevent and suppress terrorist acts...." Even prior to the coordinated terror attacks of September 11, 2001, the United States government recognized the threat of international terrorism and the need to provide solid legal mechanisms for American terror victims to file private causes of action against both those who commit international acts of terror and those who contribute to those attacks, either directly or indirectly. In addition to providing an avenue for victims of terror to receive compensation, the United States also understood that civil litigation, if used effectively, would certainly serve as a critical and necessary means of deterrence against terrorist organizations as well as those nations who sponsor terrorist groups.

For this reason, Congress expressly directed retroactive application to the Antiterrorism and Effective Death Penalty Act of 1996 (AEDPA), 8 U.S.C. § 1189, so that the law applied to any cause of action arising before or after the enactment of the AEDPA. In tandem with subsequent federal statutes dealing with terrorism civil lawsuits, this model ensures that terrorists and their supporters suffer significant financial punishment which functions both as a direct deterrence, and also as a disabling mechanism—the very core of the intent of punitive damages. Clearly, in the American justice system, the essence of punitive damages is to award the plaintiff(s) a significant money judgment in addition to actual damages against those defendants who acted with recklessness, intentional malice, or deceit. The wrongdoer is penalized by means of punitive damages in order to both deter future wrongdoing and to make a clear example to others. Nowhere is this context more applicable than in the sphere of curtailing international terrorism.

The second type of civil action associated with terrorism lawsuits are those claims brought against one of three categories of international terrorists and their sponsors: (1) purely non-State actors, individuals as well as groups; (2) States that sponsor terrorism, or their agents (Flatow Amendment); or (3) so-called non-FSIA (Foreign Sovereign Immunities Act) defendants, State actors committing acts of terrorism outside of their official capacity. Currently, under American jurisprudence, two main federal statutory frameworks exist: (1) the Flatow amendment to the Foreign Sovereign Immunities Act (FSIA), 28 U.S.C. §1605; and (2) the Antiterrorism Act (ATA), 18 U.S.C. §2333.

The so-called Flatow amendment provides that a foreign official of a designated State sponsor of terrorism, while acting within the scope of his office, can be civilly liable in an American court for violation of acts contained within the legislation. Further, as part of the 2008 Defense Authorization Act, Congress made it crystal clear that 1996 FSIA Amendments applied a statutory cause of action against the actual State that sponsored the terrorist act. Similarly, the ATA allows for private citizens to bring lawsuits for acts of international terrorism with the added deterrent goal of making it unprofitable for terrorists to solicit or maintain financial assets within the United States.

Added to the FSIA in 1996, the Flatow Amendment is codified at 28 U.S.C. § 1605A, creating an exception to foreign sovereign immunity in civil suits in which money damages are sought against a foreign State for personal injury or death that was caused by an act of "torture, extrajudicial killing, aircraft sabotage, hostage taking, or provision of material support or resources (as defined in section 2339A of Title 18) for such an act if such act or provision of material support is engaged in by an official, employee, or agent of such foreign state while acting within the scope of his or her office, employment, or agency…" or other terrorist acts. Although this exception applies only if the defendant foreign State was designated as a State sponsor of terrorism at the time the alleged acts occurred, the issue of punitive damages remains. Specifically, § 1605(A) (c) authorizes the full range of money damages which "may include economic damages, solatium, pain and suffering, and punitive damages." The Flatow Amendment provides that:

[A]n official, employee, or agent of a foreign state designated as a state sponsor of terrorism… while acting within the scope of his or her office, employment, or agency shall be liable to a United States national or the national's legal representative for personal injury or death caused by acts of that official, employee, or agent for which the courts of the United States may maintain jurisdiction under for *money damages which may include economic damages, solatium, pain and suffering, and punitive damages* if the acts were among those described in [emphasis added].

In *Flatow v. Islamic Republic of Iran*, which dealt with a suicide bomber terror attack on a bus in the Gaza Strip in 1995, the federal court recognized that special compensatory and punitive damages were legitimate deterrence considerations since terrorism was directed not just at the immediate victims, but also at their family members and the society as a whole. Again, the goal of the terrorist is to "kill one and frighten ten thousand."

The malice associated with terrorist attacks transcends even that of premeditated murder. The intended audience of a terrorist attack is not limited to the families of those killed and wounded or even just Israelis, but in this case, the American public, for the purpose of affecting United States government support for Israel and the peace process. The terrorist's intent is to strike fear not only for one's own safety, but also for that of friends and family, and to manipulate that fear in order to achieve political objectives. Thus the character of the wrongful act itself increases the magnitude of the injury. It thus demands a corresponding increase in compensation for increased injury.

In the context of punitive damages, the matter of deterrence plays a central component since the goal of punitive damages is to create within the minds of those organizations and nations that sponsor terror and torture the realistic expectation of seizure and dissemination of assets in the form of large monetary damages against them. The court in *Flatow*, the foundational terror incident which directly prompted Congress to create a new statutory cause of action, set out the standard approach in regards to calculating punitive damages:

Factors which may be considered in determining an appropriate amount of punitive damages may be grouped under a few broad headings, including: (1) the nature of the act itself, and the extent to which any civilized society would find that act repugnant; (2) the circumstances of its planning; (3) Defendants' economic status with regard to the ability of Defendants to pay; and (4) the basis upon which a Court might determine the amount of an award reasonably sufficient to deter like conduct in the future, both by the Defendants and others.

Expert testimony in *Flatow* also led to a standard calculation in awarding punitive damages three times the amount that the State which sponsors terrorism (in this case Iran) spends annually on terrorist activities. In *Flatow*, this multiplier produced a $300,000,000 punitive damages award. Again, under such a calculation punitive awards of this magnitude are designed for deterrence to: (1) deter State sponsors of terrorism, and (2) affect the ability of such nations to fund terrorist activities in the future.

The victim's family in *Flatow* was also allowed to recover compensatory damages for economic loss, pain and suffering, and solatium. The court calculated economic damages by adding the funeral bill of $4,470.00 with the loss of accretions to the estate in the amount of $1,508,750.00. The calculation for loss of accretions took into account inflation, rise in productivity, job advancement, and net earnings. Furthermore, the court awarded $1,000,000 for the three to five hours of pain and suffering the victim endured, after the terrorist attack, before she died.

The *Flatow* decision is also noted for its increased award of solatium damages which account for the additional suffering caused by the family members of a victim to a terrorist act. The court noted that "mental anguish, bereavement and grief resulting from the fact of decedent's death constitutes the preponderant element of a claim for solatium." The court then divided its solatium inquiry into determining: (1) the mental anguish suffered by the victim's family, and (2) the loss of decedent's society and comfort. Calculations for both of these damage types are fact intensive and not subject to exact models associated with economic loss.

Two main factors guided the analysis for both damage types: (1) the expected duration of the mental anguish; and (2) the nature of the relationship between the claimant and decedent. Since all acts of terrorism employ unlawful violence, the anguish of family members is prolonged well beyond what is experienced for a natural death. In turn, a more intimate family connection calls for greater levels of compensation for the victim's family member. Again, *Flatow* provides a superb standardized rubric for compensatory damages calculation.

> Numerous factors enter into this analysis, including: strong emotional ties between the claimant and the decedent; decedent's position in the family birth order relative to the claimant; the relative maturity or immaturity of the claimants; whether decedent habitually provided advice and solace to claimants; whether the claimant shared interests and pursuits with decedent; as well as decedent's achievements and plans for the future which would have affected claimants.

Unlike the FSIA, the ATA does not specify what type of damages may be awarded. Neither does it clearly define the class of potential plaintiffs. Nevertheless, by allowing the "estate, survivors, or heirs" of a U.S. national killed by an act of terrorism to sue in federal district court and to recover treble damages and attorney's fees, it is certain that the intent of the law is to maximize the punishment of the wrongdoer so that it is *punitive* in nature. In American jurisprudence, the purpose of allowing for treble damages is always punitive in nature and designed to "punish past, and to deter future, unlawful conduct." The court used a treble damages formula in assessing damages against Iran. This approach is now standard.

Rooted in a common law tort framework, the ATA has no specific requirement that those recovering be citizens of the United States themselves (the statute provides no definition for "survivors" or "heirs"), nor does it specify the types of damages. Nevertheless, in the light of the legislative history and developing case law, the 2004 case of *Ungar v. Palestinian Authority*, sets the accepted methodology in determining these matters. Yaron Ungar and his wife were killed in a drive-by shooting by terrorists on June, 9, 1996, in Israel. Yaron's family brought suit under the ATA against multiple defendants including the Palestinian Authority. The district court found that Yaron's parents and siblings qualified to bring suit as "survivors" under the wording of 18 U.S.C. §2333(a), since Congress intended to use common law tort principles to extend civil liability to terrorist acts with the widest possible effect. The use of the term "survivors" evidences the intent that immediate family members, other than heirs, may seek compensation for the loss of a loved one. Indeed, allowing siblings and parents of those killed by terrorists to recover damages serves as an additional deterrence factor to terrorism.

In reference to the issue of damages, *Ungar* held that the primary purpose of the law was to empower the victims of terrorism to the fullest extent possible. Accordingly, *Ungar* allowed for the full range of damages set out under the FSIA. Ungar's two children (heirs), parents, and siblings were all awarded damages for loss of society and companionship. The children also recovered for loss of parental guidance and parental services which Ungar could no longer provide. "These services include such tasks as babysitting, feeding, bathing, doing the laundry, getting them ready for school, and similar assistance normally performed by a parent for a child." Economic damages will ordinarily include loss of earnings and funeral costs. Similar to *Flatow*, where the court considered inflation, rise in productivity, job advancement, and net earnings in its calculations of lost earnings, the Ungar family recovered lost earnings subject to Ungar's personal consumption.

Understanding that no rigid formula exists for computing damages associated with pain and suffering, the *Ungar* court heard expert testimony giving a step-by-step analysis of the drive-by shooting to accurately determine damages for pain and suffering. The Court considered in its calculation the fact that Ungar suffered painful bullet wounds in his arm and chest before being killed by a head shot while slumped in his car seat, as well as the mental pain Ungar experienced at seeing his wife's death shortly before his own. The court awarded $500,000 for the pain and suffering. In addition, Ungar's family received losses for mental anguish (solatium) which were calculated in a similar fashion to loss of society. Ungar's children, parents and three siblings received a total of $38,803,401 in compensatory damages for all the above mentioned losses.

In *Eisenfeld v. Islamic Republic of Iran*, a case involving a 1996 Iranian State-sponsored act of terrorism carried out by the terror organization HAMAS where a bus was bombed in Jerusalem, the court cited the *Flatow* punitive damages approach and awarded the two plaintiff decedents' estate a single award of $300,000,000 ($150,000,000 each). In *Boim v. Quranic Literacy Institute and Hold Land Foundation for Relief and Development*, the parents of a U.S. citizen murdered in a terror attack in Israel by the terrorist group HAMAS sued several individuals and organizations for the loss of their son. They were awarded damages using the treble damages formula. As seen in *Boim*, bringing civil litigation against a non-State actor can involve individuals as well as groups. While many plaintiffs win by default, the defendants in *Boim* offered a spirited defense touching a number of important statutory and Constitutional issues.

BOIM v. QURANIC LITERACY INSTITUTE AND HOLY LAND FOUNDATION FOR RELIEF AND DEVELOPMENT
United States Court of Appeals for the Seventh Circuit
291 F.3d 1000 (June 5, 2002)

OPINION BY ROVNER, J

In this case of first impression, the parents of a young United States citizen murdered in Israel by Hamas terrorists have sued several individuals and organizations for the loss of their son.

Two of the organizational defendants moved to dismiss the complaint, and the district court denied the motion. In this interlocutory appeal, we are asked to consider the viability of a claim brought under the never-tested *18 U.S.C. § 2333*, which allows U.S. nationals who have been injured "by reason of an act of international terrorism" to sue therefor and recover treble damages. We affirm the district court's denial of the defendants' motion to dismiss....

I Background

David Boim was the son of Joyce and Stanley Boim, who are United States citizens. David held dual citizenship in the United States and Israel. In 1996, the Boims were living in Israel, where seventeen-year-old David was studying at a yeshiva. On May 13, 1996, David was murdered as he waited with other students at a bus stop near Beit El in the West Bank. He was struck by bullets fired from a passing car, and was pronounced dead within an hour of the shooting. His two attackers were later identified as Amjad Hinawi and Khalil Tawfiq Al-Sharif. The Palestinian Authority apprehended Hinawi and Al-Sharif, and temporarily imprisoned them in early 1997. They were released shortly thereafter, apparently pending trial. Al-Sharif subsequently killed himself and five civilians and injured 192 other people in a suicide bombing in Jerusalem on September 4, 1997. Two other suicide bombers joined him in this action. Hinawi, who confessed to participating in the shooting of David Boim, was eventually tried for David's murder by a Palestinian Authority court and was sentenced to ten years' imprisonment on February 17, 1998.

Both Hinawi and Al-Sharif were known members of the military wing of Hamas. The Boims describe Hamas as an extremist, Palestinian militant organization that seeks to establish a fundamentalist Palestinian state. The group is divided into two branches, one political and one military. The military branch receives orders and material support from the political branch. Hamas seeks to advance its political objectives through acts of terrorism and works to undermine the Middle East peace process through violent attacks on civilians. Hamas has a global presence, and terrorist operatives in Gaza and the West Bank receive their instructions, funds, weapons and practical support for their missions from Hamas organizers throughout the world. The Boims believe that Hamas has command and control centers in the United States, Britain and several Western European countries. The leaders of these control centers coordinate fundraising efforts from sympathetic parties in these various countries and then launder and channel the money to Hamas operatives in Gaza and the West Bank. They also arrange for the purchase of weapons and for the recruitment and training of military personnel. They work with local commanders in the West Bank and Gaza to plan terrorist attacks. Hamas was designated a terrorist organization by President William Jefferson Clinton in 1995 by Executive Order. In 1997, Hamas was designated a foreign terrorist organization pursuant to *8 U.S.C. § 1189*.

The Boims allege that Hamas' military wing depends on foreign contributions, with approximately one-third of its multi-million dollar annual budget coming from fund-raising in North America and Western Europe. The Boims believe that the Quranic Literacy Institute ("QLI") and the Holy Land Foundation for Relief and Development ("HLF"), along with other defendants not involved in this appeal, are the main fronts for Hamas in the United States. They allege that these organizations' allegedly humanitarian functions mask their core mission of raising and funneling money and other resources to Hamas operatives in support of terrorist activities.

QLI is an Illinois not-for-profit corporation that purports to translate and publish sacred Islamic texts, but the Boims believe it is also engaged in raising and laundering money for Hamas. QLI also employed another defendant, Mohammed Abdul Hamid Khalil Salah, nominally as a computer analyst. The FBI has seized $1.4 million in cash and property from Salah, who is the admitted United States based leader of the military branch of Hamas. He has been prosecuted for channeling money to Hamas and for recruiting, organizing and training terrorist operatives in Israel. Salah is named on a list of Specially Designated Terrorists compiled by the United States Treasury Department's Office of Foreign Assets Control.

HLF is also a not-for-profit corporation, whose ostensible mission is to fund humanitarian relief and development efforts. HLF's director has acknowledged providing money to Hamas, and the Boims allege that, although HLF purports to have a charitable purpose, its true function is to raise and channel money to Hamas for terrorist activities. The U.S. base of HLF's operations is in Texas. HLF also has offices in Jerusalem and in Illinois. HLF, QLI and the other organizational defendants are linked by interlocking directorates and by ties to Salah and Mousa Mohammed Abu Marzook, another individual defendant (not involved in this appeal) who has a leadership role in the military branch of Hamas.

According to the Boims, money flows from American contributors to Hamas in a three-step process: first, the front organizations solicit contributions; second, the leaders arrange for the money to be laundered and wired overseas; and third, Hamas operatives in Gaza and the West Bank use the money to finance terrorist activities. Because it is illegal to provide financial support to recognized terrorist groups, the money flows through a series of complicated transactions, changing hands a number of times, and being commingled with funds from the front organizations' legitimate charitable and business dealings. The funds are laundered in a variety of ways, including through real estate deals and through Swiss bank accounts. The Boims allege that money raised by HLF and QLI was transferred to Hamas terrorists using these various methods in order to finance terrorist activities. Hamas used the money raised in this way to purchase weapons to carry out terrorist attacks, including the attack on David Boim. Hamas regularly drew money from a pool of laundered funds in order to finance training, weapons purchases, lodging, false identification, communications equipment, lethal substances, explosives, personnel, transportation and other material support for terrorist operations. The Boims believe that expenditures from this pool of funds paid for the vehicle, machine guns and ammunition used to kill David Boim, and also paid for the training of Hinawi, Al-Sharif and other Hamas operatives involved in the attack on David Boim. The funds were also used to provide a stipend for Al-Sharif's family, as it is a common practice to pay the families of suicide bombers in order to encourage others to volunteer for these activities.

The Boims bring their suit against HLF, QLI and other organizational and individual defendants pursuant to *18 U.S.C. § 2333*. They charge that all of the defendants are civilly liable for David's murder. They name Hinawi and Al-Sharif as the persons who actually killed David, but allege that the other defendants aided, abetted and financed Hinawi and Al-Sharif. They assert that the organizational defendants provided material support or resources to Hamas as those terms are defined in *18 U.S.C. §§ 2339A* and *2339B*. The Boims seek compensation for the extreme physical pain David suffered before his death, and for the cost of his funeral and the loss of accretion to his estate due to his death at age seventeen. They also seek damages for their own extreme mental anguish and loss of the society of their son. They ask for $100,000,000 compensatory damages, $100,000,000 punitive damages, plus costs and attorney's fees, and request the trebling of damages pursuant to the statute.

...

The district court granted HLF and QLI's motion for a certificate of appealability, and we subsequently granted them leave to file an interlocutory appeal. See *28 U.S.C. § 1292(b)*....

In this case, the district court correctly certified three issues for appeal:

(1) Docs funding, simpliciter, of an international terrorist organization constitute an act of terrorism under *18 U.S.C. § 2331*?

(2) Does *18 U.S.C. § 2333* incorporate the definitions of international terrorism found in *18 U.S.C. §§ 2339A and 2339B*?

(3) Does a civil cause of action lie under *18 U.S.C. §§ 2331 and 2333* for aiding and abetting international terrorism?

...

II Discussion

The Boims seek to recover against HLF and QLI pursuant to 18 U.S.C. § 2333, which provides, in relevant part:

> Any national of the United States injured in his or her person, property, or business by reason of an act of international terrorism, or his or her estate, survivors, or heirs, may sue therefor in any appropriate district court of the United States and shall recover three-fold the damages he or she sustains and the cost of the suit, including attorney's fees.

18 U.S.C. § 2333(a). "International terrorism," in turn, is a defined term:
[T]he term "international terrorism" means activities that—

(A) involve violent acts or acts dangerous to human life that are a violation of the criminal laws of the United States or of any State, or that would be a criminal violation if committed within the jurisdiction of the United States or of any State;

(B) appear to be intended-

(i) to intimidate or coerce a civilian population;

(ii) to influence the policy of a government by intimidation or coercion; or

(iii) to affect the conduct of a government by assassination or kidnapping; and

(C) occur primarily outside the territorial jurisdiction of the United States, or transcend national boundaries in terms of the means by which they are accomplished, the persons they appear intended to intimidate or coerce, or the locale in which their perpetrators operate or seek asylum. *18 U.S.C. § 2331(1).* These provisions became law in 1992.

We turn now to the Boims' three theories of liability under *section 2333: (1)* that funding Hamas, without more, is an act of international terrorism because it is conduct that involves violent acts or acts dangerous to human life; (2) that funding Hamas constitutes the provision of material support or resources to a terrorist organization in violation of the criminal provisions set forth in *sections 2339A* and *2339B*, and that violations of these criminal provisions give rise to civil liability under *section 2333*; and (3) that aiding and abetting an act of terrorism gives rise to civil liability under *section 2333*.

A.

The plaintiffs' first theory is that the simple provision of funds to Hamas by QLI and HLF constitutes an act of international terrorism because it "involve[s] violent acts or acts dangerous to human life." The Boims liken payments to Hamas to murder for hire: the person who pays for the murder does not himself commit a violent act, but the payment "involves" violent acts in the sense that it brings about the violent act and provides an incentive for someone else to commit it. The Boims urge us to adopt a very broad definition of "involves" that would include any activity that touches on and supports a violent act. They argue that David's murder was indisputably a violent act, and we have no quarrel with that premise. But they further argue that the provision of money or in-kind services to persons outside the country who set up the infrastructure used to recruit and train David's murderers, buy their weapons, and compensate their families also "involves" violent acts. The defendants, in turn, urge us to read the statute to hold liable only those who actually commit a violent act.

No court has yet considered the meaning or scope of *sections 2331* and *2333*, and so we write upon a tabula rasa. The starting point in all statutory analysis is the plain language of the statute itself. *United States v. Wagner, 29 F.3d 264, 266 (7th Cir.1994).* We look to the language in order to determine what Congress intended, and we also look to the statute's structure, subject matter, context and history for this same purpose. *Almendarez-Torres v. United States, 523 U.S. 224, 228, 118 S.Ct. 1219, 140 L.Ed.2d 350 (1998)* ("We therefore look to the statute before us and ask what Congress intended....In answering this question, we look to the statute's language, structure, subject matter, context, and history—factors that typically help courts determine a statute's objectives and thereby illuminate its text."). The controversy here centers on the definition of international terrorism, and in particular on the definition of the word "involve," which is susceptible to many meanings. The statutory definition of international terrorism in *section 2331(1)* is drawn verbatim from the Foreign Intelligence Surveillance Act, *50 U.S.C. § 1801(c)* ("FISA"). No court has yet expounded on the meaning or scope of "international terrorism" as it is used in FISA either, so we are not aided by that origin. A dictionary definition of "involve" demonstrates the many levels of participation that could constitute involvement. To involve is: to enfold or envelop so as to encumber; to engage as a participant; to oblige to take part; to occupy (as oneself) absorbingly; to commit emotionally; to relate closely; to have within or as part of itself; to require as a necessary accompaniment; to have an effect on. Webster's Ninth New Collegiate Dictionary (1983). Because of these many possibilities, we agree with the district court that we must look to the structure, context and legislative history of the statute to determine what Congress intended.

The government, in its very helpful amicus curiae brief, delineates some of the legislative history of *sections 2331* and *2333*. That history, in combination with the language of the statute itself, evidences an intent by Congress to codify general common law tort principles and to extend civil liability for acts of international terrorism to the full reaches of traditional tort law. *See 137 Cong. Rec. S4511-04 (April 16, 1991)* ("The [antiterrorism act] accords victims of terrorism the remedies of American tort law, including treble damages and attorney's fees.");

Antiterrorism Act of 1990, Hearing Before the Subcommittee on Courts and Administrative Practice of Committee on the Judiciary, United States Senate, 101st Congress, Second Session, July 25, 1990 (hereafter "Senate Hearing"), *Testimony of Joseph Morris, at 136* ("[T]he bill as drafted is powerfully broad, and its intention…is to…bring [in] all of the substantive law of the American tort law system.") In particular, the statute itself contains all of the elements of a traditional tort: breach of a duty (i.e., committing an act of international terrorism); injury to the person, property or business of another; and causation (injured "by reason of"). Although the statute defines the class of plaintiffs who may sue, it does not limit the class of defendants, and we must therefore look to tort law and the legislative history to determine who may be held liable for injuries covered by the statute.

The legislative record is replete with references to the then-recent decision in *Klinghoffer v. Palestine Liberation Organization, 739 F.Supp. 854 (S.D.N.Y.1990)*, vacated, *937 F.2d 44 (2d Cir.1991). See Senate Hearing at 1, 12, 17, 79, 83, 122, 133; H.R. Rep. 102-1040, at 5 (1992); 137 Cong. Rec. S4511-04 (April 16, 1991); 136 Cong. Rec. S4568-01 (1990).* Leon Klinghoffer was a U.S. citizen who was murdered in a terrorist attack on a cruise ship in the Mediterranean Sea. The district court found that his survivors' claims were cognizable in federal court under federal admiralty jurisdiction and the Death on the High Seas Act because the tort occurred in navigable waters. *739 F.Supp. at 858-59.* The repeated favorable references to *Klinghoffer* indicate a desire on the part of Congress to extend this liability to land-based terrorism that occurred in a foreign country. *See Senate Hearing at 12, Testimony of Alan Kreczko, Deputy Legal Advisor, Department of State* ("This bill…expands the *Klinghoffer* opinion."); *H.R. Rep. 102-1040, at 5 (1992)* ("Only by virtue of the fact that the [*Klinghoffer*] attack violated certain Admiralty laws and the organization involved—the Palestinian Liberation Organization—had assets and carried on activities in New York, was the court able to establish jurisdiction over the case. A similar attack occurring on an airplane or in some other locale might not have been subject to civil action in the U.S. In order to facilitate civil actions against such terrorists the Committee [on the Judiciary] recommends [this bill]."); *137 Cong. Rec. S4511-04* (April 16, 1991), *Statement of Senator Grassley (section 2333* would "codify [the *Klinghoffer*] ruling and makes the right of American victims definitive"); *136 Cong. Rec. S4568-01 (1990).*

The statute clearly is meant to reach beyond those persons who themselves commit the violent act that directly causes the injury. The Senate report on the bill notes that "[t]he substance of [an action under *section 2333*] is not de fined by the statute, because the fact patterns giving rise to such suits will be as varied and numerous as those found in the law of torts. This bill opens the courthouse door to victims of international terrorism." *S. Rep.102-342, at 45 (1992).* This same report also remarks that the legislation, with "its provisions for compensatory damages, treble damages, and the imposition of liability at any point along the causal chain of terrorism," would "interrupt, or at least imperil, the flow of money." *Id.* at 22 (emphasis added). *See also Statement of Senator Grassley, 136 Cong. Rec. S4568-01 at S4593* ("With the enactment of this legislation, we set an example to the world of how the United States legal system deals with terrorists. If terrorists have assets within our jurisdictional reach, American citizens will have the power to seize them."); *Senate Hearing at 17, Statement of Alan Kreczko* ("[F]ew terrorist organizations are likely to have cash assets or property located in the United States that could be attached and used to fulfill a civil judgment. The existence of such a cause of action, however, may deter terrorist groups from maintaining assets in the United States, from benefitting from investments in the U.S. and from soliciting funds within the U.S."); *Senate Hearing at 79, Statement of Joseph Morris* ("[A]nything that could be done to deter money-raising in the United States, money laundering in the United States, the repose of assets in the United States, and so on, would not only help benefit victims, but would also help deter terrorism.") All of this history indicates an intent by Congress to allow a plaintiff to recover from anyone along the causal chain of terrorism.

But to the extent that the Boims urge a reading of the statute that would lead to liability for merely giving money to Hamas, a group which then sponsored a terrorist act in the manner the Boims have alleged, we agree with the district court, the defendants and the government that those allegations would be inadequate. To say that funding simpliciter constitutes an act of terrorism is to give the statute an almost unlimited reach. Any act which turns out to facilitate terrorism, however remote that act may be from actual violence and regardless of the actor's intent, could be construed to "involve" terrorism. Without also requiring the plaintiffs to show knowledge of and intent to further the payee's violent criminal acts, such a broad definition might also lead to constitutional infirmities by punishing mere association with groups that engage in terrorism, as we shall discuss later in addressing the First Amendment concerns raised here.

Additionally, the statute itself requires that in order to recover, a plaintiff must be injured "by reason of" an act of international terrorism. The Supreme Court has interpreted identical language to require a showing of proximate cause. See *Holmes v. Securities Investor Protection Corp., 503 U.S. 258, 265-68, 112 S.Ct. 1311, 117 L.Ed.2d 532 (1992)* (interpreting "by reason of" language in civil RICO provision to require a showing that the defendant's conduct proximately caused the plaintiff's injury). Foreseeability is the cornerstone of proximate cause, and in tort law, a defendant will be held liable only for those injuries that might have reasonably been anticipated as a natural consequence of the defendant's actions. *Suzik v. Sea-Land Corp., 89 F.3d 345, 348 (7th Cir.1996)*; Restatement (2d) of Torts, §§ 440-447. In the circumstances of this case, the Boims cannot show that David Boim was injured "by reason of" the defendants' payments to Hamas in the traditional tort sense of causation unless they can also show that murder was the reasonably foreseeable result of making the donation. To hold the defendants liable for donating money without knowledge of the donee's intended criminal use of the funds would impose strict liability. Nothing in the language of the statute or its structure or history supports that formulation. The government, in its amicus brief, maintains that funding may be enough to establish liability if the plaintiff can show that the provider of funds was generally aware of the donee's terrorist activity, and if the provision of funds substantially assisted the terrorist act in question. See *Halberstam v. Welch, 705 F.2d 472, 477 (D.C.Cir.1983)* (describing the standards for joint liability for tortious acts). We will consider the government's proposed standard separately in our discussion of aiding and abetting liability. For now we note only that the complaint cannot be sustained on the theory that the defendants themselves committed an act of international terrorism when they donated unspecified amounts of money to Hamas, neither knowing nor suspecting that Hamas would in turn financially support the persons who murdered David Boim. In the very least, the plaintiffs must be able to show that murder was a reasonably foreseeable result of making a donation. Thus, the Boims' first theory of liability under *section 2333*, funding simpliciter of a terrorist organization, is insufficient because it sets too vague a standard, and because it does not require a showing of proximate cause.

B.

The Boims' second theory of liability is that the defendants' violation of *sections 2339A* and *2339B*, the criminal counterparts to *section 2333*, gives rise to civil liability under *section 2333*. The Boims further contend that *sections 2339A* and *2339B* demonstrate Congress' intent to include the provision of material support to terrorist organizations in the definition of international terrorism for the purposes of *section 2333*. The district court concluded that Congress viewed violations of *sections 2339A* and *2339B* as "activities involving violent acts or acts dangerous to human life," and therefore found that violations of *sections 2339A* and *2339B* gave rise to civil liability under *section 2333*. Because much of the conduct the Boims alleged occurred before the passage of *sections 2339A* and *2339B*, however, the district court ruled that the Boims would have to rely primarily on their aiding and abetting theory.

In 1994, Congress passed *18 U.S.C. § 2339A*, which criminalizes the provision of material support to terrorists:

> Whoever, within the United States, provides material support or resources or conceals or disguises the nature, location, source, or ownership of material support or resources, knowing or intending that they are to be used in preparation for, or in carrying out, a violation of *section 32, 37, 81, 175, 351, 831, 842(m) or (n), 844(f) or (i), 930(c), 956, 1114, 1116, 1203, 1361, 1362, 1363, 1366, 1751, 1992, 2155, 2156, 2280, 2281, 2332, 2332a, 2332b, 2332c,* or *2340A* of this title or *section 46502 of title 49*, or in preparation for, or in carrying out, the concealment or an escape from the commission of any such violation, shall be fined under this title, imprisoned not more than 10 years, or both.

18 U.S.C. § 2339A(a). "Material support or resources" is a defined term:

In this section, the term "material support or resources" means currency or other financial securities, financial services, lodging, training, safehouses, false documentation or identification, communications equipment, facilities, weapons, lethal substances, explosives, personnel, transportation, and other physical assets, except medicine or religious materials. *18 U.S.C. § 2339A(b)*. Two years later, Congress extended criminal liability to those providing material support to foreign terrorist organizations:

Whoever, within the United States or subject to the jurisdiction of the United States, knowingly provides material support or resources to a foreign terrorist organization, or attempts or conspires to do so, shall be fined under this title or imprisoned not more than 10 years, or both.

18 U.S.C. § 2339B(a)(1). *Section 2339B* adopts the definition of "material support or resources" provided in *section 2339A*, and looks to *8 U.S.C. § 1189* for the definition of "terrorist organization."

HLF and QLI, of course, protest the district court's conclusion that funding may form the basis for a *section 2333* civil action if the funding meets the standards for criminal liability under *sections 2339A* or *2339B*. The defendants also fault the district court for relying on Congress' repeal of the jurisdictional immunity of a foreign state that has been designated a state sponsor of terrorism as evidence of Congressional intent to allow a *section 2333* civil action against persons who violate *sections 2339A* and *2339B*. See *28 U.S.C. § 1605(a)(7)*. HLF and QLI present a number of puzzling arguments against the Boims' theory of civil liability through violations of these criminal statutes. According to HLF and QLI, Congress neither expressly nor impliedly amended the definition of "international terrorism" when it enacted *section 2339A* and *2339B* because (1) these sections set forth criminal offenses separate from the statute making violent acts of international terrorism illegal under U.S. law; (2) these sections provide for relatively minor criminal penalties compared to the penalties for violent terrorist acts; (3) nothing in the text of either *sections 2339A* or *2339B* suggests that violations of these provisions are acts of international terrorism remediable under *section 2333*; (4) the inclusion of *sections 2339A* and *2339B* in the terrorism section of Title 18 alone does not mean that Congress intended for violations of these provisions to constitute acts of international terrorism for the purposes of *section 2333*; and (6) *section 2339B* contains a separate remedial scheme that does not include a private right of action but instead provides for civil enforcement by the United States. The defendants also argue that even if violations of *sections 2339A* and *2339B* create civil liability under *section 2333*, the Boims have insufficiently alleged violations of those criminal statutes.

Most of these arguments are tautologous. For example, *sections 2339A* and *2339B* certainly do proscribe different conduct than sections 2332, *2332a*, *2332b* and *2332d*. These latter provisions address the primary perpetrators of violent acts of terrorism, while *sections 2339A* and *2339B* apply to those persons who provide material support to the primary perpetrators of violent acts of terrorism. When it passed *sections 2339A* and *2339B*, Congress undoubtedly intended that the persons providing financial support to terrorists should also be held criminally liable for those violent acts. Indeed, as we have already noted, the Congressional record for *section 2333* indicates an intention to cut off the flow of money in support of terrorism generally. *S. Rep.102-342 at 22 (1992). Sections 2339A* and *2339B* further this goal by imposing criminal liability for financial support of terrorist activities and organizations. The fact that Congress imposed lesser criminal penalties for the financial supporters indicates perhaps that they found the financiers less dangerous or less culpable than the terrorists they finance, but it does not in any way indicate that Congress meant to limit civil liability to those who personally committed acts of terrorism. On the contrary, it would be counterintuitive to conclude that Congress imposed criminal liability in *sections 2339A* and *2339B* on those who financed terrorism, but did not intend to impose civil liability on those same persons through *section 2333*.

Section 2339A prohibits the provision of material support for an extensive list of violent crimes associated with terrorism—assassination, kidnapping, arson, destruction of aircraft—that make clear what types of conduct Congress had in mind when it defined "international terrorism" in *section 2331(1)* as not just the violent acts themselves, but also "activities that involve violent acts or acts dangerous to human life." There is no textual, structural or logical justification for construing the civil liability imposed by section 2333 more narrowly than the corresponding criminal provisions. Because Congress intended to impose criminal liability for funding violent terrorism, we find that it also intended through *sections 2333* and *2331(1)* to impose civil liability for funding at least as broad a class of violent terrorist acts. If the plaintiffs could show that HLF and QLI violated either *section 2339A* or *section 2339B*, that conduct would certainly be sufficient to meet the definition of "international terrorism" under *sections 2333* and *2331*. Such acts would give rise to civil liability under *section 2333* so long as knowledge and intent are also shown, as we shall discuss shortly in the context of aiding and abetting.

We hasten to add that, although proof of a criminal violation under *sections 2339A* or *2339B* might satisfy the definition of international terrorism under *section 2333*, such proof is not necessary to sustain a *section 2333* claim. As we discuss in the context of aiding and abetting, we believe Congress intended for civil liability for financing terrorism to sweep more broadly than the conduct described in *sections 2339A* and *2339B*. We also note that the district court seems to have inadvertently redefined the term "material" in the context of *sections 2339A* and *2339B* as meaning substantial or considerable. The statute itself defines "material support or resources" as "currency or other financial securities, financial services, lodging, training, safehouses, false documentation or identification, communications equipment, facilities, weapons, lethal substances, explosives, personnel, transportation, and other physical assets, except medicine or religious materials." *18 U.S.C. § 2339A(b)*. Thus, the term relates to the type of aid provided rather than whether it is substantial or considerable. For civil liability, *section 2333* requires that the plaintiff be injured "by reason of" the act of international terrorism. Because we believe Congress intended to import standard tort law into *section 2333*, causation may be demonstrated as it would be in traditional tort law. Congress has made clear, though, through the criminal liability imposed in *sections 2339A* and *2339B*, that even small donations made knowingly and intentionally in support of terrorism may meet the standard for civil liability in *section 2333*. Congress' goal of cutting off funding for terrorism would be seriously compromised if terrorist organizations could avoid liability by simply pooling together small donations to fund a terrorist act.

We turn finally to *28 U.S.C. § 1605(a)(7)*. In relevant part, the statute provides:

> A foreign state shall not be immune from the jurisdiction of courts of the United States or of the States in any case…in which money damages are sought against a foreign state for personal injury or death that was caused by an act of torture, extrajudicial killing, aircraft sabotage, hostage taking, or the provision of material support or resources (as defined in *section 2339A of title 18)* for such an act if such act or provision of material support is engaged in by an official, employee, or agent of such foreign state while acting within the scope of his or her office, employment, agency[.]

Contrary to the defendants' characterization, the district court did not rely solely on the passage of *section 1605(a)(7)* in finding that Congress viewed the provision of material support and resources as an act of international terrorism. After finding support in both the text and the structure of *sections 2333* and *2331* for this proposition, the court found further reasons in *section 1605(a)(7)*. As the district court noted, "Considering that Congress has permitted foreign states that have been designated state sponsors of terrorism to be sued in United States courts for violating § 2339A, it is hard to argue that Congress did not intend to include such violations in its definition of 'terrorism' under the statutory scheme." *Boim, 127 F.Supp.2d at 1016*. We take the district court to mean that section 1605(a)(7) implies a foreign state may be sued in the United States for acts that would give rise to criminal liability under *section 2339A*, not that *section 2339A* itself has a civil provision. The mechanism for suing a foreign state for these acts that would give rise to criminal liability under *section 2339A* is *section 2333* . The defendants complain that Congress did not specifically mention *section 2333* as the device by which plaintiffs might sue foreign governments for violations of *section 2339A*, but they fail to point to any other source of civil liability. We agree that Congress made clear in *section 1605(a)(7)* its intent to characterize violations of *section 2339A* as acts of international terrorism under *section 2333*.

The district court believed there was a timing problem for the Boims in making their case under these criminal provisions because much of the funding conduct allegedly committed by HLF and QLI occurred prior to the passage of *sections 2339A* and *2339B*. Indeed, Hamas was not designated a terrorist organization under section 1189 until 1997, after David's murder. Certainly HLF and QLI could not be held criminally liable for conduct that occurred before the statutes were enacted, but that argument misses the point. We are using *sections 2339A* and *2339B* not as independent sources of liability under section 2333 , but to amplify what Congress meant by "international terrorism." *Sections 2339A* and *2339B* merely lend further support to our finding that Congress considered the provision of material support to terrorists an act of international terrorism. This reading simply amplifies the conclusion we have already reached by examining the language and legislative history of *section 2333*. *Sections 2339A* and *2339B* provide criminal liability for the provision of material support, and *section 2333* provides civil liability. The Boims may thus show that QLI and HLF committed an act of international terrorism subject to civil liability under section 2333 by proving that QLI and HLF provided material support to terrorist organizations. No timing problem arises because *sections 2339A* and *2339B* merely elucidate conduct that was already prohibited by *section 2333*.

C.

We turn next to the Boims' theory that HLF and QLI may be held civilly liable under *section 2333* for aiding and abetting an act of international terrorism.

…

Finally, if we failed to impose liability on aiders and abettors who knowingly and intentionally funded acts of terrorism, we would be thwarting Congress' clearly expressed intent to cut off the flow of money to terrorists at every point along the causal chain of violence. *S. Rep. 102-342, at 22* (by imposing "liability at any point along the causal chain of terrorism, it would interrupt, or at least imperil, the flow of money."). Unlike section 10(b) where Congress' intent could be met without imposing liability on aiders and abettors, Congress' purpose here could not be met unless liability attached beyond the persons directly involved in acts of violence. The statute would have little effect if liability were limited to the persons who pull the trigger or plant the bomb because such persons are unlikely to have assets, much less assets in the United States, and would not be deterred by the statute. See *Central Bank, 511 U.S. at 188, 114 S.Ct. 1439* (policy considerations may be used to interpret the text and structure of a statute when a literal reading would lead to a result so bizarre that Congress could not have intended it). Also, and perhaps more importantly, there would not be a trigger to pull or a bomb to blow up without the resources to acquire such tools of terrorism and to bankroll the persons who actually commit the violence. Moreover, the organizations, businesses and nations that support and encourage terrorist acts are likely to have reachable assets that they wish to protect. The only way to imperil the flow of money and discourage the financing of terrorist acts is to impose liability on those who knowingly and intentionally supply the funds to the persons who commit the violent acts. For all of these distinguishing reasons, we do not think *Central Bank* controls the result here, but that aiding and abetting liability is both appropriate and called for by the language, structure and legislative history of *section 2333*.

D.

The defendants raise two First Amendment objections to this *section 2333* action against them. First, they argue that the Boims seek to hold them liable for their mere association with Hamas. Harking back to a line of cases involving the Communist party, HLF and QLI contend that, when an organization has both legal and illegal aims, a person may not be punished for mere membership in or association with that organization, but may be held civilly liable only if he or she possesses the specific intent to further the organizations' illegal purposes. Second, they contend that, to the extent the Boims' claim is founded on a violation of *section 2339B*, it cannot withstand First Amendment scrutiny because *section 2339B* fails to account for the intent and the associational rights of the contributors who donate money for humanitarian purposes. The National Coalition to Protect Political Freedom and the Center for Constitutional Rights have jointly filed an amicus brief in support of the defendants' First Amendment arguments, and we will consider their contentions as well.

1.

HLF and QLI begin their argument with the well-established proposition that the Constitution protects against the imposition of liability based solely upon association with a group. See *NAACP v. Claiborne Hardware Co., 458 U.S. 886, 920, 102 S.Ct. 3409, 73 L.Ed.2d 1215 (1982)* ("[c]ivil liability may not be imposed merely because an individual belonged to a group, some members of which committed acts of violence."); *Healy v. James, 408 U.S. 169, 185-86, 92 S.Ct. 2338, 33 L.Ed.2d 266 (1972)* ("the Court has consistently disapproved governmental action imposing criminal sanctions or denying rights and privileges solely because of a citizen's association with an unpopular organization."); *United States v. Robel, 389 U.S. 258, 265, 88 S.Ct. 419, 19 L.Ed.2d 508 (1967)* (where a statute establishes guilt by association alone, the inhibiting effect on First Amendment rights is clear); *Scales v. United States, 367 U.S. 203, 229, 81 S.Ct. 1469, 6 L.Ed.2d 782 (1961)* (a blanket prohibition of association with a group having both legal and illegal aims presents a real danger that legitimate political expression or association would be impaired). We have no quarrel with that general proposition or with its corollary, that in order to impose liability on an individual for association with a group, it is necessary to establish that the group possessed unlawful goals and that the individual held a specific intent to further those illegal aims.

…

HLF and QLI protest that the Boims have not alleged their specific intent to further the illegal activities of Hamas, and that the claim does not, therefore, survive First Amendment scrutiny. Rather, HLF complains, the Boims have simply alleged that HLF has admitted providing funds to Hamas, that HLF functions as a front organization for Hamas, that HLF raises and channels funds to Hamas to finance terrorist activities in Israel, and that HLF solicits donations over the internet. HLF protests that even if these allegations suffice to show a present intent to further terrorist acts, they do not show that HLF had that intent prior to David Boim's murder. Rather, HLF believes the Boims are lumping their organization in with other groups that may have had an intent to commit illegal acts, and that the Boims are seeking to hold them liable for their mere association with these other organizations. QLI similarly argues that the Boims have not alleged a specific intent on the part of QLI to further the illegal goals of Hamas, and that they may not be held liable for merely associating with organizations that might have intended to aid the illegal operations of Hamas.

Amici also emphasize that individuals may not be penalized for their association with a political organization that engages in both lawful and unlawful ends, absent a showing of specific intent to further the organization's illegal goals. *Claiborne Hardware, 458 U.S. at 919-20, 102 S.Ct. 3409.* The arguments of the defendants and amici beg the question, though, because *section 2333* does not seek to impose liability for association alone but rather for involvement in acts of international terrorism. The defendants nonetheless object that the definition of acts of international terrorism is so broad that they might be held liable for involvement in terrorist activity when all they intended was to supply money to fund the legitimate, humanitarian mission of Hamas or other organizations. To resolve the tension that arises when a group engages in both protected advocacy and unprotected criminal acts....Civil liability may not be imposed merely because an individual belonged to a group, some members of which committed acts of violence. For liability to be imposed by reason of association alone, it is necessary to establish that the group itself possessed unlawful goals and that the individual held a specific intent to further those illegal aims.

We have already held that the Boims may prevail on their claim by showing, among other things, that the defendants aided and abetted David's murder. This requires them to prove that the defendants knew of Hamas' illegal activities, that they desired to help those activities succeed, and they engaged in some act of helping the illegal activities. See *Zafiro, 945 F.2d at 887.* If the Boims are able to prove the defendants aided and abetted terrorist acts, liability would not offend the principles announced in Claiborne Hardware. The Boims have alleged that HLF and QLI supplied money to Hamas to fund terrorist operations, that they are "front" organizations with ostensibly legitimate purposes which are actually engaged in fund-raising and money laundering in support of terrorist activities. They have alleged that HLF and QLI provided the money to purchase the weapons and train the men who killed David Boim. HLF and QLI, of course, deny these allegations and argue that as a factual matter, Hamas is primarily a humanitarian organization, and that any money supplied to Hamas by QLI and HLF was intended to fund humanitarian efforts, not terrorism. This is a classic factual dispute, not suitable for resolution on a motion to dismiss for failure to state a claim. If the Boims are able to prove their allegations, that HLF and QLI provided legitimate-looking fronts for raising money to support the terrorist operation that resulted in David Boim's murder, their claim will not run afoul of the First Amendment. The Boims are not seeking to hold HLF and QLI liable for their mere association with Hamas, nor are they seeking to hold the defendants liable for contributing money for humanitarian efforts. Rather, they are seeking to hold them liable for aiding and abetting murder by supplying the money to buy the weapons, train the shooters, and compensate the families of the murderers. That Hamas may also engage in legitimate advocacy or humanitarian efforts is irrelevant for First Amendment purposes if HLF and QLI knew about Hamas' illegal operations, and intended to help Hamas accomplish those illegal goals when they contributed money to the organization.

...

2.

We turn next to the defendants' contention that any *section 2333* claim founded on a violation of *section 2339B* must fail because *section 2339B* violates the First Amendment. As we noted above, *section 2339B* subjects to criminal liability anyone who, within the United States or subject to the jurisdiction of the United States, knowingly provides material support or resources to a foreign terrorist organization, or attempts or conspires to do so. *18 U.S.C. § 2339B(a)(1)*. The defendants complain that, because *section 2339B* imposes liability without regard to the intent of the donor, it violates the First Amendment. They maintain that *section 2339B* unnecessarily interferes with the associational rights of contributors who donate money solely for humanitarian purposes by failing to limit liability to those who intend to support the illegal goals of an organization. They contend that *section 2339B* will chill legitimate fund-raising for humanitarian purposes if a charitable organization could be prosecuted for providing food for the needy in the Middle East that happens to make its way into the mouths of the families of terrorists. They urge us to reject the reasoning of the Ninth Circuit in *Humanitarian Law Project v. Reno, 205 F.3d 1130 (9th Cir.2000)*, cert. denied, *532 U.S. 904, 121 S.Ct. 1226, 149 L.Ed.2d 136 (2001)*, in upholding the constitutionality of section 2339B against a First Amendment challenge. They argue that *Humanitarian Law Project* is inconsistent with *Claiborne Hardware*, and that even if it is not, it is factually distinguishable from the instant case.

These arguments miss the mark because the constitutionality of *section 2339B* is not before us. The defendants have not been charged with a criminal violation of *section 2339B*. As we discussed above, *section 2339B* is relevant to the Boims' claim only to the extent that it helps define what conduct Congress intended to include in its definition of "international terrorism." *Section 2339B* provides further support to the Boims' theory that Congress meant to include funding terrorism as an act "involving" violence. It is the constitutionality of section 2333 that concerns us today, and as we have just found, funding that meets the standard for aiding and abetting terrorist acts does not offend the First Amendment. We take the defendants' argument to be that a *section 2333* claim founded solely on conduct that would render a person criminally liable under *section 2339B* would violate the First Amendment. With this refinement to the question, we turn to the Ninth Circuit's analysis of *section 2339B*.

The plaintiffs in *Humanitarian Law Project* were organizations and individuals who wished to provide money to two groups that had been designated as foreign terrorist organizations under *8 U.S.C. § 1189*. They sought a preliminary injunction barring enforcement of *section 2339B* against them, and maintained that they intended only to support the nonviolent humanitarian and political activities of the designated groups. They argued, as HLF and QLI do here, that *2339B* violates the First Amendment because it imposes liability on persons who provide material support to terrorist organizations regardless of whether the donor intends to further the unlawful goals of the organization. The plaintiffs relied on *Claiborne Hardware* for the proposition that "[f]or liability to be imposed by reason of association alone, it is necessary to establish that the group itself possessed unlawful goals and that the individual held a specific intent to further those illegal aims." *Humanitarian Law Project, 205 F.3d at 1133 (Claiborne Hardware* and the similar cases we have discussed supra apply to situations where the government seeks to impose liability on the basis of association alone, i.e., on the basis of membership alone or because a person espouses the views of an organization that engages in illegal activities. Conduct giving rise to liability under *section 2339B*, of course, does not implicate associational or speech rights. *Humanitarian Law Project, 205 F.3d at 1133*. Under *section 2339B*, and indeed under *section 2333* , HLF and QLI may, with impunity, become members of Hamas, praise Hamas for its use of terrorism, and vigorously advocate the goals and philosophies of Hamas. *Section 2339B* prohibits only the provision of material support (as that term is defined) to a terrorist organization. There is no constitutional right to provide weapons and explosives to terrorists, nor is there any right to provide the resources with which the terrorists can purchase weapons and explosives. *205 F.3d at 1133.*

Advocacy is always subject to the highest levels of scrutiny under the First Amendment, but donations are not always equivalent to advocacy and are subject to greater government regulation. In *Buckley v. Valeo, 424 U.S. 1, 96 S.Ct. 612, 46 L.Ed.2d 659 (1976),* the Supreme Court upheld the $1000 limit on political contributions to candidates for federal offices by individual donors. The Court acknowledged the expressive element of a contribution to a political campaign, noting that a contribution serves as a general expression of support for a candidate and the candidate's views, but does not communicate the underlying basis for the support. *424 U.S. at 21, 96 S.Ct. 612.* Because the expression involved in donating money "rests solely on the undifferentiated, symbolic act of contributing," the size of the donation provides only a very rough estimate of the intensity of the contributor's support for the candidate. *424 U.S. at 21, 96 S.Ct. 612.* The Court concluded that a limitation on the amount of money a person may contribute thus involved little direct restraint on the donor's political communication. Any size contribution will permit a symbolic expression of support, but a limitation on the size does not infringe the contributor's freedom to discuss issues. The Court acknowledged that the funds might be used by the candidate to present views to voters, but "the transformation of contributions into political debate involves speech by someone other than the contributor." *424 U.S. at 21, 96 S.Ct. 612.* The Court found that associational interests were also implicated because making a contribution affiliates a person with a candidate, and enables like-minded people to pool their resources to further political goals. *424 U.S. at 22, 96 S.Ct. 612.* Setting the standard for reviewing governmental regulation in this context, the Court held that "[e]ven a significant interference with protected rights of political association may be sustained if the State demonstrates a sufficiently important interest and employs means closely drawn to avoid unnecessary abridgement of associational freedoms." *424 U.S. at 25, 96 S.Ct. 612* (internal quote marks omitted).

Applying the *Buckley* standard to *section 2333* claims founded on conduct that would give rise to criminal liability under *section 2339B*, we conclude that the government's interest in preventing terrorism is not only important but paramount. *Humanitarian Law Project, 205 F.3d at 1135.* Although that interest has been made all the more imperative by the events of September 11, 2001, the terrorist threat to national security was substantial in 1992 when Congress passed *section 2333* and in 1996 when Congress passed section 2339B. That interest is unrelated to suppressing free expression. A *section 2333* suit founded on conduct violating *section 2339B* does not punish membership in a designated terrorist organization, or penalize the expression of views held by these organizations. Rather, such a suit is aimed at prohibiting the funding of violent acts that these organizations wish to carry out. *205 F.3d at 1135.*

The only remaining question is whether a *section 2333* action based on conduct that violates *section 2339B* employs means closely drawn to avoid unnecessary abridgement of associational freedoms. *Section 2339B* forbids the provision of any amount of "material support or resources" to a foreign terrorist organization. "Material support or resources" includes, among other things, money, training, weapons, lethal substances, explosives and personnel. Congress determined that "foreign organizations that engage in terrorist activity are so tainted by their criminal conduct that any contribution to such an organization facilitates that conduct." *Pub. L. 104-132, Section 301.* Terrorist organizations use funds for illegal activities regardless of the intent of the donor, and Congress thus was compelled to attach liability to all donations to foreign terrorist organizations. In order to be designated a terrorist organization, a group must engage in terrorist activity that threatens the security of United States nationals or the national security of the United States. *8 U.S.C. § 1189(a)*. "Terrorist activity" is defined, in relevant part, as unlawful activity which involves any of the following: the hijacking or sabotage of any aircraft, vessel or vehicle; the seizing, detaining or threatening to kill, injure or continue detaining an individual in order to compel a third person to do or abstain from doing any act as a condition for the release of the individual detained; a violent act upon an internationally protected person; an assassination; the use of any biological agent, chemical agent, nuclear weapon or device, or explosive or firearm, with intent to endanger the safety of one or more individuals or cause substantial damage to property. *8 U.S.C. § 1182(a)(3)(B)(ii)*. Given the stringent requirements that must be met before a group is designated a foreign terrorist organization, Congress carefully limited its prohibition on funding as narrowly as possible in order to achieve the government's interest in preventing terrorism. We note that Congress did not attach liability for simply joining a terrorist organization or zealously espousing its views. By prohibiting funding alone, Congress employed means closely drawn to avoid unnecessary abridgement of associational freedoms. A *section 2333* action founded on conduct violating *section 2339B* is sufficiently tailored to achieve an important government interest and does not run afoul of the First Amendment. *Humanitarian Law Project, 205 F.3d at 1136.*

III Conclusion

In short, we answer the three questions certified by the district court as follows: funding, *simpliciter*, of a foreign terrorist organization is not sufficient to constitute an act of terrorism under *18 U.S.C. § 2331*. However, funding that meets the definition of aiding and abetting an act of terrorism does create liability under *sections 2331* and *2333*. Conduct that would give rise to criminal liability under *section 2339B* is conduct that "involves" violent acts or acts dangerous to human life, and therefore may meet the definition of international terrorism as that term is used in *section 2333*. Finally, as we have set forth the elements of an action under *section 2333*, civil liability for funding a foreign terrorist organization does not offend the First Amendment so long as the plaintiffs are able to prove that the defendants knew about the organization's illegal activity, desired to help that activity succeed and engaged in some act of helping. The plaintiffs have not yet had an opportunity to develop the facts of their case. Today we hold that dismissal would be premature at this stage of the litigation because we can envision a set of facts in support of the claim they have alleged that would entitle them to relief.

Affirmed.

Despite the development of the current American terrorism jurisprudence, all is not well. The inability of victims to recover damages once they are awarded judgment in court stands as a major distorter of justice and deterrence. In some instances, Iran, the most notorious State-sponsor of terrorism, has removed or hidden assets from the reaches of American law. In other instances, the executive branch of the U.S. government has served to block recovery of assets under the notion that the Executive needs the flexibility to conduct foreign affairs. This occurred in both the Bush and Obama Administrations where they successfully blocked recovery initially granted by the D.C. federal district court to American POWs tortured during the 1991 Gulf War.

In *Acree v. Republic of Iraq*, the U.S. District Court for the District of Columbia not only reiterated the validity of punitive damages as a deterrence tool, it saw fit to award compensatory and punitive damages totaling over $959,000,000. In *Acree*, 17 American prisoners of war (POWs) during the 1991 Gulf War and their immediate family members sued the Republic of Iraq, its president, and its intelligence service, seeking compensatory and punitive damages for injuries suffered as a result of torture inflicted on the POWs while in Iraqi captivity between January and March 1991. In 2003, the District Court granted default judgment for the plaintiff POWs. In their complaint, "the POW plaintiffs described brutal and inhumane acts of physical and psychological torture suffered during their captivity, including severe beatings, starvation, mock executions, dark and unsanitary living conditions, and other violent and shocking acts."

The POW plaintiffs alleged that the acts of torture set forth in their complaint constituted "traditional torts of assault, battery and intentional infliction of emotional distress," and requested full compensatory and punitive damages for each of the 17 POW plaintiffs and their family members. On July 7, 2003, the court entered final judgment in favor of the plaintiffs. Based on extensive findings of fact regarding the specific injuries suffered by each plaintiff, the federal district court awarded compensatory and punitive damages to all of the POW plaintiffs and their family members totaling just under $1 billion.

11.3 Proposed International Civil Legal Model

University of Virginia School of Law international law expert, Professor John Norton Moore strongly advocates that all nations adopt a strong legal model for civil lawsuits that incorporates significant punitive damages: "It is strongly in our interest to have every nation on earth copy the 1996 FSIA amendments." Nevertheless, Moore recognizes that punitive damages are not palatable to most civil law nations and pose a significant hurdle to developing a consensus that would truly hold renegade nations accountable for acts of terrorism committed by them or their agents. Adopting an American-styled deterrence model that not only provides for citizens to be compensated for acts of terror, but also brings with it the hammer of punitive damages is simply unrealistic. If real progress is to be made toward creating a global legal framework which can act to effectively suppress the scourge of international terrorism the concept of punitive damages must be framed within the parameters of compensatory damages.

In short, even if punitive damages have to be discarded in any attempt to develop a workable model for other democracies to honor judgments rendered by fellow democracies in terror cases, American precedents in setting damage awards under compensatory concepts would still produce meaningful and effective remedies. Since legal cases involving acts of terror have parallels in common law wrongful death and injury lawsuits, a brief overview of American judgments in these areas reveals that there is still significant *punch* in the compensatory arena. A reasonable pragmatic approach in dealing with compensatory damage awards would still act as a deterrent to States that support terrorism. Although the compensatory judgments are certainly not large *vis-à-vis* punitive damages, a flood of lawsuits wait hungrily at the door for satisfaction and would certainly make up for the discrepancy in short order.

Despite the perception that American courts grant exorbitant awards in wrongful death cases, the amount of compensatory damages in most instances is both practical and reasonable. Even in what can be considered high-profile cases, the awards granted reflect a judicious approach in terms of just compensation for the wrongs inflicted. Four examples illustrate. First, a 2004 civil lawsuit from a Texas State court in Harris v. Harris (2007) dealt with a wrongful death claim where a wife killed her husband (she suspected him of having sex with another woman) by intentionally hitting him with her car and then running the vehicle over his body multiple times. The parents of the victim sued the woman for wrongful death and received $1,858,750 each for pecuniary losses, loss of companionship, and mental anguish.

Second, in perhaps the most infamous wrongful death suit in the history of the United States, the verdict against O.J. Simpson, though totaling $33.5 million, awarded compensatory damages equaling only $8.5 million. A jury found that defendant Orenthal James (O.J.) Simpson committed these homicides willfully and wrongfully, with oppression and malice.

Third, in the case of the surviving family members of American sailors killed in the 2000 al-Qa'eda terror attack on the U.S.S. Cole, in Yemen, a Virginia federal judge granted an award just under $8 million. This civil action lawsuit claimed wrongful death, intentional infliction of emotional distress, and violations under the Foreign Sovereign Immunities Act and the Death on the High Seas Act against the Republic of Sudan. The family members claimed that the Republic of Sudan was liable for damages from the attack of the U.S.S. Cole in the Port of Aden, Yemen, because it provided material support and assistance to al- Qa'eda, the terrorist organization behind the attack. The compensatory award was split between 33 family members, with the amounts ranging from $117,418 to $471,327 each.

The final example returns to the most often cited American case dealing with compensatory damages: *Flatow v. Islamic Republic of Iran*, which dealt with a suicide bomber terror attack on a bus in the Gaza Strip in 1995. *Flatow* and a line of cases following *Flatow* set out valuable considerations associated with the long standing concept of compensatory damages in common law tort which are designed to compensate not just the immediate family of the victims, but also their family members. The *Flatow* court found that the vicious nature of terrorism inflicts a unique harm which is reflected in the resulting compensatory damages.

The next step in the process of developing civil litigation as a viable tool to fight terror is to propose for adoption a United Nations protocol that will allow State Parties to honor damage awards in terrorism civil litigation suits rendered by other State Parties. In his 2010 book, *Legal Issues in the Struggle Against Terror*, John Norton Moore offers such a draft protocol. Disregarding the punitive damages set out in American legislation, Moore provides the following at proposed Article 11:

States Parties to this Protocol undertake to honor in their national legal systems judgments rendered by other States Parties under actions established consistent with this Protocol provided:
- A judge of the honoring State Party reviews the foreign judgment and determines that the judgment was fair and consistent with due process of law;
- *No State Party is required to honor damage awards, such as those for punitive damages, which are inconsistent with its own national law*; and
- No attachment or execution shall be permitted against facilities protected by diplomatic or counselor immunity, military assets, or assets held by national central banks [emphasis added].

11.4 Conclusion
The War on Terror requires the use of all available legal tools, and the application of the power of the civil justice system represents a vastly underutilized potential of great impact. Understanding that in-

ternational tort law has been around for centuries, it is imperative that the democracies of the international community take direct steps to capitalize on this essential legal tool as a weapon against terrorist States. Totalitarian regimes like Iran and North Korea are guilty of supporting terrorism and have too long been able to conceal huge financial assets within the borders and reach of many of the world's democratic States.

Apart from the fact that the attachment of assets in the United States to satisfy multi-million dollar verdicts against terror States like Iran are blocked by the Executive Branch in the interest of national security or other provisions of law, the need for an American-style civil action framework at the international level is much needed. Chief among the arguments against adopting an American-style civil action framework is the concern over punitive damages. Since punitive damages are generally not available in civil law systems and are very controversial in international practice, a proposed international protocol must limit damages to compensatory only. As discussed above, the use of compensatory damages would still deliver a significant blow to States that sponsor terrorism, particularly if the full range of compensation is provided.

A new United Nations convention on civil causes of action against States that sponsor terrorists would have as its key component an obligation on State parties to enact legislation to permit civil suits and honor the judgments issued by other States. Not only would the civil litigation serve as a permanent record of the terror act established by a competent court—an official record of condemnation—the damages awarded would serve as a deterrence to the machinations of the State that sponsored the terrorism.

At the end of the day, civil lawsuits are also intended to bring public shame within the international community to those nations who sponsor acts of terror. Since terrorist acts have long been criminalized in every democratically based legal system as well as in numerous United Nations sponsored conventions, it is essential that all democracies take the next step and develop a legal framework where the terror judgments of other democracies are given reciprocity.

11.5 Questions for Discussion

1. *Litigation as a deterrence to State-sponsored terrorism.* Some have argued that allowing civil actions against States who sponsor international terrorism is an important deterrence tool. Wendy Bay Lewis, *Civil Litigants as Citizen Diplomats*, VOIR DIRE, Spring 2003:

   > Litigation is an important weapon for several reasons. First, it opens a judicial front in the war against terrorism which supplements military, political, and economic sanctions. Second, as the result of globalization, there is an intricate network of individuals, groups, corporations, and nation-states which facilitate terrorism and make military and political measures less than adequate. Third, given the supremacy of the rule of law in a democracy, judicial outcomes eventually put pressure on the other two branches of government to be more accountable to the voters. For example, when the Pan Am plaintiffs' lawsuit initially faltered because Libya had immunity as a sovereign nation, Congress amended antiterrorism statutes to preclude immunity pleas by state sponsors of terrorism.

   On the other hand, has Congress opened the door for other nations to sue the United States for "terrorism"?

2. *What impact has the concept of civil liability against affected targets had on the development of new anti-terrorism technology?* Consider the impact of the SAFETY Act (*see* Chapter 8).

3. *Costs and Benefits.* Because enforcing a monetary judgment is often impossible, what would be the other benefits to the plaintiff of going through the process of a civil action?

Selected Bibliography

Lewis, Wendy Bay. *Civil Litigants as Citizen Diplomats*, VOIR DIRE, Spring 2003.

Moore, John Norton (ed). CIVIL LITIGATION AGAINST TERRORISM, 2004.

Murphy, John F. PUNISHING INTERNATIONAL TERRORISTS: THE LEGAL FRAMEWORK FOR POLICY INITIATIVES, 1985.

Strachman, David and James Steck. CIVIL TERRORISM LAW, 2008.

Chapter 12

Responses to Bioterrorism and the Legal Ramifications

[T]he whole people covenants with each citizen, and each citizen with the whole people, that all shall be governed by certain laws for the 'common good.'

—John Marshall Harlan II

Synopsis
12.1 Defining Bioterrorism
12.2 Government Responsibilities and Authority
12.3 The Goal of Quarantine
12.4 The Legality of Quarantine
12.5 Search and Seizure
12.6 Other Legal Issues
12.7 Questions for Discussion
Selected Bibliography

Terrorists are continuously expanding their capabilities and methods, turning to new and old tools to threaten death and chaos. The use of biological agents to cause death is so feared in the War on Terror that a new term has entered the lexicon—bioterrorism. While the use of infectious substances as a tool of terror is not new—the British were alleged to have spread smallpox to American soldiers during the War for Independence—the United States has yet to suffer a major biological attack from terrorists. Nevertheless, the potential for harm is so great that Federal, State, local and tribal government officials have expended considerable efforts to establish effective response plans and to improve preemptive tools already in place. In the event of a significant biological attack, a variety of containment procedures would most certainly be employed to prevent or slow the spread of death and disease. Such measures would include quarantine, isolation, vaccination, decontamination, destruction of infected property, eviction, specimen testing, mandatory health information disclosure, mandatory health care responses, etc. All of these measures give rise to significant policy and legal issues. The purpose of this chapter is to explore the realities of a biological attack and to examine the local, State and Federal responsibilities in preventing and reacting to the event—prevention and containment.

12.1 Defining Bioterrorism

Bioterrorism is a deadly specter that looms on the horizon. It can affect any living creature and cause mass destruction across great physical expanses. While there are a variety of definitions of the term, the best is found in the Model State Emergency Health Powers Act (MSEHPA), drafted in 2001 by the Center for Law and the Public's Health at Johns Hopkins and Georgetown Universities:

[T]he intentional use of any organism, virus, infectious substance, or biological product...to cause death, disease, or other biological malfunction in a human, an animal, a plant, or another living organism in order to influence conduct of government or to intimidate or coerce a civilian population.

Biological agents occur naturally, but may also be manufactured by Man. Not all biological agents are capable of causing death or harm; therefore, not all biological agents may be suited to function as "weapons" in a bioterrorist attack. Still, harmful biological agents can be produced and disseminated with tremendous ease and can target animals, plants, crops, and material supplies. Recognizing the vast potential for widespread harm associated with harmful biological agents, Chapter 18 of the United States Code makes the possession of biological agents or devices which may be utilized to spread biological agents a federal crime. Section 178 defines a biological agent as:

[A]ny microorganism (including, but not limited to, bacteria, viruses, fungi, rickettsiae or protozoa), or infectious substance, or any naturally occurring, bioengineered or synthesized component of any such microorganism or infectious substance, capable of causing—
    (A) death, disease, or other biological malfunction in a human, an animal, a plant, or another living organism;
    (B) deterioration of food, water, equipment, supplies, or material of any kind; or
    (C) deleterious alteration of the environment.

Bioterrorism is the poor man's "atomic bomb." The use of harmful biological agents is attractive to terrorists for a variety of reasons: (1) many biological agents can do great harm with only a small amount of material; (2) some agents may be harvested directly from the natural environment; (3) there are numerous methods of "weaponizing" the material for release into the environment; (4) it is difficult or impossible to trace the agent to its source; and (5) some harmful agents can be developed or synthesized in laboratories, stolen from company supplies or stockpiles, or genetically manipulated. In addition, biological agents are capable of changing naturally. For example, influenza is a virus that is continuously mutating and taking on new forms; most recently a form know as Avian flu originated in Asia. In short, the availability, accessibility, and alterability of certain harmful biological agents makes them a particularly dangerous weapon in the hands of terrorists.

Biological agents can be delivered to the environment utilizing a wide variety of methods. One method a terrorist may use is releasing a harmful biological agent through aerosol form in a ventilation system in a building, school, airplane, or mass transit system. Since many ventilation systems are enclosed, they contribute to the spread of the harmful material. Food and water systems are also attractive targets for biological terrorism. The consequences associated with the natural occurrence of Mad Cow disease is some indication of the panic that could quickly spread should a significant attack target the food sources of the nation. Another method of disseminating a harmful biological agent is through physical contact with the agent itself or something that is contaminated with the agent. For instance, the anthrax in the mail attacks in 2001, saw the death of at least five people (several were postal workers) when individuals came into contact with letters and envelopes containing the harmful agent. Although anthrax is not contagious, the smallpox virus is highly contagious.

Diseases that are easily spread through contact between humans, animals, or insects are known as infectious or communicable diseases. Communicable diseases are transmitted from person to person through physical contact with the infectious bacteria or virus by means of bodily fluids, coughing, sneezing, and feces. Because the virus or bacteria is easily and rapidly spread, requiring only a small quantity to infect a small portion of the population, terrorists could introduce the harmful agent and watch as it spread like wildfire. Furthermore, as an added bonus, there is always the possibility that the disease may mutate naturally and adapt to stifle vaccines. The likelihood that a terrorist could start what would become a global pandemic is not far fetched.

12.2 Government Responsibilities and Authority

The consensus among those who study the threat of a wide spread biological epidemic, whether it occurs naturally or via a terrorist, is that the United States is not prepared. Among other matters, the lack of national procedures, policies, response plans, medical facilities and medicine contribute to this assessment. On the other hand, the world community is even less prepared.

The last major pandemic to strike the globe was the Spanish flu of 1918. Incredibly, the flu killed about 500,000 in the United States and anywhere from 20 million to 50 million people worldwide! This tragic event, coupled with the use of poison gas in World War I, prompted the civilized world to realize the dangers of biological warfare and the need to prevent or limit the availability and use of these weapons of mass destruction. In 1925, the Protocol for the Prohibition of the Use in War of Asphyxiating, Poisonous or other Gases, and of Bacteriological Methods of Warfare was introduced and subsequently adopted by most of the world. The treaty prohibits the use of chemical and biological weapons in warfare, but is silent with regard to the development, manufacture, storage, and transfer of these weapons. In an effort to remedy the deficiencies of this treaty and to eliminate the existence of chemical and biological weapons entirely, the United Nations developed the 1972 Convention on the Prohibition of the Development, Production and Stockpiling of Bacteriological (Biological) and Toxin Weapons and on Their Destruction. Not only does this treaty ban all development, manufacture, storage, and transfer of biological weapons, it also mandates that all stockpiles of biological weapons and biological agents be peaceably and safely destroyed or legitimately diverted to peaceful purposes within nine months of entry into force of the treaty. The United States ratified this treaty in 1975.

At the domestic level, the federal government has concentrated efforts associated with the most harmful communicable biological agents. The federal government is authorized to take official action in response to a communicable disease only if the disease is specifically designated by Presidential executive order. Executive Order 13295, as amended by Executive Order 13375, in April 2005, lists all of the communicable diseases that mandate official action:

> Cholera, diphtheria, infectious tuberculosis, plague, smallpox, yellow fever, viral hemorrhagic fevers (Marburg, Ebola, and Congo-Crimean), Severe Acute Respiratory Syndrome (SARS), and influenza caused by novel or reemergent influenza viruses that are causing or have the potential to cause a pandemic.

The first responders to a bioterrorist attack will be local emergency room personnel, physicians, and health departments. These first responders must be trained to recognize the symptoms in sick individuals as early as possible to ensure that these listed highly communicable diseases are detected as quickly as possible.

The Constitution of the United States grants each State the power to regulate the health, safety, and welfare of its citizens. This authority is generally known as the police powers and is specifically reserved to the States by the Tenth Amendment. These powers empower the State with the ability to develop rules, regulations, policies, procedures, and plans to prepare the State's response, within its own borders, to an outbreak of a highly communicable disease. Each State operates differently to meet the needs of its citizens; as a result, each State has a slightly different response plan. However, since harmful agents do not recognize State borders, it is imperative that States adopt a standardized set of rules that will allow better cooperation and the ability of federal agencies to lend aid more efficiently. In addition, streamlined procedures, information sharing, and compatible response plans can help States and federal agencies identify biological agents that are the result of bioterrorism as opposed to disease outbreaks that are naturally occurring.

As noted, the MSEHPA was drafted to provide States with a uniformed framework for passing Emergency Health Powers Acts of their own. As of 2006, the MSEHPA has been introduced either in whole or in part in legislation in 44 States and has been enacted in whole or in part in 38 States including the District of Columbia. While the MSEHPA is not enacted verbatim in every State, the wide acceptance of many of the main principles and policies set forth in the model help to prevent conflict between State laws. Although it is beyond the scope of this chapter to detail the plans of individual States, an overview of the MSEHPA is helpful. The MSEHPA grants emergency powers to the State governor and public health officials which are subject to legislative veto. The appropriate State officials have the authority to prevent, detect, manage and contain any biological or health threats that arise within State borders. At the same time, the MSEHPA recognizes that State officials have the duty to protect individuals from undue interference with their civil rights and liberties. While the ultimate goal is to protect the health, safety, and welfare of individuals, State officials should simultaneously develop an environment that fosters respect for all social groups and individuals from every background. State police powers under MSEHPA are restricted to communicable disease outbreaks that are wholly contained within the State's borders and naturally occurring (it may take some time before a disease can be traced to a terrorist).

In September of 2003 the Turning Point Model State Public Health Act (Turning Point) was introduced as essentially an extension of the original project, MSEHPA. Like MSEHPA, Turning Point was written in order to strengthen the legal framework of public health through a collaborative process. As of 2007, Turning Point had been featured in whole or in part in 133 resolutions in 33 States. Turning Point differs from MSEHPA in that the overall goals outlined are much broader in scope. The first two purposes listed in Turning Point are:

(1) to identify and strengthen the public health infrastructure to improve the public's health through statutory reform and (2) to set a broad mission for providing essential public health services and functions principally through the efforts of state and local public health agencies in collaboration with others in the public health system.

Both Turning Point and the MSEHPA address the need for collaboration amongst all participants tending to the public health in a time of emergency.

If a naturally occurring disease spreads past a single State's borders or is introduced via foreign arrival from another country, the Centers for Disease Control (CDC), a part of the Department of Health and Human Services (HHS), has the authority to assert federal authority under Title 42 (Public Health and Welfare) U.S.C. § 264. The use of this authority is at the discretion of the Surgeon General, who must have approval of the Secretary of HHS and also may not authorize actions to address any communicable diseases other than those listed in the aforementioned Executive Orders. In the event that the

CDC takes command and control the Code of Federal Regulations (CFR) provides a variety of tools that the CDC can utilize. These are found in Parts 70 (Interstate Quarantine) and 71 (Foreign Quarantine) of Title 42 (Public Health).

While the CDC is designated as the lead agency to prevent and control the spread of the listed communicable diseases when they occur naturally, the aforementioned laws and regulations do not control in the event of a terrorist attack. The CDC would monitor public health threats, but the FBI would take the lead for crisis management. The Federal Emergency Management Agency, now part of the DHS, would coordinate the overall national response to a terror biological attack.

On February 28, 2003, President George W. Bush signed Homeland Security Presidential Directive 5 (HSPD-5) which mandated the development and implementation of a National Response Plan (NRP) that would supersede the FRP. The NRP was developed and released in 2004 and has been updated on a regular basis. The purpose of the NRP is to provide a national system for prevention, preparedness, response and recovery in the event of any national disasters, including terrorist and bioterrorist attacks. If a biological outbreak occurs in the United States, the NRP Biological Incident Annex provides the guiding procedures and policies to be followed by federal agencies in aiding State, local and tribal governments. Biological outbreaks are unique in nature as compared to most of the other possible types of national disasters. For that reason: "Actions described in [the Biological Incident] Annex take place with or without a Presidential…declaration or a public health emergency declaration by the Secretary of Heath and Human Services."

Governmental response to any biological outbreak must be timely, strong and effective. Accordingly, at the State level, the Governor has the authority to order isolation, quarantine, or social-distancing requirements to prevent the spread of certain communicable diseases. At the federal level, 42 U.S.C. § 264 empowers the Surgeon General of the United States to order "inspection, fumigation, disinfection, sanitation, pest extermination, destruction of animals or articles found to be so infected or contaminated as to be sources of dangerous infection to human beings, and other measures, as…may be necessary" to prevent the spread of any of the listed communicable diseases across State lines. In addition, § 70.6 of Title 42 of the C.F.R. authorizes the "detention, isolation, quarantine, or conditional release of individuals" when the purpose is to prevent the spread of any of the listed communicable diseases within the United States. Part 71 of Title 42 of the C.F.R. provides for the detention, isolation and quarantine of individuals, goods, animals and other items at ports and airports to prevent the introduction or spread of any of the listed communicable diseases.

12.3 The Goal of Quarantine

Quarantine is a critical tool that governmental agencies may utilize in the event of a biological outbreak to prevent the continuing spread of the subject communicable disease to new individuals. The MSEHPA defines quarantine as:

> The physical separation and confinement of an individual or groups of individuals, who are or may have been exposed to a contagious or possibly contagious disease and who do not show signs or symptoms of a contagious disease, from non-quarantined individuals, to prevent or limit the transmission of the disease to non-quarantined individuals.

By definition, quarantine may be used to restrict the movement and actions of individuals who are not yet ill, and may not ever become ill, but have been exposed to the disease. Quarantine is different from isolation, which is the isolation of individuals who have become infected or ill from the communicable disease. Obviously, the main goal of quarantine is to separate people who are potential carriers of a communicable disease from coming into contact with those individuals who have never come into contact with the disease. Utilizing quarantine prevents the spread of communicable diseases during incubation periods when individuals do not exhibit any symptoms of the illness.

The concept of quarantine is not new. For instance, the Old Testament commands the separation of lepers from the camps of the people and specifies instructions on how and when they may be returned to society. The term quarantine is derived from the Italian words *quaranta giorni*, meaning 40 days. It is believed that the Italian phrase was used to describe the practice of requiring ships that arrived in Venice from infected ports during the fourteenth century plague outbreaks to weigh anchor outside the port for forty days before the ship could dock. During the 2003 SARS (severe acute respiratory syndrome) virus outbreak, many countries implemented quarantine procedures to include Canada, China, Hong Kong, and Singapore.

Although the United States did not utilize the quarantine tool during the SARS outbreak, the President did add, by Executive Order, SARS to the list of quarantinable communicable diseases. In addition, the Executive Order also listed an extremely broad based category to cover all possible future influenza viruses: "influenza caused by novel or reemergent influenza viruses that are causing or have the potential to cause a pandemic."

12.4 The Legality of Quarantine

As noted, federal authority to establish quarantine in the event of a bioterrorist attack or biological outbreak rests in the Surgeon General and the Secretary of HHS pursuant to § 264 of Title 42 of the U.S.C., which has been conferred to the CDC. The law explicitly limits quarantine authority to those cases in which the purpose of the quarantine is to prevent the introduction, transmission, or spread of the communicable diseases set out in Executive Orders. States, through their police powers, have reserved the right to establish quarantines for communicable disease outbreaks wholly contained within the State borders and which are not the result of a terrorist attack.

Quarantine is not always a mandatory order. Several times in history, including the more recent SARS epidemic, the government has instead suggested voluntary quarantine by individuals who believe they have come in contact with the subject communicable disease. While many individuals may choose to voluntarily quarantine themselves, legal concerns do not arise from these actions. Legal concerns involving quarantine arise only when the government issues a mandatory quarantine.

The Fourteenth Amendment to the Constitution of the United States guarantees that no person shall be deprived of life, liberty, or property without due process of law. This guarantee has long protected individuals' freedom from physical restraint. The United States Supreme Court has interpreted the preservation of due process to include a balancing test that weighs private interests against government interests. In *Jacobson v. Commonwealth of Massachusetts*, 197 U.S. 11 (1905), a case involving mandatory small pox vaccinations, the Supreme Court said:

> But the liberty secured by the Constitution of the United States to every person within its jurisdiction does not import an absolute right in each person to be, at all times and in all circumstances, wholly freed from restraint. There are manifold restraints to which every person is necessarily subject for the common good. On any other basis organized society could not exist with safety to its members.

While the individual right to due process and freedom against physical restraint are not absolute, the government may not impose mandatory quarantine orders without restraint. In every instance of quarantine, the government and the courts that review governmental actions will have to weigh individual interests in privacy, freedom, and due process against the government's interests in protecting the safety and health of all citizens. In *Parham v. J.R.*, 442 U.S. 584 (1979), the Supreme Court noted: "What process is constitutionally due cannot be divorced from the nature of the ultimate decision that is being made."

The main goals of quarantine authority in United States law are constructed in ways that aim to protect individual due process to the greatest extent possible. The Supreme Court in *Goldberg v. Kelly*, 397 U.S. 254, discusses four requirements of due process: (1) reasonable and adequate notice; (2) opportunity to be heard within a reasonable manner and time; (3) available legal counsel; and (4) review of governmental actions by an impartial decision maker. Because quarantine necessarily interferes with an individual's right to be free from restraint, the government must utilize procedures that comport with these basic due process requirements.

Currently, 42 C.F.R Parts 70 and 71 lay out the federal regulations regarding quarantine and the process necessary to invoke quarantine. Specifically, § 70.6 states:

Regulations prescribed in this part authorize detention, isolation, quarantine, or conditional release of individuals, for the purpose of preventing the introduction, transmission, and spread of communicable diseases listed in an Executive Order setting out a list of quarantinable communicable diseases, as provided under section 361(b) of the Public Health Service Act.

In addition to this authority, § 70.5 provides special travel restrictions on persons who have been exposed to cholera, plague, smallpox, typhus, or yellow fever.

Even a cursory view of the matter reveals that the current laws and regulations associated with quarantine are not settled, even at the federal level. In light of these major gaps, HHS issued a Proposed Rule on November 30, 2005, for public comment. The Proposed Rule would have changed and added to 42 C.F.R. Parts 70 and 71. Under the proposed version of Part 70, federal officials would have several different types of tools—ranging in severity—to address a biological threats caused by, for example, sick airline passengers. The proposed Part 70 provided measures to address vaccination clinics, screenings, travel restrictions, and the establishment of hospitals and stations in the event of a biological outbreak. In addition to these measures, the proposed Part 70 would have established a specific process for ordering quarantine. Under the new rules, a person would only be placed under what was termed "provisional quarantine" if the responsible government official had a reasonable belief that the individual had been exposed to a quarantinable communicable disease. Generally, an individual in such a situation would have been asked to submit voluntarily to quarantine. However, if an individual refused to submit voluntarily to quarantine, the official could order provisional quarantine via written order, verbal order, or actual physical movement restrictions. Individuals could be served with provisional quarantine orders through personal service, or the government officials could post or publish the order in a noticeable location. Under the proposed rule, provisional quarantine would last only three business days. If the government wished to extend the provisional quarantine, the official must serve the individual with a written quarantine order. The written quarantine order must explain the reasonable belief that the individual is in a communicable stage of a quarantinable disease based on medical evidence and that the quarantine was necessary to prevent the spread of the disease to non-infected individuals. The quarantine order must also specify the person(s) to be quarantined, the legal basis for the quarantine, the dates of quarantine, and the location of the quarantine. Both the quarantine order and the provisional quarantine order must inform the person to be quarantined that they have the right to refuse any medical treatment offered, e.g., vaccination. In addition, the following rights are set out:

- The quarantine order must provide the person with notice that they have the right to request a hearing to review the quarantine order at any time during the quarantine.
- Following a request for a hearing, the government must hold a hearing within one business day of the request. The official will provide reasonable notice to inform the individual, designate a hearing officer to review all the evidence available to the government, and make findings to determine whether or not the quarantined individual is in a quarantinable stage of a communicable disease.
- The individual has the right to appoint a representative to provide other evidence to the hearing officer and the government must make reasonable accommodations to allow the individual to communicate with their representative.
- The hearing officer, upon reviewing all the evidence, will make a written recommendation to the government regarding release from quarantine. This final determination made by the government official is deemed to be final.
- Section 2241 of Title 28 of the U.S.C. provides that any individual that is detained may seek a writ of habeas corpus. The hearing officer is only authorized to review the factual, scientific, and medical basis for the quarantine; therefore, the writ of habeas corpus provides judicial review of the legal and constitutional concerns associated with the quarantine.

While most administrative rules are quickly proposed and adopted, these proposed rules were left in limbo for five years. It was not until March of 2010, that the Obama Administration quietly discarded the proposed rules under pressure from the American Civil Liberties Union (ACLU).

The MSEHPA provides a model quarantine process for State government officials. Under MSEHPA:

- The State officials may order a temporary quarantine or isolation by written directive.
- The temporary isolation or quarantine may not last more than ten days.
- Longer periods of quarantine require that State officials obtain a court order for quarantine or isolation. The court must hold a hearing to review the evidence presented by health officials as well as evidence provided by representatives of the quarantined or isolated persons within five days of the petition to the court.
- The court may issue a quarantine or isolation order only upon finding by a preponderance of the evidence that the quarantine or isolation is reasonably necessary to prevent the spread of the communicable disease.
- Should the court decide to issue the order, a quarantine or isolation order cannot be for a period longer than thirty days for any individual. If the State officials believe that quarantine is necessary for longer than the thirty day period, the State must file a petition for an extension, which may not last longer than thirty days.
- Individuals who are quarantined have the right to request the court show cause for the order of quarantine or isolation and why the individual should not be released. The court must

either grant or deny the petition to show cause within forty-eight hours and, if the petition is granted, must issue an order to show cause within twenty-four hours.

Like the MSEHPA, Turning Point outlines a quarantine process for individuals with notice:

The *state* or *local public health agency* may make a written petition to a *court* for an order authorizing the *isolation* or *quarantine* of an *individual* or groups of *individuals*. *The petition must include the name of the individual, the premise subject to quarantine, and the suspected contagious disease.* The petition shall be accompanied by the sworn affidavit executed by the *state* or *local public health agency* attesting to the facts asserted in the petition, together with any further information that may be relevant and material to the *court's* consideration. A hearing must be held on any petition filed pursuant to this subsection within [forty-eight hours] of filing of the petition. The *court* shall grant the petition if, by clear and convincing evidence, *isolation* or *quarantine* is shown to be reasonably necessary to prevent or limit the transmission of *contagious* or possibly *contagious disease* to others.

Turning Point follows the model quarantine process set out in MSEHPA with a few exceptions. Turning Point allows for quarantine of an individual without full notice provisions, stating:

The *state* or *local public health agency* may temporarily *isolate* or *quarantine* an *individual* or groups of *individuals* through a written directive if delay in imposing the *isolation* or *quarantine* would significantly jeopardize the agency's ability to prevent or limit the transmission of a *contagious* or possibly *contagious disease* to others.

During the quarantine or isolation period, the MSEHPA provides additional protections.

• State health officials must continuously monitor individuals for changes in their medical condition, and must release individuals immediately in the event that they are no longer in a medical state that poses a threat to others requiring quarantine or isolation.
• Isolated individuals and quarantined individuals shall be housed in separate locales.
• All quarantine and isolation measures should utilize the least restrictive means available to prevent the spread of the communicable disease.
• The State must provide food, clothing, shelter, means of communication, medical treatment, and medication in a systematic and efficient manner to all individuals in quarantine or isolation.
• All quarantine or isolation locations must be kept clean and safe.
• The State should make every effort to ensure that cultural and religious beliefs of the quarantined or isolated persons are considered.

The Supreme Court has not squarely addressed the validity of quarantine laws and procedures enacted by States to prevent the spread of communicable diseases since 1902. In 1902, the Supreme Court heard a case from Louisiana regarding a quarantine law that prohibited a French vessel from entering a port that had been quarantined due to infestation. In *Compagnie Francaise de Navigation a Vapeur v. Louisiana State Board of Health*, 186 U.S. 380 (1902), the Court held:

That from an early day the power of the States to enact and enforce quarantine laws for the safety and the protection of the health of their inhabitants has been recognized by Congress, is beyond question. That until Congress has exercised its power on the subject, such state quarantine laws and state laws for the purpose of preventing, eradicating or controlling the spread of contagious or infectious diseases, are not repugnant to the Constitution of the United States, although their operation affects interstate or foreign commerce, is not an open question.

In further examining whether such quarantine laws were unconstitutional, the Court stated:

It having been ascertained that the regulation was lawfully adopted and enforced the contention demonstrates its own unsoundness, since in the last analysis it reduces itself to the proposition that the effect of the Fourteenth Amendment was to strip the government, whether state or national, of all power to enact regulations protecting the health and safety of the people, or, what is equivalent thereto, necessarily amounts to saying that such laws when lawfully enacted cannot be enforced against person or property without violating the Constitution. In other words, that the lawful powers of government which the Constitution has conferred may not be exerted without bringing about a violation of the Constitution.

The case law regarding the quarantine of individuals is sparse because the United States has yet to face mass quarantine due to the spread of an epidemic, pandemic, or a bioterrorist attack. Clearly, the enactment of laws and regulations in the vein of the CDC's Proposed Parts 70 and 71 and the MSEHPA provide starting points from which the judicial branch can evaluate the issues.

UNITED STATES v. SHINNICK
United States District Court for the Eastern District of New York
219 F. Supp. 789 (E.D.N.Y. Aug. 2, 1963)

DOOLING, District Judge.

Petitioner, Helen Minkin, seeks on behalf of her mother, Ellen Siegel, an order, after inquiry, that respondents produce the body of relator before the court and that relator then be discharged from custody. Relator is presently being held at the United States Public Health Hospital at Stapleton, Staten Island, in this District; she is in isolation for the balance of the small pox incubation period of 14 days from July 25, 1963. She is being isolated because she was in Stockholm, a small pox infected local area, on July 25, 1963 and she did not present on arrival here from Stockholm on July 25, 1963, a valid certificate of vaccination against small pox; she stated in substance that the only vaccination to which she had reacted positively was her school entry vaccination, sixty-three years earlier; all later attempts at vaccination produced no positive reaction; the latest such 'unsuccessful' vaccination was on May 31, 1963 (Ex. 4).

The facts were found orally in tentative form at the conclusion of the hearing and that part of the hearing has been transcribed. There being no apparent dispute about the underlying facts, they are now found as transcribed with ink typographical corrections and with one material change.

The suspected small pox case in Stuttgart, a person who had been in Stockholm July 14 to 17, has now been ascertained to be a case of eczema, so that the last Stockholm case now known is that which was isolated June 22. Both counsels have supplied this datum by affidavit.

Stockholm is a small pox infected area and has been since before July 21-25, 1963 when Relator visited Stockholm (Ex. 3, 6 pp. 372, 376; 312, 328, 360). Under the International Sanitary Regulations (W H O Regulations No. 2) [FN1] Articles 3, 6 (Cf. 42 C.F. R. § 71.1(1)(0) [FN2] the declaration that a local area is infected and that it is free of local infection emanates from the health administration of the territory in which the infected local area is situated. It does not appear that others are legally competent to (as they would be hopelessly handicapped in seeking to) make a determination on such a question as whether or not Stockholm can now be regarded as not an infected local area on the basis that the last reported case went into isolation on June 22 and W H O Regulations No. 2 seems to provide for terminating a declaration of local infection twenty-eight days after the last reported case of small pox dies, recovers or is isolated; responsibility for applying that standard rests with the territorial health administration and depends on whether, also, all measures of prophylaxis have been taken and maintained to prevent recurrence of the disease. It is idle and dangerous to suggest that private judgment or judicial ipse dixit can, acting on the one datum of the date June 22 as the last identified and reported case, undertake to supercede the continuing declaration of the interested territorial health administration that Stockholm is still a small pox infected local area.

The Public Health Service Regulations do not conflict with W H O Regulations No. 2 although their arrangement is quite different. Relator did not arrive on an infected aircraft (42 C.F.R. § 71.87, W H O Reg. No. 2, Art. 84). Had she so arrived, isolation could have been directed on the basis of that fact, the authorities, however, taking into account previous vaccinations and the possibilities of her exposure to infection (42 C.F.R. § 71.87(b)(3); W H O Reg. No. 2, Art. 85 sd. 1(b). Where the aircraft is not infected, isolation may be imposed if the passenger is a 'suspect' (42 C.F.R. § 71.88; W H O Reg. No. 2, Art. 84, sd. 2). A 'suspect' is one who is considered by the health authority (medical officer in charge) as having been exposed to infection by a quarantinable disease and to be capable of spreading that disease (42 C.F.R. § 71.1(bb); W H O Reg. No. 2, Art. 1). While isolation is not to be substituted for surveillance unless the health authority considers the risk of transmission of the infection by the suspect to be exceptionally serious (42 C.F.R. § 71.70, W H O Reg. No. 2, Art. 39 sd. 2), the judgment required is that of a public health officer and not of a lawyer used to insist on positive evidence to support action; their task is to measure risk to the public and to seek for what can reassure and, not finding it, to proceed reasonably to make the public health secure. They deal in a terrible context and the consequences of mistaken indulgence can be irretrievably tragic. To supercede their judgment there must be a reliable showing of error. The words cautioning against light use of isolation are indeed strong but the three medical men who testified manifestly shared a concern that was evident and real and reasoned. [FN3] Their differentiation of the case of Mr. Siegel, Relator's husband, was forthright, reasoned and circumstantially reassuring. Their conclusion, reached in obvious good faith, cannot be challenged on the ground that they had no evidence of the exposure of Relator to the disease; they, simply, were not free and certainly not bound to ignore the facts that opportunity for exposure existed during four days in Stockholm, that no one on earth could know for fourteen days whether or not there had been exposure, and that Relator, with a history of unsuccessful vaccinations, was peculiarly in a position to have become infected and to infect others. Their action in no way discriminated against Relator or singled her out for treatment different from that accorded the few others similarly situated.

The petition for issuance of the writ is therefore denied. It is accordingly Ordered that Relator's petition be and it hereby is dismissed after hearing on the merits.

FN1. 7 United States Treaties and other International Agreements (1956) 2259-2296—cited 7 UST 2259-2296.

FN2. The Foreign Quarantine regulations (Part 71 of Title 42) appear to depend primarily from 42 U.S.C. § 264. Their adjustment to the W H O Regulations reflects, no doubt, the quasi-treaty status of regulations adopted under authority of the International Agreement creating the Organization, 62 Stat., Part 3, 2679, 2685; Congress authorized the President to accept membership and participate in the Organization 62 Stat. 441.

FN3. No negative inference, that voluntary submission to vaccination requires substitution of surveillance for isolation, can be drawn from 42 C.F.R. § 71.86(c); W H O Reg. No. 2, Art. 83, sd. 2. The regulation states one condition warranting isolation: refusal of vaccination; and one procedure available when vaccination is accepted: continued surveillance notwithstanding vaccination. The regulation does not exhaust the procedural alternatives nor straiten the authorities. Their procedure remains a function of the gravity of the situation as measured by their expert judgments dispassionately formed.

12.5 Search and Seizure

The government also has the power to search and seize personal property in the event of the emergence of a named communicable disease. The Fourth Amendment to the Constitution of the United States provides that:

> The right of the people to be secure in their persons, houses, papers, and effects, against unreasonable searches and seizures, shall not be violated, and no Warrants shall issue, but upon probable cause, supported by Oath or affirmation, and particularly describing the place to be searched, and the persons or things to be seized.

As is often repeated, the right to be free from search and seizure conducted without probable cause or warrant is not an absolute right. There are several situations in which the Supreme Court has found that a government search and seizure without warrant or probable cause does not violate the Constitution. One instance when a warrant and probable cause are not necessary is when a search and seizure is conducted with the consent of someone who is authorized to provide such consent. Accordingly, an individual may consent to the search and seizure of personal property which may be infected with biological agents.

Individuals in transit between States or at points of entry into the United States, occupy a unique position when it comes to privacy expectations. Parts 70 and 71 of 42 C.F.R. afford government officials the authority to search individuals in transit between States or individuals attempting to enter the United States from foreign countries for the purpose of determining the presence of communicable diseases. Indeed, inspections for communicable diseases are routine at all international ports of entry and are required under the CFR even without the presence of a warrant or probable cause. Courts have made it clear that by the nature of being in transit or attempting to enter or leave the United States, individuals have a reduced expectation of privacy and are subject to search and seizure of their person and effects without a warrant or probable cause. The Seventh Circuit, in *United States v. McDonald*, 100 F. 3d 1320 (1996), found that individuals who are in transit on public transportation vehicles, like a bus, train, or airplane, have a greatly reduced expectation of privacy as compared to individuals in a fixed place, like their homes. In *United States v. Berisha*, 925 F. 2d 791 (1991), the Fifth Circuit held that individuals at the border, both entering and leaving the United States, are essentially on notice that their privacy may be invaded.

Closely regulated commercial industries have also been deemed by the Supreme Court to occupy a position of reduced expectation of privacy, primarily due to the fact that the nature of the business is highly regulated by the government. In *New York v. Burger*, 482 U.S. 691 (1987), the Court set forth the standard.

> Because the owner or operator of a commercial premises in a "closely regulated" industry has a reduced expectation of privacy, the warrant and probable-cause requirements, which fulfill the traditional Fourth Amendment standard of reasonableness for a government search have lessened application in this context....This warrantless inspection...will be deemed to be reasonable only so long as three criteria are met. First, there must be a "substantial" government interest that informs the regulatory scheme pursuant to which the inspection is made. Second, the warrantless inspections must be "necessary to further [the] regulatory scheme...." Finally, "the statute's inspection program, in terms of certainty and regularity of its application, [must] provid[e] a constitutionally adequate substitute for a warrant." In other words, the regulatory statute must perform the two basic functions of a warrant: it must advise the owner of the commercial premises that the search is being made pursuant to the law and has a properly defined scope, and it must limit the discretion of the inspecting officers [citations omitted].

Finally, the requirements of the Fourth Amendment that a warrant and probable cause are necessary to conduct a search and seizure may be unnecessary if the search and seizure is conducted in an effort to prevent an imminent threat to the health or safety of the general public. The Supreme Court upheld the seizure and destruction of food that was unfit for consumption to protect the public health in *North American Cold Storage Company v. City of Chicago*, 211 U.S. 306 (1908). This decision suggests that in the event of a biological outbreak or bioterrorist attack, government officials may have a great amount of authority to inspect, seize, and destroy personal property to prevent the spread of deadly communicable diseases. As noted, current provisions exist in 42 C.F.R. Parts 70 and 71 to provide for the search and seizure of property at ports of entry, but no federal laws or regulations have been passed to grant such carte blanche authority to government officials in the event of a bioterrorist attack or biological outbreak in the United States.

12.6 Other Legal Issues

A variety of other legal concerns may arise when government officials are faced with preventative and containment measures. Officials at any level of government—federal, State, local, or tribal—may infringe on individual civil liberties. Accordingly, the full range of possible actions available to the government should be complemented by a combination of limitations, safeguards, and oversight provisions to ensure the protection of individual rights.

The MSEHPA recognizes that a major outbreak may quickly overwhelm the existing health care system of clinics and hospitals, requiring the government to procure property to provide for the care, treatment and housing of patients. In addition, the government may find it necessary to destroy entire facilities or private property and material that has become infected and poses a threat to the health of the general public. Private property may be taken by the government, even when the procurements are only utilized temporarily. However, when the government commits a taking of private property it must provide the rightful owner with just compensation. Both the MSEHPA and Turning Point suggest that the calculated compensation should include the value of the property at the eminent domain cost that would be afforded in a non-emergency setting. Recognizing the possibility that an outbreak may cause a shortage in health care facilities, Turning Point advocates forming emergency relationships with the private health care sector:

> To carry out the mission of public health, state and local public health agencies are authorized to provide or implement essential public health services and functions, including services or functions to establish formal or informal relationships with public or private sector partners within the public health system.

Government officials will also be faced with patient concerns about protecting privacy rights. The conflicting goals of protecting privacy and preventing the spread of a communicable disease must be addressed. The MSEHPA as well as the Proposed Parts 70 and 71 of 42 C.F.R. provide for the maintenance of administrative records for each patient that will combine their legal quarantine orders, challenges, as well as their entire medical records. The protection of these records and maintenance of individual privacy should also be accounted for not only during the crisis but also in the aftermath. Use of the medical records should be limited to the provision of treatment, epidemiological research, or investigation of the cause of transmission of the communicable disease on a strict need to know basis. Likewise, Turning Point recognizes that an individual's private records may be disclosed in certain situations where the public health is at stake. During a state of emergency Turning Point specifically allows the public health care agency to communicate certain information to health care providers.

Another issue of concern deals with the fact that health care providers may simply refuse to provide treatment to the infected, as occurred with some hospital personnel in Canada during the SARS outbreak in 2003. To be sure, in the event of an epidemic, pandemic, or bioterrorist attack, health care providers will be in high demand and short supply. The MSEHPA suggests that States pass laws that allow government officials to compel health care providers within the State to treat individuals who have fallen ill due to an epidemic, pandemic, or bioterrorist attack as a condition of the provider's licensing and ability to practice in that State. The MSEHPA also provides that the State officials should allow health care providers licensed in other States to assist during the crisis, in effect temporarily waiving jurisdictional and licensing concerns. Furthermore, the MSEHPA suggests that State actors, health care providers, and others providing aid and assistance during an outbreak should be afforded immunity for negligent acts or omissions. Immunity would help foster action during a crisis situation that might otherwise be hindered by fear of legal repercussions. Nevertheless, immunity should not extend to gross negligence or willful misconduct or to any individual that in some way brought about the biological emergency.

Legal concerns do not cease when an infected individual dies. The Black Death of the fourteenth century killed 25 million Europeans in just five years, with corpses playing a large role in the spread of the virus. Since disease can spread from human remains, government officials must have a process to control and dispose of human remains that prevents the spread of the communicable disease while taking into account the religious, cultural, familial, and individual beliefs of the deceased and their survivors.

Enforcement of any orders of quarantine will create a variety of problems and every mandatory quarantine order will see its violators. The MSEHPA suggests that violations pursuant to State laws should constitute a misdemeanor. Federal law, in 42 U.S.C. § 271, states that violations of the enforcement provisions for 42 U.S.C. § 264, namely 42 C.F.R. Parts 70 and 71, will give rise to a fine not more than $1,000, imprisonment for not more than a year, or both. In addition, Subsection (b) of § 271 subjects vessels that violate orders pursuant to the aforementioned code and regulations to a fine that will not be more than $5,000. While these penalties can provide a framework for how to address non-compliance with mandatory quarantine orders, lawmakers should consider unintended consequences. For example, during the 2003 SARS outbreak in Singapore, the government ordered local law enforcement not to arrest individuals engaged in some illegal activities, like quarantine violation, so as to prevent those who may have been exposed from being pushed underground.

Funding issues are also a major concern. The majority of hospitals in the United States are privately owned and are simply not equipped, staffed, or willing to stretch the capabilities of the hospital to meet the enormous needs that would occur during a major epidemic. In addition, if the epidemic strikes Mexico, the United States could expect a flood of people streaming across the border for health care. Diseases that cause such mayhem do not discriminate in victim choice. Privately owned hospitals in the United States will need major financial support from the government.

Individuals ordered to quarantine also face the possibility that they will lose their employment. Will the government compensate those who suffer financial loss due to quarantine?

In summary, a plethora of legal issues stand hungrily at the door. They will not become fully apparent until the nation is in the middle of a biological outbreak. In the ensuing chaos, the government will have to utilize all the legal tools that are currently in place and quickly develop new tools. Certainly, the government entities at all levels should plan now for the worst case scenario. The United States has managed responses to a variety of disasters in recent years, both natural and terrorist, and each new disaster brings new legal issues that require executive, legislative, and judicial attention and action. Like all issues associated with the War on Terror, the goal in addressing these issues is always to ensure that the citizens of the United States are safe from the crisis as well as from an over active governmental response.

12.7 Questions for Discussion

1. *HHS Proposed Rules.* The proposed changes to 42 C.F.R. Parts 70 and 71, published by the HHS in November 2005, not only established more detailed procedures for quarantine by the CDC, the proposed changes also established authority in the CDC to mandate a variety of measures, including: the collection of passenger information by airlines; travel permits for individuals to travel to places the CDC deems a potential threat to the health of the public; the establishment of hospitals and clinics; implementation of sanitary measures; implementation of CDC control in the event the CDC perceives local control inadequate; and special powers given to the government in time of war. In the event of a confirmed bioterrorist attack, the FBI assumes control of all government actions in response to the attack, meaning the FBI will have all of the power that the proposed changes afford the CDC. The proposed rules were dropped by the Obama Administration in 2010 over concerns that the proposed rules gave the government too much power. While the proposed regulations clearly infringe upon privacy rights what arguments exist to suggest that such rules are needed?

2. *Who oversees the government?* A bioterrorist attack on the United States would set in motion a governmental response machine that currently is not subject to oversight. Do the courts have sufficient power to oversee the executive branch to ensure that individual civil liberties are secure during the government's response to a large scale bioterrorist attack? Will the courts exercise the power they may have even if they will appear to be acting contrary to the wants of the majority?

3. *Does Executive Order 13375 go too far?* President Bush's 2005 Executive Order 13375 lists a new and extremely broad based category to cover all possible future influenza viruses: "influenza caused by novel or reemergent influenza viruses that are causing or have the potential to cause a pandemic." What impact does such a broad based category present in terms of government power?

Selected Bibliography

Department of Health and Human Services. *Control of Communicable Diseases; Proposed Rule.* Fed. Reg. 70, 229 at 71891, Nov. 30, 2005.

Department of Homeland Security. *National Response Plan* 2004.

Gosten, Lawrence O. MODEL STATE EMERGENCY HEALTH POWERS ACT, 2001.

O'Leary, N. Pieter M. *Cock-a-Doodle-Doo: Pandemic Avian Influenza and the Legal Preparation and Consequences of an H5N1 Influenza Outbreak,* HEALTH MATRIX: JOURNAL OF LAW-MEDICINE, Summer 2006.

O'Leary, N. Pieter M. *Bioterrorism or Avian Influenza: California, the Model State Emergency Health Powers Act, and Protecting Civil Liberties During a Public Health Emergency,* CALIFORNIA WESTERN L.REV., Spring, 2006.

Pimentel, David and Marcia Pimentel. *Essay: Bioweapon Impacts on Public Health and the Environment,* WILLIAM AND MARY ENVIRONMENTAL LAW AND POL. REV. Spring, 2006.

Posner, Richard A. CATASTROPHE: RISK AND RESPONSE, 2005.

Public Health Statute Modernization National Excellence Collaborative. Turning Point Model State Public Health ACT, 2003.

Rosenstein, Mark et. al. *Quarantine and Isolation: Lessons Learned from SARS.* REPORT TO THE CENTERS FOR DISEASE CONTROL AND PREVENTION, 2003.

Sutton, Victoria. LAW AND BIOTERRORISM, 2002.

Appendix A

Selected Provisions of the Charter of the United Nations

June 26, 1945, 59 Stat. 1031, T.S. 993, 3 Bevans 1153, entered into force Oct. 24, 1945.

PREAMBLE

WE THE PEOPLES OF THE UNITED NATIONS DETERMINED

- to save succeeding generations from the scourge of war, which twice in our lifetime has brought untold sorrow to mankind, and
- to reaffirm faith in fundamental human rights, in the dignity and worth of the human person, in the equal rights of men and women and of nations large and small, and
- to establish conditions under which justice and respect for the obligations arising from treaties and other sources of international law can be maintained, and
- to promote social progress and better standards of life in larger freedom,

AND FOR THESE ENDS

- to practice tolerance and live together in peace with one another as good neighbors, and
- to unite our strength to maintain international peace and security, and
- to ensure by the acceptance of principles and the institution of methods, that armed force shall not be used, save in the common interest, and
- to employ international machinery for the promotion of the economic and social advancement of all peoples,

HAVE RESOLVED TO COMBINE OUR EFFORTS TO ACCOMPLISH THESE AIMS

Accordingly, our respective Governments, through representatives assembled in the city of San Francisco, who have exhibited their full powers found to be in good and due form, have agreed to the present Charter of the United Nations and do hereby establish an international organization to be known as the United Nations.

CHAPTER I
PURPOSES AND PRINCIPLES

Article 1

The Purposes of the United Nations are:

1. To maintain international peace and security, and to that end: to take effective collective measures for the prevention and removal of threats to the peace, and for the suppression of acts of aggression or other breaches of the peace, and to bring about by peaceful means, and in conformity with the principles of justice and international law, adjustment or settlement of international disputes or situations which might lead to a breach of the peace;

2. To develop friendly relations among nations based on respect for the principle of equal rights and self-determination of peoples, and to take other appropriate measures to strengthen universal peace;

3. To achieve international cooperation in solving international problems of an economic, social, cultural, or humanitarian character, and in promoting and encouraging respect for human rights and for fundamental freedoms for all without distinction as to race, sex, language, or religion; and

4. To be a center for harmonizing the actions of nations in the attainment of these common ends.

Article 2

The Organization and its Members, in pursuit of the Purposes stated in Article 1, shall act in accordance with the following Principles.

1. The Organization is based on the principle of the sovereign equality of all its Members.

2. All Members, in order to ensure to all of them the rights and benefits resulting from membership, shall fulfill in good faith the obligations assumed by them in accordance with the present Charter.

3. All Members shall settle their international disputes by peaceful means in such a manner that international peace and security, and justice, are not endangered.

4. All Members shall refrain in their international relations from the threat or use of force against the territorial integrity or political independence of any state, or in any other manner inconsistent with the Purposes of the United Nations.

5. All Members shall give the United Nations every assistance in any action it takes in accordance with the present Charter, and shall refrain from giving assistance to any state against which the United Nations is taking preventive or enforcement action.

6. The Organization shall ensure that states which are not Members of the United Nations act in accordance with these Principles so far as may be necessary for the maintenance of international peace and security.

7. Nothing contained in the present Charter shall authorize the United Nations to intervene in matters which are essentially within the domestic jurisdiction of any state or shall require the Members to submit such matters to settlement under the present Charter; but this principle shall not prejudice the application of enforcement measures under Chapter VII.

CHAPTER II
MEMBERSHIP

Article 3

The original Members of the United Nations shall be the states which, having participated in the United Nations Conference on International Organization at San Francisco, or having previously signed the Declaration by United Nations of January 1, 1942, sign the present Charter and ratify it in accordance with Article 110.

Article 4

1. Membership in the United Nations is open to all other peace-loving states which accept the obligations contained in the present Charter and, in the judgment of the Organization, are able and willing to carry out these obligations.
2. The admission of any such state to membership in the United Nations will be effected by a decision of the General Assembly upon the recommendation of the Security Council.

Article 5

A member of the United Nations against which preventive or enforcement action has been taken by the Security Council may be suspended from the exercise of the rights and privileges of membership by the General Assembly upon the recommendation of the Security Council. The exercise of these rights and privileges may be restored by the Security Council.

Article 6

A Member of the United Nations which has persistently violated the Principles contained in the present Charter may be expelled from the Organization by the General Assembly upon the recommendation of the Security Council.

CHAPTER III
ORGANS

Article 7

1. There are established as the principal organs of the United Nations: a General Assembly, a Security Council, an Economic and Social Council, a Trusteeship Council, an International Court of Justice, and a Secretariat.
2. Such subsidiary organs as may be found necessary may be established in accordance with the present Charter.

Article 8

The United Nations shall place no restrictions on the eligibility of men and women to participate in any capacity and under conditions of equality in its principal and subsidiary organs.

CHAPTER IV
THE GENERAL ASSEMBLY

Composition

Article 9

1. The General Assembly shall consist of all the Members of the United Nations.
2. Each member shall have not more than five representatives in the General Assembly.

Functions and Powers

Article 10

The General Assembly may discuss any questions or any matters within the scope of the present Charter or relating to the powers and functions of any organs provided for in the present Charter, and, except as provided in Article 12, may make recommendations to the Members of the United Nations or to the Security Council or to both on any such questions or matters.

Article 11

1. The General Assembly may consider the general principles of cooperation in the maintenance of international peace and security, including the principles governing disarmament and the regulation of armaments, and may make recommendations with regard to such principles to the Members or to the Security Council or to both.
2. The General Assembly may discuss any questions relating to the maintenance of international peace and security brought before it by any Member of the United Nations, or by the Security Council, or by a state which is not a Member of the United Nations in accordance with Article 35, paragraph 2, and, except as provided in Article 12, may make recommendations with regard to any such questions to the state or states concerned or to the Security Council or to both. Any such question on which action is necessary shall be referred to the Security Council by the General Assembly either before or after discussion.
3. The General Assembly may call the attention of the Security Council to situations which are likely to endanger international peace and security.
4. The powers of the General Assembly set forth in this Article shall not limit the general scope of Article 10.

Article 12

1. While the Security Council is exercising in respect of any dispute or situation the functions assigned to it in the present Charter, the General Assembly shall not make any recommendation with regard to that dispute or situation unless the Security Council so requests.
2. The Secretary-General, with the consent of the Security Council, shall notify the General Assembly at each session of any matters relative to the maintenance of international peace

and security which are being dealt with by the Security Council and shall similarly notify the General Assembly, or the Members of the United Nations if the General Assembly is not in session, immediately the Security Council ceases to deal with such matters.

Article 13

1. The General Assembly shall initiate studies and make recommendations for the purpose of:
   a. promoting international cooperation in the political field and encouraging the progressive development of international law and its codification;
   b. promoting international cooperation in the economic, social, cultural, educational, and health fields, and assisting in the realization of human rights and fundamental freedoms for all without distinction as to race, sex, language, or religion.
2. The further responsibilities, functions and powers of the General Assembly with respect to matters mentioned in paragraph 1(b) above are set forth in Chapters IX and X.

Article 14

Subject to the provisions of Article 12, the General Assembly may recommend measures for the peaceful adjustment of any situation, regardless of origin, which it deems likely to impair the general welfare or friendly relations among nations, including situations resulting from a violation of the provisions of the present Charter setting forth the Purposes and Principles of the United Nations.

Article 15

1. The General Assembly shall receive and consider annual and special reports from the Security Council; these reports shall include an account of the measures that the Security Council has decided upon or taken to maintain international peace and security.
2. The General Assembly shall receive and consider reports from the other organs of the United Nations.

Article 16

The General Assembly shall perform such functions with respect to the international trusteeship system as are assigned to it under Chapters XII and XIII, including the approval of the trusteeship agreements for areas not designated as strategic.

Article 17

1. The General Assembly shall consider and approve the budget of the Organization.
2. The expenses of the Organization shall be borne by the Members as apportioned by the General Assembly.

3. The General Assembly shall consider and approve any financial and budgetary arrangements with specialized agencies referred to in Article 57 and shall examine the administrative budgets of such specialized agencies with a view to making recommendations to the agencies concerned.

Voting

Article 18

1. Each member of the General Assembly shall have one vote.

2. Decisions of the General Assembly on important questions shall be made by a two-thirds majority of the members present and voting. These questions shall include: recommendations with respect to the maintenance of international peace and security, the election of the non-permanent members of the Security Council, the election of the members of the Economic and Social Council, the election of members of the Trusteeship Council in accordance with paragraph 1(c) of Article 86, the admission of new Members to the United Nations, the suspension of the rights and privileges of membership, the expulsion of Members, questions relating to the operation of the trusteeship system, and budgetary questions.

3. Decisions on other questions, Composition including the determination of additional categories of questions to be decided by a two-thirds majority, shall be made by a majority of the members present and voting.

Article 19

A Member of the United Nations which is in arrears in the payment of its financial contributions to the Organization shall have no vote in the General Assembly if the amount of its arrears equals or exceeds the amount of the contributions due from it for the preceding two full years. The General Assembly may, nevertheless, permit such a Member to vote if it is satisfied that the failure to pay is due to conditions beyond the control of the Member.

Procedure

Article 20

The General Assembly shall meet in regular annual sessions and in such special sessions as occasion may require. Special sessions shall be convoked by the Secretary-General at the request of the Security Council or of a majority of the Members of the United Nations.

Article 21

The General Assembly shall adopt its own rules of procedure. It shall elect its President for each session.

Article 22

The General Assembly may establish such subsidiary organs as it deems necessary for the performance of its functions.

CHAPTER V
THE SECURITY COUNCIL

Article 23

1. The Security Council shall consist of fifteen Members of the United Nations. The Republic of China, France, the Union of Soviet Socialist Republics, the United Kingdom of Great Britain and Northern Ireland, and the United States of America shall be permanent members of the Security Council. The General Assembly shall elect ten other Members of the United Nations to be non-permanent members of the Security Council, due regard being specially paid, in the first instance to the contribution of Members of the United Nations to the maintenance of international peace and security and to the other purposes of the Organization, and also to equitable geographical distribution.

2. The non-permanent members of the Security Council shall be elected for a term of two years. In the first election of the non-permanent members after the increase of the membership of the Security Council from eleven to fifteen, two of the four additional members shall be chosen for a term of one year. A retiring member shall not be eligible for immediate re-election.

3. Each member of the Security Council shall have one representative.

Functions and Powers

Article 24

1. In order to ensure prompt and effective action by the United Nations, its Members confer on the Security Council primary responsibility for the maintenance of international peace and security, and agree that in carrying out its duties under this responsibility the Security Council acts on their behalf.

2. In discharging these duties the Security Council shall act in accordance with the Purposes and Principles of the United Nations. The specific powers granted to the Security Council for the discharge of these duties are laid down in Chapters VI, VII, VIII, and XII.

3. The Security Council shall submit annual and, when necessary, special reports to the General Assembly for its consideration.

Article 25

The Members of the United Nations agree to accept and carry out the decisions of the Security Council in accordance with the present Charter.

Article 26

In order to promote the establishment and maintenance of international peace and security with the least diversion for armaments of the world's human and economic resources, the Security Council shall be responsible for formulating, with the assistance of the Military Staff Committee referred to in Article 47, plans to be submitted to the Members of the United Nations for the establishment of a system for the regulation of armaments.

Voting

Article 27

1. Each member of the Security Council shall have one vote.
2. Decisions of the Security Council on procedural matters shall be made by an affirmative vote of nine members.
3. Decisions of the Security Council on all other matters shall be made by an affirmative vote of nine members including the concurring votes of the permanent members; provided that, in decisions under Chapter VI, and under paragraph 3 of Article 52, a party to a dispute shall abstain from voting.

Procedure

Article 28

1. The Security Council shall be so organized as to be able to function continuously. Each member of the Security Council shall for this purpose be represented at all times at the seat of the Organization.
2. The Security Council shall hold periodic meetings at which each of its members may, if it so desires, be represented by a member of the government or by some other specially designated representative.
3. The Security Council may hold meetings at such places other than the seat of the Organization as in its judgment will best facilitate its work.

Article 29

The Security Council may establish such subsidiary organs as it deems necessary for the performance of its functions.

Article 30

The Security Council shall adopt its own rules of procedure, including the method of selecting its President.

Article 31

Any Member of the United Nations which is not a member of the Security Council may participate, without vote, in the discussion of any question brought before the Security Council whenever the latter considers that the interests of that Member are specially affected.

Article 32

Any Member of the United Nations which is not a member of the Security Council or any state which is not a Member of the United Nations, if it is a party to a dispute under consideration by the Security Council, shall be invited to participate, without vote, in the discussion relating to the dispute. The Security Council shall lay down such conditions as it deems just for the participation of a state which is not a Member of the United Nations.

CHAPTER VI
PACIFIC SETTLEMENT OF DISPUTES

Article 33

1. The parties to any dispute, the continuance of which is likely to endanger the maintenance of international peace and security, shall, first of all, seek a solution by negotiation, enquiry, mediation, conciliation, arbitration, judicial settlement, resort to regional agencies or arrangements, or other peaceful means of their own choice.
2. The Security Council shall, when it deems necessary, call upon the parties to settle their dispute by such means.

Article 34

The Security Council may investigate any dispute, or any situation which might lead to international friction or give rise to a dispute, in order to determine whether the continuance of the dispute or situation is likely to endanger the maintenance of international peace and security.

Article 35

1. Any Member of the United Nations may bring any dispute, or any situation of the nature referred to in Article 34, to the attention of the Security Council or of the General Assembly.
2. A state which is not a Member of the United Nations may bring to the attention of the Security Council or of the General Assembly any dispute to which it is a party if it accepts in advance, for the purposes of the dispute, the obligations of pacific settlement provided in the present Charter.
3. The proceedings of the General Assembly in respect of matters brought to its attention under this Article will be subject to the provisions of Articles 11 and 12.

Article 36

1. The Security Council may, at any stage of a dispute of the nature referred to in Article 33 or of a situation of like nature, recommend appropriate procedures or methods of adjustment.

2. The Security Council should take into consideration any procedures for the settlement of the dispute which have already been adopted by the parties.

3. In making recommendations under this Article the Security Council should also take into consideration that legal disputes should as a general rule be referred by the parties to the International Court of Justice in accordance with the provisions of the Statute of the Court.

Article 37

1. Should the parties to a dispute of the nature referred to in Article 33 fail to settle it by the means indicated in that Article, they shall refer it to the Security Council.

2. If the Security Council deems that the continuance of the dispute is in fact likely to endanger the maintenance of international peace and security, it shall decide whether to take action under Article 36 or to recommend such terms of settlement as it may consider appropriate.

Article 38

Without prejudice to the provisions of Articles 33 to 37, the Security Council may, if all the parties to any dispute so request, make recommendations to the parties with a view to a pacific settlement of the dispute.

CHAPTER VII
ACTION WITH RESPECT TO THREATS TO THE PEACE, BREACHES OF THE PEACE,
AND ACTS OF AGGRESSION

Article 39

The Security Council shall determine the existence of any threat to the peace, breach of the peace, or act of aggression and shall make recommendations, or decide what measures shall be taken in accordance with Articles 41 and 42, to maintain or restore international peace and security.

Article 40

In order to prevent an aggravation of the situation, the Security Council may, before making the recommendations or deciding upon the measures provided for in Article 39, call upon the parties concerned to comply with such provisional measures as it deems necessary or desirable. Such provisional measures shall be without prejudice to the rights, claims, or position of the parties concerned. The Security Council shall duly take account of failure to comply with such provisional measures.

Article 41

The Security Council may decide what measures not involving the use of armed force are to be employed to give effect to its decisions, and it may call upon the Members of the United Nations to apply such measures. These may include complete or partial interruption of economic relations and of rail, sea, air, postal, telegraphic, radio, and other means of communication, and the severance of diplomatic relations.

Article 42

Should the Security Council consider that measures provided for in Article 41 would be inadequate or have proved to be inadequate, it may take such action by air, sea, or land forces as may be necessary to maintain or restore international peace and security. Such action may include demonstrations, blockade, and other operations by air, sea, or land forces of Members of the United Nations.

Article 43

1. All Members of the United Nations, in order to contribute to the maintenance of international peace and security, undertake to make available to the Security Council, on its call and in accordance with a special agreement or agreements, armed forces, assistance, and facilities, including rights of passage, necessary for the purpose of maintaining international peace and security.
2. Such agreement or agreements shall govern the numbers and types of forces, their degree of readiness and general location, and the nature of the facilities and assistance to be provided.
3. The agreement or agreements shall be negotiated as soon as possible on the initiative of the Security Council. They shall be concluded between the Security Council and Members or between the Security Council and groups of Members and shall be subject to ratification by the signatory states in accordance with their respective constitutional processes.

Article 44

When the Security Council has decided to use force it shall, before calling upon a Member not represented on it to provide armed forces in fulfillment of the obligations assumed under Article 43, invite that Member, if the Member so desires, to participate in the decisions of the Security Council concerning the employment of contingents of that Member's armed forces.

Article 45

In order to enable the United Nations to take urgent military measures Members shall hold immediately available national air-force contingents for combined international enforcement action. The strength and degree of readiness of these contingents and plans for their combined action shall be determined, within the limits laid down in the special agreement or agreements referred to in Article 43, by the Security Council with the assistance of the Military Staff Committee.

Article 46

Plans for the application of armed force shall be made by the Security Council with the assistance of the Military Staff Committee.

Article 47

1. There shall be established a Military Staff Committee to advise and assist the Security Council on all questions relating to the Security Council's military requirements for the maintenance of international peace and security, the employment and command of forces placed at its disposal, the regulation of armaments, and possible disarmament.
2. The Military Staff Committee shall consist of the Chiefs of Staff of the permanent members of the Security Council or their representatives. Any Member of the United Nations not permanently represented on the Committee shall be invited by the Committee to be associated with it when the efficient discharge of the Committee's responsibilities requires the participation of that Member in its work.
3. The Military Staff Committee shall be responsible under the Security Council for the strategic direction of any armed forces placed at the disposal of the Security Council. Questions relating to the command of such forces shall be worked out subsequently.
4. The Military Staff Committee, with the authorization of the Security Council and after consultation with appropriate regional agencies, may establish regional subcommittees.

Article 48

1. The action required to carry out the decisions of the Security Council for the maintenance of international peace and security shall be taken by all the Members of the United Nations or by some of them, as the Security Council may determine.
2. Such decisions shall be carried out by the Members of the United Nations directly and through their action in the appropriate international agencies of which they are members.

Article 49

The Members of the United Nations shall join in affording mutual assistance in carrying out the measures decided upon by the Security Council.

Article 50

If preventive or enforcement measures against any state are taken by the Security Council, any other state, whether a Member of the United Nations or not, which finds itself confronted with special economic problems arising from the carrying out of those measures shall have the right to consult the Security Council with regard to a solution of those problems.

Article 51

Nothing in the present Charter shall impair the inherent right of individual or collective self-defense if an armed attack occurs against a Member of the United Nations, until the Security Council has taken measures necessary to maintain international peace and security. Measures taken by Members in the exercise of this right of self-defense shall be immediately reported to the Security Council and shall not in any way affect the authority and responsibility of the Security Council under the present Charter to take at any time such action as it deems necessary in order to maintain or restore international peace and security.

CHAPTER VIII
REGIONAL ARRANGEMENTS

Article 52

1. Nothing in the present Charter precludes the existence of regional arrangements or agencies for dealing with such matters relating to the maintenance of international peace and security as are appropriate for regional action, provided that such arrangements or agencies and their activities are consistent with the Purposes and Principles of the United Nations.

2. The Members of the United Nations entering into such arrangements or constituting such agencies shall make every effort to achieve pacific settlement of local disputes through such regional arrangements or by such regional agencies before referring them to the Security Council.

3. The Security Council shall encourage the development of pacific settlement of local disputes through such regional arrangements or by such regional agencies either on the initiative of the states concerned or by reference from the Security Council.

4. This Article in no way impairs the application of Articles 34 and 35.

Article 53

1. The Security Council shall, where appropriate, utilize such regional arrangements or agencies for enforcement action under its authority. But no enforcement action shall be taken under regional arrangements or by regional agencies without the authorization of the Security Council, with the exception of measures against any enemy state, as defined in paragraph 2 of this Article, provided for pursuant to Article 107 or in regional arrangements directed against renewal of aggressive policy on the part of any such state, until such time as the Organization may, on request of the Governments concerned, be charged with the responsibility for preventing further aggression by such a state.

2. The term enemy state as used in paragraph 1 of this Article applies to any state which during the Second World War has been an enemy of any signatory of the present Charter.

Article 54

The Security Council shall at all times be kept fully informed of activities undertaken or in contemplation under regional arrangements or by regional agencies for the maintenance of international peace and security.

...

IN FAITH WHEREOF the representatives of the Governments of the United Nations have signed the present Charter.

DONE at the city of San Francisco the twenty-sixth day of June, one thousand nine hundred and forty-five.

Appendix B

Selected Provisions of the 2002 National Security Strategy of the United States of America

The great struggles of the twentieth century between liberty and totalitarianism ended with a decisive victory for the forces of freedom—and a single sustainable model for national success: freedom, democracy, and free enterprise. In the twenty-first century, only nations that share a commitment to protecting basic human rights and guaranteeing political and economic freedom will be able to unleash the potential of their people and assure their future prosperity. People everywhere want to be able to speak freely; choose who will govern them; worship as they please; educate their children—male and female; own property; and enjoy the benefits of their labor. These values of freedom are right and true for every person, in every society—and the duty of protecting these values against their enemies is the common calling of freedom-loving people across the globe and across the ages.

Today, the United States enjoys a position of unparalleled military strength and great economic and political influence. In keeping with our heritage and principles, we do not use our strength to press for unilateral advantage. We seek instead to create a balance of power that favors human freedom: conditions in which all nations and all societies can choose for themselves the rewards and challenges of political and economic liberty. In a world that is safe, people will be able to make their own lives better. We will defend the peace by fighting terrorists and tyrants. We will preserve the peace by building good relations among the great powers. We will extend the peace by encouraging free and open societies on every continent.

Defending our Nation against its enemies is the first and fundamental commitment of the Federal Government. Today, that task has changed dramatically. Enemies in the past needed great armies and great industrial capabilities to endanger America. Now, shadowy networks of individuals can bring great chaos and suffering to our shores for less than it costs to purchase a single tank. Terrorists are organized to penetrate open societies and to turn the power of modern technologies against us.

To defeat this threat we must make use of every tool in our arsenal—military power, better homeland defenses, law enforcement, intelligence, and vigorous efforts to cut off terrorist financing. The war against terrorists of global reach is a global enterprise of uncertain duration. America will help nations that need our assistance in combating terror. And America will hold to account nations that are compromised by terror, including those who harbor terrorists—because the allies of terror are the enemies of civilization. The United States and countries cooperating with us must not allow the terrorists to develop new home bases. Together, we will seek to deny them sanctuary at every turn.

The gravest danger our Nation faces lies at the crossroads of radicalism and technology. Our enemies have openly declared that they are seeking weapons of mass destruction, and evidence indicates that they are doing so with determination. The United States will not allow these efforts to succeed. We will build defenses against ballistic missiles and other means of delivery. We will cooperate with other nations to deny, contain, and curtail our enemies' efforts to acquire dangerous technologies. And, as a matter of common sense and self-defense, America will act against such emerging threats before they are fully formed. We cannot defend America and our friends by hoping for the best. So we must be prepared to defeat our enemies' plans, using the best intelligence and proceeding with deliberation. History will judge harshly those who saw this coming danger but failed to act. In the new world we have entered, the only path to peace and security is the path of action.

As we defend the peace, we will also take advantage of an historic opportunity to preserve the peace. Today, the international community has the best chance since the rise of the nation-state in the seventeenth century to build a world where great powers compete in peace instead of continually prepare for war. Today, the world's great powers find ourselves on the same side—united by common dangers of terrorist violence and chaos. The United States will build on these common interests to promote global security. We are also increasingly united by common values. Russia is in the midst of a hopeful transition, reaching for its democratic future and a partner in the war on terror. Chinese leaders are discovering that economic freedom is the only source of national wealth. In time, they will find that social and political freedom is the only source of national greatness. America will encourage the advancement of democracy and economic openness in both nations, because these are the best foundations for domestic stability and international order. We will strongly resist aggression from other great powers—even as we welcome their peaceful pursuit of prosperity, trade, and cultural advancement.

Finally, the United States will use this moment of opportunity to extend the benefits of freedom across the globe. We will actively work to bring the hope of democracy, development, free markets, and free trade to every corner of the world. The events of September 11, 2001, taught us that weak states, like Afghanistan, can pose as great a danger to our national interests as strong states. Poverty does not make poor people into terrorists and murderers. Yet poverty, weak institutions, and corruption can make weak states vulnerable to terrorist networks and drug cartels within their borders.

The United States will stand beside any nation determined to build a better future by seeking the rewards of liberty for its people. Free trade and free markets have proven their ability to lift whole societies out of poverty—so the United States will work with individual nations, entire regions, and the entire global trading community to build a world that trades in freedom and therefore grows in prosperity. The United States will deliver greater development assistance through the New Millennium Challenge Account to nations that govern justly, invest in their people, and encourage economic freedom. We will also continue to lead the world in efforts to reduce the terrible toll of HIV/AIDS and other infectious diseases.

In building a balance of power that favors freedom, the United States is guided by the conviction that all nations have important responsibilities. Nations that enjoy freedom must actively fight terror. Nations that depend on international stability must help prevent the spread of weapons of mass destruction. Nations that seek international aid must govern themselves wisely, so that aid is well spent. For freedom to thrive, accountability must be expected and required.

We are also guided by the conviction that no nation can build a safer, better world alone. Alliances and multilateral institutions can multiply the strength of freedom-loving nations. The United States is committed to lasting institutions like the United Nations, the World Trade Organization, the Organization of American States, and NATO as well as other long-standing alliances. Coalitions of the willing can augment these permanent institutions. In all cases, international obligations are to be taken seriously. They are not to be undertaken symbolically to rally support for an ideal without furthering its attainment.

Freedom is the non-negotiable demand of human dignity; the birthright of every person—in every civilization. Throughout history, freedom has been threatened by war and terror; it has been challenged by the clashing wills of powerful states and the evil designs of tyrants; and it has been tested by widespread poverty and disease. Today, humanity holds in its hands the opportunity to further freedom's triumph over all these foes. The United States welcomes our responsibility to lead in this great mission.

George W. Bush
THE WHITE HOUSE
September 17, 2002

I. Overview of America's International Strategy

Our Nation's cause has always been larger than our Nation's defense. We fight, as we always fight, for a just peace—a peace that favors liberty. We will defend the peace against the threats from terrorists and tyrants. We will preserve the peace by building good relations among the great powers. And we will extend the peace by encouraging free and open societies on every continent.

President Bush
West Point, New York
June 1, 2002

The United States possesses unprecedented—and unequaled—strength and influence in the world. Sustained by faith in the principles of liberty, and the value of a free society, this position comes with unparalleled responsibilities, obligations, and opportunity. The great strength of this nation must be used to promote a balance of power that favors freedom.

For most of the twentieth century, the world was divided by a great struggle over ideas: destructive totalitarian visions versus freedom and equality.

That great struggle is over. The militant visions of class, nation, and race which promised utopia and delivered misery have been defeated and discredited. America is now threatened less by conquering states than we are by failing ones. We are menaced less by fleets and armies than by catastrophic technologies in the hands of the embittered few. We must defeat these threats to our Nation, allies, and friends.

This is also a time of opportunity for America. We will work to translate this moment of influence into decades of peace, prosperity, and liberty. The U.S. national security strategy will be based on a distinctly American internationalism that reflects the union of our values and our national interests. The aim of this strategy is to help make the world not just safer but better. Our goals on the path to progress are clear: political and economic freedom, peaceful relations with other states, and respect for human dignity.

And this path is not America's alone. It is open to all. To achieve these goals, the United States will:

- champion aspirations for human dignity;
- strengthen alliances to defeat global terrorism and work to prevent attacks against us and our friends;
- work with others to defuse regional conflicts;
- prevent our enemies from threatening us, our allies, and our friends, with weapons of mass destruction;

- ignite a new era of global economic growth through free markets and free trade;
- expand the circle of development by opening societies and building the infrastructure of democracy;
- develop agendas for cooperative action with other main centers of global power; and
- transform America's national security institutions to meet the challenges and opportunities of the twenty-first century.

...

V. Prevent Our Enemies from Threatening Us, Our Allies, and Our Friends with Weapons of Mass Destruction

The gravest danger to freedom lies at the crossroads of radicalism and technology. When the spread of chemical and biological and nuclear weapons, along with ballistic missile technology—when that occurs, even weak states and small groups could attain a catastrophic power to strike great nations. Our enemies have declared this very intention, and have been caught seeking these terrible weapons. They want the capability to blackmail us, or to harm us, or to harm our friends—and we will oppose them with all our power.

President Bush
West Point, New York
June 1, 2002

The nature of the Cold War threat required the United States—with our allies and friends—to emphasize deterrence of the enemy's use of force, producing a grim strategy of mutual assured destruction. With the collapse of the Soviet Union and the end of the Cold War, our security environment has undergone profound transformation.

Having moved from confrontation to cooperation as the hallmark of our relationship with Russia, the dividends are evident: an end to the balance of terror that divided us; an historic reduction in the nuclear arsenals on both sides; and cooperation in areas such as counterterrorism and missile defense that until recently were inconceivable.

But new deadly challenges have emerged from rogue states and terrorists. None of these contemporary threats rival the sheer destructive power that was arrayed against us by the Soviet Union. However, the nature and motivations of these new adversaries, their determination to obtain destructive powers hitherto available only to the world's strongest states, and the greater likelihood that they will use weapons of mass destruction against us, make today's security environment more complex and dangerous.

In the 1990s we witnessed the emergence of a small number of rogue states that, while different in important ways, share a number of attributes. These states:

- brutalize their own people and squander their national resources for the personal gain of the rulers;
- display no regard for international law, threaten their neighbors, and callously violate international treaties to which they are party;
- are determined to acquire weapons of mass destruction, along with other advanced military technology, to be used as threats or offensively to achieve the aggressive designs of these regimes;
- sponsor terrorism around the globe; and
- reject basic human values and hate the United States and everything for which it stands.

At the time of the Gulf War, we acquired irrefutable proof that Iraq's designs were not limited to the chemical weapons it had used against Iran and its own people, but also extended to the acquisition of nuclear weapons and biological agents. In the past decade North Korea has become the world's principal purveyor of ballistic missiles, and has tested increasingly capable missiles while developing its own WMD arsenal. Other rogue regimes seek nuclear, biological, and chemical weapons as well. These states' pursuit of, and global trade in, such weapons has become a looming threat to all nations.

We must be prepared to stop rogue states and their terrorist clients before they are able to threaten or use weapons of mass destruction against the United States and our allies and friends. Our response must take full advantage of strengthened alliances, the establishment of new partnerships with former adversaries, innovation in the use of military forces, modern technologies, including the development of an effective missile defense system, and increased emphasis on intelligence collection and analysis.

Our comprehensive strategy to combat WMD includes:

- *Proactive counterproliferation efforts.* We must deter and defend against the threat before it is unleashed. We must ensure that key capabilities—detection, active and passive defenses, and counterforce capabilities—are integrated into our defense transformation and our homeland security systems. Counterproliferation must also be integrated into the doctrine, training, and equipping of our forces and those of our allies to ensure that we can prevail in any conflict with WMD-armed adversaries.
- *Strengthened nonproliferation efforts to prevent rogue states and terrorists from acquiring the materials, technologies, and expertise necessary for weapons of mass destruction.* We will enhance diplomacy, arms control, multilateral export controls, and threat reduction assistance that impede states and terrorists seeking WMD, and when necessary, interdict enabling technologies and materials. We will continue to build coalitions to support these efforts, encouraging their increased political and financial support for nonproliferation and threat reduction programs. The recent G-8 agreement to commit up to $20 billion to a global partnership against proliferation marks a major step forward.

- *Effective consequence management to respond to the effects of WMD use, whether by terrorists or hostile states.* Minimizing the effects of WMD use against our people will help deter those who possess such weapons and dissuade those who seek to acquire them by persuading enemies that they cannot attain their desired ends. The United States must also be prepared to respond to the effects of WMD use against our forces abroad, and to help friends and allies if they are attacked.

It has taken almost a decade for us to comprehend the true nature of this new threat. Given the goals of rogue states and terrorists, the United States can no longer solely rely on a reactive posture as we have in the past. The inability to deter a potential attacker, the immediacy of today's threats, and the magnitude of potential harm that could be caused by our adversaries' choice of weapons, do not permit that option. We cannot let our enemies strike first.

In the Cold War, especially following the Cuban missile crisis, we faced a generally status quo, risk-averse adversary. Deterrence was an effective defense. But deterrence based only upon the threat of retaliation is less likely to work against leaders of rogue states more willing to take risks, gambling with the lives of their people, and the wealth of their nations.

- In the Cold War, weapons of mass destruction were considered weapons of last resort whose use risked the destruction of those who used them. Today, our enemies see weapons of mass destruction as weapons of choice. For rogue states these weapons are tools of intimidation and military aggression against their neighbors. These weapons may also allow these states to attempt to blackmail the United States and our allies to prevent us from deterring or repelling the aggressive behavior of rogue states. Such states also see these weapons as their best means of overcoming the conventional superiority of the United States.
- Traditional concepts of deterrence will not work against a terrorist enemy whose avowed tactics are wanton destruction and the targeting of innocents; whose so-called soldiers seek martyrdom in death and whose most potent protection is statelessness. The overlap between states that sponsor terror and those that pursue WMD compels us to action.

For centuries, international law recognized that nations need not suffer an attack before they can lawfully take action to defend themselves against forces that present an imminent danger of attack. Legal scholars and international jurists often conditioned the legitimacy of preemption on the existence of an imminent threat—most often a visible mobilization of armies, navies, and air forces preparing to attack.

We must adapt the concept of imminent threat to the capabilities and objectives of today's adversaries. Rogue states and terrorists do not seek to attack us using conventional means. They know such attacks would fail. Instead, they rely on acts of terror and, potentially, the use of weapons of mass destruction—weapons that can be easily concealed, delivered covertly, and used without warning.

The targets of these attacks are our military forces and our civilian population, in direct violation of one of the principal norms of the law of warfare. As was demonstrated by the losses on September 11, 2001, mass civilian casualties is the specific objective of terrorists and these losses would be exponentially more severe if terrorists acquired and used weapons of mass destruction.

The United States has long maintained the option of preemptive actions to counter a sufficient threat to our national security. The greater the threat, the greater is the risk of inaction—and the more compelling the case for taking anticipatory action to defend ourselves, even if uncertainty remains as to the time and place of the enemy's attack. To forestall or prevent such hostile acts by our adversaries, the United States will, if necessary, act preemptively.

The United States will not use force in all cases to preempt emerging threats, nor should nations use preemption as a pretext for aggression. Yet in an age where the enemies of civilization openly and actively seek the world's most destructive technologies, the United States cannot remain idle while dangers gather. We will always proceed deliberately, weighing the consequences of our actions. To support preemptive options, we will:

- build better, more integrated intelligence capabilities to provide timely, accurate information on threats, wherever they may emerge;
- coordinate closely with allies to form a common assessment of the most dangerous threats; and
- continue to transform our military forces to ensure our ability to conduct rapid and precise operations to achieve decisive results.

The purpose of our actions will always be to eliminate a specific threat to the United States or our allies and friends. The reasons for our actions will be clear, the force measured, and the cause just.

Appendix C

War Powers Resolution

Public Law 93-148, 93rd Congress, H. J. Res. 542, November 7, 1973

Joint Resolution

Concerning the war powers of Congress and the President.

Resolved by the Senate and the House of Representatives of the United States of America in Congress assembled,

...

PURPOSE AND POLICY

SEC. 2.

(a) It is the purpose of this joint resolution to fulfill the intent of the framers of the Constitution of the United States and insure [sic] that the collective judgement of both the Congress and the President will apply to the introduction of United States Armed Forces into hostilities, or into situations where imminent involvement in hostilities is clearly indicated by the circumstances, and to the continued use of such forces in hostilities or in such situations.
(b) Under article I, section 8, of the Constitution, it is specifically provided that the Congress shall have the power to make all laws necessary and proper for carrying into execution, not only its own powers but also all other powers vested by the Constitution in the Government of the United States, or in any department or officer thereof.
(c) The constitutional powers of the President as Commander-in-Chief to introduce United States Armed Forces into hostilities, or into situations where imminent involvement in hostilities is clearly indicated by the circumstances, are exercised only pursuant to (1) a declaration of war, (2) specific statutory authorization, or (3) a national emergency created by attack upon the United States, its territories or possessions, or its armed forces.

CONSULTATION

SEC. 3.

The President in every possible instance shall consult with Congress before introducing United States Armed Forces into hostilities or into situation where imminent involvement in hostilities is clearly indicated by the circumstances, and after every such introduction shall consult regularly with the Congress until United States Armed Forces are no longer engaged in hostilities or have been removed from such situations.

REPORTING

SEC. 4.

(a) In the absence of a declaration of war, in any case in which United States Armed Forces are introduced—

(1) into hostilities or into situations where imminent involvement in hostilities is clearly indicated by the circumstances;

(2) into the territory, airspace or waters of a foreign nation, while equipped for combat, except for deployments which relate solely to supply, replacement, repair, or training of such forces; or

(3) in numbers which substantially enlarge United States Armed Forces equipped for combat already located in a foreign nation; the President shall submit within 48 hours to the Speaker of the House of Representatives and to the President pro tempore of the Senate a report, in writing, setting forth—

(A) the circumstances necessitating the introduction of United States Armed Forces;

(B) the constitutional and legislative authority under which such introduction took place; and

(C) the estimated scope and duration of the hostilities or involvement.

(b) The President shall provide such other information as the Congress may request in the fulfillment of its constitutional responsibilities with respect to committing the Nation to war and to the use of United States Armed Forces abroad

(c) Whenever United States Armed Forces are introduced into hostilities or into any situation described in sub section (a) of this section, the President shall, so long as such armed forces continue to be engaged in such hostilities or situation, report to the Congress periodically on the status of such hostilities or situation as well as on the scope and duration of such hostilities or situation, but in no event shall he report to the Congress less often than once every six months.

CONGRESSIONAL ACTION

SEC. 5.

(a) Each report submitted pursuant to section 4(a)(1) shall be transmitted to the Speaker of the House of Representatives and to the President pro tempore of the Senate on the same calendar day. Each report so transmitted shall be referred to the Committee on Foreign Affairs of the House of Representatives and to the Committee on Foreign Relations of the Senate for appropriate action. If, when the report is transmitted, the Congress has adjourned sine die or has adjourned for any period in excess of three calendar days, the Speaker of the House of Representatives and the President pro tempore of the Senate, if they deem it advisable (or if petitioned by at least 30 percent of the membership of their respective

Houses) shall jointly request the President to convene Congress in order that it may consider the report and take appropriate action pursuant to this section.

(b) Within sixty calendar days after a report is submitted or is required to be submitted pursuant to section 4(a)(1), whichever is earlier, the President shall terminate any use of United States Armed Forces with respect to which such report was submitted (or required to be submitted), unless the Congress

    (1) has declared war or has enacted a specific authorization for such use of United States Armed Forces,

    (2) has extended by law such sixty-day period, or

    (3) is physically unable to meet as a result of an armed attack upon the United States. Such sixty-day period shall be extended for not more than an additional thirty days if the President determines and certifies to the Congress in writing that unavoidable military necessity respecting the safety of United States Armed Forces requires the continued use of such armed forces in the course of bringing about a prompt removal of such forces.

(c) Notwithstanding subsection (b), at any time that United States Armed Forces are engaged in hostilities outside the territory of the United States, its possessions and territories without a declaration of war or specific statutory authorization, such forces shall be removed by the President if the Congress so directs by concurrent resolution.

CONGRESSIONAL PRIORITY PROCEDURES FOR JOINT RESOLUTION OR BILL

SEC. 6.

(a) Any joint resolution or bill introduced pursuant to section 5(b) at least thirty calendar days before the expiration of the sixty-day period specified in such section shall be referred to the Committee on Foreign Affairs of the House of Representatives or the Committee on Foreign Relations of the Senate, as the case may be, and such committee shall report one such joint resolution or bill, together with its recommendations, not later than twenty-four calendar days before the expiration of the sixty-day period specified in such section, unless such House shall otherwise determine by the yeas and nays.

(b) Any joint resolution or bill so reported shall become the pending business of the House in question (in the case of the Senate the time for debate shall be equally divided between the proponents and the opponents), and shall be voted on within three calendar days thereafter, unless such House shall otherwise determine by yeas and nays.

(c) Such a joint resolution or bill passed by one House shall be referred to the committee of the other House named in subsection (a) and shall be reported out not later than fourteen calendar days before the expiration of the sixty-day period specified in section 5(b). The joint resolution or bill so reported shall become the pending business of the House in question and shall be voted on within three calendar days after it has been reported, unless such House shall otherwise determine by yeas and nays.

(d) In the case of any disagreement between the two Houses of Congress with respect to a joint resolution or bill passed by both Houses, conferees shall be promptly appointed and the committee of conference shall make and file a report with respect to such resolution or bill not later than four calendar days before the expiration of the sixty-day period specified in section 5(b). In the event the conferees are unable to agree within 48 hours, they shall report back to their respective Houses in disagreement. Notwithstanding any rule in either House concerning the printing of conference reports in the Record or concerning any delay in the consideration of such reports, such report shall be acted on by both Houses not later than the expiration of such sixty-day period.

CONGRESSIONAL PRIORITY PROCEDURES FOR CONCURRENT RESOLUTION

SEC. 7.

(a) Any concurrent resolution introduced pursuant to section 5(b) at least thirty calendar days before the expiration of the sixty-day period specified in such section shall be referred to the Committee on Foreign Affairs of the House of Representatives or the Committee on Foreign Relations of the Senate, as the case may be, and one such concurrent resolution shall be reported out by such committee together with its recommendations within fifteen calendar days, unless such House shall otherwise determine by the yeas and nays.

(b) Any concurrent resolution so reported shall become the pending business of the House in question (in the case of the Senate the time for debate shall be equally divided between the proponents and the opponents), and shall be voted on within three calendar days thereafter, unless such House shall otherwise determine by yeas and nays.

(c) Such a concurrent resolution passed by one House shall be referred to the committee of the other House named in subsection (a) and shall be reported out by such committee together with its recommendations within fifteen calendar days and shall thereupon become the pending business of such House and shall be voted on within three calendar days after it has been reported, unless such House shall otherwise determine by yeas and nays.

(d) In the case of any disagreement between the two Houses of Congress with respect to a concurrent resolution passed by both Houses, conferees shall be promptly appointed and the committee of conference shall make and file a report with respect to such concurrent resolution within six calendar days after the legislation is referred to the committee of conference. Notwithstanding any rule in either House concerning the printing of conference reports in the Record or concerning any delay in the consideration of such reports, such report shall be acted on by both Houses not later than six calendar days after the conference report is filed. In the event the conferees are unable to agree within 48 hours, they shall report back to their respective Houses in disagreement.

INTERPRETATION OF JOINT RESOLUTION

SEC. 8.

(a) Authority to introduce United States Armed Forces into hostilities or into situations wherein involvement in hostilities is clearly indicated by the circumstances shall not be inferred—

(1) from any provision of law (whether or not in effect before the date of the enactment of this joint resolution), including any provision contained in any appropriation Act, unless such provision specifically authorizes the introduction of United States Armed

Forces into hostilities or into such situations and stating that it is intended to constitute specific statutory authorization within the meaning of this joint resolution; or

(2) from any treaty heretofore or hereafter ratified unless such treaty is implemented by legislation specifically authorizing the introduction of United States Armed Forces into hostilities or into such situations and stating that it is intended to constitute specific statutory authorization within the meaning of this joint resolution.

(b) Nothing in this joint resolution shall be construed to require any further specific statutory authorization to permit members of United States Armed Forces to participate jointly with members of the armed forces of one or more foreign countries in the headquarters operations of high-level military commands which were established prior to the date of enactment of this joint resolution and pursuant to the United Nations Charter or any treaty ratified by the United States prior to such date.

(c) For purposes of this joint resolution, the term "introduction of United States Armed Forces" includes the assignment of member of such armed forces to command, coordinate, participate in the movement of, or accompany the regular or irregular military forces of any foreign country or government when such military forces are engaged, or there exists an imminent threat that such forces will become engaged, in hostilities.

(d) Nothing in this joint resolution—

(1) is intended to alter the constitutional authority of the Congress or of the President, or the provision of existing treaties; or

(2) shall be construed as granting any authority to the President with respect to the introduction of United States Armed Forces into hostilities or into situations wherein involvement in hostilities is clearly indicated by the circumstances which authority he would not have had in the absence of this joint resolution.

SEPARABILITY CLAUSE

SEC. 9.

If any provision of this joint resolution or the application thereof to any person or circumstance is held invalid, the remainder of the joint resolution and the application of such provision to any other person or circumstance shall not be affected thereby.

EFFECTIVE DATE

SEC. 10.

This joint resolution shall take effect on the date of its enactment.

Appendix D

The United States Constitution (Selected Provisions)

We the People of the United States, in Order to form a more perfect Union, establish Justice, insure domestic Tranquility, provide for the common defence, promote the general Welfare, and secure the Blessings of Liberty to ourselves and our Posterity, do ordain and establish this Constitution for the United States of America.

Article I

Section 1

All legislative Powers herein granted shall be vested in a Congress of the United States, which shall consist of a Senate and House of Representatives.

…

Section 8

Clause 1: The Congress shall have Power To lay and collect Taxes, Duties, Imposts and Excises, to pay the Debts and provide for the common Defence and general Welfare of the United States; but all Duties, Imposts and Excises shall be uniform throughout the United States;

Clause 2: To borrow Money on the credit of the United States;

Clause 3: To regulate Commerce with foreign Nations, and among the several States, and with the Indian Tribes;

Clause 4: To establish an uniform Rule of Naturalization, and uniform Laws on the subject of Bankruptcies throughout the United States;

Clause 5: To coin Money, regulate the Value thereof, and of foreign Coin, and fix the Standard of Weights and Measures;

Clause 6: To provide for the Punishment of counterfeiting the Securities and current Coin of the United States;

Clause 7: To establish Post Offices and post Roads;

Clause 8: To promote the Progress of Science and useful Arts, by securing for limited Times to Authors and Inventors the exclusive Right to their respective Writings and Discoveries;

Clause 9: To constitute Tribunals inferior to the supreme Court;

Clause 10: To define and punish Piracies and Felonies committed on the high Seas, and Offences against the Law of Nations;

Clause 11: To declare War, grant Letters of Marque and Reprisal, and make Rules concerning Captures on Land and Water;

Clause 12: To raise and support Armies, but no Appropriation of Money to that Use shall be for a longer Term than two Years;

Clause 13: To provide and maintain a Navy;

Clause 14: To make Rules for the Government and Regulation of the land and naval Forces;

Clause 15: To provide for calling forth the Militia to execute the Laws of the Union, suppress Insurrections and repel Invasions;

Clause 16: To provide for organizing, arming, and disciplining, the Militia, and for governing such Part of them as may be employed in the Service of the United States, reserving to the States respectively, the Appointment of the Officers, and the Authority of training the Militia according to the discipline prescribed by Congress;

Clause 17: To exercise exclusive Legislation in all Cases whatsoever, over such District (not exceeding ten Miles square) as may, by Cession of particular States, and the Acceptance of Congress, become the Seat of the Government of the United States, and to exercise like Authority over all Places purchased by the Consent of the Legislature of the State in which the Same shall be, for the Erection of Forts, Magazines, Arsenals, Dock-Yards, and other needful Buildings;—And

Clause 18: To make all Laws which shall be necessary and proper for carrying into Execution the foregoing Powers, and all other Powers vested by this Constitution in the Government of the United States, or in any Department or Officer thereof.

...

Article II

Section 1

Clause 1: The executive Power shall be vested in a President of the United States of America. He shall hold his Office during the Term of four Years, and, together with the Vice President, chosen for the same Term, be elected, as follows

...

Section 2

Clause 1: The President shall be Commander in Chief of the Army and Navy of the United States, and of the Militia of the several States, when called into the actual Service of the United States; he may require the Opinion, in writing, of the principal Officer in each of the executive Departments, upon any Subject relating to the Duties of their respective Offices, and he shall have Power to grant Reprieves and Pardons for Offences against the United States, except in Cases of Impeachment.

Clause 2: He shall have Power, by and with the Advice and Consent of the Senate, to make Treaties, provided two thirds of the Senators present concur; and he shall nominate, and by and with the Advice and Consent of the Senate, shall appoint Ambassadors, other public Ministers and Consuls, Judges of the supreme Court, and all other Officers of the United States, whose Appointments are not herein otherwise provided for, and which shall be established by Law: but the Congress may by Law vest the Appointment of such inferior Officers, as they think proper, in the President alone, in the Courts of Law, or in the Heads of Departments.

...

GO. WASHINGTON—President and deputy from Virginia

[Signed also by the deputies of twelve States.]

Appendix E

Universal Declaration of Human Rights

PREAMBLE

Whereas recognition of the inherent dignity and of the equal and inalienable rights of all members of the human family is the foundation of freedom, justice and peace in the world,

Whereas disregard and contempt for human rights have resulted in barbarous acts which have outraged the conscience of mankind, and the advent of a world in which human beings shall enjoy freedom of speech and belief and freedom from fear and want has been proclaimed as the highest aspiration of the common people,

Whereas it is essential, if man is not to be compelled to have recourse, as a last resort, to rebellion against tyranny and oppression, that human rights should be protected by the rule of law,

Whereas it is essential to promote the development of friendly relations between nations,

Whereas the peoples of the United Nations have in the Charter reaffirmed their faith in fundamental human rights, in the dignity and worth of the human person and in the equal rights of men and women and have determined to promote social progress and better standards of life in larger freedom,

Whereas Member States have pledged themselves to achieve, in cooperation with the United Nations, the promotion of universal respect for and observance of human rights and fundamental freedoms,

Whereas a common understanding of these rights and freedoms is of the greatest importance for the full realization of this pledge,

Now, therefore,

The General Assembly,

Proclaims this Universal Declaration of Human Rights as a common standard of achievement for all peoples and all nations, to the end that every individual and every organ of society, keeping this Declaration constantly in mind, shall strive by teaching and education to promote respect for these rights and freedoms and by progressive measures, national and international, to secure their universal and effective recognition and observance, both among the peoples of Member States themselves and among the peoples of territories under their jurisdiction.

Article 1

All human beings are born free and equal in dignity and rights. They are endowed with reason and conscience and should act towards one another in a spirit of brotherhood.

Article 2

Everyone is entitled to all the rights and freedoms set forth in this Declaration, without distinction of any kind, such as race, colour, sex, language, religion, political or other opinion, national or social origin, property, birth or other status.
Furthermore, no distinction shall be made on the basis of the political, jurisdictional or international status of the country or territory to which a person belongs, whether it be independent, trust, non-self-governing or under any other limitation of sovereignty.

Article 3

Everyone has the right to life, liberty and security of person.

Article 4

No one shall be held in slavery or servitude; slavery and the slave trade shall be prohibited in all their forms.

Article 5

No one shall be subjected to torture or to cruel, inhuman or degrading treatment or punishment.

Article 6

Everyone has the right to recognition everywhere as a person before the law.

Article 7

All are equal before the law and are entitled without any discrimination to equal protection of the law. All are entitled to equal protection against any discrimination in violation of this Declaration and against any incitement to such discrimination.

Article 8

Everyone has the right to an effective remedy by the competent national tribunals for acts violating the fundamental rights granted him by the constitution or by law.

Article 9

No one shall be subjected to arbitrary arrest, detention or exile.

Article 10

Everyone is entitled in full equality to a fair and public hearing by an independent and impartial tribunal, in the determination of his rights and obligations and of any criminal charge against him.

Article 11

1. Everyone charged with a penal offence has the right to be presumed innocent until proved guilty according to law in a public trial at which he has had all the guarantees necessary for his defence.

2. No one shall be held guilty of any penal offence on account of any act or omission which did not constitute a penal offence, under national or international law, at the time when it was committed. Nor shall a heavier penalty be imposed than the one that was applicable at the time the penal offence was committed.

Article 12

No one shall be subjected to arbitrary interference with his privacy, family, home or correspondence, nor to attacks upon his honour and reputation. Everyone has the right to the protection of the law against such interference or attacks.

Article 13

1. Everyone has the right to freedom of movement and residence within the borders of each State.

2. Everyone has the right to leave any country, including his own, and to return to his country.

Article 14

1. Everyone has the right to seek and to enjoy in other countries asylum from persecution.

2. This right may not be invoked in the case of prosecutions genuinely arising from non-political crimes or from acts contrary to the purposes and principles of the United Nations.

Article 15

1. Everyone has the right to a nationality.

2. No one shall be arbitrarily deprived of his nationality nor denied the right to change his nationality.

Article 16

1. Men and women of full age, without any limitation due to race, nationality or religion, have the right to marry and to found a family. They are entitled to equal rights as to marriage, during marriage and at its dissolution.

2. Marriage shall be entered into only with the free and full consent of the intending spouses.

3. The family is the natural and fundamental group unit of society and is entitled to protection by society and the State.

Article 17

1. Everyone has the right to own property alone as well as in association with others.

2. No one shall be arbitrarily deprived of his property.

Article 18

Everyone has the right to freedom of thought, conscience and religion; this right includes freedom to change his religion or belief, and freedom, either alone or in community with others and in public or private, to manifest his religion or belief in teaching, practice, worship and observance.

Article 19

Everyone has the right to freedom of opinion and expression; this right includes freedom to hold opinions without interference and to seek, receive and impart information and ideas through any media and regardless of frontiers.

Article 20

1. Everyone has the right to freedom of peaceful assembly and association.

2. No one may be compelled to belong to an association.

Article 21

1. Everyone has the right to take part in the government of his country, directly or through freely chosen representatives.

2. Everyone has the right to equal access to public service in his country.

3. The will of the people shall be the basis of the authority of government; this will shall be expressed in periodic and genuine elections which shall be by universal and equal suffrage and shall be held by secret vote or by equivalent free voting procedures.

Article 22

Everyone, as a member of society, has the right to social security and is entitled to realization, through national effort and international co-operation and in accordance with the organization and resources of each State, of the economic, social and cultural rights indispensable for his dignity and the free development of his personality.

Article 23

1. Everyone has the right to work, to free choice of employment, to just and favourable conditions of work and to protection against unemployment.

2. Everyone, without any discrimination, has the right to equal pay for equal work.

3. Everyone who works has the right to just and favourable remuneration ensuring for himself and his family an existence worthy of human dignity, and supplemented, if necessary, by other means of social protection.

4. Everyone has the right to form and to join trade unions for the protection of his interests.

Article 24

Everyone has the right to rest and leisure, including reasonable limitation of working hours and periodic holidays with pay.

Article 25

1. Everyone has the right to a standard of living adequate for the health and well-being of himself and of his family, including food, clothing, housing and medical care and necessary social services, and the right to security in the event of unemployment, sickness, disability, widowhood, old age or other lack of livelihood in circumstances beyond his control.

2. Motherhood and childhood are entitled to special care and assistance. All children, whether born in or out of wedlock, shall enjoy the same social protection.

Article 26

1. Everyone has the right to education. Education shall be free, at least in the elementary and fundamental stages. Elementary education shall be compulsory. Technical and professional education shall be made generally available and higher education shall be equally accessible to all on the basis of merit.

2. Education shall be directed to the full development of the human personality and to the strengthening of respect for human rights and fundamental freedoms. It shall promote understanding, tolerance and friendship among all nations, racial or religious groups, and shall further the activities of the United Nations for the maintenance of peace.

3. Parents have a prior right to choose the kind of education that shall be given to their children.

Article 27

1. Everyone has the right freely to participate in the cultural life of the community, to enjoy the arts and to share in scientific advancement and its benefits.

2. Everyone has the right to the protection of the moral and material interests resulting from any scientific, literary or artistic production of which he is the author.

Article 28

Everyone is entitled to a social and international order in which the rights and freedoms set forth in this Declaration can be fully realized.

Article 29

1. Everyone has duties to the community in which alone the free and full development of his personality is possible.

2. In the exercise of his rights and freedoms, everyone shall be subject only to such limitations as are determined by law solely for the purpose of securing due recognition and respect for the rights and freedoms of others and of meeting the just requirements of morality, public order and the general welfare in a democratic society.

3. These rights and freedoms may in no case be exercised contrary to the purposes and principles of the United Nations.

Article 30

Nothing in this Declaration may be interpreted as implying for any State, group or person any right to engage in any activity or to perform any act aimed at the destruction of any of the rights and freedoms set forth herein.

Appendix F

International Covenant on Civil and Political Rights

Adopted and opened for signature, ratification and accession by General Assembly resolution 2200A (XXI) of 16 December 1966.

Entry into force 23 March 1976, in accordance with Article 49

PREAMBLE

The States Parties to the present Covenant,

Considering that, in accordance with the principles proclaimed in the Charter of the United Nations, recognition of the inherent dignity and of the equal and inalienable rights of all members of the human family is the foundation of freedom, justice and peace in the world,

Recognizing that these rights derive from the inherent dignity of the human person,

Recognizing that, in accordance with the Universal Declaration of Human Rights, the ideal of free human beings enjoying civil and political freedom and freedom from fear and want can only be achieved if conditions are created whereby everyone may enjoy his civil and political rights, as well as his economic, social and cultural rights,

Considering the obligation of States under the Charter of the United Nations to promote universal respect for, and observance of, human rights and freedoms,

Realizing that the individual, having duties to other individuals and to the community to which he belongs, is under a responsibility to strive for the promotion and observance of the rights recognized in the present Covenant,

Agree upon the following articles:

Part I

Article 1

1. All peoples have the right of self-determination. By virtue of that right they freely determine their political status and freely pursue their economic, social and cultural development.

2. All peoples may, for their own ends, freely dispose of their natural wealth and resources without prejudice to any obligations arising out of international economic co-operation, based upon the principle of mutual benefit, and international law. In no case may a people be deprived of its own means of subsistence.

3. The States Parties to the present Covenant, including those having responsibility for the administration of Non-Self-Governing and Trust Territories, shall promote the realization of the right of self-determination, and shall respect that right, in conformity with the provisions of the Charter of the United Nations.

Part II

Article 2

1. Each State Party to the present Covenant undertakes to respect and to ensure to all individuals within its territory and subject to its jurisdiction the rights recognized in the present Covenant, without distinction of any kind, such as race, colour, sex, language, religion, political or other opinion, national or social origin, property, birth or other status.

2. Where not already provided for by existing legislative or other measures, each State Party to the present Covenant undertakes to take the necessary steps, in accordance with its constitutional processes and with the provisions of the present Covenant, to adopt such laws or other measures as may be necessary to give effect to the rights recognized in the present Covenant.

3. Each State Party to the present Covenant undertakes:

    (a) To ensure that any person whose rights or freedoms as herein recognized are violated shall have an effective remedy, notwithstanding that the violation has been committed by persons acting in an official capacity;

    (b) To ensure that any person claiming such a remedy shall have his right thereto determined by competent judicial, administrative or legislative authorities, or by any other competent authority provided for by the legal system of the State, and to develop the possibilities of judicial remedy;

    (c) To ensure that the competent authorities shall enforce such remedies when granted.

Article 3

The States Parties to the present Covenant undertake to ensure the equal right of men and women to the enjoyment of all civil and political rights set forth in the present Covenant.

Article 4

1. In time of public emergency which threatens the life of the nation and the existence of which is officially proclaimed, the States Parties to the present Covenant may take measures derogating from their obligations under the present Covenant to the extent strictly required by the exigencies of the situation, provided that such measures are not inconsistent with their other obligations under international law and do not involve discrimination solely on the ground of race, colour, sex, language, religion or social origin.

2. No derogation from articles 6, 7, 8 (paragraphs I and 2), 11, 15, 16 and 18 may be made under this provision.

3. Any State Party to the present Covenant availing itself of the right of derogation shall immediately inform the other States Parties to the present Covenant, through the intermediary of the Secretary-General of the United Nations, of the provisions from which it has derogated and of the reasons by which it was actuated. A further communication shall be made, through the same intermediary, on the date on which it terminates such derogation.

Article 5

1. Nothing in the present Covenant may be interpreted as implying for any State, group or person any right to engage in any activity or perform any act aimed at the destruction of any of the rights and freedoms recognized herein or at their limitation to a greater extent than is provided for in the present Covenant.

2. There shall be no restriction upon or derogation from any of the fundamental human rights recognized or existing in any State Party to the present Covenant pursuant to law, conventions, regulations or custom on the pretext that the present Covenant does not recognize such rights or that it recognizes them to a lesser extent.

Part III

Article 6

1. Every human being has the inherent right to life. This right shall be protected by law. No one shall be arbitrarily deprived of his life.

2. In countries which have not abolished the death penalty, sentence of death may be imposed only for the most serious crimes in accordance with the law in force at the time of the commission of the crime and not contrary to the provisions of the present Covenant and to the Convention on the Prevention and Punishment of the Crime of Genocide. This penalty can only be carried out pursuant to a final judgement rendered by a competent court.

3. When deprivation of life constitutes the crime of genocide, it is understood that nothing in this article shall authorize any State Party to the present Covenant to derogate in any way from any obligation assumed under the provisions of the Convention on the Prevention and Punishment of the Crime of Genocide.

4. Anyone sentenced to death shall have the right to seek pardon or commutation of the sentence. Amnesty, pardon or commutation of the sentence of death may be granted in all cases.

5. Sentence of death shall not be imposed for crimes committed by persons below eighteen years of age and shall not be carried out on pregnant women.

6. Nothing in this article shall be invoked to delay or to prevent the abolition of capital punishment by any State Party to the present Covenant.

Article 7

No one shall be subjected to torture or to cruel, inhuman or degrading treatment or punishment. In particular, no one shall be subjected without his free consent to medical or scientific experimentation.

Article 8

1. No one shall be held in slavery; slavery and the slave-trade in all their forms shall be prohibited.

2. No one shall be held in servitude.

3. (a) No one shall be required to perform forced or compulsory labour;

   (b) Paragraph 3(a) shall not be held to preclude, in countries where imprisonment with hard labour may be imposed as a punishment for a crime, the performance of hard labour in pursuance of a sentence to such punishment by a competent court;

   (c) For the purpose of this paragraph the term "forced or compulsory labour" shall not include:

   (i) Any work or service, not referred to in subparagraph (b), normally required of a person who is under detention in consequence of a lawful order of a court, or of a person during conditional release from such detention;

   (ii) Any service of a military character and, in countries where conscientious objection is recognized, any national service required by law of conscientious objectors;

   (iii) Any service exacted in cases of emergency or calamity threatening the life or well-being of the community;

   (iv) Any work or service which forms part of normal civil obligations.

Article 9

1. Everyone has the right to liberty and security of person. No one shall be subjected to arbitrary arrest or detention. No one shall be deprived of his liberty except on such grounds and in accordance with such procedure as are established by law.

2. Anyone who is arrested shall be informed, at the time of arrest, of the reasons for his arrest and shall be promptly informed of any charges against him.

3. Anyone arrested or detained on a criminal charge shall be brought promptly before a judge or other officer authorized by law to exercise judicial power and shall be entitled to trial within a reasonable time or to release. It shall not be the general rule that persons awaiting trial shall be detained in custody, but release may be subject to guarantees to appear for trial, at any other stage of the judicial proceedings, and, should occasion arise, for execution of the judgement.

4. Anyone who is deprived of his liberty by arrest or detention shall be entitled to take proceedings before a court, in order that court may decide without delay on the lawfulness of his detention and order his release if the detention is not lawful.

5. Anyone who has been the victim of unlawful arrest or detention shall have an enforceable right to compensation.

Article 10

1. All persons deprived of their liberty shall be treated with humanity and with respect for the inherent dignity of the human person.

2. (a) Accused persons shall, save in exceptional circumstances, be segregated from convicted persons and shall be subject to separate treatment appropriate to their status as unconvicted persons;

(b) Accused juvenile persons shall be separated from adults and brought as speedily as possible for adjudication.

3. The penitentiary system shall comprise treatment of prisoners the essential aim of which shall be their reformation and social rehabilitation. Juvenile offenders shall be segregated from adults and be accorded treatment appropriate to their age and legal status.

Article 11

No one shall be imprisoned merely on the ground of inability to fulfil a contractual obligation.

Article 12

1. Everyone lawfully within the territory of a State shall, within that territory, have the right to liberty of movement and freedom to choose his residence.

2. Everyone shall be free to leave any country, including his own.

3. The above-mentioned rights shall not be subject to any restrictions except those which are provided by law, are necessary to protect national security, public order (ordre public), public health or morals or the rights and freedoms of others, and are consistent with the other rights recognized in the present Covenant.

4. No one shall be arbitrarily deprived of the right to enter his own country.

Article 13

An alien lawfully in the territory of a State Party to the present Covenant may be expelled therefrom only in pursuance of a decision reached in accordance with law and shall, except where compelling reasons of national security otherwise require, be allowed to submit the reasons against his expulsion and to have his case reviewed by, and be represented for the purpose before, the competent authority or a person or persons especially designated by the competent authority.

Article 14

1. All persons shall be equal before the courts and tribunals. In the determination of any criminal charge against him, or of his rights and obligations in a suit at law, everyone shall be entitled to a fair and public hearing by a competent, independent and impartial tribunal established by law. The press and the public may be excluded from all or part of a trial for reasons of morals, public order (ordre public) or national security in a democratic society, or when the interest of the private lives of the parties so requires, or to the extent strictly necessary in the opinion of the court in special circumstances where publicity would prejudice the interests of justice; but any judgement rendered in a criminal case or in a suit at law shall be made public except where the interest of juvenile persons otherwise requires or the proceedings concern matrimonial disputes or the guardianship of children.

2. Everyone charged with a criminal offence shall have the right to be presumed innocent until proved guilty according to law.

3. In the determination of any criminal charge against him, everyone shall be entitled to the following minimum guarantees, in full equality:
    (a) To be informed promptly and in detail in a language which he understands of the nature and cause of the charge against him;
    (b) To have adequate time and facilities for the preparation of his defence and to communicate with counsel of his own choosing;
    (c) To be tried without undue delay;
    (d) To be tried in his presence, and to defend himself in person or through legal assistance of his own choosing; to be informed, if he does not have legal assistance, of this right; and to have legal assistance assigned to him, in any case where the interests of justice so require, and without payment by him in any such case if he does not have sufficient means to pay for it;
    (e) To examine, or have examined, the witnesses against him and to obtain the attendance and examination of witnesses on his behalf under the same conditions as witnesses against him;
    (f) To have the free assistance of an interpreter if he cannot understand or speak the language used in court;
    (g) Not to be compelled to testify against himself or to confess guilt.

4. In the case of juvenile persons, the procedure shall be such as will take account of their age and the desirability of promoting their rehabilitation.

5. Everyone convicted of a crime shall have the right to his conviction and sentence being reviewed by a higher tribunal according to law.

6. When a person has by a final decision been convicted of a criminal offence and when subsequently his conviction has been reversed or he has been pardoned on the ground that a new or newly discovered fact shows conclusively that there has been a miscarriage of justice, the person who has suffered punishment as a result of such conviction shall be compensated according to law, unless it is proved that the non-disclosure of the unknown fact in time is wholly or partly attributable to him.

7. No one shall be liable to be tried or punished again for an offence for which he has already been finally convicted or acquitted in accordance with the law and penal procedure of each country.

Article 15

1. No one shall be held guilty of any criminal offence on account of any act or omission which did not constitute a criminal offence, under national or international law, at the time when it was committed. Nor shall a heavier penalty be imposed than the one that was applicable at the time when the criminal offence was committed. If, subsequent to the commission of the offence, provision is made by law for the imposition of the lighter penalty, the offender shall benefit thereby.

2. Nothing in this article shall prejudice the trial and punishment of any person for any act or omission which, at the time when it was committed, was criminal according to the general principles of law recognized by the community of nations.

Article 16

Everyone shall have the right to recognition everywhere as a person before the law.

Article 17

1. No one shall be subjected to arbitrary or unlawful interference with his privacy, family, home or correspondence, nor to unlawful attacks on his honour and reputation.

2. Everyone has the right to the protection of the law against such interference or attacks.

Article 18

1. Everyone shall have the right to freedom of thought, conscience and religion. This right shall include freedom to have or to adopt a religion or belief of his choice, and freedom, either individually or in community with others and in public or private, to manifest his religion or belief in worship, observance, practice and teaching.

2. No one shall be subject to coercion which would impair his freedom to have or to adopt a religion or belief of his choice.

3. Freedom to manifest one's religion or beliefs may be subject only to such limitations as are prescribed by law and are necessary to protect public safety, order, health, or morals or the fundamental rights and freedoms of others.

4. The States Parties to the present Covenant undertake to have respect for the liberty of parents and, when applicable, legal guardians to ensure the religious and moral education of their children in conformity with their own convictions.

Article 19

1. Everyone shall have the right to hold opinions without interference.

2. Everyone shall have the right to freedom of expression; this right shall include freedom to seek, receive and impart information and ideas of all kinds, regardless of frontiers, either orally, in writing or in print, in the form of art, or through any other media of his choice.

3. The exercise of the rights provided for in paragraph 2 of this article carries with it special duties and responsibilities. It may therefore be subject to certain restrictions, but these shall only be such as are provided by law and are necessary:

    (a) For respect of the rights or reputations of others;

    (b) For the protection of national security or of public order (ordre public), or of public health or morals.

Article 20

1. Any propaganda for war shall be prohibited by law.

2. Any advocacy of national, racial or religious hatred that constitutes incitement to discrimination, hostility or violence shall be prohibited by law.

Article 21

The right of peaceful assembly shall be recognized. No restrictions may be placed on the exercise of this right other than those imposed in conformity with the law and which are necessary in a democratic society in the interests of national security or public safety, public order (ordre public), the protection of public health or morals or the protection of the rights and freedoms of others.

Article 22

1. Everyone shall have the right to freedom of association with others, including the right to form and join trade unions for the protection of his interests.

2. No restrictions may be placed on the exercise of this right other than those which are prescribed by law and which are necessary in a democratic society in the interests of national security or public safety, public order (ordre public), the protection of public health or morals or the protection of the rights and freedoms of others. This article shall

not prevent the imposition of lawful restrictions on members of the armed forces and of the police in their exercise of this right.

3. Nothing in this article shall authorize States Parties to the International Labour Organization Convention of 1948 concerning Freedom of Association and Protection of the Right to Organize to take legislative measures which would prejudice, or to apply the law in such a manner as to prejudice, the guarantees provided for in that Convention.

Article 23

1. The family is the natural and fundamental group unit of society and is entitled to protection by society and the State.
2. The right of men and women of marriageable age to marry and to found a family shall be recognized.
3. No marriage shall be entered into without the free and full consent of the intending spouses.
4. States Parties to the present Covenant shall take appropriate steps to ensure equality of rights and responsibilities of spouses as to marriage, during marriage and at its dissolution. In the case of dissolution, provision shall be made for the necessary protection of any children.

Article 24

1. Every child shall have, without any discrimination as to race, colour, sex, language, religion, national or social origin, property or birth, the right to such measures of protection as are required by his status as a minor, on the part of his family, society and the State.
2. Every child shall be registered immediately after birth and shall have a name.
3. Every child has the right to acquire a nationality.

Article 25

Every citizen shall have the right and the opportunity, without any of the distinctions mentioned in article 2 and without unreasonable restrictions:
(a) To take part in the conduct of public affairs, directly or through freely chosen representatives;
(b) To vote and to be elected at genuine periodic elections which shall be by universal and equal suffrage and shall be held by secret ballot, guaranteeing the free expression of the will of the electors;
(c) To have access, on general terms of equality, to public service in his country.

Article 26

All persons are equal before the law and are entitled without any discrimination to the equal protection of the law. In this respect, the law shall prohibit any discrimination and guarantee to all persons equal and effective protection against discrimination on any ground such as race, colour, sex, language, religion, political or other opinion, national or social origin, property, birth or other status.

Article 27

In those States in which ethnic, religious or linguistic minorities exist, persons belonging to such minorities shall not be denied the right, in community with the other members of their group, to enjoy their own culture, to profess and practice their own religion, or to use their own language.

Part IV

Article 28

1. There shall be established a Human Rights Committee (hereafter referred to in the present Covenant as the Committee). It shall consist of eighteen members and shall carry out the functions hereinafter provided.
2. The Committee shall be composed of nationals of the States Parties to the present Covenant who shall be persons of high moral character and recognized competence in the field of human rights, consideration being given to the usefulness of the participation of some persons having legal experience.
3. The members of the Committee shall be elected and shall serve in their personal capacity.

...

Part V

Article 46

Nothing in the present Covenant shall be interpreted as impairing the provisions of the Charter of the United Nations and of the constitutions of the specialized agencies which define the respective responsibilities of the various organs of the United Nations and of the specialized agencies in regard to the matters dealt with in the present Covenant.

Article 47

Nothing in the present Covenant shall be interpreted as impairing the inherent right of all peoples to enjoy and utilize fully and freely their natural wealth and resources.

Part VI

Article 48

1. The present Covenant is open for signature by any State Member of the United Nations or member of any of its specialized agencies, by any State Party to the Statute of the International Court of Justice, and by any other State which has been invited by the General Assembly of the United Nations to become a Party to the present Covenant.

2. The present Covenant is subject to ratification. Instruments of ratification shall be deposited with the Secretary-General of the United Nations.

3. The present Covenant shall be open to accession by any State referred to in paragraph 1 of this article.

4. Accession shall be effected by the deposit of an instrument of accession with the Secretary-General of the United Nations.

5. The Secretary-General of the United Nations shall inform all States which have signed this Covenant or acceded to it of the deposit of each instrument of ratification or accession.

Article 49

1. The present Covenant shall enter into force three months after the date of the deposit with the Secretary-General of the United Nations of the thirty-fifth instrument of ratification or instrument of accession.

2. For each State ratifying the present Covenant or acceding to it after the deposit of the thirty-fifth instrument of ratification or instrument of accession, the present Covenant shall enter into force three months after the date of the deposit of its own instrument of ratification or instrument of accession.

Article 50

The provisions of the present Covenant shall extend to all parts of federal States without any limitations or exceptions.

Article 51

1. Any State Party to the present Covenant may propose an amendment and file it with the Secretary-General of the United Nations. The Secretary-General of the United Nations shall thereupon communicate any proposed amendments to the States Parties to the present Covenant with a request that they notify him whether they favour a conference of States Parties for the purpose of considering and voting upon the proposals. In the event that at least one third of the States Parties favours such a conference, the Secretary-General shall convene the conference under the auspices of the United Nations. Any amendment adopted by a majority of the States Parties present and voting at the conference shall be submitted to the General Assembly of the United Nations for approval.

2. Amendments shall come into force when they have been approved by the General Assembly of the United Nations and accepted by a two-thirds majority of the States Parties to the present Covenant in accordance with their respective constitutional processes.

3. When amendments come into force, they shall be binding on those States Parties which have accepted them, other States Parties still being bound by the provisions of the present Covenant and any earlier amendment which they have accepted.

Article 52

Irrespective of the notifications made under article 48, paragraph 5, the Secretary-General of the United Nations shall inform all States referred to in paragraph I of the same article of the following particulars:

(a) Signatures, ratifications and accessions under article 48;

(b) The date of the entry into force of the present Covenant under article 49 and the date of the entry into force of any amendments under article 51.

Article 53

1. The present Covenant, of which the Chinese, English, French, Russian and Spanish texts are equally authentic, shall be deposited in the archives of the United Nations.

2. The Secretary-General of the United Nations shall transmit certified copies of the present Covenant to all States referred to in article 48.

Appendix G

President George W. Bush's Letter to Congress on American Response to Terrorism

Office of the Press Secretary
October 9, 2001

President's Letter to Congress on American Response to Terrorism

Text of a Letter from the President to the Speaker of the House of Representatives and the President Pro Tempore of the Senate
October 9, 2001

Dear Mr. Speaker: (Dear Mr. President:)

At approximately 12:30 p.m. (EDT) on October 7, 2001, on my orders, U.S. Armed Forces began combat action in Afghanistan against al Qaida terrorists and their Taliban supporters. This military action is a part of our campaign against terrorism and is designed to disrupt the use of Afghanistan as a terrorist base of operations.

We are responding to the brutal September 11 attacks on our territory, our citizens, and our way of life, and to the continuing threat of terrorist acts against the United States and our friends and allies. This follows the deployment of various combat-equipped and combat support forces to a number of locations in the Central and Pacific Command areas of operations, as I reported to the Congress on September 24, to prepare for the campaign to prevent and deter terrorism.

I have taken these actions pursuant to my constitutional authority to conduct U.S. foreign relations as Commander in Chief and Chief Executive. It is not possible to know at this time either the duration of combat operations or the scope and duration of the deployment of U.S. Armed Forces necessary to counter the terrorist threat to the United States. As I have stated previously, it is likely that the American campaign against terrorism will be lengthy. I will direct such additional measures as necessary in exercise of our right to self-defense and to protect U.S. citizens and interests.

I am providing this report as part of my efforts to keep the Congress informed, consistent with the War Powers Resolution and Public Law 107-40. Officials of my Administration and I have been communicating regularly with the leadership and other members of Congress, and we will continue to do so. I appreciate the continuing support of the Congress, including its enactment of Public Law 107-40, in these actions to protect the security of the United States of America and its citizens, civilian and military, here and abroad.

Sincerely,
GEORGE W. BUSH

Appendix H

Treaty Providing for the Renunciation of War as an Instrument of National Policy (Kellogg-Briand Pact)

Signed in Paris, August 27, 1928

Entered into force 24 July 1929

The President of the German Reich, the President of the United States of America, His Majesty the King of the Belgians, the President of the French Republic, His Majesty the King of Great Britain Ireland and the British Dominions beyond the seas, Emperor of India, His Majesty the King of Italy, His Majesty the Emperor of Japan, the President of the Republic of Poland, the President of the Czechoslovak Republic.

Deeply sensible of their solemn duty to promote the welfare of mankind; Persuaded that the time has come when a frank renunciation of war as an instrument of national policy should be made to the end that the peaceful and friendly relations now existing between their peoples may be perpetuated;

Convinced that all changes in their relations with one another should be sought only by pacific means and be the result of a peaceful and orderly process, and that any signatory Power which shall hereafter seek to promote its national interests by resort to war should be denied the benefits furnished by this treaty;

Hopeful that, encouraged by their example, all the other nations of the world will join in this humane endeavor and by adhering to the present treaty as soon as it comes into force bring their peoples within the scope of its beneficent provisions, thus uniting the civilized nations of the world in a common renunciation of war as an instrument of their national policy;

Have decided to conclude a treaty and for that purpose have appointed as their respective plenipotentiaries:

The President of the German Reich: Dr. Gustav Stresemann, Minister for Foreign Affairs;

The President of the United States of America: The Honorable Frank B. Kellogg, Secretary of State;

His Majesty the King of the Belgians: Mr. Paul Hymans, Minister for Foreign Affairs, Minister of State;

The President of the French Republic: Mr. Aristide Briand, Minister for Foreign Affairs;

His Majesty the King of Great Britain, Ireland and the British Dominions beyond the seas, Emperor of India: For Great Britain and Northern Ireland and all parts of the British Empire which are not separate members of the League of Nations: The Right Honourable Lord Cushendun, Chancellor of the Duchy of Lancaster, Acting Secretary of State for Foreign Affairs;

For the Dominion of Canada: The Right Honourable William Lyon Mackenzie King, Prime Minister and Minister for External Affairs;

For the Commonwealth of Australia: The Honourable Alexander John McLachlan, Member of the Executive Federal Council;

For the Dominion of New Zealand: The Honourable Sir Christopher James Parr, High Commissioner for New Zealand in Great Britain;

For the Union of South Africa: The Honourable Jacobus Stephanus Smit, High Commissioner for the Union of South Africa in Great Britain;

For the Irish Free State: Mr. William Thomas Cosgrave, President of the Executive Council;

For India: The Right Honourable Lord Cushendun, Chancellor of the Duchy of Lancaster, Acting Secretary of State for Foreign Affairs.

His Majesty the King of Italy: Count Gaetano Manzoi, His Ambassador Extraordinary and Plenipotentiary at Paris;

His Majesty the Emperor of Japan: Count Uchida, Privy Councillor;

The President of the Republic of Poland: Mr. A. Zaleski, Minister for Foreign Affairs;

The President of the Czechoslovak Republic: Dr. Eduard Benes, Minister for Foreign Affairs;

who, having communicated to one another their full powers found in good and due form have agreed upon the following articles:

Article 1

The high contracting parties solemnly declare in the names of their respective peoples that they condemn recourse to war for the solution of international controversies, and renounce it as an instrument of national policy in their relations with one another.

Article 2

The high contracting parties agree that the settlement or solution of all disputes or conflicts of whatever nature or of whatever origin they may be, which may arise among them, shall never be sought except by pacific means.

Article 3

The present treaty shall be ratified by the high contracting parties Named in the preamble in accordance with their respective constitutional requirements, and shall take effect as between them as soon as all their several instruments of ratification shall have been deposited at Washington.

This treaty shall, when it has come into effect as prescribed in the preceding paragraph, remain open as long as may be necessary for adherence by all the other Powers of the world. Every instrument evidencing the adherence of a Power shall be deposited at Washington and the treaty shall immediately upon such deposit become effective as between the Power thus adhering and the other Powers parties hereto.

It shall be the duty of the Government of the United States to furnish each government named in the preamble and every government subsequently adhering to this treaty with a certified copy of the treaty and of every instrument of ratification or adherence. It shall also be the duty of the Government of the United States telegraphically to notify such governments immediately upon the deposit with it of each instrument of ratification or adherence. In faith whereof the respective Plenipotentiaries have signed this Treaty in the French and English languages both texts having equal force, and hereunto affix their seals.

Appendix I

DOD Department of Defense Directive Number 2310.01E September 5, 2006

SUBJECT: The Department of Defense Detainee Program

References:

(a) DoD Directive 2310.01, "DoD Program for Enemy Prisoners of War (EPOW) and Other Detainees," August 18, 1994 (hereby canceled)

(b) DoD Directive 5101.1, "DoD Executive Agent," September 3, 2002

(c) Secretary of Defense Memorandum, "Office of Detainee Affairs," July 16, 2004 (hereby superseded)

(d) DoD Directive 2311.01E, "DoD Law of War Program," May 9, 2006

(e) through (k), see Enclosure 1

1. REISSUANCE AND PURPOSE

This Directive:

1.1. Reissues Reference (a) to revise policy and responsibilities within the Department of Defense (DoD) for a Detainee Program to ensure compliance with the laws of the United States, the law of war, including the Geneva Conventions of 1949, and all applicable policies, directives, or other issuances, consistent with References (d) through (k).

1.2. Re-designates, according to Reference (b), the Secretary of the Army as the DoD Executive Agent for the Administration of Department of Defense Detainee Operations Policy.

1.3. Supersedes Reference (c) and establishes the responsibilities of the Under Secretary of Defense for Policy (USD(P)) as the lead proponent in developing, coordinating, and implementing policies and guidance pertaining to detainee operations.

2. APPLICABILITY

2.1. This Directive applies to:

2.1.1. The Office of the Secretary of Defense (OSD), the Military Departments, the Chairman of the Joint Chiefs of Staff, the Combatant Commands, the Office of the Inspector General of the Department of Defense, the Defense Agencies, the DoD Field Activities, and all other organizational entities in the Department of Defense (hereafter collectively referred to as the "DoD Components").

2.1.2. DoD contractors assigned to or supporting the DoD Components engaged in, conducting, participating in, or supporting detainee operations.

2.1.3. Non-DoD personnel as a condition of permitting access to internment facilities or to detainees under DoD control.

2.1.4. All detainee operations conducted by DoD personnel (military and civilian), contractor employees under DoD cognizance, and DoD contractors supporting detainee operations.

2.2. This Directive applies during all armed conflicts, however such conflicts are characterized, and in all other military operations.

3. DEFINITIONS

Terms used in this Directive are defined, and are to be interpreted, in accordance with U.S. law and the law of war. Specific terms found in this directive are provided in Enclosure 2.

4. POLICY

It is DoD policy that:

4.1. All detainees shall be treated humanely and in accordance with U.S. law, the law of war, and applicable U.S. policy.

4.2. All persons subject to this Directive shall observe the requirements of the law of war, and shall apply, without regard to a detainee's legal status, at a minimum the standards articulated in Common Article 3 to the Geneva Conventions of 1949 (References (g) through (j),full text of which is found in Enclosure 3), as construed and applied by U.S. law, and those found in Enclosure 4, in the treatment of all detainees, until their final release, transfer out of DoD control, or repatriation. Note that certain categories of detainees, such as enemy prisoners of war, enjoy protections under the law of war in addition to the minimum standards prescribed in Common Article 3 to References (g) through (j).

4.3. Captured or detained persons will be removed as soon as practicable from the point of capture and transported to detainee collection points, holding areas, or other detention locations operated by the DoD Components.

4.4. Detainees and their property shall be accounted for and records maintained according to applicable law, regulation, policy, or other issuances.

4.4.1. Detainees shall be assigned an Internment Serial Number (ISN) as soon as possible after coming under DoD control, normally within 14 days of capture. DoD Components shall maintain full accountability for all detainees under DoD control.

4.4.2. Detainee records and reports shall be maintained, safeguarded, and provided to USD(P) and other DoD Components as appropriate.

4.5. No person subject to this Directive shall accept the transfer of a detainee from another U.S. Government Department or Agency, coalition forces, allied personnel, or other personnel not affiliated with the Department of Defense or the U.S. Government, except in accordance with applicable law, regulation, policy, and other issuances.

4.6. No detainee shall be released or transferred from the care, custody, or control of a DoD Component except in accordance with applicable law, regulation, policy, and other issuances.

4.7. Where doubt exists as to the status of a detainee, the detainee's status shall be determined by a competent authority.

4.8. Detainees under DoD control who do not enjoy prisoner of war protections under the law of war shall have the basis for their detention reviewed periodically by a competent authority.

4.9. All persons subject to this Directive shall:

4.9.1. Receive instruction and complete training, commensurate with their duties, in the laws, regulations, policies, and other issuances applicable to detainee operations, prevention of violations of same, and the requirement to report alleged or suspected violations thereof that arise in the context of detainee operations.

4.9.2. Receive instruction and complete training in advance of conducting, participating in, or supporting detainee operations, and annually thereafter. Training requirements and certifications of completion shall be documented according to applicable law and policy.

4.10. All persons subject to this Directive shall report possible, suspected, or alleged violations of the law of war, and/or detention operations laws, regulations, or policy, for which there is credible information, or conduct, during military operations other than war, that would constitute a violation of law or policy if it occurred during an armed conflict, in accordance with References (d) and (k).

4.11. The International Committee of the Red Cross (ICRC) shall be allowed to offer its services during an armed conflict, however characterized, to which the United States is a party.

5. RESPONSIBILITIES

5.1. The USD(P) shall:

5.1.1. Review, ensure coordination of, and approve all implementing policies or guidance to the DoD Detainee Program, including all detainee matters involving interaction between the Department of Defense and other U.S. Government Departments or Agencies.

5.1.2. Review, ensure coordination of, and approve all implementing policy or guidance developed pursuant to this Directive by DoD Components. DoD Components will forward copies of such documents to USD(P) for review prior to issuance.

5.1.3. Serve as the principal DoD interlocutor with the ICRC and develop policy and procedures to ensure the proper and timely reporting of ICRC communications to appropriate DoD and U.S. Government officials.

5.2. The Under Secretary of Defense for Personnel and Readiness (USD(P&R)) shall:

5.2.1. Develop and oversee policy to ensure education and training programs satisfy DoD Component requirements in the areas of language, culture, customs, and related matters and to assure that persons subject to this directive have been provided requisite training, knowledge, and skills necessary to perform detainee operations duties.

5.2.2. Ensure the Assistant Secretary of Defense for Health Affairs develops policies, procedures, and standards for medical program activities and issues DoD instructions consistent with this Directive for medical program activities required by the DoD Detainee Program.

5.2.3. Ensure the Assistant Secretary of Defense for Reserve Affairs develops policies, procedures, and standards for Reserve Components and issues DoD Instructions consistent with this Directive for National Guard and Reserve activities required for the DoD Detainee Program.

5.3. The Under Secretary of Defense for Acquisition, Technology, and Logistics (USD(AT&L)) shall:

5.3.1. Establish policies and procedures, in coordination with USD(P), the General Counsel, and the appropriate DoD Components, to ensure all DoD contracts pursuant to which contractor employees interact with detainees include a requirement that such contractor employees receive training regarding the international obligations and laws of the United States applicable to detention operations.

5.3.2. Ensure contractor employees accompanying DoD Components in conducting, participating in, or supporting detainee operations complete training and receive information on the law, regulations, and policies applicable to detention operations, and the requirements to report possible, suspected, or alleged violations that arise in the context of detention operations, in accordance with References (d) and (k).

5.4. The Under Secretary of Defense for Intelligence (USD(I)) shall:

5.4.1. Exercise primary responsibility for developing policy pertaining to DoD intelligence interrogations, detainee debriefings, and tactical questioning according to Reference (k).

5.4.2. Act as primary liaison between the Department of Defense and other agencies of the Intelligence Community on intelligence matters pertaining to detainees.

5.5. The General Counsel of the Department of Defense shall coordinate with the Department of Justice and other agencies regarding detainee-related litigation matters and on matters pertaining to detainees who may be U.S. citizens, dual-nationals with U.S. citizenship, or U.S. resident aliens, as appropriate.

5.6. The Heads of the DoD Components shall ensure that all personnel are properly trained and certified in detainee operations commensurate with their duties, maintaining records of such training and certification.

5.7. The Secretary of the Army is hereby designated as the Executive Agent for the Administration of Department of Defense Detainee Operations Policy and in that role shall:
5.7.1. Ensure all Executive Agent responsibilities and functions for the administration of DoD detainee operations policy are assigned and executed according to Reference (b) and this Directive.

5.7.2. Develop and promulgate guidance, regulations, and instructions necessary for the DoD-wide implementation of detainee operations policy in coordination with USD(P).

5.7.3. Communicate directly with the Heads of the DoD Components as necessary to carry out assigned functions. The Chairman of the Joint Chiefs of Staff shall be informed of communications to the Commanders of the Combatant Commands.

5.7.4. Designate a single point of contact within the Department of the Army for detainee operations policy, who shall also provide advice and assistance to USD(P).

5.7.5. Plan for and operate a national-level detainee reporting center and its elements (e.g., theater and lower levels) to account for detainees. Coordinate with USD(P) to provide reports on detainee operations to the Secretary of Defense and others as appropriate.

5.7.6. Recommend DoD-wide detainee operations-related planning and programming guidance to the USD(P), USD(AT&L), USD(I), USD(P&R), the Under Secretary of Defense (Comptroller), the Assistant Secretary of Defense for Networks and Information Integration, the Director of Program Analysis and Evaluation, and the Chairman of the Joint Chiefs of Staff. Provide information copies of such guidance to the Secretaries of the Military Departments.

5.7.7. Establish detainee operations training and certification standards, in coordination with the Secretaries of the Military Departments and the Joint Staff.

5.7.8. Develop programs to ensure all DoD detainee operations policy; doctrine; tactics, techniques, and procedures; and regulations or other issuances are subject to periodic review, evaluation, and inspection for effectiveness and compliance with this Directive.

5.8. The Chairman of the Joint Chiefs of Staff shall:

5.8.1. Provide appropriate oversight to the Commanders of the Combatant Commands to ensure their detainee operations policies and procedures are consistent with this Directive.

5.8.2. Designate a single point of contact within the Joint Staff for matters pertaining to the implementation of this Directive.

5.8.3. Ensure that operational exercises routinely test the capabilities of the DoD Components to conduct, participate in, and support detainee operations, consistent with this Directive.

5.9. The Commanders of the Combatant Commands shall:

5.9.1. Plan, execute, and oversee Combatant Command detainee operations in accordance with this Directive and implementing issuances.

5.9.2. Develop programs and issue appropriate guidance and orders implementing this Directive. All such programs and guidance shall be subjected to periodic review and evaluation for compliance and efficacy.

5.9.3. When detainee internment facilities, holding areas, collection points, or interrogation facilities are in their area of responsibility:

5.9.3.1. Ensure procedures are established for the treatment of detainees consistent with this Directive.

5.9.3.2. Ensure detainees are provided with information, in their own language, concerning the rights, duties, and obligations of their detention, which may include applicable provisions of the Geneva Conventions.

5.9.3.3. Ensure periodic unannounced and announced inspections of internment facilities, including temporary holding areas and collection points, are conducted to provide continued oversight of detainee operations.

6. EFFECTIVE DATE

This Directive is effective immediately.

Gordon England
Deputy Secretary of Defense
DEFINITIONS

E2.1. Detainee. Any person captured, detained, held, or otherwise under the control of DoD personnel (military, civilian, or contractor employee). It does not include persons being held primarily for law enforcement purposes, except where the United States is the occupying power. A detainee may also include the following categories:

E2.1.1. Enemy Combatant. In general, a person engaged in hostilities against the United States or its coalition partners during an armed conflict. The term "enemy combatant" includes "both" "lawful enemy combatants" and "unlawful enemy combatants."

E2.1.1.1. Lawful Enemy Combatant. Lawful enemy combatants, who are entitled to protections under the Geneva Conventions, include members of the regular armed forces of a State party to the conflict; militia, volunteer corps, and organized resistance movements belonging to a State party to the conflict, which are under responsible command, wear a fixed distinctive sign recognizable at a distance, carry their arms openly, and abide by the laws of war; and members of regular armed forces who profess allegiance to a government or an authority not recognized by the detaining power.

E2.1.1.2. Unlawful Enemy Combatant. Unlawful enemy combatants are persons not entitled to combatant immunity, who engage in acts against the United States or its coalition partners in violation of the laws and customs of war during an armed conflict. For purposes of the war on terrorism, the term Unlawful Enemy Combatant is defined to include, but is not limited to, an individual who is or was part of or supporting Taliban or al Qaeda forces or associated forces that are engaged in hostilities against the United States or its coalition partners.

E2.1.2. Enemy Prisoner of War. Individuals under the custody and/or control of the Department of Defense according to Reference (g), Articles 4 and 5.

E2.1.3. Retained Person. Individuals under the custody and/or control of the Department of Defense according to Reference (g), Article 33.

E2.1.4. Civilian Internee. Individuals under the custody and/or control of the Department of Defense according to Reference (h), Article 4.

E2.2. <u>Law of War</u>. That part of international law that regulates the conduct of armed hostilities and occupation. It is often called the "law of armed conflict" and encompasses all international law applicable to the conduct of hostilities that is binding on the United States or its individual citizens, including treaties and international agreements to which the United States is a party (e.g., the Geneva Conventions of 1949), and applicable customary international law.

E3. <u>ENCLOSURE</u> 3

ARTICLE 3 COMMON TO THE GENEVA CONVENTIONS OF 1949
E3.1. The text of Common Article 3 to the Geneva Conventions of 1949 is as follows:

In the case of armed conflict not of an international character occurring in the territory of one of the High Contracting Parties, each Party to the conflict shall be bound to apply, as a minimum, the following provisions:

(1) Persons taking no active part in the hostilities, including members of armed forces who have laid down their arms and those placed *hors de combat* by sickness, wounds, detention, or any other cause, shall in all circumstances be treated humanely, without any adverse distinction founded on race, colour, religion or faith, sex, birth or wealth, or any other similar criteria.

To this end, the following acts are and shall remain prohibited at any time and in any place whatsoever with respect to the above-mentioned persons:

(a) violence to life and person, in particular murder of all kinds, mutilation, cruel treatment and torture;

(b) taking of hostages;

(c) outrages upon personal dignity, in particular humiliating and degrading treatment;

(d) the passing of sentences and the carrying out of executions without previous judgment pronounced by a regularly constituted court, affording all the judicial guarantees which are recognized as indispensable by civilized peoples.

(2) The wounded and sick shall be collected and cared for.

An impartial humanitarian body, such as the International Committee of the Red Cross, may offer its services to the Parties to the conflict.

The Parties to the conflict should further endeavour to bring into force, by means of special agreements, all or part of the other provisions of the present Convention.
The application of the preceding provisions shall not affect the legal status of the Parties to the conflict.

E4. <u>ENCLOSURE</u> 4

DETAINEE TREATMENT POLICY

E4.1. In addition to the requirements in paragraph 4.2 and Enclosure 3, DoD policy relative to the minimum standards of treatment for all detainees in the control of DoD personnel (military, civilian, or contractor employee) is as follows:

E4.1.1. All persons captured, detained, interned, or otherwise in the control of DoD personnel during the course of military operations will be given humane care and treatment from the moment they fall into the hands of DoD personnel until release, transfer out of DoD control, or repatriation, including:

E4.1.1.1. Adequate food, drinking water, shelter, clothing, and medical treatment;

E4.1.1.2. Free exercise of religion, consistent with the requirements of detention;

E4.1.1.3. All detainees will be respected as human beings. They will be protected against threats or acts of violence including rape, forced prostitution, assault and theft, public curiosity, bodily injury, and reprisals. They will not be subjected to medical or scientific experiments. They will not be subjected to sensory deprivation. This list is not exclusive.

E4.1.2. All persons taken into the control of DoD personnel will be provided with the protections of Reference (g) until some other legal status is determined by competent authority.

E4.1.3. The punishment of detainees known to have, or suspected of having, committed serious offenses will be administered in accordance with due process of law and under legally constituted authority.

E4.1.4. The inhumane treatment of detainees is prohibited and is not justified by the stress of combat or deep provocation.

Appendix J

Selected List of Charged/Convicted "Islamic" Terrorists in Federal Courts 2002-2010

Name	Court	Description of Charges/Convictions
2010		
Abdow Munye Abdow	District of Minnesota	Abdow Munye Abdow pled guilty to making a false statement to an FBI agent about who was in the car with him on a drive from Minnesota to Las Vegas. Abdow was convicted of obstructing an FBI and grand jury investigation into the recruitment of young men in the U.S. to train and fight extremist groups in Somalia.
Umar Farouk Abdulmutallab, (also known as Umar Abdul Mutallab) and Omar Farooq al-Nigeri	Eastern District of Michigan	Umar Farouk Abdulmutallab was charged with attempted use of a weapon of mass destruction and attempted murder of 289 people. He failed in his attempt to detonate plastic explosives on a Northwest Airlines flight from Amsterdam to Detroit, Michigan.
Hor I. Akl and Amera A. Akl	Northern District of Ohio	Toledo couple, Hor Akl and spouse, Amera Akl, were arrested and charged with conspiring to provide material support to Hizballah, with conspiring to money laundering, and committing arson in an insurance fraud scheme. The couple attempted to smuggle money to Lebanon in hollow sections of a vehicle that would be shipped overseas. Others involved in the plan included Mrs. Akl's brother and Mr. Akl's brother, who resides in Lebanon and owns a recreational facility where Hezbollah is allegedly allowed to meet.

Name	Court	Description of Charges/Convictions
Mohamed Mahmood Alessa and Carlos Eduardo Almonte	District of New Jersey	Mohamed Mahmood Alessa and Carlos Eduardo Almonte, also known as the Jersey Jihadists, were accused of trying to join terrorist group Al-Shabaab and charged with conspiring to murder, kidnap, and maim persons outside the United States. They were stopped at the Kennedy airport where they were about to board separate flights to Cairo, allegedly en route to Somalia for training with militant Somali Islamic group Al-Shabaab.
Amina Farah Ali and Hawo Mohamed Hassan	District of Minnesota	Amina Farah Ali and Hawo Mohamed Hassan were charged with one count of conspiracy to provide material support to Al-Shabaab. Ali also faces 12 substantive counts of providing material support to Al-Shabaab, while Hassan has three additional charges of making false statements.
Abdul Tawala Ibn Ali Alishtari aka Michael Mixon	Eastern District of New York	Abdul Tawala Ibn Ali Alishtari aka Michael Mixon, a bank underwriter, was convicted of knowingly financing terrorism, conspiring to commit wire fraud, and stealing millions from investors. Aqueel Khan the Mosque founder of the Islamic Center of Queens aka Masjid al-Fatima is also listed as the Chief Financial Officer of at least one of the Florida corporations set up by Alishtari.
Viktor Bout	Southern District of New York	Viktor Bout, an international arms dealer and Russian native, was indicted by federal authorities on a series of charges, including counts of illegally purchasing U.S. cargo planes to ferry weapons to warring parties and regimes in Africa and the Middle East. U.S. is still trying to extradite Bout from Thailand to New York. His alleged American co-conspirator, Richard Chichakli, remains at large.
Barry Walter Bujol, Jr.	Southern District of Texas	Barry Walter Bujol, Jr. was charged with attempting to provide material support to a terrorist organization and aggravated identity theft. Bujol attempted to provide material support to al-Qa'eda in the Arabian Peninsula in the form of personnel, currency, pre-paid phone cards, mobile telephone SIM cards, global positioning system receivers, public access-restricted U.S. military publications, a military-issue compass and other materials. He also possessed and used a false government-issued identification card.

Name	Court	Description of Charges/Convictions
Zachary Chesser	Eastern District of Virginia	Zachary Chesser was indicted for attempting to provide material support to terrorist group Al-Shabaab. In the complaint, he made various attempts to travel to Somalia to join and train with Al-Shabaab.
Richard Ammar Chichakli	Southern District of New York	Richard Ammar Chichakli, a Vietnam veteran and American citizen, was accused of co-conspiracy with Viktor Bout. The "Merchant of Death," Viktor Bout, and his reputed chief financial manager, Richard Chichakli, have been indicted in Federal Court in New York for conspiracy to violate the IEEPA, money laundering conspiracy, and wire fraud conspiracy.
Colleen Renee "Fatima" LaRose, aka Jihad Jane	Eastern District of Pennsylvania	Colleen LaRose, also known as "Fatima LaRose" or "Jihad Jane," was charged with conspiracy to provide material support to terrorists, conspiracy to kill in a foreign country, making false statements to a government official, and attempted identity theft. She recruited men from several countries via the Internet to wage violent jihad in South Asia and Europe. She was also allegedly part of a plot to kill a Swedish cartoonist, who made fun of Prophet Mohammad. Her trial was postponed by a federal judge due to complexities of the case.
Shaker Masri	Northern District of Illinois	Shaker Masri was charged with knowingly attempting to provide material support and resources to a designated foreign terrorist organizations, al-Qaeda and Al-Shabaab, and attempting to provide material support through the use of a weapon of mass destruction.
Khalid Ouazzani	District of Kansas	Khalid Ouazzani, a naturalized U.S. citizen, was charged with and plead guilty to financing terrorism, money laundering and bank fraud. He sent funds to al-Qa'eda in 2007 and 2008.
Jamie Paulin-Ramirez	Eastern District of Pennsylvania	Jamie Paulin-Ramirez was accused of an online plot to attend a terror training camp that supports violent jihad, or Muslim holy war.
Nadia Piroska Maria Rockwood	District of Alaska	Nadia Piroska Maria Rockwood pled guilty to making false statements to the FBI. She carried a list of specific targets for terrorism made by Paul Rockwood, her husband.

Name	Court	Description of Charges/Convictions
Paul Gene Rockwood, Jr.	District of Alaska	Paul Gene Rockwood, Jr. pled guilty to making false statements involving domestic terrorism. Paul Rockwood, Jr. researched targets for terrorism and created a list, which he gave to his wife, Nadia Piroska Maria Rockwood. The list was confiscated by the FBI, and Paul lied about creating the list and its purpose, among other things.
Faisal Shahzad	Southern District of New York	Faisal Shahzad pled guilty to attempting to use a weapon of mass destruction in the failed New York City Times Square car bombing. Shahzad was charged with five counts of terrorism-related crimes: attempting to use a weapon of mass destruction; attempting to kill and maim people in the U.S.; using and carrying a destructive device; transporting an explosive device and; attempting to damage building, vehicles, and other property.
Hosam Maher Husein Smadi	Northern District of Texas	Hosam Maher Husein Smadi, a 19-year old Jordanian, was charged with attempted use of a weapon of mass destruction; he pled guilty to the 2009 attempted bombing of a downtown Dallas skyscraper. The weapon of mass destruction he attempted to use was actually a decoy device given to him by an undercover FBI agent, which Smadi placed downtown Dallas with the intent of killing hundreds, if not thousands, of people.
Lynn Stewart, Ahmed Abdel Sattar, and Mohammed Yousry	Southern District of New York	Lynn Stewart was sentenced to ten years in prison for aiding convicted terrorist Sheik Omar Abdel Rahman's communication from prison to his terrorist group, the Islamic Group. In 2005, Stewart and co-defendants Ahmed Abdel Sattar and Mohammed Yousry were found guilty of all seven counts against them – including providing material support to a terrorist group, conspiracy to kill and kidnap individuals in a foreign country, conspiracy to defraud the United States and making false statements.
2009		
Akram Musa Abdallah	District of Arizona	Akram Musa Abdallah (a.k.a. Abu Saiaf) was accused of lying to authorities about his involvement in fundraising for the Holy Land Foundation, an Islamic charity alleged to have provided financial support to Hamas. Abdallah pleaded guilty to making false statements to the FBI and was sentenced.

Name	Court	Description of Charges/Convictions
Abdikadir Ali Abdi	District of Minnesota	Abdikadir Ali Abdi was charged with providing material support to a terrorist organization and conspiring to kill, maim, kidnap or injure people outside the U.S. He recruited young Somalis in Minneapolis to join Al-Shabaab and facilitated travel to Somalia. He still remains at large.
Khalid Abshir	District of Minnesota	Khalid Abshir was charged with conspiring to provide material support to terrorists and foreign terrorist organizations; conspiracy to kill, kidnap, maim and injure persons abroad; possessing and discharging a firearm during a crime of violence; and solicitation to commit a crime of violence along with Ahmed Ali Omar, Zakaria Maruf, Mohamed Hassan and Mustafa Salat. He left Minneapolis for Somalia to fight with Al-Shabaab and remains at large.
Salah Osman Ahmed	District of Minnesota	Salah Osman Ahmed pled guilty to providing material support for terrorism and conspiracy to kill and/or maim in a foreign country. He left Minneapolis to join Al-Shabaab.
Zubair Ahmed and Khaleel Ahmed	Northern District of Ohio	Zubair Ahmed and Khaleel Ahmed pled guilty to conspiracy to provide material support to terrorists and travel abroad to murder or maim U.S. military forces in Iraq or Afghanistan.
Abdisalan Hussein Ali	District of Minnesota	Abdisalan Hussein Ali was charged with providing material support to a terrorist organization and conspiring to kill, maim, kidnap or injure people outside the U.S. He recruited young Somalis in Minneapolis to join Al-Shabaab and facilitated travel to Somalia. He still remains at large.
Wesam al-Delaema	District of Columbia	Wesam al-Delaema was convicted of conspiring to murder Americans overseas by planting roadside bombs targeting U.S. soldiers in Iraq and by demonstrating on video how these explosives could be detonated to destroy American vehicles.
Ali Al-Marri	Central District of Illinois	Ali Al-Marri pled guilty to conspiracy to provide material support to al-Qa'eda. Al-Marri attended terrorist training camps where he learned the al-Qa'eda tradecraft and was dispatched by al-Qa'eda to carry out terrorist objectives in America.

Name	Court	Description of Charges/Convictions
Farah Mohamed Beledi	District of Minnesota	Farah Mohamed Beledi was charged with providing material support to a terrorist organization and conspiring to kill, maim, kidnap or injure people outside the United States. He still remains at large.
Daniel Boyd	Eastern District of North Carolina	(North Carolina Group) –Daniel Boyd was charged with conspiracy to murder abroad, providing material support to a terrorist group and weapon charges. He was involved in the plot to commit acts of violence in Israel and Kosovo. He was also charged with plotting an attack on U.S. military personnel at the Quantico Marine Base, as well as recruiting young people to travel overseas in order to kill them. He is the father of Dylan and Zakariya Boyd.
Dylan Boyd	Eastern District of North Carolina	(North Carolina Group) – Dylan Boyd was charged with conspiracy to murder abroad, providing material support to a terrorist group and weapon charges. He was involved in the plot to commit acts of violence in Israel and Kosovo. He is the son of Daniel Boyd.
Zakariya Boyd	Eastern District of North Carolina	(North Carolina Group) – Zakariya Boyd was charged with conspiracy to murder abroad, providing material support to a terrorist group and weapon charges. He was involved in the plot to commit acts of violence in Israel and Kosovo. He is the son of Daniel Boyd.
Roya Rahmani, Alireza Mohammadmoradi, Moustafa Ahmady, Hossein Afshari, Hassan Rezaie, Navid Taj, and Mohammad Omidvar	Central District of California	Roya Rahmani, Alireza Mohammadmoradi, Moustafa Ahmady, Hossein Afshari, Hassan Rezaie, Navid Taj, and Mohammad Omidvar pled guilty to federal charges of providing material support to terrorists. The group was convicted of engaging in fundraising activities on behalf of the MEK, a designated foreign terrorist organization.
James Cromitie, David Williams, Onta Williams, Laguerre Payen	Southern District of New York	James Cromitie, David Williams, Onta Williams and Laguerre Payen, were arrested on charges arising from a plot to detonate explosives near a synagogue in Bronx, New York and to shoot Stinger surface-to-air guided missiles at military planes located at the National Guard Base at Stewart Airport in Newburgh, New York. All were charged in an eight-count indictment.

Name	Court	Description of Charges/Convictions
Cabdulaahi Ahmed Faarax	District of Minnesota	Cabdulaahi Ahmed Faarax was charged with providing material support to a terrorist organization and conspiring to kill, maim, kidnap or injure people outside the United States. He recruited young Somalis in Minneapolis to join Al-Shabaab and facilitated travel to Somalia. He still remains at large.
Ahmed Khalfan Ghailani	Eastern District of New York	Ahmed Khalfan Ghailani, an al-Qa'eda militant, was charged with crimes associated with the 1998 bombings of American embassies in Tanzania and Kenya. He was captured in 2004, held as an enemy combatant by the CIA and transferred in 2006 to the naval base at Guantánamo Bay, Cuba.
Omar Hammami	Southern District of Alabama	Omar Hammami was indicted on three counts of providing material support to terrorism. He joined Al-Shabaab in Somalia and made terrorism recruitment videos. He is still at large.
Nidal Hasan	United States Military Court	Nidal Hasan was charged with murder and attempted murder for the Fort Hood shootings and is awaiting trial.
Kamal Hassan	District of Minnesota	Kamal Hassan pled guilty to providing material support to terrorism. He left Minneapolis for Somalia to join Al-Shabaab.
Mohamed Abdullahi Hassan	District of Minnesota	Mohamed Abdullahi Hassan was charged with conspiracy to provide material support to terrorists and foreign terrorist organizations; conspiracy to kill, kidnap, maim and injure persons abroad; possessing and discharging a firearm during a crime of violence; and solicitation to commit a crime of violence along with Khalid Abshir, Ahmed Ali Omar, Zakaria Maruf, and Mustafa Salat. He left Minneapolis for Somalia and fought with Al-Shabaab. He still remains at large.
Mohammad Omar Aly Hassan	Eastern District of North Carolina	Mohammad Omar Aly Hassan was charged with conspiracy to murder abroad, providing material support to a terrorist group and weapon charges. He was involved in the plot to commit acts of violence in Israel and Kosovo.

Name	Court	Description of Charges/Convictions
David Coleman Headley	Northern District of Illinois	David Coleman Headley was charged with and is awaiting trial for conspiracy to murder and maim abroad, conspiracy to bomb a public place abroad, murder of U.S. nationals abroad, and for providing material support to foreign terrorist organizations. He was part of the plot to kill Danish newspaper editors and conspired to execute the Mumbai attacks.
Shukri Abu Baker, Ghassan Elashi, Mufid Abdulqader, Mohammed El Mezain and Abdulrahman Odeh	Northern District of Texas	Shukri Abu Baker, Ghassan Elashi, Mufid Abdulqader, Mohammed El Mezain and Abdulrahman Odeh, five leaders of the Holy Land Foundation, once the largest Muslim charity in the United States, were convicted for their role in funneling more than $12 million to the Hamas terror organization.
Abdiweli Yassin Isse	District of Minnesota	Abdiweli Yassin Isse was charged with, among other things, conspiring to and providing material support to Al-Shabaab and conspiring to kill, maim and injure persons abroad. He left Minneapolis for Somalia and fought with Al-Shabaab. He still remains at large.
Abdifatah Yusuf Isse	District of Minnesota	Abdifatah Yusuf Isse pled guilty to providing material support for terrorism and conspiracy to kill and maim in a foreign country. He urged violence against the United States on al-Qa'eda videotapes.
Oussama Kassir	Southern District of New York	Oussama Kassir was convicted of charges related to his participation in an effort to establish a jihad training camp in Oregon and his operation of several terrorist web sites containing instructions on how to make bombs and poisons. Kassir was found guilty of all 11 charges against him, including providing material support to al-Qa'eda and distributing information on explosives and weapons of mass destruction.
Betim Kaziu	Eastern District of New York	Betim Kaziu was charged with and is awaiting trial for conspiracy to provide material support for terrorism and for conspiring to commit murder abroad. He attempted to join a group related to al-Qa'eda and sought military training.

Name	Court	Description of Charges/Convictions
Narseal Batiste, Patrick Abraham, Stanley Grant Phanor, Burson Augustin, and Rothschild Augustine, Naudimar Herrera	Southern District of Florida	Narseal Batiste, Patrick Abraham, Stanley Grant Phanor, Burson Augustin, and Rothschild Augustine were sentenced in Miami to federal prison terms. They were convicted of multiple charges that included conspiring to provide material support to the al-Qa'eda terrorist organization and conspiracy to levy war against the United States by discussing and planning attacks on targets including the Sears Tower in Chicago, the FBI building in Miami, and other federal buildings in Florida. A sixth man, Naudimar Herrera, was acquitted on all counts.
Zakaria Maruf	District of Minnesota	Zakaria Maruf was charged with conspiracies to provide material support to terrorists and foreign terrorist organizations; conspiracy to kill, kidnap, maim and injure persons abroad; possessing and discharging a firearm during a crime of violence; and solicitation to commit a crime of violence. He left Minneapolis for Somalia and fought with Al-Shabaab. He still remains at large.
Tarek Mehanna	District of Massachusetts	Tarek Mehanna was charged with and is awaiting trial for conspiracy to provide material support to terrorists. He plotted to bomb a mall in Boston, Massachusetts, and targets abroad.
Omer Abdi Mohamed	District of Minnesota	Omer Abdi Mohamed was charged with providing material to support a terrorist organization and conspiring to kill, maim, kidnap or injure people outside the United States. He left Minneapolis for Somalia and fought with Al-Shabaab. He still remains at large.
Jehad Serwan Mostafa, aka "Ahmed" aka "Emir Anwar" aka "Anwar"	Southern District of California	Jehad Serwan Mostafa was indicted on three counts of providing material support to the terrorist organization and conspiracy to provide material support to terrorists. He is accused of working with Al-Shabaab.
Abdulhakim Mujahid Muhammad	District of Arkansas	Abdulhakim Mujahid Muhammad was charged with 15 counts of terrorist acts; he shot military recruiters in Little Rock, Arkansas.
Abduwali Abdukhadir Muse	Southern District of New York	Abduwali Abdukhadir Muse was charged with participating in the hijacking of the Maersk Alabama container ship in the Indian Ocean.

Name	Court	Description of Charges/Convictions
Patrick Nayyar and Conrad Mulholland	Southern District of New York	Patrick Nayyar and Conrad Mulholland were charged with trying to provide weapons, ammunition, and vehicles to the Lebanese militant group Hezbollah. He was indicted along with Conrad Stanisclaus Mulholland for providing material support to terrorism.
Mohammad Zaki Amawi, Marwan Othman El-Hindi, and Wassim I. Mazloum	Northern District of Ohio	Mohammad Zaki Amawi, Marwan Othman El-Hindi, and Wassim I. Mazloum, three Ohio residents, were convicted of conspiring to commit terrorist acts against Americans overseas, including U.S. military personnel in Iraq, and conspiring to provide material support to terrorists.
Ahmed Ali Omar	District of Minnesota	Ahmed Ali Omar was charged with conspiracies to provide material support to terrorists and foreign terrorist organizations; conspiracy to kill, kidnap, maim and injure persons abroad; possessing and discharging a firearm during a crime of violence; and solicitation to commit a crime of violence along with Khalid Abshir, Zakaria Maruf, Mohamed Hassan and Mustafa Salat. He left Minneapolis for Somalia and fought with Al-Shabaab. He still remains at large.
Mahamud Said Omar	District of Minnesota	Mahamud Said Omar was charged with providing material support to a terrorist organization. He recruited young Somalis in Minneapolis to join Al-Shabaab, and purchased weapons in Somalia for Minneapolis recruits.
Christopher Paul	Southern District of Ohio	Christopher Paul was convicted of conspiring to use explosives against targets in Europe and the U.S. Paul joined al-Qa'eda in the early 1990s and fought in Afghanistan and Bosnia.
Tahawwur Hussain Rana	Northern District of Illinois	Tahawwur Hussain Rana was charged with and is awaiting trial for providing material support to terrorism. He was part of the plot to kill Danish newspaper editors and conspired to execute the Mumbai attacks.
Ehsanul Islam Sadequee and Syed Haris Ahmed	Northern District of Georgia	Ehsanul Islam Sadequee and Syed Haris Ahmed were convicted of conspiring to provide material support to terrorists.

Name	Court	Description of Charges/Convictions
Mustafa Salat	District of Minnesota	Mustafa Salat was charged with conspiracies to provide material support to terrorists and foreign terrorist organizations; conspiracy to kill, kidnap, maim and injure persons abroad; possessing and discharging a firearm during a crime of violence; and solicitation to commit a crime of violence along with Khalid Abshir Ahmed Ali Omar, Zakaria Maruf, and Mohamed Hassan. He left Minneapolis for Somalia and fought with Al-Shabaab. He still remains at large.
Hysen Sherifi	Eastern District of North Carolina	(North Carolina Group) – Hysen Sherifi was charged with conspiracy to murder abroad, providing material support to a terrorist group and weapon charges. He was involved in the plot to commit acts of violence in Israel and Kosovo.
Anes Subasic	Eastern District of North Carolina	(North Carolina Group) – Anes Subasic was charged with conspiracy to murder abroad, providing material support to a terrorist group and weapon charges. He was involved in the plot to commit acts of violence in Israel and Kosovo.
Bryant Neal Vinas	Eastern District of New York	Bryant Neal Vinas pled guilty to conspiracy to murder U.S. nationals and providing material support to al-Qa'eda. He joined al-Qa'eda and participated in a rocket attack in Afghanistan.
Mohammed Warsame	District of Minnesota	Mohammed Warsame pled guilty to conspiracy to provide material support to al-Qa'eda, admitting that he attended al-Qa'eda training camps, sent money from Canada to one of his former training camp commanders, and exchanged messages with individuals associated with al-Qa'eda once in Minnesota.
Kobie Diallo Williams	Southern District of Texas	Kobie Diallo Williams was convicted of conspiring to unlawfully possess firearms by an alien and supporting the Taliban. Williams, also known as Abdul Kabir, conspired with three other foreign nationals to train with firearms in preparation to join the Taliban "to engage in battlefield jihad."
Ziyad Yaghi	Eastern District of North Carolina	(North Carolina Group) – Ziyad Yaghi was charged with conspiracy to murder abroad, providing material support to a terrorist group, and weapon charges. He was involved in a plot to commit acts of violence in Israel and Kosovo.

Name	Court	Description of Charges/Convictions
Najibullah Zazi	Southern District of New York	Najibullah Zazi was charged with conspiring to use a weapon of mass destruction as part of an al-Qa'eda plot to bomb targets in the United States. He attended terrorist training camp and assembled bomb making materials in Colorado.
2008		
Mohamad Ibrahim Shnewer, Dritan Duka, Shain Duka, Eljvir Duka, and Serdar Tatar	District of New Jersey	Mohamad Ibrahim Shnewer, brothers Dritan Duka, Shain Duka and Eljvir Duka, and Serdar Tatar were convicted of plotting to kill U.S. soldiers in an armed attack on the military base in Fort Dix, New Jersey.
Mohammed Jabarah	Southern District of New York	Mohammed Jabarah was convicted of terrorism charges stemming from his participation in a plot to bomb U.S. embassies in Singapore and the Philippines. Jabarah trained in al-Qa'eda camps in Afghanistan and spent time with Osama bin Laden, to whom he swore an oath of allegiance.
Hassan Abu Jihaad	District of Connecticut	Hassan Abu Jihaad, a former member of the U.S. Navy, was convicted of providing material support to terrorists and delivering classified information on the movements of a U.S. Navy battle group to Azzam Publications, a London-based organization alleged to have provided material support to persons engaged in terrorism.
Derrick Shareef	Northern District of Illinois	Derrick Shareef was convicted of attempted use of a weapon of mass destruction in connection with setting off hand grenades at a shopping mall in Rockford, Illinois in 2006.
Aafia Siddiqui	Eastern District of New York	Aafia Siddiqui was charged with and is awaiting trial for the attempted murder of U.S. military personnel in Afghanistan at an Afghan police station. She went missing while visiting Pakistan in 2003, but was detained in Afghanistan in 2008.
Mohammad Amawi, Marwan El-Hindi and Wassim Mazloum	Northern District of Ohio	Mohammad Amawi, Marwan El-Hindi and Wassim Mazloum were convicted of conspiracy to commit terrorist acts against Americans overseas, including U.S. armed forces in Iraq, and conspiracy to provide material support to terrorists. Amawi and El-Hindi were also convicted of distributing information regarding suicide bomb vests and Improvised Explosive Devices.

Name	Court	Description of Charges/Convictions
2007		
Tahmeed Ahmad	Southern District of Florida	Tahmeed Ahmad was charged with and is awaiting trial for assaulting a U.S. government employee. He charged a U.S. Air Reserve base with crude explosives and butcher knives, chanting "Death to America." He was under supervision by a psychiatric hospital at the time of the attack and had been on a terrorist watch list.
Kevin James, Levar Washington, Gregory Patterson (California Prison Plot)	Central District of California	Kevin James, who formed a radical Islamic organization while in California state prison, and two of his recruits, Levar Washington and Gregory Patterson, were convicted of conspiracy to attack U.S. military facilities and Jewish facilities in Los Angeles.
Russell Defreitas	Eastern District of New York	Russell Defreitas was charged with conspiracy to cause death, serious bodily injury and extensive destruction. He planned to blow up fuel tanks at JFK Airport.
Paul Hall	District of Connecticut	Paul Hall was convicted of providing material support for terrorism, passing classified information, and receiving military training. He passed information on ship movements to a group supporting terrorism. Prior to this, he was in the U.S. Navy.
Daniel Joseph Maldonado	Southern District of Texas	Daniel Joseph Maldonado pled guilty to receiving military training from foreign terrorist organization and conspiring to use explosive device outside the U.S. He received terrorist training in Somalia.
Ahmed Mohamed	Southern District of New York	Ahmed Mohamed pled guilty to providing material support to terrorists. He made videos showing how to assemble rockets.
Jose Padilla, Adham Hassoun and Kifah Jayyousi	Southern District of Florida	Jose Padilla, Adham Hassoun and Kifah Jayyousi were convicted of conspiracy to murder, kidnap and maim individuals in a foreign country, conspiracy to provide material support, and providing material support to terrorists.
Sulejmen Talovic		Sulejmen Talovic was killed when he opened fire in a Utah shopping mall.
Houssein Zorkot	Eastern District of Michigan	Houssein Zorkot was charged and is awaiting trial for possession of a loaded firearm and a felony firearm offense. Zorkot was arrested for having an AK-47 under his coat. He also operated a Hezbollah-praising website with a post entitled, "The Start of My Personal Jihad (in the U.S.)."

Name	Court	Description of Charges/Convictions
2006		
Adam Gadahn	Central District of California	Adam Gadahn was charged with treason, as he urged violence against the United States on al-Qa'eda video tapes. He still remains at large.
Naveed Haq	Western District of Washington	Naveed Haq was convicted of murder and attempted murder after he opened fire at a Seattle-area Jewish organization.
Adnan Babar Mirza	Southern District of Texas	Adnan Babar Mirza was charged with conspiracy to contribute services to Taliban and weapons charges. He had trained with and was sending money to Taliban with intent to fight U.S. troops in Afghanistan.
Zacarias Moussaoui	Eastern District of Virginia	Zacarias Moussaoui was convicted of various terrorism violations, admitting that he conspired with al-Qa'eda to hijack and crash planes into prominent U.S. buildings as part of the 9/11 attacks.
Muhammed Taheri-Azar	Central District of California	Muhammed Taheri-Azar pled guilty to attempted 1st degree murder. He drove a van through the University of North Carolina campus, injuring several students.
2005		
Ahmed Omar Abu Ali	Eastern District of Virginia	Ahmed Omar Abu Ali was convicted on all counts of an indictment charging him with, among other violations: two counts of providing material support to terrorists, two counts of providing material support to a terrorist organization (al-Qa'eda), one count of contributing goods and services to al-Qa'eda, and one count of receiving services from al-Qa'eda. The following additional charges were added later: conspiracy to assassinate the president, conspiracy to hijack aircraft, conspiracy to destroy aircraft, and providing material support to al-Qa'eda.
Mahmud Faruq Brent al-Mutazzim	Eastern District of New York	Mahmud Faruq Brent al-Mutazzim pled guilty to providing material support to a foreign terrorist organization. He trained with Lashkar-e-Taiba in Pakistan.
Hamid Hayat	Eastern District of California	Hamid Hayat was convicted of providing material support to terrorists and false statements. He received terrorist training in Pakistan and admitted returning to U.S. to engage in violence.

Name	Court	Description of Charges/Convictions
Kifah Jayyousi	Southern District of Florida	Kifah Jayyousi was convicted of conspiracy to murder, kidnap and maim overseas; providing material support for terrorists; and conspiracy to provide material support for terrorists. He operated as an al-Qa'eda support cell, and planned to send material support/commit attacks overseas. He was convicted with Jose Padilla.
Hammad Sammana	Central District of California	Hammad Sammana was charged with conspiracy to levy war against the U.S. and conspiracy to kill foreign officials. He planned on attacking U.S. military facilities, Israeli government facilities, and Los Angeles-area synagogues.
Tarik Shah	Eastern District of New York	Tarik Shah pled guilty to conspiring to provide material support to al-Qa'eda. He agreed to train al-Qa'eda fighters in martial arts.
2004		
Nuradin Abdi	Southern District of Ohio	Nuradin Abdi pled guilty to providing material support to terrorism. He helped Iyman Faris with the Brooklyn Bridge plot.
Ali Al-Timimi	Eastern District of Virginia	Ali Al-Timimi was convicted of counseling and inducing others to use and carry firearms and explosives, wage war, and aid a foreign terrorist organization. He was a cleric who incited members of a northern Virginia group to take up arms and attend training camps.
Ryan Anderson	United States Military Court	Ryan Anderson was convicted of seeking to aid the enemy in time of war and attempted espionage. He attempted to pass intelligence about tanks on to al-Qa'eda.
Mohammed Babar	Southern District of New York	Mohammed Babar pled guilty to conspiring to provide and providing material support to terrorists. He provided bomb making material and night-vision goggles, in addition to funding to al-Qa'eda and the Taliban. He also provided support to a United Kingdom fertilizer bomb plot.
Ruben Shumpert	Western District of Washington	Ruben Shumpert was convicted of handgun and counterfeiting charges. The Seattle barber was convicted of non-terrorism offenses, but allegations were that radical rhetoric pervaded his shop. He jumped bail prior to sentencing and ended up in Somalia where he was rumored to have been killed.

Name	Court	Description of Charges/Convictions
Shahawar Matin Siraj	Eastern District of New York	Shahawar Matin Siraj was convicted of conspiracy to damage or destroy a subway station by means of an explosive. He planned on bombing Herald Square in Manhattan.
2003		
Muhammed Aatique	Eastern District of Virginia	(Northern Virginia "paintball" group) Muhammed Aatique pled guilty to aiding and abetting others to conduct military operations with firearms against Americans. He attended terrorist training camps abroad; trained by playing paintball.
Hammad Abdur-Raheem	Eastern District of Virginia	(Northern Virginia "paintball" group) Hammad Abdur-Raheem pled guilty to conspiracy to provide material support to a foreign terrorist organization (Lashkar-e-Taiba). He attended terrorist training camps abroad and trained by playing paintball.
Ibrahim al-Hamdi	Eastern District of Virginia	(Northern Virginia "paintball" group) Ibrahim al-Hamdi pled guilty to weapons and explosives charges. He helped other northern Virginia "paintball" group gain access to terrorist training.
Hasan Akbar	Military Court	Hasan Akbar was convicted (court martial) of premeditated murder and attempted premeditated murder. He killed two fellow soldiers in a surprise grenade attack.
Yassin Arif	Northern District of New York	Yassin Arif was convicted of conspiring to aid a terrorist group, providing support for weapons of mass destruction, money laundering, and supporting a foreign terrorist organization. He was a part of the Albany sting operation to assassinate a Pakistani United Nations ambassador.
Jeffrey Leon Battle	District of Oregon	(Portland Seven Cell) Jeffrey Leon Battle pled guilty to conspiracy to levy war against the U.S., conspiracy to contribute services to al-Qa'eda and the Taliban, and conspiracy to providing material support to al-Qa'eda. He tried several times to join al-Qa'eda/Taliban in Afghanistan.
Ahmed Abrahim Bilal	District of Oregon	(Portland Seven Cell) Ahmed Abrahim Bilal pled guilty to conspiracy to levy war against the U.S., conspiracy to contribute services to al-Qa'eda and the Taliban, and conspiracy to provide material support to al-Qa'eda. He tried several times to join al-Qa'eda/Taliban in Afghanistan.

Name	Court	Description of Charges/Convictions
Muhammad Ibrahim Bilal	District of Oregon	(Portland Seven Cell) Muhammad Ibrahim Bilal pled guilty to conspiracy to levy war against the U.S., conspiracy to contribute services to al-Qa'eda and the Taliban, and conspiracy to provide material support to al-Qa'eda. He tried several times to join al-Qa'eda/Taliban in Afghanistan.
Ali Asad Chandia	Eastern District of Virginia	(Northern Virginia "paintball" group) Ali Asad Chandia was convicted of providing material support to Lashkar-e-Taiba. He attended terrorist training camps abroad and trained by playing paintball.
Seifullah Chapman	Eastern District of Virginia	(Northern Virginia "paintball" group) Seifullah Chapman was convicted of conspiracy to provide material support to a foreign terrorist organization, Lashkar-e-Taiba. He attended terrorist training camps abroad and trained by playing paintball.
Iyman Faris	Eastern District of Virginia	Iyman Faris pled guilty to providing material support to a designated foreign terrorist organization. He planned to bomb the Brooklyn Bridge.
Patrice Lumumba Ford	District of Oregon	(Portland Seven Cell) Patrice Lumumba Ford pled guilty to conspiracy to levy war against the U.S., conspiracy to contribute services to al-Qa'eda and the Taliban, and conspiracy to provide material support to al-Qa'eda. He tried several times to join al-Qa'eda/Taliban in Afghanistan.
Khwaja Mahmood Hasan	Eastern District of Virginia	(Northern Virginia "paintball" group) Khwaja Mahmood Hasan pled guilty to conspiracy to provide material support to a foreign terrorist organization, Lashkar-e-Taiba. He attended terrorist training camps abroad and trained by playing paintball.
Maher Mofeid Hawash	District of Oregon	(Portland Seven Cell) Maher Mofeid Hawash pled guilty to conspiracy to levy war against the U.S., conspiracy to contribute services to al-Qa'eda and Taliban, and conspiracy to provide material support to al-Qa'eda.
Mohammed Hossein	Northern District of New York	Mohammed Hossein was convicted of conspiring to aid a terrorist group, provide support for weapons of mass destruction, money laundering, and supporting a foreign terrorist organization. He was a part of the Albany sting operation to assassinate a Pakistani United Nations ambassador.

Name	Court	Description of Charges/Convictions
Masoud Ahmad Khan	Eastern District of Virginia	(Northern Virginia "paintball" group) Masoud Ahmad Khan was convicted of conspiracy to provide material support to a foreign terrorist organization (Lashkar-e-Taiba). He attended terrorist training camps abroad and trained by playing paintball.
Yong Ki Kwon	Eastern District of Virginia	(Northern Virginia "paintball" group) Yong Ki Kwon pled guilty to conspiracy to commit an offense against the U.S. and weapons charges. He attended terrorist training camps abroad and trained by playing paintball.
Uzair Paracha	Southern District of New York	Uzair Paracha was convicted of providing and conspiracy to provide material and financial support to a foreign terrorist organization, and conspiracy to make or receive contribution to/from al-Qa'eda. He helped smuggle Majid Khan into the U.S. and moved between the U.S. and Pakistan frequently, but spent most of his life in Pakistan.
Randall Royer	Eastern District of Virginia	(Northern Virginia "paintball" group) Randall Royer pled guilty to weapons and explosives charges. He helped other northern Virginia "paintball" group members gain access to terrorist training camps.
Habis Abdulla al Saoub	District of Oregon	(Portland Seven Cell) Habis Abdulla al Saoub joined the Taliban and was killed fighting in Afghanistan.
Donald Thomas Surratt	Eastern District of Virginia	(Northern Virginia "paintball" group) Donald Thomas Surratt pled guilty to conspiracy to commit an offense against the U.S. and weapons charges. He attended terrorist training camps abroad and trained by playing paintball.
2002		
Mukhtar al-Bakri	Western District of New York	(Lackawanna Six) Mukhtar al-Bakri pled guilty to providing material support to al-Qa'eda. al-Bakri attended terrorist training camp in Pakistan/Afghanistan.
Sahim Alwan	Western District of New York	(Lackawanna Six) Sahim Alwan pled guilty to providing material support to al-Qa'eda. Alwan attended terrorist training camp in Pakistan/Afghanistan.
Charles Bishop		Charles Bishop flew a Cessna aircraft into a downtown Tampa skyscraper. He was killed during the incident and left a suicide note which praised Osama bin Laden.

Name	Court	Description of Charges/Convictions
Kemal Derwish	Western District of New York	Kemal Derwish was recruited by Lackawanna Six. He left the U.S. in 2001 and was killed in Yemen by a U.S. missile strike.
Jaber A. Elbaneh	Western District of New York	Jaber A. Elbaneh was convicted in absentia for providing material support to al-Qa'eda. Elbaneh attended terrorist training camp in Pakistan/ Afghanistan as a member of the Lackawanna group, but never returned to the U.S. from Afghanistan. He is currently detained in Yemen where he was convicted of conspiring to blow up an oil facility.
Faysal Galab	Western District of New York	(Lackawanna Six) Faysal Galab pled guilty to providing material support to al-Qa'eda. Galab attended terrorist training camp in Pakistan/Afghanistan.
Yahya Goba	Western District of New York	(Lackawanna Six) Yahya Goba pled guilty to providing material support to al-Qa'eda. Goba attended terrorist training camp in Pakistan/Afghanistan.
Hesham Mohamed Hadayet	Central District of California	Hesham Mohamed Hadayet was killed when he opened fire at El Al ticket counter at Los Angeles International Airport.
Shueyb Mossa Jokhan	Southern District of Florida	Shueyb Mossa Jokhan was charged with conspiracy to destroy property with explosives and fire. He planned on bombing electric plants, National Guard armory, and Jewish sites in southern Florida. He dropped out of the conspiracy weeks into plot.
Lee Boyd Malvo	District of Maryland	Lee Boyd Malvo was convicted of capital murder. Muhammad was a Washington D.C.-area sniper who killed at least ten people.
Imran Mandhai	Southern District of Florida	Imran Mandhai was charged with conspiracy to destroy property with explosives. He planned on bombing electric plants, a National Guard armory, and Jewish sites in southern Florida.
Shafal Mosed	Western District of New York	(Lackawanna Six) Shafal Mosed pled guilty to providing material support to al-Qa'eda. Mosed attended terrorist training camp in Pakistan/Afghanistan.
John Allen Muhammad	Eastern District of Virginia	John Allen Muhammad was convicted of capital murder. Muhammad was a Washington D.C. area sniper who killed at least ten people.

Name	Court	Description of Charges/Convictions
Semi Osman	Western District of Washington	Semi Osman was indicted and pled guilty to weapons possession and immigration charges, though prosecution sought a sentence only appropriate in terrorism-linked immigration cases. Osman was deported. He was suspected as part of the cell that attempted to set up a terrorist training camp in Oregon at instruction of Abu Hamza al-Masri, and pled to lesser charge.
Yasein Taher	Western District of New York	(Lackawanna Six) Yasein Taher pled guilty to providing material support to al-Qa'eda. Taher attended terrorist training camp in Pakistan/Afghanistan.
James Ujaama	Eastern District of New York	James Ujaama was charged with providing material support to terrorists. He set up a terrorist training camp in Oregon at the instruction of Abu Hamza al-Masri. He initially pled guilty to lesser charges, but violated parole and pled guilty to original charges.

About the Author

Jeffrey F. Addicott is a Distinguished Professor of Law and the Director of the Center for Terrorism Law at St. Mary's University School of Law (www.stmarytx.edu/ctl) in San Antonio, Texas, where he teaches a variety of courses to include National Security Law and Terrorism Law. An active duty Army officer in the Judge Advocate General's Corps for twenty years (he retired in 2000 at the rank of Lieutenant Colonel), Professor Addicott spent a quarter of his career as the senior legal advisor to the United States Army's Special Forces. An internationally recognized authority in terrorism law, Professor Addicott not only lectures and participates in professional and academic organizations both in the United States and overseas, he is a frequent contributor to national and international media outlets.

Foreign presentations include numerous professional lectures at universities and government institutions in India, Colombia, Peru, Ukraine, Germany, France, Austria, Canada, Thailand, Japan, Honduras, Haiti, Egypt, Kuwait, Panama, Guatemala, Albania, Okinawa, Cuba, South Korea, England, Mexico, Sweden, Ireland, Scotland, Greece, Israel, Russia, and Uruguay. Presentations in the United States include over 500 appearances at universities, public and private State and Federal institutions, as well as more than 2,000 appearances on radio, print, and television broadcasts to include the *New York Times*, *Miami Herald*, *Dallas Star-Tribune*, *San Antonio Express-News*, *Los Angeles Times*, *Chicago Tribune*, *Washington Times*, *Wall Street Journal*, FOX News Channel, MSNBC, CNN, ABC, PBS, NBC, CBS, NPR, BBC, and al-Jazeera.

Professor Addicott is a prolific author, publishing over twenty books, articles, and monographs on a variety of legal topics. Among his many contributions to the field, Professor Addicott pioneered the teaching of law of war and human rights courses to the militaries of numerous nascent democracies in Eastern Europe and Latin America. For these efforts he was awarded the Legion of Merit, named the "Army Judge Advocate of the Year" and honored as a co-recipient of the American Bar Association's Hodson Award.

Dr. Addicott served as the Associate Dean for Administration and Finance at St. Mary's University School of Law (2006-2007). He is also the 2007 recipient of St. Mary's University Alumni Association's "St. Mary's University School of Law Distinguished Faculty Award." Lieutenant Colonel Addicott (U.S. Army, ret.) served in senior legal positions in Germany, Korea, Panama, and throughout the United States. Professor Addicott holds a Doctor of Juridical Science (SJD) and Master of Laws (LLM) from the University of Virginia School of Law. He also received a Master of Laws (LLM) from the Judge Advocate General's School, a Juris Doctor (JD) from the University of Alabama School of Law and a bachelor of arts with "Honors in Government" (BA) from the University of Maryland.

Index